Petrels, Albatrosses, and
Storm-Petrels of North America

Petrels, Albatrosses, and Storm-Petrels of North America: *A Photographic Guide*

Steve N. G. Howell

In collaboration with J. Brian Patteson,

Kate Sutherland,
and Debra L. Shearwater

PRINCETON UNIVERSITY PRESS • PRINCETON AND OXFORD

Requests for permission to reproduce material from this
work should be sent to Permissions, Princeton University
Press

Published by Princeton University Press,
41 William Street, Princeton, New Jersey 08540

In the United Kingdom: Princeton University Press,
6 Oxford Street, Woodstock, Oxfordshire OX20 1TW

press.princeton.edu

Library of Congress Cataloging-in-Publication Data
Howell, Steve N. G.
  Petrels, albatrosses, and storm-petrels of North America :
a photographic guide / Steve N. G. Howell ; in collabora-
tion with J. Brian Patteson, Kate Sutherland, and Debra L.
Shearwater.
     p. cm.
  Includes index.
  ISBN 978-0-691-14211-1 (cloth : alk. paper) 1. Pro-
cellariidae—Identification. 2. Procellariidae—Pictorial
works. I. Patteson, J. Brian. II. Shearwater, Debra. III.
Title.
  QL696.P665H69 2012
  598.4'2—dc22   2011003912

British Library Cataloging-in-Publication Data is
available

This book has been composed in Adobe Caslon
and Trade Gothic

Printed on acid-free paper. ∞
Printed in Singapore

10 9 8 7 6 5 4 3 2 1

Dedicated to David G. Ainley and the late Larry B. Spear

And to the memory of my brother, Chris (Dave) Howell (1947–2011)

The cure for anything is salt water—sweat, tears, or the sea

—*Isak Dinesen*

CONTENTS

LIST OF SPECIES COVERED

Petrels (P1–P40)

Albatrosses (A1–A11)

Storm-Petrels (S1–S19)

PREFACE

A nyone you meet on the street has probably heard of an albatross, but ask them about a Least Storm-Petrel or a Sooty Shearwater—these birds might as well be from Mars. Two-thirds of the surface of our planet is water, yet it's really another world with its own inhabitants. The oceans have long held grip on the human psyche, epitomizing the last wilderness, a watery world that can never be tamed: from the voyages of Captain Cook to Moby Dick, sea monsters, and the Bermuda Triangle, the oceans are rich in history and mystery. Yet most people have never been even a few miles offshore, let alone experienced the magic of the open ocean.

Unlike people, the world's petrels, albatrosses, and storm-petrels—collectively termed *tubenoses* because their nostrils are encased in tube-like structures on the bill—are at home in the oceans. Tubenoses are among the most remarkable yet least known of all birds, living as they do in a constantly changing environment, in a world where people struggle even to stand without falling over. Largely because of logistical difficulties—such as spending time at sea, or visiting remote islands where tubenoses breed—our knowledge of tubenose identification, distribution, biology, and taxonomy lags well behind what we know of most landbirds. Even the breeding grounds of some locally common species remain unknown, such as of the Elliot's Storm-Petrels that follow every tourist boat in the supposedly well-researched Galapagos Islands.

The ocean is increasingly recognized as the last birding frontier, and every trip offshore can produce surprises and new information—it's exciting out there. More and more pelagic trips are being arranged from different parts of North America, and, together with bird observations gathered on research cruises, the frontiers are receding slowly. With more interest and more knowledge should come more understanding, more love, and a commitment to conserve ocean ecosystems—and thus ourselves.

Approximately 70 species of tubenoses (of 140+ species worldwide) occur or have occurred in North America, here defined as waters within 370 km (200 nautical miles) of land (or otherwise-agreed international border) from Alaska and Canada south to the Caribbean and Panama. "Approximately" reflects the dynamic taxonomic status of several groups, such as albatrosses and, especially, storm-petrels.

W. B. Alexander pioneered the modern seabird field guide with his *Birds of the Ocean*, published in 1928. Although rudimentary by today's standards, Alexander's work stood essentially alone for about 50 years, when a few other guides appeared, among them the charmingly titled *A Field Guide to the Seabirds of Britain and the World* (Tuck & Heinzel 1978). Other important works on seabirds, relating mainly to distribution and taxonomy, include L. M. Loomis's report on tubenoses collected on the 1905–1906 California Academy of Sciences' expedition from California to the Galapagos Islands (Loomis 1918), Robert Cushman Murphy's classic two-volume work, *Oceanic Birds of South America* (1936), and the Smithsonian Institution's report on seabirds in the central and eastern Pacific Ocean (King 1974a). The nascent pelagic dreams of birders were kindled with the publication in 1983 of Peter Harrison's classic *Seabirds: An Identification Guide*, followed in 1987 by his photographic guide (Harrison 1987). Pioneering regional guides included Rich Stallcup's *Ocean Birds of the Nearshore Pacific* (1990). Together these books helped fuel growing numbers of pelagic trips off both coasts of North America. For those curious about how seabirding developed in North America, I recommend the article "A Brief History of Pelagic Birding in North America" (Shearwater 2004). For those with a deeper interest in tubenoses I also recommend recent monographs by John Warham on the petrels (Warham 1990, 1996) and by W.L.N. Tickell on the albatrosses (Tickell 2000). Other recent works include Brooke's (2004) family guide to the Procellariiformes, but there is still no good modern identification guide to the world's tubenoses.

Despite a growing interest by birders and ongoing research by various scientists, a modern-style identification guide for North American seabirds has also been lacking. This guide aims to help fill that gap, at least for tubenoses. There is still much to learn, however. For example, increasing conservation interest in Black-footed and Steller's albatrosses has not been paralleled by simple studies to establish the plumage sequences of these birds. If even a fraction of the budget spent on bureaucratic oversight of conservation efforts were spent on identification studies, the seasonal at-sea distributions of different ages (and perhaps sexes) of these majestic but threatened species might be known, which could be of value to their conservation. And if we know so little of birds as grand and iconic as albatrosses, imagine what else remains to be learned. That's part of the magic of pelagic birding, knowing that there is always so much more to see, to learn, to wonder about. I hope this guide helps synthesize present knowledge of tubenose identification while admitting that there are many more waves to crest before we have clear view of how to identify tubenoses at sea.

ACKNOWLEDGMENTS

The vast resource of museum specimens is often overlooked by birders, yet has been largely responsible for the text and illustrations of most field guides that we all use and take for granted. This book could not have been written without reference to museum specimens, and for their generous assistance I thank personnel at the California Academy of Sciences (CAS; John P. Dumbacher, Maureen Flannery, Becky Morin, Kathleen Berge), the Museum of Vertebrate Zoology, University of California, Berkeley (MVZ; Carla Cicero), the North Carolina State Museum of Natural Sciences (NCSM; Rebecca Desjardins, John A. Gerwin, H. Douglas Pratt), the British Museum, Tring (BM; Mark Adams, Robert Prys-Jones, Hein Van Grouw), the San Diego Natural History Museum (SDNHM; Philip Unitt), the National Museum of Natural History (Smithsonian Institution), Washington, D.C. (USNM; James Dean, Storrs Olson), the American Museum of Natural History, New York (AMNH; Paul Sweet), the Natural History Museum of Los Angeles County (Kimball L. Garrett, Kathy Molina), and the Santa Barbara Museum of Natural History (Paul Collins, Krista Fahy). I am also grateful to the Macaulay Library of Natural Sounds (LNS), Cornell Laboratory of Ornithology, Ithaca, New York (Jessie H. Barry), for access to voice recordings.

Over the years I have met many people on boats around the world, far too many to remember or thank here, and I apologize to those I have neglected to mention. For company in the field, thoughtful discussions, responses to questions, assistance in museum collections, and hospitality while visiting far-flung sites and museums I thank David G. Ainley, George L. Armistead, Lisa T. Ballance, Chris Benesh, Dominique Besson, Mark J. Billings, Russ Bradley, Matt Brady, Edward S. Brinkley, Dennis Buurmann/Albatross Encounter (New Zealand), Rachel T. Buxton, Jamie Cameron, Steven W. Cardiff, Anthony Collerton, the late Luke Cole, Chris Collins, Elaine Cook, Chris Corben, Jim Danzenbaker, Mike Danzenbaker, Judy Davis, Alan R. Dean, Don Doolittle, Sam Droege, Ann Dunham, Jon Dunn, Richard A. Erickson, Jon Feenstra, Dick Filby, Bob Flood, Ted Floyd, Michael P. Force (with information gleaned during cruises supported by the Protected Resources Division, Southwest Fisheries Science Center, La Jolla, California, and directed by Lisa T. Ballance), Russell Fraker, Peter A. Fraser, Kimball L. Garrett, Greg Gillson, Jennifer Green, Robb Hamilton, Phil Hansbro, Hiroshi Hasegawa, Scott and Claudia Hein, Hendrik Herlyn, Michelle Hester/Oikonos, Peter Hodum, Alan Hopkins, Lisa Hug, Terry Hunefeld, Ali Ijoob, Greg D. Jackson, Alvaro Jaramillo, Oscar Johnson, Nina Karnovsky, Michelle Kappes, Kim Kreitinger, Paul E. Lehman, Ron LeValley, Les and Cindy Lieurance, Kirsten Lindquist, Mark W. Lockwood, Richard Lowe, Tony Marr, Charlene McAllister, Guy McCaskie, Steven W. McConnell, Todd McGrath, Bert McKee, Ken Morgan, Joseph Morlan, Maura Naughton, Dick Newell, Michael O'Brien, Storrs L. Olson, J. Brian Patteson, Kenneth Petersen, Robert L. Pitman, Richard F. Porter, Peter Pyle, Danny I. Rogers, Marc Romano, Kayo J. Roy, Rodney Russ, Shirley Russ, Aaron Russ, and Nathan Russ/Heritage Expeditions (New Zealand), Matt Sadowski, Debi Shearwater, Hadoram Shirihai, Dave Shoch, Chris Sloan, the late Larry B. Spear, Brian L. Sullivan, Kate Sutherland, Scott, Linda, and Ryan Terrill, Bernie Tershy, Bryan Thomas, David Vander Pluym, David and Kelley Ward, Sarah Warnock, Pete Warzybok, Sophie Webb, Henri Weimerskirch, David B. Wingate, and Chris Wood.

In particular, Debi Shearwater of *Shearwater Journeys* (California) and J. Brian Patteson of *Seabirding* (North Carolina) have enabled me frequent access to the marine realm, and Will Russell and all in the WINGS office have helped over the years in many ways. All at Point Reyes Bird Observatory (PRBO), particularly the Palomarin Field Station, were supportive throughout; I thank Geoff Geupel, Tom Gardali, and Renée Cormier for helping to maintain this productive work environment, and Will Lewis and Amber Wingert for helping me finish the manuscript.

Information on status and distribution was gathered primarily from regional, national, state, provincial, and more local published works on distribution (see Geographic References, pp. 476–479); reports in *North American Birds* (and its predecessors *Audubon Field Notes* and *American Birds*), which are abbreviated as NAB, AFN, or AB, followed by volume number, page number(s), and year of publication, e.g., NAB 63:502, 2010; and summaries in the *Birds of North America* series. I attempted to include information published (which does not include internet websites) at least through 2009, but it is inevitable that some records were overlooked; nonetheless, patterns of distribution and seasonal occurrence are at least broadly outlined. The following persons kindly reviewed introductory material, species accounts, and status accounts, and commented on photo captions: David G. Ainley, Edward S. Brinkley, the late Luke Cole, Elaine Cook, Michael P. Force, Diana Humple, Paul E. Lehman, Kirsten Lindquist, Bruce Mactavish, J. Brian Patteson, Peter Pyle, Patricia Shanks, and Debi Shearwater.

And lastly, but obviously not least, a photographic guide would be nothing without photographs. I am indebted to the following for providing images for review: George L. Armistead (GLA), Malcolm and Michael Boswell (M&MB), Robin W. Baird/www.cascadiaresearch.org (RWB), Edward S. Brinkley, Chris Collins/birdsandwildlife.com (CC), Mike Danzenbaker/avesphoto.com (MD), Ryan DiGaudio (RDiG), Don Doolittle, Annie B. Douglas/www.cascadiaresearch.org (ABD), Seamus Enright (SE), Kieran Fahy (KF), Phil Hansbro (PH), Bill Henry/Island Conservation, Michelle Hester/Oikonos, Marshall J. Iliff (MJI), Alvaro Jaramillo (AJ), Ron LeValley/levalleyphoto.com (RLeV), Kirsten Lindquist (KL), Gerard Lillie, Todd McGrath (TMcG), Bruce Mactavish (BM), Killian Mullarney (KM), Michael O'Brien, Michael O'Keeffe (MO'K), Tony Palliser (TP), J. Brian Patteson/www.patteson.com (JBP), Kenneth Petersen (KP), Robert L. Pitman (RLP), Eric W. Preston/ericpreston.com (EWP), Michael L. P. Retter, Matt Sadowski (MS), Ben Saenz, Debi Shearwater/www.shearwaterjourneys.com (DS), Mark Stackhouse, Brian L. Sullivan (BLS), Kate Sutherland (KS), Sophie Webb (SW), Pete Warzybok/PRBO Conservation Science (PW), and Daniel L. Webster/www.cascadiaresearch.org (DLW). Ian Lewington kindly provided illustrations to supplement the photos.

HOW TO USE THIS BOOK

When opening any bird guide there's an overwhelming urge to look at the pictures, or to check the text to answer a specific question. The introduction is often skipped, and maybe never read. However, to get the most out of this book I recommend taking a little time to read the introduction, which covers a number of subjects important to understanding tubenoses and their habitats, and which will help you develop skills for identifying what you see.

FORMAT OF THE SPECIES ACCOUNTS

The species recorded in North America (including two, Solander's Petrel and Madeiran Storm-Petrel, presumed to occur but as yet unconfirmed) are here broken down into three main groups (petrels, albatrosses, and storm-petrels), with each group subdivided for identification purposes: large shearwaters, small shearwaters, Atlantic gadfly petrels, Pacific gadfly petrels, other petrels, North Pacific albatrosses, vagrant albatrosses, white-rumped storm-petrels, dark-rumped storm-petrels, and distinctive storm-petrels (see List of Species Covered, p. xi). Each group is introduced by a summary of its characters, at times with overviews and photos treating some of the more challenging identifications, followed by individual species accounts. Species accounts comprise an introductory section and a field identification section, followed by photos with annotated captions.

First a species' English and scientific names are given. Few groups of birds have experienced a more checkered taxonomic history than tubenoses, and their wide-ranging habits have further resulted in the application of numerous different English names in different countries. I prefer to retain names that evoke a sense of ocean exploration and discovery, with alternative names noted when relevant. For albatrosses I have mostly followed the names used by Tickell (2000), which are well reasoned and appropriate, and most petrels, shearwaters, and storm-petrels have agreed-upon names in recent literature.

After the names come values for length (L), wingspan (WS), tail length, and sometimes other values that may be helpful for identification, such as bill length for albatrosses and shearwaters, tail graduation for petrels (distance from tip of longest central feather to tip of shortest outer feather), and depth of tail fork for storm-petrels. These standardized measurements were taken by me from museum specimens and from freshly dead birds collected by the late Larry Spear. Length (tip of bill to tip of tail) was measured from birds laid on their backs, with due regard to different styles of specimen preparation. Wingspans for some species were estimated from a ratio of wing chord to wingspan derived from closely related (usually congeneric) species. For example, for most *Pterodroma* petrels the wing chord is about 30% of the wingspan, for Tahiti Petrel (with a longer humerus) it is about 27.5%, for the even longer-armed *Phoebastria* albatrosses it is around 23.5%, and for the shorter-armed *Oceanodroma* storm-petrels it is around 34%.

Although these measurements provide a guide to the relative sizes of each species, at least equally important is having an idea of a bird's mass (Tables 1–2). Mass, however, can vary greatly within a species, depending on factors such as age, foraging experience, migration status, and breeding status. Differences in mass can affect flight manner. For example, adult Short-tailed Shearwaters fattened up in late summer prior to migration south from Alaska (weighing up to 800 g) fly rather differently from lean, immature Short-tailed Shearwaters wintering off California (weighing perhaps 500 g). Also important is the relationship between wing area and body mass (known as wing-loading), which can indicate how different species may fly in different wind speeds. Heavy-bodied species with a relatively small wing area have high wing-loading, whereas lighter-bodied species with a larger wing area have low wing-loading (see Flight Manner, pp. 24–28).

Table 1. Comparison of wingspan (in cm, see p. xvii) and mass (in g) for selected North American petrels (approximate mean mass given in parentheses after each species name, for quick comparison). Some sources unhelpfully give only means with standard deviation (SD); in the latter case I have taken the mean ± 2 SDs to approximate the range for 95% of the sample (indicated by 95% noted after range). When known, data from beachcast birds were avoided. Such birds can be emaciated and atypical of birds likely to be seen at sea; e.g., mass for Audubon's Shearwater (NCSM specimens) varies from 99–128 g (beachcast) to 138–253 g (at sea); and for adult White–chinned Petrels mass ranges from 665 g (beachcast) to 1885 g at the breeding colony! (Marchant & Higgins 1990). There can also be a difference between nonbreeding or immature birds at sea and breeding adults at a colony (which may be fattened in preparation for incubation spells, or filled with food for their young); e.g., 12 Kermadec Petrels at sea weighed 315–434 g (Spear et al. 1992) whereas 7 breeding adults at a colony weighed 370–590 g (Marchant & Higgins 1990).

	Wingspan	Mass (sample size)
Large Shearwaters		
Sooty Shearwater (800 g)	97–106	666–978 (100)[11]
Short-tailed Shearwater (625 g)	91–99	460–800 (184)[11]
Flesh-footed Shearwater (625 g)	109–116	533–692 (13)[11]
Pink-footed Shearwater (725 g)	110–118	576–879 (93)[1,6,12]
Buller's Shearwater (425 g)	96–104	339–499 (120)[11]
Wedge-tailed Shearwater (400 g)	99–109	300–512 (81)[13]
Streaked Shearwater (500 g)	103–113	440–538 (4)[11]
Great Shearwater (850 g)	108–116	715–950 (14)[3]
Cory's Shearwater (850 g)	113–124	605–1060 (488)[2]
Scopoli's Shearwater (650 g)	110–121	486–768 (115; 95%)[14]
Small Shearwaters		
Audubon's Shearwater (200 g)	65–74	138–253 (100)[1]
Barolo Shearwater (175 g)	58–61	140–211 (157)[2]
Manx Shearwater (450 g)	75–84	335–545 (183)[3,4]
Newell's Shearwater (375 g)	77–85	340–411 (35)[5]
Townsend's Shearwater (300 g)	76–83	256–358 (10)[6,7]
Black-vented Shearwater (450 g)	78–86	332–545 (258)[8]
Galapagos Shearwater (180 g)	63–70	123–230 (78)[9]
Christmas Shearwater (350 g)	83–90	260–455 (89)[10]
Atlantic Gadfly Petrels		
Black-capped Petrel (475 g)	98–105	350–590 (40)[1]
Bermuda Petrel (250 g)	85–92	246 (1)[15]
Desertas Petrel (325 g)	87–97	275–355 (17)[16]
Trinidade Petrel (350 g)	94–102	305–392 (7)[1,17]

Table 1. *cont.* Comparison of wingspan and mass for selected North American petrels

	Wingspan	Mass (sample size)
Pacific Gadfly Petrels		
Cook's Petrel (180 g)	76–82	112–250 (12)[11]
Stejneger's Petrel (140 g)	70–76	114–167 (47)[13]
Mottled Petrel (325 g)	84–92	205–441 (146)[11]
Hawaiian Petrel (450 g)	94–104	355–540 (157; 95%)[18]
Galapagos Petrel (425 g)	99–110	309–515 (115; 95%)[19]
Juan Fernandez Petrel (450 g)	103–114	310–555 (198)[13]
Murphy's Petrel (375 g)	89–97	335–423 (7)[13]
Kermadec Petrel (450 g)	97–106	315–590 (19)[11,13]
Herald Petrel (275 g)	90–97	237–320 (13)[13]
Tahiti Petrel (400 g)	101–108	315–506 (140)[13]
Other Petrels		
Atlantic Northern Fulmar (725 g)	101–115	560–1050 (86)[20]
Pacific Northern Fulmar (650 g)	95–110	445–787 (134)[20]
Parkinson's Petrel (725 g)	112–123	587–855 (20)[11]
Bulwer's Petrel (110 g)	63–68	75–139 (547)[2,11]

[1]NCSM specimens, [2]Monteiro et al. 1996, [3]Cramp & Simmons 1977, [4]Ainley et al. 1997, [5]Lee 1995, [6]Binford 1989, [7]Jehl 1982, [8]Keitt et al. 2000b, [9]Harris 1969a, [10]Seto 2001, [11]Marchant & Higgins 1990, [12]Guicking et al. 2004, [13]Spear et al. 1992, [14]Thibault & Bretagnolle 1998, [15]Wingate 1972, [16]Zino & Zino 1986, [17]USNM specimens, [18]Simons & Hodges 1998, [19]Tomkins & Milne 1991, [20]Hatch & Nettleship 1998.

Table 2. Comparison of wingspan (in cm, see p. xvii) and mass (in g) for selected North American storm-petrels (approximate mean mass given in parentheses after each species name, for quick comparison). See comments for **Table 1.**

	Wingspan	Mass (sample size)
White-rumped storm-petrels		
Wilson's (39 g)	36–42	27–50 (208)[1,2]
Fuegian [Wilson's] (31 g)	34–38	28–34 (7)[2]
European (28 g)	35–37	18–38 (165)[3]
Grant's [Band-rumped] (49 g)	45–51	36–67 (729)[4]
Monteiro's [Band-rumped] (45 g)	44–50	33–58 (229)[4]
Madeiran [Band-rumped] (45 g)	43–48	35–55 (72)[5]
Darwin's [Band-rumped] (43 g)	45–50	31–54 (137)[6]
Leach's (N Atlantic) (46 g)	45–50	38–55 (82)[7]
Leach's (California) (42 g)	44–48	31–50 (1043)[8]
Peruvian [Wedge-rumped] (23 g)	33–37	19–27 (6)[9]
Galapagos [Wedge-rumped] (27 g)	36–40	19–35 (131)[6]

Table 2. *cont.* Comparison of wingspan and mass for selected North American storm-petrels

	Wingspan	Mass (sample size)
Dark-rumped storm-petrels		
Black (62 g)	50–55	46–77 (162)[10,11,12]
Least (18 g)	32–36	14–22 (17)[10,11]
Ashy (38 g)	40–45	33–42 (20)[10]
Chapman's [Leach's] (36 g)	44–48	29–42 (78)[10]
Markham's (54 g)	49–54	49–59 (214; 95%)[13]
Tristram's (90 g)	52–57	66–112 (246)[14]
Swinhoe's (43 g)	45–50	39–47 (6)[15]
Distinctive storm-petrels		
Fork-tailed (Aleutians) (65 g)	45–52	49–82 (424)[16]
Fork-tailed (Washington) (56 g)	43–49	45–67 (422)[16]
White-faced (N Atlantic) (54 g)	40–45	39–69 (69)[3,5]
White-faced (*maoriana*) (50 g)	38–42	40–62 (100)[1]

[1]Marchant & Higgins 1990, [2]Spear & Ainley 2007, [3]Cramp & Simmons 1977, [4]Monteiro et al. 2006, [5]Robertson & James 1988, [6]Harris 1969b, [7]Huntington et al. 1996, [8]Harris 1974, [9]Bernal et al. 2006, [10]Crossin 1974, [11]Binford 1989, [12]Ainley & Everett 2001, [13]J. Jahnke, unpubl. data, [14]Slotterback 2002, [15]Bretagnolle et al. 1991, [16]Boersma & Silva 2001.

Photos of each species are then listed, including reference to photos elsewhere in the book (such as the Introduction). After an identification summary, three introductory sections provide background information for each species, followed by characters that relate directly to field identification; last in each account is a series of photos with annotated captions.

Identification Summary The key points for identifying a species are given here, such as geographic range, habitat, structural characters, plumage features, and flight manner. In some cases you may need to refer to more detailed information in the Similar Species section. Alternate common names may also be mentioned here. For species that occur regularly north of Mexico, an introductory photo is included after the identification summary.

Taxonomy This includes a brief notation about subspecies (if any), taxonomic relationships, and differing treatments. If no subspecies are recognized for a species, then it is termed *monotypic*.

Names The origin of scientific names is explained, if known, and also sometimes the common name if its derivation is not obvious.

Status and Distribution The world range of each species is summarized first for context, starting with conservation categories ranging from Least Concern through Near Threatened, Vulnerable, and Endangered to Critically Endangered (with some species classified as Data Deficient) from Birdlife International (2010a); species not recognized by that source are noted as such. The term *endemic breeder* indicates the species breeds only in the region, although nonbreeding birds may range outside the region. Then follows more detailed information for the North American region on breeding and nonbreeding ranges, migration routes and timing, and vagrant occurrences, divided when relevant into Pacific and Atlantic regions. Information on status and distribution was gathered from published and unpublished sources (see

Acknowledgments); references are cited mainly for specific (usually exceptional) records or for information not included in, or subsequent to, the main references consulted (see pp. 476–479). Acceptance criteria for records vary among sources and the accounts here are intended to provide an overview of each species' distribution and patterns of occurrence, not a comprehensive treatise listing (or evaluating) every known record. Seasonal ranges given for breeding (from modal egg-laying to fledging), migration, and nonbreeding occurrences are broad-brush and should be viewed as such; more detailed information can be found in regional and species-specific sources. Terms for abundance used include *rare*: occurs annually but in small numbers; *casual* or *very rare*: on average, less than annual in occurrence, but fitting a pattern of known occurrence; *exceptional*, or *accidental*: of extremely rare occurrence, including records that do not conform to presently understood patterns of vagrancy. Abundance in an area often varies between years and over longer cycles, so status sections should be interpreted with this in mind—what is common in some years can be rare or absent in other years. See p. 457 for an explanation of how geographic terms (e.g., Atlantic Canada, the West Coast) are defined.

Maps Maps are included for all species that occur regularly. Specific breeding sites are not mapped except for very localized species, and arrows may indicate primary migration routes. Maps do not generally show areas where a species is rare or casual (e.g., Short-tailed Shearwater off west Mexico); such information may be summarized by a sentence or two accompanying the map, and details of rare occurrence are summarized in the status and distribution sections.

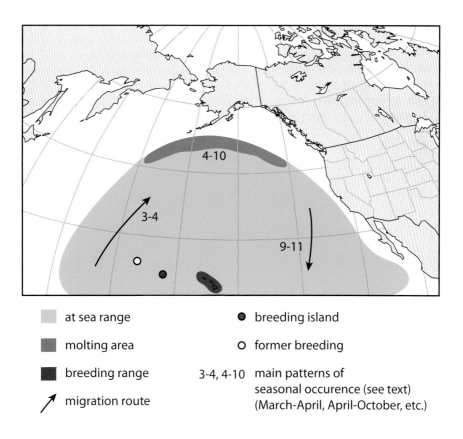

at sea range   ● breeding island

molting area   ○ former breeding

breeding range   3-4, 4-10   main patterns of seasonal occurence (see text) (March-April, April-October, etc.)

↗ migration route

Field Identification
The following sections cover aspects relating more directly to field identification. I have at-sea experience, usually extensive, with all but one of the taxa covered in this guide, and much of the identification-related information is derived from my own experience; when this is not the case, other sources are cited.

Similar Species This section highlights distinguishing features of the species in question relative to potentially similar species. Features useful for identification are often relative and require some experience to use in the field. Additional identification features can be found in the detailed descriptions and photo captions. Similar species are listed in a subjective order from most similar and most likely to overlap through least similar and least likely to occur together.

Habitat and Behavior A summary of habitat and behavior emphasizes features relevant to identification. Most of this information comes from my own observations, supplemented by literature summaries (especially Marchant and Higgins 1990, Poole and Gill 1992–2002); sources for other data are given. Few flight manners are species-specific and all should be interpreted in relation to wind speed, wind direction, and behavior (see Flight Manner, pp. 24–28). As a rule, calm to light winds translate to about 0–12 knots (sea states 0–3 on the Beaufort Scale, as modified by Petersen; see Huler 2004); moderate winds to about 15–25 knots (Beaufort 4–5), and strong winds to about 25–40 knots (Beaufort 6–8), above which watching tubenoses at sea on most ships tends to be exhilarating rather than objective. Voice is usually noted only for species that breed in the region.

Description In most tubenoses except albatrosses the ages and sexes look similar, and a single description covers all plumages. In species with age-related variation, adults are described first, followed by juveniles and any subsequent immature stages. Plumage cycles are used to allow comparisons among all species (see Molts, Plumages, and Aging, pp. 38–45); the first cycle indicates a juvenile until the start of its second prebasic molt, when it enters the second cycle. Descriptions are based largely upon museum specimens, supplemented by field observations and photos.
The legs and feet of some species are described as, e.g., "pinkish overall," which indicates that the outer or hind edges of the legs and toes are variably blackish; the legs and feet of gadfly petrels described as "bicolored" indicate that the legs and bases of the feet are pale (pinkish or bluish), whereas the tips of the feet are black (see Leg and Foot Color, p. 36).

Molt Molt is usually most apparent among the primaries where it is termed *wing molt*. Wing molt timing often differs by age groups, which is noted if data are available; information is often provisional, however (*provisional data are indicated in italics*). Wing molt data were derived mostly from specimens, at-sea observations, and peer-reviewed literature (in particular, Cramp and Simmons 1977, Marchant and Higgins 1990). Molt information provided by Pyle (2008) is a mix of scientific study and conjecture, but unfortunately the two are rarely if ever distinguished and no direct citations are provided; where information herein agrees with Pyle (2008) this had to be determined by laboriously revisiting the literature and specimen collections, in conjunction with my own at-sea observations. Where information differs from, or supplements, the three sources noted above, this is indicated by citations of relevant publications, museum collections (especially CAS, MVZ, NCSM, and USNM), and specific field observations, often supported by some of the photos included herein. Careful observers can still contribute considerably to an understanding of molt timing, which can be helpful in species identification (see Molts, Plumages, and Aging, pp. 38–45).

Notes Notes sometimes expand upon unpublished data noted in the species accounts. Full citations for published works can be found in the Literature Cited section (pp. 463–479).

Photos Each species is shown in a series of photos placed at the end of each species account, with captions that highlight identification criteria for each species and plumage. Photos were selected to show a representative range of plumages, with an emphasis on birds of typical appearance. When ages are distinguishable, adults are shown first, then juveniles and any subsequent immature ages. For species of regular or almost annual occurrence in the U.S. and Canada, one or two "character sketch" images are included near the start of an account, showing species in typical situations or with other species for comparison. In the series of photos, birds in flight (dorsal, then ventral) are generally shown first, followed by birds at rest and then images showing the species with other species.

WHAT ARE TUBENOSES?

In traditional classifications such as that of the American Ornithologists' Union (AOU) (1998), tubenoses are a well-defined group of seabirds that comprise the order Procellariiformes, and are so-named because their nostrils are encased in tube-like structures on the bill. Tubenoses are represented by up to five families worldwide: northern storm-petrels, southern storm-petrels, albatrosses, petrels (including shearwaters), and diving-petrels (a southern hemisphere family not covered in this guide, and sometimes merged with the petrels). Based upon DNA studies, Sibley and Monroe (1990) treated all of the tubenoses as a single family (Procellariidae) within the superfamily Procellarioidea, which also includes frigatebirds, penguins, and loons.

Tubenoses occur all over the world's oceans and vary in appearance from the tiny, swallow-like storm-petrels to the great albatrosses, among the largest of flying birds, with wingspans approaching 3.5 m (almost 12 feet)! Wings range from relatively broad and rounded in some storm-petrels to long, narrow, and pointed in the majority of species. Tails mostly range from squared to graduated, but several storm-petrels have forked tails. All tubenoses have 10 functional primaries and most have 12 rectrices (fulmars have 14, giant-petrels 16); the number of secondaries ranges from 11–13 in storm-petrels to 25–38 in albatrosses.

Bills vary from fairly short in storm-petrels to long and substantial in albatrosses, and all have hooked tips and are covered by distinct horny plates. The nostrils of albatrosses are mounted in small tubes on either side of the bill, whereas in petrels and storm-petrels they are fused into a tube on top of the bill base (Figs 1–2). Tubenoses drink saltwater and excrete

Fig 1. On albatrosses, such as this Black-footed Albatross, the nostril tubes lie on either side of the bill (cf. Fig 2). SNGH. Off Bodega Bay, California, 14 Aug 2007.

Fig 2. On petrels, such as this Sooty Shearwater, the nostrils open in a double-barreled tube at the base of the culmen (cf. Fig 1). SNGH. Off Monterey, California, 11 May 2008.

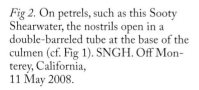

surplus salt in solutions that leak out of the nostril tubes. All species have short legs and webbed feet, with the hind toe absent (in albatrosses) to greatly reduced (in petrels and storm-petrels); the toes of burrowing species in particular have strong and sharp claws. Tubenoses have a well-developed olfactory bulb and use smell to find food and help locate their burrows in the dark (the plumage of most petrels and storm-petrels has a distinctive musky odor, which pervades their nests). It has even been found that adults of some species can distinguish by smell their own burrows from those of their neighbors (Bonadonna et al. 2003).

The plumage of tubenoses is dense and waterproof, hued in blacks, grays, browns, and whites. Some species are all-dark whereas others are strikingly patterned, with contrasting white uppertail coverts (as in some storm-petrels) or bold underwing markings (as in some petrels). The bills of most smaller species are black or dark, but some larger species, especially albatrosses, have brightly colored bills; the legs and feet of most species are blackish or pinkish overall.

Sexes appear alike in plumage although in some of the large albatrosses males more quickly develop "adult" plumage—a male Snowy [Wandering] Albatross 5 years old may be as white as a female 20 years old (Prince et al. 1997). In general, males average larger in albatrosses and petrels, whereas females average larger in storm-petrels. This is rarely apparent at sea except perhaps in bill depth or, with some albatrosses, in the bulk and width of the head (females having more slender heads). In most species the fledglings appear indistinguishable from adults, which is something to be thankful for in terms of at-sea identification. Appreciable age-related variation in appearance is largely limited to albatrosses. Molt in tubenoses is relatively poorly known. Most tubenoses do not molt their wings while breeding, and the time available for molt can be as little as a few months between successive breeding seasons. Thus, particularly among albatrosses, molt can involve novel strategies that allow the maximum number of primaries to be replaced in a short period. As adults, all tubenoses have one molt per cycle (a cycle for most species being a year), which, especially in larger species, is often incomplete, with not all remiges being replaced in a single cycle (see Molts, Plumages, and Aging, pp. 38–45). Because flight is so important to tubenoses, some species will skip a year of breeding to catch up on their molt rather than risk another season with impaired flight capabilities.

Except for the diving-petrels, which have sacrificed wing area to allow them to dive better (like northern hemisphere auks), tubenoses are generally accomplished fliers—as they have to be to live in such an open and windy environment (see Flight Manner, pp. 24–28). All rest on the sea surface, and many species dive well for food (especially shearwaters). Most tubenoses are migratory to some degree. These migrations vary from poorly understood shorter-distance dispersals to spectacular transequatorial odysseys.

Life at sea is all about finding food, which is patchy, mobile, and unpredictable (see Ocean Habitats, pp. 5–13). Tubenoses can survive fairly long periods without feeding and have a great ability to lay down subdermal fat for insulation, which helps them through fasting periods such as incubation (spells of which can last 3–4 weeks in albatrosses). Tubenoses find their food by sight and smell, and they forage by day and night (some food items perform vertical migrations, and only approach the surface at night); the main food groups are squid, fish, and crustaceans such as krill. Feeding strategies include scavenging, seizing prey near the surface, diving to depths of 50 m or more, and even pirating other species. Scavenging is a common form of feeding for many tubenoses, such as Tahiti Petrel and storm-petrels (Fig 3). This is why fish-oil slicks (which mimic dead fish) are successful in attracting certain tubenoses, notably petrels and storm-petrels, which can detect smells from miles away. Some fishing operations, mainly in productive temperate waters, provide large quantities of offal. Albatrosses and fulmars can gather in hundreds or even thousands to eagerly consume this "free food" (free in the myopic, human short term). In fact, the best way to find albatrosses in some areas is to locate active fishing boats. However, the practice of setting baited hooks (such as the thousands used by

Fig 3. Many species of tubenoses, here a Black-capped Petrel and a Wilson's Storm-Petrel, scavenge dead squid and fish, which can be detected from miles away courtesy of an acute sense of smell. SNGH. Off Hatteras, North Carolina, 15 Aug 2009.

Fig 4. Pink-footed Shearwaters over Humpback Whale. Several species of petrels feed in association with whales and dolphins, presumably scavenging spillage and scraps. SNGH. Off Monterey, California, 26 Sep 2008.

long-line fishing operations) without protecting them from hungry tubenoses causes countless birds to take the bait and drown—a major source of mortality for some species, particularly albatrosses, and a serious conservation issue that is beginning to be addressed.

In tropical waters, schools of dolphin and tuna chase schools of fish to the surface, allowing many tubenoses to feed on the smaller fish being pursued as well as on left-over scraps. For example, Juan Fernandez Petrels and Wedge-tailed Shearwaters (along with Sooty Terns and numerous other species) feed over yellowfin tuna in the tropical Pacific Ocean (Spear et al. 2007), Parkinson's Petrels often scavenge in association with dolphins off Middle America (Pitman & Ballance 1992), and Pink-footed Shearwaters often forage over whales or schools of dolphins off California (pers. obs.; Fig 4).

Fig 5. Hybrid Laysan x Black-footed Albatross with plumage pattern superficially suggesting Galapagos Albatross. RdG. Midway Atoll, Hawaii, 28 Dec 2006.

All tubenoses nest on or under ground, typically on islands that are (or were) free from predators, and most species are colonial. Long-distance migrants and species breeding at high latitudes tend to be more synchronized in their breeding, whereas tropical species and shorter-distance migrants tend to have more protracted and less synchronized cycles. A high degree of philopatry characterizes tubenoses, and young birds generally return to their natal islands for breeding; when breeding islands are at carrying capacity, however, young birds may range widely in search of suitable new breeding sites. Larger species such as albatrosses and fulmars are diurnal at the breeding grounds and nest on the surface, whereas most smaller species are nocturnal and nest in burrows or crevices, coming and going at night to avoid predators such as hawks, falcons, gulls, and skuas.

The ocean is not a gentle or forgiving mother, and tubenoses need to know what they're doing before they start breeding. All species have a conservative reproductive strategy characterized by late maturity, low reproductive rates, and long life spans. The typical age of first breeding in tubenoses ranges from 4–5 years in storm-petrels to 6–13 years in albatrosses, some of which can live for 50 or more years. Prebreeding birds visit colonies for a few years before settling, and arrive earlier each year as they get older to develop long-lasting monogamous pair bonds. Breeders usually return at least one or two months before egg-laying, to bond with their mates and refurbish the nest site. A prelaying exodus, or "honeymoon" period, when birds leave the nesting grounds for 2–4 weeks, is characteristic of tubenoses and most apparent in species with synchronized breeding systems. During this time the egg is developed and birds store food reserves for incubation spells. Incubation for the single white egg ranges from about 6–8 weeks in storm-petrels to 9–11 weeks in albatrosses. Fledging requires from around 7–10 weeks in storm petrels to 20–40 weeks in albatrosses, and nestlings are adapted to survive weeks without food while their parents roam the oceans. In the largest albatrosses, more than a year is required for a breeding cycle and so these birds only breed every other year. Hybrid tubenoses—derived from two species interbreeding—appear to be very rare, and the only well-documented ones that occur in the region are those between Black-footed and Laysan albatrosses (Fig 5). Even so, these are sufficiently rare that most birders will never see one.

The voices of tubenoses are unmusical and heard mostly at or near the breeding grounds. They comprise a variety of brays, whinnies, purring chatters, whistles, moans, and sometimes other-worldly shrieks and screams. Periods of loud calling over storm-petrel colonies in the middle of the season, after laying or hatching, may be due largely to the presence of prebreeding immatures. Calls, in conjunction with ritualized display postures and bouts of bill-clapping in some species, serve important social functions during courtship, territorial disputes, and

4

arguments over food. Calls are of limited value for identification except at night on the breeding grounds when, e.g., they enable different species of storm-petrels to be distinguished. An excellent reference to the sounds of tubenoses in the Northeast Atlantic is the Sound Approach guide by Magnus Robb and colleagues (Robb et al. 2008).

OCEAN HABITATS

As with all birds, habitat is a key to understanding patterns of distribution and occurrence. We all readily recognize grasslands, marshes, conifer forests, and such on land, but what of marine habitats? The oceans are not simply wet and salty but instead they comprise many habitats usually invisible to the human eye (Figs 6–7). On land, these habitats would be as different as deserts are from rainforests, and at sea they are *mobile* deserts and rainforests! Both large-scale and small-scale physical processes in the ocean can change the habitat in an area overnight, as many people who have taken pelagic trips on two consecutive days to the same area can attest. We are a long way from understanding, let alone predicting, many of the large-scale, let alone small-scale, changes to which seabirds respond. The following is a simplified overview of the oceans as they relate to habitat for seabirds, particularly tubenoses.

Figs 6–7. Like many wide-ranging tubenoses, Great Shearwaters encounter varied sea conditions in their annual cycle, from mountainous southern seas near the breeding islands (sea-surface temperature 10°C) to the Gulf Stream in glassy calm (sea-surface temperature 27°C). Note the retained juvenile outermost primary cutting the water, identifying a second-cycle bird. SNGH. South Atlantic (45°S, 21°W), 6 Apr 2009, and off Hatteras, North Carolina, 26 May 2008.

Current Systems (Fig 8a–8b)

Oceans and seas are the contiguous saltwater masses that cover about 70% of the Earth's surface. They surround and define land masses and are dynamic water bodies within which patterns of predictable circulation can be identified at different depths. Ocean currents are the dominant feature of surface movement and they broadly correspond to the direction of prevailing winds, which themselves are a consequence of the easterly direction of the Earth's rotation, solar heating, and the torque of the Coriolis force.

This means that at the large scale of ocean basins the prevailing winds (and currents) are easterly (flowing from east to west) in tropical latitudes, westerly in mid-temperate latitudes, and easterly again at high latitudes. Conversely, the continental coasts have an overall north-south orientation. Thus, in the Americas, westward-flowing equatorial currents driven by the easterly Trade Winds push water away from Pacific coasts but toward Atlantic coasts, whereas eastward-flowing mid-latitude currents driven by prevailing westerly winds push water toward Pacific coasts and away from Atlantic coasts.

The Coriolis force lends a clockwise direction to mid-latitude water mass circulations in the northern hemisphere and a counterclockwise direction in the southern hemisphere. Consequently, in low to mid-latitudes there is a flow of relatively cold, higher-latitude water toward the equator along the eastern edges of the oceans, forming eastern boundary currents such as the California Current and Humboldt (or Peru) Current. Conversely, relatively warm tropical water flows away from the equator along the western edges of the oceans, forming western boundary currents such as the Gulf Stream and Kuroshio Current. At high latitudes, the current patterns reverse with the reversal of prevailing winds, and relatively warm water flows north into the Gulf of Alaska as the Alaska Current, while cold water flows south from the Davis Strait as the Labrador Current. To maintain equilibrium (all of the westward-flowing tropical water has to be replaced somehow), roughly along the equator there is an eastward-flowing current (the Equatorial Counter Current) that transports water back across the oceans between the North Equatorial and South Equatorial currents.

In addition to these major current systems there are numerous smaller-scale currents. In the Pacific, e.g., on reaching the American mainland the Equatorial Counter Current splits into the relatively warm, and usually weak, north-flowing Costa Rica Current and the south-flowing, somewhat submerged Peru Undercurrent. In the North Pacific, the Alaska Current curves around to form a westward-flowing current along the south side of the Aleutians, but some water splits off to enter the eastern Bering Sea (through Unimak Pass) and circulate in a clockwise gyre over the continental shelf.

The inherently dynamic nature of ocean water masses means that currents vary in their strength and position (even on a daily basis), but the broad patterns are consistent and helpful to have in mind when considering seabird distribution.

Thermoclines, Upwelling, and Fronts

The oceans are not uniform in nature, and within them we can distinguish distinct water masses by characteristics such as their density, which is a product of temperature and salinity. Temperature is the feature most easily appreciated by humans, although salinity may be more important in defining habitats for marine organisms. The bottom line is that the interactions of different water masses affect biological productivity. When organisms in the sea die they sink, taking the nutrients needed for photosynthesis into the cooler, deeper ocean waters. But photosynthesis can occur only in surface waters to the depth of sunlight penetration. Thus biological productivity depends in part on forces that bring nutrient-rich cooler waters into the zone where photosynthesis can occur.

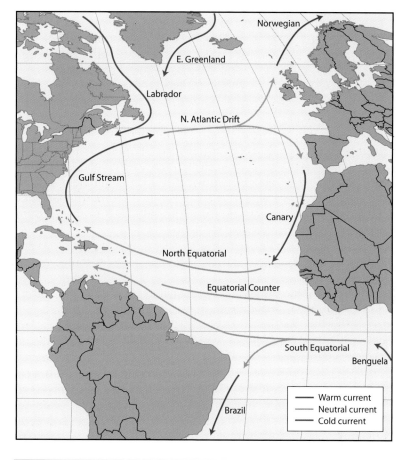

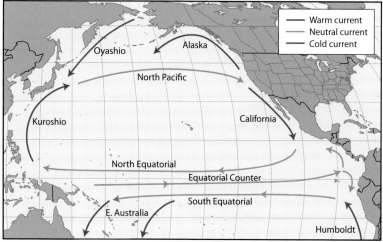

Fig 8a–8b. An overview of ocean currents relating to North American waters (warm, neutral, and cold are relative terms for the prevailing currents). At mid-latitudes, warm currents such as the Gulf Stream flow away from the equator along eastern coasts, whereas cold currents, such as the California Current, flow toward the equator along western coasts.

Thermoclines. Productivity can often be inferred by looking at the nature of the temperature gradient between warmer surface waters and cooler subsurface waters, which is called a thermocline. This gradient may be abrupt (a strong thermocline) or diffuse (a weak thermocline), and it can be nearer to (shallow) or farther from (deep) the sea surface.

For example, strong, deep thermoclines indicate little mixing of the cooler, nutrient-rich subsurface waters with the warmer, nutrient-poor surface waters. Ocean areas with these characteristics tend to be biologically unproductive, like the vast areas of "blue water" in the tropical and subtropical Central Atlantic and Central Pacific oceans, which are effectively marine deserts. Some species, such as Bulwer's Petrel, seem adapted to roam these deserts in search of food, but in general such areas are poor in seabird life. The much-publicized El Niño events that cause periodic food-web crashes in the Humboldt and California currents occur when the thermocline deepens; this happens when the Trade Winds slacken, which allows warm surface water that has been pushed to the western Pacific to slop back to the east and intrude over cooler water masses.

Weak and shallow thermoclines, on the other hand, indicate mixing of water masses, so that nutrients and sunlight combine. Hence there is increased food productivity, which extends through the food web to seabirds. Such mixing occurs where cool subsurface waters are drawn toward the surface (or upwelled) and where different water masses meet (at fronts).

Upwelling can occur in a number of ways. For example, where surface waters have a tendency to diverge, the "space" thus created may be filled by upwelling of cooler subsurface waters. Waters along the equator are relatively cool for this reason, because the Trade Winds driven by the Coriolis force tend to push the surface water north and south away from the equator. Upwelling also occurs when subsurface currents hit rises in the seafloor and are forced upward, so that nutrient-rich waters may be pushed into the sunlight zone, e.g., over seamounts, submarine canyon walls, and the continental shelf break. Tidally induced currents can also contribute significantly to upwelling among islands and over continental shelf waters, such as at Georges Bank, between Cape Cod and Nova Scotia, and in Hecate Strait, inshore of the Queen Charlotte Islands off British Columbia, where large numbers of Sooty Shearwaters gather to molt (Fig 9).

The best-known types of upwelling are the wind-driven systems associated with eastern boundary currents such as the California and Humboldt currents, which are rich feeding grounds for seabirds. But even in these areas productivity is cyclic because wind direction and strength vary, often on a seasonal basis. Upwelling can be greatly suppressed if the prevailing winds simply aren't blowing, but then even a day or two of strong winds can generate significant upwelling.

The frictional drag of wind on the ocean surface, combined with the Coriolis force, means that water flows at an angle to the wind direction: water angles to the right in the northern hemisphere, to the left in the southern hemisphere. Thus, in spring and summer (mainly March to August) the prevailing northwest winds along the Pacific coast from Oregon to California cause surface water to flow to the "right," or offshore, and cool subsurface water upwells at the coast to take its place before being similarly conveyed offshore. Two other areas of seasonal Pacific coastal upwelling in North America are around the Gulf of Tehuantepec, in southern Mexico (mainly October to March), and in the Gulf of Panama (mainly January to April), where strong winds funnel across the land isthmuses from the Gulf of Mexico and Caribbean; large numbers of Black and Least storm-petrels occur in both areas at these seasons. During El Niño events the deepened thermocline means that warm, nutrient-depleted water upwells instead of cold water, and marine productivity is greatly reduced even with upwelling.

Fronts represent the meeting of different water masses. They are three-dimensional systems, and the depth to which they extend in the water column varies with their scale and with local conditions. They can be large scale, as between the Labrador Current and Gulf Stream

Fig 9. Sooty Shearwaters gather locally in swarming masses off the West Coast to feed in food-rich waters that fuel their wing molt. SNGH. Monterey Bay, California, 24 Jul 2008.

Fig 10. Few ocean fronts are as abrupt as the break between the cold green Labrador Current (at back, around 5°C) and the warm blue Gulf Stream (in front, around 16°C and warming rapidly away from the front). Food items, and thus birds (such as these Dovekies *Alle alle*), often concentrate along such fronts. SNGH. Off Hatteras, North Carolina, 14 Feb 2010.

(Fig 10), or small scale, such as the passes between some Aleutian Islands where North Pacific and Bering Sea water masses are mixed by tidal-current action that also promotes local upwelling; many Short-tailed Shearwaters gather to molt in these productive areas.

The relatively shallow waters over the continental shelf usually differ from deeper offshore waters in temperature and salinity (e.g., shelf waters are fed by freshwater runoff from land and are mixed more by tidal action); these water masses meet and mix at what are known as shelf-break fronts, areas of generally high productivity. Upwelling fronts occur when cool,

Fig 11. Sargassum weed and associated tubenose prey items concentrate at fronts between different water masses along the edges of the Gulf Stream. SNGH. Off Hatteras, North Carolina, 26 May 2007.

upwelled water flowing offshore sinks where it meets warmer, less dense water; plankton are usually concentrated at upwelling fronts, which are often good for birds. The shelf-break front and upwelling fronts often lie over the continental shelf break, where current-driven upwelling can further enhance productivity—so it is not surprising that the shelf break is usually a good area for seabirds and seabirding.

Other, usually short-lived, fronts are the locally wind-driven or tidally driven convergences marked by strips of glassy, slick-like water dotted with lines of debris and weed (Fig 11), among which are fish eggs, gelatinous zooplankton, and other biological matter. Off California in fall these small-scale fronts often attract Buller's and other shearwaters, phalaropes, Long-tailed Jaegers, and Xantus' Murrelets. Off the southeastern U.S. in summer they are good areas to find Audubon's and other shearwaters, and Bridled and other terns. Internal waves (subsurface waves that generate vertical undulations in the thermocline) are another physical phenomenon that helps explain the small-scale patchiness of seabirds within larger-scale water masses, as noted for Black-capped Petrels off the southeastern U.S. (Haney 1987a).

Habitat Associations

For tubenoses, at-sea habitat translates largely to food. But food in the oceans is not evenly spread, and it is also dynamic in its distribution: trying to predict details of tubenose distribution patterns at sea is a little like trying to predict exactly when and where it will rain. Still, as with climatic zones on land, broad-scale marine habitat zones can be identified. Characteristics of marine habitats are rather different from those we associate with habitats on land, and include sea-surface temperature and salinity, thermocline depth and strength, ocean depth (such as over or offshore of the continental shelf), and even wind strength and wind direction. For example, albatrosses need sufficient wind speeds to support their flight, and they avoid areas with persistently low winds or calm conditions.

Within broader-scale habitats there are hotspots that concentrate food and are favored by seabirds, and by birders. For example, in the Cordell Bank National Marine Sanctuary, off the central California coast, the outer boundary of the wind-driven upwelling system corresponds with the shelf-break front and is enhanced by tidally induced and subsurface current upwellings; this all results in a productive area where 25 species of tubenoses, including 5 albatrosses, have been recorded.

As with terrestrial habitats, the avifaunas of marine habitats vary seasonally. The California Current system is a well-studied example. In spring and summer, persistent northwest winds from Oregon to central California drive the upwelling of cool, nutrient-rich, south-flowing waters that support a large avifauna of locally breeding and migrant seabirds. With changing atmospheric conditions in fall, the northwest winds decrease in both strength and persistence, the upwelling productivity is reduced, and warmer oceanic water moves onshore (mainly during August to October, when several warmer-water seabirds expand their ranges northward). The winter climate that follows is characterized by southerly winds, which allow the relatively warm, northward-flowing, and usually subsurface Davidson Current to dominate inshore marine waters during November to March (when productivity is reduced and fewer tubenoses occur), before the northwest winds return in spring.

Different habitats show varying degrees of overlap. In the Pacific Ocean, Wahl et al. (1989) found that the high-temperature/high-salinity avifauna of the subtropical North Pacific overlapped little with the three colder water/lower-salinity avifaunas to the north and east, which had numerous species in common. Habitats can also be interpreted differently. For example, Gould and Piatt (1993) recognized 3 avifaunas (comprising 14 species guilds) within the 2 offshore North Pacific avifaunas identified by Wahl et al. (1989). Tables 3–4 list the broad-scale distribution of tubenose avifaunas in North American waters during spring to fall.

Table 3. Simplified overview of Pacific Ocean habitat associations for regularly occurring petrels, albatrosses, and storm-petrels in North American waters from spring through fall (roughly Apr–Oct). BERS: Bering Sea region; NOPA: North Pacific (e to se Alaska); INCC: Inshore California Current (coastal upwelling zone out to shelf break, n to Vancouver Island); OFCC: Offshore California Current (seaward of the main upwelling and shelf break); INTP: Inshore Tropical Pacific (inshore waters out to the shelf break); OFTP: Offshore Tropical Pacific (offshore from the shelf break). [G]Also in Gulf of California; [S]Southern section (s of cen California); [N]Northern section (n of cen California). X: primary habitat associations and commoner species; x: smaller numbers occur or species generally uncommon to rare.

	BERS	NOPA	INCC	OFCC	INTP	OFTP
Sooty Shearwater		X	X[G]	x		
Short-tailed Shearwater	X	X	x			
Flesh-footed Shearwater		x	x	x		
Pink-footed Shearwater		x	X[G]	X		
Buller's Shearwater		x	X	X		
Wedge-tailed Shearwater					X	X
Manx Shearwater		x	x			
Townsend's Shearwater					X	x
Black-vented Shearwater			X[S,G]	X		
Galapagos Shearwater					X	
Christmas Shearwater					X	x
Cook's Petrel		x		X		
Mottled Petrel	X	X				
Hawaiian Petrel				X		
Galapagos Petrel						X
Juan Fernandez Petrel						X
Murphy's Petrel		x		X		
Kermadec Petrel						X

Table 3.*cont.* Simplified overview of Pacific Ocean habitat

	BERS	NOPA	INCC	OFCC	INTP	OFTP
Herald/Henderson Petrel						x
Tahiti Petrel						X
Northern Fulmar	X	X	x	X		
Parkinson's Petrel						X
Black-footed Albatross	x	X	X	X		
Laysan Albatross	X	X	x	X		
Steller's Albatross	X	x	x	x		
Wilson's Storm-Petrel			x			
Leach's Storm-Petrel		X		X		X
Wedge-rumped Storm-Petrel					X	X
Black Storm-Petrel			X[S,G]		X	
Least Storm-Petrel			X[S,G]		X	
Ashy Storm-Petrel			X	x		
Markham's Storm-Petrel						X
Fork-tailed Storm-Petrel	X	X	X[N]	X[N]		
	BERS	NOPA	INCC	OFCC	INTP	OFTP

Table 4. Simplified overview of Atlantic Ocean habitat associations for regularly occurring petrels, albatrosses, and storm-petrels in North American waters from spring through fall (roughly Apr–Oct). LABC: Labrador Current (cooler waters); GULS: Gulf Stream (warmer waters). [G]Also in Gulf of Mexico; [C]Also in Caribbean. X: primary habitat associations and commoner species; x: smaller numbers occur or species generally uncommon to rare.

	LABC	GULS
Sooty Shearwater	X	x
Great Shearwater	X	x
Cory's Shearwater		X[G,C]
Audubon's Shearwater		X[G,C]
Manx Shearwater	X	x
Black-capped Petrel		X[C]
Bermuda Petrel		x
Cape Verde/Desertas Petrel		x
Trinidade Petrel		x
Northern Fulmar	X	

12

Table 4. *cont.* Simplified overview of Atlantic Ocean habitat

	LABC	GULS
Wilson's Storm-Petrel	X	X
Leach's Storm-Petrel	X	x
Grant's [Band-rumped] Storm-Petrel		X[G]
White-faced Storm-Petrel		x
	LABC	**GULS**

PHYLOGENY, BIOGEOGRAPHY, AND VAGRANCY

The habitats described above help explain seabird distributions as we see them today. But environments are nothing if not dynamic, and a longer-term view of tubenose distributions is also of interest in understanding present-day patterns and perhaps in predicting future trends. The origins of tubenoses are shrouded in the mists of prehistoric time, but different lines of evidence agree on a common ancestor for penguins, tubenoses, and loons (Cracraft 1981, Olson 1985, Sibley & Alquist 1990). The fossil record also indicates that the tubenose families recognized today were distinct some 30 million years ago, and that most modern genera existed around 10 million years ago (Brooke 2004).

The times and rates of evolution for different groups of tubenoses are contentious, but the order likely originated in the southern hemisphere along the shores of a fragmenting Gondwanaland. It appears that storm-petrels split first from the ancestral tubenose lineage, followed by the albatrosses, and then the ancestor of petrels and diving-petrels, with the diving-petrels having diverged relatively recently (Harper 1978, Nunn & Stanley 1998; Fig 12).

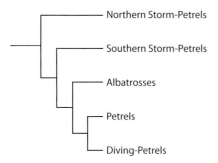

Northern Storm-Petrels

Southern Storm-Petrels

Albatrosses

Petrels

Diving-Petrels

Fig 12. Relationships among present-day tubenose families (from Nunn & Stanley 1998); the earliest branching was northern storm-petrels, followed by southern storm-petrels and albatrosses.

Until much more work is undertaken, unraveling the geographic origins of different families and genera of tubenoses will remain controversial. Islands and shores of the proto-Pacific Ocean seem likely candidates, however, given that the Indian Ocean and Atlantic Ocean did not open up until the plates of Gondwanaland diverged. Certainly, the modern-day breeding distributions of tubenoses are heavily weighted to the Pacific and to the southern hemisphere. Tubenoses, however, are tied to oceanic habitats, not to land, and their present-day breeding distributions may simply reflect the nearest predator-free land masses as much as any biogeographic ties to the immediately surrounding seas.

Tubenose distributions are ever-changing over different time scales, and what we see today are relics of a richer, more diverse bygone era. For example, the fossil record indicates that around 2–4 million years ago up to five species of albatrosses roamed the North Atlantic, where none is regular today, and there was even a breeding population of Steller's Albatrosses on Bermuda! (Olson & Rasmussen 2001). Even in our lifetimes we can see changes. For example, Northern Fulmars and Manx Shearwaters spread across the North Atlantic from western Europe to North America in the 1960s and 1970s and, as I write this, Manx Shearwaters appear to be colonizing the North Pacific. Laysan Albatrosses have colonized islands off west Mexico since the 1980s, apparently because their Hawaiian nesting grounds reached carrying capacity so that young were forced to roam in search of new lands. Given the strong philopatry of breeding adult tubenoses, the pioneering movements of young birds have likely resulted in range shifts and expansions. New colonizations need not always be driven by increasing populations: steadily rising sea levels during past eras would have reduced the area of nesting grounds and caused a steady shift in breeding distributions (or extinctions, if no alternative breeding sites could be found). Something similar may be happening today on islands where burgeoning fur seal populations appear to be limiting albatross nesting sites (such as of Snowy [Wandering] Albatross on South Georgia, and of Salvin's Albatross on the Bounty Islands).

The occurrences of vagrant tubenoses visiting islands beyond their breeding range are noteworthy events in the birding world, but might some be precursors of range changes that will span thousands of years? Could they be inexorable responses to climatic change? Or are they simply random events? Examples include Black-browed Albatross and Barolo Shearwater in Britain, Wedge-rumped Storm-Petrel and Cory's Shearwater off Baja California, Mexico, Salvin's Albatross in Hawaii, Trinidade Petrel in the West Indies, and Bermuda Petrel in the Azores.

Of the 70 or so tubenose species recorded in North America, only 16 breed in the region covered in this guide; about 36 are regular or probably regular nonbreeding visitors (some occurring in only very small numbers) from breeding grounds as distant as Hawaii, Japan, Australia, New Zealand, Chile, Antarctica, Europe, and the South Atlantic; and about 17 appear to be vagrants. Most vagrants originate from habitats similar to those found in the region: 12 species (9 albatrosses, 2 petrels, 1 storm-petrel) come from temperate and subtropical latitudes of the southern hemisphere, whereas only 5 species (1 albatross, 2 petrels, 2 storm-petrels) come from tropical regions and subtropical northern latitudes adjacent to the region. Thus, in temperate waters off California you are more "likely" to encounter species of temperate southern hemisphere waters (such as Gray-faced [Great-winged] Petrel) than to find species that occur much closer but over tropical and subtropical waters (such as Kermadec Petrel).

TAXONOMY AND AN IDENTIFICATION FRAMEWORK

Taxonomy is the science of classification and it allows us to place birds within a frame of reference. Birds, like all living organisms, are classified by a hierarchal system. The category most familiar to birders is that of a *species*, and an important category just above the species level is the *genus*; a subgenus is a grouping between the levels of genus and species. Each genus (and subgenus) has certain shared characteristics, an appreciation of which can be helpful in identification. For example, Leach's Storm-Petrel, like other members of the genus *Oceanodroma*, has relatively narrow and angled wings with a long arm, whereas Wilson's Storm-Petrel, like other members of the genus *Oceanites*, has relatively broad-based and straight wings with a short arm.

Each described organism on Earth has a scientific name, which is italicized and comprises its genus name (capitalized) and species name (lowercase). Variation within a species, if noticeable and correlated with geographic populations, may be expressed by means of *subspecies* (also called races); species with recognized subspecies are termed *polytypic*. A species is *monotypic* if no subspecies are recognized. A subspecies name is the third and last part (also termed an epithet, or trinomial) of the scientific name. With few exceptions, the first-described population retains the same subspecies epithet as the species epithet, and is known as the nominate subspecies. For example, the nominate subspecies of Northern Fulmar is *Fulmarus glacialis glacialis* (often abbreviated to *Fulmarus g. glacialis*), which breeds in the North Atlantic, while the subspecies *Fulmarus glacialis rodgersii* breeds in the North Pacific and can be classified as:

> Class: Aves
> Order: Procellariiformes
> Family: Procellariidae
> Genus: *Fulmarus*
> Species: *glacialis*
> Subspecies: *rodgersii*

The classification of tubenoses has followed a long and tortuous path, with much debate about whether separate populations are species or subspecies. Many taxa, populations, or even color morphs were originally described as separate species. A conservative period followed, with some rather extreme lumping based largely on philosophical grounds rather than new data. Thus, e.g., Murphy (1952) subsumed eight taxa of shearwaters as one, the Manx Shearwater (all eight are now considered full species again).

Like all traditional classifications, that of tubenoses has relied heavily on plumage patterns and external morphology. Recent genetic studies have repeatedly shown, however, that some taxa may diverge yet show little external evidence of their genetic separation, whereas distantly related taxa can converge in appearance and morphology. An example of the former situation occurs with different populations of Band-rumped Storm-Petrel, which may comprise as many as 10 species worldwide, with 4 in the northeastern Atlantic alone (Robb et al. 2008). An excellent example of the latter situation is the Little Shearwater/Audubon's Shearwater complex, which traditionally has been considered to comprise two widespread but rather variable species: the higher-latitude Little Shearwater, with a shorter tail and white undertail coverts, and the lower-latitude Audubon's Shearwater, with a longer tail and dark undertail coverts. Austin et al. (2004) showed that this complex comprises multiple species, and that one population of "Little" Shearwater from the North Atlantic is actually an "Audubon's" Shearwater! An interesting parallel in morphological variation occurs in the Manx Shearwater complex, such as between the higher-latitude Manx (with a shorter tail and white undertail coverts) and the lower-latitude Townsend's Shearwater (with a longer tail and dark undertail coverts).

As well as finding that traditional morphology does not necessarily reflect relationships, genetic studies have revealed a trend for geographic clades, whereby a presumed ancestor colonized an area and then diversified. Examples include the North Pacific clade of *Phoebastria* albatrosses, and the North Atlantic clade comprising Audubon's, Boyd's, and Barolo shearwaters, with the last-named resembling the southern hemisphere Little Shearwater complex (Austin et al. 2004). A further complication is that specimens may look similar in a museum tray whereas the birds in life (and genetically) are quite different. An example is the Fea's Petrel complex, which is part of a North Atlantic clade (including Black-capped and Bermuda petrels) and not closely related to the southern hemisphere Soft-plumaged Petrel (Nunn & Stanley 1998), with which Fea's was lumped for many years based on superficial similarities.

As new information becomes available, subspecies are being elevated to species rank (such as Hawaiian and Galapagos petrels; AOU 2002), cryptic species are being identified (such as Henderson Petrel; Brooke & Rowe 1996), and some distinct taxa even remain to be named (such as Grant's [Band-rumped] Storm-Petrel). Thus, taxonomy within the tubenoses remains dynamic—and often controversial, such as proposals to elevate all albatross taxa to the level of species. In birds as site-faithful as albatrosses every island population could, in theory, evolve into a species: witness the coexistence of Desertas [Fea's] and Zino's petrels in the Madeira archipelago, and the differences found among populations of Galapagos Petrels from different islands in the Galapagos archipelago (Tomkins & Milne 1991). The difficulty, for humans, lies in determining how differentiated insular populations have become—which should be recognized as species and which should not?

Despite the state of flux in tubenose taxonomy and nomenclature, the classification of the American Ornithologists' Union *Checklist of North American Birds* (and subsequent supplements) is particularly anachronistic and is not followed here. Instead, I have tried to pick a realistic course through various taxonomic papers (Austin 1996, Austin et al. 2004, Chambers et al. 2009, Harper 1978, Imber 1985, Nunn & Stanley 1998, Viot et al. 1993), but I acknowledge the fluid state of tubenose taxonomy. One recent review of taxonomy and nomenclature in tubenoses as a whole (Penhallurick & Wink 2004) contained numerous flaws (Rheindt & Austin 2005) and has not been generally accepted. Another review (Kennedy & Page 2002) represented an exercise in statistics more than an advance in taxonomy.

Tubenoses have been traditionally divided into four families: albatrosses, petrels, diving-petrels, and storm-petrels (Figs 13–15). Recent studies, however, suggest it is more realistic to treat diving-petrels as a subfamily within petrels, and to consider storm-petrels as two families (see Fig 12). Some features of each genus or subgenus within these families are described below (at least for species recorded in North America). In the species accounts these families and genera are subdivided into groups convenient for field identification, which do not necessarily reflect taxonomic relationships.

Fig 13. Black-footed Albatross and Chapman's [Leach's] Storm-Petrel are examples of the larger and smaller tubenoses; both scavenge together at squid and fish carcasses. SNGH. Off San Diego, California, 25 Aug 2009.

Fig 14. Although large for a petrel, this Pink-footed Shearwater is dwarfed by a Black-footed Albatross (an adult with extensively white uppertail coverts), which is relatively small for an albatross. SNGH. Off Monterey, California, 21 Sep 2007.

Fig 15. The small size of Wilson's Storm-Petrel is readily appreciated with a Cory's Shearwater for scale. SNGH. Off Hatteras, North Carolina, 31 May 2007.

Family Procellariidae: Petrels

Petrels, which include shearwaters, are a well-defined family of tubenoses, but over the years they have been divided into many different groups by different authors. There is increasing agreement that both the fulmar clade (represented in the northern hemisphere by one species, with six other species in five genera inhabiting the cold Southern Ocean) and the *Pterodroma* clade are distinct monophyletic groups. Other relationships are less clear, including those of the shearwaters and the genera *Procellaria*, *Bulweria*, and *Pseudobulweria* (as well as of some southern hemisphere genera unrecorded in North America). Genetic studies confirm that the traditional *Puffinus* shearwaters are not monophyletic (Austin 1996, Nunn & Stanley 1998). Thus the larger "*Puffinus*" shearwaters are treated here in the genus *Ardenna*, with *Puffinus* reserved for the smaller shearwaters, which share a common ancestor with *Calonectris*. Fig 16 shows a provisional phylogeny of present-day petrel genera recorded in North America. The following genera occur in North American waters, listed here in the sequence of three main groups used for identification (shearwaters, gadfly petrels, and other petrels).

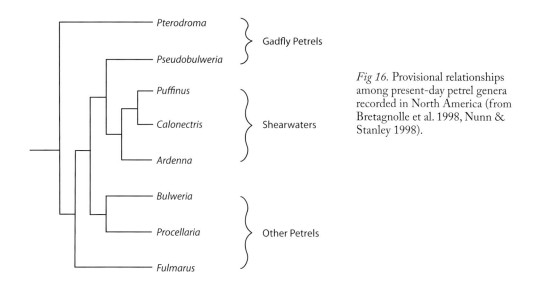

Fig 16. Provisional relationships among present-day petrel genera recorded in North America (from Bretagnolle et al. 1998, Nunn & Stanley 1998).

Shearwaters comprise three genera worldwide, all found in the region: *Ardenna*, *Calonectris*, and *Puffinus*. Gadfly petrels in the region comprise two genera: *Pterodroma* and *Pseudobulweria*. Other petrels in the region involve three genera: *Fulmarus*, *Procellaria*, and *Bulweria*.

Genus *Ardenna*. Seven species of large shearwaters, all of which occur in the region; six breed in the southern hemisphere and migrate to the northern hemisphere to molt, and one (Wedge-tailed) breeds and ranges in the tropics. This genus might best be considered as multiple genera, but it is recognized here provisionally to highlight that these large shearwaters are not closely related to true *Puffinus*. Bills are relatively slender, varying from blackish to pink with a black tip, and legs and feet are pink to dusky overall. Plumage is all-dark or bicolored. Wedge-tailed and Buller's are a distinctive pair that can be recognized in the subgenus *Thyellodroma*, differing from other species in lighter build, relatively broader wings, and longer, strongly graduated tails, which combine to give them a buoyant flight manner befitting their lower-latitude distribution. Typical *Ardenna* are heavier bodied with shorter tails and narrower and stiffer wings, and inhabit higher latitudes with stronger winds. For species identification note flight manner, overall plumage pattern, tail shape, head and neck patterns, bill color and size, and underwing pattern.

Genus *Calonectris*. Four species (all recorded in the region) of large shearwaters with long and overall pale bills, broad wings, and medium-long graduated tails. All breed in warm subtropical waters of the northern hemisphere and further differ from *Ardenna* in having longer and heavier bills, rounded tarsi, lighter skeletons, and more marked sexual dimorphism (male bills being 5–13% longer than those of females). For species identification check head and neck pattern, bill color, and underwing pattern.

Genus *Puffinus*. At least 26 species (taxonomy is vexed) of small to very small shearwaters. That only eight species have been recorded in the region reflects the relatively sedentary habits of many taxa. *Puffinus* shearwaters are widespread in tropical and mid-latitudes. Most species are bicolored, dark above and white below, although two are dark overall, including Christmas Shearwater, which traditionally has been associated with the larger shearwaters. Bills are dark overall, and legs and feet mostly pinkish to pale bluish. Similarities in plumage patterns have clouded the determination of species limits, and it is likely that more species await recognition, or even formal discovery. For species identification note overall structure (especially tail length), head and neck pattern, undertail-covert pattern, underwing pattern, and bill size.

Genus *Pterodroma*. Approximately 30 species (taxonomy is vexed) widespread in tropical and subtropical latitudes. They are often simply called pterodromas in birding talk, or known as gadfly petrels because of their impetuous flight manner. In North American waters at least 15 species of gadfly petrels have been recorded. Gadflies are small to medium-sized petrels that range from all-dark to bicolored, with dark upperparts and white underparts; the upperparts of several species have a blacker M pattern. The bills are black, notably stout on larger species but relatively slender on some of the smaller species; the wings are generally long, relatively narrow, and pointed, characteristically held pressed slightly forward, crooked at the carpals, and flexed; the tails are slightly to distinctly graduated, varying from medium-short and relatively squared to medium-long and tapered; the toes do not project in flight and usually the feet are hidden in the plush undertail coverts; legs and feet vary from all-dark to pale pinkish or pale bluish with black distal toes and webbing. The genus may include multiple genera, but data are not available to resolve relationships for all species. For species identification note overall size (small, medium, or large), head and neck pattern, underwing pattern, flight manner, and bill size.

Genus *Pseudobulweria*. Four or more poorly known tropical species of medium-sized petrels with very stout black bills, long wings, and medium-long graduated tails. One distinctive species (Tahiti Petrel) occurs in the region and has very long narrow wings and overall dark plumage with a contrasting white belly and undertail coverts.

Genus *Fulmarus*. These are two species (one in the region) of fairly large petrels with stout pale bills, fairly broad and stiffly held wings, and medium-short, slightly graduated tails. Fulmars inhabit cold temperate waters, often scavenge at fishing boats, and are readily identifiable.

Genus *Procellaria*. Five species of fairly large petrels that breed in the southern hemisphere, four of which (including the two species recorded in North America) have predominantly blackish plumage and blackish legs and feet, and are sometimes called "black petrels." *Procellaria* bills are pale yellowish overall with well-defined plates and tend to be slightly stouter than shearwater bills; their wings are long and fairly broad, and the tails medium-short and graduated (the toes can project in flight). For species identification note bill size and pattern, overall size (relative to other species), and any white markings on the chin or head.

Genus *Bulweria*. Two distinctive tropical species (one recorded in the region) of small to medium-sized petrels with stout black bills, long narrow wings, and long, strongly graduated tails usually held closed in a point. Plumage is all-dark with a paler ulnar band, a pattern recalling some large northern storm-petrels.

Family Diomedeidae: Albatrosses

Albatrosses form a well-defined family and differ from other tubenoses in their generally larger size and in having nostril tubes on either side of the bill (see Fig 1). A well-reasoned and widely accepted review by Nunn et al. (1996) identified four recent genera of albatrosses (Fig 17), all of which have occurred in North America: the North Pacific *Phoebastria* (short-tailed albatrosses) and three southern hemisphere genera: *Diomedea* (great albatrosses), *Thalassarche* (mollymawks), and *Phoebetria* (sooty albatrosses). Moreover, Robertson and Nunn (1998) recommended that 24 albatross species be recognized, a leap from the 12–13 species traditionally recognized and one that has yet to be universally accepted. Although most if not all of these "new" species are probably valid, it is not always possible to distinguish them at sea.

Fig 17. Relationships among present-day albatross genera (from Nunn & Stanley 1998).

Genus *Phoebastria*. Four species of small to medium-large albatrosses with relatively short wings, relatively short tails (the feet project in flight unless pulled in), and generally dull-patterned bills. Ages differ little in three species but strongly in Steller's Albatross. For species identification check overall color pattern, and bill size and color. Three species occur regularly in North America; one is a vagrant.

Genus *Diomedea*. A complex of seven taxa (five Wandering Albatrosses and two Royal Albatrosses). These are the largest albatrosses, with huge bodies, very long and narrow wings, relatively short tails (the feet project in flight unless pulled in), and pale pink bills. Ages differ greatly in Wandering Albatrosses, but little in Royals. For species identification check head and body pattern, upperwing pattern, tail pattern, and details of bill pattern and structure. Northern hemisphere records are exceptional and all are of Wandering Albatross taxa, with only three records in the region, all from the Pacific.

Genus *Thalassarche*. Mollymawks are small to fairly large albatrosses with relatively short wings, relatively long tails (the feet do not project in flight), and brightly patterned bills. Ages differ in appearance; most species attain adult-like plumage aspect in 2–3 years, with fully adult bill pattern taking 4–5 years or longer to develop. For species identification check head and neck pattern, bill color and pattern, underwing pattern, and degree of contrast between hindneck and back. Six taxa of *Thallasarche* have occurred in North American waters.

Genus *Phoebetria*. Two species of striking, all-dark, angular albatrosses with long pointed wings and tails and dark bills; one has occurred as a vagrant in North America. Their flight is often spectacular, with higher sailing glides and steeper arcs than other albatrosses, and the wings are typically crooked strongly. Ages differ slightly in appearance. For species identification check overall plumage contrast, head and bill shape, and bill pattern.

Family Hydrobatidae: Northern Storm-Petrels

Storm-petrels appear to be the earliest divergences from the ancestral tubenose lineage and traditionally have been treated as well-defined southern and northern subfamilies. Recent genetic evidence, however, suggests these are better considered distinct families (Nunn & Stanley 1998; see Fig 12), and they are treated here as such. Only 3–4 genera (but 24 or more taxa, at least 19 of which have occurred in North American waters) are recognized among northern storm-petrels.

Genus *Hydrobates*. Comprises two taxa (British and Mediterranean storm-petrels) sometimes treated as separate species. *Hydrobates* are distinctive tiny storm-petrels with relatively rounded wings, a slightly rounded tail, bright white rump band, white underwing stripe, and hurried flight.

Genus *Oceanodroma*. The largest genus of northern storm-petrels, comprising 18+ taxa worldwide (one presumed recently extinct), with 12+ found in the Pacific, 4+ in the Atlantic, and 2 in both oceans. *Oceanodroma* differ from southern storm-petrels in their longer-armed, more crooked, and relatively narrower wings, and in their shorter legs and smaller feet, which are not habitually used to kick off from the sea surface; the bill, legs, and feet are black. *Oceanodroma* are medium-sized to large storm-petrels with relatively squared heads and relatively long tails, which are forked or notched; the tarsus is usually shorter than the middle toe, and there is often a strong gray gloss to the fresh dorsal plumage.

Six *Oceanodroma* taxa are dark-rumped (Ashy, Chapman's, Markham's, Tristram's, Swinhoe's, and the extralimital Matsudaira's), as are some Townsend's [Leach's]; 9+ taxa are white-rumped (5+ taxa in the Band-rumped complex plus Leach's, Ainley's [Leach's], the extinct Guadalupe, and some Townsend's), and 3 are handsomely patterned and distinctive (2 subspecies of Fork-tailed, plus Hornby's). The Band-rumped Storm-Petrel complex may be distinct enough to comprise its own genus, *Thalobata* (Penhallurick & Wink 2004), and the strikingly distinct Hornby's Storm-Petrel has yet to be investigated genetically. For at-sea identification note overall size, flight manner (relative to wind conditions), tail length and shape, and details of any white rump patches and pale upperwing bands. Bill size and shape can be helpful for identification, and are best evaluated from photos.

Genus *Halocyptena*. This includes at least four taxa of the eastern Pacific (Least, Black, and two Wedge-rumped taxa), all of which have at times been subsumed into *Oceanodroma* but which are distinct enough to warrant separation (Nunn & Stanley 1998). Relative to *Oceanodroma*, *Halocyptena* have small, rounded heads, long legs (tarsus usually longer than middle toe), short tails, sooty plumage (with only a slight gray sheen dorsally in fresh plumage), and deep wingbeats. They often feed and raft in fairly tight-knit groups, and patter over food much like Wilson's or European storm-petrels. Two taxa of *Halocyptena* (Least and Black) are all-dark, whereas the two Wedge-rumped taxa (which might best be treated as separate species) are white-rumped.

Family Oceanitidae: Southern Storm-Petrels

The southern storm-petrels are outwardly more diverse than are northern storm-petrels, with 17 taxa in 5 genera (5–6 taxa of 3 genera have occurred in North American waters). Relative to northern storm-petrels the southern genera have short-armed, relatively broad wings well suited for sailing, and longer legs and bigger feet often used to kick off from the sea surface. As among northern storm-petrels there are some well-marked subspecies, a few of which might better be treated as species (such as northern hemisphere White-faced Storm-Petrels, and all taxa of White-bellied Storm-Petrel).

Genus *Oceanites*. Four or more taxa (two of which, Wilson's and Fuegian [Wilson's], have been recorded in the region) make up this genus of small storm-petrels; all four taxa might better be considered full species but critical studies are lacking. These species have almost triangular wings, slightly rounded tails, and yellowish foot webbing. All have white uppertail coverts and differ mainly in underpart patterning and size.

Genus *Fregetta*. Six or seven taxa (one recorded in the region) of medium-sized to fairly large and broad-winged storm-petrels that suggest *Oceanites* in shape but differ in their broader toes and spade-like claws. All have white uppertail coverts (except some "dark-rumped" White-bellied in polymorphic populations) and white bellies.

Genus *Pelagodroma*. The six taxa of White-faced Storm-Petrel (2–3 recorded in the region) are medium-large storm-petrels with broad, slightly paddle-shaped wings, broad cleft tails, and long legs that often dangle as birds sail-kick along low over the sea.

FIELD IDENTIFICATION OF TUBENOSES

Although what follows may seem an almost overwhelming amount of information to digest, there's no rush. Time spent watching tubenoses and gaining experience is a key to identifying them with confidence. And still, even the most experienced observers can be fooled by observations out of context, or by factors such as atypical lighting, molt, or calm winds for a bird usually seen under windy conditions. As with identifying all birds, a synthesis of characters is important. Don't rely on a single field mark and be especially aware of how flight manner can vary depending on a bird's behavior and on wind strength and direction.

Fine-level details, such as those you might see on shorebirds when studying them with a telescope, are rarely helpful (or even visible) on tubenoses under at-sea conditions, and identification usually rests on size, structure, flight manner, overall plumage pattern, and sometimes other details such as bill structure or foot color. Digital photos can help resolve fine-level details retrospectively. Habitat can also be important (see Ocean Habitats, pp. 5–13), as can an evaluation of environmental conditions such as lighting and distance.

The following sections discuss various things that can aid in at-sea identification of tubenoses, and they provide background to put your observations in context. Armed with this information you are in a position not only to identify the birds you see but to contribute to knowledge about tubenose identification and distribution.

Age, Sex, Individual, and Geographic Variation

When identifying any group of birds it is helpful to know how much inherent variation there is. The good news is that the appearance of most tubenoses varies relatively little with season (except for the effects of wear and fading; see below), and there is no distinct age-related variation in plumage aspect except for some albatrosses (and the extralimital giant-petrels). Thus, at sea, a juvenile female Leach's Storm-Petrel looks like a 20-year-old male Leach's Storm-Petrel. Among albatrosses and petrels, males average larger and bigger billed than females

Fig 18. The relatively stout bill of this Sooty Shearwater (which has recently completed its molt and looks fattened up for migration) suggests an adult male (cf. Fig 19). SNGH. Off Monterey, California, 27 Sep 2008.

Fig 19. The relatively slender bill of this Sooty Shearwater (which has yet to complete its molt) suggests an immature, likely female (cf. Fig 18); such birds can be mistaken for Short-tailed Shearwater but still have a longer and bigger bill than that species, as well as different overall structure and underwing pattern. SNGH. Off Monterey, California, 27 Sep 2008.

(e.g., Einoder et al. 2008), whereas in storm-petrels females average larger, and adults average stouter billed than juveniles, although rarely does this play into identification (Figs 18–19).

Individual variation among some species can be considerable, however, as with a few dimorphic and polymorphic species of shearwaters and petrels, and as with rump patterns in the Leach's Storm-Petrel complex. Even among species that are usually considered rather uniform in appearance there can be appreciable variation in appearance, compounded by molt and plumage wear (Figs 20–23).

Leucistic tubenoses (i.e., birds with white or pale patches where the plumage should be dark) are sometimes seen and can be puzzling (Figs 24–25), whereas albinos (all-white birds with pink bills) are rare and look odd enough to stand out as abnormal. Melanistic tubenoses (i.e., birds with abnormal dark pigmentation) are rare, and melanism has only been reported in a few species of shearwaters (Davis & Packer 1972, Bried et al. 2005, Howell 2007b). In cases of leucisim and melanism, check structure and flight manner to resolve identifications.

Some species of tubenoses exhibit geographic variation that may be consistent enough for subspecies to be distinguished, such as by differences in wing length or bill size, less often by slight differences in plumage patterns. Whether one treats such populations as species or subspecies is a matter of opinion (see Taxonomy and an Identification Framework, pp. 14–21). For the 70 or so species treated here, geographic variation at the level of described subspecies (some of which may prove to be species) is recognized in 2 species of shearwaters (Audubon's,

Fig 20. Sooty Shearwater with unusually white underwings and virtually unstreaked primary coverts. The underwing pattern of most Sooties falls between this extreme and Fig 21. SNGH. Off Monterey, California, 1 Oct 2006.

Fig 21. Sooty Shearwater with unusually dark underwings (cf. Fig 20). SNGH. Off Bodega Bay, California, 12 Jul 2007.

Fig 22. Fresh-plumaged juvenile Sooty Shear-waters, somewhat lean after their transequatorial migration, look rather different from older birds completing their molt (cf. Fig 23). SNGH. Off Hatteras, North Carolina, 29 May 2008.

Fig 23. Completing its molt (the tail is not fully grown), this fresh-plumaged adult Sooty Shear-water is fattening up for migration (cf. Fig 22). SNGH. Off Monterey, California, 14 Sep 2008.

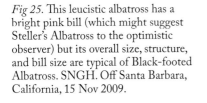

Fig 24. Leucistic tubenoses, like this Ashy Storm-Petrel, can be puzzling and sometimes exhibit patterns that suggest other (much rarer!) species. DLS. Off Santa Cruz, California, 5 Oct 2008.

Fig 25. This leucistic albatross has a bright pink bill (which might suggest Steller's Albatross to the optimistic observer) but its overall size, structure, and bill size are typical of Black-footed Albatross. SNGH. Off Santa Barbara, California, 15 Nov 2009.

Wedge-tailed), 3 petrels (Kermadec, Tahiti, Northern Fulmar), and 5 storm-petrels (Wilson's, Leach's, Wedge-rumped, Fork-tailed, White-faced).

Flight Manner

Tubenoses are usually seen in flight or on the water. Although on-the-water behaviors may at times be helpful for identification, *it is flight manner that defines most tubenoses* (Fig 26). The following is an overview of this essential aspect of tubenose identification, but there is no substitute for at-sea experience when it comes to learning how different species fly. In general, flying tubenoses are either foraging, transiting (moving to and from feeding and nesting areas, including migration), or taking evasive action (freak-out flight) in response to ships or predators such as skuas.

Many tubenoses are highly accomplished fliers largely because they need to travel long distances in search of food. This is due partly to the limited number of predator-free nesting sites, which do not always adjoin the best feeding areas, and partly to the inherently shifting character of marine habitats. The different wing morphologies and flight manners of tubenoses correlate strongly to life history traits such as geographic distribution, colony location, dispersal distances, and foraging behavior (Spear & Ainley 1997).

In general, flight manner relates to wind direction, wind strength, bird behavior, and wing morphology. Wing morphology can be described by two ratios: wing-loading (body mass

Fig 26. In moderate to strong winds, Sooty Shearwaters often tower in high arcs and race across the sky, whereas in calm conditions, or when molting, they usually fly low to the water (Fig 29). SNGH. Off Monterey, California, 26 Sep 2008.

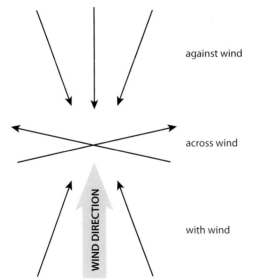

against wind

across wind

WIND DIRECTION

with wind

Fig 27. Diagrammatic representation of flight directions relative to wind direction. The main directions are into the wind (when birds often tack and stay fairly low) and across the wind (when birds can sail and wheel, at times very high above the sea, especially with the wind from slightly behind). Few birds fly with the wind blowing directly from behind.

relative to wing area) and aspect ratio (wing length divided by width). Lighter-bodied and broader-winged birds have lower wing-loading and lower aspect ratios, and they fly more buoyantly than do heavier-bodied and narrow-winged birds, which have higher wing-loading and higher aspect ratios.

The flight of tubenoses can be likened to sailing, but unlike inert canvas sails the birds use the undersides of their wings as sentient, self-adjusting sails to catch and manage the wind. In general, there are three modes of flight relative to wind direction—into the wind, across the wind, and with the wind (Fig 27). Unlike ships, however, birds don't have sails that can catch the wind when it blows from directly behind and so they tend to avoid this flight direction. Using the wind to sail is more energy-efficient than wing-flapping, particularly for heavy-bodied birds, which helps explain, e.g., why present-day albatrosses occur mainly in the windy Southern Ocean, where there is an uninterrupted 360° flow of wind around the planet, and not in the relatively confined North Atlantic Ocean.

To conserve energy, transiting birds generally flap as little as possible and sail directly across the wind or sail in a zigzag manner with the wind (as a sailing vessel jibes) or into the wind (as a sailing vessel tacks). Foraging birds may need to travel less quickly if they are seeking food visually and so they often fly into the wind, which usually involves slower flight with more prolonged flapping and shorter glides.

The most efficient flight is across the wind, by *dynamic sailing* (also called dynamic soaring). This flight mode can be seen in almost all tubenoses from Leach's Storm-Petrel to Wandering Albatross. When employed with maximum efficiency, as done by albatrosses in windy regions, birds can fly for hours without flapping, as follows. While flying across and slightly into the wind a bird tilts its underside up into the wind, the undersides of the wings catch the wind, and the bird sails up. At some point gravity will limit the height of the climb (birds climb higher in windier conditions). At the apex of the climb the bird tips its wings down so the wind flows across the uppersurface of the wings, and the bird glides down to near the sea surface. Then it tilts again and catches the wind to sail up, then glide down, on and on. If the wind is not strong enough, or the flight direction is not perfectly matched to wind direction, the bird often compensates or corrects by flapping a little at the bottom of the glide or even in the climb; in contrast, a ship's sails flap, or luff, when not fully filled with wind, which is an indication for the sailor to adjust the sails.

Sometimes a bird levels out at the apex of the climb and glides along high up, at other times it stalls and flaps at the apex before gliding down, perhaps to adjust its direction. Between arcs a bird often glides and banks low over the sea for some distance before sailing up again, so the flight progression is not simply a straightforward rollercoaster. Often the climb is steeper than the descent, and the apparent flight path (e.g., steepness of climb) will depend on the angle of the observer relative to the bird's flight direction. For example, a bird flying perpendicular to an observer's line of vision will show a "truer" path than one that is flying toward or away from the observer.

Because a bird rises with its underside facing into the wind, if it is downwind of you when it rises you see its underparts on the climb; but the reverse will be true if it is upwind, when its upperparts face you as it sails up (Fig 28). Thus, if a large shearwater downwind of you sails up and looks all-dark (i.e., on the underside) then it could be a Flesh-footed; but if a large shearwater upwind of you sails up and looks all-dark then you are seeing the upperparts, which

Fig 28. Birds flying across the wind that are downwind of an observer will bank up into the wind and show their underside as they climb, tip at the top of the arc, and show their upperside on the descent. Conversely, birds upwind of an observer on the same flight path will show their upperside on the climb and underside on the descent. Also note the steeper and shorter arcs of Black-capped Petrel (upper image) vs. the lower and longer arcs of the heavy-bodied Cory's Shearwater (lower image).
© Ian Lewington. Also cf. Fig 29.

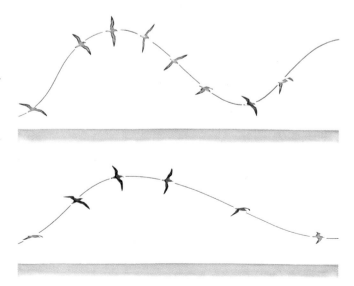

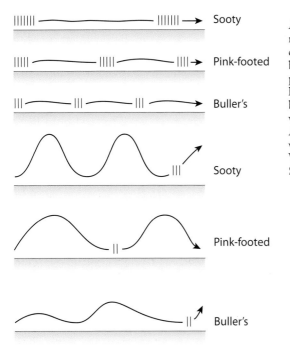

Fig 29. Diagrammatic representation of flight manners of Sooty, Pink-footed, and Buller's shearwaters in calm and strong winds (short vertical lines represent bursts of wingbeats). In calm, the heavy-bodied Sooty proceeds with hurried bursts of deep wingbeats followed by relatively long, low glides, whereas the light-bodied Buller's proceeds with a few quick, flicking wingbeats followed by relatively short, buoyant glides. Across a strong wind, Sooty towers high and steeply whereas Buller's wheels relatively low to the water. With its intermediate wing-loading, Pink-footed Shearwater flies between these extremes.

are uninformative (at least for Pink-footed vs. Flesh-footed). All else being equal, birds with higher wing-loading (e.g., Sooty Shearwater, Great Shearwater, Mottled Petrel) wheel higher and more steeply than birds with lower wing-loading (e.g., Buller's Shearwater, Cory's Shearwater, Galapagos Petrel). Also, when a bird tacks it tends to stay lower than when it jibes or sails across the wind.

In calm or light winds, flight manner can be very different from when it's windy. Many species (especially albatrosses and species with high wing-loading) track winds and do their best to avoid becoming becalmed, when they often simply sit on the water and wait for wind. Thus, migrating Sooty Shearwaters track winds around the Pacific and fly about 65,000 km on their round-trip migration (Shaffer et al. 2006), a distance more than 3 times greater than that offered by a direct route to and from their breeding and nonbreeding areas. Other species of generally calmer tropical waters have low wing-loading and are better suited to fly with less wind, e.g., Bulwer's Petrel. The structural and aerodynamic characteristics of Bulwer's Petrel and Sooty Shearwater, which represent extremes, are common to species in tropical and temperate regions, respectively (Spear & Ainley 1998). Basically, tropical tubenoses range widely over warmer, food-poor environments with lower wind speeds and feed mainly by seizing more mobile prey from the surface, for which a lighter body and broader wings are well suited. Conversely, temperate tubenoses inhabit colder, windier environments with food-rich areas, where they dive for less mobile prey, for which a heavier body and narrower wings are better suited.

In calm conditions, shearwaters usually fly low over the surface by bursts of flapping interspersed with short glides, sometimes seeming to glide low over the surface on a cushion of air trapped under the wings. Species with lower wing-loading (such as Buller's Shearwater) flap less quickly, glide more frequently, and have an easier, more buoyant flight; species with a higher wing-loading (such as Sooty Shearwater) flap quicker, glide less frequently (but often for longer distances), and have a more labored, hurried flight (Fig 29). Thus these two species, which have similar total lengths and wingspans, fly quite differently because of their different morphology.

In winds of 25–30 knots and greater, almost all species of shearwaters and petrels can wheel high and exhibit the classic rollercoaster flight associated with *Pterodroma* petrels. However, only those species with high wing-loading (such as Sooty Shearwater and Mottled Petrel) seem to cut the winds and tower comfortably, whereas species with lower wing-loading (e.g., Buller's Shearwater and Fea's Petrel) tend to stay lower, presumably because their lighter bodies and bigger wings make it more difficult for them to control high flight in strong winds. Low wing-loading also makes birds disproportionately susceptible to being swept inland by tropical storms; hence relatively large numbers of *Pterodroma* petrels compared to shearwaters turn up inland in eastern North America after hurricanes.

So, next time you're on a pelagic trip, or even watching tubenoses from shore, don't just identify the species and move on. Watch the way a bird flies and relate it to the wind speed, wind direction, and behavior—and soon a whole new world of field marks may open up to you.

Environmental Factors

Factors that work directly on the bird include bleaching (color loss through exposure to sunlight), wear (the physical abrasion of feathers), and discoloration from staining, such as from petroleum oil spills. Indirect environmental factors, which affect what an observer sees, or believes he or she sees, include lighting, distance, and wind conditions.

Bleaching and wear work together to cause the deterioration of feathers so that plumage needs to be replaced by molt (see Molts, Plumages, and Aging, pp. 38–45). The most extreme cases of bleaching are usually apparent on birds in their second plumage cycle, when retained juvenile feathers can be very bleached or worn (see P37a.6). In most tubenoses, bleaching and wear can cause birds to look odd, or atypical, but generally not to the extent that species identification is a problem. An exception might be that of bleached Ashy Storm-Petrels, which can look unusually pale in strong sunlight and thus might be mistaken for Fork-tailed Storm-Petrels.

In general, and given the same lighting conditions, fresher feathers are grayer and often look reflective, or frosty, whereas worn feathers tend to be browner and duller, without strong sheens. Observers familiar with a species in worn plumage may be surprised to see how different it appears in fresh plumage; e.g., fresh and frosty Pink-footed Shearwaters have been mistaken for Buller's Shearwaters, and Buller's Shearwaters in worn plumage look rather different than they do in fresh plumage (Figs 30–31).

The importance of lighting and distance to evaluating an observation at sea cannot be overemphasized (Figs 32–35). Most tubenose misidentifications result from misjudging size, which is all too easy without familiar frames of reference, or from illusions resulting from a combination of distance and lighting. The best lighting is with the sun relatively high in the sky (more than 45° above the horizon) and at one's back, preferably with high clouds to reduce glare; cloudier skies and paler gray seas are best for spotting birds, but patterns and colors can be difficult to discern; partly blue skies and seas allow patterns and colors to be seen (and are better for photography), but birds are more difficult to spot against such backgrounds. Bright overcast skies tend to shadow underwings and increase the apparent width of black underwing margins (such as on *Pterodroma* petrels). Conversely, low-angle sun early and late in the day heightens contrast, and sun glare often bleeds out white areas and makes them appear more extensive (Fig 36), such as those on underwing margins or the rump patches of storm-petrels; this is particularly true when observers are close to the sea surface such as on smaller boats. Thus, e.g., Black-vented Shearwaters early and late in the day can appear bright "black-and-white" and be mistaken for Manx Shearwaters (Fig 37); or Pink-footed Shearwaters can appear to have dark caps and bright white underwings, inviting confusion with Buller's Shearwater. Given low-angle sun in mostly cloudy to overcast conditions a Leach's Storm-Petrel appears black with a bright white uppertail-covert band, but under high-angle sun with high clouds and

Fig 30. Buller's Shearwater in fresh plumage, showing the bright pattern familiar to West Coast pelagic birders. SNGH. Off Monterey, California, 22 Sep 2007.

Fig 31. Buller's Shearwater in worn plumage, appearing much browner and less contrasting than typical of West Coast migrants. SNGH. South Island, New Zealand, 27 Mar 2008.

diffuse light the same bird appears warm dark brown, and dusky markings may be apparent on the duller-looking white uppertail coverts. Moreover, a bird's position relative to the sun angle and to an observer can cause its appearance and color tones to change in a matter of seconds (Figs 38–39).

All observers have a distance beyond which they cannot identify a bird, and this distance generally increases with experience. However, most observers tend to underestimate distance and believe, e.g., that a bird 500 m distant is only 200–300 m away; clearly, this will have implications for judging size or for believing what features should be visible at a given distance. If a bird is simply too far away to identify, then there is little to be gained by watching it. Remember, distance is the great deceiver and imagination the great receiver—more can be learned by studying closer birds. Conversely it is very helpful to watch, say, a close Pink-footed Shearwater or Great Shearwater and follow it into the distance. At the limits of visibility it will still be the same species, even though you can no longer see the features you used to identify it when it was close. In this way you can absorb subtleties of flight manner, shape, and overall pattern, which can improve your pelagic birding skills greatly.

Size judgment of birds at sea, particularly lone birds, can be difficult at best. Even very experienced observers can be fooled easily by a lone bird, especially one out of context. The sea has no yardsticks, and estimating wave and swell heights at a distance is fraught with potential for misjudgment. If you watch seabirds from different size vessels then you will also need to calibrate your size impressions for the size of a vessel and your height above the sea. For example, from a small boat in gentle seas a Black-footed Albatross can look really big to an observer low to the water, as might even be true of a Black Storm-Petrel in calm conditions. But from high up on a larger vessel, the same albatross can look deceptively small, especially if viewed against a seascape of big swells and impressive waves, and the storm-petrel might not even be visible. Fog decreases the visible horizon, which can increase the apparent size of a bird.

Wind is another important environmental factor that relates to at-sea identification of tubenoses—as well as to their distribution. For example, wind is actually a "habitat" favored by albatrosses and other heavy-bodied species that experience difficulty flying in calm conditions. Wind speed and relative direction can greatly affect how a bird flies (see Flight Manner, above), not to mention how well an observer can see and watch a bird if he or she is being buffeted and coated with salt spray!

Appearance and Topography

Being able to accurately describe and understand what you see are essential steps in any identification process. Because good close-range views of many tubenoses tend to be brief, observers should learn to appreciate the overall structure and plumage patterns of birds viewed at a distance before worrying about details such as how deeply a tail may be forked.

Overall Size and Structure

Even without other species for comparison it is relatively easy in almost all cases to place a tubenose into the category of small (storm-petrel), medium (petrel/shearwater), or large (albatross) (see Figs 13–15). Finer-level distinctions within these groups can be more difficult but are often a fundamental first step in any species-level identification. Such evaluations are best achieved with other species for comparison. For example, a lone Black-vented Shearwater might be confused with the much larger Pink-footed Shearwater based simply on similarities in plumage pattern, but the size difference would be apparent if the species were together or if another known species were present for comparison, such as a Sooty Shearwater (bigger than Black-vented, smaller than Pink-footed).

Fig 32. In low-angle backlighting, the white underwing panels of a Sooty Shearwater are muted but nonetheless contrast distinctly with the dark remiges (cf. Figs 33–35). SNGH. Off Bodega Bay, California, 24 Sep 2006.

Fig 33. In low-angle lighting, only minutes after Fig 32 was taken, the white underwing panels of a Sooty Shearwater flash bright silvery white and the whole bird appears paler overall (cf. Figs 36–37). SNGH. Off Bodega Bay, California, 24 Sep 2006.

Fig 34. Even in light fog and low-angle lighting the white underwing panels of a Sooty Shearwater can be striking (cf. Figs 32–33, 35). SNGH. Off Bodega Bay, California, 24 Sep 2006.

Fig 35. In thicker fog, the white underwing panels of a Sooty Shearwater can disappear altogether (cf. Figs 32–34). Notice the overall dark aspect, relatively slim body, and narrow wings, which distinguish this silhouette from that of a Northern Fulmar. SNGH. Off Bodega Bay, California, 24 Sep 2006.

Fig 36. Two light morph Wedge-tailed Shear-waters showing how direct sunlight and a slight difference in angle can wash out the contrast between the white coverts and "dark" remiges. SNGH. Western Pacific, 20°N, 147°E, 19 Apr 2007

Fig 37. Bright, low-angle sunlight can transform the normally muted plumage contrasts of a Black-vented Shearwater into a contrasting pattern that could suggest Manx, Newell's, or Townsend's shearwaters. Note lack of a discrete dark thigh patch, dusky markings on undertail coverts. SNGH. Off Baja California, Mexico, 12 Sep 2006.

Figs 38–39. These two images of an individual juvenile White-faced Storm-Petrel in fresh plumage, taken within a minute of each other, illustrate how lighting can dramatically—and quickly—change apparent plumage tones. SNGH. Off Hatteras, North Carolina, 28 Jul 2007.

Structural features that lend tubenoses distinctive shapes are their wing length and wing width, tail length and shape, head size and shape, and body size relative to wing area. Such differences are not always conveyed easily by standard measurements. Although simple linear measurements of Buller's Shearwater (L 43–45.5 cm, WS 96–104 cm) and Sooty Shearwater (L 43–45.5 cm, WS 97–106 cm) almost completely overlap, these two species are quite different in shape because Buller's has a longer neck, longer tail (115–135 mm vs. 83–97 mm in Sooty), and distinctly broader wings, and it weighs much less (around 425 g vs. 800 g for Sooty).

At sea it is often difficult to disassociate size, structure, and behavior because, all else being equal, larger birds have slower wingbeats than do smaller birds. However, failure to uncouple these aspects can sometimes compromise size perceptions, particularly if comparisons are made with different wind speeds or even wind directions. For example, in calm or light winds, or even when flying into a moderate wind, the languid flapping of a Black Storm-Petrel translates to "large size." But when the same bird is sailing quickly across moderate winds it may give only occasional, relatively quick and shallow wingbeats, which can cause it to appear smaller, more like a Chapman's Storm-Petrel.

If confronted by an unfamiliar tubenose, try to evaluate its overall structure in terms of wing length relative to wing width, tail length relative to wing width (is the tail longer or shorter than the width of the wings at the body?), and head and neck projection relative to tail projection (is the head and neck projection forward of the wings shorter than, longer than, or similar to the tail projection behind the wings?). Other structural characters (see below) can be helpful, such as forehead shape (gently sloping, steep, bulbous, etc.), bill shape (relatively thick, slender, long, etc.), and tail shape (squared, strongly graduated, deeply forked, slightly notched, etc.), but these details should be built upon the overall shape.

Plumage Patterns

For better or worse, most tubenoses are hued in shades of blackish, dark brown, gray, and white, and most are either dark above and white below, or all-dark. Dark areas tend to be blacker or grayer when fresh and then fade to browner, and their apparent tones can be greatly affected by lighting: dark browns look cold and blackish in overcast lighting but warm and even gingery in bright sunlight (see P6.11–P6.12). The dark undersides of the remiges and greater coverts on several species have a reflective sheen, the strength of which varies greatly with angle of lighting.

On any unfamiliar all-dark tubenose check for any underwing flashes and any other areas of contrast, as well as noting overall structure and bill color. On "black-and-white" tubenoses check the width and distribution of any dark underwing margins (beware of lighting effects) and the color of the undertail coverts (dark or white?). The pattern and extent of dark on the head and neck sides is also helpful for distinguishing some species (such as Hawaiian and Galapagos petrels, or Townsend's and Galapagos shearwaters) but has to be evaluated carefully. As viewed from above, dark head and neck sides often appear as a cowl or a bulge on the chest sides, but viewed from below the same pattern can appear as a shallow dark cap (see P28.2 vs. P28.7); a good side-on view is best for determining head and neck patterns.

On storm-petrels, it can be important to note the shape and size of the pale upperwing band and the shape and extent of any white rump patch. For example, on Leach's Storm-Petrel the upperwing band tends to widen toward the front edge of the wing and it usually reaches the wing bend; on Grant's [Band-rumped] Storm-Petrels the ulnar band is shorter, is more even in width, and usually does not reach the wing bend. The white rump patch on Leach's is often longer than wide, is slightly U-shaped, and does not wrap around the sides of the undertail coverts; the white band on Grant's [Band-rumped] is typically wider than long, tends to be more parallel sided, and wraps around to the lateral undertail coverts.

Topography

An understanding of topography is important for being able to describe accurately what you see. Tubenoses have the same general structure as most birds, but some of the proportions differ, especially the wings of longer-winged species. The general features of tubenose topography are shown in Figs 40–46.

Tubenoses on the water look very different from tubenoses in flight (Figs 42–43). On a swimming tubenose you basically see the head, neck, chest, flanks, "upperparts" (including the closed wings and the tail), and undertail coverts. The undertail coverts of most tubenoses are notably long and full, covering much of the tail. The wings are folded so that mostly what you see are the coverts (which cloak the secondaries) and the projecting tips of the outer primaries, which lie over the tail. On longer-winged species with a long humerus (see below), the elbow sticks up and creates a variable hump on the back.

Unlike most birds we see every day (such as songbirds, gulls, and ducks), many of the larger tubenoses (especially albatrosses) have a relatively long humerus (the upper arm bone). This results in a "double-jointed" wing, with a bend at the elbow (between the humerus and ulna) as well as the usual bend at the wrist (between the carpal joint, where the primaries are attached, and the ulna, where the secondaries are attached) (Fig 42). At the other extreme among tubenoses, the southern storm-petrels (such as Wilson's) have a short ulna, which results in an almost triangular, swallow-like wing shape.

Tubenoses have ten *primaries* (p), or primary flight feathers. These are attached to the hand bones and are numbered outward. Thus p1 is the short innermost primary and p10 the long outermost primary. As the wing closes, the bases of outer primaries slide under the inner primaries and the primaries overall slide under the secondaries and tertials. Mostly what you see of the primaries on a closed wing is the tips of the outer primaries. The *wing projection* is the projection of the wingtip beyond the tail tip, which can be helpful for some identifications. When evaluating wing structure, beware of pitfalls provided by birds that are molting their outer primaries; e.g., a Sooty Shearwater with the outer primaries not fully grown can look relatively short- and blunt-winged, inviting confusion with Short-tailed Shearwater.

The *secondaries* (s), or secondary flight feathers, are attached to the ulna bone of the forearm. Secondaries vary in number among species (from 11 in small storm-petrels to 38 in large albatrosses) and are numbered inward; thus s1 is the outermost, adjacent to p1. The innermost secondaries are called tertials, which are elongated feathers that act as coverts for the closed wing.

On most birds the humerus bone is short and any feathers associated with it are small and not really noticeable; thus the tertials slide under and merge with the scapulars where the wing meets the body. However, because long-winged birds such as albatrosses have a long humerus they have an "extra" stretch of wing, which lies between the secondaries (and their coverts) and the scapulars. The *humerals* are the long, fairly strong wing feathers that fill the "gap" between the secondaries and the scapulars (the tertials slide under them), and they are overlain by humeral coverts (Fig 42).

The *greater secondary upperwing coverts* (often just called greater coverts) mostly or completely conceal the secondaries on resting birds (Fig 43). The coverts immediately above the greater coverts are usually termed *median coverts*. (For simplicity I follow this convention here, but note that "median coverts" are not homologous feather groups across species: on tubenoses they are ostensibly a second row of greater coverts while on songbirds they are simply the largest lesser coverts.)

The *scapulars* are a group of feathers that originate from a point at the base of the humerus. They fan out to protect the base of the wings at rest and form a seamless join between the wings and body in flight (Figs 41–42).

Fig 40. Juvenile Sooty Shearwater. Note how p10 is appreciably narrower and more tapered than the other primaries, something common to many juvenile petrels and albatrosses. SNGH. Off Cape Hatteras, North Carolina, 25 May 2009.

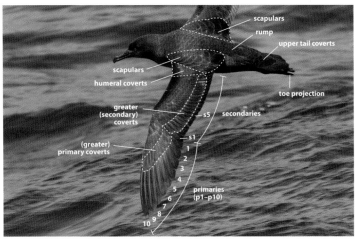

Fig 41. Sooty Shearwater. Subtle contrasts between fresher secondaries and relatively faded primaries and greater coverts indicate a bird older than its first cycle (when all wing feathers would be juvenile, with comparable wear). SNGH. Off Monterey, California, 11 May 2008.

Fig 42. Adult Steller's Albatross. Compare wing anatomy with Fig 43. SNGH. Torishima, Japan, 1 May 2008.

Fig 43. Adult Steller's Albatross. Note how the tertials and humerals bunch up on the closed wing (cf. Fig 42). SNGH. Torishima, Japan, 1 May 2008.

The tails of most tubenoses consist of 12 *rectrices* (r) (the singular of which is *rectrix*), six on each side of the midpoint. Rectrices are numbered outward from the central rectrix (r1) to the outermost rectrix (r6) on each side of the tail (Fig 42). Tail shape and length can be of use in tubenose identification, as well as whether or not the toes project beyond the tail tip. Note, though, that all species can pull in their feet under the relatively long and plush under-tail coverts so that no toes (and no toe projection) are apparent (Fig 44).

In most albatrosses and petrels the tail is slightly to strongly graduated (with the outer feathers progressively shorter), the most extreme examples being the long and strongly gradu-ated tails of Wedge-tailed Shearwater, Bulwer's Petrel, and the sooty albatrosses (genus *Phoe-betria*). Tail shape differences among storm-petrels can be helpful for identification but always be aware of how molt and how the tail is held can affect tail shape. For example, if the lon-gest outer rectrices of an Ashy Storm-Petrel are missing, then its tail may look squared or even rounded, inviting confusion with Least Storm-Petrel (see S11.3); or if the outer rectrices of a Leach's Storm-Petrel are worn or molting, its tail can look fairly squared, similar to a Grant's [Band-rumped] Storm-Petrel (see S5.5). Also note that a spread tail can appear relatively squared or rounded, but the same tail held closed can show a notch or shallow fork.

Bill Structure and Color

The bill of a tubenose is covered by a set of horny plates (Fig 43), which are easily seen on spe-cies such as Northern Fulmar and albatrosses. Bill size and shape can be important in tuben-ose identification. Obvious differences are those between the relatively thick bills of medium-sized and larger *Pterodroma* petrels and the relatively slender bills of shearwaters. More subtle differences, best evaluated from photos, are those between the relatively small, slender bill of Ashy Storm-Petrel and the bigger, stouter bill of Black Storm-Petrel. When making some judgments, note that male albatrosses and petrels tend to have slightly longer and deeper, or stronger, bills than females, and that immatures tend to have more slender bills than do adults (see Figs 18–19).

Bill coloration and pattern can be important for identifying some albatrosses and petrels (all storm-petrels and gadfly petrels have basically all-black bills). For example, an easy way to pick out a Flesh-footed Shearwater sitting among Sooty Shearwaters is to look for a bright pink, black-tipped bill (vs. the all-dark bill of a Sooty). Among mollymawks, details of bill color and pattern can be essential for age and species identification. More subtle differences in bill color probably remain to be described and evaluated, such as among the small shearwaters; if such differences prove consistent, they may be invaluable in tricky identifications and may be documented with good photos.

Leg and Foot Color

Details of leg and foot color can be useful for identification but are rarely visible at sea, although they may be captured by photos. In many cases, the feet are tucked into the under-tail coverts and simply not visible. On shearwaters with mostly pinkish or bluish legs and feet the outer or rear edges of the legs and toes are often blackish, which can greatly affect one's perception of leg color (Fig 46). On many gadfly petrels the legs and basal portions of the feet are pinkish or bluish whereas the distal portions of the toes and webs are black, almost as if they have been dipped in ink. On some taxa of small shearwaters, age-related changes in foot color have been suggested (Bretagnolle & Attié 1996), and such variation should be investi-gated further.

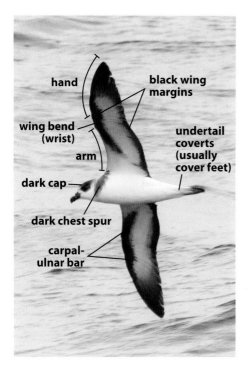

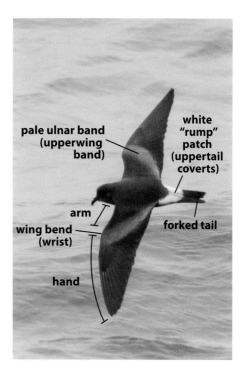

Fig 44. Black-capped Petrel. SNGH. Off Hatteras, North Carolina, 23 May 2008.

Fig 45. Leach's Storm-Petrel. SNGH. Off Santa Barbara, California, 25 Jul 2009.

Fig 46. Several shearwater species, including Buller's Shearwater, have bicolored legs and feet, with the outer and hind portions being black, the inner and front portions pinkish. SNGH. North Island, New Zealand, 26 Mar 2007.

Molts, Plumages, and Aging

Feathers are not permanent—they wear out and need to be replaced. Molt is simply the normal and regular growth of feathers, by which plumages are attained. As a rule, tubenoses do not molt when they are breeding, and immatures and nonbreeding adults molt earlier than do adults (Figs 47–50). The prebasic molt of breeders can be shorter and finish earlier than that of nonbreeders (as in southern-breeding transequatorial migrants; Figs 47, 49) or can be more protracted and finish later (as in northern hemisphere residents and northern-breeding transequatorial migrants; Figs 48, 50).

Fig 47. Provisional wing molt schedules for Sooty Shearwater; some postjuvenile molts occur in northern hemisphere (N Hem) but PB2 can start (and perhaps complete?) in first southern hemisphere (S Hem) summer. Green indicates first prebasic (PB1 = prejuvenile) molt in nest; orange indicates subsequent wing molts (PB2 = second prebasic, PB = later prebasic molts); paler tones indicates plumages. Great Shearwater (and perhaps other transequatorial-migrant *Ardenna*) may be similar.

Months=	J	F	M	A	M	J	J	A	S	O	N	D
S Hem		PB1				Juvenile = First Basic						
S Hem	PB2, some may complete in south					Second Basic						
S/N Hem		PB2, suspending for northward migration?				Second Basic						
N Hem			PB nonbreeders					Adult Basic				
N Hem				PB breeders				Adult Basic				

Fig 48. Provisional wing molt schedules for Northern Fulmar; see Fig 47 for key.

A	M	J	J	A	S	O	N	D	J	F	M
		PB1				Juvenile = First Basic					
	PB2					Second Basic					
			PB nonbreeders						Adult Basic		
				PB breeders, possibly suspends over winter							

Fig 49. Provisional wing molt schedules for Wilson's Storm-Petrel; see Fig 47 for key; blue indicates (complete) preformative molt. Most postjuvenile molts occur in northern hemisphere but preformative molt can suspend to finish in first southern hemisphere summer.

	J	F	M	A	M	J	J	A	S	O	N	D
S/N/S Hem			PB1			Juvenile= First Basic			Preformative Molt			
N Hem	Formative Plumage						PB2			Second Basic		
N Hem					PB nonbreeders					Adult Basic		
N Hem						PB breeders				Adult Basic		

Fig 50. Provisional wing molt schedules for Leach's Storm-Petrel; see Fig 47 for key.

	M	J	J	A	S	O	N	D	J	F	M	A
N Hem			PB1				Juvenile= First Basic					
N (S) Hem			PB2, some probably complete in south				Second Basic					
N/S Hem					PB nonbreeders					Adult Basic		
N/S Hem						PB breeders, may suspend for southward migration						

Noting the proportions of molting birds and how far their primary molt has progressed (see below) and nonmolting birds (in worn and fresh plumage, if possible) can provide important information on molt timing, molt duration, and age composition of a population. For example, second prebasic molts start earlier than subsequent prebasic molts except in Wilson's Storm-Petrel, which has a complete preformative molt. Under at-sea conditions it can be difficult to distinguish fresh juveniles from birds that have recently completed molt. For example, some fresh-plumaged Northern Fulmars in October or Black-capped Petrels in August may be juveniles or perhaps in fresh second basic plumage.

As well as aiding in age determination, wing molt timing may also be helpful for species identification if similar-looking species breed at different seasons, as do Cape Verde [Fea's], Desertas [Fea's], and Zino's petrels (Howell & Patteson 2007).

The most conspicuous molt tends to be in the wings, especially among the primaries, and with practice observers should find primary molt quite easy to see and record (Figs 51–58). Among petrels and storm-petrels the primary molt starts with p1 or p2 (NCSM specimens of Black-capped Petrel, and see P20.7; also Pyle 2008) and proceeds out to p10 (the extent to which molt initiates with p1 rather than p2 has yet to be investigated critically). In these species I find it helpful to score wing molt in the field by how far it has progressed in the primaries: are there missing or growing feathers in the inner (p1-p4), middle (p5-p7), or outer (p8-p10) primaries?

Often the inner 3–4 primaries are dropped almost simultaneously, so that there is an obvious gap in the inner wing (Figs 51–52, 55); the middle primaries tend to be molted gradually, 1–2 at a time; the outer primaries may be molted gradually or, in some species, may all be growing at once, which can compromise flight for a short period. Species that molt several outer primaries at once tend to do so because they have only a limited time available for molt, such as long-distance migrants (e.g., Great and Sooty shearwaters) or species with a short period between breeding seasons (e.g., Black-footed Albatross); these birds may feed intensively and fast while molting, and also tend to congregate in food-rich areas where they don't need to fly great distances.

When wing molt has progressed to around p4-p5, many species (such as Black-capped Petrel, Pink-footed Shearwater, and Wilson's Storm-Petrel) synchronously shed most or all of the greater upperwing secondary coverts; species with white bases to the secondaries often show white upperwing stripes at this stage of molt, before the coverts grow out and cover the white bases (Fig 52). The primary coverts are usually molted sequentially, along with each corresponding primary.

The secondaries tend to start molt from at least three points: from s1 and s5 inward and from one or two points among the inner secondaries. The secondaries usually start molt after primary molt has progressed out to the middle primaries. This means birds older than 1 year can often be distinguished by slight contrast between the fresher outer secondaries and the variably worn primaries (and greater coverts); on juvenile birds all feathers grow simultaneously and there is no strong contrast (see Figs 40–41; also see Pyle 2008). Tail molt usually occurs toward the end of, or after completion of, primary molt, and starts with the central rectrix (r1) or sometimes the outermost (r6); r5 is often the last feather to grow.

Albatrosses have novel wing molt strategies (Howell 2006c, Howell 2010b, Rohwer & Edwards 2006), with the primaries being split into two series: p8-p10 molt outward as a series (annually in *Phoebastria*; biennially in southern hemisphere genera), whereas the middle primaries appear to molt inward from p7, perhaps in stepwise waves.

Age Terminology and Plumage Cycles

In this book I use the Humphrey-Parkes (H-P) system of naming molts and plumages, which is based upon plumage cycles and the concept of homology (Howell et al. 2003, 2004,

Fig 51. Sooty Shearwater. In a pattern shared with many other species, most petrels shed their inner primaries almost synchronously, creating a fairly large and obvious gap in the trailing edge of the wing. SNGH. Off Monterey, California, 11 May 2008.

Fig 52. Sooty Shearwater. When molt reaches the middle primaries being shed, most or all of the greater coverts are shed synchronously. This often results in a white stripe on the upperwing, produced by exposed bases to the secondaries. SNGH. Off Monterey, California, 11 May 2008.

Fig 53. Sooty Shearwater. After the new inner primaries and greater coverts grow, molt progresses through the middle and outer primaries (p6 is just starting to grow here). Unlike the greater secondary coverts, primary coverts grow sequentially. Molt in the secondaries proceeds inward from both s1 and s5 (the latter feather replaced on this bird), and outward from the tertials. SNGH. Off Monterey, California, 11 May 2008.

Fig 54. Sooty Shearwater. Molt progresses through the middle and outer primaries as the upperwing coverts, secondaries (s1 and the innermost ss have been shed), and some body feathers are renewed. SNGH. Off Monterey, California, 11 May 2008.

Fig 55. Wilson's Storm-Petrel. As with Sooty Shearwater, the inner primaries usually drop almost synchronously. This bird shows asymmetrical wing molt (not that rare in Wilson's Storm-Petrel): on the far wing, p1-p2 are growing, p3-p4 and the greater coverts have been shed; on the near wing, p1-p3 are new, p4 and the greater coverts are growing, p5 has been shed. SNGH. Off Hatteras, North Carolina, 25 May 2009.

Fig 56. Most adult Wilson's Storm-Petrels complete wing molt by early Sep (compare with Figs 57–58); this bird is growing p9, with p10 shed, and is also molting its secondaries. SNGH. Off Hatteras, North Carolina, 17 Aug 2009.

Fig 57. Wilson's Storm-Petrel is unusual in having a preformative wing molt, which usually starts in late summer or fall, when adults are completing their wing molt (see Figs 49, 56), and may be suspended over southward migration to complete in the southern summer (see Fig 58). SNGH. Off Hatteras, North Carolina, 16 Aug 2009.

Fig 58. Wilson's Storm-Petrel in later stages of presumed preformative wing molt, with p9-p10 old and p8 growing. Such birds presumably complete this molt by austral mid-summer and are in mostly fresh plumage when they migrate north in Apr–May. SNGH. North Island, New Zealand, 8 Nov 2008.

Humphrey & Parkes 1959). In the H-P system only molts produce plumages (plumages are not attained by wear), and the word *plumage* refers to a coat of feathers not to the appearance of the feathers; thus there is a one-to-one correlation of plumages to molts. A plumage cycle (often shortened simply to cycle) runs from a given plumage or molt to the next occurrence of the same plumage and molt. The first plumage cycle extends from the acquisition of juvenile plumage (equivalent to first basic plumage; Howell et al. 2003) to the start of the second prebasic molt. In most tubenoses the juvenile plumage is often not distinguishable in the field from that of older immatures or adults, and molt timing (see Figs 47–50) or state of plumage (fresh or worn) may be the only clues to aging.

Basic and Formative Plumages

As adults, all birds follow a fundamentally similar pattern of plumage succession and have a molt by which most or all of their feathers are replaced. The plumage attained by this complete molt is called *basic plumage* because that's what it is—a bird's basic plumage. The molt by which basic plumage is attained is the *prebasic molt*. In most adult tubenoses the basic plumage cycle is about 12 months long, i.e., an annual cycle. The prebasic wing molt of tubenoses typically occurs between breeding seasons, although molt of body feathers often starts when birds are nesting. Some birds (but no tubenoses, as far as known) have a second plumage added into their basic cycle. This added plumage is called an *alternate plumage*: it alternates with the basic plumage, and it is attained by a *prealternate molt*.

Most species of tubenoses appear to molt straight from juvenile (first basic) into second basic plumage at about 1 year of age. A few species, however, appear to have a novel molt added into their first cycle (i.e., a molt with no counterpart in subsequent cycles); this is called the *preformative molt,* which produces formative plumage. The preformative molt is usually limited to head and body feathers but is complete in Wilson's Storm-Petrel. In *Phoebastria* albatrosses and several species of shearwaters, the body molt starting within 6–8 months of fledging may be a preformative molt but seems more likely to be the start of the protracted second prebasic molt (offsetting the molt of head and body feathers from that of flight feathers would reduce energy demands for when the all-important remiges are replaced). After the first cycle, molts of prebreeding immatures are much like those of breeding adults but average earlier, are more protracted, and, in larger species such as albatrosses, are often more extensive among the primaries and secondaries. This is because the immatures have more time to molt than do breeders, which have only a relatively short period for wing molt between breeding seasons.

Molt Strategies of Tubenoses

The molt strategies of a bird reflect a finely honed balance with other aspects of its lifecycle—mainly breeding and migration—in combination with food availability, environmental conditions, foraging experience, fitness, and the overall size of an individual bird. The main requirement for molt is sufficient and predictable food, which tends to be more abundant in the temperate northern hemisphere during the northern summer. This helps explain why several southern-breeding species (such as Great and Sooty shearwaters) undertake long transequatorial migrations to molt in North American waters at this season; the North Pacific albatrosses also molt in this season. First-year individuals, which are not breeding, typically molt earlier than do adults.

As noted under Flight Manner (pp. 24–28), tubenoses of tropical latitudes tend to have lower wing-loading and range widely over warmer, food-poor environments, whereas tubenoses of temperate habitats tend to have higher wing-loading and inhabit windier, food-rich environments. Tropical tubenoses (such as Wedge-tailed Shearwater and Black-capped Petrel) also tend to have more protracted wing molts during which they maintain good flight capabilities, whereas temperate tubenoses (such as Short-tailed Shearwater and Mottled Petrel) often have relatively rapid wing molts during which they may be temporarily almost flightless but can dive for concentrated prey that fuels a quick molt; reduced wing area during molt may even improve diving proficiency in shearwaters because these birds flap their wings underwater.

Within tubenoses that molt regularly in North American waters, four groups can be identified in terms of breeding latitudes and migrations (Table 5). Like most attempts to draw lines on natural processes these groups do not indicate clear-cut differences, and some species are grouped as subjective best fits.

A. *Northern Residents.* Relatively few species remain year-round in the temperate and subtropical northern oceans, and those that do molt after breeding. The smaller species, petrels and storm-petrels, have protracted wing molts that start in late summer and continue gradually over the winter or may be suspended in mid-winter before completing in spring. The second prebasic molt occurs earlier, mostly during the northern summer when food is plentiful (Fig 48).

The North Pacific albatrosses are a subset of northern residents, but because of their large size they do not have sufficient time to replace all of their flight feathers in the few months available between the protracted breeding seasons. They have compensated for this with a novel strategy whereby the heavily worn outer three primaries are replaced every year, but the less exposed inner and middle primaries are usually replaced over two or more years. In some cases a bird may be unable to replace enough primaries between successive breeding seasons and it will skip a year of breeding to catch up with its molt (Langston & Rohwer 1996). These albatrosses undergo wing molt in late summer and fall, which corresponds to seasonal peaks in food abundance.

B. *Northern Migrants* breed in temperate or subtropical northern latitudes and withdraw to tropical or southern latitudes in the nonbreeding season. Their molts may be suspended for migration, such as with Cory's Shearwater and Leach's Storm-Petrel, which start primary molt while nesting and complete it in winter (Ainley et al. 1976, Monteiro et al. 1996). The second prebasic molt occurs earlier, mostly during the northern summer period of food abundance (Fig 50).

C. *Tropical Migrants* breed in tropical or subtropical latitudes and often range to food-rich areas within the tropics or subtropics to molt, sometimes traveling considerable distances in longitude (such as Wedge-tailed Shearwaters that migrate from Hawaii to western Mexico); several species (such as Parkinson's and Juan Fernandez petrels) are transequatorial migrants, but not to the extent of species in Group D. Mostly these species molt in the "summer season" of either hemisphere (March–September in the northern, September–March in the southern), but there are several exceptions in these relatively aseasonal environments. A notable exception is Murphy's Petrel, which appears to molt in the subtropical North Pacific during mid-winter. At least two species occurring in the region (Galapagos Petrel and Galapagos Shearwater) molt year-round, reflecting their year-round breeding schedules. The second prebasic molt generally appears to start a month or two earlier than the adult prebasic molt.

D. *Southern Migrants* are species that migrate from southern temperate or subtropical waters (where they breed) to northern temperate or subtropical waters to molt in the food-rich northern summer (Figs 47, 49). Generally these species have a relatively quick wing molt. The second prebasic molt strategy is variable: some birds molt in the southern hemisphere in late summer, before migrating north; some may spend their first year in the northern hemisphere and molt there slightly earlier than do the adults; and some start molt in the southern hemisphere and suspend it to complete in the northern hemisphere summer. Perhaps because of its relatively weak juvenile plumage, in combination with its long migrations, Wilson's Storm-Petrel has a complete preformative molt, which occurs slightly later than the adult prebasic molt (Fig 49). This strategy parallels that of other transequatorial migrants, such as Long-tailed Jaeger and South Polar Skua.

Table 5. Molt strategies of selected petrels, albatrosses, and storm-petrels that occur in the region (see p. XX). Group A: northern residents; prebasic wing molt in n fall through winter; molt incomplete and mainly during fall in albatrosses. Group B: n migrants; prebasic wing molt mainly in n winter on tropical or s nonbreeding grounds. Group C: tropical migrants; prebasic wing molt mainly in tropical or subtropical latitudes. Group D: austral migrants; prebasic wing molt mainly in temperate latitudes during n summer.

	A	B	C	D
Sooty Shearwater				X
Short-tailed Shearwater				X
Flesh-footed Shearwater				X
Pink-footed Shearwater				X
Buller's Shearwater				X
Wedge-tailed Shearwater			X	
Great Shearwater				X
Cory's Shearwater		X		
Scopoli's Shearwater		X		
Manx Shearwater		X		
Townsend's Shearwater			X	
Black-vented Shearwater			X	
Galapagos Shearwater			X	
Christmas Shearwater			X	
Black-capped Petrel			X	
Bermuda Petrel			X	
Desertas/Cape Verde Petrel			X	
Trinidade Petrel			X	
Cook's Petrel			X	
Mottled Petrel				X
Hawaiian Petrel			X	
Galapagos Petrel			X	
Juan Fernandez Petrel			X	
Kermadec Petrel			X	
Herald/Henderson Petrel			X	
Tahiti Petrel			X	
Northern Fulmar	X			
Parkinson's Petrel			X	
Black-footed Albatross	X			
Laysan Albatross	X			
Steller's Albatross	X			
Wilson's Storm-Petrel				X
Leach's Storm-Petrel		X		

Table 5. *cont.* Molt strategies of selected petrels, albatrosses, and storm-petrels

	A	B	C	D
Townsend's [Leach's] Storm-Petrel		X		
Grant's [Band-rumped] Storm-Petrel			X	
Darwin's [Band-rumped] Storm-Petrel			X	
Wedge-rumped Storm-Petrel			X	
Black Storm-Petrel		X		
Least Storm-Petrel		X		
Ashy Storm-Petrel	X			
Markham's Storm-Petrel			X	
Fork-tailed Storm-Petrel	X			
White-faced Storm-Petrel			X	

HOW TO SEE TUBENOSES

Seeing tubenoses is as easy as getting on a boat and taking what is known as a pelagic trip, or simply "a pelagic." And some tubenoses can even be seen from shore, although usually not as well as they can from a boat. That said, a few tips may be helpful if you've never been on a pelagic or have tried only one or two. Because you'll be on a moving platform at all times, pelagic birding is some of the most challenging birding there is. As on land there will be slower birding days, and even on great days there will be slower periods. The number of bird species on a pelagic day trip may be only in the order of 12–20 (with perhaps only 4–10 tubenoses), but they'll include some good birds. Given the manageable number of species you can easily review the possibilities beforehand. So when somebody shouts out "Flesh-footed Shearwater" or "Fea's Petrel!" you have an image of what you are looking for and can pick out the right bird, which may simply fly by the boat once and be gone. You can determine which species might be seen by looking at trip reports from pelagics taken in the same area and season in earlier years; reports are usually available on websites maintained by pelagic trip operators. As with birding tours on land, if you're going on a pelagic it's good to pick a reputable company with experienced leaders who can help you see the birds and explain how to identify them. Word of mouth among the birding community is a good way to learn which are the best pelagic operators.

Good waterproof binoculars and a rainguard are important. You don't want to test the waterproofing of your binoculars at sea, but it's better to be prepared. Telescopes and tripods are not practical except on larger vessels (such as big ferries or cruise ships) and mainly in calmer seas. Obviously they're really helpful if you're watching from shore. Good 8-power or 7-power binoculars are better at sea than 10-power; the lower magnifications have a wider, brighter, and deeper field of view and are easier to hold steady—all big advantages on a moving platform while watching moving subjects over a moving surface. That said, a lot of watching from boats is best done with the naked eye, at least until you feel comfortable being on a moving platform. Think about trying to watch birds using binoculars from the back of a pickup truck driving down a dirt road—using your naked eye is a lot easier. However, when the boat stops, or birds are close, then this is the time to use your binoculars to get a good view of things.

Books could be written on the dos and don'ts of pelagic birding, but the best way to learn is to take a few trips. The following is some advice gleaned from years of pelagic trips (and see Howell 2007a). On the boat find a place with a wide field of view, sheltered from any wind buffeting, and not looking into the sun; this is not always possible, but aim for the best combination of these factors. From high up on a larger ship you can see farther and not lose sight of birds behind waves, but it can be difficult to spot birds against the ocean. Being nearer the sea surface it is easier to spot birds as they wheel above the horizon and to discern whether wingbeats are shallow or deep, but it is also easy to lose sight of birds behind waves. If you want help from leaders or more experienced birders stay fairly close to them—words can be hard to hear on a boat, birds often don't stay around long, and leaders tend to stand in the best places to see from.

Polarized sunglasses help greatly in cutting down glare, and sunscreen is a good idea, even on partly cloudy days, because reflection from the sea can be strong. Earplugs can be helpful if the boat has loud engines. Keep a dry cloth or tissues handy in a Ziploc bag for wiping off your lenses, which can be licked first to remove salt and avoid scratching. A cube or two of ice from an ice-chest is good for rinsing your hands and face of saltwater, and also refreshing. After a pelagic it's good to rinse off any salt spray residue with freshwater, to prolong the functional life of your optics.

Seasickness? If you've never been on a boat don't assume you'll get seasick, particularly if you take the following precautions. I think it's better to try a short trip free from drugs, as some seasickness medications can make you queasy, dry mouthed, and sleepy, none of which is likely to enhance your experience. Instead, get a good night's sleep; stay outside with a breeze in your face; watch the horizon; don't read or look down (review species you might see the day before—there aren't that many); and use your binoculars only to look at birds you can see with the naked eye. It's helpful to keep food and water on your person to avoid going into the cabin; eat light meals and keep something in your stomach during the trip. Some people find saltine crackers or ginger cookies are good to munch on; I find grapes and other sharp tastes, like mints, more refreshing. Standing all day at sea can be tiring, and on longer trips you can lie down or sit down and take naps.

One possibility for seeing pelagic species well on land is to follow the paths of tropical storms and seek birds pushed onshore or inland to reservoirs. In the East, hurricanes can carry birds inland as far as the eastern Great Lakes and also up the Mississippi watershed from the Gulf of Mexico. In the West, storms can sweep birds up into the Gulf of California and on to the Salton Sea (where at least eight species of tubenoses have been recorded; Patten et al. 2003) or other water bodies such as Lake Havasu on the Arizona/California border (Jones 1999).

CONSERVATION

Tubenose numbers today are a mere fraction of what they once were—before humans brought non-native mammals (including themselves) to former seabird havens across the planet. Of the 70 or so tubenose species recorded in the region, about one-third qualify as vulnerable or endangered globally due to human activities, past or present (Birdlife International 2010a). We should all be familiar with the decimation of whale stocks worldwide caused by hunting, but the fates of tubenoses have been no less dramatic. Pelagic trips out of California only 150 years ago could have encountered tens or hundreds of Steller's Albatrosses, perhaps even hundreds of Guadalupe Storm-Petrels—we can only imagine. Trips out of North Carolina at that time might have found thousands of Black-capped Petrels, hundreds of Desertas Petrels—and maybe even hundreds of Jamaican Petrels. We can only hope that someone writing 50 or 100 years from now will not be lamenting the loss of Townsend's Shearwater (Fig. 59), or of the great albatrosses, whose populations are in rapid decline. As whaling should be viewed in its historical context, the introduction of non-native mammals to islands was, for the most part, inadvertent. But by now we should have learned.

Fig 59. Townsend's Shearwater may today breed on only one island off Mexico, where it is preyed upon by feral cats. Without prompt action this rapidly declining species may become extinct in our lifetime. On this date, fresh plumage indicates a juvenile—confirmation that at least one pair bred successfully in 2010. MS. Baja California Sur, 20 Aug 2010.

Seabird conservation and study have traditionally focused on the breeding grounds, because birds are easiest to study there. The study of tubenoses at sea, where they spend most of their lives, involves numerous logistical factors that have limited this area of research. But problems at sea are also great, and understanding all aspects of a species' life history is necessary if we are to have any hope of conserving it. Likewise, an understanding of the entire marine environment, not just birds, is critical to maintaining the health of our planet.

Threats to Seabirds

Seabirds such as tubenoses are long-lived and adapted to periodic natural phenomena such as ocean food-web crashes, from which their populations recover over time. But the addition of human-induced mortality when seabird populations are at a naturally low ebb could push some species over the edge. Human-caused threats to seabirds can be divided broadly into competition and contamination. Competition includes the impact of fisheries and the modification of nesting habitats. Contamination includes the effects of oil, plastics, and other chemicals in the ocean, the effects of lights on vessels at night, and the impacts of introduced (non-native) species on nesting grounds.

Fisheries impact birds by overfishing stocks that are a resource shared by humans and seabirds; by causing seabird mortality as incidental catch (or "bycatch") through gill-netting, long-lining, or other fishing activities; and by wholesale marine habitat destruction, such as caused by bottom-trawling for fish, which effectively strip-mines the ocean floor. It has been calculated that around 1500 square km (580 square miles) of deep ocean floor are hit by trawls each day—*for every breath we take, an area covering 10 football pitches is stripped of its fish and invertebrates* (Roberts 2007:340); this short-term greed is not sustainable, its consequences are to the detriment of humans and seabirds alike. On land, seabird nesting sites can be built upon for homes or businesses, or altered for human recreational pursuits. The effects of oil and other chemical spills on seabirds should be well known, and the washing ashore of unsightly oiled birds on recreational beaches has forced this problem into our conservation consciousness. The effects of plastics in the sea are more insidious: small pieces of plastic look much like the food items of many tubenoses and are eaten by mistake. The plastics do not break down in the birds' stomachs but accumulate so that there is no room for food or liquid—and the birds die with a full stomach (Fig 60). At night, many seabirds are attracted to lights much as happens with moths and candles. If brightly lit vessels are anchored near nesting islands, the decks can become littered with birds (Fig 61), many of which become soiled or crawl off and die in corners.

Seabirds tend to nest on or under the ground and they seek predator-free islands on which to nest. Enter humans, with their rats, cats, dogs, mongooses, and other species that prey on adult and nestling seabirds. Thus, millions of seabirds have been killed worldwide and perhaps hundreds of islands made uninhabitable for nesting. Rabbits, goats, sheep, and other species trample nest burrows and modify habitat through overgrazing, which destabilizes soil. And introduced plants can grow up and cover areas with dense vegetation, making them unsuitable for birds that require open ground for nesting. Two tubenose species endemic to the region covered by this guide have become extinct in the past 100 years—the Jamaican Petrel and the Guadalupe Storm-Petrel. Both are apparently gone forever, killed on their nesting grounds by cats and other introduced mammals.

It's not all doom and gloom, though. With increased awareness and education, in tandem with regulation and restoration, seabird population declines are slowing and some species may even be increasing. The concept of marine reserves and protected areas, where fish stocks have a chance to recover and ecosystems can regenerate, is slowly catching on—but whereas about 12% of the Earth's land area is contained in protected areas, the corresponding figure for the sea is only about 0.6% (Roberts 2007:374). Fishermen don't want seabirds on hooks that could catch fish, and many are adopting techniques that reduce or eliminate seabird bycatch. The *Save the Albatross* campaign (www.savethealbatross.net) has been prominent in highlighting this worldwide issue. On islands where tubenoses and other seabirds nest, conservation groups (such as Island Conservation, www.islandconservation.org, and its sister organization Conservación de Islas) are working to eliminate non-native animals and plants so that seabird populations have a chance to recover or recolonize. Seabird and marine conservation awareness has come a long way in the past 50 years, but it still has a much longer way to go.

Seabirds as Indicators

Humans have relatively coarse-grain environmental filters, particularly with respect to the ocean; we are, after all, ostensibly terrestrial mammals. Our attempts to understand marine processes rely on a limited number of variables that we can measure, and as far as oceanography goes we're little more than dilettantes, albeit technologically sophisticated ones. Seabirds, on the other hand, are professionals—they feed and breed in the oceanic environment for a living, and if they fail, they die. If enough of them die it could be a sign that humans will soon follow along the road to extinction.

Monitoring seabird population trends can give us an index of marine ecosystem health, and seabird populations are easier to see and to study than fish and other organisms that lie below the inscrutable ocean surface. A fundamental first step in studying any organism is the ability to identify and name it. Hopefully this guide will aid in the identification, appreciation, monitoring, and conservation of tubenoses.

Fig 60. Plastics and other trash in the ocean can be mistaken for prey by albatrosses and fed to their young, whose stomachs become so full of plastics (which cannot be digested and passed through the system) that there is no room for real food. Thus, many juvenile Laysan and Black-footed albatrosses starve to death with a full stomach. After their bodies rot away, all that remains is a pile of bottle tops, fishing lures, and other agents of death. RdG. Midway Atoll, Hawaii, 3 Jan 2007.

Fig 61. Like moths drawn to a candle, seabirds (such as these Fork-tailed Storm-Petrels) are attracted to lights on ships, perhaps a form of night-blindness, and seem unable to leave the ring of light surrounding a vessel. Many cannot take off again or crawl into oily nooks and crannies where they starve to death. Untold thousands of seabirds probably die each year in this way (in this instance the birds were safely removed and released). KL. Off Aleutian Islands, Alaska, 1 Aug 2003.

etrels, which include shearwaters, comprise about 100 species of medium-sized to large pelagic birds found throughout the world's oceans (Figs 62–64). About 40 species have occurred in the region. Ages appear similar in all but giant-petrels (unrecorded in North America); sexes are similar but males average larger and often have bigger bills. Plumages are colored in black, dark browns, grays, and white, often in striking patterns, and several species are polymorphic. Bills are black in many species, gray in some, and pale yellowish or pinkish overall in others; legs and feet vary from black to pale pinkish or pale bluish overall. Molts are often not well known in terms of their timing and relationship to age and breeding status. Some species may have a partial preformative molt, and prebasic molts are typically complete, although some species do not always renew all secondaries and wing coverts annually.

For identification purposes, the species treated here are broken into three main groups: shearwaters, gadfly petrels, and other petrels. Shearwaters are further subdivided into large shearwaters (genera *Ardenna* and *Calonectris*) and small shearwaters (genus *Puffinus*), and gadfly petrels into Atlantic and Pacific species.

Fig 62. Larger gadfly petrels, such as this Black-capped Petrel (left), differ from shearwaters, such as Cory's Shearwater (right), in having a thicker, shorter bill and steeper forehead. SNGH. Off Hatteras, North Carolina, 5 Aug 2007.

Fig 63. Dark shearwaters and gadfly petrels can appear rather similar to one another but show characteristic shearwater vs. petrel differences, including flight manner not apparent in photos. On this juvenile Sooty Shearwater (aged by fresh plumage on this date), note the relatively long head/neck projection with a long slender bill, and fairly straight-held wings (cf. Fig 64). SNGH. Off Hatteras, North Carolina, 22 May 2007.

Fig 64. Dark morph Trinidad Petrel. Compared to Sooty Shearwater (Fig 63), note relatively short head/neck projection and short thick bill, slightly broader and more crooked wings; also note mid-primary molt (almost all Sooties off the East Coast in the spring are not in wing molt). SNGH. Off Hatteras, North Carolina, 23 May 2007.

SHEARWATERS

Shearwaters often comprise the predominant tubenoses seen on North American pelagic trips, and some species can be seen readily from shore, at times in thousands. Different species often associate together when feeding and resting (Figs 65–66), which can be helpful for identification. Shearwaters occur worldwide in tropical and mid-latitudes, with two species of *Ardenna* ranging seasonally into the cold high latitudes favored by fulmarine petrels. Three genera are recognized (see Taxonomy and an Identification Framework, pp. 14–21).

Large Shearwaters: Genera *Ardenna* and *Calonectris*

All 11 species of large shearwaters worldwide have occurred in North American waters—7 species in the s-breeding genus *Ardenna* and 4 in the n-breeding genus *Calonectris* (Figs 67–68). *Ardenna* are large migratory shearwaters that breed mostly in temperate and subtropical waters of the s hemisphere, with one species also in the tropics. All seven species have occurred in the Pacific and four in the Atlantic. In the Pacific region of North America, Buller's, Pink-footed, Flesh-footed, Sooty, and Short-tailed shearwaters are regular nonbreeding visitors, Wedge-tailed breeds in Mexico, and Great is a vagrant. In the Atlantic region, Great and Sooty shearwaters are regular nonbreeding visitors, Buller's and Short-tailed are vagrants.

Fig 65. Shearwaters often raft in mixed-species flocks. This group comprises one small species (Black-vented) and three large species (two Pink-footed, right center; a Buller's, front bird; and a Sooty, front left). SNGH. Off Monterey, California, 15 Oct 2006.

Fig 66. Off the East Coast, flocks of shear-waters can also include both small and large species. This group comprises one small species (Audubon's) and three large species (three Cory's, right center; a Sooty, back right; and a Great, far left). SNGH. Off Hatteras, North Carolina, 6 Jun 2009.

Ardenna shearwaters are rather variable in external appearance and may comprise more than one genus. They have narrow to fairly broad wings, variably graduated tails, relatively slender bills that vary from dark overall to pink with a black tip, and pale pinkish to dusky legs and feet. Their wingbeats are generally stiff and their flight is notably less agile than that of gadfly petrels. Most *Ardenna* species are relatively heavy bodied and dive well, for which their laterally compressed tarsi are suited. Dives are from the surface or heights of 3–5 m above the surface at about a 45˚ angle; underwater the feet and partially extended wings aid in propulsion and maneuvering. The relatively heavy-bodied and narrower-winged Sooty and Short-tailed are quite proficient divers that can reach depths of 50–70 m. Great, Pink-footed, and Flesh-footed can dive fairly well but usually less frequently and for shorter periods than Sooty, and these three species in particular are attracted to fishing boats. The lighter-bodied and broader-winged Buller's and Wedge-tailed rarely submerge completely and obtain their food at or near the surface. Three species are dark overall, three are bicolored, and one is dimorphic.

Calonectris are large migratory shearwaters of warmer inshore waters. They are the only large shearwaters that breed in the subtropical and temperate n hemisphere, three species in the ne Atlantic, one in the nw Pacific; all have been recorded as nonbreeding visitors to North American waters. In the Atlantic, Cory's and Scopoli's shearwaters are regular visitors and Cape Verde Shearwater is a vagrant; in the e Pacific, Streaked is very rare and Cory's a vagrant.

Fig 67. Large shearwaters mostly can be separated into dark-bellied and white-bellied species, as with these Short-tailed (behind) and Pink-footed shearwaters. SNGH. Off Monterey, California, 21 Sep 2007.

Fig 68. The two common, white-bellied large shearwaters off the East Coast are Great (left) and Cory's. As well as differences in size, head pattern, and plumage tones (such as dark vs. white undertail coverts), note longer, thicker neck, bigger head, and stout bill of Cory's. SNGH. Off Hatteras, North Carolina, 27 May 2007.

Calonectris shearwaters have broad wings, graduated tails, big pale bills (5–13% larger on males than females), and pale pinkish legs and feet. The light-boned structure and rounded tarsi of *Calonectris* species are reflected in their languid flight, with unhurried wingbeats and frequent glides, and in their predominantly surface feeding, although Cory's (at least) can dive deep on occasion (E. S. Brinkley, pers. comm.). *Calonectris* mainly feed over schooling fish and dolphins, and they tend not to be attracted to boats. The upperparts are gray-brown overall and the underparts bright white.

For species identification of large shearwaters note flight manner, overall plumage pattern, tail length and shape, any head and neck patterns, bill color and size, and underwing pattern. The commonest and most challenging identification problems among large shearwaters lie with Sooty vs. Short-tailed shearwaters in the Pacific (Figs 69–77) and with Cory's and Scopoli's shearwaters in the Atlantic (Figs 78–81). At long range, separation of Great and Cory's can also be challenging, and an appreciation of structural characters and flight manner is important (Figs 82–83).

Fig 69. Sooty Shearwater in fresh plumage. Notoriously similar to Short-tailed Shearwater, differing in structure and underwing pattern (cf. Figs 71–72). Note relatively long neck, sloping forehead, long bill (cf. Fig 70). SNGH. Off Bodega Bay, California, 30 Sep 2007.

Fig 70. Short-tailed Shearwater in fresh plumage. Notoriously similar to Sooty Shearwater, differing in structure and underwing pattern (cf. Figs 71–72); both species can show toes projecting beyond the tail tip. Note relatively short neck, rounded forehead, small bill (cf. Fig 69). SNGH. Off Bodega Bay, California, 20 Nov 2010.

Fig 71. Sooty Shearwater. Note long head/neck projection with relatively long bill, wings held fairly straight, and contrast between pale panel on underwing coverts and dark primary bases (cf. Fig 72). SNGH. Lima, Peru, 16 Sep 2007.

Fig 72. Short-tailed Shearwater. Note relatively short neck, steep forehead, and small bill, plus slightly crooked wings and pale from underwing coverts bleeding to primary bases (cf. Fig 71). Apparent darkness of head and body plumage varies with lighting and wear. SNGH. Western Pacific, 23°N 144°E, 20 Apr 2007.

Fig 73. Confiding Sooty Shearwaters that scavenge around boats in fall off the West Coast are sometimes mistaken for Short-tailed Shearwaters. On this Sooty (with retarded wing molt, with old p10), note relatively long bill and overall elongated shape (cf. Figs 74–76). SNGH. Off Monterey, California, 15 Sep 2008.

Fig 74. Short-tailed Shearwater in fresh plumage, recently having completed molt. Compared to Sooty Shearwater (cf. Fig 73), note more compact shape, relatively big head, and small bill. MJI. Aleutians, Alaska, 11 Sep 2006.

Fig 75. Sooty Shearwater. Note long bill and overall elongated shape (cf. Figs 73–74, 76). SNGH. South Island, New Zealand, 27 Mar 2008.

Fig 76. (Below left) Short-tailed Shearwater. Note same features as Fig 74 (cf. Figs 73, 75). MJI. Aleutians, Alaska, 11 Sep 2006.

Fig 77. (Below) Differences in overall shape, head shape, and bill size, along with overall smaller size than adjacent Sooty Shearwaters (readily apparent in the field) point to the back bird being a Short-tailed Shearwater, but could it be a small female Sooty? In some cases, specific identity is best left undetermined. SNGH. Off Bodega Bay, California, 26 April 2010.

Fig 78. Cory's Shearwater. Note dark primaries, relatively large head and bill (cf. Fig 79). SNGH. Off Hatteras, North Carolina, 29 May 2008.

Fig 79. Scopoli's Shearwater. Note white tongues on outer primaries, relatively small head and bill (cf. Fig 78). SNGH. Off Hatteras, North Carolina, 6 Jun 2009.

Fig 80. Cory's Shearwater in mid-primary molt. Some Cory's show white tongues on p9-p8, but p10 typically is dark (cf. Fig 81). SNGH. Off Hatteras, North Carolina, 21 Aug 2009.

Fig 81. Scopoli's Shearwater with inner primary molt. Note extensive white tongues on outer primaries (cf. Fig 80). Relatively large bill suggests male (cf. relatively small bill of presumed female Cory's in Fig 80). SNGH. Off Hatteras, North Carolina, 16 Aug 2009.

Fig 82. Cory's Shearwater. Note broad wings held slightly crooked, bright white body and underwing coverts, head pattern, and stout pale bill (cf. Fig 83). SNGH. Off Hatteras, North Carolina, 21 May 2008.

Fig 83. Great Shearwater. Compared to Cory's, note relatively narrow wings held straighter, smaller head with slender bill, and dark markings on body and underwing coverts (cf. Fig 82). SNGH. Off Hatteras, North Carolina, 6 Jun 2009.

P1. SOOTY SHEARWATER *Ardenna grisea*

L 43–45.5 cm, WS 97–106 cm, tail 83–97 mm (graduation 20–30 mm), bill 38–47 mm
Figures 2, 9, 18–23, 26, 29, 32–35, 40–41, 47, 51–54, 63, 65–66, 69, 71, 73, 75, 77, P1.1–P1.10, P3.1, P8.1, P8.14, P14.1

Identification Summary Pacific and Atlantic; prefers cooler waters and often seen from shore. A fairly large shearwater with narrow pointed wings, a fairly short tail, and a heavy, almost cigar-shaped body. Dark sooty brown overall with conspicuous whitish panel on underwing coverts. Flight fast, with quick wingbeats and short glides in light winds, high and steep wheeling in strong winds. Glides on slightly bowed wings with wingtips often curled up slightly.

P1.1. A typical group of Sooty Shearwaters completing primary molt; note dark bellies, contrasting whitish underwing panels. SNGH. Off Monterey, California, 25 Jul 2008.

Taxonomy Monotypic.

Names *Ardenna* (some ancient authors use *Artenna*) is perhaps derived from the Latin *ardens*, meaning "ardent or burning bright." Ulisse Aldrovandi (*Ornithologiae tomus tertius*, 1603) interprets the reference to shearwaters' flaming or glowing eyes, from Pliny the Elder (*Historia Naturalis*), as pertaining to the actual appearance of the eyes, though Pliny's reference may be to the fierce appearance, with flaming eyes, of Diomedes' soldiers, who in Greek mythology transformed into seabirds; *grisea* means "gray," in reference to the sooty plumage tones.

Status and Distribution Near Threatened. Breeds (mid-Nov to late Apr) off e Australia, New Zealand, and s South America, ranges n (mainly Apr–Oct) to n Atlantic and n Pacific oceans. A figure-eight migration route proposed for trans-Pacific migrants by Spear and Ainley (1999a) has been confirmed recently by satellite tagging (Shaffer et al. 2006): thus, some birds track favorable winds from New Zealand e to Humboldt Current (Jan–Apr?), thence nw across equator to North Pacific (Mar–May), thence e to California Current region (May–Oct), and finally sw back across equator and on to New Zealand (Aug–Dec). Others spend nonbreeding period (May–Oct) mainly off Japan and Kamchatka or in Gulf of Alaska region (Shaffer et al. 2006). Particularly when Humboldt

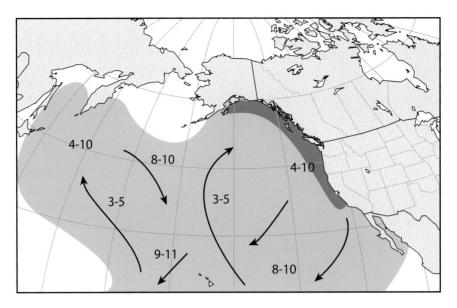

Sooty Shearwater (Pacific). Rare off western Mexico and Central America.

Current productivity is reduced, South American birds may follow this same route, with last leg being a return from sw Pacific back e to South America. Breeding birds may have a more direct trans-Pacific migration than prebreeders (Spear & Ainley 1999a).

Pacific. Generally a common to locally abundant migrant and nonbreeding visitor (mainly Apr–Oct) from Gulf of Alaska s to California, arrivals being slightly later northward and departures slightly later southward. Arrivals off West Coast apparent in Mar, with peak numbers May–Aug from cen California (where daily counts in places such as Monterey Bay are often 100,000–500,000 birds) n to Gulf of Alaska; small numbers (mainly juveniles?) occur w into Aleutians but are lost amid the millions of Short-tailed Shearwaters there. Molting birds often concentrate at food-rich locations during May–Aug, e.g., Hecate Strait, British Columbia, and Monterey Bay, California. After molting, breeders quickly depart in Aug, but nonbreeders remain common through Sep and (at least n to Oregon) into Oct, when a second marked departure occurs; small numbers remain into Nov, with stragglers n as far as British Columbia into mid-Dec. Uncommon to rare and local during Dec–Feb from cen California n to Washington, before the first migrants return in Mar–Apr. Often seen from shore (mainly Jul–Oct), at times in swarms of thousands, and in some years birds range into inland marine waters of Washington. Breeding adults depart colonies mid-Apr and probably arrive off West Coast by early May; first juveniles noted California early Jun and more numerous there Sep–Nov (CAS specimens), suggesting these birds may have ranged farther n and be moving back s in fall.

Off s California and nw Mexico, patterns mirror those to the n but the species is generally less common in these warmer waters. Can be locally fairly common (mainly Apr–Sep) in Gulf of California and off n Baja California and s California; at least formerly, most common off s California in May, when waters there cooler (Ainley 1976). Wanders very rarely into San Francisco Bay, and exceptional (late Apr to mid-Aug) inland in Southwest, mainly at Salton Sea.

Off Mexico and Central America status poorly known, and these warm, often windless waters are outside main migration track. Uncommon to rare off w Mexico (perhaps mainly Mar–Apr and Sep–Oct) and n Central America, but reported as sporadically common (mainly May–Oct) off Costa Rica and Panama, perhaps birds moving n in food-poor years from Humboldt Current.

Recent warming trends in California Current since about 1990 have resulted in a 90% decline in numbers of Sooty Shearwaters off w North America (Oedekoven et al. 2001, Veit et al. 1997); birds are presumed to have shifted to more pelagic waters of w and cen North Pacific, where there has been compensatory cooling of waters (Spear & Ainley 1999a). Decline has been most marked off s California, e.g., San Diego County, where Unitt (2004:110) noted that "Few changes in bird distribution have been as sudden and dramatic as

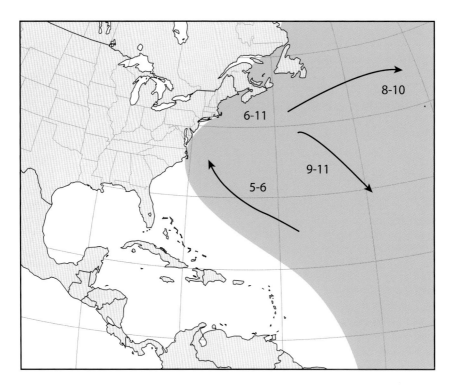

Sooty Shearwater (Atlantic). Very rare in Gulf of Mexico and Caribbean.

the Sooty Shearwater's desertion of the ocean off southern California"—daily counts in 1970s ran from hundreds to 10,000 birds, but by 1990s a typical count was fewer than 10 birds.

Atlantic. Generally a fairly common to locally common migrant and nonbreeding visitor (mainly Jun–Sep) to cooler waters off New England and Atlantic Canada, n to se Baffin Island (rare in Gulf of St. Lawrence) and sw Greenland (mid-Jul to mid-Sep), where increasing in recent years (D. Boertmann, pers. comm.). Off-shore migrant (mid-May to Jul, mainly late May to mid-Jun) from n West Indies to North Carolina (i.e., mostly avoiding South Atlantic Bight); spring movement past Bermuda mid-Apr to mid-Jun (mainly mid-late May). Prefers cooler inshore waters off North Carolina, where often seen from shore rather than in warm Gulf Stream offshore. Arrivals off New England are mid-late May into Jun, with peak numbers Jun–Jul (daily counts can reach low thousands off Massachusetts) before birds presumably move n or into ne Atlantic; a second influx of presumably southbound birds appears to occur off Northeast in late Sep to mid-Nov (daily counts in low hundreds off Massachusetts), with stragglers into Dec; exceptionally Jan–Apr. Very rare in fall off Atlantic coast s of New England, and exceptional Dec–Apr. Very rare in w Caribbean and Gulf of Mexico (year-round records, but mainly May–Aug, often dead or dying birds onshore). Exceptional inland (early Sep) after hurricanes in New York and North Carolina; an inland report from Alabama (AOU 1998) is unsubstantiated.

FIELD IDENTIFICATION

Similar Species This frequently common species should be learned well, as it provides numerous pitfalls for incautious observers. The only truly similar species is Short-tailed Shearwater—beware that Sooty Shearwater also has a short tail and often shows projecting toes. Several other species might be mistaken for Sooty Shearwater, and vice versa. Note especially the narrow, pointed wings and spindle-shaped body of Sooty, which has a higher wing-loading than any other shearwater; thus Sooty has quick, fairly deep, fluid wingbeats in calm conditions but it arcs high and steeply in strong winds.

Pacific. *Short-tailed Shearwater* (May–Sep in Alaska, mainly Oct–Nov and into winter off West Coast) slightly smaller (often appreciable when the two species are together) and shorter winged with smaller and more slender bill, accentuated by slightly steeper forehead; note, though, that female Sooties (especially juveniles) have smaller and more slender bills than males. Short-tailed usually appears shorter necked than Sooty, with head/neck projection forward of wings less than rump/tail projection behind wings (thus, ironically, Short-tailed can look relatively long tailed); Sooty has longer head/neck projection and longer bill, about the same as rump/tail projection. This difference recalls that between shorter-necked Arctic Tern and Long-tailed Jaeger vs. longer-necked Common Tern and Parasitic Jaeger.

Short-tailed has lower wing-loading and thus more buoyant and more maneuverable flight (especially in light to moderate winds) than heavy-bodied Sooty. Short-tailed flies with snappier wingbeats, more buoyant glides on slightly arched wings that do not curl up strongly at tips, and holds wings slightly more crooked. Heavy-bodied Short-taileds in migration often fly with quicker wingbeats and steeper, quicker arcs than Sooty. Beware that Sooties completing molt of outer primaries (mainly in Jul–Aug) have shorter and blunter-tipped wings that invite confusion with Short-tailed.

Plumage aspect of Sooty and Short-tailed can be ostensibly identical, but underwing pattern often differs (beware the effects of lighting). Underwings of Short-tailed typically have a whitish to pale brownish underwing panel (usually duller than Sooty, but bright silvery white in some lights), which is more even in width, especially across secondary coverts, than flared wedge on Sooty; pale underwing panel of Short-tailed typically does not contrast strongly with undersides of primaries (vs. distinct contrast typical of Sooty); and primary coverts of Short-tailed lack distinct darker shaft streaks of Sooty. As a rule, if you *think* you see a Short-tailed off the West Coast in Sep–Oct, it's much more likely a Sooty—a real Short-tailed often stands out as quite distinct (in flight manner and structure) to observers familiar with Sooty.

Christmas Shearwater (tropics) darker overall and distinctly smaller with longer tail, shorter black bill, and more buoyant gliding between bursts of hurried wingbeats; lacks pale underwing panels but greater coverts and primaries can reflect silvery in sunlight.

Dark morph *Wedge-tailed Shearwater* (tropics) has small light body and big, broad-based wings—almost the structural opposite to Sooty; consequently Wedge-tailed has low wing-loading and very different, buoyant flight—as well as having long tapered tail (beware that Sooty can appear long tailed, especially in photos) and small,

relatively "pin-headed" front end. On the water, look for Wedge-tailed's long neck, small head, long tail.

Flesh-footed Shearwater (widespread) larger and broader winged with bright pink, black-tipped bill; flight generally unhurried and quite different from Sooty, and lacks silvery-white underwing panels. On the water, Flesh-footed usually looks darker and more chocolate-brown (vs. slightly paler, sooty gray-brown of Sooty), sits higher, and has blockier head.

Dark morph *Northern Fulmar* (cool temperate waters) often paler overall, medium-dark ashy gray vs. dark sooty brown of Sooty, and this color (or tonal) difference is appreciable under almost all conditions; however, some dark fulmars (mainly in Aleutians) are as dark as Sooties. Fulmars are broader winged and broader tailed, with looser wingbeats of wings held stiffly and straight out from body, and have stout pale bill obvious at closer range. Some heavily worn fulmars flap atypically fast in calm or light winds, which can suggest flight manner of Sooty.

Murphy's Petrel (offshore) smaller but bigger headed, with longer tail and stouter black bill. Murphy's has more buoyant flight with snappier wingbeats, and glides on slightly arched and crooked wings. Murphy's has strong gray gloss and dark *M* on upperparts in fresh plumage, variable white throat patch (often noticeable), and dark underwing coverts (but bases to primary coverts and primaries often reflect silvery white). On the water, Murphy's sits higher and looks bigger headed with shorter, stouter black bill offset by whitish throat.

Dark *jaegers* on the water have longer and relatively thicker-based necks, generally sit higher (more like gulls), and have different bill shapes.

Atlantic. See above for dark morph *Northern Fulmar* (rare in the Atlantic) and dark jaegers.

Trinidade Petrel (offshore Gulf Stream) has slightly shorter head projection with thicker black bill, slightly broader wings, and lower wing-loading. In light to moderate winds, Trinidade flies with deep but relatively measured wingbeats and buoyant glides on slightly arched and crooked wings; in stronger winds it arcs more gracefully and buoyantly and has a snappier, more maneuverable demeanor. Back of Trinidade Petrel often has a gray gloss and underwings are silvery white mainly on primary bases. On the water, Trinidade sits higher and has a longer neck (more like a jaeger) and shorter black bill.

Habitat and Behavior (see Fig 29, p. 27) Pelagic but often seen from shore, at times in swarms of thousands off West Coast. Favors cooler waters of the shelf (especially with tidal fronts), shelf break, and other areas of upwelling, such as offshore banks. Associates readily with other shearwaters when feeding and rafting, also with mixed-species feeding flocks that include gulls, cormorants, pelicans, and terns. Feeds by diving while swimming as well as by shallow-angle plunging from a few meters above the surface, and generally not attracted to scavenge or follow boats. Molting and staging birds fly reluctantly when well fed, and often patter frantically or dive to avoid boats; conversely, the lighter-bodied Pink-footed and, especially, Buller's shearwaters usually take flight much more readily when approached. Large flocks seen from shore off California are usually pure Sooties (with occasional Pink-footed or Manx shearwaters among them), and dense rafts of birds can look like oil slicks on the sea.

In calm to light winds flies low with fairly quick, deep, and fluid wingbeats interspersed with short glides on slightly bowed wings that often curl up at the tips; occasionally catches lift from large swells to make low, wheeling arcs. In moderate to strong winds, often wheels high and steeply, much like gadfly petrels, and with little flapping. Flight manner also reflects body weight, with fattened premigrating birds having a much higher wing-loading (and faster flight) then lighter, oversummering or overwintering immatures, which can appear more buoyant. Wings usually held straight out from body or only slightly crooked, but feeding birds over schooling fish can weave erratically with deep wingbeats of strongly crooked wings.

Description A fairly large and heavy-bodied shearwater with narrow pointed wings, medium-short tail. Bill slender and fairly long (shorter and slimmer on females); toes often project beyond short tail but more usually pulled in. At rest, wings project slightly beyond tail tip. High wing-loading. Leucism noted regularly in this species, such as birds with cleanly demarcated white heads or white back patches.

Ages similar but juveniles fresh in May–Jul when most older birds are in wing molt. Dark sooty gray-brown overall, head and upperparts slightly darker and chin often slightly paler; looks black overall in gloomy conditions but in sun underparts can appear warm brown, especially birds in worn plumage. Some birds have contrasting whitish throat offset by dark hood, and underbody can also be dusky pale gray (mainly

in worn plumage). Upperwings of fresh plumage have a sheen often most distinct on secondaries, which can appear as a narrow silvery trailing edge to wings. Underwings have variable whitish panel across median and greater coverts narrowest near body and broadest across primary coverts, where typically forms a broad rounded border in contrast to dark undersides of primaries; in bright sun, however, undersides of fresh primaries can also reflect silvery. Underwing panel variable but usually distinct, often looking silvery white when lit by bright sun but can be inconspicuous when shadowed; rarely dingy grayish white overall, but always with dark or dusky shaft streaks to greater primary coverts. Birds molting inner to middle primaries (mainly Mar–May) often have whitish stripe across upperwing. Bill dark grayish, legs and feet dusky flesh to grayish.

Hybrids Presumed with Short-tailed Shearwater (Kuroda 1967).

Molt (see Fig 47, p. 38) Off West Coast, adult wing molt Apr/early Jun–Aug/Sep; mainly May–Aug on presumed breeding adults, which often have p8-p10 growing simultaneously in late Jul–Aug (molt thus compressed in timing relative to PB2); tail molt mainly May–Sep. A few (sick?) birds are still molting outer primaries and tail Oct–Dec. In North Pacific, PB2 wing molt and wing molt of some prebreeders (perhaps PB3 and some PB4) mainly Feb/Mar–Jun/Jul, with p9-p10 often not shed until adjacent inner feather mostly grown; tail molt Feb–Aug. PB2 wing molt of birds in s hemisphere may be earlier (Jan–May), when many birds reported molting in Bass Strait (Marchant & Higgins 1990:633). Variable head and body molt on first-year birds in Sep–Nov or later (often visible as dark blotching on faded underparts) may be PF molt or start of protracted PB2 (body molt of adults starts Dec on breeding grounds).

In North Atlantic, most summering birds off Atlantic Canada are not in wing molt (Brown 1988), as is true of more than 99% of migrants off North Carolina in late May–Jun, which appear to be in fresh plumage, presumably juveniles and perhaps some birds with recently completed PB2 (NCSM specimens, pers. obs.). Birds in mid-primary molt found locally off Newfoundland in early Jun 2010 (B. L. Sullivan, photos) may have been on an adult schedule, and more study is needed of molt timing off the Northeast.

P1.2. Sooty Shearwater in fresh plumage (secondaries often reflect silvery when fresh). Note dark sooty plumage, relatively long and slender dark bill. SNGH. Off Bodega Bay, California, 30 Sep 2007.

P1.3. Sooty Shearwater in fresh plumage. Apparent darkness of plumage varies appreciably with lighting (cf. P1.2); toes often project beyond tail tip, as here, or can be pulled in (cf. P1.2). SNGH. Off Monterey, California, 26 Sep 2008.

P1.4. Sooty Shearwater starting inner primary molt and showing classic underwing pattern. SNGH. Off Monterey, California, 11 May 2008.

P1.5. Underwing pattern of Sooty Shearwater highly variable, and appearance greatly influenced by lighting. Bottom wing of this bird appears much like Short-tailed Shearwater but top wing more like Sooty; also note long bill. SNGH. Off Hatteras, North Carolina, 29 May 2008.

P1.6. Sooty Shearwater with relatively muted underwing pattern that could suggest Short-tailed Shearwater; heavy dark shaft streaks in primary coverts rarely if ever shown by Short-tailed. Also note large bill, probably indicating male; head often appears darker than body (cf. P1.4–P1.5). SNGH. Off Monterey, California, 26 Sep 2008.

P1.7. Atypically faded Sooty Shearwater with extensive white underwing panels. Note overall structure and long slender bill. SNGH. Off Monterey, California, 23 Sep 2007.

P1.9. Juvenile Sooty Shearwater in uniformly fresh plumage (cf. P1.10), perhaps having fledged only about two months earlier. SNGH. Off Hatteras, North Carolina, 24 May 2007.

P1.8. Viewed head-on or going away, as here, long narrow wings of Sooty Shearwater often sweep up at tips (cf. P2.13). SNGH. Off Hatteras, North Carolina, 29 May 2008.

P1.10. Sooty Shearwater in mid-primary molt, with p5 shed to reveal dark basal portion of p6 (cf. P1.9). SNGH. Off Monterey, California, 11 May 2008.

P2. SHORT-TAILED SHEARWATER *Ardenna tenuirostris*
L 40.5–43 cm, WS 91–99 cm, tail 74–87 mm (graduation 15–20 mm), bill 29–35 mm
Figures 67, 70, 72, 74, 76–77, P2.1–P2.15

Identification Summary Pacific and Bering Sea; prefers cooler waters. A medium-sized shearwater with narrow wings, fairly short neck, and fairly small, slender bill. Dark sooty brown overall with variable paler panel on underwing coverts. Flight fast but maneuverable with slightly snappy wingbeats and buoyant glides in light winds, high and steep wheeling in strong winds. Glides on slightly arched wings.

P2.1. Short-tailed Shearwaters gather to molt in food-rich northern waters, which they often share with Humpback Whales. MJI. Aleutians, Alaska, 11 Sep 2006.

Taxonomy Monotypic.

Names For *Ardenna*, see under Sooty Shearwater; *tenuirostris* means "slender-billed," and this species was formerly known as Slender-billed Shearwater.

Status and Distribution Least Concern. Breeds (late Nov to late Apr) off s Australia, ranges (mainly May–Oct) to n Pacific and Bering Sea.
    Pacific. Generally a common to locally abundant migrant and nonbreeding visitor (mainly May–Oct) to Bering Sea region, and uncommon to locally fairly common (mainly Nov–Feb) off the West Coast. Arrivals in s Bering Sea can be as early as mid-late Apr, but most arrive May–Jun. Locally abundant in Bering Sea, Aleutians (especially Unimak Pass), and Bering Strait during Jun–Sep, with smaller numbers (perhaps mainly juveniles?) ranging n into Chukchi Sea (e to Barrow, where recorded late Jul to mid-Nov). Adults depart late Aug–Sep after molting (arriving on breeding grounds in late Sep–Oct), and nonbreeders move later, with most withdrawing s in Oct, and stragglers into Nov. Off St. Lawrence Island, large numbers arrive offshore by late Aug (very rare there in May–Jun) and stage through early Oct (daily counts in excess of 1 million birds). Small numbers occur in se Alaska, but status in e Aleutians and Gulf of Alaska clouded by abundance there of Sooty Shearwaters.

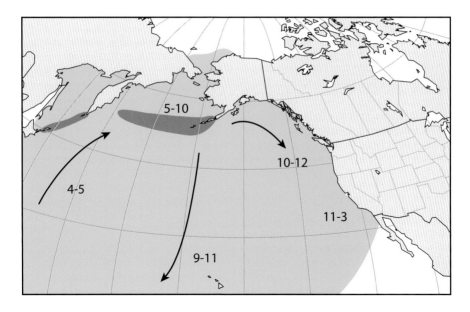

Off British Columbia recorded late Apr to late Feb (mainly May–Nov), generally uncommon or rare, but occasionally locally abundant in late spring and late autumn, presumably birds at the edge of the main migration tracks. Off the West Coast s to cen California, very rare or exceptional in Aug–Sep (exceptionally late Jul in Washington), with main numbers (often a few hundred, exceptionally a few thousand daily in Washington) in Oct–Dec, and smaller numbers (tens to a few hundred daily) remaining through Mar; much interannual variation, with larger numbers generally in cold-water years. A few linger into Apr–May, especially in cold-water years, and in some years birds range to inland marine waters of Washington. Very rare (mainly Nov–Mar) s to nw Mexico, including Gulf of California; beached carcass in Guerrero (Oct 1972) is southernmost record. A report from Costa Rica requires verification.

Atlantic. Exceptional: one seen off Virginia (Jan 1998; Brinkley et al. 2001) and one moribund in Gulf of Mexico off Florida (Jul 2000; Kratter & Steadman 2003). Also one beached specimen from Brazil (May 2005; Souto et al. 2008).

FIELD IDENTIFICATION

Similar Species Sooty Shearwater is notoriously similar to Short-tailed; see discussion of other potentially similar species (e.g., Northern Fulmar) under Sooty Shearwater. To identify Short-tailed, note especially its medium-size, snappy wingbeats, and buoyant gliding, as well as an even-width pale underwing panel.

Sooty Shearwater (widespread, but rare in w Aleutians) larger (often appreciable when the two species are together), longer necked, and longer winged, with longer and slightly stouter bill accentuated by more sloping forehead; note that female Sooty has smaller and more slender bill than male. Sooties completing molt of outer primaries (mainly in Jul–Aug) have shorter and blunter-tipped wings, inviting confusion with Short-tailed. Sooty has higher wing-loading and thus a less buoyant and heavier flight (especially in light to moderate winds) than lighter-bodied Short-tailed. Sooty flies with deeper, stronger, and more fluid wingbeats and less buoyant glides on slightly bowed wings that often curl up at tips. Underwings of Sooty have flared, silvery-whitish panel broadest on primary coverts and typically contrasting with dark primaries (vs. duller, more even-width panel of Short-tailed that does not contrast strongly with underside of primaries), and primary coverts have distinct darker shaft streaks. As a rule, if you *think* you see a Short-tailed off the West Coast in Sep–Oct, it's far more likely a Sooty—a real Short-tailed often stands out as quite distinct (in flight manner and structure) to observers intimately familiar with Sooty.

Christmas Shearwater (tropics) smaller and darker overall with slightly longer tail (toes do not project) and less slender black bill; lacks pale underwing panels but greater coverts and primaries can reflect silvery in sunlight.

Murphy's Petrel (offshore) slightly smaller and bigger headed with longer tail and stouter black bill. Murphy's has a more buoyant flight with snappier wingbeats, and glides on slightly arched and crooked wings. Murphy's has strong gray gloss and dark *M* on upperparts in fresh plumage, variable white throat patch (often noticeable), and dark underwing coverts (but bases to primary coverts and primaries often reflect silvery white). On the water, Murphy's sits higher and looks bigger headed with stouter black bill offset by whitish throat.

Habitat and Behavior Pelagic but often seen from shore in w Alaska, at times in swarms of thousands. Favors cooler waters of the shelf (especially tidal fronts in passes and straits between islands), shelf break, and other areas of upwelling, such as offshore banks. Associates readily with other shearwaters when feeding and rafting, also with mixed-species feeding flocks that include gulls, cormorants, and terns. Feeds by diving while swimming as well as by shallow-angle plunging from 3–5 m above the surface; birds off West Coast more prone than Sooty Shearwater to scavenge and follow boats. Molting and staging birds fly reluctantly when well fed, and often patter frantically or dive to avoid boats.

In calm to light winds flies low with fairly quick and slightly snappy wingbeats interspersed with buoyant glides on slightly arched wings; more maneuverable than Sooty Shearwater, particularly noticeable when the two species are feeding together. In moderate to strong winds, often wheels high and steeply, much like gadfly petrel, and with little flapping. Flocks of heavy-bodied Short-taileds in migration fly purposefully with quick, fairly deep wingbeats and steep, fairly fast arcs, passing through an area rapidly.

Description A medium-sized and fairly heavy-bodied shearwater with narrow wings, medium-short tail; plumage sometimes considered dimorphic with respect to underwing pattern, the differences apparently not correlated with age or wear (Loomis 1918, Marchant & Higgins 1990), but intermediate patterns exist and thus not truly dimorphic. Bill slender and medium-length; toes often project beyond short tail but more usually are pulled in. At rest, wings project slightly beyond tail tip. Moderate wing-loading.

Ages similar but juveniles fresh in May–Jul when older birds are worn or in wing molt. Dark sooty gray-brown overall, head and upperparts slightly darker; looks black overall in gloomy conditions but in sun underparts can appear warm brown, especially on birds in worn plumage. Some birds (usually those with whitish underwing panels) have whitish throat patch of variable extent, which often contrasts with dark hood. Upperwings of fresh plumage have a sheen often most distinct on secondaries, which can appear as a narrow silvery trailing edge to wings. Darkest birds (commonest) have underwings uniform brownish overall, whereas palest birds (less common) have contrasting grayish-white panel across median and greater coverts, typically fairly even in width. The two extremes are bridged by intermediates with pale brown to whitish underwing panels. In bright sun, undersides of primaries can flash bright silvery and blend with underwing panels. Bill dark grayish, legs and feet dusky flesh to grayish.

Presumed first-cycle birds in Sep–Nov (at least) can have contrasting dark head and faded underparts with scattered dark feathers perhaps indicating molt.

Hybrids Presumed with Sooty Shearwater (Kuroda 1967).

Molt Adult wing molt rapid, mainly May–late Jul/early Sep, probably starting earlier in nonbreeders, with a few (sick?) birds still molting outer primaries and tail off West Coast in Oct–Dec (Loomis 1918, CAS specimens). Timing (and location) of PB2 wing molt apparently unknown (information in Pyle 2008 speculative), perhaps mainly Jan–May in s hemisphere, Apr–Aug in n hemisphere, or some combination of these two schedules.

P.2.2. Short-tailed Shearwater. Note relatively compact shape and short head/neck projection with small bill; toe tips here project just beyond tail tip. SNGH. Western Pacific, 27°N 142°E, 15 May 2011.

P2.3. Short-tailed Shearwater in fresh plumage. Note relatively compact shape, but not especially short tail projection, and small bill. SNGH. Off Bodega Bay, California, 20 Nov 2010.

P2.4. Short-tailed Shearwater. Top wing shows classic, muted underwing pattern relative to Sooty Shearwater; contrast between primary coverts and primary bases on bottom wing suggests Sooty but muted; also note plain primary coverts (no dark shaft streaks), even-width pale panel on secondary coverts. SNGH. Off Bodega Bay, California, 20 Nov 2010.

P2.5. Short-tailed Shearwater showing classic underwing pattern with pale panel on underwing coverts not contrasting strongly with primary bases. SNGH. Off Bodega Bay, California, 6 Feb 2007.

P2.6. Short-tailed Shearwater in worn plumage (outer primaries heavily frayed). Note how paler underwing panel bleeds from coverts to primaries. SNGH. Western Pacific, 31°N 137°E, 24 Apr 2007.

P2.7. Short-tailed Shearwater with mid-primary molt. Besides overall shape, note even-width pale panel across secondary coverts. SW. Aleutians, Alaska, 20 Jun 2009.

P2.8. Short-tailed Shearwater in fresh plumage, thus presumably a juvenile on this date (cf. P2.7). Note classic shape, with crooked wings and short head/neck projection, plus even-width pale panel across secondary coverts. Contrasting dark head often shown by Short-tailed but also shown by Sooty Shearwater. SW. Aleutians, Alaska, 4 Jul 2009.

P2.9. Short-tailed Shearwater in fresh plumage. Straight-winged pose suggests Sooty Shearwater but note even-width whitish panel on secondary coverts, lack of contrast between primary bases and coverts, relatively short wings. MJI. Aleutians, Alaska, 10 Sep 2006.

P2.10. In bright light, Short-tailed Shearwater often shows contrasting silvery underwing flashes that invite confusion with Sooty Shearwater. Besides differences in overall structure, note fairly even width of silvery panels and that they bleed into the primaries. SNGH. Western Pacific, 13°N 149°E, 17 Apr 2007.

P2.12. Short-tailed Shearwater. Apparent brightness of underwing panels varies greatly with lighting (cf. P2.11 of same individual taken two minutes earlier). SNGH. Off Monterey, California, 21 Sep 2007.

P2.11. In some lights, even Short-tailed Shearwaters with whitish underwing panels can appear dark-winged, as here (cf. P2.12 of same individual). However, some Short-tailed do have an extensively and smoothly dark underwing pattern, much like this. Note classic shape, with short head/neck projection, small bill. SNGH. Off Monterey, California, 21 Sep 2007.

P2.14. Short-tailed Shearwater. Note compact shape, rounded head, "cute" face, and small bill; SNGH. Off Bodega Bay, California, 20 Nov 2010.

P2.13. Head-on, Short-tailed Shearwater often shows distinctly arched wings suggesting a gadfly petrel rather than the long wings with swept-up tips typical of Sooty Shearwater (cf. P1.8). SNGH. Off Bodega Bay, California, 20 Nov 2010.

P2.15. Short-tailed Shearwaters, like Sooties, often gather in dense, slick-like flocks when molting and feeding. MJI. Aleutians, Alaska, 11 Sep 2006.

P3. FLESH-FOOTED SHEARWATER *Ardenna carneipes*
L 45–48 cm, WS 109–116 cm, tail 108–122 mm (graduation 25–30 mm), bill 38–45 mm
Figures P3.1–P3.11, P38.4, P38.5

Identification Summary Pacific. A large, all-dark shearwater with a bright pink bill tipped black. Similar to much commoner Pink-footed Shearwater in size, shape, and flight manner.

P3.1. Off the West Coast, Flesh-footed Shearwater (left-hand dark-bodied bird) is most often seen singly among flocks of other species, here with Pink-footed Shearwaters, one Sooty Shearwater (top right), and an immature gull (back right). Note dark underwing coverts, pink bill and legs of Flesh-footed. SNGH. Off Bodega Bay, California, 14 Aug 2007.

Taxonomy Monotypic. Birds breeding in e Australia and New Zealand average larger than those breeding in w Australia and have been separated as subspecies *hullianus* (Mathews 1934), but mensural differences slight and species usually considered monotypic (e.g., Marchant & Higgins 1990).

Names For *Ardenna*, see under Sooty Shearwater; *carneipes* means "flesh-footed," in reference to the pink feet.

Status and Distribution Least Concern. Breeds (Nov–Apr) in s Indian Ocean and sw Pacific Ocean; birds from the latter area range to waters off w North America.
 Pacific. Generally a rare to seasonally uncommon nonbreeding visitor (mainly May–Nov) off

w North America from Gulf of Alaska s to nw Mexico. A slight peak in records off California and Washington in late Apr–May suggests arrival of migrants at that time, and most numerous off West Coast in Sep–Nov (peaking earlier off Washington, later off s California, indicative of southward migration). In the s, reported off nw Mexico Jan–Jul (perhaps mainly Mar–May; Radamaker & McCaskie 2006), exceptionally (May) in Gulf of California. In the n, casual in Gulf of Alaska (Jul–early Sep; probably regular, but few observers) and rare to uncommon off British Columbia (May–mid-Oct, most numerous Jun–Sep). Recorded off cen and s California in all months (very rare Jan–Mar), and very rare n (Dec–Mar) to Washington. Occurrence patterns mirror other austral-breeding shearwaters

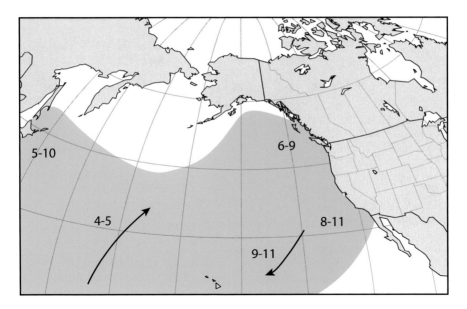

and migration may follow clockwise path typical of many species in the region.

Scarcest off California in cold-water years (Ainley 1976), and may have increased slightly off cen California since mid-1990s, perhaps reflecting a regional ocean warming trend (cf. regional decline of Sooty Shearwaters, which prefer cooler waters).

FIELD IDENTIFICATION

Similar Species Although Flesh-footed is a fairly distinctive shearwater, pitfalls are provided by dark Northern Fulmar, by other dark shearwaters, and (off Middle America) by Parkinson's Petrel. Perhaps the most likely confusion species off California is immature Heermann's Gull, especially when birds are on the water.

Immature *Heermann's Gull* shares similar size, overall dark-brown coloration, and black-tipped pinkish bill, and often sits with inshore flocks of shearwaters. Heermann's has thinner neck, smaller head with low, sloping forehead, duller pinkish bill (without tubes), and black legs.

Dark morph *Northern Fulmar* stockier and usually paler overall, dark ashy gray to gray-brown rather than dark chocolate-brown, with shorter and broader wings, stiffer wingbeats, and thicker, pale-tipped bill.

Sooty Shearwater on the water is smaller headed, shorter necked, and slightly paler and grayer overall with dark bill (can reflect pale silvery in sunlight). In flight, Flesh-footed readily distinguished by heavier build, dark underwings, relatively leisurely flight, black-tipped pink bill.

Pink-footed Shearwater has rare dark morph, which may not always be separable from Flesh-footed. In general, Pink-footed looks slightly bulkier and broader winged than slightly rangier and narrower-winged Flesh-footed, and bill averages duller pinkish; some dark morphs slightly paler and grayer than Flesh-footed (i.e., upperparts typical in tone of Pink-footed, rather than darker brown of Flesh-footed).

Dark morph *Wedge-tailed Shearwater* more lightly built with relatively bigger wings (thus, lower wing-loading) held more crooked, longer neck, smaller head, and longer, more strongly graduated tail (birds molting longest rectrices can be easily mistaken for Flesh-footed); thinner bill varies from grayish to pinkish with a dark tip, strongly resembling Flesh-footed. Wedge-tailed typically slightly paler overall and, especially at a distance, underwing usually appears more evenly toned, whereas coverts of Flesh-footed often appear dark, contrasting with reflectively pale remiges. With birds on the water note lighter build, longer neck, and longer tail of dark Wedge-tailed. In calm to light winds, Wedge-tailed has an easier, more buoyant flight with more-prolonged glides on slightly arched wings that tend to be pushed forward and crooked back at the carpals; in moderate to strong winds, wheels lower than heavier-bodied Flesh-footed.

Parkinson's Petrel slightly bulkier, shorter tailed, and blacker overall, dark-tipped bill slightly shorter, stouter, and pale-greenish (not pink), and feet black. On the water, long wings of Parkinson's project well past relatively short tail, unlike short wing projection of relatively long-tailed Flesh-footed.

Dark jaegers on the water have longer and relatively thicker-based necks, gull-like bills.

Habitat and Behavior Prefers warm-temperate waters, and usually found in association with more numerous Pink-footed and Sooty shearwaters. Generally pelagic, and very rarely seen from shore. Attracted to boats usually only briefly, but will scavenge fairly aggressively at fishing boats discarding offal. Usually encountered singly but, at least in Oct–Nov off California, loose groups of 10 or more birds can be found among flocks of other shearwaters.

Flight much like Pink-footed Shearwater: in calm to light winds generally unhurried with easy wingbeats and buoyant low glides on slightly bowed wings; in moderate to strong winds can fly fast and wheel high, suggesting a large gadfly petrel. In powered flight, such as when chasing around with other birds over food, can suggest a jaeger.

Description A large shearwater with medium-width wings and medium-length, slightly graduated tail; moderate wing-loading.

Ages similar but juveniles fresh in Apr–Jul when older birds are worn or molting. Plumage blackish brown to dark chocolate-brown overall, primaries appearing slightly blacker at rest; paler tips to scapulars create pale scalloping. Undersides of greater coverts and remiges have a reflective sheen and often appear paler, at times silvery, when caught by the light. Bill pink with a dark tip, legs and feet pink overall.

On the water. Dark chocolate-brown overall, back with paler scalloping; pink bill tipped black.

Molt Adult wing molt mainly Apr–Aug, earlier in nonbreeders than breeders. PB2 wing molt perhaps mainly Jan–Jun but few data.

P3.2. Flesh-footed Shearwater. Note overall dark plumage, broad wings, and black-tipped pink bill. SNGH. North Island, New Zealand, 31 Mar 2008.

P3.3. Flesh-footed Shearwater. Note broad wings, all-dark plumage, and pink bill; perhaps not separable in this image from extremely rare dark morph of Pink-footed Shearwater. SNGH. Off Monterey, California, 15 Sep 2008.

P3.4. Flesh-footed Shearwater. Note broad wings, all-dark plumage, pink bill and feet (often pulled into undertail coverts and not visible). TMcG. Off Fort Bragg, California, 18 Oct 2009.

P3.5. (Below) Shape of distant wheeling Flesh-footed Shearwater is subtly but distinctly different from Sooty Shearwater (see Fig 71), as is its flight manner. SNGH. Off Bodega Bay, California, 20 Nov 2010.

P3.6. (Below right) Besides pink bill, note big wings and typically darker plumage aspect of Flesh-footed relative to Sooty Shearwater. SNGH. South Island, New Zealand, 28 Mar 2008.

P3.7. This image shows well the differences between Flesh-footed Shearwater (right) and Pink-footed Shearwater. Flesh-footed typically darker above (pale bill contrasts more strongly on darker head) and appears narrower winged. SNGH. Off Monterey, California, 24 Sep 2007.

P3.8. Flesh-footed Shearwater is longer necked and larger headed than Sooty Shearwater; also note pink bill, pale scalloping on back. SNGH. North Island, New Zealand, 8 Nov 2008.

P3.9. Size and shape of Flesh-footed Shearwater ostensibly identical to much commoner but white-bellied Pink-footed Shearwater (behind). SNGH. Off Bodega Bay, California, 13 Oct 2006.

P3.10. Flesh-footed Shearwater (at back) similar in coloration to first-year Heermann's Gull. As well as tubenose bill, note larger size and darker plumage of the shearwater. SNGH. Off Monterey, California, 15 Sep 2008.

P3.11. Flesh-footed Shearwater (left) similar in size to California Gull, with which it associates readily when resting. SNGH. Off Monterey, California, 24 Sep 2007.

P4. PINK-FOOTED SHEARWATER *Ardenna creatopus*

L 45–48 cm, WS 110–118 cm, tail 106–124 mm (graduation 25–30 mm), bill 40–46 mm
Figures 4, 14, 65, 67, P3.1, P3.7, P3.9, P4.1–P4.16, P5.1, P5.9, P7.1, P7.8, P7.10, P7.11. P8.15

Identification Summary Pacific. A large, fairly heavy-bodied shearwater with broad wings and medium-length, slightly graduated tail. Upperparts gray-brown, underparts white with dark undertail coverts. Bill pinkish with dark tip, feet pink.

P4.1. A typical flock of Pink-footed Shearwaters flushing off the water with an adult Western Gull. Note variation in underwing pattern. SNGH. Off Bodega Bay, California, 14 Aug 2007.

Taxonomy Monotypic.

Names For *Ardenna*, see under Sooty Shearwater; *creatopus* means "flesh-footed," in reference to the pink feet.

Status and Distribution Vulnerable. Breeds (Dec–May) off Chile on Juan Fernandez Islands and Isla Mocha, ranges n (mainly Apr–Oct) to n and e Pacific, although some of population remains year-round in Humboldt Current off South America.

    Pacific. Generally a common to fairly common nonbreeding visitor (mainly Apr–Oct) off w North America (from British Columbia to Mexico). Migrates n well offshore from Chile (thus unrecorded Panama and rare Costa Rica, in vicinity of Cocos Island), becoming fairly common offshore n from Guatemala. Occurs off Mexico year-round where commonest Mar–May and Aug–Nov, least numerous Dec–Jan; irregularly uncommon to fairly common (Feb–Oct) in Gulf of California. Fairly common to locally and seasonally common (mainly Apr–Oct; first arrivals off s California in early Mar) from California n to British Columbia, with main arrival off California in Apr–May, Washington in May, and British Columbia in May–Jun; rare n to Gulf of Alaska (mid-May to mid-Sep), possibly very rare w to Aleutians and s Bering Sea (Gibson & Byrd 2007, Gould et al. 1982). Withdraws s during Aug–Nov. Peak numbers off coastal California occur Aug–Oct, suggesting northward spring movement occurs farther offshore (where birds favor warmer waters, which usually move nearer to shore in fall) and is less concentrated. Small numbers remain off West Coast n to Washington during Dec–Mar.

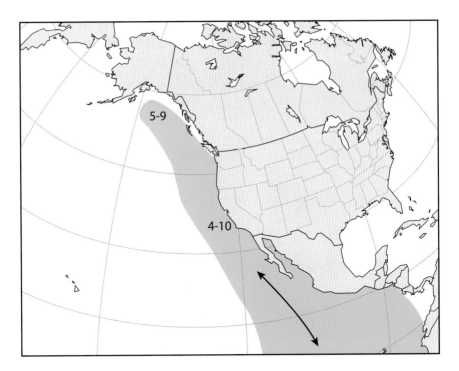

FIELD IDENTIFICATION

Similar Species This common and somewhat variable large shearwater should be learned well. Off the West Coast no similar species occur regularly, but off Mexico beware light morph Wedge-tailed Shearwater. Also beware that steadily flapping Pink-footeds can look surprisingly jaeger-like and molting birds often show white upperwing flashes—but usually on the secondary coverts, not the primary bases. See under Flesh-footed Shearwater for separation from dark morph Pink-footed. Also see Cory's Shearwater, a vagrant to e Pacific.

Because of vagaries of distance and lighting, Pink-footed is frequently mistaken for other species. For example, although Pink-footed's upperparts usually look medium gray-brown they range in appearance (because of light angle and freshness of plumage) from dark chocolate-brown to ashy or even frosty gray, often with a blacker M pattern and paler secondaries.

Buller's Shearwater has bright white underparts, sharply contrasting dark cap, and boldly patterned upperparts. However, with low-angle sunlight reflecting off the sea, such as occurs in early morning, Pink-footed's underparts can appear gleaming white and head somewhat capped, inviting confusion with Buller's. Also note that fresh-plumaged Pink-footed shows variable dark M pattern on upperparts, which could

suggest Buller's. On backlit birds plumage details not always easy to discern, so attention should be paid to shape and flight manner. Buller's is slightly smaller and more lightly built with more buoyant flight, lighter wingbeats, and slightly longer, more graduated tail. In calm to light winds, Buller's flies with slightly quicker wingbeats and longer glides on slightly arched wings (vs. Pink-footed's slightly slower and deeper wingbeats, with shorter glides on slightly bowed wings); in moderate to strong winds, Buller's typically wheels fairly low to the water, whereas Pink-footed often arcs high (see Fig 29, p. 27).

Light morph *Wedge-tailed Shearwater* more lightly built with relatively bigger wings (thus, lower wing-loading) often held crooked, longer neck, smaller head, and longer, more strongly graduated tail; thinner bill grayish or pinkish with darker tip, and especially in bright light could be mistaken for pink bill of Pink-footed. Wedge-tailed often looks whiter below (especially on bases of underwings) with a cleaner-cut dark cap (vs. dark head sides typical of Pink-footed). In calm to light winds, Wedge-tailed has an easier, more buoyant flight with more-prolonged glides on slightly arched wings that tend to be pushed forward and crooked back at the carpals (held straighter on Pink-footed); in moderate to strong winds, tends to wheel lower but snappier than heavier-bodied Pink-footed, and more strongly crooked wings of Wedge-tailed often appear narrow and rakish (despite being broad) than broad, straighter-held wings of Pink-footed.

Black-vented Shearwater (Mexico and California) much smaller but plumage pattern similar overall to Pink-footed. Black-vented has slender dark bill and flies with hurried wingbeats and short glides; in strong winds can wheel fairly high but usually more steeply and with shorter wavelength arcs than Pink-footed. On the water, Black-vented often looks darker and more uniform above, with paler or whitish flanks, whereas Pink-footed tends to be browner above, usually with some paler scalloping, and pale brownish flanks do not contrast as strongly with back.

Habitat and Behavior (see Fig 29, p. 27) Prefers warm-temperate waters, and occurs from shelf to pelagic waters. Generally pelagic but can be seen from land, especially with onshore winds; e.g., southbound migrants may be seen from headlands of s California and Baja California. Often feeds and rafts (sometimes in thousands) with other shearwaters, albatrosses, and gulls, and readily attracted to fishing boats discarding offal; dives for food are usually shallow and not long duration. Loose flocks (usually of 10–100 birds off California) regularly forage over schools of dolphins. Foraging birds often utter nasal bleating and squawking calls. Flight in calm to light winds generally unhurried with easy, fairly deep wingbeats and short glides on slightly bowed wings. In light to moderate winds often flies with low, long-wavelength wheeling arcs. In moderate to strong winds can fly fast and wheel high, suggesting a large *Pterodroma* petrel. Feeding birds over schooling fish can weave erratically with deep wingbeats of crooked wings and quick dashes to seize prey near the surface.

Description A large, fairly heavy-bodied shearwater with large head, relatively broad wings, and medium-length, slightly graduated tail; moderate wing-loading.

Ages similar but juveniles fresh in May–Jul when older birds worn or molting.

Light morph. Head, neck sides, and upperparts medium-dark gray-brown with darker flight feathers; worn-plumaged birds look darker and browner overall, whereas upperparts of fresh-plumaged birds have an ashy-gray sheen and variable dark M pattern, often with secondaries and greater coverts looking frosty at some angles. Variable paler edgings to upperparts most pronounced on scapulars, which often look pale-scalloped. Throat, foreneck, and underbody white with dark brown undertail coverts and variable brown mottling on flanks; some birds (< 1%) have extensively white undertail coverts, the lateral and longest feathers barred dark brown to solidly dark. Underwings white with dark remiges, blackish leading edge to the primary coverts, and variable dark spotting and coarse streaking on primary coverts, lesser coverts, and axillars; whitest portion of underwing is a broad panel across greater and median coverts. Many birds have white throat and underparts freckled and vermiculated dusky, most heavily marked birds with mostly dark underwings and dusky (not white) underbody. Molting birds (mainly Apr–Jun) often show white stripe on upperwing. Bill pinkish with dark tip, legs and feet pink overall.

On the water. Gray-brown overall; white throat, foreneck, and chest often inconspicuous unless seen from the front, when birds appear white chested.

Dark morph (very rare; ≤ 0.1% of population). Dark gray-brown to brown overall, including underbody and underwing coverts. Bill and legs as light morph.

Molt Adult wing molt mainly Apr–Aug, earlier in nonbreeders than breeders. PB2 wing molt perhaps mainly Jan–Jun but few data. Molt of head and back feathers on some birds in Oct–Dec (CAS specimens) may be PF molt or start of PB2 molt.

P4.2. Pink-footed Shearwaters. Note broad wings, pink bill, smudgy demarcation between dark brownish upperparts and white underparts. Worn plumage and incoming new scapulars on this date indicate first-year bird (cf. P4.3). SNGH. Off Monterey, California, 15 Oct 2006.

P4.3. In bright light, upperparts of Pink-footed Shearwater (especially in fresh plumage, as here) can show variable darker M pattern (cf. P4.2, P4.4). SNGH. Off Santa Cruz, California, 12 Oct 2008.

P4.4. (Above) Typical Pink-footed Shearwater in fresh plumage. SNGH. Off Monterey, California, 15 Sep 2008.

P4.5. (Above right) Pink-footed Shearwater with outer primary molt; note how fresh greater coverts appear contrastingly silvery gray. SNGH. Off Bodega Bay, California, 12 Jul 2007.

P4.6. (Right) Some Pink-footed Shearwaters are extensively dusky below and might be mistaken for Flesh-footed Shearwater. Relative to Flesh-footed, this bird is broad winged, gray toned, and has a dull pinkish bill—all features pointing to Pink-footed. SNGH. Off Monterey, California, 15 Sep 2008.

P4.7. Bright patterning of fresh-plumaged Pink-footed Shearwater can suggest Wedge-tailed (cf. P6.10) or even Buller's Shearwater. Pink-footed readily distinguished in the field by larger size, bulky body, shorter tail, and large head with pink bill. SNGH. Off Monterey, California, 25 Sep 2008.

P4.8. Head-on, note pink bill, brownish head not contrasting strongly with white throat. SNGH. Off Monterey, California, 24 Sep 2007.

P4.9. Typical Pink-footed Shearwater, showing eponymous pink feet; underwing pattern highly variable (cf. P4.10–P4.12). SNGH. Off Monterey, California, 15 Sep 2008.

P4.10. Pink-footed Shearwater with very clean white body and underwings (cf. P4.9, P4.11–4.12). SNGH. Off Monterey, California, 27 Sep 2008.

P4.11. Pink-footed Shearwater in mid-primary molt, with extensive dusky markings on body and underwings. SNGH. Off Monterey, California, 11 May 2008.

P4.12. Pink-footed Shearwaters this dark are rare and can be puzzling, but nothing else looks particularly similar. SNGH. Off Monterey, California, 28 Sep 2008.

P4.13. A typical flock of Pink-footed Shearwaters, here resting with a single Buller's Shearwater (left front) and a South Polar Skua (at back). SNGH. Off Monterey, California, 14 Sep 2008.

P4.14. Amount of white visible on resting Pink-footed Shearwaters (two back birds at left, and far right bird) varies greatly with angle and posture. Sleeping birds can suggest a Great Shearwater (front left bird), which has cleaner dark cap, whiter neck sides, and often shows stronger pale scalloping on back. SNGH. Off Bodega Bay, California, 26 Apr 2010.

P4.15. Pink-footed Shearwater similar in overall plumage pattern to much smaller Black-vented Shearwater (right). Black-vented has slender dark bill, whiter sides than Pink-footed, and often appears darker capped. SNGH. Off Monterey, California, 15 Oct 2006.

P4.16. Compared to these Wedge-tailed Shearwaters, Pink-footed (left center) is larger and bulkier with a thick neck, large head, and stout bill. SNGH. Oaxaca, Mexico, 16 Dec 2008.

P5. BULLER'S SHEARWATER *Ardenna bulleri*
L 43–45.5 cm, WS 96–104 cm, tail 115–136 mm (graduation 50–60 mm), bill 38–45 mm
Figures 29–31, 46, 65, P4.13, P5.1–P5.11, P7.1, P7.11, P8.14, P37a.1

Identification Summary Pacific. A fairly large, smartly patterned, and ostensibly unmistakable shearwater. Gray above with clean-cut dark cap, blackish M pattern, and pale-silvery panel on the greater coverts; bright white below. Flight buoyant and graceful, usually fairly low over the water.

P5.1. Buller's Shearwater often flies in fairly close-knit, choreographed flocks, here joined by two Pink-footed Shearwaters (top center). SNGH. Off Bodega Bay, California, 9 Oct 2006.

Taxonomy Monotypic.

Names For *Ardenna*, see under Sooty Shearwater; *bulleri* and the English name commemorate the New Zealand ornithologist Sir W. L. Buller (1838–1906).

Status and Distribution Vulnerable. Breeds (late Nov–Mar) in n New Zealand, ranges to temperate Pacific waters off South America (mainly Mar–Jul) and North America (mainly Aug–Oct). Migration routes and location of prebasic molt not well known; birds in wing molt off Chile in Mar–Jul perhaps prebreeding immatures.

    Pacific. Generally a fairly common nonbreeding visitor off the West Coast (mainly Sep–Oct). Departs New Zealand in Feb–Mar and moves n to subarctic waters of n Pacific (mainly 40–50°N) by Jun–Jul (Wahl 1985); spreads e through Aug but mainly well offshore, whence adults return to New Zealand by Sep.

    Rare to uncommon and irregular off West Coast in mid-Jun to Jul, increasing in Aug (occasional influxes off cen California in mid-Aug may be staging adults; pers. obs.[1]), with main arrival (nonbreeders) in Sep. Peak numbers off West Coast mid-Sep to mid-Oct, with stragglers into Dec, exceptionally Jan. Considerable interannual variation in numbers related to oceanic conditions; numbers off Washington decreased markedly after 1977 (Wahl and Tweit 2000), but off cen California may have increased since late 1980s, perhaps linked to an overall ocean warming trend. Farther n, considered uncommon or rare off s Alaska (late Apr to late Sep), but few observers in that region. Some northbound birds (juveniles and prebreeding immatures?) may wander n along Pacific coast of the Americas, accounting for Jun–Sep records off n

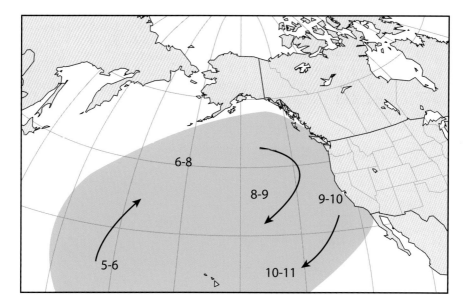

Middle America, in Gulf of California, and a sick bird at Salton Sea in Aug 1966.

Atlantic. Exceptional (Oct 1984) off New Jersey.

FIELD IDENTIFICATION

Similar Species Unlikely to be confused if seen well, but at a distance or in certain lighting conditions several pitfalls exist. In bright sun, beware of the effects of lighting on larger and heavier-bodied *Pink-footed Shearwater* (which see). On the water, sharply black-capped and white-sided appearance can suggest stockier *Great Shearwater* and even *Manx Shearwater*; Great is browner overall with deeper cap, more extensively white hindneck, scaly brown back, dark undertail coverts; Manx is smaller (but size harder to judge on swimming birds than on flying birds) and more compact with shorter bill, blackish upperparts. Light morph *Wedge-tailed Shearwater* in fresh plumage can have frosty-edged greater coverts, pale-edged scapulars, darker M pattern above, and even dark-capped appearance, all suggesting Buller's; note browner upperparts of Wedge-tailed, deeper cap to well below eyes, and dingier underparts with broad dark wing margins and dark undertail coverts.

Plumage pattern of Buller's suggests various gadfly petrels, especially much smaller Stejneger's, but upperparts of Buller's more contrasting, with broad pale panel on greater coverts; gadfly petrels relatively larger headed (the larger species with thicker black bills) and fly with more strongly arcing flight. Stejneger's is small and snappy vs. large

and leisurely Buller's. Overeager observers could confuse Buller's with Cook's Petrel, but this brain fart should be fleeting given the very different sizes and flight manners of the two species. Juan Fernandez Petrel similar in size but has longer and narrower wings, white forehead, blackish eye patch, and more uniform upperwings (gray back is palest area of upperparts, vs. broad pale greater-covert panel on Buller's); note thicker black bill and stronger flight.

Habitat and Behavior (see Fig 29, p. 27) Pelagic, favoring warm-temperate waters from shelf to offshore, and often concentrating at temperature fronts. Singles may be seen alone or among flocks of other shearwaters, especially Pink-footed, but more often gregarious, found in loose to fairly tight aggregations feeding over the ocean or rafting in flocks that number tens to hundreds of birds (occasionally thousands in Sep–Oct). Feeds by wheeling, dashing, and skittering over the surface, seizing prey near the surface and rarely if ever submerging completely. Notable for aerobatic "ballets," whereby tens to hundreds of birds wheel in formation, alternately flashing upper-sides then undersides.

Flight buoyant and generally low, with shallow, slightly flicking wingbeats and frequent glides on wings pressed slightly forward and crooked. Even in moderate to strong winds does not usually wheel very high or steeply, unlike heavier-bodied Pink-footed Shearwater and gadfly petrels.

Description A fairly large, lightly built shearwater with fairly long neck and small head, broad-based wings, and medium-long, distinctly graduated tail; low wing-loading.

Adult. Upperparts gray with dark slaty cap, black tail (central rectrices relatively truncate), and bold blackish M pattern with contrasting pale-gray outer greater coverts, which in fresh plumage often appear as broad silvery panel on upperwings. In gloomy conditions, contrast on upperparts subdued but still apparent at moderate range. Patterns and contrast notably duller when plumage worn and brown-toned (mainly Mar–Apr, when unrecorded in the region). Throat, foreneck, and underparts clean white; narrow black trailing edge to underwing and even narrower leading edge visible only at close range. Bill dark gray with blacker tip, legs and feet pinkish overall.

First cycle. Following presumed PF molt of head and upperparts, first-cycle birds in fall often show slight contrast between fresh gray (or mixed gray-and-brown) back and faded browner upperwings (including tertials); tail browner in fall than adult and central rectrices relatively tapered.

On the water. Throat, foreneck, chest, sides, and undertail coverts bright white, contrasting with dark cap and hindneck, dark chest spur (when neck hunched), gray back, and blackish wings.

Molt Adult wing molt probably Mar–Aug and PB2 wing molt Jan–Jun, but few data; some individuals off California finish growth of p10 and inner secondaries in Aug–Sep (pers. obs.[2]). Apparent PF molt of head and back mostly completed by Sep (CAS specimens).

Notes 1. Daily counts of 900–1000 birds, 12 Aug 2001, 18 Aug 2003, vs. usual daily maxima in August of 10–100 birds. 2. Photo of 13 Sep bird growing p10, with inner secondaries molting.

P5.2. Buller's Shearwater in fresh plumage. Unmistakable if seen well. SNGH. Off Bodega Bay, California, 9 Sep 2008.

P5.3. Plumage of Buller's Shearwater suggests several gadfly petrels; besides differences in size and flight manner, note small head and slender bill of Buller's. SNGH. Off Santa Cruz, California, 12 Oct 2008.

P5.4. Even in fog, striking plumage pattern of Buller's Shearwater is usually discernable. SNGH. Off Bodega Bay, California, 7 Oct 2008.

P5.5. Contrasting pale gray and black pattern of Buller's Shearwater, even flying away, should be unmistakable (cf. P4.7). SNGH. Off Monterey, California, 24 Sep 2007.

P5.6. Head-on, note cleanly demarcated black cap (with white teardrop), clean white underwings with narrow dark trailing edge. SNGH. Off Monterey, California, 24 Sep 2007.

P5.7. As well as clean white underparts, note fairly broad wings and long, wedge-shaped tail of this Buller's Shearwater. SNGH. Off Santa Cruz, California, 12 Oct 2008.

P5.8. Buller's Shearwater has a low wing-loading and often flies low over the waves. SNGH. Off Bodega Bay, California, 17 Oct 2008.

P5.9. Compared to Pink-footed Shearwater (right), Buller's is slightly smaller, more lightly built, and has gleaming, clean white underparts. SNGH. Off Monterey, California, 24 Sep 2007.

P5.10. Contrasting black-and-white head and neck pattern of swimming Buller's Shearwater can suggest appreciably smaller Manx Shearwater. Among other things, Manx lacks white teardrop and contrasting gray back, has much shorter tail. SNGH. Off Monterey, California, 14 Sep 2008.

P5.11. Buller's Shearwaters occasionally climb out of the water to rest on floating kelp mats. SNGH. Off Bodega Bay, California, 17 Oct 2008.

P6. WEDGE-TAILED SHEARWATER *Ardenna pacifica*

L 43–47 cm, WS 99–109 cm, tail 129–147 mm (graduation 55–60 mm), bill 36–44 mm
Figures 36, P4.16, P6.1–P6.20, P7.9, P14.15, P17.16, P18.14–P18.15, P19.9–P19.10

Identification Summary Tropical Pacific, very rare off West Coast. A fairly large, lightly built, and small-headed shearwater with broad-based wings and long graduated tail often held closed in a point. Dimorphic and variable: dark morph dark gray-brown overall with pale scalloping on scapulars; light morph gray-brown above, white below. Bill grayish to pinkish with dark tip. Flight buoyant with frequent glides on slightly arched wings.

Taxonomy Morphological variation complex and in need of study. Murphy (1951) documented increasing average size in wing, tarsus, and culmen from w to e among 10 populations from Indian Ocean to cen Pacific, as well as an increase in average size from equatorial to subtropical populations both to n and s. He distinguished slightly longer-winged birds breeding mostly in Kermadec Islands as nominate *pacificus*, with other populations referred to the subspecies *chlororhynchus*. Whether differences among dark morphs off Mexico (between sooty-grayish birds with grayish bills and chocolate-brown birds with pinkish bills) have taxonomic significance is unknown (study needed).

Names For *Ardenna*, see under Sooty Shearwater; *pacifica* refers to the Pacific Ocean, where this species is widespread.

Status and Distribution Least Concern. Widespread in tropical Pacific and Indian oceans; breeding seasons vary (mainly Jun–Nov in n populations, Nov–Jun in s hemisphere). In the Pacific, light morphs generally commoner in subtropical n latitudes, and dark morphs commoner in tropical and s latitudes, the Mexican population being an exception to this rule.

  Pacific. Local breeder (late May/Jun–Nov) on Isla San Benedicto, Revillagigedo Islands, Mexico (about 1000 pairs, 90% or more dark morph). Fairly common to locally and seasonally common nonbreeding visitor to tropical waters off Middle America. During Nov–Jun, light morphs (presumed from Hawaii) fairly common to common n to around 20°N; during Jul–Oct, smaller numbers off Middle America but locally common (at least in some years) around tip of Baja California Peninsula (mostly presumed nonbreeders from Hawaiian population). Dark morphs generally uncommon (usually only 2–10% of population, pers. obs.) off Middle America (Jan–Dec, most numerous Jun–Sep; King 1974b); based on wing molt timing, some dark morphs in summer off Mexico originate from equatorial populations

(pers. obs.). Overall movement of Pacific breeding birds may follow a counterclockwise route, migrating e along the Equatorial Counter Current and returning w along the North Equatorial Current (King 1974b). Most reports of Wedge-taileds off Costa Rica and Panama are Jan–Mar, although coverage there is irregular.

  Regular range extends n to around 24°N, off s Baja California Peninsula. Very rare (late Mar–Apr, late Aug–Oct) off West Coast, and exceptional at Salton Sea (late Jul). In U.S., spring birds and Salton Sea bird have been dark morphs, whereas fall records both light and dark, with light morphs perhaps more frequent.

FIELD IDENTIFICATION

Similar Species Wedge-tailed is a fairly distinctive species with a light build, small head (often appears "pin-headed"), broad-based wings, long tail, and buoyant flight. However, vagrants could be overlooked easily among large flocks of Sooty and Pink-footed shearwaters, and flying birds can be confused with Pink-footed, Flesh-footed, and even Buller's shearwaters. Note that Wedge-tailed's bill can be contrastingly pale (even pinkish) with a dark tip, and that molting birds have shorter and broader-looking tails than nonmolting birds.

  Dark morph. On the water, *Sooty Shearwater* is stockier and shorter necked, lacking long tail projection of Wedge-tailed, and its bill often looks smaller and slimmer. In flight, Sooty is the opposite of Wedge-tailed—narrow-winged and heavy-bodied with hurried wingbeats and, in windy conditions, steep wheeling. If size is misjudged, dark Wedge-tailed can suggest much smaller *Bulwer's Petrel*, which has quicker flight manner, usually shows distinct pale ulnar bands on upperwing.

  Flesh-footed Shearwater larger, bulkier, and bigger headed with more evenly broad wings, a shorter, less graduated tail (molting Wedge-tailed can appear similar), and thicker bill, which is pink with a blackish tip (beware that Wedge-tailed can have a dark-tipped pinkish bill). Flesh-footed

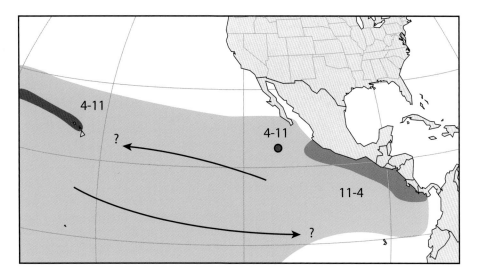

Wedge-tailed Shearwater. Very rare north to California, exceptional to Washington.

generally darker overall than Wedge-tailed, but can appear similar in some lights. Especially at a distance, underwing of Wedge-tailed usually appears more evenly toned, whereas coverts of Flesh-footed often appear contrasting darker than reflectively pale remiges. Wedge-tailed has more buoyant flight with wings pressed slightly forward and crooked, recalling Buller's Shearwater, and can show pale ovals on lores.

Light morph. *Pink-footed Shearwater* similar in plumage to light morph Wedge-tailed but larger, bulkier, and bigger headed with more evenly broad wings, a shorter, less graduated tail (molting Wedge-tailed can appear similar), and thicker bill, which is pink with a blackish tip. Wedge-tailed has a more buoyant flight with wings pressed slightly forward and crooked, recalling Buller's Shearwater. Wedge-tailed also has a more extensively white throat and usually a capped appearance, and typically lacks extensive dark smudging on flanks and underwing coverts. On the water, Wedge-tailed smaller in direct comparison, with longer neck, smaller head, and long tail; typically shows more white on throat and sides.

Buller's Shearwater has bold-patterned upperparts that can be hinted at by fresh-plumaged *Wedge-tailed*; note shallower and more contrasting dark cap of Buller's and extensively bright white underparts with narrow dark wing margins, white undertail coverts.

Streaked Shearwater (vagrant) slightly larger and noticeably broader winged, with paler and grayer upperparts, a white-headed appearance, and overall brighter white underparts, including undertail coverts.

Distant Wedge-taileds seen poorly might suggest large gadfly petrels, especially Hawaiian or Galapagos petrels, but Wedge-tailed is larger with lower-wheeling flight, diffuse dark cap, dark undertail coverts.

Habitat and Behavior Pelagic, over warm tropical waters from inshore to offshore, especially in association with schools of dolphin and yellowfin tuna. Feeds over the shelf with other shearwaters, boobies, and terns, and over deeper pelagic waters with Sooty Terns and Juan Fernandez Petrels. Nests on San Benedicto in burrows dug in compacted ash, and a nocturnal visitor to the island (Apr–Sep, or later). Calls from burrow (Apr–May at least) are eerie, drawn-out, rising and falling wailing moans, usually in series of two and three, e.g., *ouwhh 'oahh ouwhh*, and variations.

Flight typically unhurried with wings pressed forward slightly and crooked; wingbeats usually shallow and easy, interspersed with buoyant glides. In moderate to strong winds may glide and wheel for prolonged periods but typically does not bank steeply and wheel high like heavier-bodied species. In powered flight, such as feeding or avoiding a skua, wingbeats deep and slightly floppy, and can dash erratically over schooling fish, skittering on the water and seizing prey near the surface, rarely if ever submerging completely.

Description A fairly large but lightly built shearwater with relatively long neck, small head, broad-based wings, and long, strongly graduated tail often held closed in a point. At rest, tail typically projects beyond wingtips. Ages similar.

Light morph. Head and upperparts dark gray-brown to brown, darker on flight feathers, with variable pale scalloping on scapulars (duller in fresh plumage) and greater coverts (brighter and often frosty gray in fresh plumage); head sometimes appears dark capped (cap below eye level). Throat, foreneck, and underparts white with mostly dark undertail coverts; body rarely freckled and washed dusky ("intermediate morph"). Underwings white with dark remiges, a dark leading edge to primary coverts, a narrow dark leading edge to secondary coverts, and sometimes a variable dark ulnar bar and dusky axillars; heavily marked birds have mostly dark underwing with a broad whitish central panel. Bill grayish to pale pinkish with dark tip, legs and feet pinkish overall.

On the water. Throat, foreneck, and chest white, contrasting with dark cap, hindneck, and chest sides; upperparts dark brown with variable pale scalloping and blacker flight feathers; sides whitish or variably washed and mottled dusky, thigh patch and undertail coverts mostly dark.

Dark morph. Dark sooty brown to brown overall (can appear fairly warm brown in sunlight), paler below and darker on flight feathers, with variable pale scalloping on scapulars and greater coverts. Lores sometimes paler, showing as pale ovals at base of bill, and rarely throat can be contrastingly whitish. Underwings often show a broad paler central panel across greater coverts and primary bases. Bill grayish to pink with black tip, legs and feet pinkish overall.

Molt Adult wing molt timing varies with population. Mexican and Hawaiian birds in wing molt mainly Sep–Apr, with immatures earlier than breeders; tail molt occurs late in period of primary molt (King 1974b). Wing molt of equatorial populations mainly Apr–Sep, with immatures earlier than breeders. First-years, at least of n breeding populations, have head and body molt (Jun–Aug?) that may be PF or start of protracted PB2 (study needed; cf. P6.4, P6.18).

P6.1. Light morph Wedge-tailed Shearwater showing classic shape with big broad wings, long tapered tail, small head; pale feather tips on upperparts form distinct pale scalloping in fresh plumage (cf. P6.3). SNGH. Western Pacific, 24°N 143°E, 29 Apr 2008.

P6.2. Light morph Wedge-tailed Shearwater. Note long angular wings with pale-tipped greater coverts, tapered tail, slender gray bill. SNGH. Western Pacific, 20°N 146°E, 20 Apr 2008.

P6.3. Light morph Wedge-tailed Shearwater in worn plumage, with most pale tips to upperparts lost (cf. P6.1, P6.4). SNGH. Oaxaca, Mexico, 15 Dec 2008.

P6.4. Light morph Wedge-tailed Shearwater with two generations of scapulars, perhaps a first-cycle bird (note uniformly worn upperwing coverts) with preformative body molt. SNGH. Baja California Sur, Mexico, 20 Aug 2010.

P6.5. Light morph Wedge-tailed Shearwater in fresh plumage, with distinct pale tips to upperparts, strikingly pale bill (cf. P6.3). SNGH. Western Pacific, 20°N 146°E, 20 Apr 2008.

P6.6. Typical light morph Wedge-tailed Shearwater, with outer primary molt. Note broad wings, tapered tail, dark but smudgily demarcated cap, slender gray bill. SNGH. Oaxaca, Mexico, 8 Mar 2007.

P6.7. Typical light morph Wedge-tailed Shearwater. Note shape, dark cap, slender bill. SNGH. Western Pacific, 24°N 143°E, 28 Apr 2008.

P6.8. Light morph Wedge-tailed Shearwater with extensive dusky markings on underparts suggesting pattern of Pink-footed Shearwater. SNGH. Baja California Sur, Mexico, 20 Aug 2010.

P6.9. Dusky-bodied or "intermediate" Wedge-tailed Shearwaters, like this, are very much in the minority among birds found in the region. MS. Baja California Sur, Mexico, 20 Aug 2010.

P6.10. Light morph Wedge-tailed Shearwater in fresh plumage (cf. P4.7, P5.5), with distinct pale tips to upperparts; squared-looking tail tip may indicate central rectrices not fully grown. SNGH. Western Pacific, 20°N 146°E, 20 Apr 2007.

P6.11. Dark morph Wedge-tailed Shearwater. In bright sun, underparts can appear warm gingery brown (cf. P6.12). SNGH. Western Pacific, 23°S 166°E, 8 Apr 2008.

P6.12. Dark morph Wedge-tailed Shearwater. In overcast conditions, underparts can appear cold gray-brown (cf. P6.11). SNGH. Western Pacific, 23°S 166°E, 31 Mar 2007.

P6.13. (Above left) Some dark morph Wedge-tailed Shearwaters are overall chocolate-brown and can have a pink, black-tipped bill, inviting confusion with Flesh-footed Shearwater. Note long tapered tail, mid-primary molt on this date. SNGH. Oaxaca, Mexico, 18 Dec 2008.

P6.14. (Above) Some dark morph Wedge-tailed Shearwaters are overall sooty brown, have a grayish bill, and, especially during molt, can show whitish underwing patches, inviting confusion with Sooty Shearwater. Note long tail, pink legs and feet, mid-primary molt on this date. SNGH. Oaxaca, Mexico, 18 Dec 2008.

P6.15. (Left) Dark morph Wedge-tailed Shearwater. Note classic shape with broad wings, long tapered tail, small head. Equatorial populations (which are mainly dark morph) breed at opposite season to north-tropical populations; hence worn plumage on this date (cf. P6.5). SNGH. Western Pacific, 23°S 166°E, 8 Apr 2008.

P6.16. Light morph Wedge-tailed Shearwater. Note long neck, small head, and long tail; bill coloration variable (cf. P6.17). SNGH. Oaxaca, Mexico, 18 Dec 2008.

P6.17. Light morph Wedge-tailed Shearwater. Note long tapered tail, broad pale tips to scapulars; bill coloration variable (cf. P6.16). SNGH. Oaxaca, Mexico, 8 Mar 2007.

P6.18. Presumed first-cycle light morph Wedge-tailed Shearwater (note uniformly worn upperwing coverts); new back feathers may reflect preformative molt (cf. P6.4). SNGH. Baja California Sur, Mexico, 20 Aug 2010.

P6.19. Dark morph Wedge-tailed Shearwater. Plumage tones and long gray bill suggest Sooty Shearwater, but note lighter build with longer neck, long tapered tail. SNGH. Oaxaca, Mexico, 16 Dec 2008.

P6.20. Off Middle America, Wedge-tailed Shearwaters (one dark morph, on left) often associate in mixed-species feeding flocks with Brown Boobies (taking off behind). SNGH. Oaxaca, Mexico, 16 Dec 2008.

P7. STREAKED SHEARWATER *Calonectris leucomelas*

L 45–52 cm, WS 103–113 cm, tail 130–145 mm (graduation 40–50 mm), bill 45–55 mm
Figures P7.1–P7.10

Identification Summary Pacific. Very rare fall visitor (mainly to California). A medium-large, rangy shearwater with broad wings, a fairly long graduated tail, long neck, and small head. Gray-brown above and white below with distinctive white face, pale scalloping on back, and large dark patches on underprimary coverts. Shape and buoyant flight suggest Buller's Shearwater or Wedge-tailed Shearwater rather than the heavier-bodied Pink-footed; moderate wing-loading.

P7.1. Streaked Shearwater (back right) with Pink-footed Shearwaters, Western Gulls, and a Buller's Shearwater (back left). White face of Streaked can be striking in bright light; also note gray-green bill, white flanks and undertail coverts. SNGH. Off Monterey, California, 15 Oct 2006.

Taxonomy Monotypic.

Names *Calonectris* means "beautiful swimmer"; *leucomelas* means "black-and-white," presumably in reference to the strongly bicolored plumage.

Status and Distribution Least Concern. Breeds (May–Nov) in nw Pacific, ranging s (mainly Nov–Feb) to n Australia and rarely the n Indian Ocean; very rare in e Pacific.
    Pacific. Very rare visitor (mid-Aug to mid-Oct) off Oregon and California, perhaps becoming slightly more frequent in recent years; exceptional inland in n California (Aug 1993) and Wyoming (desiccated carcass found Jun 2006; Faulkner

2007), perhaps linked to tropical cyclones tracking through the n Pacific.

FIELD IDENTIFICATION

Similar Species A distinctive large shearwater, but beware of leucistic individuals of other shearwater species that might show a white face. Besides the white face, note Streaked's long neck; small head with a long and slender pale bill; broad wings and fairly long wedge-shaped tail; pale-scalloped back; and bright white underparts with a variable dark patch on underprimary coverts. On the water, perhaps as likely to be mistaken for a first-year *California Gull* as for another species of shearwater: note long neck and small head, which are extensively white. Some California birds have been molting middle primaries; in Sep–Oct this should attract attention because Pink-footed and Buller's shearwaters have completed wing molt by that time.

Pink-footed Shearwater bulkier and thicker necked with bigger head and shorter, less strongly graduated tail; has generally dingier underparts with dark mottling and dark undertail coverts, and pink bill with black tip. At a distance in good light, back of Streaked usually appears paler and grayer than dark brown typical of Pink-footed.

Buller's Shearwater shares Streaked's bright white underparts and easy, buoyant flight, but has quicker, flicking wingbeats (not languid and heavy like Streaked) and distinctly different plumage.

Light morph *Wedge-tailed Shearwater* (vagrant to West Coast) slightly smaller and appreciably narrower winged, with darker and browner upperparts, a dark-capped appearance, and overall dingier underparts with dark on leading edge of underwings, dark distal undertail coverts.

Cory's Shearwater (vagrant to e Pacific) shares overall *Calonectris* shape, languid flight, and bright white underparts but larger and bulkier with bigger head, gray-brown head and neck, stout yellowish bill.

Habitat and Behavior Inshore waters over shelf and shelf slope, usually with Pink-footed and Buller's shearwaters, but also associates readily with mixed-species feeding flocks that include gulls, cormorants, and other species. Several birds have been attracted to flocks of birds following boats that were chumming.

Flight in light to moderate winds languid and buoyant with easy, fairly loose wingbeats and low wheeling glides on flexed or slightly arched wings, recalling Buller's or Wedge-tailed shearwaters rather than heavier Pink-footed. Sails higher in stronger winds, more so than Buller's but not as high as Pink-footed.

Description Large and rangy with fairly broad-based wings and medium-long graduated tail often held closed in a point; long neck and relatively small head often lend somewhat gawky appearance. Bill fairly long and slender. Fairly low wing-loading.

Ages similar. Head, foreneck, and underparts white, the crown and head sides with variable dark slaty spotting and streaking (hence the species' name) often setting off a white eye ring. Underwings white with dark remiges, variable dark marks on primary coverts (typically a broad dark panel on median underprimary coverts, but some birds have mostly white coverts), and sometimes a diffuse, dark-streaked ulnar bar; despite having a broad dark trailing edge, the underwings can appear overall bright white at medium to long range. Upperparts medium-dark gray-brown with darker flight feathers and whitish scalloping (lost by wear) on back, rump, and uppertail coverts (broadest on longest and lateral uppertail coverts). Legs and feet pinkish overall; bill pale fleshy gray to pale greenish with a dusky subterminal mark.

On the water. Head and neck extensively white with broad dark hindneck shawl, upperparts dark with pale scalloping; sides and undertail coverts white with variable brown thigh strap.

Molt Adult wing molt perhaps mainly Nov–Mar and PB2 wing molt Sep–Jan, but few data. Head and body molt apparently precedes wing molt, as in Cory's Shearwater, and some California birds in Sep–Oct had fresh head and upperpart feathers with distinct whitish tipping but had not started wing molt.

P7.2. Streaked Shearwater. Note white face, dark hindneck, and long, broad tapered tail. Prominence of patterning on upperparts varies greatly with lighting (cf. P7.3). SNGH. Miyake Jima, Japan, 3 May 2008.

P7.3. Streaked Shearwater. Prominence of patterning on upperparts varies with lighting (cf. P7.2) and also with wear. SNGH. Miyake Jima, Japan, 3 May 2008.

P7.4. Streaked Shearwater is a distinctive species. Bill color varies from pale gray-green to dirty pale pinkish. SNGH. Off Monterey, California, 15 Oct 2006.

P7.5. Streaked Shearwater. Some birds have coarse white spotting on head; dark markings on underwing coverts variable (cf. P7.6–P7.7). SNGH. Miyake Jima, Japan, 3 May 2008.

P7.6. Streaked Shearwater. Ostensibly unmistakable if seen well. SNGH. Off Monterey, California, 15 Oct 2006.

P7.7. Extent of dark markings on underwing coverts of Streaked Shearwater variable (cf. P7.5–P7.6); this is a lightly marked individual. Also note bright white underparts, long tapered tail. SNGH. Miyake Jima, Japan, 3 May 2008.

P7.8. Streaked Shearwater. White head markings variable. Note bright white body and underwing coverts, pale grayish bill. SNGH. Western Pacific, 23°N 144°E, 21 Apr 2007.

P7.9. Streaked Shearwater (right) with light morph Wedge-tailed Shearwater. Note larger size and greater bulk of Streaked, plus its clean white axillars and undertail coverts, dark primary coverts. SNGH. Torishima, Japan, 1 May 2008.

P7.10. Streaked Shearwater (center) with Heermann's Gull (back left), Western Gull (back right), and Brandt's Cormorant. Long neck and small head of Streaked can lend it a rather gull-like aspect. SNGH. Off Monterey, California, 30 Sep 2006.

P7.11. Streaked Shearwater (front) with Buller's and Pink-footed shearwaters. As well as white face and gray-green bill, note white flanks and undertail coverts. SNGH. Off Monterey, California, 15 Oct 2006.

P8. GREAT SHEARWATER *Ardenna gravis*
L 45–49 cm, WS 108–116 cm, tail 106–124 mm (graduation 25–30 mm), bill 43–50 mm
Figures 6–7, 66, 68, 83, P4.14, P8.1–P8.16, P9.1, P9.11, P10.1, P14.1

Identification Summary Atlantic (very rare Pacific). A large, distinctive shearwater, dark brown above and white below, with a contrasting dark cap, long black bill, dark smudging on belly and underwing coverts. Often has been called Greater Shearwater in North America.

P8.1. Great Shearwaters (left, and back right, wings raised) often scavenge at fishing boats, here with two Pomarine Jaegers and a Sooty Shearwater. SNGH. Off Hatteras, North Carolina, 25 May 2007.

Taxonomy Monotypic.

Names For *Ardenna*, see under Sooty Shearwater; *gravis* means "heavy," although this species is no heavier (and no greater) than several other species of *Ardenna*.

Status and Distribution Least Concern. Breeds (Nov–May) on islands in s Atlantic Ocean, ranges n (mainly May–Nov) to n Atlantic; very rare (Jan–Dec) in e Pacific (Chile and North America).

    Atlantic. Fairly common to locally common nonbreeding visitor (mainly Jun–Nov) to waters off e North America. Migrates north (May–Jun) from s Atlantic breeding grounds, passing Bermuda in numbers (with a peak there in late May–Jun) and arriving off the Carolinas in mid-May

to early Jun. Most move n to molt in more productive cooler waters from New England n to Atlantic Canada (ranging n to waters off se Baffin Island and s Greenland), where commonest Jun–early Nov, at times with flocks numbering hundreds of thousands. Birds remaining off the Carolinas in Jun–Aug are mainly nonmolting juveniles and second-cycle birds completing outer primary molt (NCSM specimens). Most birds apparently move e into n Atlantic (with some recorded off w Europe) before heading s, while others move s (Sep–Nov, with stragglers into Dec) off e North America, although generally rare s of the Carolinas. Casual, but perhaps increasing, in winter and early spring (Jan–Apr) off East Coast, n to Nova Scotia, exceptionally Newfoundland (B. Mactavish, pers. comm.).

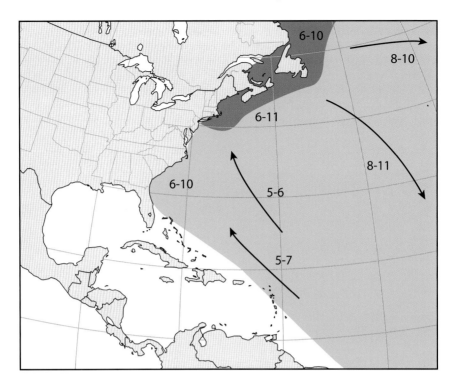

Great Shearwater. Very rare in Gulf of Mexico and North Pacific.

Apparently an uncommon to fairly common (but probably under-recorded) migrant (mainly May–Jul) off Lesser Antilles and n West Indies, and uncommon (mainly Jun–Oct) off se U.S. Very rare in Gulf of Mexico (mainly late Jun–Oct, stragglers into Dec) w to Texas. Mid-summer records from Florida and Gulf of Mexico often involve dead or dying birds found onshore.

Casual inland (mainly Aug–Sep) in e U.S. from Florida n to New England, exceptionally w to e Great Lakes (Ontario Birds 16:58, 1998) and Tennessee (NAB 60:82, 2006), mainly after tropical cyclones.

Pacific. Very rare visitor, mainly since 1990s (mainly Aug–Oct; also late Nov–Apr off California) from Gulf of Alaska (Aug 2001; Pearce 2002) s to cen California.

FIELD IDENTIFICATION

Similar Species Great Shearwater is a distinctive species when seen well. Distant birds might be confused with other tubenoses, however, and vagrants should always be studied carefully.

Atlantic. *Cory's Shearwater* (favors warmer waters but often seen in association with Great) is larger and broader winged with a big yellowish bill visible at moderate range. Cory's has more languid wingbeats of slightly arched wings, which usually rise higher above the body, and has more buoyant flight with more-prolonged gliding in calm to light winds. In strong winds, Great often towers more steeply (recalling Sooty Shearwater) whereas Cory's wheels high but less steeply, and with longer-wavelength arcs. Cory's is paler gray-brown above and cleaner white below, and lacks strong plumage contrasts of Great; some (mainly first-cycle?) Cory's have darker face and head that might suggest capped appearance of Great.

Black-capped Petrel smaller and more boldly patterned, only likely to be mistaken for Great Shearwater if seen poorly. Note large white upper-tail-covert patch of Black-capped and more buoyant flight.

Pomarine and Parasitic jaegers on the water usually appear longer necked, and neck often washed yellowish; note shorter bills, also the pinkish bill base and deeper cap of Pomarine. In windy conditions jaegers can wheel like shearwaters but generally have more crooked wings, dark underwings, and white primary flashes. Molting shearwaters often show white upperwing flashes but these are usually on secondary bases, not primaries.

Pacific. Buller's Shearwater slightly smaller and more lightly built but at rest on the water could suggest Great Shearwater. Great is overall browner and more uniform above (Buller's has a gray back) with dark undertail coverts (white on Buller's), deeper and more evenly demarcated cap, which extends well below eyes, and more extensive white on neck sides. Also see jaegers (above).

Habitat and Behavior Favors cooler waters over continental shelf, shelf slope, and banks, but migrates through warm waters. Generally pelagic, although not far offshore, and may be seen from land during windy conditions or storms. Often associates with other shearwaters, Wilson's Storm Petrels, and gulls; scavenges aggressively at fishing boats, where dives readily. Some vagrants in the Pacific have been with large flocks of shearwaters on the water, others have been attracted to boats but have not associated strongly with other shearwaters. Foraging birds often utter nasal bleating and squawking calls.

In calm to light winds, flies with fairly stiff wingbeats (mainly below the body plane), short glides, and low arcing on slightly bowed wings held out fairly straight from the body. In moderate to strong winds arcs higher and flaps less, at times wheeling steeply in strong winds.

Description A large shearwater with medium-width wings, a slightly graduated tail, and fairly long, slender hooked bill; moderate wing-loading.

Adult. Upperparts dark brown to gray-brown with darker remiges, clean-cut brownish-black cap offset by narrow whitish hindcollar, and white distal uppertail coverts that typically form a contrasting white band above blackish tail. Pale grayish to gray-brown edgings to upperparts lend a scalloped appearance obvious at close range and boldest on scapulars (duller and browner in fresh fall plumage, bolder and whiter in spring and early summer). Throat, neck, and underparts white with variable dark-brown belly patch (often best seen on birds banking away), mostly dark-brown undertail coverts, and dark-brown neck spur forward of wings. Underwings white with broad dark trailing edge, narrow blackish leading edge to primary coverts, and variable dark spotting and coarse streaking on primary coverts, lesser coverts, and axillars. Molting birds (mainly Jun–Jul) often have a white stripe across upperwing on secondary bases. Bill blackish, legs and feet pink overall.

Immature. Juvenile (Jun–Nov in n hemisphere) similar to adult but lacks whitish hindcollar, the cap and hindneck evenly dusky dark brown or cap contrastingly darker (especially when hindneck faded in fall); plumage fresh in Jun–Jul but often faded and worn by Sep–Nov, when pale tips to juvenile back feathers bleach to whitish (adult tips fresher and duller at this season). First-summer (second-cycle) birds in May–Aug have cap and hindneck pattern varying from adult-like to juvenile-like, and often retain one or more abraded juvenile outer primaries into Jul, rarely Aug or later. Dark belly patch reduced in worn plumage and virtually absent on some birds in Oct–Dec. Birds in May–Jun with very faded, worn greater coverts and primaries contrasting with fresh blackish secondaries may be second-summer individuals that completed PB2 early.

On the water. Neck, chest, and sides white with contrasting dark cap, variable brownish on hindneck; dark upperparts and dark undertail coverts; slender blackish bill.

Molt Adult wing molt of breeders fairly rapid in n hemisphere (late May–early Aug); presumed prebreeders still molting outer primaries through Sep. Variable PF molt of head and back feathers may occur Jul–Sep (needs confirmation). PB2 wing molt starts Jan–Mar in s hemisphere, perhaps completing by Apr–May on some birds, before migration, but most birds complete outer primary molt during Jun–Aug in n hemisphere, with some not completing until Oct (NCSM specimens, pers. obs.).

P8.2. Great Shearwater in fresh plumage, recently having completed prebasic molt. Unmistakable if seen well, note contrasting blackish cap, scaly dark-brown upperparts, slender black bill. SNGH. Off Monterey, California, 15 Oct 2006.

P8.3. Adult Great Shearwater completing prebasic molt, with three outer primaries growing simultaneously (outer primaries typically grow sequentially in second prebasic molt, which usually completes earlier; cf. P8.4–P8.5). BM. Newfoundland, Canada, 14 Aug 2006.

P8.4. (Above) Timing of prebasic molt on this Great Shearwater retarded for second cycle (P8.5), advanced for breeding adult (P8.3); together with heavily worn (second basic?) outer primaries, may indicate third cycle. SNGH. Off Hatteras, North Carolina, 1 Jun 2008.

P8.5. (Above right) Great Shearwater completing second prebasic molt (p10 growing); plumage aspect not distinguishable from adult but molt completes earlier (cf. P8.3). SNGH. Off Hatteras, North Carolina, 23 May 2007.

P8.6. (Right) Juvenile Great Shearwater. Besides uniformly fresh plumage on this date, strong brown wash to hindneck typical of juveniles (cf. P8.2–P8.5). SNGH. Off Hatteras, North Carolina, 6 Jun 2009.

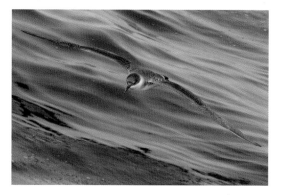

P8.7. Great Shearwater. Head-on, note contrasting dark cap (including forehead), typically incomplete white collar (cf. Black-capped Petrel, P20.14). SNGH. Off Hatteras, North Carolina, 22 May 2007.

P8.8. Great Shearwater. Going away, note scaly gray-brown upperparts, well-demarcated white band at base of tail (cf. P9.9). SNGH. Off Hatteras, North Carolina, 30 May 2007.

P8.9. Second-cycle Great Shearwater (p9-p10 are frayed juvenile feathers). Dark markings on belly and underwing coverts variable (cf. P8.10–P8.11). SNGH. Off Hatteras, North Carolina, 30 May 2007.

P8.10. Juvenile Great Shearwater (note sharply pointed p10) showing minimal dark markings on underwing coverts; belly not fully visible at this angle. SNGH. Off Hatteras, North Carolina, 4 Aug 2007.

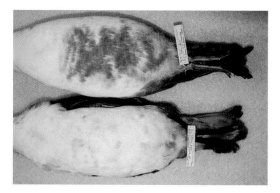

P8.11. Variation in dark belly markings on Great Shearwater. Upper bird (NCSM 4472; 7 Jun) is typical, lower bird (NCSM 5896; 14 Oct) shows how some first-year birds become by late fall, with dark tips mostly worn off. SNGH. Specimens from North Carolina.

P8.12. Rafting Great Shearwaters typically exhibit a strongly contrasting black-and-white appearance at a distance (cf. P9.1). BM. Newfoundland, Canada, 14 Aug 2006.

P8.13. Juvenile Great Shearwater, as here, typically has browner hindneck and paler cap than adult. SNGH. Off Hatteras, North Carolina, 4 Aug 2007.

P8.14. Great Shearwater (left) is larger and bulkier than Buller's Shearwater (right), with a more contrasting dark cap and typically a bold white band at the base of its shorter, broader tail. SNGH. New Zealand, 35°S 174°E, 20 Apr 2011.

P8.15. Great Shearwater is similar in size and overall shape to Pink-footed Shearwater (right). SNGH. Off Bodega Bay, California, 26 Apr 2010.

P8.16. Compared with Great Shearwater (right), dark-faced Black-capped Petrel is smaller and stockier with large white rump patch, white forehead, thicker bill. SNGH. Off Hatteras, North Carolina, 6 Jun 2009.

The Cory's Shearwater complex comprises three taxa that breed in the ne Atlantic and Mediterranean: Cory's Shearwater (*C. borealis*), breeding on Atlantic islands off nw Africa; Scopoli's Shearwater (*C. diomedea*), breeding in the Mediterranean; and Cape Verde Shearwater (*C. edwardsii*), breeding on the Cape Verde islands, off West Africa (Figs 84–87). The first two species are regular nonbreeding visitors to North American waters; the last is an exceptional vagrant there.

Patteson and Armistead (2004) discussed the taxonomic history of the distinctive Cape Verde Shearwater, whose appearance in life (as opposed to in a museum tray) was highlighted only recently (Porter et al. 1997), and this taxon is now usually afforded species status. Cory's and Scopoli's shearwaters appear more similar to one another than to Cape Verde, but differ appreciably in plumage, morphology, voice (Bretagnolle & Lequette 1990), and genetics (Randi et al. 1989, Wink et al. 1993). Very limited (and perhaps only recent) interbreeding may occur between Scopoli's and immigrant Cory's in the Mediterranean (Thibault & Bretagnolle 1998), but the two taxa nonetheless appear distinct enough to treat as separate species (Robb et al. 2008, van den Berg 2006).

Fig 84. Scopoli's Shearwater (left) and Cory's Shearwater (right), identified in flight by underwing pattern (see P10.6 of same individuals). Resting birds often not safely distinguished but note larger darker head and deeper bill of Cory's. SNGH. Off Hatteras, North Carolina, 5 Aug 2007.

Fig 85. Cory's Shearwater (identified in flight by underwing pattern). Resting birds often not safely distinguished from Scopoli's but note relatively large head (cf. Fig 86); bill size may indicate female. SNGH. Off Hatteras, North Carolina, 17 Aug 2009.

Fig 86. Scopoli's Shearwater (identified in flight by underwing pattern). Resting birds often not safely distinguished from Cory's but note small head, which can make bill appear relatively large (cf. Fig 85). SNGH. Off Hatteras, North Carolina, 16 Aug 2009.

Fig 87. Cape Verde Shearwater. Slightly smaller and lighter in build than Cory's or Scopoli's, with darker and browner head and neck, typically dusky pinkish bill. KM. Cape Verde Islands, 25 Mar 2007.

P9. CORY'S SHEARWATER *Calonectris [diomedea] borealis*

L 48–56 cm, WS 113–124 cm, tail 121–144 mm (graduation 25–35 mm), bill 50–60 mm
Figures 15, 17, 62, 66, 68, 78, 80, 82, 84, 85, P9.1–P9.11, P10.1, P10.6, P20.19, P40.10

Identification Summary Atlantic, over warmer waters. The largest shearwater, with broad wings and a long stout bill. Gray-brown above and white below, with a big yellowish bill; underside of outer primaries dark or with variable whitish tongues. Flight unhurried with languid wingbeats and easy glides. Does not scavenge at boats.

P9.1. Rafts of Cory's Shearwaters show varying degrees of bright white but generally lack the strongly contrasting effect of Great Shearwaters (cf. P8.12); given this flock size, some Scopoli's Shearwaters are likely mixed in. Can you spot the two Great Shearwaters in this group? Look for the contrasting blackish caps. SNGH. Off Hatteras, North Carolina, 21 Aug 2009.

Taxonomy Monotypic. See introduction to the Cory's Shearwater complex (pp. 105–106). Slight differences in size exist among some populations (Granadeiro 1993).

Names *Calonectris* means "beautiful swimmer," and *borealis* "northern." The English name commemorates U.S. ornithologist Charles B. Cory (1857–1921).

Status and Distribution Least Concern. Breeds (May–Oct) in subtropical ne Atlantic, ranges widely in Atlantic from e North America (mainly May–Oct) to South America and South Africa (mainly Nov–Feb).

Atlantic. Fairly common to locally common nonbreeding visitor (mainly May–Nov) to warmer waters from Florida (commonest Sep–Nov) and Bahamas n to waters s of Cape Cod (where commonest Jul–Oct; extreme dates off Massachusetts early Apr and mid-Dec), ranging n irregularly (mainly Jul–Oct in warm-water years) to waters s of Nova Scotia and Newfoundland (B. Mactavish, pers. comm.), casually to Gulf of Maine. Uncommon to rare offshore in Gulf of Mexico (May–Nov, mainly Jul–Sep) w to Texas, especially along the shelf break. Poorly known off Greater and Lesser Antilles: uncommon to fairly common (May–Jul) off Lesser Antilles (where casual Nov–Apr), and casual (Sep–Oct) in s Caribbean. Very

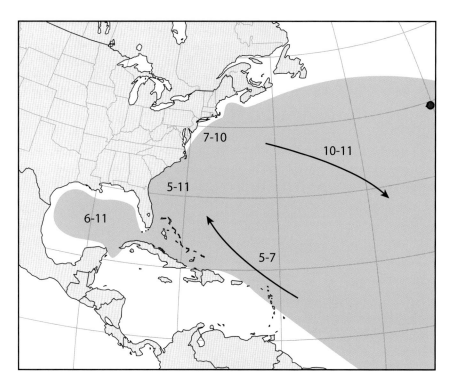

Cory's Shearwater. Very rare in southern Caribbean; exceptional in North Pacific. Scopoli's Shearwater appears to have same distribution.

rare inland after tropical cyclones (mainly Sep) from Virginia n to Massachusetts, exceptionally to Oklahoma (NAB 63:113, 2009). Most if not all North American records are of immatures and nonbreeding birds.

Pacific. Exceptional off cen California (Aug 2003), and vocalizing on land (mainly Mar–Oct) at the Coronado Islands, Baja California, in 2005–2007 (NAB 59:658, 2006; NAB 60:441, 2007; NAB 61:515, 533, 2008).

FIELD IDENTIFICATION

Similar Species Cory's and Scopoli's shearwaters are a distinctive species-pair, but at long range or under poor viewing conditions they might be confused with other species such as Great Shearwater. Distant wheeling birds might suggest large *Pterodroma* petrels, but the arcs of Cory's are typically lower and less towering. The main difficulty lies in distinguishing Cory's from Scopoli's, which may be possible given good views. Also see Cape Verde Shearwater (fall vagrant off the East Coast).

Atlantic. *Scopoli's Shearwater* averages smaller and more lightly built with narrower wings, smaller head, and slimmer bill. Beware, though, that both species exhibit marked sexual dimorphism, so small female Cory's overlaps in bill size with male Scopoli's; moreover, because Scopoli's has a smaller head its bill can look disproportionately large. Under comparable conditions, the flight of Scopoli's is lighter and less lumbering than Cory's, with slightly quicker wingbeats.

Pattern on undersides of the primaries, especially p10, may be best plumage feature to distinguish these two species at sea, but more work is needed. On Scopoli's, bases to primaries (including p10) typically have distinct and fairly long white tongues on inner webs, which project into dark wingtip; on Cory's, primaries are solidly dark or have variable white tongues, but with little or no white visible on p10 beyond tips of primary coverts. Overall effect on typical Cory's is of an evenly rounded white/dark covert/primary border, whereas on typical Scopoli's the border is more jagged and diffuse. However, some birds may not be safely ascribed to either species on the basis of underwing pattern (Howell & Patteson 2008a). Fairly good views are needed to evaluate underwing pattern (which is often best seen on photos); beware that shadowing can make Scoploi's appear dark under the primaries, whereas reflective sunlight can bleach out contrast on Cory's and make the primary bases appear pale.

Proposed differences in upperpart tone and neck contrast (Gutierrez 1998) may be more helpful for breeding adults than for nonbreeding immatures, which comprise most or all of the North American population. For example, fading of weaker juvenile feathers can make Cory's appear paler above, and ongoing head and neck molt could make Scopoli's appear darker above.

Great Shearwater, the only other large white-bellied shearwater regular in Atlantic region, is slightly smaller and narrower winged than Cory's, with stiffer wingbeats that have a lower upstroke; lacks languid flight typical of Cory's in calm to light winds. Sailing Greats in windy conditions tend to hold their wings straighter, less pressed forward and crooked, and have slightly quicker, stiffer wingbeats. Great has dark brown upperparts with contrasting dark brown cap, white neck sides, more contrasting white uppertail-covert band, and slender black bill. Variable dark mottling on belly and underwing coverts of Great usually visible at closer range.

Immature *Northern Gannet* or boobies in the distance are perhaps as likely to be mistaken for Cory's as is anything else, but they have thick necks and long head and bill projections.

Distant *Northern Fulmar* in bad light could suggest Cory's to an inexperienced observer, but note the fulmar's straighter wings and its stiffer and more hurried wingbeats.

Pacific. Observers from Atlantic often find that *Pink-footed Shearwater* suggests Cory's, and vagrant Cory's could be overlooked as, or among flocks of, Pink-footed. Given a good view, these two species appear distinct, however. Cory's is larger, longer necked, and bigger billed (evident in direct comparison), and also can look paler and warmer brown on hindneck and upperparts. Cory's has white undertail coverts whereas Pink-footed has mostly dark undertail coverts, which helps greatly with birds on the water. In flight, cleaner white underwings of Cory's are another feature and it often shows a whitish band on uppertail coverts; bill color and pattern are diagnostic given good views. Flight of Cory's is more buoyant than heavier flight of Pink-footed.

Habitat and Behavior Warmer waters from inshore to offshore. Regularly seen from shore off the Atlantic coast, especially when following warm water and schooling fish inshore. Off the Atlantic coast mostly associated with Gulf Stream, where birds often concentrate at fronts, especially along Gulf Stream's inshore edge (Haney & McGillivray 1985); in Gulf of Mexico off Texas, favors fronts over the shelf break and offshore banks (Pulich 1982). Often feeds over dolphins and schools of bait fish with terns, Audubon's Shearwaters, and other birds; will follow boats for short periods but does not usually come in close and scavenge aggressively as do Great Shearwaters. Foraging birds often utter nasal bleating calls. California vagrant was with a large raft of Pink-footed, Buller's, and Sooty shearwaters.

In light to moderate winds, flight generally unhurried with languid wingbeats and buoyant glides on slightly arched or bowed wings that are pressed forward and crooked slightly; wingbeats relatively loose with a fairly pronounced, arched upstroke; in moderate to strong winds can fly fast and wheel high, but usually not as steep or quickly as Great Shearwater. Feeding birds scavenge or splash and skitter on the surface; rarely seen diving in the region.

Description The largest shearwater; wings broad and tail graduated; bill stout to medium-stout and long with a hooked tip; moderate wing-loading. Melanistic individuals occur very rarely (Bried et al. 2005).

Ages similar. Head, neck sides, and upperparts gray-brown to brown (often looking relatively warm brown in sunlight) with darker flight feathers; head and back often slightly paler and grayer, contrasting with darker and browner upperwings, which in some lights show darker M pattern; back feathers, especially scapulars, have paler tips that form variable scalloping, boldest when tips bleach to whitish; longest uppertail coverts usually have some whitish, extensive on some birds (especially bleached first-cycle birds?), which forms variable U-shaped band at base of tail. In first-year birds, molt can include variable amount of head and back, and some first-cycle birds in May–Jun have dark face contrasting with bleached pale nape (faded juvenile feathering). Throat, foreneck, and underparts bright white. Underwings white with dark remiges (typically little or no white on exposed bases of primaries, and border between coverts and primaries evenly rounded), a narrow dark leading edge to primary coverts, very fine dark leading edge to secondary coverts, and sometimes a narrow, diffuse, dark-streaked ulnar bar; despite having a broad dark tip and trailing edge, the underwings appear bright white overall at medium to long range. Even at fairly close range, reflected sunlight can wash out undersides to primaries and reduce contrast between white primary coverts and dark primaries; and some birds have moderate whitish tongues on outer primaries, especially p9. Legs and feet pinkish overall; bill fleshy yellow to yellowish (brighter orange-yellow on some breeding adults, not found in region) with dark subterminal mark; perhaps averaging duller and more greenish yellow on first-year birds.

On the water. Head, hindneck, chest sides, and back grayish to gray-brown, usually contrasting with dark brown wings and tail; foreneck, chest, sides, and undertail coverts white with variable brown thigh strap.

Molt Adult wing molt Sep/Oct–Feb/Mar, starts around hatching (Monteiro et al. 1996). PB2 and molts of prebreeders and nonbreeders occur earlier. Nonbreeding (including first-cycle) birds off North America start primary molt mid-July to mid-Oct, probably complete Dec–Feb after leaving the region; tail molt of these birds mainly Aug–Nov; adults complete tail molt by Mar. Head and body molt often precedes wing molt, occurs mainly Apr/Jun–Aug/Oct (NCSM specimens, Monteiro et al. 1996); first-cycle birds off North Carolina often have a few to most of feathers on head and upperparts fresh in May–Jun (molted Jan–May?), perhaps a PF molt or the start of a protracted PB2 molt (needs study).

P9.2. Cory's Shearwater. Note gray head and neck, stout yellow bill with black subterminal band, broad wings, long tapered tail. Tone of upperparts varies with lighting (cf. P9.3). SNGH. Off Hatteras, North Carolina, 25 May 2008.

P9.3. Cory's Shearwater. Tone of upperparts varies with lighting (cf. P9.2); extent of whitish on uppertail coverts variable but not as well-defined as on Great Shearwater (cf. P8.8, P9.9). SNGH. Off Hatteras, North Carolina, 1 Jun 2007.

P9.4. Presumed first-summer Cory's Shearwater (cf. P9.5), showing contrast between faded (juvenile) hind-neck and darker incoming (second basic?) head feathers. SNGH. Off Hatteras, North Carolina, 25 May 2007.

P9.5. Cory's Shearwater with strongly bleached upper back. Relatively faded inner primaries and greater coverts contrast with fresher and darker outer primaries and dark secondaries, indicating a bird older than one year (cf. uniform upperwings of P9.4). SNGH. Off Hatteras, North Carolina, 25 May 2010.

P9.6. Head-on, Cory's Shearwater characteristically shows plain gray head and big yellow bill (cf. P8.7). SNGH. Off Hatteras, North Carolina, 24 May 2007.

P9.7. Cory's Shearwater in fresh plumage. Note brownish-gray head and neck, classic dark underside to primaries (cf. P9.8). Relatively small, dull bill might suggest Cape Verde Shearwater (cf. P11.8), but note evenly and extensively grayish head and neck. SNGH. Off Hatteras, North Carolina, 27 May 2007.

P9.8. Presumed first-summer Cory's Shearwater, showing contrast between faded hindneck and darker incoming head feathers. Whitish tongues on p9-p8 and limited whitish on p10 base appear to lie within variation shown by Cory's. SNGH. Off Hatteras, North Carolina, 28 May 2007.

P9.9. Going away, Cory's Shearwater often shows some whitish on uppertail coverts, but not as well-defined as Great Shearwater (cf. P8.8). SNGH. Off Hatteras, North Carolina, 27 May 2007.

P9.10. Sleeping Cory's Shearwater can appear quite contrastingly patterned on head and neck; also note large head relative to body (cf. P4.14). SNGH. Madeira, eastern Atlantic, 16 May 2010.

P9.11. Cory's Shearwater (left) and Great Shearwater. As well as head and bill patterns, note narrower, straighter wings of Great, which typically appears darker above (especially in fall when many Cory's are in wing molt). SNGH. Off Hatteras, North Carolina, 16 Aug 2009.

P10. SCOPOLI'S SHEARWATER *Calonectris [diomedea] diomedea*

L 44–49 cm, WS 110–121 cm, tail 117–135 mm (graduation 25–35 mm), bill 35–55 mm
Figures 79, 81, 84, 86, P10.1–P10.6

Identification Summary Atlantic, over warmer waters. A large shearwater with broad wings and a long stout bill. Gray-brown above and white below, with a big yellowish bill and white basal tongues on undersides of outer primaries. Flight unhurried with languid wingbeats and easy glides. Considered conspecific with Cory's Shearwater by AOU (1998).

P10.1. Scopoli's Shearwater (center right) often appears appreciably smaller and smaller billed than Cory's Shearwater (back three birds), more similar in overall size to Great Shearwater (far left) or even Sooty Shearwater (front right). SNGH. Off Hatteras, North Carolina, 2 Jun 2010.

Taxonomy Monotypic. See introduction to the Cory's Shearwater complex (pp. 105–106). Slight differences in size exist among some populations (Granadeiro 1993).

Names *Calonectris* means "beautiful swimmer"; *diomedea* may refer to the Greek warrior Diomedes, whose companions transformed into seabirds, or perhaps to the Diomedes Islands in the Adriatic Sea. English name (pronounced Scópoli) commemorates Italian zoologist Giovanni Antonio Scopoli (1723–1788), who described this species in 1769.

Status and Distribution Not recognized by Birdlife International (2010a). Breeds (May–Oct) in Mediterranean, ranges widely in Atlantic from e North America (mainly May–Oct) to South Africa and perhaps South America (mainly Nov–Feb).

Atlantic. Uncommon to rare nonbreeding visitor (mainly May–Oct) to warmer waters from Florida n to New England, and in Gulf of Mexico off Texas. Likely occurs throughout North American range of Cory's Shearwater, which is much more numerous. Off North Carolina in May–Jun, no more than 5–10% of *Calonectris* shearwaters appear to be Scopoli's, but in Aug perhaps as many as 10–15% may be Scopoli's (pers. obs.).

FIELD IDENTIFICATION

Similar Species Resembles a smaller, more lightly built Cory's with narrower wings, a smaller head and bill, and distinct white basal tongues under the primaries (especially p10). See under Cory's Shearwater and Howell and Patteson (2008a) for identification criteria relative to Cory's and to other potential confusion species.

Habitat and Behavior Warmer waters from inshore to offshore. Study needed to determine any habitat differences relative to Cory's Shearwater, with which Scopoli's often occurs. Behavior much like Cory's Shearwater but flight lighter and less lumbering, with slightly quicker wingbeats that may at times suggest Great Shearwater.

Description A large shearwater with broad wings, a graduated tail, and fairly stout bill with a hooked tip; moderate wing-loading.

Ages similar. Head, neck sides, and upperparts gray-brown with darker flight feathers; head and back often slightly paler and grayer, contrasting with darker and browner upperwings, which in some lights show darker M pattern; back feathers, especially scapulars, have paler tips that form variable scalloping, boldest when tips bleach to whitish; longest uppertail coverts usually have some whitish, extensive on some birds (especially bleached first-cycle birds?), which forms a variable U-shaped band at base of tail. In first-year birds, molt can include variable amount of head and back, and some first-cycle birds in May–Jun have dark face contrasting with bleached pale nape (faded juvenile feathering). Throat, foreneck, and underparts bright white. Underwings white with dark remiges except for variable white tongues on exposed bases of primaries, narrow dark leading edge to primary coverts, a very fine dark leading edge to secondary coverts, and sometimes a narrow, diffuse, dark-streaked ulnar bar. Legs and feet pinkish overall; bill fleshy yellow to yellowish with dark subterminal mark; perhaps averaging duller and more greenish on first-year birds.

On the water. Head, hindneck, chest sides, and back grayish to gray-brown, usually contrasting with dark brown wings and tail; foreneck, chest, sides, and undertail coverts white with variable brown thigh strap.

Molt Molt appears to be much like that of Cory's Shearwater, perhaps averaging earlier but with much overlap (NCSM specimens). Nonbreeding (including first-cycle) birds off North America start primary molt mid-July to mid-Oct, probably complete Dec–Feb after leaving the region; tail molt of these birds mainly Aug–Nov. First-cycle birds off North Carolina often have a few to most of feathers on head and upperparts fresh in May–Jun (molted Jan–May?), perhaps a PF molt or the start of a protracted PB2 molt (needs study).

P10.2. Scopoli's Shearwater. Averages narrower wings and smaller head than Cory's Shearwater. SNGH. Off Hatteras, North Carolina, 23 May 2008.

P10.3. Scopoli's Shearwater. Presumed first-summer showing bleached hindneck also often shown by Cory's. Relatively small head of Scopoli's often makes bill seem large. SNGH. Off Hatteras, North Carolina, 6 Jun 2009.

P10.4. Scopoli's Shearwater, perhaps a male given relatively large bill. Probably not safely separable in this image from Cory's, but identified carefully in the field by underwing pattern. SNGH. Off Hatteras, North Carolina, 23 May 2008.

P10.5. (Above) Presumed Scopoli's Shearwater with poorly marked primaries (Cory's not known to show this much white on p10, but study needed on variation in both species). SNGH. Off Hatteras, North Carolina, 2 Jun 2008.

P10.6. (Left) Scopoli's Shearwater (right) and Cory's Shearwater showing typical underwing patterns; differences in head and bill size not obvious in this image but see Fig 84 of same individuals. SNGH. Off Hatteras, North Carolina, 5 Aug 2007.

P11. CAPE VERDE SHEARWATER *Calonectris edwardsii*

L 42–47 cm, WS 101–112 cm, tail 115–130 mm (graduation 30–35 mm), bill 40–45 mm
Figures 87, P11.1–P11.10

Identification Summary Atlantic vagrant. A medium-large, rangy shearwater with broad wings, a long graduated tail, long neck, and small head. Dark gray-brown above and white below, with a dusky pinkish bill. Shape, plumage, and flight manner all suggest Wedge-tailed Shearwater as much as the bulkier Cory's Shearwater.

Taxonomy Monotypic. See introduction to the Cory's Shearwater complex (pp. 105–106).

Names *Calonectris* means "beautiful swimmer"; *edwardsii* commemorates the French zoologist Alphonse Milne-Edwards (1835–1900), who in 1883 led an expedition to the Cape Verde Islands, during which this species was collected.

Status and Distribution Near Threatened. Breeds (Jun–Nov) in Cape Verde Islands, ranges to coastal waters off West Africa and s to Brazil.
    Atlantic. Exceptional or very rare visitor (Aug–Oct, at least) off East Coast, recorded from North Carolina (Patteson & Armistead 2004) and reported from Maryland (NAB 61:47, 2007).

FIELD IDENTIFICATION

Similar Species A fairly distinctive species, but could be overlooked as Cory's Shearwater or Scopoli's Shearwater if not seen clearly.
    Cory's Shearwater appreciably larger and bulkier with broader wings, bigger, more bulbous head, and a bigger, brighter yellowish bill (beware that bill on some immature Cory's can be quite dull, at times approaching brightest Cape Verde). Cory's usually has a paler and grayer cast to head and rarely looks as capped as Cape Verde.
    Scopoli's Shearwater closer in size to Cape Verde but still larger, differs in same respects as Cory's, plus having white tongues on undersides of primaries.
    Great Shearwater slightly larger and stockier with stiffer wings, a contrasting dark cap, slender black bill, dark on underwing coverts, belly, and undertail coverts.
    The chances of a *Wedge-tailed Shearwater* reaching the Atlantic seem slim, but the light morph of this tropical Pacific species shares appreciable similarities in appearance with Cape Verde Shearwater. Wedge-tailed is smaller and lighter in build with a slightly longer, slimmer, and more strongly graduated tail, a smaller gray to dusky pinkish bill (that can appear reflectively pale in bright light, often with a distinct dark tip), and dark distal undertail coverts.

Habitat and Behavior Warmer waters, where likely to be found in association with Cory's Shearwaters. Behavior similar to Cory's Shearwater but flight a little lighter, less lumbering, and wings tend to be crooked more strongly.

Description Medium-large and rangy with fairly broad-based wings and a medium-long graduated tail; long neck and relatively small head often lend a somewhat gawky appearance. Bill fairly long and relatively slender; probably has moderate to fairly low wing-loading.
    Ages similar. Head, neck sides, and upperparts medium-dark, cold gray-brown to brown with darker flight feathers; head often slightly darker than hindneck, creating a capped appearance; back often slightly paler and grayer than upperwings, which can show darker M pattern; back feathers, especially scapulars, have paler tips that form variable scalloping, boldest in worn plumage; longest uppertail coverts usually have some white, which forms narrow *U*-shaped band at base of tail. Throat, foreneck, and underparts clean white. Underwings white with dark remiges (no white on exposed bases of primaries), narrow dark leading edge to primary coverts, very fine dark leading edge to secondary coverts, and sometimes a narrow, diffuse, dark-streaked ulnar bar. Legs and feet pinkish overall; bill pale fleshy gray to grayish (rarely appearing pale pinkish or even yellowish green in bright sun) with dark subterminal mark.
    On the water. Head, hindneck, chest sides, and back gray-brown to brown, usually contrasting with darker brown wings and tail; throat, foreneck, chest, sides, and undertail coverts white with a variable brown thigh strap.

Molt Adult wing molt perhaps mainly Nov–Mar, with molt of prebreeders and nonbreeders starting earlier, and PB2 wing molt perhaps Aug–Nov (needs study); in Oct off Senegal, many birds in mid-primary molt (Porter et al. 1997).

P11.1. Cape Verde Shearwater. Resembles lightly built Cory's with slender dull bill, darker cap. KM. Cape Verde Islands, 25 Mar 2007.

P11.2. Cape Verde Shearwater. Tone of upperparts varies with lighting (cf. P11.1, P11.3); white band on tail coverts often narrower and more clean-cut than Cory's, resembling Great Shearwater. KM. Cape Verde Islands, 25 Mar 2007.

P11.3. Cape Verde Shearwater. Tone of upperparts varies with lighting (cf. P11.1–11.2); can show contrasting dark M pattern and dark cap, as here. SNGH. Cape Verde Islands, 16 Apr 2005.

P11.4. Cape Verde Shearwater. Contrast of darker cap varies with wear and lighting; also note dirty pale bill with dark subterminal band. SNGH. Cape Verde Islands, 16 Apr 2005.

P11.5. Cape Verde Shearwater. Resembles lightly built Cory's with slender dull bill, darker cap; averages more dusky smudging on sides. KM. Cape Verde Islands, 25 Mar 2007.

P11.6. Cape Verde Shearwater. In some lights can show a strong dark cap, but cap not as clean-cut as Great Shearwater. KM. Cape Verde Islands, 25 Mar 2007.

P11.7. Cape Verde Shearwater. Relative to Cory's Shearwater note darker head and bill. Superficially similar light morph Wedge-tailed Shearwater has dark undertail coverts, lacks contrasting dark band on bill. SNGH. Cape Verde Islands, 16 Apr 2005.

P11.8. Cape Verde Shearwater. Bill color varies from pale pinkish gray to pale gray-green, with blackish subterminal band. KM. Cape Verde Islands, 25 Mar 2007.

P11.9. Cape Verde Shearwaters in fresh plumage. Note contrasting dark head, variable bill coloration. KM. Cape Verde Islands, 25 Mar 2007.

P11.10. Cape Verde Shearwater in worn plumage (right; other photos show mid-primary molt) with Cory's Shearwaters. Note smaller size, distinctive plumage and bill of Cape Verde. JBP. Off Hatteras, North Carolina, 15 Aug 2004.

Small Shearwaters: Genus *Puffinus*

This genus includes at least 26 species of worldwide distribution, breeding mainly in tropical and mid-latitudes, with 8 species recorded in North America. In the Atlantic region, Audubon's Shearwater breeds in the Caribbean and Manx in the Northeast, while Barolo Shearwater is a very rare nonbreeding visitor. In the Pacific region, Black-vented and Townsend's shearwaters breed in Mexico; Galapagos and Christmas shearwaters are regular nonbreeding visitors to tropical waters; Manx is an increasingly regular visitor to the North Pacific; and Newell's Shearwater is a vagrant.

Puffinus shearwaters have narrow to fairly broad wings, variably graduated tails, relatively slender bills that are gray to blackish overall, and legs and feet that range from pink and pale bluish to dusky overall. Their wingbeats are generally stiff and hurried, almost fluttery in some species, and birds tend to fly low to the water, wheeling high only in strong winds. Most *Puffinus* are relatively heavy bodied and dive well, for which their laterally compressed tarsi are well suited. Like *Ardenna* shearwaters, *Puffinus* dive from the surface or heights of 3–5 m above the surface at about a 45° angle, and underwater they use their feet and partially extended wings to maneuver. They feed singly or in groups and generally are independent, even wary, of boats. Seven species in the region are bicolored, one is all-dark.

For species identification note overall structure (especially tail length), head and neck pattern, under-tail-covert pattern, underwing pattern, and bill size. The commonest identification challenges (see Figs 88–100) involve Manx and Audubon's off the East Coast, and Black-vented, Manx, Townsend's, Galapagos, and the vagrant Newell's off the Pacific coast.

Fig 88. From left to right, comparison of overall size and undertail-covert pattern of Manx, two Audubon's (note variation in undertail coverts), Boyd's (relatively long tail with dark distal coverts), and Barolo (relatively short tail with white coverts) shearwaters. SNGH. NCSM specimens 10112 (Manx, North Carolina), 10756 (Audubon's, U.S. Virgin Islands), 16617 (North Carolina), 19853 (Cape Verde Islands), 14894 (no location).

Fig 89. In moderate to strong winds, Manx Shearwater often towers steeply. Note narrow wings, relatively short tail with white undertail coverts, dark face (cf. Fig 89). SNGH. Off Hatteras, North Carolina, 6 Jun 2009.

Fig 90. Audubon's Shearwater. Note light build, thick blackish underwing margins, dark underside to long tail, whitish spectacles (cf. Fig 88). SNGH. Off Hatteras, North Carolina, 6 Jun 2009.

Fig 91. Manx Shearwater. Note stocky body, relatively narrow wings with narrow dark underwing margins, and toes projecting beyond tail tip (cf. Fig 91). SNGH. Off Monterey, California, 15 Oct 2006.

Fig 92. Audubon's Shearwater. Note slender body, relatively broad dark underwing margins, and toes falling short of tail tip (cf. Fig 90). SNGH. Off Hatteras, North Carolina, 26 May 2009.

121

Fig 93. Audubon's Shearwater (upper two skins) is slightly larger and bigger billed than Boyd's Shearwater (lower skin), as yet unrecorded in North America. Some populations of Audubon's are strikingly black faced (top bird), lacking white spectacles typical of Audubon's seen off the East Coast. SNGH. NCSM specimens 10756 (top; U.S. Virgin Islands, 10 Aug 1984), 16617 (middle, North Carolina, 22 Jul 1990), 14893 (bottom, Cape Verde Islands, 16 May 1922).

Fig 94. Manx Shearwater. Note stocky shape with relatively short tail, white undertail coverts, head and neck pattern (cf. Fig 95). Extent of dark underwing markings varies individually, and contrast between coverts and remiges varies with lighting (cf. P14.7). SNGH. Off Monterey, California, 25 Sep 2008.

Fig 95. Black-vented Shearwater in slightly worn plumage. Note brownish head and neck sides, dark undertail coverts, and relatively rangy build (cf. Fig 94); extent of dark underwing markings variable, this bird being heavily marked with dusky. SNGH. Oaxaca, Mexico, 17 Dec 2008.

Fig 96. Variation (left to right) in pattern of undertail coverts on Townsend's, Newell's, and Manx shearwaters (upper figures show minimum extent of black, lower figures maximum black). Extent of distal black under the tail (value X) measures 43–72 mm on Townsend's, 20–46 mm on Newell's, and 4–21 mm on Manx (from Howell et al. 1994).

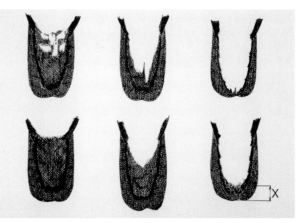

Fig 97. Audubon's Shearwater. Note pale spectacles, long tail with dark distal undertail coverts (cf. Fig 98). SNGH. Off Hatteras, North Carolina, 16 Aug 2009.

Fig 98. Manx Shearwater. Note dark face, short tail with bright white undertail coverts (cf. Fig 97). SNGH. Oaxaca, Mexico, 17 Dec 2008.

Fig 99. Galapagos Shearwater. Note clean-cut black/white contrast on head and neck, relatively short tail, and dark undertail coverts. SNGH. Oaxaca, Mexico, 17 Dec 2008.

Fig 100. Black-vented Shearwater. Note dirty brownish head and hind neck, long bill, and dark undertail coverts. SNGH. Oaxaca, Mexico, 8 Mar 2007.

123

The taxonomy of small black-and-white shearwaters worldwide is in a state of flux. Audubon's Shearwater has been considered a species of pantropical distribution, with numerous disparate subspecies in the Atlantic, Indian, and Pacific oceans (Murphy 1927). However, Austin et al. (2004) showed that this view was based on convergent morphology and plumage, and that many of the populations traditionally lumped as Audubon's Shearwater are distinct species not closely related to Audubon's; they identified a well-defined "true" Audubon's clade as comprising birds breeding in the Caribbean region and on the Macaronesian islands off nw Africa.

The nomenclature and characters of Audubon's Shearwater itself are also vexing. The type locality for *Puffinus lherminieri* is "ad ripas Antillarum" = shores of the Antilles (Lesson 1839), which has been restricted to Guadeloupe Island, in the Lesser Antilles, where l'Herminier resided and likely obtained the type specimen (Hellmayr & Conover 1948). The AOU (1998), however, restricted the type locality of *lherminieri* to "Straits of Florida," although this does not fit in the context of l'Herminier's travels and instead likely refers to the type of *Puffinus auduboni* (Finsch 1872), which is from "Cape Florida." The type specimen of *auduboni* (Zoological Museum of Berlin #13634) agrees in appearance with birds from the Bahamas, to which it likely pertains on geographic grounds. More recently, the taxon *loyemilleri* was described from islets off the Caribbean coast of w Panama (Wetmore 1959); *loyemilleri* resembles *auduboni* in plumage but averages smaller.

At least some populations of Audubon's Shearwater from the Lesser Antilles look distinct from both *auduboni* and *loyemilleri*, being blacker above and in the face, and averaging more extensively black undertail coverts (Figs 92–93). These plumage differences may simply reflect individual variation, although they recall species-level differences in other *Puffinus* (such as those between Newell's and Townsend's shearwaters) and raise the possibility that more than one species of "Audubon's Shearwater" may exist in the Caribbean region. A critical review of variation in Audubon's Shearwater is needed, although without recourse to the type specimen of *lherminieri* (present whereabouts unknown; S. L. Olson, pers. comm.), the nomenclatural cluster that is Audubon's Shearwater is difficult to resolve.

The Audubon's Shearwater complex is provisionally treated here as three species (Robb et al. 2008, Olson 2010; Table 6): Audubon's Shearwater (perhaps three taxa, *lherminieri*, *auduboni*, and *loyemilleri*), breeding in Caribbean region; Boyd's Shearwater (*P. boydii*), breeding on the Cape Verde islands, off West Africa (formerly Bermuda; Olson 2010); and Barolo Shearwater (*P. baroli*), breeding in n Macaronesian Islands (and itself perhaps including multiple taxa). Audubon's Shearwater breeds in the region and ranges as a regular nonbreeding visitor to waters off e North America; Barolo is a casual or very rare visitor to waters off e North America; and Boyd's may have wandered into the region from Bermuda, although there are no confirmed North American records.

Table 6. Measurements (in mm) of specimens of Galapagos Shearwater and taxa in the Audubon's Shearwater complex. Wing chord = unflattened, culmen = exposed culmen; I measured all specimens except *loyemilleri*. The 2 juvenile NCSM specimens from U.S. Virgin Islands (Figs 88, 93) have wing chord 195–196 mm, tail 82–83 mm, culmen 28–29 mm, tarsus 40–41 mm. CAS = California Academy of Sciences; NCSM = North Carolina State Museum; USNM = U.S. National Museum of Natural History; YPM = Yale Peabody Museum; BM = British Museum of Natural History.

Taxon	Wing chord	Tail	Culmen	Tarsus	Source
Galapagos					
n = 30	178–192	63–72	25–30	33–36	CAS
Audubon's					
20 "*lherminieri*"	192–210	83–91	27–32	39–42	NCSM
11 *loyemilleri*	185–195	81–88	27–31	38–40	Wetmore 1965

Table 6. *cont.* Measurements (in mm) of specimens of Galapagos Shearwater and taxa in the Audubon's Shearwater complex.

Taxon	Wing chord	Tail	Culmen	Tarsus	Source
Boyd's					
n = 20	174–188	73–80	23–28	36–38	USNM, YPM
Barolo					
n = 18	165–183	67–79	24–28	36–39	BM, USNM

P12. AUDUBON'S SHEARWATER *Puffinus lherminieri*

L 30–33 cm, WS 65–74 cm, tail 81–91 mm (graduation 20–25 mm), bill 27–32 mm
Figures 66, 90, 92, 97, P12.1–P12.15

Identification Summary Atlantic. A small bicolored shearwater of warm waters in the Caribbean region and Gulf Stream. Blackish brown above, white below with variable dark on undertail coverts, clean-cut dark cap and neck sides with variable whitish spectacles. Flight low and fluttering with buoyant glides on slightly arched wings.

P12.1. Audubon's Shearwater often forages around golden mats of sargassum weed. SNGH. Off Hatteras, North Carolina, 6 Jun 2009.

Taxonomy See introduction to Audubon's Shearwater complex. Two subspecies recognized here, pending examination of larger samples from Lesser Antilles.

P. [l.] lherminieri. Breeds locally in Lesser Antilles and Bahamas, formerly Bermuda. Averages larger (wing 192–210 mm, tail 83–91 mm). May comprise two taxa (study of known breeding populations needed): *P. [l.] auduboni* of Bahamas

(Bahama Shearwater): upperparts browner, face typically with whitish spectacles, undertail coverts often with extensive white basally. *P. [l.] lherminieri* of Lesser Antilles (Antillean Shearwater): upperparts blacker, face blackish overall, undertail coverts blackish overall.

P. [lherminieri] loyemilleri. Breeds on islets off Panama and Venezuela. Plumage like "*auduboni*" but averages smaller (wing 185–195 mm, tail 81–88 mm). Without explanation, Van Halewyn and Norton (1984) attributed birds at Isla Providencia to this taxon (*contra* Wetmore 1965), and considered subspecies of Venezuelan birds unknown or "intermediate?"

Names *Puffinus* derives from puffin, a name that in English now refers to auks in the genus *Fratercula*, and its attribution to shearwaters may reflect some historical misunderstanding; *lherminieri* commemorates French naturalist Félix Louis l'Herminier (1779–1833), who presumably obtained the type specimen during his residence on Guadeloupe; and *loyemilleri* honors U.S. paleornithologist Loye Holmes Miller (1874–1970). The English name commemorates French bird artist John James Audubon (1785–1851).

Status and Distribution Least Concern, although numbers off the East Coast have declined dramatically in recent years, suggesting a review of conservation status is warranted. Breeds (mainly Jan/Mar–May/Jul) as follows: *P. [l.] lherminieri* widely in Bahamas and from islets e of Puerto Rico through Lesser Antilles to islets off Tobago and (perhaps this taxon?) on islets off Isla Providencia; *P.[l.] loyemilleri* on islets off w Panama and n Venezuela (Wetmore 1965). Recently extirpated as a breeder from Bermuda (Van Halewyn & Norton 1984).

Atlantic. At-sea ranges of different populations not well known. Fairly common to locally common (Mar–Aug) in waters around Bahamas, where apparently uncommon in winter. Birds breeding in e Caribbean considered mostly sedentary (Van Halewyn & Norton 1984), but abundance distinctly seasonal in some areas (e.g., mainly Apr–Jul off Guadeloupe; Levesque & Yésou 2005). In s and w Caribbean (presumed *loyemilleri*) ranges (year-round?) from Costa Rica e to Venezuela, at least rarely to Guyana (Wetmore 1965). Rare (taxon unknown) off e Yucatan Peninsula (Mar–Oct) and off Cuba (Feb–May, at least).

In North America, birds presumed from Bahamas historically fairly common to common (late Apr–early Nov; peak numbers Jun–Sep, when juveniles disperse n), but apparently declining. In recent years, fairly common to uncommon over Gulf Stream waters from Florida (where rare or uncommon, Nov–Mar) to North Carolina (where rare into Dec–Jan; Lee 1988). Uncommon to rare (late Jun–Sep, mainly Jul–Aug) n to s New England, casually to s Nova Scotia. The single specimen from Canada (inland in Ontario, Sep 1975) has been attributed to *loyemilleri* (Godfrey 1986). Very rare onshore and inland after tropical cyclones (Jul–Sep) from the Carolinas n to Massachusetts, exceptionally inland to Kentucky (NAB 59:555, 607, 2006). In Gulf of Mexico, uncommon to locally fairly common nonbreeding visitor offshore (Apr–early Nov, mainly Aug–Sep) w to Texas.

FIELD IDENTIFICATION

Similar Species The only other small black-and-white shearwater regular in range of Audubon's is Manx Shearwater. Note Audubon's lighter build with relatively broader wings, longer tail, dark distal undertail coverts, and often a whiter face. Beware of distant Audubon's wheeling high in windy conditions (nicknamed *Pseudodroma* petrels), when they can suggest smaller gadfly petrels; arcs of Audubon's tend to be not as steep (especially in the ascent) or quick and controlled as gadfly petrels, and Audubon's often flaps a few times before the peak of the arc. Also note the possibility of vagrant Barolo and Boyd's shearwaters.

Manx Shearwater (cooler waters) slightly larger and stockier overall (averaging 450 g vs. 200 g in Audubon's), with relatively longer, narrower, and more pointed wings, shorter tail (with white undertail coverts), shorter neck, and higher wing-loading. Manx has stronger, more confident wingbeats and, in calm to light winds, glides less buoyantly on slightly bowed wings; in moderate to strong winds, Manx often wheels high and steeply (recalling Sooty Shearwater), whereas Audubon's tends to fly lower to the water or wheel in shallower arcs.

In general, Manx looks black-faced with a whitish hook cutting up behind dark auriculars, unlike the white-faced look of Audubon's, which has shallower, cleaner-cut dark cap (often with whitish spectacles). Some populations of Audubon's (e.g., in Lesser Antilles) have blacker faces, more like Manx, but these also have extensively black undertail coverts. Undertail coverts of Manx are white (with projecting black thigh patch), reaching nearly to tip of short tail, whereas always black (at least distally) on Audubon's, which lacks the effect of a distinct black thigh patch projecting

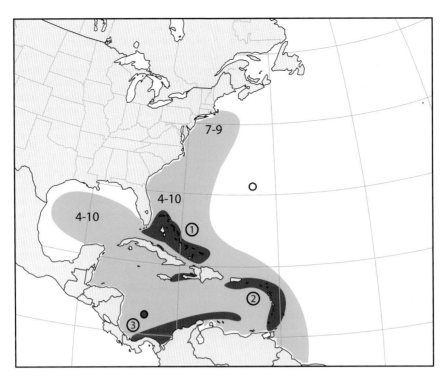

Audubon's Shearwater. 1) = *"auduboni"*; 2) = *lherminieri*; 3) = *loyemilleri*.

into the white. On resting Audubon's, however, extensive white on basal undertail coverts can produce a white-vented appearance; note Audubon's long rear end (tail projects beyond wingtips) vs. relatively sawn-off rear-end of resting Manx (wingtips project slightly beyond short tail).

Slaty-blackish upperparts of Manx can be helpful relative to browner upperparts of Audubon's, but beware the effects of lighting and note that faded first-cycle Manx (such as off the e U.S. in May–Sep) have relatively brownish upperparts, whereas fresh-plumaged Audubon's (such as juveniles in Jun–Oct) are relatively blackish above. Primaries of Manx dark gray below (often reflecting as silvery), vs. solidly blackish on Audubon's. Thus underwing of Manx often looks whiter overall (especially on leading edge) whereas underwing of Audubon's has broad dark margins.

Barolo Shearwater (very rare off e North America) smaller with shorter bill, shorter tail (Audubon's can look shorter tailed during molt, mainly Aug–Oct), white undertail coverts, and overall whitish to slaty-gray undersides to primaries (underwings usually appear white to silvery gray with variable blackish trailing edge, but darker birds similar to Audubon's); upperparts in fresh plumage (May–Jan) slaty blackish. Dark on head of Barolo usually extends down to upper edge

of eye (vs. lower edge on Audubon's). Although Audubon's can appear white-faced (especially in bright light), it does not match Barolo classic look of a beady dark eye in a white face. Whitish tips to greater and median coverts of adult Barolo striking in fresh plumage (mainly Aug–Feb), sometimes suggesting a pale trailing edge to wing, especially when secondaries are fresh and reflect as silvery. Legs and feet of Barolo typically grayish blue. Flight of Barolo usually faster and more hurried, with quicker wingbeats and shorter glides, likely to be apparent in direct comparison but beware that flight manner is affected greatly by behavior, wind direction, and wind speed.

Boyd's Shearwater (breeds Jan–Jun on Cape Verde Islands and formerly Bermuda, unrecorded North America; Figs 88, 93, P12a.1) has plumage, structure, and flight manner much like Audubon's (pers. obs.) but smaller overall (L 28–30 cm, WS 60.5–65 cm, tail 73–80 mm [graduation 12–18 mm], bill 23–28 mm), which might be apparent given direct comparison, at least with extremes. On average, Boyd's shows more extensive whitish around its eyes, including behind the eyes (hence, eye sometimes stands out on pale face, recalling Barolo Shearwater; on Audubon's, most white on face is forward of eyes). Legs and feet grayish blue overall. In-hand examination and measurements are required, on current knowledge, to confirm identification.

Habitat and Behavior Pelagic, over warmer waters. Can be seen from shore in breeding range, exceptionally from shore off East Coast during storms. Favors waters over the shelf slope where found singly or more often in flocks, at times in hundreds. Often in same areas as Bridled Terns along weed lines at ocean fronts in Gulf Stream. Associates readily with mixed-species feeding flocks that include other shearwaters, terns, and boobies. Nests in rock crevices, among rubble, and in burrows dug in soil. At night on breeding grounds gives a rhythmic, wheezy, fairly rapid-paced bleating call of 4–5 syllables, usually repeated several times in quick succession: *h'whieh-whieh huhr, h'whieh-whieh huhr…*, or *wh'whieh-whieh h'hr*, etc. (LNS 42998), with higher-pitched calls probably being males and lower, more gravelly calls females.

In calm to light winds, flight typically low over the water, with quick, fluttering wingbeats interspersed with buoyant glides on slightly arched wings, the head sometimes raised slightly; flying across moderate to strong winds can wheel high, inviting confusion with smaller gadfly petrels. Feeding birds often submerge their heads to peer under weed mats, skitter and splash over the surface, and make shallow dives.

Description A small, lightly built shearwater with relatively broad wings, long tail, relatively small head and long neck; feet do not project beyond tail tip in flight. On the water, wingtips fall well short of long tail tip.

Ages similar but juveniles fresh in May–Aug when older birds worn or molting. Upperparts, including sides of head to lower edge of eye, brownish black (browner when faded, mainly May–Aug); dark/white border on head and neck fairly clean-cut but auriculars often freckled whitish and eye crescents white, creating variable white spectacles; on some birds, dark eyes stand out in white face. Dark on sides of neck forms variable bulge, or spur, forward of wings. Greater upperwing coverts (especially distally) often slightly paler and browner than rest of upperparts, sometimes appearing as dull paler panel or band contrasting with black secondaries. White saddlebags highly variable, prominent on many birds but absent on others. Underparts white with blackish undersides to remiges, variable blackish leading wedge on underwing (usually moderate and distinct), and variably extensive blackish on undertail coverts: most Bahama birds have basal 25–65% of undertail-covert area white, whereas some birds (populations?) from Lesser Antilles have undertail coverts almost solidly blackish (Fig 88). Axillars vary from white overall to variably marked with dusky. Bill bluish gray with blackish tubes, culmen, and variably extensive tip; legs and feet pink overall in adults, but on some birds (probably juveniles) legs and toes can be bluish, with webs pinkish (S. E. Finnegan, photos; Austin et al. 2004, also see Bretagnolle & Attié 1996).

On the water. Blackish above and white below with white sides; undertail coverts blackish, at least distally.

Molt In birds off the East Coast, adult wing molt starts late Jun–Jul, completes late Sep–Oct; tail molt mainly Sep–Oct (NCSM specimens), PB2 wing molt starts mainly May–Jun, usually completes by Aug. Molt timing of other populations not known but likely similar given broadly similar breeding schedules.

P12.2. Classic Audubon's Shearwater. Note white spectacles, relatively broad wings, and long tail. Tarsus of this individual is pale pinkish but foot webbing is bluish white. SNGH. Off Hatteras, North Carolina, 26 May 2008.

P12.3. Audubon's Shearwater. Compared to Manx Shearwater, note lighter build, relatively broad wings, and long broad tail (cf. P14.2). SNGH. Off Hatteras, North Carolina, 6 Jun 2009.

P12.4. Audubon's Shearwater can have face and neck pattern recalling Manx, but note broad wings, long broad tail, blackish distal undertail coverts. SNGH. Off Hatteras, North Carolina, 23 May 2008.

P12.5. Audubon's Shearwater sometimes flies with head slightly raised. Note long tail with dark undertail coverts; white saddlebags variable (cf. P12.3, P12.6). SNGH. Off Hatteras, North Carolina, 23 May 2008.

P12.6. Audubon's Shearwater. Note long broad wings and tail; this individual has prominent whitish saddle-bags (cf. P12.3, P12.5). SNGH. Off Hatteras, North Carolina, 27 Jul 2007.

P12.7. Audubon's Shearwater. Extent of black underwing margins somewhat variable (cf. Fig 89); note pale bluish on feet. SNGH. Off Hatteras, North Carolina, 26 May 2008.

P12a.1. Boyd's Shearwater. Slightly smaller and shorter billed than Audubon's, but no consistent plumage differences are known. KM. Cape Verde Islands, 25 Mar 2007.

P12.8. Audubon's Shearwater with mid-primary molt and secondary molt. Extent of dark on sides of neck varies with wear and angle of viewing (cf. P12.4, P12.7, P12.9). SNGH. Off Hatteras, North Carolina, 2 Jun 2008.

P12.9. In worn plumage, dark neck sides of Audubon's Shearwater can be greatly reduced (cf. P12.8). SNGH. Off Hatteras, North Carolina, 26 May 2009.

P12.10. Blackish tones of fresh-plumaged Audubon's Shearwater rather different from brown tones typical of worn plumage (cf. P12.8–P12.9). Note long tail with dark distal undertail coverts. SNGH. Off Hatteras, North Carolina, 27 May 2007.

P12.11. Audubon's Shearwater. Note long tail projecting beyond wingtips, white spectacles, and typical feeding habitat. SNGH. Off Hatteras, North Carolina, 26 May 2008.

P12.12. Audubon's Shearwater. Undertail coverts often white basally but always dark distally; note long tail, face pattern. SNGH. Off Hatteras, North Carolina, 6 Jun 2009.

P12.13. In worn plumage, face of Audubon's Shearwater can be extensively whitish, inviting confusion with rare Barolo Shearwater, but note long bill and tail. SNGH. Off Hatteras, North Carolina, 26 May 2007.

P12.14. Audubon's Shearwaters flying across moderate to strong winds often wheel fairly high, and distant birds have been nicknamed *Pseudodroma* petrels for their passing resemblance to smaller gadfly petrels, especially Bermuda Petrel (cf. P21.11). SNGH. Off Hatteras, North Carolina, 31 May 2010.

P12.15. Undertail coverts of Audubon's Shearwaters off North Carolina vary from solidly blackish (less common) to having extensive white basally (most frequent). SNGH. NCSM specimens 8102 (upper), 8101 (lower), both collected 11 Aug 1981. Also see Fig 88.

P13. BAROLO SHEARWATER *Puffinus baroli*

L 26–28 cm, WS 58–61 cm, tail 67–79 mm (graduation 12–17 mm), bill 24–28 mm
Figures 88, P13.1–P13.5

Identification Summary Casual or very rare visitor (Aug–Sep) from n Macaronesian islands in e Atlantic. A very small black-and-white shearwater with a whitish face, medium-length tail, mostly white undertail coverts, and hurried flight low to the water. In fresh plumage, note distinct whitish tips to greater and median coverts. Formerly considered a subspecies of Little Shearwater (*P. assimilis*).

Taxonomy Taxonomy of small black-and-white shearwaters worldwide is vexed, but *P. baroli* is here considered a monotypic species. Based on external appearance, *baroli* was traditionally considered a disjunct subspecies of s hemisphere Little Shearwater, but genetic study reveals it is part of a North Atlantic clade together with Audubon's Shearwater (see introduction to Audubon's Shearwater complex).

Within the Audubon's Shearwater clade, Caribbean birds (including nominate *lhermin-ieri*) comprise one group, and Macaronesian birds (*baroli* and *boydi*) a second (Austin et al. 2004). The British Ornithologists' Union (Sangster et al. 2005) has split the latter pair as a separate species, Macaronesian Shearwater (*P. baroli*, including subspecies *baroli* and *boydi*). Onley and Scofield (2007), supposedly following the recommendations of Sangster et al. (2005), treated *boydi* as a subspecies of Audubon's, and *baroli* as a separate species, Macaronesian Shearwater. Hazevoet (1995) treated *boydi* as a separate species, which he called Cape Verde Little Shearwater.

Given differences between *baroli* and *boydi* in morphology, vocalizations, and plumage (*baroli* resembles traditional Little Shearwater, *boydi* resembles traditional Audubon's Shearwater), both are here treated as separate species: Barolo Shearwater (*P. baroli*) and Boyd's Shearwater (*P. boydi*), as done elsewhere (Olson 2010, Robb et al. 2008). Further study may even reveal that cryptic species exist among populations of Barolo Shearwater (see Description, below).

Names *Puffinus* derives from puffin (see under Audubon's Shearwater); *baroli* and the English name commemorate the Marquis Carlo Tancredi Falletti di Barolo (1783–1838), philanthropist mayor of Turin and/or his wife, the Marquise Giulietta Francesca Falletti di Barolo (1785–1864). Has also been called Barolo's Shearwater, but Barolo refers to a location, not a person, and Barolo Shearwater is now used (see *Dutch Birding* 32:50, 2010).

Status and Distribution Not recognized by Birdlife International (2010a). Breeds (Jan–May/Jun) in n Macaronesian islands, from Canaries n to Azores, where considered relatively sedentary, with adults often returning to burrows from Aug onward (Monteiro et al. 1996). Postbreeding dispersal n (Jun–early Oct, mainly Aug) to Bay of Biscay (Martin & Rowlands 2001), casual elsewhere (Apr–Oct) in nw Europe (Lewington et al. 1991).

Atlantic. Probably under-recorded, and perhaps a very rare nonbreeding visitor in fall (late Jul–early Oct) off Atlantic Canada and New England. First North American record was a specimen from Sable Island, Nova Scotia, on 1 Sep 1896 (Dwight 1897); a second specimen reported from South Carolina (probably in Aug 1883; Peters 1924) is actually an Audubon's Shearwater (MCZ specimen #220051). No other verifiable records for more than 100 years. Four birds have been seen since 2000: three birds s of Sable Island in late Sep 2003 (NAB 58:31, 2004), and one in late Aug 2007 about 135 km se of Nantucket, Massachusetts (NAB 62:40, 190). Lee (1988) summarized numerous other claims (mainly Aug–Mar) off e North America, but none is adequately documented.

FIELD IDENTIFICATION

Similar Species Seen well, Barolo Shearwater is a distinctive species, but any suspected vagrant should be distinguished with care from larger Audubon's and Manx shearwaters (see distinguishing characters under those species). Note Barolo's small size, medium-length tail, white face and undertail coverts, whitish-tipped greater and median upperwing coverts (of adults), and hurried flight; underwing varies from whitish overall (whiter than Manx) to having broad dark margins (recalling Audubon's).

Boyd's Shearwater (L 28–30 cm, WS 60.5–65 cm, tail 73–80 mm; Figs 88, P12a.1 [graduation 12–18 mm], bill 23–28 mm) breeds Feb–Jun on

Cape Verde Islands and could occur as a vagrant off the East Coast. Similar in size to Barolo but averages longer tailed, with a darker face and dark undertail coverts; thus looks like a small Audubon's Shearwater. Both have mostly bluish legs and feet (beware that Audubon's can have bluish legs).

Habitat and Behavior Pelagic, favoring warm-temperate waters. The first North American record was of a bird that struck the lighthouse on Sable Island (Nova Scotia). At-sea ecology poorly known, but around nesting islands may be a pelagic rather than inshore feeder, found singly or in loose groups, unlike Boyd's Shearwater, flocks of which often feed inshore with Cory's Shearwaters around nesting islands (pers. obs.).

Flight similar to Audubon's Shearwater, but quicker-looking under comparable conditions, with hurried wingbeats and shorter glides; sometimes lifts its head in flight, in a manner recalling Red-throated Loon.

Description A very small, fairly compact shearwater with relatively short and slightly rounded wings, medium-length tail, and fairly slender bill; feet do not project beyond tail tip in flight. On the water, wingtips probably fall about even with tail tip.

Adult. Upperparts, including sides of head to upper edge of eye, slaty blackish (browner when worn, mainly Apr–Jun); dark/white border on head and neck fairly distinct (sharpness often accentuated by bright lighting at sea), but area around eye and upper auriculars often freckled dark.

Dark on sides of neck forms a variable bulge forward of wings. Whitish tips to greater and median upperwing coverts show as distinct lines in fresh plumage (mainly Aug–Feb), weakest and often worn away in Mar–Jul. White saddlebags variable, typically moderate, sometimes extensive. Underparts clean white with variable underwing pattern. Classic birds (BM specimens from Porto Santo, Great Salvage, and Deserta Grande) have underwings mostly bright white with fairly broad dark trailing edge and narrow, dark leading edge. Underwings of some birds (especially those of Canary Islands; BM specimens) have dark gray remiges and relatively thick blackish leading edge. Undertail coverts white (can be obscured by extended feet), usually with some dark markings on lateral and longest undertail coverts. Bill dark grayish to blackish with variable blue-gray at base and on sides; legs and feet grayish blue overall.

First cycle. Juveniles fresh in May–Aug (when older birds worn or molting), lack white tips to median coverts; narrow paler tips to greater coverts, when present, dull gray to whitish (BM specimens).

On the water. Blackish above and white below with white sides and undertail coverts, note white face, small bill.

Molt Adult wing molt of Azores breeders mainly May–Aug, with tail molt Aug (Monteiro et al. 1996); PB2 wing molt can be expected slightly earlier (perhaps Mar/Apr–Jun/Jul, but study needed). The Sable Island specimen was molting body and rectrices in early Sep (Dwight 1897), perhaps a prebreeding bird completing prebasic molt.

P13.1. Barolo Shearwater (same bird as P13.2). Note striking whitish tips to upperwing coverts (typical of fresh-plumaged adult) and white face. MJI. Off Massachusetts, 25 Aug 2007.

P13.2. Barolo Shearwater. Whitish tips to upperwing coverts often appear as frosty trailing edge to innerwing; also note white saddlebags. MJI. Off Massachusetts, 25 Aug 2007.

P13.3. Barolo Shearwater in worn plumage (same bird as P13.5). Note face pattern, overall shape, and relatively small fine bill. SNGH. Madeira, eastern Atlantic, 15 May 2010.

P13.4. Barolo Shearwater. Note white undertail coverts, extensively white underwings (cf. P13.5). KM. Azores, eastern Atlantic, 27 May 2007.

P13.5. Barolo Shearwater (same bird as P13.3). Some populations (undescribed taxa?) have extensive dark underwing margins much like Audubon's Shearwater (cf. P13.4); note white undertail coverts, small fine bill. SNGH. Madeira, eastern Atlantic, 15 May 2010.

P14. MANX SHEARWATER *Puffinus puffinus*

L 31–35 cm, WS 75–84 cm, tail 68–79 mm (graduation 10–15 mm), bill 31–38 mm
Figures 88, 89, 91, 94, 96, 98, P14.1–P14.16

Identification Summary Atlantic (common) and Pacific (rare). A small, brightly patterned black-and-white shearwater. Black above and white below with relatively short tail and white undertail coverts; on the water note white sides and undertail coverts. Flight fast and low with quick, stiff wingbeats; glides on slightly bowed wings, wheels steeply in windy conditions.

P14.1. Manx Shearwater (back) often occurs off the Northeast in the same areas as Great Shearwater (right) and Sooty Shearwater (left). Note small size, short tail, and strongly contrasting head pattern of Manx. MJI. Off Cape Cod, Massachusetts, 30 Jun 2007.

Taxonomy Monotypic. Murphy (1952) subsumed seven disparate worldwide taxa as subspecies of Manx Shearwater, but these are now all treated as species.

Names *Puffinus* derives from puffin (see under Audubon's Shearwater); Manx means "of the Isle of Man," in the Irish Sea, where this species breeds.

Status and Distribution Least Concern. Breeds (Apr–Sep) in ne Atlantic Ocean (mainly British Isles) n to Iceland, s to Canary Islands, since 1970s off ne North America. Winters (Oct–Feb) mainly in South Atlantic (10–50°S off Brazil and Argentina), n locally to se U.S.; recent colonist of ne Pacific (since mid-1970s).

    Atlantic. Considered casual in North America by AOU (1957) but off Atlantic coast has increased dramatically since then, with a marked increase since late 1960s and 1970s. Breeds locally (May–Sep) from s Newfoundland (breeding first

confirmed 1977) s to Maine (breeding first confirmed 2009; NAB 63:570, 2009) and Massachusetts (breeding first confirmed 1973); breeding population small and apparently not growing, and most birds off the Northeast appear to be nonbreeders (Robertson 2002).

    Uncommon to locally fairly common spring migrant (Feb–May) off Lesser Antilles, Bermuda, and Atlantic coast n from North Carolina, peaking in Mar off Guadeloupe, mid-Mar off Bermuda, and arriving in Apr off New England. Uncommon to locally fairly common in summer (May–Sep) off ne North America, n to Newfoundland, e.g., daily counts up to 200 birds off Massachusetts in Jul. Ranges regularly into Gulf of Maine but rare in Gulf of St. Lawrence. Departure from Northeast mainly Sep–Oct, with stragglers off New England through Nov, and uncommon to fairly common fall transient (Sep–Nov) s to North Carolina. Nonbreeding immatures summer (May–Sep) off mid-Atlantic coast and se U.S., casually in Caribbean.

135

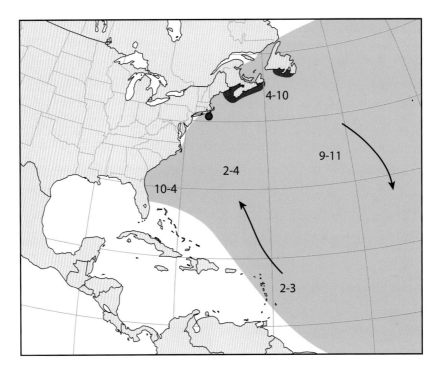

Rare to locally uncommon winter resident (Nov–Jan) off se U.S. (Lee 1995), n to Virginia, casual n in mid-winter (Dec–Jan) to Massachusetts. Casual or very rare (mainly Nov–Mar) in Caribbean, w to Belize (beached carcass in Feb), e to Lesser Antilles, s to Panama (moribund on shore, Jan; NAB 57:270, 2003) and (mainly Aug–Feb) in Gulf of Mexico (w to Texas, where most records are of dead and dying birds).

Casual inland to e Great Lakes (Aug–early Nov; all records since 2000); exceptional in w Montana (Jun 2004; NAB 58:403–404, 2004).

Pacific. First detected in ne Pacific mid-1970s, with a marked increase in mid-1990s, and rare but regular with records year-round by 2000 (Mlodinow 2004). Possibility of breeding should be investigated at sites such as Triangle Island, British Columbia (calling bird found there in burrow, Jul 1994; Mlodinow 2005), and Middleton Island, Alaska.

Recorded in summer (May–early Sep) from British Columbia n to Gulf of Alaska, casually to se Bering Sea. Better known off West Coast, where rare but increasing visitor (mid-Feb to early Nov, mainly Apr–Aug) off Washington (first recorded 1990) and Oregon (first recorded 1998); and (year-round, mainly Aug–Oct) off California (first recorded 1993), with winter records n to vicinity of Monterey Bay. Very rare in winter (Nov–Feb?) s to Oaxaca, Mexico (NAB 63:331, 2009).

FIELD IDENTIFICATION

Similar Species In the Atlantic, main confusion risk is Audubon's Shearwater. In the Pacific, off California can be seen with Black-vented Shearwater; also occurs rarely in range of Townsend's and Galapagos shearwaters. Two other small bicolored shearwaters of e Atlantic might occur as vagrants to North American waters: Yelkouan Shearwater (*P. yelkouan*) and Balearic Shearwater (*P. mauretanicus*), both breeding in Mediterranean and ranging to ne Atlantic; see Bourne et al. (1988) and Gutiérrez (2004) for identification of these species relative to Manx.

Atlantic. *Audubon's Shearwater* (warmer waters) slightly smaller, more lightly built (averages about 200 g vs. 450 g of Manx) and rangier overall, with relatively shorter, broader, and more rounded wings, longer and more strongly graduated tail (with blackish distal undertail coverts), longer neck, and lower wing-loading. Audubon's has weaker, more fluttery wingbeats and, in calm to light winds, glides more buoyantly and on slightly arched wings; in moderate to strong winds, Audubon's wheels lower and less steeply than Manx.

Audubon's from the Bahamas (which occur off e U.S.) have a cleaner-cut and shallower dark cap (with whitish mottling around eyes, which often creates thin spectacles), lacking Manx's white hook behind dark auriculars; thus Audubon's typically looks "white-faced" and Manx "black-faced."

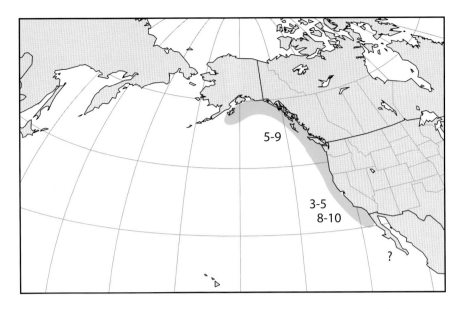

5-9

3-5
8-10

?

Undertail coverts of Audubon's are always black-ish at least distally, showing as a broad blackish tip to underside of tail. However, on resting birds the extensive white on basal undertail coverts can produce white-vented appearance; note head and neck patterns plus Audubon's long rear end (tail projects beyond wingtips) vs. relatively sawn-off rear-end of resting Manx (wingtips project slightly beyond short tail).

Brownish cast to upperparts of Audubon's can be helpful relative to slaty-blackish upperparts of Manx, but beware the effects of lighting and note that faded first-cycle Manx (such as off the e U.S. in May–Sep) have relatively brownish upperparts whereas fresh-plumaged Audubon's are relatively blackish above. Underwing of Audubon's has broader, dark margins, especially on leading edge.

Some Caribbean populations of Audubon's are blacker above than Bahamas birds and have blacker faces, more like Manx, but these also have extensively black undertail coverts and otherwise seem typical of Audubon's in size, shape, and (pre-sumably) flight manner.

Barolo Shearwater (very rare off Northeast) distinctly smaller (appears two-thirds the size of Manx in direct comparison) and lighter bodied with shorter, more rounded wings, proportion-ately longer tail, and smaller, more slender bill. Flight appears quicker, with hurried wingbeats, and generally low to the water with short glides and little banking. Dark on head of Barolo comes down only to upper edge of eyes, so that dark eyes typically stand out in whiter face, whereas Manx has dark face and auriculars, with whitish hook behind, and dark wedge on neck sides. In

fresh plumage (mainly Aug–Feb), adult Barolo has prominent whitish tips to greater and median upperwing coverts, which often appear as a pale panel on trailing edge of wing.

Pacific. *Black-vented Shearwater* (mainly s California and Mexico) slightly larger, bigger-tailed, and longer-billed than Manx, which can be apparent in direct comparison. Despite its slightly larger size, Black-vented tends to have a more fluttery and hurried flight than Manx, with slightly looser wingbeats that suggest Audubon's Shearwater, rather than the stronger, stiffer wing-beats of Manx.

Under most conditions, Black-vented identi-fied readily by dark brown (not blackish) upper-parts, diffusely dusky head and neck sides, and dark distal undertail coverts; also usually lacks distinct white saddlebags typically shown by Manx, but some well-marked Black-vented overlap poorly marked Manx. Under some conditions, how-ever, such as backlighting, bright seas with high contrast, or dull and overcast conditions, upper-parts of Black-vented can appear blackish and in strong sun (especially early and late in the day) underparts can flash bright white, inviting con-fusion with Manx; moreover, the head sides of Black-vented are often washed out in bright sun and can appear to have a contrasting dark cap. Structure and flight manner can be helpful under such conditions, but also look for Black-vented's eponymous dark undertail coverts (which often appear as a broad dark tip to the undertail), and note that cap of Manx extends lower in face and typically is offset by a contrasting white hook at rear, forward of contrasting dark wedges on neck sides (any hook on Black-vented tends to be diffuse and not contrasting).

Although distinctly larger, *Buller's Shearwater* (mainly Aug–Oct off West Coast) perhaps as likely to be confused with Manx as is Black-vented. Buller's shares a clean blackish cap and bright white neck and sides, and on the water can be confused with Manx, when size not always easy to determine. Buller's is longer necked and longer billed, and gray back contrasts with black wings. As soon as a bird takes off, languid flight of Buller's is very different from hurried flight of Manx, and the problem should vanish.

Townsend's Shearwater (w Mexico) has slightly smaller bill and relatively longer tail (toes do not project beyond tail tip) and lower wing-loading; best distinguished by longer tail and black undertail coverts (Fig 96), apparent in flight and on the water. Manx Shearwaters molting longest undertail coverts can have relatively extensive black undertail, and beware of dark-looking feet of Manx not being tucked in. Undersides of primaries on Townsend's are blackish, typically contrasting strongly with white coverts; those of Manx are dark gray, often reflecting as silvery so that the primary bases do not contrast distinctly with white underwing coverts, but beware of the effects of lighting. Manx averages more whitish freckling in face and often shows narrow whitish line across base of bill; forehead of Townsend's is solidly black. White thigh patch (saddlebags) of Townsend's average more prominent than on Manx, but variable in both species and probably unreliable for specific identification. Flight of Townsend's often more buoyant than Manx, but take into account wind speed and other conditions.

Galapagos Shearwater (e Pacific n to Mexico) appreciably smaller with relatively broader, more rounded wings, longer and broader tail, and more hurried, fluttering flight with buoyant glides on slightly arched wings. Galapagos has a cleaner-cut and less extensive dark cap (lacking a white "hook" behind the auriculars) and hindneck, and lacks the white saddlebags typically shown in flight by Manx. On the water, Manx shows extensive white flanks, set off by dark spur on chest sides, whereas Galapagos typically sits lower in the water and shows less extensive and less contrasting white, often with dusky mottling and streaking.

Newell's Shearwater (exceptional in s California) has longer tail and broader wings, lower wing-loading, black distal undertail coverts (Fig 96), and clean-cut black-and-white face pattern, often with white teardrop visible at close range. Flight more buoyant and less powerful than heavy-bodied Manx.

Habitat and Behavior Pelagic but also seen from land off both coasts, mainly in windy conditions off the Atlantic coast. Favors cooler inshore waters over the continental shelf and shelf slope. Usually associates readily with other shearwaters and with mixed-species feeding flocks, but single birds also occur alone or sometimes do not associate strongly with other shearwaters. Off the Northeast in summer occurs in groups (up to 50 or more birds) or singly, elsewhere more often found singly or with a few birds in loose association, such as northbound migrants. Feeds while swimming by pattering and diving after prey. Nests in burrows dug in soil. At night on breeding grounds gives strangled, rhythmic, moaning and wailing calls, repeated several times in fairly rapid succession in flight and from burrow, with males being higher and more shrieky than females (Robb et al. 2008). Calls typically 4–5 syllables, the first note slightly emphatic, the last throaty and not always audible at a distance, usually repeated in rhythmic series: *kéh-keh keh-hohrr, kéh-keh keh-hohrr …* or *kéh-keh kóh-oh-ohrr…*, etc.

In calm to light winds, flight typically fast and low over the water, with bursts of fairly rapid, stiff wingbeats interspersed with short glides on slightly bowed wings; in moderate to strong winds, often wheels high and steeply, at times recalling Sooty Shearwater.

Description A small, fairly stocky, bicolored shearwater with long narrow wings and relatively short tail; in flight, tips of toes often project slightly beyond tail tip, or feet are pulled in and not visible. On the water, wingtips typically project slightly beyond tail. A melanistic individual has been found (Davis & Packer 1972).

Ages similar but juveniles fresh in Sep–Dec when older birds worn or molting. Upperparts, including sides of head to below eye, black to blackish, extending down as a distinct wedge on neck sides; black/white border on head and neck freckled, or smudged (not clean-cut), typically with a distinct pale hook behind auriculars and often a narrow whitish line across base of bill. Particularly in worn and bleached plumage (mainly Sep–Dec) some birds have relatively extensive whitish speckling and mottling in lores and an overall frosty-faced look. Dark on sides of neck typically forms a large wedge forward of wings. White saddlebags usually distinct in flight (but can be poorly defined). Underparts clean white with dark gray underside to remiges (often reflecting as silvery) and narrow black leading edge to underwing; variable blackish marks on lesser underwing coverts may form a weak ulnar bar visible at close range. Variable dark distal marks on axillars appear not to be a reliable indicator of age (*contra* Baker 1993, Pyle 2010; cf. P14.8 of bird older than 1 year, with truncate axillars boldly tipped black). Undertail coverts white or with limited blackish tipping. Faded plumage (especially first-cycle birds in May–Aug) notably browner above, and molting birds can show a whitish band across upperwing coverts, mainly when inner and middle primaries are in molt (usually Sep–Dec). Bill dark gray to blackish, legs and feet pinkish overall.

On the water. Black above and white below with striking white sides, prominent white undertail-covert wedge reaching to or just short of tail tip.

Molt Adult wing molt Sep/Nov–Dec/Mar, being earlier in nonbreeding birds and shorter-distance migrants; tail molt occurs at or following end of primary molt. PB2 wing molt probably Aug/Sep–Nov/Dec. A variable PF molt, including head, body, and tail, apparently occurs Nov–Mar (Lee & Haney 1996).

P14.2. Upperparts of Manx Shearwater typically appear blackish, as here, but tone varies greatly with lighting and wear (cf. P14.2–P14.3); note blackish face with white notch behind cheeks, narrow whitish line across base of bill. Contrast between blacker body and browner upperwings represents interrupted second prebasic molt or preformative molt (study needed). BM. Newfoundland, Canada, 29 Jul 2009.

P14.3. In bright light, Manx Shearwater in worn plumage can appear strikingly brown above (cf. P14.2); note stocky shape, face and neck pattern. SNGH. Off Hatteras, North Carolina, 24 May 2007.

P14.4. Manx Shearwater in worn plumage, starting primary molt (same bird as P14.9). Plumage tones suggest Black-vented Shearwater but note relatively short tail, distinct white notch behind dark cheeks. EWP. Off Monterey, California, 13 Sep 2008.

P14.5. Manx Shearwater showing classic face pattern, with whitish hook behind dark cheeks, pale line above gape. Note toes projecting beyond tail tip. SNGH. Madeira, eastern Atlantic, 14 May 2010.

P14.6. Compare stocky shape, relatively short tail, and relatively small wings of this Manx Shearwater with rangier Audubon's (cf. P12.3–P12.6). SNGH. Madeira, eastern Atlantic, 16 May 2010.

P14.7. Medium-gray underside to primaries of Manx Shearwater apparent in good light, but often appears blackish (cf. P14.8). Note black thigh patch offsetting white saddlebags. SNGH. Madeira, eastern Atlantic, 14 May 2010.

P14.8. Manx Shearwater. Note face pattern, white undertail coverts, black thigh patch. Dark markings on underwing variable, this bird being near the dark extreme (cf. P14.7, P14.9). BLS. Off Hatteras, North Carolina, 5 Jun 2005.

P14.9. Manx Shearwater in worn plumage, starting primary molt (same bird as P14.4). Note stocky shape, relatively short tail with white undertail coverts, face pattern. EWP. Off Monterey, California, 13 Sep 2008.

P14.10. Manx Shearwater sometimes looks dark hooded, suggesting Black-vented Shearwater; note white undertail coverts. SNGH. Madeira, eastern Atlantic, 15 May 2010.

P14.11. Flying away, Manx Shearwater typically shows distinct white saddlebags, and trailing feet can create the impression of dark undertail coverts. SNGH. Oaxaca, Mexico, 17 Dec 2008.

P14.12. Manx Shearwater often shows variable whitish eye ring. Note white undertail coverts, short tail; relatively short bill may indicate female. KM. Ireland, 6 Sep 2007.

P14.13. Blackish distal area under tail here about the maximum for Manx Shearwater, perhaps produced by misarranged and somewhat worn undertail coverts; relatively long but slender bill may indicate first-year male (cf. P14.12). SNGH. Off Hatteras, North Carolina, 5 Jun 2010.

P14.14. Manx Shearwater (right) with Black-vented Shearwater. Note strongly contrasting plumage and white undertail coverts of Manx. SNGH. Off Monterey, California, 15 Oct 2006.

P14.15. Compare size, structure, and plumage patterns of Manx Shearwater (center) with Wedge-tailed Shearwater (left) and Galapagos Shearwater (right). SNGH. Oaxaca, Mexico, 17 Dec 2008.

P14.16. Manx Shearwater in fresh plumage (upper) is distinctly black faced. However, birds in heavily worn and bleached plumage (mainly Sep–Dec) can be whitish faced (lower); this white-faced appearance can be exaggerated by bright lighting. SNGH. NCSM specimens (off North Carolina).

P15. NEWELL'S SHEARWATER *Puffinus newelli*
L 35–38 cm, WS 77–85 cm, tail 77–89 mm (graduation 12–20 mm), bill 30–35 mm
Figures 96, P15.1–P15.5

Identification Summary Accidental visitor to California, from Hawaii. A small bicolored shearwater, black above and white below. Note relatively long tail with black distal undertail coverts, sharply clean-cut black-and-white division on sides of head and neck. Flight fast and low with quick, stiff wingbeats; glides on slightly bowed wings, wheels steeply in windy conditions.

Taxonomy Monotypic. Sometimes treated as conspecific with Townsend's Shearwater (AOU 1998), but better treated as a separate species: differences between Townsend's and Newell's in plumage (Howell et al. 1994), morphology (Ainley et al. 1997, Bourne et al. 1988), breeding chronology (Ainley et al. 1997), and at-sea ecology (Spear et al. 1995) are comparable to or greater than those among other small shearwater species.

Names *Puffinus* derives from puffin (see under Audubon's Shearwater); *newelli* and the English name commemorate Brother Matthias Newell (1854–1939), a missionary to Hawaii.

Status and Distribution Endangered. Breeds (Jun–Oct) in Hawaii, ranges at sea mainly e and s of Hawaiian islands.
    Pacific. Accidental (early Aug 2007) in s California (Unitt et al. 2009). May range to waters in vicinity of Clipperton Atoll (Pitman 1986).

FIELD IDENTIFICATION

Similar Species Similar to Townsend's Shearwater; see criteria discussed under that species for separation from Galapagos and Black-vented shearwaters (taking into account the longer tail, white basal undertail coverts, and lack of dark speckling on the face of Newell's).
    Manx Shearwater (Pacific coast of North America) has heavier body, narrower wings, and shorter tail with white undertail coverts that extend to near tail tip (Fig 96); underside of Manx's primaries silvery gray rather than blackish, and black/white division on sides of head typically smudgy and not clean-cut.

Townsend's Shearwater (w Mexico) slightly smaller with lower wing-loading, slightly shorter tail, all-black undertail coverts (Fig 96), and smudgy border between blackish head sides and white throat.

Habitat and Behavior Pelagic, usually offshore. Flight tends to be more buoyant, less heavy-bodied than Manx Shearwater, and may wheel less steeply than Manx in windy conditions.

Description A small bicolored shearwater with a fairly long tail; feet do not project beyond tail tip in flight. On the water, tail tip typically projects slightly beyond wingtips.
    Ages similar but juveniles fresh in Oct–Feb when older birds worn or molting. Upperparts, including sides of head to below eye, black, extending down as partial collar on neck sides; black/white border on head and neck clean-cut, typically with a white subocular teardrop and white hook behind auriculars. White saddlebags usually prominent in flight (but can be poorly defined). Underparts clean white with blackish underside to remiges, black leading edge to underwing, and blackish distal undertail coverts. Variable blackish marks on lesser underwing coverts form a small ulnar bar, visible at close range. Faded plumage (especially first-cycle birds in May–Aug) may be browner above, and some birds show narrow whitish tips to greater coverts. Bill dark gray to blackish, legs and feet pinkish overall.
    On the water. Black above and white below with white sides, black distal undertail coverts.

Molt Wing molt mainly Jul–Feb (King & Gould 1967); within this span PB2 presumably earlier (probably Jul–Nov) and adult molt later (Oct–Feb).

143

P15.1. Newell's Shearwater. Compared to Manx, note cleanly demarcated black/white face, relatively large wing area, long tail. DLW. Hawaii, 27 Jun 2008.

P15.2. Newell's Shearwater, showing well its long tail. Some birds have whitish tips to greater coverts, perhaps an indication of age (study needed). DLW. Hawaii, 26 Apr 2009.

P15.3. White saddlebags of Newell's Shearwater average larger than Manx; also note long tail and big wings, which suggest Audubon's Shearwater (cf. P12.6). RWB. Hawaii, 25 Jul 2008.

P15.4. Newell's Shearwater (same bird as P15.3). Note long tail with black distal coverts, relatively thick and contrasting blackish wing margins (resembling Audubon's rather than Manx), cleanly demarcated black/white face. RWB. Hawaii, 25 Jul 2008.

P15.5. Newell's Shearwater. Note same features as P15.4. DLW. Hawaii, 26 Apr 2009.

P16. TOWNSEND'S SHEARWATER *Puffinus auricularis*

L 32–35 cm, WS 76–83 cm, tail 71–83 mm (graduation 7–15 mm), bill 29–34 mm
Figures 59, 96, P16.1

Identification Summary Pacific (endemic to Mexico). A small bicolored shearwater, black above and white below. Note freckled border on sides of head, medium-long tail with black undertail coverts; on water, note extensive and clean white sides. Flight fast and low with quick wingbeats and fluid upstroke, glides on slightly bowed wings.

Taxonomy Monotypic. Murphy (1952) subsumed seven disparate worldwide taxa (including Townsend's) as subspecies of Manx Shearwater, but these are all now usually treated as species. See discussion under Newell's Shearwater.

Names *Puffinus* derives from puffin (see under Audubon's Shearwater); *auricularis* presumably refers to the dark-freckled auriculars. The English name commemorates Charles H. Townsend (1859–1944), the U.S. ornithologist who described this species.

Status and Distribution Critically Endangered. Endemic. Breeds or bred (Jan–Jul, Jehl 1982) only on three of Mexico's Revillagigedo Islands: on Clarion Island (extirpated in 1980s by introduced mammals; Howell & Webb 1989, Santaella & Sada 1991), San Beneditco Island (eradicated in 1952 by volcanic eruption, small numbers may have recolonized in 1990s but status uncertain; Pitman & Ballance 2002), and Socorro (persists on higher slopes but preyed upon by feral cats). Population in early 1990s estimated at 46,000 birds (Spear et al. 1995), which could translate to about 10,000 breeding pairs, but recent unsuccessful searches off Oaxaca (where formally numerous at times) suggest population is declining (pers. obs.), and fewer than 100 pairs located in 2008 (Birdlife International 2010b).

Pacific. Breeders range over waters around Revillagigedo Islands (Nov–Jun), also n to around 23˚N (off s Baja California Peninsula) and e to waters off w Mexico. Formerly present year-round (commonest Apr–Oct) from Baja California Sur s to Oaxaca, occasionally at least to El Salvador (Jehl 1982, Spear et al. 1995), now apparently only rare (and irregular?) s to Oaxaca (pers. obs.).

FIELD IDENTIFICATION

Similar Species Two other small bicolored shearwaters (Galapagos and Black-vented) occur regularly in the range of Townsend's, but are relatively distinctive given good views. Newell's Shearwater (accidental in the region) and Manx Shearwater (very rare in range of Townsend's) are more similar, and should be distinguished with care (see under those species; also see Howell et al. 1994).

Galapagos Shearwater (e Pacific n to Mexico) often in feeding or loafing flocks with Townsend's, is smaller with shorter, more rounded wings but proportionately longer bill; often appears slightly browner above. In prolonged flight, note more hurried, fluttering wingbeats of Galapagos, but feeding birds of both species often make short, rapid flights that are similar. Galapagos has cleaner-cut and less extensive dark cap (lacking a white "hook" behind the auriculars) and hindneck, lending it a whiter-faced aspect, whereas head and neck sides of Townsend's are more extensively blackish, not clean-cut from the white throat and foreneck. In flight Galapagos often looks relatively longer necked and holds its head slightly raised, usually lacks white saddlebags, and often has broader, dark leading edge to underwing and dark on axillars and flanks. On the water, Townsend's shows extensive white flanks set off by dark spur on chest sides, whereas Galapagos typically sits lower and shows less extensive and less contrasting white, often with dusky mottling and streaking.

Black-vented Shearwater (w Mexico and California) favors inshore waters and is slightly larger and bulkier overall, with longer and heavier bill, slightly more rounded wings, and more fluttery, less snappy flight. Under most conditions, Black-vented is identified readily by its dark brown (not blackish) upperparts, diffusely dusky head and neck sides, lack of sharply contrasting white saddlebags, and dark-tipped axillars. Faded first-cycle Townsend's (mainly in Mar–Apr) can appear relatively brownish above with a less sharply defined face pattern and might be mistaken for Black-vented. Beware that Black-vented often shows moderately distinct white saddlebags and, under some conditions, such as backlighting, bright seas with high contrast, or dull and overcast conditions, upperparts can appear blackish, while in strong sun (especially early and late in the day) underparts can flash bright white,

145

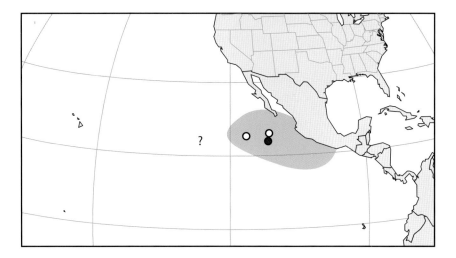

inviting confusion with Townsend's; furthermore, head sides of Black-vented often washed out in bright sun, when can appear dark capped. Structure and flight manner can be helpful under such conditions; also note that dark undertail coverts of Black-vented are usually less extensive, and that dark cap of Townsend's extends lower in face.

Habitat and Behavior Pelagic, usually near land only during breeding season, when rafts gather offshore in late afternoon. Off Mexican mainland, foraging birds concentrate over eastern slope of Middle American trench; relative to Newell's Shearwater, Townsend's favors cooler, more upwelled waters associated with lower wind speeds (Spear et al. 1995). Often in feeding flocks with other shearwaters, boobies, terns, etc. Nests in burrows dug in soil. At night on breeding grounds gives gruff, throaty, slightly braying two- to three-syllable phrases, *ahr eh, ahr eh...*, or *ahr ah-ah, ahr ah-ah...*, typically repeated a few times in slightly intensifying series (L. F. Baptista, tape); calls at colony may suggest chorusing chachalacas (*Ortalis*).

In calm to light winds, flight typically fast and low over the water, with bursts of fairly rapid, stiff wingbeats interspersed with glides on slightly bowed wings, the upstroke relatively high and smooth; sometimes glides for 100–200 m or longer. Flying across moderate to strong winds, wheels in shallow arcs interspersed with quick flaps, and sometimes wheels high and fairly steeply.

Description A small bicolored shearwater with a medium-long tail; feet do not project beyond tail tip in flight. On the water, tail tip typically projects slightly beyond wingtips.

Ages similar but juveniles fresh in Jul–Oct when older birds worn or molting. Upperparts, including sides of head to below eye, black to blackish, extending down as a partial collar on neck sides; black/white border on head and neck freckled, or smudged (not clean-cut), and typically with a messy whitish hook behind auriculars. White saddlebags usually prominent in flight (but can be poorly defined). Underparts clean white with blackish underside to remiges, black leading edge to underwing, and solidly blackish undertail coverts. Variable blackish marks on lesser underwing coverts form a small ulnar bar visible at close range. Faded plumage (especially first-cycle birds in Mar–Jun) notably browner above. Bill dark gray to blackish above, blue-gray below with dark tip, legs and feet pinkish overall.

On the water. Black above and white below with white sides, extensively black undertail coverts.

Molt Wing molt mainly late Apr–Nov (Binford 1989, Howell & Engel 1993, Jehl 1982); within this span PB2 presumably earlier (probably late Apr–Aug) and adult molt later (probably Jul–Oct/Nov).

P16.1. Townsend's Shearwater, and comparison with Newell's, Manx, and Black-vented shearwaters.
© Ian Lewington. On Townsend's note relatively long tail, extensively black undertail coverts, smudgy black/white division on head sides. Newell's has white basal undertail coverts, clean-cut black/white division on head sides (with whitish teardrop often apparent at close range). Manx has shorter tail, extensively white undertail coverts (but smaller white saddlebags), subtly different face pattern. Black-vented slightly larger and bulkier with longer bill, dark brownish upperparts (beware, however, of lighting and wear), smudgy brownish head sides. See text and photos of other species for further information.

P17. BLACK-VENTED SHEARWATER *Puffinus opisthomelas*
L 35.5–38 cm, WS 78–86 cm, tail 70–83 mm (graduation 15–20 mm), bill 35–41 mm
Figures 37, 95, 100, P4.15, P14.14, P17.1–P17.16, P18.13

Identification Summary Pacific (Mexico and California). A small bicolored shearwater, dark brown above and white below, with dark undertail coverts. Sides of head and neck brownish, not sharply demarcated from white underparts; some birds become notably bleached and white-headed in winter. Flight hurried and low with fluttery wingbeats; glides on slightly bowed wings and wheels fairly steeply in windy conditions.

P17.1. Black-vented Shearwaters commonly occur in flocks and often can be seen from shore. SNGH. Off San Diego, California, 4 Oct 2008.

Taxonomy Monotypic. Murphy (1952) subsumed seven disparate worldwide taxa (including Black-vented) as subspecies of Manx Shearwater, but these are now all treated as species.

Names *Puffinus* derives from puffin (see under Audubon's Shearwater); *opisthomelas* can be translated as "black rear" and presumably refers to the species' dark undertail coverts.

Status and Distribution Near Threatened. Endemic. Local breeder (Mar–Aug) on islands off cen Pacific coast of Baja California Peninsula, mainly on Natividad Island (about 76,500 pairs), also on San Benito Islands (a few hundred pairs), and offshore rocks at Guadalupe Island (a few hundred pairs) (Keitt et al. 2000b).

Pacific. Main pelagic range is inshore waters from vicinity of breeding islands n to Point Conception, California. Typically fairly common to common around breeding islands year-round (least numerous Sep–Nov), but numbers there may decline in warm-water years. Postbreeding dispersal begins Jul–Aug and main numbers off s California occur Sep–Dec, with smaller numbers irregularly appearing in Jul or Aug and lingering into Mar or Apr. Strongest incursions are in warm-water years such as during El Niño events, when thousands occur regularly n to Monterey Bay (mainly Oct–Dec, smaller numbers casually from Jul–Aug and into Mar–Apr), and small numbers casually (mainly Oct–Jan) n to Sonoma County, exceptionally to s British Columbia.

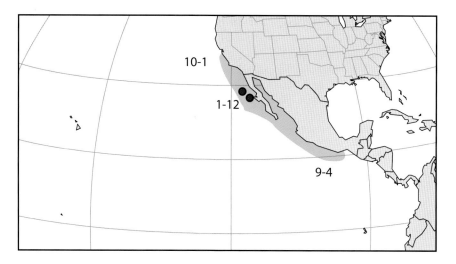

10-1

1-12

9-4

Black-vented Shearwater. Rare and irregular in winter south to Central America, north to northern California.

Uncommon to fairly common but irregular nonbreeding visitor (mainly Sep–Apr) s to Oaxaca (pers. obs.), irregularly uncommon to common in Gulf of California (Jun–Feb, mainly Jul–Nov), and irregularly (Oct–Nov, at least) s in small numbers off Central America, to Costa Rica (Sullivan 2009). Exceptional inland in sw Arizona (Sep 1997) after a tropical storm (Jones 1999).

FIELD IDENTIFICATION

Similar Species Three other small bicolored shearwaters (Manx, Townsend's, and Galapagos) occur regularly in range of Black-vented, but all three have darker and more sharply contrasting dorsal plumage, especially on the head and neck, and Manx has a shorter tail with white undertail coverts. See under Manx and Townsend's shearwaters for details.

Galapagos Shearwater (e Pacific n to Mexico) favors warmer waters. Distinctly smaller with shorter, more rounded wings and clean-cut dark cap and hindneck contrasting strongly with extensively white throat and foreneck. Upperparts darker, blackish brown in fresh plumage with narrow pale tips to greater coverts; underwings often with extensive dusky on leading edge.

Pink-footed Shearwater much larger and bulkier with stout black-tipped pink bill, but plumage similar to Black-vented, and these two can be confused if scale is misjudged. Pink-footed typically flies with slow, unhurried wingbeats and leisurely glides, but in windy conditions both Pink-footed and Black-vented can wheel behind a boat in a similar manner and cause more than momentary confusion. On the water, Black-vented often looks darker and more uniform above, with more contrasting whitish flanks, whereas Pink-footed tends to be browner above, usually with some paler scalloping, and pale brownish flanks do not contrast strongly with back.

Habitat and Behavior Inshore waters, mainly within 25 km of shore, but locally ranges 100 km or more offshore and breeds offshore on Guadalupe Island. Often seen from land, at times in thousands or tens of thousands, streaming past or feeding in flocks that may be just beyond the surf. Associates readily with other shearwaters, and with mixed-species feeding and loafing flocks of gulls, terns, pelicans, and other waterbirds. Nests in burrows dug in soil, also locally in rock crevices. At night on breeding grounds gives rough, strangled moans with a slightly hissing quality, often repeated a few times with a slightly pulsating rhythm, *whóhr kuh, whóhr kuh, whóhr kuh,* ...

In calm to light winds, flight typically fast and low over the water, at times almost fluttery, with bursts of hurried, slightly loose wingbeats interspersed with short glides on slightly bowed wings; in light to moderate winds glides can be longer with shallow wheeling, and in moderate to strong winds can wheel and even tower high and fairly steeply, often stalling and flapping at the top of a climb. Feeds by plunging from low flight, diving from the surface, and skittering over the surface; dives regularly to 20–30 m, rarely 50 m (Keitt et al. 2000a).

Description A small bicolored shearwater with medium-length tail and relatively long bill; toe tips can project past tail in flight. On the water, wingtips typically fall about even with or slightly beyond tail tip. Leucism not rare (Garrett 1990; pers. obs.), and a melanistic specimen exists (Howell 2007b).

Ages similar but juveniles fresh in Aug–Sep when most older birds worn or molting. Head, neck sides, and upperparts blackish brown (grayer when fresh, warmer brown when worn, and usually with distinct brown tones in sunlight); head darkest on forecrown, and brownish on head sides and neck often fades in fall (mainly Aug–Nov), contrasting with dark cap and dark back; some birds have whole head and neck strongly bleached whitish in fall and early winter. Throat, foreneck, and underbody white, some birds with extensive dusky mottling and scalloping over throat and foreneck, and many birds with dusky mottling on flanks. Undertail coverts dark sooty brown (often mixed with white on shorter coverts); in flight, underside of tail often appears to have a broad blackish tip. Underwings white with blackish-brown remiges, variably dark greater coverts (often dark overall), variable dusky leading edge, and variable dark tips to axillars (often showing as distinct diagonal dark bar). Dark distal marks on axillars may not be helpful for aging (*contra* Pyle 2010; more study needed). Small white thigh patches can show as saddlebags in flight, but usually poorly contrasting. Bill gray, sometimes with the mandible paler; legs and feet pinkish overall.

On the water. Dark brown crown and upperparts, paler brownish neck sides, variable white on foreneck and chest, whitish sides, mostly dark undertail coverts.

Molt Adult wing molt mainly Jun/Jul–Oct/Nov; perhaps more protracted in food-poor years such as during El Niño events. Overlap of wing molt and breeding rare among shearwaters, but reduced wing area may facilitate deeper diving during chick-rearing period (Keitt et al. 2000a). Tail molt occurs at or following completion of primary molt, ending Jan–Feb on latest birds. Timing of PB2 molt needs study; wing molt of some birds wintering off sw Mexico starts Feb–Mar (pers. obs.) and thus could complete by Jun; other birds may molt later (Apr–Aug?).

P17.2. Black-vented Shearwater completing primary molt. Note dirty brownish face pattern, relatively long slender bill, brown undertail coverts. SNGH. Off San Diego, California, 4 Oct 2008.

P17.3. Black-vented Shearwater. Upperparts can appear fairly warm brown in some lights (cf. P17.2). SNGH. Off San Diego, California, 8 Mar 2009.

P17.4. Black-vented Shearwater with inner primary molt, presumably a first-year bird on this date; note face pattern and long bill. SNGH. Oaxaca, Mexico, 8 Mar 2007.

P17.5. Black-vented Shearwater. Dark brown above with dirty brownish head pattern, long gray bill; toes often project beyond tail. SNGH. Off San Diego, California, 6 Mar 2010.

P17.6. Black-vented Shearwater in fresh plumage can show whitish tips to greater coverts; whitish saddle-bags rarely more prominent than this. SNGH. Off San Diego, California, 4 Oct 2008.

P17.7. Dark underwing markings of Black-vented Shearwater rather variable, as is extent of dusky on neck (cf. P17.8–P17.10). SNGH. Off San Diego, California, 7 Mar 2010.

P17.8. Black-vented Shearwater with relatively clean white underwings. TMcG. Off San Diego, California, 13 Apr 2005.

P17.9. Black-vented Shearwater with outer primary molt, worn head and neck, mixed generations of secondaries. SNGH. Off San Diego, California, 4 Oct 2008.

P17.10. Black-vented Shearwater in fresh plumage, with relatively contrasting dark cap (cf. P17.9). TMcG. Off San Diego, California, 22 Nov 2008.

P17.11. Black-vented Shearwater. Banking away, note dark undertail coverts but clean white flanks and base to underwing (cf. P17.12). SNGH. Off San Diego, California, 4 Oct 2008.

P17.12. Black-vented Shearwater is superficially similar to much larger and broader-winged Pink-footed Shearwater (left) but has clean white flanks and base to underwing, slender dark bill. SNGH. Off Monterey, California, 15 Oct 2006.

P17.13. Black-vented Shearwater (left of center) with flock of smaller and more contrastingly patterned Galapagos Shearwaters; note dusky brown head and neck sides of Black-vented. SNGH. Oaxaca, Mexico, 18 Dec 2008.

P17.14. Black-vented Shearwater (left) is appreciably larger than Galapagos Shearwater (right, whose small size is exaggerated by greater distance from camera). On Black-vented note dusky brown head and neck sides, long gray bill. SNGH. Oaxaca, Mexico, 16 Dec 2008.

P17.15. Black-vented Shearwater is much smaller than this first-cycle Western Gull; note extensively (but dirty) whitish basal undertail coverts on the shearwater. SNGH. Off San Diego, California, 4 Oct 2008.

P17.16. Head and neck of Black-vented Shearwater (front, with light morph Wedge-tailed Shearwater behind) can bleach to strikingly whitish in mid-winter (perhaps only in first-year birds). SNGH. Oaxaca, Mexico, 18 Dec 2008.

P18. GALAPAGOS SHEARWATER *Puffinus subalaris*

L 28–31 cm, WS 63–70 cm, tail 63–72 mm (graduation 10–15 mm), bill 25–30 mm
Figures 99, P14.15, P18.1–P18.15, S9.10

Identification Summary Pacific. A very small bicolored shearwater of warm waters off Middle America. Brownish black above, white below with dark undertail coverts, clean-cut dark/white cap and neck sides. On the water, white sides not bright and contrasting. Flight low and fluttering with buoyant glides on slightly arched wings. Formerly considered a subspecies of Audubon's Shearwater.

Taxonomy Taxonomy of small black-and-white shearwaters worldwide vexed. Galapagos Shearwater has been treated as a subspecies of Audubon's Shearwater but it is morphologically distinct and better considered a separate species, a conclusion supported by genetic analysis (Austin et al. 2004). Although considered monotypic, Galapagos Shearwater shows appreciable variation in plumage and vocalizations (see below), suggesting some populations warrant species status. Measurements of wing chord, tail, and culmen among "white-winged" and "dark-winged" birds do not differ appreciably (CAS specimens), but more study is needed.

Names *Puffinus* derives from puffin (see under Audubon's Shearwater); *subalaris* refers to "under the wings," perhaps in reference to an individual with dark underwings.

Status and Distribution Not recognized by Birdlife International (2010a). Breeds year-round on Galapagos Islands, with a cycle averaging nine months (four for breeding, five for molt) and local synchrony on islands (Snow 1965); ranges at sea mainly to the n, from Panama to Mexico, very rarely to mainland Ecuador.

Pacific. Fairly common to uncommon nonbreeding visitor (year-round) from Gulf of Panama (rarely ranging into Panama Bay) n at least to s Jalisco (around 20˚N); local concentrations up to 4000 birds off Guatemala (Jehl 1974), and of 12,000–15,000 birds off s Mexico (Dec 2008, pers. obs.; P18.4) may be irregular events driven by food crashes farther s. Favors inshore waters but has been found well out to sea and at Clipperton Atoll.

FIELD IDENTIFICATION

Similar Species Two other small bicolored shearwaters (Townsend's and Black-vented) occur regularly in the range of Galapagos off Mexico. Also see Manx and Newell's shearwaters (potential vagrants in range of Galapagos).

Townsend's Shearwater (mainly Mexico) often seen in feeding flocks with Galapagos, is slightly larger with longer wings and tail but proportionately smaller bill, often appears blacker above. In prolonged flight, note less hurried and more fluid wingbeats of Townsend's, with stronger upstroke, but feeding birds of both species often make short, rapid flights that are similar. Townsend's has messier and more extensive blackish cap (often with whitish "hook" behind auriculars) and hindneck, lending it a dark-faced aspect, whereas head and neck sides of Galapagos more extensively white with clean-cut blackish cap and hindneck; small whitish supraorbital mark on Galapagos visible at close range. In flight Galapagos often looks relatively longer necked and holds its head slightly raised, usually lacks white saddlebags, and often has broad dark leading edge to underwing and dark on axillars and flanks. On the water, Townsend's shows extensive white flanks, set off by dark spur on the chest sides, whereas Galapagos typically sits lower and shows less extensive and less contrasting white, often with dusky mottling and streaking.

Black-vented Shearwater (mainly Mexico) favors cooler waters. Distinctly larger with longer wings, less buoyant flight. Upperparts browner with messy brownish sides to head and neck, typically cleaner white leading edge to underwing.

Habitat and Behavior Pelagic, but locally can be seen from shore. Favors warmer waters over the shelf slope and submarine canyons. Found singly or more often in flocks, at times in hundreds, sometimes thousands, and associates readily with mixed-species feeding flocks that include other shearwaters, boobies, and terns.

In calm to light winds, flight typically low over the water, with quick, fluttering wingbeats interspersed with short buoyant glides on slightly arched wings, the head often raised slightly above the body plane; flying across moderate to strong winds, sometimes wheels in shallow arcs, and can wheel high and fairly steeply in strong winds, although tends to stay fairly low to the water. Feeding birds skitter and splash over the surface,

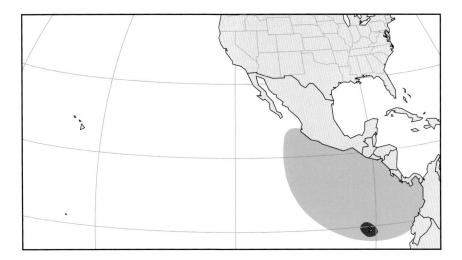

making shallow pursuit dives and often pushing their faces underwater while swimming.

Often utters hoarse grunts and slightly shrieky quacks in feeding and squabbling interactions. Rafting birds on occasion appear to sing in courtship. One song type is a three-syllable, hoarse clucking *cáh-ah-hooh...*, repeated rhythmically a few times in short series (higher- and lower-pitched songs presumably reflecting different sexes); another song type is a distinctly different four-syllable, hollow rhythmic clucking *h'kuk-á-waoh...*, also repeated a few times in short series. Other vocalizations heard from rafts of birds include a screechy whistled *shiih-shiih-shiihr*, repeated.

Description A very small shearwater with a relatively big bill, slightly rounded wings, and medium-length tail; feet do not project beyond tail tip in flight. On the water, wingtips typically fall about even with or slightly beyond tail tip.

Ages similar. Upperparts, including sides of head to just below eye, brownish black (browner when worn); dark/white border on head and neck clean-cut, and narrow whitish eye crescents form narrow spectacles; some individuals also have whitish speckling in lores; pale face markings often reduced to almost absent in "dark-winged" birds. Dark on sides of neck forms variable bulge forward of wings. Variable paler tips (dull brownish gray to whitish) to greater and median upperwing coverts and scapulars palest when bleached but reduced or lost by wear. Underparts white with solidly brownish-black undertail coverts, often some dark mottling on flanks. Underwings vary from white overall with blackish undersides to remiges, reduced dusky markings on axillars and coverts, and a narrow, dark leading edge ("white-winged" types) to extensively mottled blackish and dusky on axillars and coverts ("dark-winged" types). Bill dark grayish overall with paler bluish to blue-gray mandible, at least basally; legs and feet pinkish overall.

On the water. Blackish above and white below, with sides often mottled dark brownish and not sharply contrasting white; undertail coverts extensively blackish.

Molt Given year-round breeding, wing molt presumably can occur year-round.

P18.1. Galapagos Shearwater is a very small, bicolored shearwater once treated as a subspecies of Audubon's Shearwater. Note clean dark/white division on sides of head and neck, variable pale spectacles. SNGH. Oaxaca, Mexico, 17 Dec 2008.

P18.2. Galapagos Shearwater can show pale tips to upperwing coverts in fresh plumage. Note resemblance to Audubon's Shearwater of North Atlantic, but Galapagos is smaller and shorter tailed. SNGH. Oaxaca, Mexico, 17 Dec 2008.

P18.3. Galapagos Shearwaters commonly fly low over the water, often with their head and neck raised. SNGH. Oaxaca, Mexico, 15 Dec 2008.

P18.4. Galapagos Shearwaters gather locally in flocks of thousands, often fairly close to shore. SNGH. Oaxaca, Mexico, 17 Dec 2008.

P18.5. Underwing coverts of Galapagos Shearwater vary from white to blackish (cf. P18.6–P18.10). SNGH. Oaxaca, Mexico, 15 Dec 2008.

P18.6. Galapagos Shearwaters with extensively white underwing coverts also tend to have distinct white spectacles. SNGH. Oaxaca, Mexico, 15 Dec 2008.

P18.7. Galapagos Shearwater with overall white underwing coverts. Note classic shape, with deep chest and raised head. SNGH. Oaxaca, Mexico, 14 Dec 2008.

P18.8. Galapagos Shearwaters with overall blackish underwing coverts also tend to have indistinct white spectacles. SNGH. Oaxaca, Mexico, 14 Dec 2008.

P18.9. "Black-winged" Galapagos Shearwater with outer primary molt. Different songs among Galapagos Shearwaters suggest more than one species is involved, perhaps correlating to underwing pattern. SNGH. Oaxaca, Mexico, 15 Dec 2008.

P18.10. Some Galapagos Shearwaters don't fit neatly into "white-winged" and "black-winged" categories but instead have dusky underwing coverts. SNGH. Oaxaca, Mexico, 14 Dec 2008.

P18.11. Galapagos Shearwater (probably "black-winged" based on face pattern; cf. P18.12) has a relatively long bill for a small shearwater. SNGH. Oaxaca, Mexico, 17 Dec 2008.

P18.12. "White-winged" Galapagos Shearwater (underwings seen in flight). Note relatively long bill, bold white spectacles (cf. P18.11), and fairly clean-cut black/white head and neck. SNGH. Oaxaca, Mexico, 16 Dec 2008.

P18.13. Galapagos Shearwaters readily rest with Black-vented Shearwater (two birds here, center right), which is larger with diffuse brownish head/neck pattern. SNGH. Oaxaca, Mexico, 17 Dec 2008.

P18.14. Very small size of Galapagos Shearwater can be appreciated here in comparison with light morph Wedge-tailed Shearwater. SNGH. Oaxaca, Mexico, 17 Dec 2008.

P18.15. Galapagos Shearwaters have been noted on several occasions to successfully solicit facial preening from much larger Wedge-tailed Shearwaters, as here, but have not been seen to reciprocate. SNGH. Oaxaca, Mexico, 18 Dec 2008.

P19. CHRISTMAS SHEARWATER *Puffinus nativitatus*
L 33–36 cm, WS 83–90 cm, tail 85–94 mm (graduation 20–25 mm), bill 25–34 mm
Figures P19.1–P19.9

Identification Summary Pacific. Warm tropical waters; often with mixed-species feeding flocks. A small, all-dark shearwater akin to the Manx Shearwater complex, which it somewhat resembles in size, shape, and flight manner. Flight usually low, quick wingbeats interspersed with buoyant glides.

Taxonomy Monotypic.

Names *Puffinus* derives from puffin (see under Audubon's Shearwater); *nativitatus* refers to Christmas Island, Pacific Ocean, where the type specimen was collected.

Status and Distribution Least Concern. Breeds (seasons vary; Apr/May–Sep/Oct in Hawaii, Nov–Mar off Chile) from nw Hawaiian Islands s and e to Easter Island. Ranges in tropical cen and e Pacific Ocean.

Pacific. Not well known. Uncommon to fairly common nonbreeding visitor (Mar–Sep, at least) from w Panama Bight n to w Mexico, around 18˚N (Howell & Engel 1993, Pitman 1986, Spear & Ainley 1999b; NAB 62:487, 2008), rare n (Aug–Oct, at least) to around 23˚N off tip of Baja California Peninsula (NAB 64:158, 2010; pers. obs., Aug 2010; P19.3, P19.7).

FIELD IDENTIFICATION

Similar Species Note small size, all-dark plumage, and flight typical of small shearwaters such as Manx or Black-vented. With potential vagrants, beware the possibility of melanistic, heavily pigmented, or even oiled individuals of other small shearwater species. A melanistic Black-vented Shearwater collected in Monterey Bay was initially thought to be a Christmas Shearwater (Howell 2007b).

Dark morph *Herald Petrel* (and Henderson Petrel; both well offshore) similar in overall color but slightly larger and longer winged with thicker bills. Flight more relaxed, buoyant and wheeling on arched and slightly crooked wings, lacking bursts of rapid, stiff wingbeats.

Sooty Shearwater (little overlap in region) distinctly larger with narrower and more pointed wings, shorter tail (toes often project), a longer, grayish bill, and grayer (less chocolate-brown) plumage; underwings usually show conspicuous silvery-white flashes across the coverts. Flight faster with stronger deeper flaps in calm to light winds, higher arcing in strong winds.

Short-tailed Shearwater (little or no overlap in region) larger with narrower and more pointed wings, shorter tail (toes often project), slightly longer, grayish bill, and grayer (less chocolate-brown) plumage; underwings often show a pale panel across the coverts.

Murphy's Petrel (well offshore, not known to overlap in region) slightly larger, stockier, and longer-winged with a bigger head and thick bill; plumage steely gray overall with a white throat patch, and flies with snappier wingbeats and, in windy conditions, higher wheeling arcs.

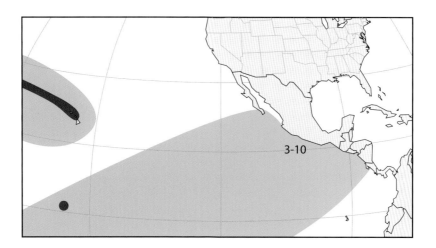

Habitat and Behavior Pelagic over warmer waters, especially over the shelf break. Associates readily with mixed-species feeding flocks of other shearwaters (off Mexico with Wedge-tailed, Townsend's, Black-vented, and Galapagos shearwaters), boobies, and terns.

In calm to moderate winds typically flies low with quick, stiff wingbeats interspersed with buoyant glides on slightly flexed wings, little wheeling. In moderate to strong winds, can wheel fairly high much like other small shearwaters.

Description A small, all-dark shearwater with fairly low wing-loading, bluntly pointed wings, medium-long and graduated tail, and medium-length bill; feet do not project beyond tail tip in flight.

Ages similar. Dark chocolate-brown overall, slightly darker on head and upperparts and occasionally with slightly paler, grayish throat; undersides of primaries and greater primary coverts can reflect dull to fairly bright silvery, depending on light angle. Bill black, legs and feet dusky brownish.

Molt Adults presumably molt mainly in nonbreeding season, and immatures earlier; hence wing molt for Hawaiian birds may be expected Jun/Sep–Oct/Feb. Thus, birds molting inner to middle primaries off Mexico in Mar–May and fresh-plumaged in Aug (P19.1–P19.4) probably have an equatorial or s hemisphere breeding schedule and do not originate from Hawaii.

P19.2. Shape of Christmas Shearwater rather similar to Newell's and Townsend's shearwaters but plumage all-dark; note long broad tail relative to larger and narrower-winged Sooty and Short-tailed shearwaters. SNGH. Oaxaca, Mexico, 8 Mar 2007.

P19.1. Christmas Shearwater with mid-primary molt (p6–p10 old). Note dark sooty brown plumage, relatively long broad tail, small head, slender bill. Molt timing suggests these birds originate from the tropical South Pacific. SNGH. Oaxaca, Mexico, 8 Mar 2007.

P19.3. Christmas Shearwater in fresh plumage. Note dark sooty brown plumage, including underwing coverts; also slender black bill. MS. Baja California Sur, Mexico, 20 Aug 2010.

P19.4. Underwings of Christmas Shearwater are all-dark but remiges can reflect silvery in some lights, and paler stripes can be produced by molt, as here. SNGH. Oaxaca, Mexico, 8 Mar 2007.

P19.5. Christmas Shearwater has a buoyant flight and often glides on slightly arched wings. Note slender bill relative to dark-bodied gadfly petrels. SNGH. Oaxaca, Mexico, 8 Mar 2007.

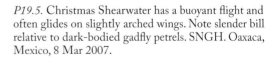

P19.6. Overall shape and coloration of Christmas Shearwater rather similar to Henderson Petrel (cf. P35b.3), from which best separated by flight manner and slender bill. SNGH. Oaxaca, Mexico, 8 Mar 2007.

P19.7. Christmas Shearwater in fresh plumage. Note dark sooty brown plumage, graduated tail tip, slender black bill. MS. Baja California Sur, Mexico, 20 Aug 2010.

P19.8. Christmas Shearwater has longer-tailed aspect and often a squarer head than larger Sooty and Short-tailed shearwaters, which favor cold temperate waters; also note glossy black bill. SNGH. Oaxaca, Mexico, 8 Mar 2007.

P19.9. Christmas Shearwater with Wedge-tailed Shearwaters is appreciably smaller; also note slender black bill. SNGH. Oaxaca, Mexico, 8 Mar 2007.

P19.10. Christmas Shearwater (below) shares buoyant flight and arched wings with Wedge-tailed Shearwater (above) but is appreciably smaller and darker. SNGH. Oaxaca, Mexico, 8 Mar 2007.

GADFLY PETRELS

The term *gadfly petrel* usually refers to birds in the genus *Pterodroma* (Fig 101). These are birds of the high seas and include some of the most accomplished, graceful, and seemingly uninhibited fliers among birds. Of about 30 *Pterodroma* species worldwide, 15 have been recorded in North American waters (see introductory sections to Atlantic Gadfly Petrels, p. 164, and Pacific Gadfly Petrels, p. 195). Several other petrels may also be termed gadfly petrels, including species in the genus *Pseudobulweria* (which has at times been merged with *Pterodroma*); one such species (Tahiti Petrel) occurs in the region.

The wings of gadfly petrels are generally long, relatively narrow, and pointed, characteristically held pressed slightly forward, crooked, and flexed or bowed at the carpals, producing a somewhat more curved and graceful aspect than the stiffer and straighter wings typical of shearwaters (see Figs 63–64). Gadflies also differ from shearwaters in their steeper foreheads (housing well-developed olfactory lobes), and medium-sized to large species have appreciably thicker bills than shearwaters (see Fig 62). Bills are black, and feet are all-dark or bicolored (pink or bluish basally, blackish distally). From below, long, plush undertail coverts cover most of the tail and the feet are held in during flight. The tails of gadflies often have some white basally, at least on the inner webs of the outer rectrices, whereas shearwater tails tend to be all-dark. Several gadflies show a contrasting M pattern across their upperparts, and species with mostly white underwings have variable black underwing

Fig 101. Among Atlantic gadfly petrels recorded in North American waters, Black-capped Petrel (left) is appreciably larger than the other species, as seen here in comparison with light morph Trinidade Petrel (right). SNGH. Off Hatteras, North Carolina, 23 May 2007.

margins. At sea gadflies are often solitary, and they tend not to form large flocks as is common with some shearwaters. Many species feed at night and early or late in the day, when they tend to be most active, and their bills are well suited for tearing squid, an important food item. All species seemingly can be attracted to ships, at least briefly, but generally birds soon veer away and do not accompany vessels, except perhaps near nesting islands. Although the textbook gadfly flight involves a fast and wheeling rollercoaster progression with no or little flapping (the genus name means "winged runner"), this usually only applies to birds flying across moderate to strong winds. Flight into moderate to strong winds can be fairly low and water-hugging, and in calm to light winds gadflies often travel low, with bursts of unhurried to fairly quick, easy flaps of flexed wings, long glides, and little or no wheeling. At other times in calm conditions they can fly at moderate heights with a disconcertingly direct, flapping, almost jaeger-like progression. In general, smaller species (such as Cook's Petrel) have quicker wingbeats and often appear to fly more quickly and erratically than larger species (such as Black-capped Petrel), which actually may be moving faster, their easier-looking flight belying their speed. Wing-loading is also an important consideration: species with a higher wing-loading (heavier bodies and smaller wing areas, such as Murphy's and Mottled petrels) appear to fly more quickly and impetuously, with shorter-wavelength and more steeply rising arcs than species with lower wing-loading (such as Desertas [Fea's] and Herald petrels), which have a more leisurely and buoyant flight, with generally longer-wavelength and less towering arcs.

Many gadfly petrels are notoriously difficult to identify at sea. The most important points to check are overall plumage patterns, head and neck patterns, underwing patterns, and flight manner; aspects of structure (such as bill size) can also be helpful but use of such features requires at least some comparative experience, and preferably a series of photos.

Atlantic Gadfly Petrels

At least five species of *Pterodroma* petrels have been recorded in North American Atlantic waters, and at least four have been seen in the same day off North Carolina. The commonest and most "familiar" species is the large and distinctive Black-capped Petrel, which breeds in the Caribbean and may comprise more than one species. Three or four other medium-sized gadfly species are rare but regular nonbreeding visitors recorded from May to Sep: Bermuda, Deserta's [Fea's], Cape Verde [Fea's], and Trinidade petrels; and Zino's Petrel has been recorded at least once.

Identification challenges among the four regular and conventionally recognized species (Black-capped, Bermuda, Fea's, and Trinidade Petrels) are relatively slight, assuming a bird is seen fairly well, but some pitfalls exist (Figs 102–108). However, at-sea identification of species in the Fea's Petrel complex (Desertas, Cape Verde, and Zino's petrels) is more challenging (Figs 109–114; see Shirihai 2010b), and if Black-capped Petrel comprises multiple species then more work will be needed (Howell & Patteson 2008b).

Fig 102. Black-capped Petrel. Typical white-faced individual with relatively narrow black underwing margins. SNGH. Off Hatteras, North Carolina, 2 Jun 2008.

Fig 103. Black-capped Petrel. Typical black-faced individual with thick black underwing margins. SNGH. Off Hatteras, North Carolina, 30 Jul 2007.

Fig 104. Bermuda Petrel. Distinguished from larger and bulkier Black-capped Petrel by dark cowl and relatively fine bill. SNGH. Off Hatteras, North Carolina, 2 Jun 2008.

Fig 105. (Below left) Bermuda Petrel with inner primary molt. Distinctive even at long range; note dark cowl, limited white on rump (cf. Fig 106). SNGH. Off Hatteras, North Carolina, 29 May 2009.

Fig 106. (Below) Even at long range, darkest-faced Black-capped Petrels distinguished from Bermuda Petrel (cf. Fig 105) by larger size, large and gleaming white rump patch; also typically differ in having white neck sides. SNGH. Off Hatteras, North Carolina, 2 Jun 2010.

Fig 107. Bermuda Petrel. Head-on, note the dark hood contrasting with the paler back, but some Fea's Petrels can appear very similar (cf. Fig 108). SNGH. Off Hatteras, North Carolina, 23 May 2009.

Fig 108. Head-on, some Fea's Petrels with relatively dark crown (like this bird) appear very similar to Bermuda Petrel (cf. Figs 107, 109). SNGH. Off Hatteras, North Carolina, 1 Jun 2010.

Fig 109. Head-on, typical Fea's Petrel has concolorous gray head and back (cf. Figs 108, 110). SNGH. Off Hatteras, North Carolina, 24 May 2007.

Fig 110. Head-on, Zino's Petrel (shown here) perhaps not safely separable from Fea's Petrel (Fig 109) but has smaller, narrower bill and often a short white eyebrow offsetting wedge-shaped eye mask, thus suggesting Cook's Petrel. SNGH. Madeira, eastern Atlantic, 15 May 2010.

166

Fig 111. Fea's Petrel differs from Zino's primarily in larger head and stouter bill (cf. Fig 112); often has a relatively messy and large rounded black eye patch. SNGH. Off Hatteras, North Carolina, 27 May 2009.

Fig 112. Zino's Petrel differs from Fea's in smaller head and bill (cf. Fig 111); often has a sharply defined, wedge-shaped black eye mask. SNGH. Madeira, eastern Atlantic, 15 May 2010.

Fig 113. Fea's Petrel differs from Zino's in larger head and stouter bill, which, with relatively messy black eye patch, often creates a relatively brutish expression (cf. Fig 114). Note how wingtip shape varies greatly with angle of viewing as well as with wind speed and bird behavior (cf. Fig 114). SNGH. Off Hatteras, North Carolina, 1 Jun 2010.

Fig 114. Zino's Petrel differs from Fea's in its smaller head and bill, which, with clean face pattern, often creates relatively gentle expression (cf. Fig 113). SNGH. Madeira, eastern Atlantic, 15 May 2010.

P20. BLACK-CAPPED PETREL *Pterodroma hasitata*

L 38–45 cm, WS 98–105 cm, tail 125–140 mm (graduation 35–50 mm)
Figures 3, 44, 62, 101–103, 106, P20.1–P20.19

Identification Summary Atlantic and Caribbean, warm water. May comprise at least two species-level taxa (see below). This large, stocky, boldly patterned *Pterodroma* is essentially a "flying field mark," with its bold black-and-white patterning. In particular, note the large white "rump" patch (mainly the upper-tail coverts and tail base), white underparts with broad black wing margins, and variable head and neck patterning.

P20.1. Essentially a flying field mark, white-faced Black-capped Petrel is readily identified even at long range; note especially the large white rump patch. SNGH. Off Hatteras, North Carolina, 5 Jun 2009.

Taxonomy Traditionally considered monotypic, but three types distinguished by Howell and Patteson (2008b) may comprise two or more species (see Description). Most birds can be allocated into slightly larger white-faced types, which average an earlier molt timing (and earlier breeding?), and slightly smaller black-faced types, which average a later molt timing (and later breeding?). Other variations exist, and these so-called intermediate types may collectively represent immatures of white-faced types, variation within black-faced types, and perhaps additional populations. More study is needed. Dark-faced types may breed mainly on Hispaniola (and Jamaica?), with white-faced types in the Lesser Antilles (on Dominica, at least) but critical study is needed. Jamaican Petrel (*P. caribbaea*) has been treated as conspecific

with Black-capped Petrel (AOU 1998) and is presumed extinct (see Appendix A).

Names *Pterodroma* means "winged runner," in reference to the notably swift flight of petrels in this genus; *hasitata* apparently refers to the uncertainty, or hesitation, of the person who described the species.

Status and Distribution Endangered. Endemic breeder. Local breeder (apparently Nov/Dec–Apr/May) in mountains of sw Hispaniola (Haiti and adjacent Dominican Republic), where breeding population perhaps in the order of 600–2000 pairs (Lee 2000). Formerly bred abundantly in Lesser Antilles (on Guadeloupe, Dominica, and possibly Martinique), but predation by humans

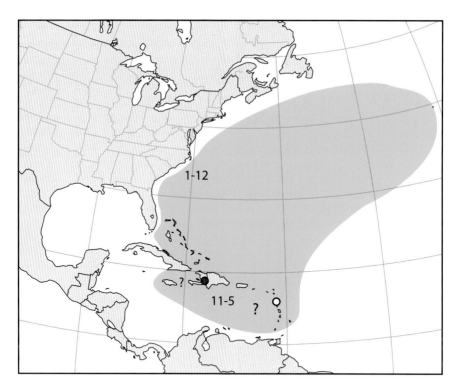

and other non-native mammals, earthquake, and perhaps volcanic eruption combined to extirpate most or all of these populations by mid-1800s; some birds may persist on Dominica (Collar et al. 1992, Lee 2000). Breeding in Cuba unsubstantiated, with numbers off the se coast of Cuba presumed to be foraging from nearby colonies on Hispaniola (Lee & Viña 1993, but see NAB 58:293, 2004), and recently found off Jamaica, where may breed (Shirihai et al. 2010b). Ranges at sea in w Atlantic n to Gulf Stream waters off U.S., and s to n coast of South America; very rare (Feb–May) in ne Atlantic (Howell 2002, Robb et al. 2008). White-faced types tend to be relatively more numerous off North Carolina in May, whereas in Jul–Aug black-faced types are much commoner (Howell & Patteson 2008b).

Atlantic. Year-round nonbreeding visitor to Gulf Steam waters from Florida to North Carolina (mainly 27–36°N; Haney 1987b), and probably n to Virginia. Most abundant off n Georgia and s South Carolina, where upwelling greatest (Haney 1987b). Main route to and from Gulf Stream may be n of Bahamas, where most of relatively few records are Jan–May (White 2004). Best known off North Carolina, where fairly common to common May–Oct, although with high counts also in Dec (perhaps reflecting prelaying exodus). Apparent rarity n of North Carolina reflects, at least in part, the distance offshore of the Gulf Stream, which cannot be reached easily by observers. Very rare (mainly Jul–Aug, when waters are warmest) n to waters s of Nova Scotia (see Brinkley & Patteson 1998 for pelagic records n of North Carolina), with hurricane-blown birds (mainly Aug–Sep) very rare on shore n to Massachusetts, and inland from w Florida n to e Great Lakes and w to Kentucky.

Very rare in Gulf of Mexico (mainly Apr–Jul) from Florida Keys w to Texas. Perhaps regular (mainly Nov–May?) in e Caribbean, off Lesser Antilles and n coast of Colombia and Venezuela, but few recent records (Collar et al. 1992). An Aug report from Costa Rica is hypothetical.

FIELD IDENTIFICATION

Similar Species Black-capped Petrel is a distinctive species only likely to be confused in flight if seen poorly, such as in bad lighting or at a distance. In combination with its large size (for a *Pterodroma*) and stocky shape, note large white uppertail-covert patch, visible at long range. On the water, cf. Great Shearwater and light morph jaegers; swimming petrels usually flush at a distance, whereas shearwaters often allow close approach.

Great Shearwater larger (in direct comparison, Black-capped looks about 75–80% the size of Great Sheawater) with slender black bill, shallower forehead, only a narrow white crescent at base of tail, brown (often scaly) upperparts, and dark cap reaching base of bill (forehead white on Black-capped). Great's flight less buoyant, with wings held straighter.

Bermuda Petrel smaller and slimmer with narrower wings, a relatively longer, narrower tail, and smaller, slimmer bill; seen head-on or from above, as likely to be confused with Fea's Petrel. Bermuda has narrow white rump band restricted to basal uppertail coverts, dark gray tail, and dark cowl, with extensive dark on neck sides; the black carpal-ulnar band on underwing averages thicker than Black-capped. Bermuda's flight often looks quick relative to unhurried Black-capped, and usually it wheels lower to the water. Beware especially of dark-faced Black-capped Petrels, which, except for the large white rump patch, overall look as much like Bermuda Petrel as they do white-faced Black-capped. Worn and faded Bermuda Petrels can have a messy but distinct white hind-collar (perhaps mainly first-year birds in wing molt, Jun–Aug).

Habitat and Behavior Pelagic away from breeding grounds, but occurs seasonally (Nov–Mar) close inshore along se coast of Cuba (Lee & Viña 1993). Favors warm waters along w edge of Gulf Stream, especially areas of upwelling associated with eddies and seafloor topography (Haney 1987b). Found singly or in loose foraging or rafting aggregations, typically of 5–20 birds. Associates readily with mixed-species feeding flocks, in summer with shearwaters and terns, in winter with Herring Gulls and Black-legged Kittiwakes (Haney 1987b); at times also rafts in loose association with those species. Does not usually follow ships and seems wary of coming close to vessels, but will scavenge on occasion; resting birds on the water usually do not allow close approach and flush at a distance. Nests in burrows dug in soil, colonies restricted to remote forested limestone cliffs. At night on breeding grounds gives fairly short, braying moans, each ending with an emphatic muted squeak and at times repeated fairly rapidly; also longer, slightly disyllabic wailing moans without an emphatic ending (LNS 139296). Occasionally heard at sea off North America, particularly in fall and winter or when squabbling over food, when birds can utter a bleating or croaking *waaahh* or *aaa-aw* (Haney 1987b).

Flight buoyant and strong, the wings pushed forward, crooked at the carpals, and flexed, as is typical of medium-sized and large gadfly petrels.

In calm to light winds, fairly deep, quick, and clipped wingbeats alternate with leisurely buoyant glides, occasional banking, and low wheeling; at times flies steadily with smooth deep flapping (recalling a large jaeger), and feeding birds often fly erratically with deep, powerful wingbeats, swooping over the surface to snatch prey. In moderate to strong winds, flight fast and strong but unhurried, varies from a low weaving and rolling progression (mainly into the wind) to classic roller-coaster flight of high, towering arcs (mainly across the wind), with longer wavelength and more prolonged peaks than smaller Atlantic gadfly petrels; birds loop back easily on their track when foraging and can hang at the peak of an arc. Freak-out flight of deep wingbeats and erratic swerving usually short-lived, birds soon adjusting to a buoyant wheeling and circling.

Description Large, thick-necked, and full-chested gadfly petrel with very stout bill (less stout on juveniles) and fairly broad, medium-length graduated tail. Moderate wing-loading.

White-faced types. Ages similar but juveniles in fresh plumage during late May–Jul when older ages worn or molting, and perhaps averaging darker-faced (needs study). Head, neck, and underparts white with fairly small blackish cap split by distinct white supercilium (black eye stands out in white face on well-marked birds); sides of chest forward of wing with variable, usually narrow, dark spur or partial collar (thickest in fresh plumage, mainly fall into winter, weakest and sometimes almost absent in spring). Hindneck typically white, forming distinct collar that offsets black cap. In fresh plumage, some birds have slight dusky clouding on auriculars and hindneck, but unlikely to be noticeable at sea. Underwings white with broad black margins; carpal-ulnar bar narrower and mixed with white on whitest-headed birds; underside of remiges blackish overall.

Upperparts dark brownish gray (looking black at any distance), with extensively white uppertail coverts and tail base, broadly black-tipped tail. Upperparts darker and browner when worn (e.g., May–Jul), with subtle blacker M pattern most distinct in fresh plumage, when upperparts have variable, sometimes surprisingly strong, gray sheen; back often appears slightly paler and grayer than upperwings. Birds molting inner to middle primaries (mainly Apr–Jun) often show bold white upperwing stripe. Bill black, legs and feet bicolored pinkish and black.

On the water. Bright black and white. Black cap often looks small on large white head and neck.

Dark-faced types. Ages similar but juveniles in fresh plumage during Jun–Aug when older ages worn or molting. Relative to white-faced types, larger black cap typically extends over auriculars, hindneck brownish (wearing and fading to white on some birds, mainly in spring), and dark spur at chest sides thick and conspicuous (least extensive in worn plumage, mainly in spring). Black underwing margins average thicker, the greater coverts often with dark centers; some birds have short white tongues projecting into outer primaries (these may occur on white-faced types but this not yet confirmed).

On the water. Contrast subdued relative to white-faced types, with extensive black cap and brownish nape reducing the white area apparent.

Intermediate types. Some birds have larger black caps than typical white-faced types but smaller than typical black-faced types; such birds usually have obvious white hindcollars and their dark chest spurs tend to be intermediate in extent. Whether these birds represent age- or sex-related variation, individual variation in one or both types, or perhaps a different population remains to be elucidated.

Molt Timing among different populations and age classes needs study; averages earlier in white-faced types by about a month (Howell & Patteson 2008b). Adult wing molt mainly May/Jun–Aug/Sep, PB2 wing molt probably late Mar/Apr–Jul/Aug (NCSM specimens; pers. obs.).

P20.2. Typical white-faced Black-capped Petrel—unmistakable; note inner primary molt. SNGH. Off Hatteras, North Carolina, 20 May 2007.

P20.3. White-faced Black-capped Petrel in fresh plumage (note pale tips to greater coverts), perhaps a juvenile. SNGH. Off Hatteras, North Carolina, 16 Aug 2009.

P20.4. White-faced Black-capped Petrel with inner primary molt; very stout bill suggests a male. SNGH. Off Hatteras, North Carolina, 30 May 2008.

P20.5. Dark-faced Black-capped Petrel with inner primary molt. Note thick dark chest spur (cf. P20.3, P20.11–P20.12). SNGH. Off Hatteras, North Carolina, 27 Jul 2007.

P20.6. Dark-faced Black-capped Petrel with mid-primary molt. Besides larger size, distinguished from Bermuda Petrel by heavy bill, large white rump patch. SNGH. Off Hatteras, North Carolina, 27 Jul 2007.

P20.7. Intermediate Black-capped Petrel with inner primary molt, some new gray feathers on back; note p1 is still old while p2-p3 have been shed. SNGH. Off Hatteras, North Carolina, 6 Jun 2009.

P20.8. Intermediate Black-capped Petrel in worn plumage; contrast between dark secondaries (fresher) and faded greater coverts (older) indicates a bird older than its first cycle. SNGH. Off Hatteras, North Carolina, 21 May 2008.

P20.9. Dark-faced Black-capped Petrel in overall worn plumage (thus, whitish necked); p1 shed at start of primary molt. SNGH. Off Hatteras, North Carolina, 31 May 2007.

P20.10. Dark-faced Black-capped Petrel in worn plumage, but with some new gray feathers on hindneck and back; fairly even wear on upperwings may indicate first-year bird (cf. P20.7–P20.8). SNGH. Off Hatteras, North Carolina, 21 May 2008.

P20.11. Typical white-faced Black-capped Petrel (cf. P20.12–P20.13) with inner primary molt. SNGH. Off Hatteras, North Carolina, 23 May 2007.

P20.12. Intermediate Black-capped Petrel (cf. P20.11, P20.13) with inner primary molt (same bird as P20.17). SNGH. Off Hatteras, North Carolina, 28 May 2007.

P20.13. Dark-faced Black-capped Petrel (cf. P20.11–P20.12) with inner primary molt and very extensive dark underwing margins. SNGH. Off Hatteras, North Carolina, 2 Jun 2008.

P20.14. White-faced Black-capped Petrels head-on show striking white hindcollar; also note white forehead, cf. P8.7. SNGH. Off Hatteras, North Carolina, 23 May 2007.

P20.15. Comparison of classic white-faced (left) and dark-faced Black-capped Petrels. Note face patterns, extent of chest spur, and more advanced primary molt of white-faced bird. SNGH. Off Hatteras, North Carolina, 27 Jul 2007.

P20.16. White-faced Black-capped Petrel (left) typically shows extensive white when sitting on water, whereas dark-faced birds much less striking. SNGH. Off Hatteras, North Carolina, 5 Aug 2007.

P20.17. Intermediate Black-capped Petrel (same bird as P20.12). SNGH. Off Hatteras, North Carolina, 28 May 2007.

P20.18. Dark-faced Black-capped Petrel in worn plumage. SNGH. Off Hatteras, North Carolina, 28 Jul 2007.

P20.19. Black-capped Petrels, like this white-faced bird, often associate on the water with appreciably larger Cory's Shearwater. SNGH. Off Hatteras, North Carolina, 27 Jul 2007.

P21. BERMUDA PETREL (CAHOW) *Pterodroma cahow*
L 35–38 cm, WS 85–92 cm, tail 110–124 mm (graduation 45 mm)
Figures 104–105, 107, P21.1–P21.11

Identification Summary Atlantic, warm water. Rare but increasing, this medium-sized, lightly built petrel is usually distinctive if seen well: note the long tail, gray to gray-brown upperparts with a cowl, narrow whitish band on uppertail coverts, and thick black underwing margins.

P21.1. Bermuda Petrel often seems to appear fairly close to a boat and pass by quickly, but is a distinctive-looking species. Note the dark cowl, relatively slender bill, and dark tail. SNGH. Off Hatteras, North Carolina, 28 May 2008.

Taxonomy Monotypic.

Names *Pterodroma* means "winged runner"; *cahow* and the alternative English name describe how the bird sounded to early settlers on Bermuda.

Status and Distribution Endangered. Breeds (Jan–early Jun) on islets in Castle Harbor, e Bermuda (formerly common and more widespread on Bermuda), and ranges at sea (presumably) over subtropical waters of e Atlantic. One bird found Nov 2002 in a burrow on Azores, e Atlantic (Bried & Magalhaes 2004), returned through 2006 (Gantlett 2007). Believed extinct from mid-1600s until 1900s (with nesting grounds rediscovered in 1951), Bermuda Petrel has been the subject of an intense conservation campaign. From

18 pairs producing 8 fledglings in 1962, population increased to 70 pairs and 39 fledglings in 2003 (NAB 57:417, 2003), and to 90 pairs and 47 chicks in 2009 (NAB 63:519, 2009), likely translating to a population of about 500 birds.

Atlantic. Rare nonbreeding visitor (late May to mid-Aug) to Gulf Stream waters off North Carolina, although first recorded there as recently as 1993 (Wingate et al. 1998); a fresh-plumaged bird (apparently juvenile) was photographed about 290 km off Massachusetts, in Jun 2009 (NAB 63:570, 2009), and satellite tagging indicates the species ranges n to waters off Atlantic Canada (NAB 63:570, 2009); may also range over w edge of Gulf Stream s to n Florida. Concentration of late May records off North Carolina reflects large number of pelagic trips at that time, and does not necessarily

176

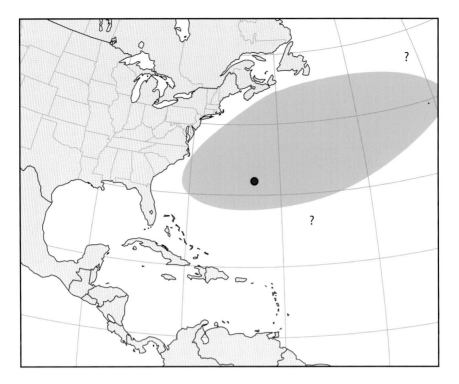

represent true seasonal occurrence. Reports off North Carolina from Apr and Dec (Lee 1984, 1987) suggest year-round presence in the region.

FIELD IDENTIFICATION

Similar Species Bermuda Petrel is a relatively distinctive species at sea, although identification criteria were not established until recently (Wingate et al. 1998). It is a medium-sized *Ptero-droma*, as likely to be confused with similarly proportioned Fea's Petrel as with larger and stockier Black-capped Petrel.

Fea's Petrel and *Zino's Petrel* usually have distinctive dark underwings contrasting with white body, and pale gray uppertail coverts and tail, but fresh-plumaged Bermuda can be disconcertingly gray above with a blackish M pattern, and Zino's with extensively white underwings can almost match the pattern of Bermuda. Moreover, when flying head-on or against the light, the size, shape, and head pattern of Fea's and Zino's are similar to Bermuda, although Bermuda typically has a darker cowl contrasting more strongly with the back. Watch for distinctive underwing and rump patterns, and also note thicker bill of Fea's.

Black-capped Petrel larger and stockier with broader wings, broader tail, thicker bill, and much larger white patch on uppertail coverts. Many Black-capped also have bold white hindcollar, but some have a dusky hindneck, inviting confusion with Bermuda. More extensive dark head markings of Bermuda typically appear as a dark cowl or hood, with little contrast between blackish crown and slaty hindneck, and no contrast between hindneck and back; variable whitish hook projects up behind blackish auriculars; on dark Black-capped, the black cap typically contrasts noticeably with paler hindneck, and there is more extensive white on neck sides. Head patterns can be quite similar, however, and worn and faded Bermudas (in Jun–Aug, at least) can have white hindneck collar. Darkest Black-capped also tend to have thick black underwing margins, similar to Bermuda, and both species can have 1–2 isolated black spots on outer primary coverts. Black-capped often towers high and can be seen at long range, whereas Bermuda tends to wheel lower and is often not detected until close to the boat.

Trinidade Petrel (light morph) might be confused briefly with Bermuda, given a poor view. Note that Trinidade has all-dark upperparts and a dark chest, its underwings have more extensive black carpal-ulnar bar and dark axillars, and undertail coverts usually have some dark markings.

Habitat and Behavior Pelagic, over warm waters along w edge of Gulf Stream, especially over submarine topography such as the shelf break.

Off North Carolina, as likely to be seen alone as in loose association with Black-capped Petrels, with which it can be found foraging and loafing. At night on breeding grounds gives a drawn-out, slightly eerie moan ending with an abrupt gulp or muted squeak and usually repeated 1–4 times (LNS 117645); higher-pitched calls may be males.

In calm to light winds, flight buoyant and quick, with easy, slightly clipped wingbeats and low wheeling. In moderate to strong winds wheels higher, although typically lower and less steeply than Black-capped Petrel, but can tower high and loop when maneuvering over food. Flight similar overall to Fea's Petrel but more buoyant and less zippy than narrower-winged Trinidade Petrel.

Description Medium-sized, lightly built gadfly petrel with fairly narrow wings and long tapered tail. Low wing-loading.

Ages similar but juveniles fresh in Jun–Sep when older ages worn or molting. Blackish crown and auriculars merge into slaty-gray to gray hind-neck, neck sides, and upperparts, which show variable blackish M pattern (bright and quite contrasting on some fresh-plumaged juveniles) and usually a narrow whitish band on base of upper-tail coverts (indistinct at a distance, and essentially lacking in some birds, which have rump and tail all-dark; Wingate et al. 1998). Upperparts appreciably browner when worn, as often the case with postjuvenile plumages in May–Jul. Lores, throat, and underparts white, underwings with broad blackish margins including thick carpal-ulnar bar. Inner webs of outer rectrices mostly white and tipped dusky. Bill black, legs and feet bicolored pinkish and black.

On the water. Dark overall with white lores, throat, and foreneck, white sides and undertail coverts.

Molt Poorly known but, given breeding chronology, adult wing molt probably May/Jun–Aug/Sep, PB2 wing molt probably Apr–Aug. Several birds seen off North Carolina in late May have been molting middle primaries, whereas others have not been in wing molt.

P21.2. Upperparts of Bermuda Petrel are dark slaty gray in fresher plumage, in some lights with a blacker M pattern (but cf. P21.3). Note narrow white rump band relative to Black-capped Petrel as well as narrow wings, dark cowl, slender bill. SNGH. Off Hatteras, North Carolina, 27 May 2005.

P21.3. Same Bermuda Petrel as P21.2, photographed with different equipment and illustrating how apparent plumage tones can vary greatly. JBP. Off Hatteras, North Carolina, 27 May 2005.

P21.4. Bermuda Petrel. In worn plumage, upperparts of Bermuda Petrel often appear dark brown (cf. P21.2). Distinguished from darkest Black-capped Petrel (cf. P20.6) by lighter build, dark cowl, limited white on rump. SNGH. Off Hatteras, North Carolina, 23 May 2009.

P21.5. Bermuda Petrel in heavily worn plumage can have white hindneck collar (cf. P25.5); distinguished from Black-capped Petrel by smaller bill, limited white on rump. JBP. Off Hatteras, North Carolina, 3 Jul 2005.

P21.6. In fresh plumage (on this date presumably a juvenile), Bermuda Petrel can be relatively pale gray above with a bold blackish M pattern suggesting Fea's Petrel. Note narrow white rump band, overall structure. PED. Off Cape Cod, Massachusetts, 28 Jun 2009.

21.7. Bermuda Petrel (same bird as P21.2). Relative to darkest Black-capped Petrel (cf. P20.5), note light build, small bill, neck pattern. SNGH. Off Hatteras, North Carolina, 27 May 2009.

P21.8. Underwing pattern of Bermuda Petrel somewhat variable (cf. P21.7, P21.9); note dark cowl, primary molt. SNGH. Off Hatteras, North Carolina, 29 May 2009.

P21.9. Wheeling high and going away, dark cowl of Bermuda Petrel can appear as a dark cap; note light build, relatively small bill. SNGH. Off Hatteras, North Carolina, 29 May 2009.

P21.10. In fresh plumage (same bird as P21.6), sides of neck on some Bermuda Petrels can be gray, suggesting Fea's Petrel in pattern rather than forming the dark cowl more typical of a Bermuda (cf. P21.8). Note underwing pattern, but cf. Zino's Petrel. PED. Off Cape Cod, Massachusetts, 28 Jun 2009.

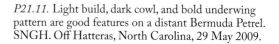

P21.11. Light build, dark cowl, and bold underwing pattern are good features on a distant Bermuda Petrel. SNGH. Off Hatteras, North Carolina, 29 May 2009.

P22A. CAPE VERDE [FEA'S] PETREL *Pterodroma [feae] feae*
P22B. DESERTAS [FEA'S] PETREL *Pterodroma [f.] desertae*
L 35.5–38 cm, WS 87–97 cm, tail 104–115 mm (graduation 30–35 mm)
Figures 108–109, 111, 113, P22.1–P22.13

Identification Summary Atlantic, warm water. Rare visitor off East Coast. Medium-sized, lightly built petrel. Note blackish underwings contrasting with white body, gray upperparts with blackish M pattern, pale gray uppertail coverts and tail. The name Fea's Petrel (pronounced Fay-a's, where fay rhymes with say) refers collectively to both taxa.

P22.1. The white body/dark underwing contrast on Fea's Petrel is a striking field mark even at moderate to long range. SNGH. Off Hatteras, North Carolina, 27 May 2009.

Taxonomy Vexed. Fea's Petrel (both taxa) and Zino's Petrel were long considered conspecific with s hemisphere Soft-plumaged Petrel (*P. mollis*); see Harrop (2004) and Patteson and Brinkley (2004) for a review of this convoluted taxonomic history.

The two taxa of Fea's Petrel differ in measurements (mainly bill size), vocalizations, genetics, and breeding season (see below), and are perhaps best treated as separate species (Jesus et al. 2009, Robb et al. 2008). They are lumped in this account simply because it is unclear how they can be distinguished at sea except perhaps by molt timing (see below).

P.[f.] feae (Cape Verde Petrel; breeds late Dec–early Jun on Cape Verde Islands; 500–1000 pairs; Ratcliffe et al. 2000). Averages smaller (especially in bill). Bill length 27–31 mm; depth at base

12.1–14.8 mm; depth at gonys 10.7–13.8 mm (Shirihai et al. 2010a). Adult wing molt mainly May–Sep.

P. [f.] desertae (Desertas Petrel; breeds late Jul–early Jan in the Desertas Islands, Madeira archipelago; 170–260 pairs; Birdlife International 2004). Averages larger (especially bill depth). Bill length 27–34 mm; depth at base 12.5–17.5 mm; depth at gonys 10.7–14.2 mm (Shirihai et al. 2010a). Adult wing molt mainly Dec–May.

Names *Pterodroma* means "winged runner"; *feae* commemorates the Italian zoologist Leonardo Fea (1852–1903), who visited the Cape Verde Islands in 1897–1898, during which the type specimen was procured; *desertae* refers to the Desertas Islands (which include Bugio) in the Madeira archipelago. Although the name Bugio Petrel was

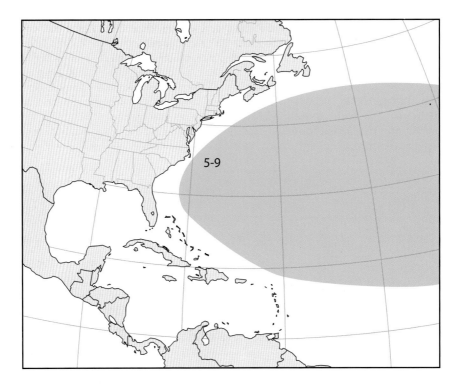

5-9

suggested recently for *desertae* (Jesus et al. 2009), the English name Desertas Petrel has been in use for some time and is retained here. Some authors (e.g., Shirihai et al. 2010a) use the name Fea's Petrel specifically for (nominate) *feae* and Desertas Petrel for *desertae*, an ambiguity I prefer to avoid.

Status and Distribution Near Threatened. Breeds Cape Verde Islands and Madeira (see Taxonomy), ranges at sea in n Atlantic, regularly w to e U.S. (mainly May–Aug), increasingly n to Britain (mainly Jul–Sep; Steele 2006). May also breed in Azores, where status unclear (Monteiro & Furness 1995).

    Atlantic. Rare nonbreeding visitor (mid-May to mid-Sep, at least) to Gulf Stream waters off North Carolina, where now annual and perhaps increasing (first recorded 1981); casual (probably under-recorded) n to Virginia (early Sep), exceptionally n to Nova Scotia (Jul 1997; Hooker & Baird 1997); also a late Sep report from South Carolina (NAB 58:59, 2004) and a Nov 1984 report off Georgia (Haney et al. 1993). Exceptional inland (Sep 1996) in Virginia following Hurricane Fran. Based on molt timing, North American records during May–Jun may involve both Cape Verde Petrels (starting primary molt; Howell & Patteson 2007; P22.13) and Desertas Petrels (birds apparently completing molt with growth of rectrices; pers. obs.; P22.4).

FIELD IDENTIFICATION

Similar Species. No reliable features (besides perhaps wing molt timing) separate Desertas Petrel and Cape Verde Petrel at sea (Shirihai et al. 2010a), and the species pair is treated here simply as "Fea's Petrel." Identification of a medium-sized, lightly built gadfly petrel off the East Coast as either Fea's Petrel or Zino's Petrel is usually fairly easy if a bird is seen reasonably well: note white body contrasting with dark underwings, gray upperparts with blackish M pattern, and contrasting pale gray uppertail coverts and tail.

    Distant *Black-capped Petrel* (much larger and bulkier) on occasion can appear to have dark underwings, depending on lighting. Distant Fea's Petrel, while striking from below, tends to disappear when viewed from above—gray upperparts blend into the ocean, unlike bright black-and-white pattern of Black-capped Petrel seen from above. Some light morph *Trinidade Petrels* might be confused with Fea's if seen poorly or briefly from below, but note Trinidade's dark chest, usually some dark on undertail coverts, and all-dark upperparts. Particularly if seen poorly, confusion also possible with *Bermuda Petrel* (which see). Main concerns when identifying Fea's Petrel come from Zino's Petrel and perhaps Soft-plumaged Petrel (one recent report from Norway; Catley 2009).

Zino's Petrel (one fall record off North Carolina) slightly smaller and more lightly built than Fea's (175–280 g vs. 245–428 g; Shirihai et al. 2010a), with slimmer bill. Blocky head and stout bill of Fea's can often be discerned at sea, whereas Zino's has smaller, more gentle-looking head and smaller bill that can even suggest cookilaria petrels (bill length 22–29 mm, depth at base 10–12.6 mm, depth at gonys 7.9–14 mm; Shirihai et al. 2010a). Wings of Fea's relatively longer and more pointed (Zino et al. 2008), but bill size and shape may be most objective features by which to distinguish these species. Bill of Fea's (especially Desertas Petrel) is more evenly deep throughout, whereas shallower bill of Zino's is often slightly pinched-in immediately distal to nostril tubes, subtly different from "meat cleaver" bill of Fea's. Flight of Zino's may be a little more fluttery and maneuverable when feeding, but critical observations of the two species in similar conditions are few. No plumage features have been found to separate these two species consistently, but Zino's often has a fairly broad whitish underwing stripe not matched by Fea's (Shirihai et al. 2010a). Moreover, face of Fea's often has larger, more diffuse, and rounder black eye patch, which, with stout bill, often creates a rather brutish look. In contrast, Zino's more often has smaller, more wedge-shaped black eye patch offset by variable whitish supercilium, which, with slender bill, often lends a gentler look to the face. Molt timing also likely to be helpful (see Molt, below); in particular, any bird with molt of inner primaries in fall should be scrutinized.

Soft-plumaged Petrel (unrecorded North America; L 35.5–37 cm, WS 84–92 cm, tail 107–117 mm [graduation 25–30 mm]; P22a.1) fatter bodied and shorter necked with shorter and narrower wings better suited to the windy Southern Ocean. Soft-plumaged often appears big headed compared to Fea's, which accentuates its slightly smaller bill. It has a broader, less strongly graduated tail not contrastingly paler than gray back,

and a plover-like dark chest band, which is usually complete and often creates a dark-hooded appearance; some birds have partial chest bands that may overlap heavily marked Fea's Petrel. The white basal patch on the leading edge of the underwing is typically smaller and spotted with dusky on Soft-plumaged, larger and more cleanly white on Fea's. In moderate to strong winds, Soft-plumaged towers more steeply and confidently than Fea's Petrel, often holding its wings crooked.

Habitat and Behavior Pelagic over warmer waters, especially along w edge of Gulf Stream over submarine topography such as canyons, which contribute to upwelling. As likely to be seen alone as in loose association with Black-capped Petrels, with which it may be found foraging and loafing, and sometimes attracted briefly to ships.

In calm to light winds, flight buoyant and quick, with easy, slightly clipped to languid deep wingbeats and low wheeling. In moderate to strong winds wheels higher, although typically lower and less steeply than Black-capped Petrel; but can tower high and loop when maneuvering over food. Flight similar to Bermuda Petrel but more buoyant and less zippy than narrower-winged Trinidade Petrel.

Description Medium-sized, lightly built gadfly petrel with fairly narrow wings and fairly long tapered tail. Low wing-loading. No plumage characters are known to separate Cape Verde and Desertas petrels, but average differences exist in some characters (see Shirihai et al. 2010a).

Ages similar. Blackish eye patch merges into gray crown, hindneck, and neck sides (which form a variable cowl, rarely a partial collar, forward of wings); upperparts gray with usually distinct blackish M pattern; back often appears paler and grayer in contrast to dark upperwings, and upperparts appear browner overall when worn. Uppertail coverts and tail contrastingly pale gray (in some lights can appear similar in tone to back, in

Table 7. Provisional wing molt timings for Cape Verde, Desertas, and Zino's petrels (modified from Howell & Patteson 2007); *italics* indicate provisional dates.

| | Approximate Breeding Schedule[1] | | | No primary molt | | |
	Return	Laying	Fledging	Primary Molt	Adults[2]	Juvs
Cape Verde	*Oct*	Dec	May	*Mar/Jun–Jul/Sep*	*Oct–Mar*	May–*Mar*
Desertas	May	Jul	Jan	*Nov/Feb–Mar/May*	*Jun–Nov*	Jan–*Nov*
Zino's	Apr	May	Oct	*Sep/Nov–Dec/Feb*	*Mar–Aug*	Oct–*Aug*

[1] From Zino & Zino 1986, Snow & Perrins 1998. [2] Birds older than first year.

others appear almost silvery whitish). Inner webs of outer rectrices mostly white and freckled dusky. White underparts contrast with dark slaty underwings, whose apparent pattern varies greatly with lighting. Overall the underwings are dark slaty (appearing black at any distance) with a white wedge on the inner lesser coverts and a broad black carpal-ulnar bar; paler bases of greater primary coverts and secondary coverts often show as a pale gray to whitish midwing stripe or as a pale crescent on the primary bases. Some birds show gray mottling or barring along body sides, and exceptionally some Cape Verde Petrels have almost a gray breast band with slaty gray flanks and gray-mottled belly and undertail coverts (Gutiérrez & González-Solis 2009, Hazevoet 1995). Bill black, legs and feet bicolored pinkish and black.

On the water. Face, throat, and foreneck white with contrasting gray cowl; upperparts dark gray or brownish gray, sides and undertail coverts white.

Molt (see Table 7) Wing molt timings in Table 7 indicate start and end ranges, modified slightly from Howell and Patteson (2007); *provisional data* are indicated in italics. Thus Cape Verde Petrel is hypothesized to start primary molt between Mar and Jun, and complete between Jul and Sep; within this span, immatures molt earlier than breeding adults. The ranges given are in need of confirmation, and molt timings can also be expected to vary in accord with breeding seasons, which still remain poorly known (especially among Cape Verde Petrels) and may show some interannual variation.

P22.2. Gray upperparts of Fea's Petrel show variable darker M pattern but lack white on rump; contrast of pale tail varies greatly with lighting. SNGH. Off Hatteras, North Carolina, 27 May 2009.

P22.3. Fresh-plumaged Fea's Petrel, perhaps completing body molt (cf. P22.4); contrast and extent of dark on head vary greatly with lighting. SNGH. Off Hatteras, North Carolina, 1 Jun 2010.

P22.4. Mostly fresh-plumaged Fea's Petrel apparently completing prebasic molt (note tail molt, contrast between fresh gray and worn brown back feathers). Given the date, perhaps a Desertas Petrel. SNGH. Off Hatteras, North Carolina, 30 May 2008.

P22.5. In poor lighting, upperparts of Fea's Petrel can appear uniform and might invite confusion with similarly proportioned Bermuda Petrel; even in this view note stout bill, and head appears paler than Bermuda. SNGH. Off Hatteras, North Carolina, 30 May 2007.

P22.6. Classic Fea's Petrel (same bird as P22.2). Compared to Soft-plumaged Petrel (P22a.1), note relatively slim body and large wing area as well as neck pattern, extensive white on leading edge of wing, large bill. SNGH. Off Hatteras, North Carolina, 27 May 2009.

P22a.1. Classic Soft-plumaged Petrel. Compared to Fea's Petrel, note thickset body, broader tail, relatively narrow wings (typically held crooked like this), chest pattern, reduced white on leading edge of wing. SNGH. Macquarie Island, Australia, 16 Nov 2008.

P22.7. A rather messy-looking Fea's Petrel (same bird as P22.4); note thick bill and variation in neck pattern, cf. P22.6. SNGH. Off Hatteras, North Carolina, 30 May 2008.

P22.8. A typical view of Fea's Petrel veering away. Even at this angle the very stout bill is apparent. SNGH. Off Hatteras, North Carolina, 31 May 2007.

P22.9. Some Fea's Petrels, like this bird, have a partial dark chest band overlapping in pattern with poorly marked Soft-plumaged Petrel. SNGH. Off Hatteras, North Carolina, 1 Jun 2007.

P22.10. In some lights, face and crown of Fea's Petrel can appear contrastingly blackish and underwings relatively pale silvery. SNGH. Off Hatteras, North Carolina, 31 May 2007.

P22.11. A typical view of Fea's Petrel heading away; note gray upperparts with blackish M pattern, pale gray tail. SNGH. Off Hatteras, North Carolina, 24 May 2007.

P22.12. At a distance, upperparts of Fea's Petrel show little contrast and often blend fairly well against the sea. SNGH. Off Hatteras, North Carolina, 22 May 2009.

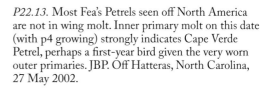

P22.13. Most Fea's Petrels seen off North America are not in wing molt. Inner primary molt on this date (with p4 growing) strongly indicates Cape Verde Petrel, perhaps a first-year bird given the very worn outer primaries. JBP. Off Hatteras, North Carolina, 27 May 2002.

P23. ZINO'S PETREL *Pterodroma madeira*
L 34–36 cm, WS 83–88 cm, tail 100–110 mm
Figures 110, 112, 114, P23.1–P23.5

Identification Summary One fall record off North Carolina. Medium-sized, lightly built petrel, very similar to Fea's Petrel but differing in lighter build, finer bill, molt timing, and, in some birds, underwing pattern.

Taxonomy. See under Fea's Petrel.

Names *Pterodroma* means "winged runner"; *madeira* refers to the only island where the species breeds. The English name commemorates Paul Alexander Zino and his son Francis Zino, who between them rediscovered the bird and continue to work on protecting it.

Status and Distribution Endangered. Breeds (mid-May to early Oct) on island of Madeira, ranges at sea (presumably) in n Atlantic.
   Atlantic. One photographed off North Carolina (mid-Sep 1995; P23.5) is the only confirmed North American record, but pelagic coverage in fall (when Zino's may be most likely to occur) is relatively sparse, and the species may prove to be a very rare fall visitor to U.S. waters.

FIELD IDENTIFICATION

Similar Species See under Fea's (= Cape Verde/Desertas) Petrel for similar species, and features to help separate Fea's and Zino's at sea.
   An underappreciated pitfall is separation of white-winged Zino's from fresh-plumaged Bermuda Petrel, perhaps especially some juveniles of the latter species (mainly Jun–Sep, when Zino's are slightly to distinctly worn) that have a contrasting blackish *M* on gray upperparts. Check for whitish rump band of Bermuda versus pale gray rump and tail of Zino's, but be aware of how molt and wear could affect such features. Also note different wing molt timings: Sep–Feb for Zino's, Apr–Sep for Bermuda.

Habitat and Behavior Much as Fea's Petrel, but flight under similar conditions may be a little more buoyant and wingbeats a little quicker, or more fluttery.

Description Medium-sized, lightly built gadfly petrel with fairly narrow wings and fairly long tapered tail. Low wing-loading.
   Ages similar. Blackish eye patch merges into gray crown, often sharply defined forward of eyes and bordered above by narrow white supercilium; gray hindneck and neck sides form variable cowl; upperparts gray with usually distinct blackish M pattern; back often appears paler and grayer in contrast to dark upperwings, and upperparts appear browner overall when worn. Uppertail coverts and tail contrastingly pale gray (in some lights can appear similar in tone to back, in others appear almost silvery whitish). Inner webs of outer rectrices mostly white and freckled dusky. White underparts contrast with variably dark underwings: some birds have overall dark slaty underwings like Fea's Petrel, others show a broad whitish median stripe across median and greater coverts, offsetting black carpal-ulnar band. Exceptionally, underwings white overall with a broad black carpal-ulnar band (Shirihai et al. 2010a), perhaps only on aberrant birds. Some birds have gray mottling or barring along body sides. Bill black, legs and feet bicolored pinkish and black.
   On the water. Face, throat, and foreneck white with contrasting gray cowl; upperparts dark gray or brownish gray, sides and undertail coverts white.

Molt (see Table 7) Wing molt occurs in nonbreeding season, mainly Sep/Nov–Dec/Feb, probably averaging earlier on immatures and nonbreeders (Howell & Patteson 2007).

P23.2. Plumage of Zino's Petrel is basically identical to Fea's Petrel, but note relatively small head and fine bill. SNGH. Madeira, eastern Atlantic, 15 May 2010.

P23.1. Zino's Petrel. Note relatively slim build, small head, and fine bill compared to Fea's Petrel. SNGH. Madeira, eastern Atlantic, 14 May 2010.

P23.3. On Zino's Petrel, pale central portion of underwing often highlights thick black carpal-ulnar bar, but some have overall dark underwings like Fea's Petrel (cf. Figs 113–114). SNGH. Madeira, eastern Atlantic, 15 May 2010.

P23.4. Broad whitish median underwing stripe appears to be quite frequent on Zino's Petrel but has not been found on Fea's Petrel. Also note small head, fine bill, and whitish eyebrow, which recall delicate Cook's Petrel more than brutish Fea's Petrel. SNGH. Madeira, eastern Atlantic, 14 May 2010.

P23.5. Overall structure, slender bill, underwing pattern, and molt timing combine to document this bird as the first North American record of Zino's Petrel. JBP. Off Hatteras, North Carolina, 16 Sep 1995.

P24. TRINIDADE PETREL *Pterodroma arminjoniana*
L 36–39 cm, WS 94–102 cm, tail 108–116 mm (graduation 20–25 mm)
Figures 64, 101, P24.1–P24.11

Identification Summary Atlantic, warm water. Rare visitor off East Coast. A medium-sized, narrow-winged petrel of highly variable appearance. Dark morph commonest in North American waters: dark brown overall, usually with white flashes across underside of primaries and underwing coverts. Intermediate and light morphs have throat and underparts pale brown to white, and often show extensive white on underwings. Formerly known as Herald Petrel (see Taxonomy).

P24.1. At a distance, Trinidad Petrel (here a dark morph) might be mistaken for Sooty Shearwater. Note shorter neck, more crooked and slightly broader wings, silvery white on primary bases (rather than coverts). Also note mid-primary molt (almost all Sooties off the East Coast are not in wing molt) and that head is darker than body. SNGH. Off Hatteras, North Carolina, 29 May 2009.

Taxonomy Vexed. Light and dark morphs were originally described as separate species (Arminjon's and Trinidad petrels, respectively), as was an intermediate morph (Wilson's Petrel) and a striking leucistic oddball (see review by Patteson & Brinkley 2004). Later, all were considered conspecific and further merged with Herald Petrel (*P. heraldica*) of the Pacific (Murphy & Pennoyer 1952). Most authors now consider Herald Petrel to be a separate species, and Herald Petrels in the Pacific may comprise two cryptic species (Brooke & Rowe 1996).

Given this state of affairs, the highly variable Atlantic Ocean birds (at present considered a single monotypic species) may comprise more than one species, as suggested by possible segregation of types by habitat and season. Thus, in mid-Sep, Wilson (1904) reported that the dark birds

(Trinidade Petrels) were nesting higher on the cliffs and away from the light birds, and the light birds he collected (on fresh eggs) were described as Wilson's Petrel (Sharpe 1904). In early Apr, Murphy (1915) found only light birds (Arminjon's Petrels) and dark birds (Trinidade Petrels) but no Wilson's Petrels. All authors report light birds as being commoner than dark at the island, yet dark birds predominate off North America whereas for 400 km to the s of the island Murphy (1915) saw only light birds. Critical study is needed to resolve these conundra. Conversely, Trinidade Petrels breeding on Round Island, in the Indian Ocean, appear to be hybridizing extensively with Kermadec Petrels (Brown et al. 2010).

Names *Pterodroma* means "winged runner"; *arminjoniana* commemorates Vice Admiral Vittorio

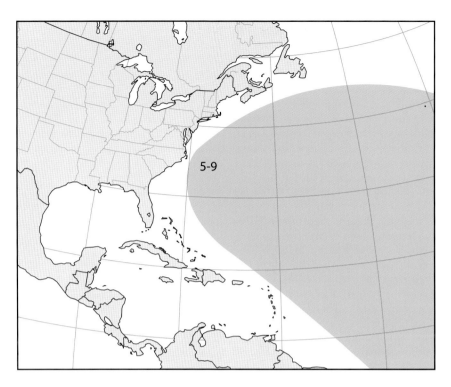

Arminjon (1830–1897) who, on the vessel *Magenta* (for which the Magenta Petrel *P. magentae* is named) made the first Italian circumnavigation of the world. Trinidade is a common English spelling of the main island where this species breeds; the island's Portuguese name, Trindade, is provided in some English references but, confusingly, is identical to the Portuguese name for the much larger and well-known island of Trinidad, which lies off the coast of Venezuela.

Status and Distribution Vulnerable. Breeds in South Atlantic far off e Brazil, on Trinidade (mainly Sep/Nov–Feb/Mar; Birdlife International 2000, Murphy 1936) and Martin Vas islands, and in Indian Ocean on Round Island, off Mauritius (perhaps bimodally, mainly Oct–Feb, Apr–Aug; Gill et al. 1970). Ranges into subtropical n Atlantic (mainly May–Sep).

Atlantic. Rare nonbreeding visitor (mid-May to late Sep) to Gulf Stream waters off North Carolina, where now annual (first recorded 1978); casual (probably under-recorded) s to Georgia (early Jul) (Brinkley & Patteson 1998) and n to Virginia (late Sep). Casual following hurricanes (Jul–Sep) over inshore waters and inland in Virginia and New York. Exceptional in Caribbean (prospecting on land) at Culebra, Puerto Rico (Gochfeld et al. 1988). Numbers seen off North Carolina have declined since the mid-2000s, perhaps indicative of cyclic changes in ocean conditions or perhaps of problems on the breeding islands.

FIELD IDENTIFICATION

Similar Species Like most gadfly petrels, a fairly distinctive bird when seen well, but confusion risks include Sooty Shearwater (most Trinidade Petrels off North Carolina are dark morphs) and jaegers. With white-bodied birds seen poorly, also cf. Fea's and Bermuda petrels (note dark undertail coverts of Trinidade Petrel, usually easy to see on a bird flying away, vs. white on Bermuda and Fea's).

Sooty Shearwater has relatively smaller head and shorter tail; white underwing flashes are across coverts, not primary bases. In calm to light winds, Sooty flies with quick, stiff wingbeats and wings held straighter out from body, slightly bowed, and often curled up at tips; Trinidade Petrel more comfortable-looking, with deep, easy wingbeats and buoyant glides on crooked, flexed wings. Both species can tower steeply in windy conditions, particularly Sooty, but Trinidade again appears more controlled and buoyant, easily able to change direction, stall at the peak of a climb, or slice up and down as if just for the hell of it. At closer range, note thicker black bill of Trinidade, vs. slender bill of Sooty. Ashy-gray bloom on upperparts of Trinidade Petrel's can sometimes be seen at moderate to long range, when Sooties look simply dull blackish or dark brown.

Jaegers (particularly immatures with little or no tail projection) wheeling high in windy conditions could be mistaken for Trinidade Petrel, and a steadily flapping petrel well above the water (usually in calm conditions) could be mistaken for jaeger. Jaegers have relatively shorter and broader wings, with white flashes on upsides of primaries, head and neck projection more tapered (or pin-headed), and wingbeats typically more gull-like.

Kermadec Petrel (postulated but unconfirmed in Atlantic region) slightly larger and bulkier with broader wings and shorter, less graduated tail. Plumage polymorphism in Kermadec roughly parallels Trinidade Petrel, but all plumages of Kermadec have distinct white primary shafts on upperwing (sun reflecting off Trinidade Petrel can create this effect, albeit briefly, as seen in some photos).

Habitat and Behavior Pelagic, over warm waters along w edge of Gulf Stream. As likely to be seen alone as in association with other species such as Black-capped Petrels, with which it can be found foraging and loafing. Sometimes appears to be attracted to ships, which it may circle once or twice before heading off.

In calm to light winds, flies with easy, deep, almost languid wingbeats and buoyant glides low to the water, the wings slightly arched; in purposeful flight, latent power in strong deep wingbeats is released and speed picks up several notches, when may suggest a jaeger. Sometimes in calm or light winds flies fairly high above the water with fairly steady wingbeats and short glides. In moderate to strong winds, flight generally a little zippier than broader-winged Fea's and Bermuda petrels, often wheeling steeply in high arcs, at times almost flipping back on itself and arcing up and down with a vertical slicing action; at other times wheels fairly low, especially when flying into the wind.

Description Medium-sized, narrow-winged, slim-bodied, and fairly small-headed gadfly petrel with medium-long tail. Fairly low wing-loading. Complex plumage variation, with different morphs and variants having been described as four or more species (see Taxonomy). Off North Carolina, light morphs comprise up to about 20% of observations overall. Ages similar.

Dark morph. Some birds dark sooty brown overall, slightly darker on head and upperparts which, especially in fresh plumage, often have an ashy sheen (surprisingly noticeable, even at

moderate range) and muted blacker M pattern. Other birds, fairly common off North Carolina, have chest and belly slightly but appreciably paler, grayish brown (and sometimes mottled whitish, visible at closer range). Underwings dark with variable white to silvery-white panels or flashes across median coverts, greater coverts (especially dark-tipped primary coverts), and primary bases. "Dark-winged" types (up to about 10% of birds off North Carolina) similar to darkest dark morph but underside of coverts and primaries reflective ashy gray overall, with no white (e.g., Gochfeld et al. 1988). Bill black, legs and feet usually all-black or dark brownish gray with black distal toes and webs, rarely sharply bicolored like light morph; legs and feet blackish on dark-winged types.

Light morph. Upperparts similar to dark morph or slightly paler and warmer. Head and chest dark brown to dark ashy gray, usually with whitish throat patch set off by chest band, but a few birds appear solidly dark hooded. Underparts white with dark undertail coverts, sometimes with dark mottling on flanks; whitish bases to outer rectrices unlikely to be visible at sea. Striking but variable black-and-white underwing pattern dominated by broad black carpal-ulnar band, dark axillars, and broad white panel extending across greater and median coverts to primary bases; wingtips and trailing edge dark, and leading edge with narrow, dark-bordered white patagial strip. Some birds have black-tipped primary coverts and greatly reduced white median underwing panel. "Dark-winged" types (rare off the East Coast) have underparts washed dusky grayish, and underwing dark overall, with reflective ashy gray to gray-brown greater coverts and primaries (e.g., figure 4 of Brinkley & Patteson 2004). Trinidade Petrels from Indian Ocean often have barred or vermiculated grayish chest band, something not noted in Atlantic birds but common in Herald Petrels of the Pacific. Bill black, legs and feet bicolored black and bluish white to pinkish.

Hybrids Trinidade Petrels breeding on Round Island, Indian Ocean, appear to be hybridizing extensively with Kermadec Petrels (Brown et al. 2010).

Molt Wing molt perhaps mainly Mar–Aug in Atlantic. Off North Carolina, many birds (dark and light morph) in late May are molting middle to outer primaries (from p3 to p9 growing, but usually p8 or p9), whereas most birds in Aug show no signs of primary molt or are completing growth of outer primaries (pers. obs.).

P24.2. Dark morph Trinidad Petrel in mid-primary molt (same bird as P24.6). Note overall shape, thick bill. SNGH. Off Hatteras, North Carolina, 23 May 2007.

P24.3. Dark morph Trinidad Petrel. By fall, most birds have completed wing molt, as here. SNGH. Off Hatteras, North Carolina, 5 Aug 2007.

P24.4. Upperparts of light morph Trinidad Petrel (same bird as P24.10) average paler than dark morph. SNGH. Off Hatteras, North Carolina, 23 May 2007.

P24.5. Dark morph Trinidad Petrel in mid-primary molt, with uniformly dark chocolate-brown head and body (cf. P24.6). SNGH. Off Hatteras, North Carolina, 31 May 2007.

P24.6. Many dark morph Trinidad Petrels have head and body slightly paler than underwing coverts (cf. P24.5). SNGH. Off Hatteras, North Carolina, 23 May 2007.

P24.7. Dark morph Trinidad Petrel completing primary molt (p10 growing). Head often slightly darker than underparts. SNGH. Off Hatteras, North Carolina, 23 May 2007.

P24.8. Intermediate morph Trinidad Petrels, like this individual, are rare off the East Coast; note similarity in plumage to jaegers. SNGH. Off Hatteras, North Carolina, 24 May 2007.

P24.9. Typical light morph Trinidad Petrel in outer primary molt; also note tail molt, which tends to occur toward end of complete molt. SNGH. Off Hatteras, North Carolina, 23 May 2003.

P24.10. Light morph Trinidad Petrel with extensive white underwings (same bird as P24.4). Uniformly fresh plumage suggests a juvenile. SNGH. Off Hatteras, North Carolina, 23 May 2007.

P24.11. Light morph Trinidad Petrel in mid-primary molt. Dark head and mostly dark underwings of this individual are a rare combination of features among birds off the East Coast. SNGH. Off Hatteras, North Carolina, 24 May 2007.

Pacific Gadfly Petrels

Some 12 species of gadfly petrels have been recorded off the Pacific coast of the region, 6 of them n of Mexico: Cook's and Mottled petrels are regular austral migrants (mainly Apr–Nov), Hawaiian is a regular visitor (May–Sep), Murphy's and Stejneger's are irregular migrants (mainly Mar–May and Nov, respectively), and Great-winged is a vagrant. Off Middle America, the warm-water offshore avifauna includes Juan Fernandez, Galapagos, Kermadec, Herald, Tahiti, and presumably Henderson petrels.

Identifying Pacific Gadfly Petrels at Sea

Several serious identification challenges exist among Pacific gadflies, and much work remains to be done. In many cases, species identification under at-sea conditions will not be possible, especially for birds not seen close or well. In terms of at-sea identification in the region, three groups can be recognized: small white-bellied species (subgenus *Cookilaria*), medium-large white-bellied species, and medium-large dark-bellied species.

Cookilaria petrels (or simply cookilarias) are small, snappy, fast-flying gadfly petrels with white underparts and a dark M pattern on gray upperparts; all breed only in the Pacific. At sea it is convenient to refer to all nine of the small gray-backed *Pterodroma* petrels as *Cookilaria*. Some authors limit the subgenus *Cookilaria* to blue-footed species with relatively slim bills and narrow black underwing margins, thus excluding the stockier, broader-billed, and pink-legged Bonin (*P. hypoleuca*), Chatham (*P. axillaris*), and Black-winged (*P. nigripennis*) petrels.

The two cookilarias recorded in the region are Cook's and Stejneger's petrels, although several other species range into the e tropical Pacific and may occur at least occasionally over waters off Middle America, where observers are few. For observers unfamiliar with gadfly petrels, Mottled Petrel should also be considered as an identification contender (Figs 115–116). For cookilaria identification check head and neck patterns, head/back contrast, and underwing pattern. Additional characters are bill size and shape, contrast of upperwing pattern, tail pattern, and, with experience, structure and flight manner. See Roberson and Bailey (1991a, b) and Spear et al. (1992) for more information on cookilaria identification and distribution.

Medium-sized and large gadfly petrels can be considered as white-bellied and dark-bellied, the latter being all-dark below. Regardless of plumage patterns, overall structure and flight manner are important identification features. As a rule, the relatively heavy-bodied species (such as Murphy's, Mottled, and Hawaiian petrels) have relatively narrower wings and a higher, stronger, and more bounding flight in windy conditions, whereas the lighter-bodied species (such as Henderson, Herald, and Galapagos petrels) have relatively broader wings and a lower, more leisurely and buoyant flight.

Medium-large white-bellied gadflies in the region are Hawaiian, Galapagos, and Juan Fernandez petrels (Figs 117–126), light morphs of Kermadec and Herald petrels, and the relatively distinctive Mottled and Tahiti petrels. Overall plumage pattern, underwing pattern, structure, bill size, and flight manner are important for species identification.

Medium-large, dark-bellied gadflies in the region include Murphy's, dark morph Kermadec, and Henderson/dark morph Herald, plus the vagrant Gray-faced [Great-winged] Petrel; Solander's Petrel probably also occurs. Structure, bill size, plumage contrast (such as head vs. back, body vs. underwings), underwing pattern, and flight manner are important for species identification (Figs 127–134).

Fig 115. Cook's Petrel in fresh plumage. A typical view, flying away. Note long narrow wings, relatively small head, concolorous gray head and back, dark tail tip. SNGH. Off Bodega Bay, California, 28 Aug 2009.

Fig 116. Mottled Petrel in fresh plumage. Stockier-bodied than Cook's, with thicker neck, larger head, and thicker bill. Also note contrasting pale trailing edge to wings, plain gray tail. SNGH. West-southwest of Campbell Island, New Zealand, 17 Nov 2008.

Fig 117. Hawaiian Petrel in slightly worn plumage, thus brownish above. Note head pattern, relatively slender bill, relatively narrow wings (cf. Fig 118). DLW. Hawaii, 15 Jul 2008.

Fig 118. Galapagos Petrel in relatively fresh plumage, thus with gray tones to back. At this angle, head pattern looks very similar to Hawaiian Petrel but blackish mask though eye slightly deeper; also note relatively stout bill, broad wings (cf. Figs 117, 119). AJ. Galapagos Islands, Ecuador, 13 Aug 2009.

Fig 119. Juan Fernandez Petrel in relatively fresh plumage. Note relatively pale gray upperparts, diffuse dark cap, gray sides of chest (cf. Figs 117–118). AJ. Juan Fernandez Islands, Chile, 26 Nov 2005.

Fig 120. Hawaiian Petrel. Note shallow dark cap with white notch behind cheeks, thick black underwing margins (cf. Figs 121–122). Also note relatively stocky body and narrow wings compared to Galapagos Petrel (Fig 121). M&MB. Off Fort Bragg, California, 13 Aug 2006.

Fig 121. Galapagos Petrel. Note dark hood, dark smudge on flanks, relatively broad dark trailing edge to secondaries, and relatively slim body and broad wings compared to Hawaiian Petrel (cf. Fig 120). GLA. Galapagos Islands, Ecuador, 21 Jul 2005.

Fig 122. Juan Fernandez Petrel with mid-primary molt. Note head pattern, extensively white underwings, big bill (cf. Figs 120–121). RLeV. Eastern tropical Pacific, 14 Apr 2006.

Fig 123. Hawaiian Petrel with relatively extensive dark hood, but less so than Galapagos Petrel; also note clean white flanks, relatively small head and bill (cf. Fig 124). DLW. Hawaii, 15 Jul 2008.

Fig 124. Galapagos Petrel. Note extensive dark hood, dark smudge on flanks, relatively large head and bill (cf. Fig 123). AJ. Galapagos Islands, Ecuador, 19 Jun 2007.

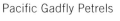

Fig 125. Hawaiian Petrel. Upperparts in worn plumage often appear chocolate-brown; note extensive white in lower face, relatively narrow wings (cf. Fig 126). SNGH. Off Santa Barbara, California, 6 Sep 2006.

Fig 126. Galapagos Petrel. Note extensive dark hood, big wings (cf. Fig 125). GLA. Galapagos Islands, Ecuador, 19 Aug 2006.

Fig 127. Murphy's Petrel in fairly fresh plumage. Compared to Solander's (Fig 128), note lighter build, narrow wings, shorter neck, smaller head and bill, reflective silvery sheen on primaries but plain gray greater primary coverts. CC. Pitcairn Islands, Central South Pacific, 9 Jun 2006.

Fig 128. Solander's Petrel in worn plumage. Note heavy build, broad wings, large head and bill, bold double white wing flash with relatively restricted white on p10 (cf. Figs 127, 129). PH. New South Wales, Australia, 25 Oct 2003.

Fig 129. Dark morph Kermadec Petrel. Note brown plumage tones, fairly stocky body, relatively broad wings and short tail (tail projection less than, or about equal to, width of wings at body), bold double white wing flash with relatively extensive white on p10 (cf. Figs 128, 130). CC. Pitcairn Islands, Central South Pacific, 15 Jun 2006.

Fig 130. Dark morph Herald Petrel or Henderson Petrel; strong contrast between dark hood and paler body may indicate Herald (rather than more uniformly dark Henderson) but study needed. Note brown plumage tones, fairly slim body, relatively narrow wings and long tail (tail projection often greater than width of wings at body), reflective silvery flashes on underwing (cf. Figs 127, 129). AJ. Easter Island, Chile, 16 Feb 2009.

Fig 131. Murphy's Petrel in slightly worn plumage, but still with distinct gray gloss to upperparts. Smaller and slighter in build than Solander's Petrel, but still relatively stocky; note relatively small bill, whitish mottling in face mainly on throat (cf. Fig 132). PH. Oeno Island, Central South Pacific, 4 Oct 2005.

Fig 132. Solander's Petrel in fresh plumage, thus with strong silvery sheen to upperparts. Note broad wings, long broad tail, stout bill, and contrasting dark hood with whitish mottling mainly in lores (cf. Fig 131). PH. New South Wales, Australia, 30 Mar 2003.

Fig 133. Solander's Petrel. Compared to Gray-faced Petrel (Fig 134), note gray sheen on wings and tail, bold double white wing flash, and white mottling in face mainly above bill. PH. New South Wales, Australia, 10 Apr 2004.

Fig 134. Gray-faced Petrel. Compared to Solander's Petrel (Fig 133), note dark brown plumage tones, lack of bold white flashes on underside of primaries, smoother whitish mottling in face often more extensive below bill. SNGH. North Island, New Zealand, 30 Mar 2008.

P25. COOK'S PETREL *Pterodroma cookii*
L 30.5–34 cm, WS 76–82 cm, tail 86–97 mm (graduation 15–23 mm)
Figures 115, P25.1–P25.15

Identification Summary Pacific. A small, fast-flying petrel with long narrow wings, bright white underparts, and a blackish M pattern on gray upperparts. Gray crown and hindneck same tone as back.

P25.1. In strong winds, Cook's Petrel often towers high in classic rollercoaster arcs, but it can also stay low, especially when flying into the wind. At such times, its gray-and-white plumage tones can be difficult to see against gray-and-white ocean. SNGH. Off Santa Barbara, California, 25 Jul 2009.

Taxonomy Monotypic.

Names *Pterodroma* means "winged runner"; *cookii* and the English name commemorate British explorer and navigator James Cook (1728–1779).

Status and Distribution Vulnerable. Breeds (Nov–Mar) New Zealand. Nonbreeding range (mainly Mar–Oct) in ne Pacific, with smaller numbers ranging to w South America.

Pacific. Fairly common to common nonbreeding visitor (mainly Mar–Sep, with small numbers Oct–Feb) off Baja California (mainly 20–30˚N), less commonly n to cen California (with peak numbers off California in Jul–Aug) and very rare n to Washington. Unknown numbers occur Jun–Aug (and perhaps into Oct or later?) in n cen Pacific (Bartle et al. 1993), when at least casual in Gulf of Alaska and s of Aleutians; whether these birds represent a different population or age class from Baja California and California birds is unknown. Probably uncommon to fairly common transient (mainly Mar–Apr, Sep–Nov) s to Clipperton, with Oct–early Dec records from vicinity of Revillagigedo Islands and Clipperton.

Occurrence off West Coast somewhat irregular, with California being at n edge of main nonbreeding range. Most California records are Apr–Sep (especially in warmer-water years) and mainly 75 km or more offshore, beyond cooler inshore waters. Presumed immatures and nonbreeders are rare well offshore into Oct–Dec, and storm-driven singles (early to mid-Dec) have been found onshore and inland in Washington and British Columbia (NAB 62:466, 2008). Casual inland at Salton Sea (Jul–early Aug).

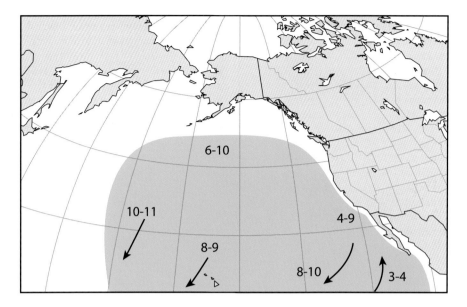

FIELD IDENTIFICATION

Similar Species Cook's Petrel is the "default" cookilaria in the region, with other species being rare or of hypothetical occurrence. Note long narrow wings, concolorous gray crown and back (beware differences between worn and fresh plumage). Identification to level of cookilaria should be straightforward, but cf. Mottled Petrel and beware misjudging size on much larger and broad-winged Buller's Shearwater.

Stejneger's Petrel (very rare off California) has slightly shorter, broader-looking wings, slightly shorter bill, and more contrasting upperparts, with brighter, bluish gray back. Stejneger's has contrasting dark cap, especially noticeable in profile or from below (more blended from above), and more contrasting M pattern above. Cook's in some lights, and particularly in worn plumage, can appear dark capped, but cap usually appears as a "flat cap" lacking hooked-down rear edge typical of Stejneger's.

Black-winged Petrel (*P. nigripennis*; L 30.5–33 cm, WS 73–78.5 cm, tail 95–111 mm [graduation 20–25 mm]; P25b.1–P25b.2) may range rarely to warmer waters well off Middle America, and is slightly broader winged and longer tailed than Cook's, with shorter and broader bill. Black-winged has gray partial collar on neck sides forward of wings; from above, upperparts slightly darker with more contrastingly pale tail; from below, note thick black underwing margins (shadowed Cook's at moderate range can appear to have thicker margins; Howell et al. 1996); legs and feet bicolored pale pinkish and black.

De Filippi's Petrel (*P. defilippiana*; L 30–33 cm, WS 74–80 cm, tail 97–108 mm [graduation 23–27 mm]; P25a.1–P25a.3) of Humboldt Current region and a potential vagrant n to waters off s Central America, is slightly stockier and broader winged than Cook's, with slightly longer tail. De Filippi's has stouter bill and larger black eye patch, which appear as two relatively bold black spots on head, and gray from hindneck extends down as a partial collar forward of wings. Tail of De Filippi's broader and typically all-gray, lacking blackish tip of Cook's, and wing molt mainly Nov–Mar. See Howell et al. (1996) for more details.

Very similar *Pycroft's Petrel* (*P. pycrofti*; L 28.5–31 cm, WS 69–73 cm, tail 89–99 mm [graduation 17–25 mm]; P25c.1–P25c.2) ranges in tropical e Pacific to around 110°W (Spear et al. 1992) and might wander very rarely to the region. Pycroft's averages smaller and often looks shorter-necked and chestier than Cook's with relatively shorter wings; flight sometimes appears more fluttery and buoyant than Cook's (cf. difference between Short-tailed and Sooty shearwaters, with Cook's being more like Sooty, Pycroft's more like Short-tailed). Plumages very similar, but Pycroft's has slightly more extensive gray on sides of head and neck (sometimes looking cowled), typically lacks distinct white eyebrow that often offsets dark beady eye of Cook's, and has slightly smaller bill.

Habitat and Behavior Pelagic, over warm temperate waters. Found singly or in loose to fairly dense feeding and rafting aggregations that locally may number hundreds of birds, such as off the cen Baja California Peninsula, where Cook's

Petrels often occur in association with Chapman's [Leach's] Storm Petrels.

Birds in heavy wing molt with large gaps in inner to middle primaries (mainly Apr–May) have more hurried wingbeats and bounding glides that may suggest Sooty Shearwater, but fuller-winged birds are less hurried and more buoyant. In calm to light winds, flight often low to the surface with buoyant glides on bowed wings interspersed with bursts of quick, flicking wingbeats and occasional low wheeling. In moderate to strong winds, flight faster and more erratic, with higher and steeper wheeling, short bursts of flickering stiff wingbeats; in strong winds at times almost flips back on itself and arcs up and down with a vertical slicing action.

Description Small snappy gadfly petrel with relatively long narrow wings and a medium-short tail. Moderate wing-loading.

Ages similar but juveniles fresh in Mar–Jun when most older birds worn or in wing molt. Crown, hindneck, chest sides, and upperparts medium-pale gray with small blackish eye patch, white forehead, and narrow white supercilium; moderately contrasting blackish M pattern duller in worn plumage, when head and back also appear browner and duskier; inner rectrices darker distally, usually forming distinct dark tail tip, outer rectrices white (white rarely visible unless tail spread) with dense dark freckling on outer webs. From below usually looks "flat-capped" but viewed from above, gray chest sides often bulge down forward of the wings. Underparts clean white (flashing bright in the sun) with narrow black wing margins usually inconspicuous; when shadowed, however, underwing margins can appear relatively bold other than at close range. Birds in inner to mid-primary molt (mainly Mar–Apr) often show white stripe across upperwing. Legs and feet bicolored pale bluish and black.

Molt Wing molt mainly Mar–Aug, with adults Apr/May–Jul/Aug; tail molt occurs at or following completion of primary molt, mainly Jul–Oct (rarely later).

25.2. As with other small gadfly petrels, shape of Cook's Petrel varies greatly with flight manner, wind speed, and wind direction; this bird is flying across a moderately strong wind (cf. P25.3). SNGH. Off Bodega Bay, California, 12 Aug 2009.

P25.3. This Cook's Petrel is wheeling gently in light winds (cf. P25.2). Note distinct white eyebrow, relatively long slender bill. SNGH. North Island, New Zealand, 8 Nov 2008.

P25.4. In worn plumage and poor light, Cook's Petrel can appear surprisingly dark above (cf. fresh plumage, P25.3). SNGH. North Island, New Zealand, 1 Apr 2008.

P25.5. In heavily worn plumage, hindneck of Cook's Petrel (as with other similarly plumaged gadflies) can wear and fade to whitish; also note exaggerated white eyebrow (cf. fresh plumage, P25.3). SNGH. North Island, New Zealand, 1 Apr 2008.

P25.6. Cook's Petrel in worn plumage, appearing darker and smoother gray above than in fresh plumage (cf. P25.7). SNGH. North Island, New Zealand, 31 Mar 2008.

P25.7. Cook's Petrel completing wing molt (p10 not fully grown). Note distinct white eyebrow, beady black eye, slender bill. SNGH. Off Santa Barbara, California, 25 Jul 2009.

P25a.1. De Filippi's Petrel with mid-primary molt. Compared to Cook's Petrel, note molt timing (cf. P25.12), heavy bill, large blackish eye patch, and lack of dark tail tip (cf. P25.6–25.7). SW. Eastern Pacific, 13°S 90°W, 11 Oct 2006.

P25b.1. Black-winged Petrel. Compared to Cook's Petrel, note broader wings, duskier back, head pattern, and bigger bill (cf. P25.6–25.7). SNGH. Western Pacific, 33°S 172°E, 4 Apr 2008.

P25.8. Cook's Petrel in fresh plumage, presumably a juvenile on this date (cf. P25.4–P25.5). Note pale gray head and back, contrasting plumage pattern; no dark tail tip apparent at this distance. SNGH. North Island, New Zealand, 3 Apr 2008.

P25.9. Cook's Petrel in fairly fresh plumage. Note relatively long neck, small head, long slender bill; dusky tail tip poorly marked on this individual (cf. P25a.2, P25c.1). SNGH. North Island, New Zealand, 8 Nov 2008.

P25a.2. De Filippi's Petrel in fairly fresh plumage (probably a juvenile on this date). Note stocky build, heavy bill, distinct white notch behind dark eye patch, plain gray tail (cf. P25.9, 25c.1). SNGH. Valparaíso, Chile, 30 Oct 2007.

P25c.1. Pycroft's Petrel in fairly fresh plumage. Note relatively short neck, puffy head, and head pattern, with diffuse blackish eye patch blending into medium-gray cowl (cf. P25.9, 25a.2). SNGH. North Island, New Zealand, 8 Nov 2008.

P25.10. Cook's Petrel in fairly fresh plumage. Note relatively long neck, small head, long slender bill, and head pattern (cf. P25.11, 25c.2). SNGH. North Island, New Zealand, 8 Nov 2008.

P25.11. Cook's Petrel in worn plumage. Note how wear, combined with angle of lighting, can make head appear contrastingly dark (cf. P25.10). SNGH. North Island, New Zealand, 31 Mar 2008.

P25c.2. Pycroft's Petrel in fairly fresh plumage. Note relatively plump shape, short neck, slender bill, and head pattern (cf. P25.10, P25c.1). SNGH. North Island, New Zealand, 8 Nov 2008.

P25b.2. Thick black underwing margins of Black-winged Petrel are striking; also note distinct gray neck spur (cf. P25.10–P25.11, P25b.1). SNGH. Western Pacific, 26°S 167°E, 7 Apr 2008.

207

P25.12. Cook's Petrel with outer primary molt. Note long neck, small head, slender bill, and face pattern (cf. P25a.3). TMcG. Baja California, Mexico, 5 Jul 2006.

P25a.3. De Filippi's Petrel. Note stocky build, large head and bill, distinctive neck pattern (cf. P25.12). SNGH. Valparaíso, Chile, 30 Oct 2007.

P25.13. At some angles, such as with birds flushing off the water, Cook's Petrel can show dark wedge on sides of neck; note bold white eyebrow, relatively slender bill, molt timing (outer primaries completing growth). SNGH. Off Santa Barbara, California, 25 Jul 2009.

P25.14. Head and neck pattern of Cook's Petrel varies individually as well as with wear and lighting, some birds being appreciably darker capped than others. SNGH. Off Santa Barbara, California, 25 Jul 2009.

P25.15. On the water, Cook's Petrel shows clean white sides, variable gray chest spur; note face pattern and long slender bill (cf. P27.11). SNGH. Off Santa Barbara, California, 25 Jul 2009.

P26. STEJNEGER'S PETREL *Pterodroma longirostris*

L 29–31.5, cm, WS 70–76 cm, tail 90–107 mm (graduation 18–27 mm)
Figures P26.1–P26.8

Identification Summary Pacific. Very rare off California. A sharply marked *Cookiliaria* with contrasting upperparts, a dark slaty cap that hooks down on the neck sides, and typical snappy flight. Pronounced "Stein-eh-grr's."

Taxonomy Monotypic.

Names *Pterodroma* means "winged runner"; *longisrostris* means "long-billed"; the English name commemorates Norwegian naturalist Leonhard Stejneger (1851–1943).

Status and Distribution Vulnerable. Breeds (Dec–Apr) on Juan Fernandez Islands, Chile. Nonbreeding range (mainly May–Oct) in nw Pacific; casual or very rare in ne Pacific and (mainly Nov–Jan) sw to New Zealand.
　Pacific. Very rare nonbreeding visitor (Apr–Nov) off California. Records in Apr and mid-May (M. P. Force, pers. comm.; N. Black, photos[1]) may involve juveniles that wandered n up the "wrong" side of the Pacific, whereas mid-Oct to early Dec records (from n California s to vicinity of Clipperton) may involve southbound migrants (mainly immatures?) spreading out at e edge of the migration track. Also a few Jul–Aug reports off California, but none substantiated by photos.
　Atlantic. A decomposing carcass of uncertain provenance found on the Texas coast (Sep 1995) is attributed to this species (Lockwood & Freeman 2004).

FIELD IDENTIFICATION

Similar Species A distinctive species, assuming good views are obtained and size is not misjudged (cf. much larger Buller's Shearwater, which has similar plumage pattern).
　Cook's Petrel slightly larger with longer and narrower wings, relatively shorter tail, slightly longer bill, and less contrasting upperparts. Cook's has medium-pale gray crown and hindneck, but can appear dark capped (rarely almost blackish) in some lights, especially when worn; in direct flight, cap of Cook's lacks hooked-down rear edge typical of Stejneger's.
　Gould's (White-winged) Petrel (*P. leucoptera*; L 30.5–33 cm, WS 72–79 cm, tail 88–102 mm

[graduation 19–25 mm]; P26a.1–P26a.2) ranges in tropical e Pacific to around 100°W (Spear et al. 1992) and might wander rarely to the region. Slightly larger than Stejneger's, with slightly longer neck, bigger bill, distinctly thicker black underwing margins, and more extensive blackish cowl that contrasts strongly with white forehead (suggesting Galapagos Petrel), unlike dark cap of Stejneger's. Legs and feet bicolored pale bluish and black.

Habitat and Behavior Pelagic. Likely to be encountered singly, alone or in loose association with Cook's Petrels. Flight overall like Cook's Petrel but tends to be a little zippier and more maneuverable.

Description Small snappy gadfly petrel with narrow wings and medium-length tail. Fairly low wing-loading.
　Ages similar but juveniles fresh in Apr–Jul when most older birds are worn or in wing molt. Upperparts medium bluish gray (darker and browner when worn) with a distinct blackish M pattern and blackish tail tip; hindneck and crown darker, slaty gray, merging with black eye patch to form a contrasting dark cap best appreciated in profile. Cap contrasts with white forehead, and white from throat hooks up behind black auriculars, setting off dark partial collar forward of wings. Underparts clean white (flashing bright in the sun) with narrow black wing margins, which appear bolder when wings are shadowed; outer rectrices dark with white freckling on inner webs. Birds in inner to mid-primary molt (mainly Apr–May, unrecorded off North America) often show white stripe across upperwing. Legs and feet bicolored pale bluish and black.

Molt Wing molt mainly Mar/May–Jun/Aug, with presumed PB2 completing Jun, adult wing molt completing Aug (Marchant & Higgins 1990).

Note 1. 12 May 2003, Monterey Bay; initially reported as a "Dark-rumped Petrel" and not accepted as any species by state committee, despite diagnostic photos.

P26.1. Stejneger's Petrel. Note white notch behind dark cap, boldly contrasting blackish M pattern (cf. P25.2–P25.3); white at tail tip represents misarranged feathers. SE. Aisén, Chile, 5 Feb 2009.

P26.2. Even at moderate range, upperparts of Stejneger's Petrel are appreciably more contrasting than Cook's Petrel; in particular, note dark head and tail tip. SE. Aisén, Chile, 5 Feb 2009.

P26a.1. Gould's Petrel. Compared to Stejneger's Petrel, note extensive black hood, darker and less contrasting upperparts. SNGH. Western Pacific, 23°S 166°E, 1 Apr 2007.

P26.3. Stejneger's Petrel. Note distinctive head pattern, brightly contrasting upperparts. MO'K. Aisén, Chile, 5 Feb 2009.

P26.4. Stejneger's Petrel. Note white notch behind dark cap, relatively short head/neck projection. AJ. Juan Fernandez Islands, Chile, 26 Nov 2005.

P26.5. Stejneger's Petrel. Note white notch behind dark cap, extensively white underwings. MO'K. Aisén, Chile, 5 Feb 2009.

P26.6. Stejneger's Petrel. Note distinctive head/neck pattern, overall structure, and extensively white underwings. SE. Aisén, Chile, 5 Feb 2009.

P26.7. Stejneger's Petrel. Note same features as P26.6, and cf. P26a.2. KF. Aisén, Chile, 5 Feb 2009.

P26a.2. Gould's Petrel. Compared to Stejneger's Petrel, note extensive dark hood, relatively long head/neck projection, bolder black underwing margins. SNGH. Western Pacific, 33°S 172°E, 4 Apr 2008.

P26.8. Banking away, the usually distinctive head and neck pattern of Stejneger's Petrel is not always apparent; this bird's pattern suggests Cook's Petrel (cf. P25.11). SE. Aisén, Chile, 5 Feb 2009.

P27. MOTTLED PETREL *Pterodroma inexpectata*

L 32–36 cm, WS 84–92 cm, tail 96–108 mm (graduation 25–30 mm)
Figures 116, P27.1–P27.11

Identification Summary Pacific, over cooler waters. A distinctive, medium-sized, fat-bodied, and fairly short-tailed gadfly petrel with high wing-loading. Slightly larger but distinctly heavier-bodied than *Cookilaria* petrels, with extensively dark belly, broad black carpal-ulnar bar on silvery-white underwing, and frosty gray trailing triangle on upperwing. A strong and fast flier.

P27.1. Ventral pattern of Mottled Petrel often striking at long range; in particular, note silvery-white underwings with thick black ulnar bar, contrast between dark belly and white undertail coverts. SNGH. Snares Islands, New Zealand, 11 Nov 28.

Taxonomy Monotypic.

Names *Pterodroma* means "winged runner"; *inexpectata* apparently refers to the unexpected joy this species brought to its describer. Mottled refers to the scaly aspect to the back (hence the species' old name of Scaled Petrel).

Status and Distribution Near Threatened. Breeds (Dec–May) s New Zealand, ranges n (mainly May–Oct) to temperate North Pacific.
   Pacific. Migrates n across cen Pacific (Feb–Jun), occasionally ranging to waters off West Coast (mainly late Feb–Apr), especially in cold-water years (Ainley & Manolis 1979); commoner northward, exceptionally with hundreds off British Columbia in late Apr. Nonbreeding range (May–Oct, mainly Jun–Oct) from s Bering Sea (to 59°N) through Aleutians to Gulf of Alaska,

mainly well offshore (Bartle et al. 1993), with southward withdrawal mainly Sep–Oct, although probably some linger later in North Pacific.
   Irregularly fairly common southbound migrant (late Oct–Dec, mainly mid-Nov to mid-Dec) off West Coast (sometimes hundreds in early Dec, perhaps mainly in cold-water years), occurring farther offshore southward, and usually beyond 370 km by s California; presumably these are immatures migrating later and on a broader front than breeding adults. Beach-washed birds may be found at any season, including mid-summer.
   Atlantic. Exceptional inland in New York (early Apr 1880).

FIELD IDENTIFICATION

Similar Species A distinctive species from both above and below. The pattern on the underparts

212

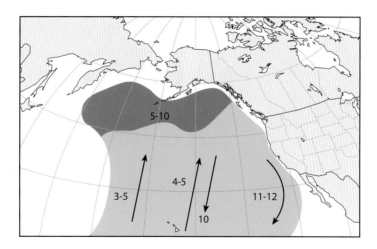

is diagnostic, given the potential exception of another species with an oiled belly, and the pale trailing triangle on the upperwings is also distinctive and can be an arresting feature in some lights.

Cookilaria petrels (such as Cook's) smaller and slimmer-bodied with narrower wings,; their snappier flight is more erratic in moderate to strong winds; their white underparts gleam at long range, and upperwings lack frosty pale trailing triangle. Cook's also has narrower-looking tail tipped blackish. On the water at moderate range, Cook's and Mottled can look similar but note white sides and slightly build of Cook's; also, Mottled usually appears more hooded, or cowled, with contrasting white forehead blaze, whereas Cook's has more extensive white on throat and foreneck.

Murphy's Petrel has slightly longer, narrower wings and longer tail. Plumage all-dark, but in dull light or strong backlighting Mottled can appear dark overall, even on the underparts unless these are seen at the right angle; note stouter bill and white undertail coverts of Mottled.

Habitat and Behavior Pelagic, over cooler waters. Migrating birds may be seen singly or in pulses of birds passing through an area; elsewhere found singly or in small flocks (up to 20 or so birds), at times associating loosely with other seabirds such as Short-tailed Shearwaters.

In calm to light winds, sometimes flies with long, low glides (barely above the surface in glassy calm) and bursts of quick flapping; at other times flies high above the horizon, flapping steadily and recalling a jaeger. In moderate to strong winds flies across the wind in high bounding and wheeling arcs with little or no flapping; at other times may wheel relatively low, especially when flying into the wind.

Description Medium-sized, fat-bodied gadfly petrel with a fairly short broad tail and high wing-loading.

Ages similar but juveniles (May–Jul at least) average broader scaly white edgings to upperparts and have more extensive whitish on outer rectrices (Marchant & Higgins 1990). Head and upperparts smoky gray with variable blacker eye patch (sometimes quite contrasting); uppertail coverts and tail slightly paler; inner webs of outer rectrices with limited to extensive white freckling. Back in fresh plumage has gray sheen, the feathers with dark shaft streaks, dark subterminal marks, and narrow whitish tips. Blackish M pattern above sets off contrasting paler hindwing panel from secondaries across inner primaries. Throat and underparts white with extensive sooty gray belly patch that sets off bright white undertail coverts; dark from hood sometimes projects down to surround white throat, and chest sometimes scalloped dusky; thus, from above, can appear all-dark with white throat patch. Underwings silvery white with thick black carpal-ulnar bar and narrow, dark trailing margins. Bill black, legs and feet bicolored pale pinkish and black.

On the water. Sooty gray overall with white throat set off by dark cowl, white undertail coverts and dark sides.

Molt Adult wing molt in North Pacific mainly May–Aug; molt of prebreeders perhaps more protracted (some Nov birds off California completing tail molt; Loomis 1918). PB2 wing molt probably mainly Jan–May in s hemisphere (Murphy & Pennoyer 1952), although some may molt later (Feb/Mar–Jun/Jul) in n hemisphere, paralleling the molt of Sooty Shearwater, another transequatorial migrant.

P27.2. In fresh plumage, upperwings of Mottled Petrel show distinct silvery panel on trailing edge; also note stocky shape. SNGH. West-southwest of Campbell Island, New Zealand, 17 Nov 2008.

P27.3. Mottled Petrel. Note stocky shape, contrasting pale trailing edge to wings, plain gray tail; depending on light, head often appears darker than back. SNGH. Northeast of Bounty Islands, New Zealand, 21 Nov 2008.

P27.4. Mottled Petrel. Note stocky shape, silvery panel on trailing edge of upperwing, contrast between dark belly and white undertail coverts. SNGH. Snares Islands, New Zealand, 11 Nov 2008.

P27.5. Mottled Petrel. Note contrast between dark belly and white undertail coverts, silvery trailing edge to upperwing. SNGH. East-northeast of Campbell Island, New Zealand, 19 Nov 2008.

P27.6. Seen well, Mottled Petrel is basically unmistakable. SNGH. West-southwest of Campbell Island, New Zealand, 17 Nov 2008.

P27.7. In strong winds, Mottled Petrel often towers high overhead, showing off its striking underparts. SNGH. North Island, New Zealand, 8 Nov 2008.

P27.8. In poor lighting, Mottled Petrel often appears surprisingly dark and can be mistaken for all-dark petrels. Note thick neck, stocky shape, relatively small wings. SNGH. North Island, New Zealand, 8 Nov 2008.

P27.9. Mottled Petrel. Dark belly patch variable in extent; note striking underwing pattern, contrasting white undertail coverts. MJI. West of Aleutians, 2 2 Sep 2008.

P27.10. Head-on, Mottled Petrel can appear dark overall with bright white face. SNGH. Northeast of Bounty Islands, New Zealand, 21 Nov 2008.

P27.11. Mottled Petrel. Note stocky shape, fairly dark head, dusky mottling on sides (cf. P25.15). SNGH. West-southwest of Campbell Island, New Zealand, 17 Nov 2008.

P28. HAWAIIAN [DARK-RUMPED] PETREL *Pterodroma sandwichensis*

L 37.5–40 cm, WS 94–104 cm, tail 125–142 mm (graduation 50–55 mm)
Figures 117, 120, 123, 125, P28.1–P28.8

Identification Summary Pacific, subtropical waters off West Coast. A medium-large, lightly built, long-tailed gadfly petrel formerly united with Galapagos Petrel (*P. [p.] phaeopygia*) as Dark-rumped Petrel (see Taxonomy). Upperparts dark with white forehead blaze set off by blackish cap, underparts white with thick black underwing margins.

P28.1. Relatively heavy body and narrow wings of Hawaiian Petrel are well suited to the windy North Pacific (Galapagos Petrel inhabits less windy tropical regions, for which its lighter body and broader wings are more efficient). SNGH. Off Bodega Bay, California, 12 Aug 2009.

Taxonomy AOU (2002) split Hawaiian and Galapagos populations of "Dark-rumped Petrel" (*P. phaeopygia*) as separate species, Hawaiian Petrel (*P. sandwichensis*) and Galapagos Petrel (*P. phaeopygia*), based on two published studies (Browne et al. 1997, Tomkins & Milne 1991). However, Tomkins and Milne (1991) reported statistically significant differences in time of breeding, morphology, egg size, and vocalizations among populations on different islands *within the Galapagos*, and only noted in passing that the vocalizations of Hawaiian birds were quite different; no relevant data were offered. Browne et al. (1997) reported some statistically significant genetic differences between Hawaiian and Galapagos birds; they painfully elaborated the obvious yet misrepresented the magnitude of morphological differences, and their conclusions are difficult to interpret in terms of biological significance. Notwithstanding these publications, it seems reasonable to treat Hawaiian and Galapagos populations as different species, as done here.

In the meantime, populations of each taxon breeding on different islands in their respective archipelagos show differences (Ainley 2009, Tomkins & Milne 1991), suggesting that multiple cryptic species might be involved! Thus, these could be the pelagic, nocturnal-breeding counterparts to the iconic Darwin's finches.

Names *Pterodroma* means "winged runner"; *sandwichensis* and the English name refer to the

216

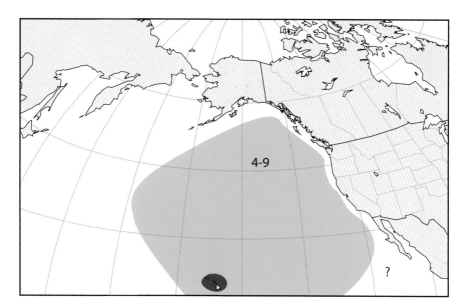

Hawaiian Islands (formerly the Sandwich Islands), where this species breeds.

Status and Distribution Vulnerable. Breeds (late Apr–Oct on Maui, returning late Feb) in Hawaii; ranges n and e in tropical and subtropical Pacific to 50˚N and to offshore California, and s rarely to equator.

Pacific. Rare nonbreeding visitor (May to mid-Sep, mainly Jul–Aug) off the West Coast. Recent reports of Dark-rumped Petrel s of the Baja California Peninsula (NAB 59:154, 2005) lie in area of potential overlap between Hawaiian and Galapagos petrels.

FIELD IDENTIFICATION

Similar Species Dark-rumped Petrels (Hawaiian and Galapagos combined) are fairly distinctive: note their medium-large size and long tail, bold white forehead blaze set off by blackish cap or hood, dark upperparts, and white underparts with thick blackish underwing margins. A few pitfalls should still be considered, however. Then, distinguishing Hawaiian Petrel from Galapagos Petrel remains a challenge (see below).

Pink-footed Shearwater is much larger and bulkier with broad wings, a shorter and broader tail, slender bill (pink with a dark tip), smudgy dark head lacking white forehead blaze, and dark undertail coverts. Flight lacks the easy buoyancy of Dark-rumped, but can wheel high and fairly steeply in windy conditions.

Light morph *Wedge-tailed Shearwater* has broader, often more strongly crooked wings, longer neck, and small head with slender grayish bill, dark cap without white forehead, and dark undertail coverts. Its buoyant flight lacks the easy bounding grace of Dark-rumped.

Juan Fernandez Petrel when worn can appear brown above, and fresh-plumaged Dark-rumped has gray sheen with blacker M pattern that might suggest Juan. Juan is larger (and slightly broader winged than Hawaiian Petrel) with paler gray hindneck and back, more contrasting black mask, and overall white underparts that lack broad black wing margins (beware that some Hawaiian Petrels have relatively narrow black underwing margins); in poor lighting, however, when no plumage features are apparent, Juan and Dark-rumped can look similar and are not always safely distinguished at a distance.

Inexperienced observers might confuse much smaller *Stejneger's Petrel* and *Gould's Petrel* (unrecorded in the region) with Dark-rumped, but these have shorter and narrower wings, shorter tails, relatively small bills, and snappier flight that is more erratic in moderate to strong winds. Both have grayer upperparts with a bolder black M pattern, and shorter, black-tipped gray tail; Gould's has blackish cowl recalling Galapagos Petrel, whereas Stejneger's has dark slaty cap.

Bonin Petrel (L 29–31.5 cm, WS 72–78 cm, tail 102–116 mm [graduation 39–45 mm]; P28a.1–28a.3) ranges in cen and w North Pacific, and seems a potential vagrant to North American waters. Smaller and more compact than Hawaiian Petrel but with similar pattern to upperparts, although dark hood more extensive and paler uppertail coverts contrast with blackish tail; striking and diagnostic underwing pattern clinches identification.

If a Dark-rumped Petrel is encountered, the most useful at-sea plumage feature to distinguish between Hawaiian and Galapagos appears to be head pattern; other things to check are underwing pattern, flank pattern, bill size, and overall shape and flight manner (Force et al. 2007).

Relative to Hawaiian Petrel, *Galapagos Petrel* is lighter bodied and broader winged, with a blackish cowl or hood (depth of cap or hood below eye typically greater than eye depth, rather than similar to or less than eye depth on Hawaiian) that typically cuts diagonally across sides of head and neck, often with less contrast between blackish auriculars and darker gray to gray-brown neck sides, and typically has little or no white cutting up behind auriculars (shown by many but not all Hawaiian). Pattern thus reminiscent of Gould's Petrel (whereas pattern on Hawaiian Petrel recalls Juan Fernandez Petrel). Some heavily pigmented Galapagos Petrels even have dusky scalloping on the neck sides, which can form a partial collar.

Observers very familiar with one or both forms may notice that Hawaiian Petrel appears a little smaller and has a "zippier" flight than larger and more leisurely Galapagos Petrel. Galapagos Petrel averages bigger billed than Hawaiian, which may be helpful with good photos of extremes, but bill measurements overlap and are difficult to appreciate at sea. Underwing of Galapagos may have broader, dark trailing edge (reflecting its wider wings; but juvenile Hawaiian can be similar), and often has noticeable dark flank markings. Birds in heavy wing molt during Mar–Jun are likely to be Galapagos Petrels (see Molt, below).

Habitat and Behavior Pelagic, over offshore subtropical and tropical waters, typically in areas with a deeper thermocline and higher wind speeds than areas favored by Galapagos Petrel (Spear et al. 1995). Usually found singly, as likely to be alone as with mixed-species feeding flocks of other petrels, shearwaters, and terns, often over schooling yellowfin tuna.

Flight easy and buoyant, much like Juan Fernandez Petrel but can appear quicker and more maneuverable. In calm to light winds, flight leisurely, meandering or weaving low over the water with easy clipped wingbeats, buoyant glides on flexed wings, and low wheeling arcs. In moderate to strong winds flight across the wind fast and wheeling, with higher arcs and no flapping or short bursts of a few quick flaps; at other times wheels fairly low, especially when flying into the wind.

Description Medium-large gadfly petrel with long narrow wings, relatively long tapered tail, and fairly stout bill. Fairly low wing-loading.

Ages similar but juveniles fresh in Oct–Dec when most older birds are worn or in wing molt. Variation not well known, and possibility of inter-island variation has not been elucidated. Blackish cap typically contrasts with medium-gray neck sides and blends into grayish hindneck; cap demarcation on head and neck sides fairly level (mainly as viewed from below), or white from throat cuts up behind cap and gray from neck bulges down forward of wings; forehead white, rarely with a few blackish spots. Upperparts slaty grayish with frosty sheen and paler tips to back in fresh plumage, and variable blacker M pattern; upperparts become darker, browner, and more uniform with wear; white mottling sometimes apparent on uppertail coverts is exposed white feather bases. Underparts white with broad blackish wing margins rarely difficult to discern because of sun glare: wingtips and trailing edge to wings blackish, grading to dusky gray on primary bases, which sometimes have whitish basal tongues; broad black carpal-ulnar bar fades out before reaching body; black trailing edge to wings may be thicker on juvenile (P28.5); some birds have limited dusky smudging on hind flanks. Outer rectrices dark with some white at base of inner webs. Bill black, legs and feet flesh bicolored pale pinkish and black.

On the water. Blackish cap and dark hindneck contrast with white forehead, lores, and foreneck; upperparts dark slaty gray to gray brown, contrasting with white chest, sides, and undertail coverts.

Molt Adult wing molt presumably Oct–Feb; immatures and prebreeders probably molt earlier, perhaps Aug/Oct–Nov/Jan.

P28.2. Hawaiian Petrel in fairly worn plumage, showing brown tones to upperparts; note distinctive head pattern. M&MB. Off Fort Bragg, California, 13 Aug 2006.

P28.3. Hawaiian Petrel in fresh plumage (presumably a juvenile on this date) showing gray tones to upperparts and contrasting dark head; also note fairly uniform rump and tail. ABD. Hawaii, 13 Dec 2009.

P28.4. Hawaiian Petrel in fairly worn plumage. Note long narrow wings, long graduated tail, small head with dark cap. SNGH. Off Bodega Bay, California, 12 Aug 2009.

P28a.1. Bonin Petrel is slightly smaller and stockier than Hawaiian Petrel with more contrasting upperparts, especially in fresh plumage (here in worn plumage but note pale uppertail coverts; cf. P28.3–P28.4). SNGH. Western Pacific, 24°N 143°E, 29 Apr 2008.

P28a.2. Bonin Petrel slightly smaller and stockier than Hawaiian Petrel with more contrasting upperparts (note pale uppertail coverts), extensive dark cowl (cf. P28.4). SNGH. Western Pacific, 26°N 142°E, 22 Apr 2007.

P28.5. Hawaiian Petrel in fresh plumage (presumably a juvenile on this date). Note distinctive head pattern; extent of blackish underwing markings variable; greater underwing coverts of juvenile may average shorter and narrower than adult, producing broader dark trailing edge to secondaries (cf. P28.6–P28.8). DLW. Hawaii, 28 Oct 2009.

P28.6. Hawaiian Petrel. Note how head pattern varies individually as well as with wear and angle of viewing (cf. P28.5, P28.7). SNGH. Off Bodega Bay, California, 12 Aug 2009.

P28.7. (Above) When Hawaiian Petrel is wheeling overhead, its dark cap often appears less extensive than when viewed in profile (cf. P28.5–P28.6). SNGH. Off Santa Barbara, California, 6 Sep 2006.

P28a.3. (Above right) Despite somewhat similar appearance to Hawaiian Petrel when viewed from above, Bonin Petrel has a striking and diagnostic underwing pattern (cf. P28.7). SNGH. Western Pacific, 26°N 142°E, 22 Apr 2007.

P28.8. Head and neck pattern of Hawaiian Petrel on the water is subtly different from Galapagos Petrel (cf. P29.10); note less extensive blackish cheeks of Hawaiian. DLW. Hawaii, 28 Oct 2009.

P29. GALAPAGOS [DARK-RUMPED] PETREL *Pterodroma phaeopygia*

L 39.5–42 cm, WS 99–110 cm, tail 130–155 mm (graduation 53–60 mm)
Figures 118, 121, 124, 126, P29.1–P29.10

Identification Summary Pacific, tropical waters off Middle America. A medium-large, lightly built, long-tailed gadfly petrel until recently united with Hawaiian Petrel (*P. [p.] sandwichensis*) as Dark-rumped Petrel (see Taxonomy under Hawaiian Petrel). Dark upperparts with white forehead blaze set off by a blackish hood, white underparts with thick black underwing margins.

Taxonomy See under Hawaiian Petrel.

Names *Pterodroma* means "winged runner"; *phaeopygia* means "dusky, or dark-brown, rumped."

Status and Distribution Critical. Breeds (egg-laying Nov–Aug, fledging Jun–Mar; varies among islands, Tomkins & Milne 1991) in Galapagos; ranges in tropical Pacific to 20°N and 20°S, and w along the equator to around 120°W.

   Pacific. Rare nonbreeding visitor (year-round, perhaps mainly Feb–Oct) off Middle America n to around 20°N (Pitman 1986, Spear et al. 1995). Recent reports of Dark-rumped Petrel s of the Baja California Peninsula (NAB 59:154, 2005) lie in area of potential overlap between Hawaiian and Galapagos petrels.

FIELD IDENTIFICATION

Similar Species See under Hawaiian Petrel. The main difficulty lies in distinguishing Hawaiian from Galapagos petrels, for which criteria were proposed recently (Force et al. 2007). The most useful feature appears to be head and neck pattern combined with overall structure; see under Hawaiian Petrel for other potential differences.

   Relative to Galapagos Petrel, *Hawaiian Petrel* is slightly heavier bodied and narrower winged (thus with higher wing-loading), with blackish cap (vs. more extensive hood of Galapagos) that typically contrasts more with grayer neck sides; there can be a fairly level demarcation across sides of head and neck (mainly as viewed from below), or white from throat cuts up behind cap and gray from neck bulges down forward of wings. Head pattern of Hawaiian can suggest Juan Fernandez Petrel. Many Galapagos Petrels have distinct dark marks on their sides, whereas Hawaiian typically is clean white below or rarely shows dusky flank smudging (which may be farther back on body than dark marks on typical Galapagos).

Habitat and Behavior Pelagic, over offshore tropical waters, typically in areas with a shallower thermocline and lower wind speeds than areas favored by Hawaiian Petrel (Spear et al. 1995). Habits much like Hawaiian Petrel (which see) but lower wing-loading results in more leisurely, less towering flight.

Description Medium-large gadfly petrel with long narrow wings, relatively long tapered tail, and stout bill. Low wing-loading.

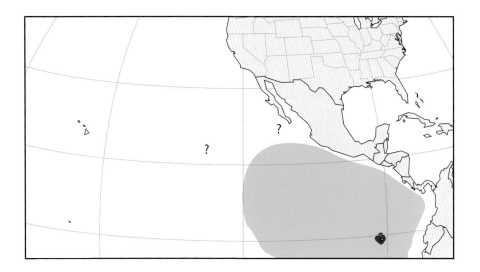

Ages similar. Blackish cowl, or hood, typically cuts diagonally across sides of head and neck, contrasting poorly with dark gray to gray-brown neck sides, and with little or no white cutting up behind auriculars. Some heavily pigmented birds have dusky scalloping on neck sides that can form partial collar; forehead varies from clean white to spotted blackish. Upperparts slaty grayish with frosty sheen and paler tips to back in fresh plumage, and variable blacker M pattern; upperparts become darker, browner, and more uniform with wear; white mottling sometimes apparent on uppertail coverts is exposed white feather bases. Underparts white with broad blackish wing margins rarely difficult to see because of sun glare: wingtips and trailing edge to wings blackish, grading to dusky gray on primary bases, which sometimes have whitish basal tongues; broad black carpal-ulnar bar fades out before reaching body; flanks typically with variable dark markings. Outer rectrices dark with some white at base of inner webs. Bill black, legs and feet flesh bicolored pale pinkish and black.

On the water. Blackish hood and dark hindneck contrast with white forehead, lores, and foreneck; upperparts dark slaty gray to gray brown, contrasting with white chest, sides, and undertail coverts.

Molt Because of protracted breeding seasons, wing molt probably occurs year-round.

P29.1. Galapagos Petrel in slightly worn plumage, thus with brownish upperparts. Note big, long wings, long tapered tail, blackish cowl. GLA. Galapagos Islands, Ecuador, 21 Jul 2009.

P29.2. Galapagos Petrel with mid-primary molt and fresh (gray-fringed) back feathers. Note big long wings relative to Hawaiian Petrel (cf. P28.4). MD. Galapagos Islands, Ecuador, 12 Nov 2006.

P29.3. Galapagos Petrel. Note overall dark upperparts, long tapered tail, blackish cowl, fairly heavy bill; some birds show variable white patches on uppertail coverts. GLA. Galapagos Islands, Ecuador, 24 Jul 2009.

P29.4. Galapagos Petrel. Note long narrow wings, long tapered tail, overall dark upperparts with black cowl. AJ. Galapagos Islands, Ecuador, 11 Aug 2009.

P29.5. Galapagos Petrel in fresh plumage, with contrast between blackish cowl and gray back (cf. P28.1–P28.2); white mark in wing is a misarranged feather. GLA. Galapagos Islands, Ecuador, 24 Jul 2009.

P29.6. Galapagos Petrel. From below, note bold patterning with extensive blackish hood. Much smaller Gould's Petrel similar from below (cf. P26a.2) but typically has narrower black wing margins, lacks dark on flanks, and more compact overall with relatively shorter tail. GLA. Galapagos Islands, Ecuador, 24 Jul 2009.

P29.7. Galapagos Petrel showing extensive dark cowl (cf. P28.6); also note dark flank patch. GLA. Galapagos Islands, Ecuador, 24 Jul 2009.

P29.8. Extent of hood and of dark underwing and flank markings on Galapagos Petrel notably variable, to some degree reflecting differences between populations on different islands. GLA. Galapagos Islands, Ecuador, 24 Jul 2009.

P29.9. Galapagos Petrels on the water are strikingly patterned—note white face contrasting with blackish cowl. GLA. Galapagos Islands, Ecuador, 19 Aug 2006.

P29.10. Head and neck pattern of Galapagos Petrel on the water is subtly different from Hawaiian Petrel (cf. P28.8). MD. Galapagos Islands, Ecuador, 14 Nov 2006.

P30. JUAN FERNANDEZ PETREL *Pterodroma externa*

L 42–45 cm, WS 103–114 cm, tail 125–143 mm (graduation 35–45 mm)
Figures 119, 122, P30.1–P30.11

Identification Summary Pacific, over tropical waters. A large gadfly petrel with long wings and a fairly long tapered tail; plumage suggests cookilaria petrels in overall pattern. Grayish above with a blackish mask and blackish M pattern (sometimes a white hindneck), bright white below with a restricted blackish carpal-ulnar bar. Buoyant, wheeling flight.

Taxonomy Monotypic. Has been considered conspecific with White-necked Petrel (*P. cervicalis*) of w Pacific, but these two are now generally treated as distinct species.

Names *Pterodroma* means "winged runner"; *externa* refers to the outside, or external, island in the Juan Fernandez archipelago, where this species breeds.

Status and Distribution Vulnerable. Breeds (Dec–May) on Juan Fernandez Islands, Chile; ranges n (mainly Apr–Oct) to 25°N in North Pacific, rarely to 42°N in cen Pacific (M. P. Force, pers. comm.).
   Pacific. Fairly common to common nonbreeding visitor (mainly Apr–Oct, smaller numbers Nov–Mar) far off Middle America n to around 10°N and to waters around Clipperton Atoll; uncommon to locally fairly common (late May–Aug at least, probably Apr–Oct) n to around 20°N, and uncommon to rare in these waters Nov–Mar, exceptionally recorded within 5 km of shore off Colima, Mexico, Feb 1999 (Howell 2004).

FIELD IDENTIFICATION

Similar Species Juan Fernandez Petrel (or simply "Juan") is a large, fairly distinctive *Pterodroma*, gray above with a blackish M pattern (and sometimes a white hindneck), bright white below with a restricted blackish carpal-ulnar bar. Might be confused with Buller's Shearwater or, if size is badly misjudged, with much smaller *Cookilaria* petrels. Also see light morph Wedge-tailed Shearwater.
   Buller's Shearwater similar in size and has superficially gadfly-like patterning, but blackish cap reaches to bill (no white forehead) and upperwings have contrasting broad pale panel on greater coverts. Buller's also has broader wings, longer neck, smaller head, and slender bill, all quite different from Juan; Buller's buoyant flight lacks confident, higher wheeling of gadfly petrels.
   Hawaiian and Galapagos petrels slightly smaller. In fresh plumage their upperparts have gray sheen with blacker M pattern that might suggest Juan.

Juan is larger and slightly broader winged than Hawaiian, with paler gray hindneck and back, a more contrasting black mask, and overall white underparts that lack broad black wing margins; in poor lighting, however, when no plumage features are apparent, these species can appear similar and are not always safely distinguished at a distance.
   Cookilaria petrels much smaller, shorter winged, and shorter tailed, with smaller bills and quicker, snappier flight that is notably more erratic in moderate to strong winds. Cook's has pale gray cap with no distinct black eye patch, Stejneger's has dark slaty cap that often appears to cut down on neck sides forward of wings.
   White-necked Petrel (breeds Dec–Jun in Kermadec Islands, ranges into cen Pacific, L 41–44 cm, WS 103–110 cm, tail 125–135 mm [graduation 30–35 mm]; P30a.1–P30a.3) may occur off Middle America, but no confirmed records (perhaps most likely Apr–Oct). Size, shape, and flight manner all much like Juan although tail less graduated; can be difficult to distinguish from white-necked Juans, which are quite frequent (Spear et al. 1992). White-necked Petrel has sooty-black cap (cap and eye patch similarly dark) that contrasts more sharply with white hindneck; underwings have more-extensive dark edging, with black lesser primary coverts (perhaps matched by some first-cycle Juans?); mostly white outer rectrices are vermiculated dusky (whitish with broad, well-marked blackish tips on Juan), and dusky chest side smudges average larger than on Juan.

Habitat and Behavior Pelagic, over tropical and subtropical waters. Found singly or in loose foraging or rafting aggregations, in the region typically of 5–20 birds. Associates readily with mixed-species feeding flocks of other petrels, shearwaters, and terns, often over schooling yellowfin tuna.
   In calm to light winds flight leisurely, meandering or weaving low over the water with easy, clipped wingbeats, buoyant glides, and low wheeling arcs, the flexed wings pressed forward and slightly crooked at the carpals. Feeding birds often fly erratically with deep, powerful wingbeats, swooping over the surface to snatch prey,

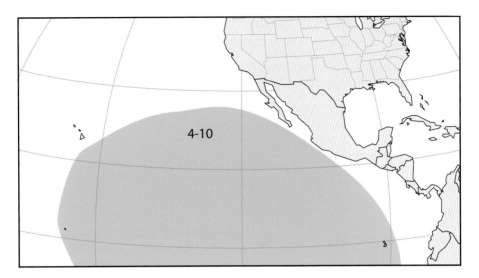

including flyingfish taken in mid-air. In moderate to strong winds flight across the wind fast and wheeling, with high arcs and no flapping or short bursts of a few quick flaps; at other times wheels fairly low, especially when flying into the wind.

Description Large gadfly petrel with long pointed wings, fairly long tapered tail, and stout bill. Medium wing-loading.

Ages similar but juveniles fresh in May–Aug when most older birds worn or in wing molt. Crown, hindneck, and upperparts gray (darker and browner when worn) with a darker cap and black eye patch, blackish M pattern, and slaty gray tail; white mottling sometimes apparent on uppertail coverts is exposed white feather bases. Gray back often appears contrastingly paler than dark upperwings, especially in strong light.

Underparts bright white with black tips to primaries, a very narrow black trailing edge, and variable black carpal mark. Carpal mark varies from simply a spot or droplet to a short bar, and lesser primary coverts white or with some dark markings; juveniles may average more extensive black carpal-ulnar bar (study needed). Outer rectrices broadly tipped blackish, with clean-cut white bases to inner webs. Some worn and molting birds (mainly Oct–Dec) have hindneck mottled to extensively white (Spear et al. 1992). Bill black, legs and feet bicolored pale pinkish and black.

On the water. Dark above with white neck, dark cap, and variable gray on hindneck (can be mostly white); sides and undertail coverts white.

Molt Wing molt mainly Apr–Sep.

P30.2. Compared to small gadfly petrels with similar plumage patterns, Juan Fernandez Petrel has relatively longer, bigger wings, a stout bill, and often shows white mottling on uppertail coverts. SW. Eastern Pacific, 8°N 97°W, 21 Oct 2006.

P30.1. Juan Fernandez Petrel is a large gadfly petrel with very long wings, variable dark cap (cf. P30.2–P30.5), and dark M pattern above. SW. Eastern Pacific, 15°N 157°W, 1 Nov 2005.

P30.3. (Above) Juan Fernandez Petrel in fresh plumage with unusually even gray hindneck and blackish cap (cf. P30.1–P30.2, P30.4–P30.6). AJ. Juan Fernandez Islands, Chile, 26 Nov 2005.

P30.4. (Above right) Juan Fernandez Petrel showing contrast between fresh gray back feathers and worn brown upperwings; note head pattern, big bill. RLeV. Eastern tropical Pacific, 14 Apr 2006.

P30.5. (Right) In worn plumage, perhaps mainly first-year birds, Juan Fernandez Petrel can show variable white hindneck, at times more extensive and clean-cut than shown here. SW. Eastern Pacific, 14°N 116°W, 30 Nov 2006.

P30.6. Juan Fernandez Petrel with inner primary molt. White stripe on upperwing made up of bases of secondaries exposed by shed greater coverts; note gray hindneck, diffuse blackish cap (cf. P30a.1). RLeV. Eastern tropical Pacific, 16 Apr 2006.

P30a.1. White-necked Petrel starting inner primary molt. Note relatively thick neck and large head with well-defined white hindcollar and black cap (cf. P30.6). RLeV. Eastern tropical Pacific, 10 Apr 2006.

P30.7. Juan Fernandez Petrel with mid-primary molt; note grayish hindneck, sooty cap (cf. P30a.2). RLeV. Eastern tropical Pacific, 15 Apr 2006.

P30a.2. White-necked Petrel. Note well-defined black cap and white hindneck (cf. P30.7). SNGH. North Island, New Zealand, 31 Mar 2008.

P30.8. Juan Fernandez Petrel with mid-primary molt. Note shape, bright white underwings with only a small black carpal spot (cf. P30a.3); some individuals, like this, have relatively white faces. RLeV. Eastern tropical Pacific, 15 Apr 2006.

P30a.3. White-necked Petrel. Note well-defined black cap and dark chest spur, relatively extensive black on underwings (cf. P30.9). SNGH. North Island, New Zealand, 31 Mar 2008.

P30.9. Juan Fernandez Petrel with mid-primary molt. Note big wings, relatively small head and long tapered tail, distinctive head/neck pattern, and extensively white underwings. RLeV. Eastern tropical Pacific, 15 Apr 2006.

P30.10. Juan Fernandez Petrel with outer primary molt. Note overall shape, head/neck pattern, extensively white underwings. SW. Eastern Pacific, 9°N 121°W, 9 Aug 2006.

P30.11. Juan Fernandez Petrel with mid-primary molt. Head-on, note head/neck pattern, big wings that are mostly white below. RLeV. Eastern tropical Pacific, 14 Apr 2006.

P31. MURPHY'S PETREL *Pterodroma ultima*

L 34.5–37 cm, WS 89–97 cm, tail 105–120 mm (graduation 30–35 mm)
Figures 127, 131, P31.1–P31.11

Identification Summary Pacific. A medium-sized, fairly stocky-bodied subtropical gadfly petrel with fairly narrow wings, medium-long tail, and fairly high wing-loading. Flight bounding in windy conditions. Plumage dark grayish overall (glossy gray above in fresh plumage with a darker hood and blackish M pattern above) with silvery flashes under primaries.

P31.1. Murphy's Petrel is a medium-sized, dark-bellied gadfly petrel that arcs steeply in strong winds. Note silvery underwing flashes, extensive whitish mottling on throat, and relatively small bill. MS. Northern California, 29 Apr 2008.

Taxonomy Monotypic.

Names *Pterodroma* means "winged runner"; *ultima* refers to the (mistaken) belief that this species would be the last species of *Pterodroma* to be described. The English name commemorates U.S. ornithologist Robert Cushman Murphy (1887–1973).

Status and Distribution Near Threatened. Breeds (mainly Jun–Dec, perhaps varying among islands and between years) in tropical s-cen Pacific Ocean, ranging (mainly Nov–May) to ne Pacific and (Jul–Aug, at least) to waters off w South America (pers. obs.).
    Pacific. Apparently an irregular nonbreeding visitor (perhaps year-round) from California n to Gulf of Alaska, but mainly well offshore.

Most frequently recorded Feb–Jun (mainly Apr–May) from California to British Columbia, with hundreds found some years off California in mid-Apr to early May, but few to none in other years when birds may be farther offshore. Birds completing primary molt in Mar–Apr, and in fresh plumage Apr–May, suggest these are returning s to the breeding islands. Very rare off West Coast in Jul–early Dec (M. P. Force, pers. comm.; NAB 60:127, 2006; Pyle 2006), presumably nonbreeding immatures. Northernmost records are in Jul far offshore (beyond 370 km) in Gulf of Alaska (to 54°N) (Bailey et al. 1989). Records e of Hawaii are mainly Oct–Dec, including apparent northbound migrants (pers. obs.). This suggests postbreeding migration into n cen Pacific, with numbers of birds seen off the West Coast being an irregular phenomenon at the edge of the main

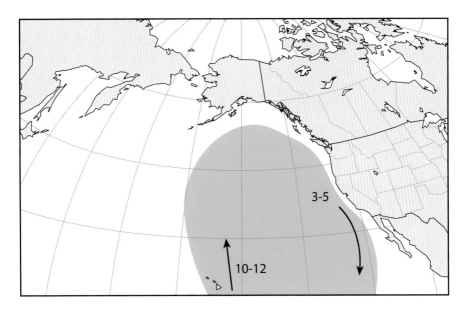

loop for birds returning s after molting, and with immatures lingering later (a pattern similar to that of Buller's and Short-tailed shearwaters). A Mar–Nov counterclockwise loop migration in the e and cen n Pacific has also been suggested (Bartle et al. 1993), but seems contrary to molt and breeding cycles.

FIELD IDENTIFICATION

Similar Species This is the "expected" dark gadfly petrel off the West Coast, but separation from larger Solander's Petrel (status in region unclear) is notoriously problematic under at-sea conditions and for observers unfamiliar with one or both species; also see dark morph Kermadec and Herald petrels (of tropical waters).

Sooty and Short-tailed shearwaters larger overall and heavier bodied with smaller heads, slender bills, narrower wings, and shorter tails. Both lack buoyant and bounding flight of Murphy's. Sooty in particular has hurried wingbeats, and holds its wings straighter and slightly bowed; in calm to light winds it flies with hurried, almost urgent flaps that course through the whole wing as it tries to stay aloft, and its glides are low and usually level; Murphy's Petrel, by contrast, is comfortable and buoyant even in light winds. In windy conditions, Sooties often wheel steeply but lack the confident grace of gadfly petrels. Any silvery-white underwing flashes on the shearwaters are concentrated across the coverts, not the primary bases. On the water, shearwaters often sit lower and more hunched, and look smaller headed.

Solander's Petrel larger overall (a large *Pterodroma*, vs. the medium-sized Murphy's) with longer wings and a bigger bill. Flight typically less bounding, with lower, more measured wheeling in longer-wavelength arcs. Plumage similar to Murphy's but Solander's hood darker, with noticeable contrast also on underparts (may be matched by worn Murphy's), and underwing has bold double white flashes (on primaries and primary coverts) that are usually visible at long range and not reflective, as is typical of Murphy's (but Murphy's in some lights can show similar underwing pattern). Whitish around bill base of Solander's often as extensive above bill as on chin (mainly on chin in Murphy's). Until variation in underwing pattern of Murphy's is studied critically, at-sea identification of some birds will remain problematic.

Christmas Shearwater (tropics) slightly smaller, shorter-winged, and more lightly built with a smaller head and slender bill; plumage dark chocolate-brown overall; flies with quick stiff wingbeats and buoyant glides mostly low to the water.

Habitat and Behavior Pelagic, mainly over subtropical waters. Found singly or in aggregations up to tens of birds, such as migrating or resting on the water, when can associate loosely with other species such as Sooty Shearwaters.

In calm to light winds, flies with easy, fairly quick, and flicking wingbeats and buoyant wheeling glides low to the water, the slightly arched wings pressed forward and slightly crooked. Sometimes in calm or light winds flies up to 10 m or so above the water on a level course with fairly steady wingbeats and short glides, when may suggest a jaeger. In moderate to strong winds, flight strong and fast, often bounding high in steep wheeling arcs across the wind, at times almost flipping upside down at the top of a climb; at other times wheels fairly low, especially when flying into the wind.

Description A medium-sized, fairly plump-bodied gadfly petrel with fairly narrow wings and medium-long tail. Relatively high wing-loading.

Ages similar but juveniles fresh in Nov–Dec when adults at their most worn. Dark sooty gray overall with glossy gray sheen to back and greater coverts strongest in fresh plumage (Mar–Aug at least); browner overall when worn. Head and neck often look darker from above, creating a variable hooded effect, and variable whitish throat patch usually apparent at closer range; some birds have whitish scalloping or mottling on the forehead, but this is less extensive than white throat patch, and some birds have whitish so limited that unlikely to be visible at sea. Dark M pattern on upperwings can be seen even at moderate to long range in good light. Underwings dark with variable paler to silvery-white flash across primary bases (usually poorly contrasting in dull conditions, striking in bright or high-contrast lighting, and tending to blend outward to tips rather than being sharply defined) and less so on secondary bases; can show reflective whitish crescent across bases of primary coverts. Bill black, legs and feet bicolored pale pinkish and black.

On the water. Dark grayish overall with variable whitish throat patch.

Molt Wing molt probably occurs mainly Oct–Apr but few data. Beached birds in North America have been completing wing molt in Mar (Bailey et al. 1989) and most birds seen off California in Apr–May appear to be in fresh plumage or with p10 growing in late Apr (CAS specimen 84182).

P31.2. Murphy's Petrel in fairly fresh plumage, thus with strong gray tones above and distinct darker hood. Compared to Solander's Petrel, note relatively small wings, short thick neck, small bill. CC. Pitcairn Islands, Central South Pacific, 15 Jun 2006.

P31.3. Even in rather worn plumage, Murphy's Petrel typically shows gray sheen above; molt contrasts in secondaries indicate a bird older than its first cycle (cf. P31.4). Also note stocky shape with thick neck, relatively small bill. PH. Oeno Island, Central South Pacific, 4 Oct 2005.

P31.4. Murphy's Petrel in uniformly fresh plumage (presumably a juvenile on this date) showing strong silvery sheen to upperparts. Note stocky shape, extensive whitish on throat, relatively small bill. ABD. Hawaii, 20 Dec 2009.

P31.5. In some lights, like this, Murphy's Petrel shows a variable dark M pattern above; also note contrast between fresh gray and worn brown feathers on back. MS. Northern California, 24 Apr 2008.

P31.6. Thick neck of Murphy's Petrel often makes head appear relatively small; note relatively small bill, extent of whitish on face (some birds have essentially no white on face). PH. Oeno Island, Central South Pacific, 4 Oct 2005.

P31.7. In even lighting, underparts of Murphy's Petrel appear overall similar in tone, or with head and neck only subtly darker; silvery underwing flashes typically stronger on primaries than on primary coverts (cf. P31.8–P31.10). CC. Pitcairn Islands, Central South Pacific, 11 Jun 2006.

P31.8. Murphy's Petrel. Note stocky shape with relatively small head, fairly even-toned underparts. Silvery underwing flashes here resemble Solander's Petrel but relatively muted (cf. P32.5–P32.8). MS. Northern California, 29 Apr 2008.

P31.9. Murphy's Petrel, presumed juvenile (same bird as P31.4). Compared to Solander's Petrel, note extensive white on throat, dull primary coverts. ABD. Hawaii, 20 Dec 2009.

P31.10. Depending on lighting, Murphy's Petrel can appear strongly dark-hooded; note muted silvery wing flashes (cf. P32.5–P32.8). CC. Pitcairn Islands, Central South Pacific, 9 Jun 2006.

P31.11. Murphy's Petrel in slightly worn plumage. Note relatively small bill, extensive whitish mottling on face, including throat (some birds have almost no white and appear dark-faced in the field). PH. Oeno Island, Central South Pacific, 4 Oct 2005.

P32. SOLANDER'S PETREL *Pterodroma solandri*

L 43–46 cm, WS 100–107 cm, tail 120–130 mm (graduation 30–35 mm)
Figures 128, 132–133, P32.1–P32.10

Identification Summary North Pacific; status in North American waters unclear (see Status and Distribution). A large subtropical *Pterodroma* resembling Murphy's Petrel in plumage but with bigger wings, thicker head/neck projection, very stout bill.

Taxonomy Monotypic.

Names *Pterodroma* means "winged runner"; *solandri* and the English name commemorate D. C. Solander (1733–1782), the Swedish botanist who accompanied James Cook on his first voyage. Also known as Providence Petrel, as it enabled the former penal colony on Norfolk Island to survive a famine; the petrel has since been exterminated from the island by feral pigs.

Status and Distribution Vulnerable. Breeds (May–Nov) in subtropical sw Pacific Ocean, ranging (mainly Nov–May) to nw Pacific. Nonbreeding immatures may wander into North American waters but more study needed.

Pacific. A bird photographed about 45 km w of Vancouver Island, British Columbia, 6 Oct 2009 (NAB 64:186 2010), shows an underwing pattern like Solander's Petrel but its overall structure and bill size appear more like Murphy's Petrel; expert opinion is divided on this bird's identity. Other reports of Solander's in the region come from waters s of the Aleutians and in n Gulf of Alaska (Aug 1994; M. P. Force, pers. comm.), Washington (Sep 1983; Wahl et al. 2005), and Oregon (Apr 1994; M. P. Force, pers. comm.); none is substantiated with satisfactory photos, and separation from Murphy's Petrel is notoriously problematic. For example, a photo from n California suggested to be Solander's (Pyle 2006) appears to show a Murphy's Petrel. Just outside U.S. waters, several Solander's Petrels were photographed w of the Aleutians in Sep 2006 (M. J. Iliff, pers. comm.), and it seems only a matter of time before an unequivocal North American occurrence is substantiated.

FIELD IDENTIFICATION

Similar Species An enigmatic species to most North American observers, having a long history of being confused with similarly plumaged Murphy's Petrel; also see dark morph Kermadec and Herald petrels (of more tropical waters).

Murphy's Petrel somewhat smaller and slighter (a medium-sized *Pterodroma*, vs. the large Solander's) with smaller, narrower wings and smaller, slimmer bill; size of lone birds, however, can be difficult to judge. Flight typically more bounding, less measured, with higher and more impetuous wheeling in moderate to strong winds. Plumage similar to Solander's but not as strongly dark-hooded (especially below) and underwing typically lacks bold and well-defined double white flashes (but can appear similar to Solander's depending on lighting, and variation in underwing pattern of Murphy's not well known); whitish around bill base of Murphy's tends to be more extensive on chin than above bill.

Sooty and Short-tailed shearwaters are heavier bodied with smaller heads, slender bills, narrower wings, and shorter tails. Both lack the buoyant flight of Solander's. Except in strong winds, both fly with bursts of quick wingbeats; in windy conditions Sooty often wheels steeply but lacks the confident grace of *Pterodroma* petrels. Any silvery-white underwing flashes on the shearwaters are concentrated across the coverts, not the primary bases.

Gray-faced Petrel similarly large and dark with whitish around base of bill but chestier in build, with slightly bigger bill, slightly broader wings, and shorter tail. Plumage dark sooty brown overall, lacking gray sheen or any M pattern; underwings lack bold double white flashes but remiges sometimes reflect dull silvery in bright light.

Habitat and Behavior Pelagic, mainly over subtropical waters. Found singly or in loose aggregations of a few birds; might associate with other species but as likely to be found alone.

In calm to light winds, flies with easy, powerful wingbeats and buoyant wheeling glides low to the water. In moderate to strong winds, flight strong and fast, often bounding fairly high in wheeling, long-wavelength arcs across the wind; at other times stays fairly low, especially when flying into the wind.

Description A large, fairly heavy-bodied gadfly petrel with big, long wings and medium-long tail. Moderate wing-loading.

Ages similar but juveniles fresh in Nov–Dec when adults at their most worn. Dark sooty gray overall with glossy gray sheen to back and greater coverts strongest in fresh plumage (Feb–Jul at least); browner overall when worn. Head and neck darkest, creating a hooded effect most pronounced in worn plumage (mainly Aug–Dec); variable whitish patch around base of bill usually more extensive above (especially in lores) than below bill. Dark M pattern on upperwings can be seen even at moderate to long range in good light. Underwings dark with bold, well-defined silvery-white double-flash across bases of primaries and primary coverts. Bill black, legs and feet blackish overall or with some yellowish basally.

On the water. Dark grayish overall with thick bill, variable whitish patch around base of bill.

Molt Wing molt of breeding adults presumably Oct/Nov–Feb/Mar; PB2 wing molt may occur Aug–Dec, but no data.

P32.1. Solander's Petrel in fresh plumage with strong silvery sheen to upperparts. Compared to Murphy's Petrel, note big wings, longer and more evenly thick head/neck projection, stout bill, blackish hood. PH. New South Wales, Australia, 10 Apr 2004.

P32.2. Solander's Petrel in fresh plumage. Lighting greatly affects intensity of silvery sheen on upperparts (cf. P32.1, P32.3). At this angle, extent of whitish in face not appreciably different from Murphy's Petrel; note stout bill. PH. New South Wales, Australia, 10 Apr 2004.

P32.3. (Above) Solander's Petrel in fresh plumage. Lighting greatly affects intensity of silvery sheen on upperparts, which here appear muted (cf. P32.1–P32.2). PH. New South Wales, Australia, 30 Mar 2003.

P32.4. (Above right) Solander's Petrel in worn plumage. Relatively brown-toned, with gray sheen reduced (cf. P32.1–P32.3). Compared to Murphy's Petrel, note big wings, longer and more evenly thick head/neck projection, stout bill. TP. New South Wales, Australia, 21 Oct 2007.

P32.5. (Right) Solander's Petrel. At some angles, wings can appear relatively narrow, suggesting Murphy's Petrel; note dark hood, double white wing flashes, stout bill, face pattern. PH. New South Wales, Australia, 9 Apr 2004.

P32.6. Solander's Petrel in fresh plumage (cf. P32.7). Note long broad wings with bold double white flashes, dark hood, whitish around base of bill most prominent on lores. PH. New South Wales, Australia, 30 Mar 2003.

P32.7. Solander's Petrel in worn plumage (cf. P32.6). Note big wings with prominent double white flashes, contrasting dark hood, relatively long and thick head/neck projection, stout bill (cf. P31.7). TP. New South Wales, Australia, 21 Oct 2007.

P32.8. Solander's Petrel in somewhat worn plumage (cf. P32.6–P32.7). Note face pattern, big bill, underwing pattern, overall structure. PH. New South Wales, Australia, 16 Aug 2003.

P32.9. Even at long range, double white wing flashes of Solander's Petrel are often striking, especially in bright light; also note long body, big long wings, contrasting dark hood. SNGH. Western Pacific, 23°S 166°E, 1 Apr 2007.

P32.10. Besides larger size and bulk, Solander's Petrel on the water distinguished from Murphy's by appreciably stouter bill; also, whitish on face tends to be more extensive above bill than below, the reverse of Murphy's. TP. New South Wales, Australia, 12 Oct 2001.

P33. GRAY-FACED [GREAT-WINGED] PETREL *Pterodroma [macroptera] gouldi*
L 42–45 cm, WS 105–113 cm, tail 122–140 mm (graduation 25–35 mm)
Figures 134, P33.1–P33.5

Identification Summary Pacific; accidental off California. A large, all-dark gadfly petrel with a very stout black bill; whitish face recalls Black-footed Albatross.

Taxonomy Morphological differences between the two described taxa of Great-winged Petrel are greater than between some recognized species of *Pterodroma*. Thus, Great-winged Petrel is treated here as two species, as also done by Onley and Scofield (2007). Measurements below are from Murphy and Pennoyer (1952).

P. [m.] gouldi (Gray-faced Petrel) breeds New Zealand, ranges in sw Pacific w at least to Australia. Averages larger (wing chord 305–330 mm, tail 122–140 mm), bill stouter (bill depth 12–13.5 mm), tail less strongly graduated (25–30 mm), moderate to extensive whitish to pale grayish around base of bill, and black eye patch small.

P. [m.] macroptera (Great-winged Petrel) breeds s Indian and s Atlantic oceans, ranges from s Atlantic e to s Australia. Averages smaller (wing chord 298–319 mm, tail 105–125 mm), bill less stout (bill depth 11.2–12.1 mm), tail more strongly graduated (30–35 mm), reduced whitish to pale brownish around base of bill, and black eye patch larger.

Names *Pterodroma* means "winged runner"; *macroptera* means "big-winged" and *gouldi* commemorates English naturalist John Gould (1804–1881).

Status and Distribution Least Concern. Breeds (May–Nov) New Zealand. Ranges in sw Pacific, mainly s of 30˚S; unrecorded in e South Pacific (Marchant & Higgins 1995).

Pacific. Accidental (Jul–Aug 1996, Oct 1998) off cen California, perhaps the same bird (*P. [m.] gouldi*) involved in both records.

FIELD IDENTIFICATION

Similar Species A distinctive species about the size of Flesh-footed Shearwater. Note large size, long wings, buoyant flight, all-dark plumage, and very stout black bill. Whitish face of *gouldi* can suggest Black-footed Albatross. Also see Kermadec and Herald petrels of generally warmer tropical waters.

Murphy's Petrel (the "expected" dark *Pterodroma* off the West Coast) is smaller with proportionately shorter wings and longer tail, and a smaller bill. Its higher wing-loading results in more bounding, impetuous flight. Especially in fresh plumage, Murphy's has glossy gray upperparts with distinct blackish M pattern; whitish on throat can suggest Gray-faced from below, but Murphy's lacks extensive white on forehead.

Flesh-footed Shearwater similarly dark brown overall but slender bill bright pink with black tip, flight generally heavier and lower, but in moderate to strong winds can wheel high and suggest a gadfly petrel.

Sooty and Short-tailed shearwaters heavier bodied with smaller heads, slender bills, narrower wings, and shorter tails. Both lack buoyant flight of Gray-faced. Except in strong winds, both fly with bursts of quick wingbeats; in windy conditions Sooty often wheels steeply but lacks the confident grace of *Pterodroma* petrels. Any silvery-white underwing flashes on the shearwaters are concentrated across the coverts, not the primary bases.

Solander's Petrel similarly large and dark with whitish around base of bill, but less chesty in build, with slightly smaller bill, slightly narrower wings, and longer tail; underwings have bold double white flashes (on primaries and primary coverts) usually visible at long range. Especially in fresh plumage, Solander's has glossy gray upperparts with distinct blackish M pattern and dark hood.

Habitat and Behavior Pelagic, over subtropical waters. May be found alone or with other species, and at times scavenges from fishing boats where associates with gulls, other petrels, shearwaters, etc.

In calm to light winds, flight fairly buoyant with prolonged gliding and long-wavelength wheeling arcs interspersed with languid flapping, the flexed wings pressed forward and crooked at the carpals. In moderate to strong winds, flies with high, wheeling arcs, at times pausing at the apex of a climb before sweeping down strongly.

Description Large, long-winged gadfly petrel with medium-length tail and very thick bill. Fairly low wing-loading.

Ages similar. Blackish brown overall, fresh plumage glossier with a slight grayish bloom above, and worn plumage browner overall; whitish to dull pale grayish around base of bill usually distinct, often forming conspicuous white frontal "blaze" from forehead to throat. Head and chest often appear slightly darker than underparts. In bright light, underwings often show dull silvery flash across primary bases, and upperparts rarely show faint darker M pattern. Bill black, legs and feet blackish.

On the water. Dark sooty brown overall with very thick bill, whitish blaze around base of bill.

Molt Wing molt in s hemisphere mainly Nov–Apr (Marchant & Higgins 1990); a California bird growing p10 in mid-Oct suggests its molt had switched to n hemisphere schedule (pers. obs.).

P33.2. Gray-faced Petrels in fresh plumage. Extent of eponymous "gray face" rather variable. SNGH. New Zealand, 33°S 172°E, 4 Apr 2008.

P33.1. Gray-faced Petrel in fresh plumage. Note dark chocolate-brown plumage without distinct gray tones, prominent whitish around base of bill. SNGH. North Island, New Zealand, 31 Mar 2008.

P33.3. (Right) Head-on, whitish face of Gray-faced Petrel can be striking and may recall Black-footed Albatross. SNGH. New Zealand, 31°S 170°E, 29 Mar 2008.

P33.4. (Below) In some lights, Gray-faced Petrel appears vaguely hooded. Underwings are dark overall but, like many species, primaries can flash silvery in bright light. SNGH. Southwest of Chatham Islands, New Zealand, 22 Nov 2008.

P33.5. Gray-faced Petrel. Note dark brown plumage without distinct gray tones, very stout bill. SNGH. North Island, New Zealand, 31 Mar 2008.

P34. KERMADEC PETREL *Pterodroma neglecta*

L 37–40 cm, WS 97–106 cm, tail 101–113 mm (graduation 5–15 mm)
Figures 129, P34.1–P34.14

Identification Summary Pacific. A medium-large, fairly thickset, polymorphic gadfly petrel with long, fairly broad wings, relatively short squared tail, and fairly low wing-loading. Plumage strongly recalls jaegers and skuas. Upperwings dark with white primary shafts, underwings dark with bold white flashes on primaries and primary coverts. Dark morph brown overall. Light morph has head and underparts whitish overall, or head and chest variably dark, with partial to complete dark chest band; some birds have dusky-washed underparts.

Taxonomy Two subspecies described, not distinguishable at sea. Nominate *neglecta* (breeds widely) averages smaller (wing chord 274–305 mm, tail 92–107 mm); subspecies *juana* (breeds Juan Fernandez and other islands off Chile) averages larger (wing chord 290–309 mm, tail 101–113 mm) (Murphy & Pennoyer 1952). Within breeding populations, dark morphs predominate in e Pacific, with light morphs commoner in sw Pacific.

Names *Pterodroma* means "winged runner"; *neglecta* refers to how the type specimen had been mislabeled and neglected for nine years before being recognized as a distinct species. The English name refers to the subtropical Kermadec Islands, n of New Zealand, where the species breeds commonly.

Status and Distribution Least Concern. Breeds (mainly Nov–May but locally year-round) in subtropical South Pacific and ranges n to 40°N in cen Pacific. Recently reported nesting in Indian Ocean (Brooke et al. 2000); reports of a South Atlantic population (Imber 2004) require verification (Tove 2005).

Pacific. Uncommon nonbreeding visitor (late Feb–Oct at least) off Middle America, n to around 20°N. About 80% of birds in this region are dark morph (pers. obs.; M.P. Force, pers. comm.; L.B. Spear, pers. comm.).

Atlantic. A record accepted as Kermadec Petrel from Pennsylvania (Heintzelman 1961, AOU 1998) may be of this species or of Trinidade Petrel (Hess 1997).

FIELD IDENTIFICATION

Similar Species Kermadec's plumage is as similar to skuas and jaegers as to other petrels; in particular, birds sitting on the water with nothing for scale can be hard to distinguish from skuas until they take flight. Most similar petrel is Herald Petrel (following account, which see for differences). All shearwaters and petrels in molt may show white wing flashes but these are usually on secondary bases or coverts, or limited to one white stripe in the primaries.

Jaegers (particularly immatures with little or no tail projection) wheeling high in windy conditions can be mistaken for Kermadec Petrel, and a steadily flapping petrel well above the water (usually in calm conditions) could be mistaken for a jaeger. Jaegers have longer necks, more tapered head and neck projections, wingbeats typically more gull-like with wings more crooked, and bills lack raised tubes at base. Immature jaegers often have barred underwings, adults have projecting central rectrices.

Dark morph. *South Polar Skua* much larger and chunkier overall with shorter and broader wings, bolder white wing flashes above, and a more powerful, flapping flight; on the water skuas often look thicker necked but, when size cannot be judged, Kermadecs can be mistaken easily for skuas.

Christmas Shearwater (tropical waters) slightly smaller and more lightly built with a longer tail and slender bill, lacks white primary flashes (but underside of primaries can reflect silvery). Flight generally lower with bursts of rapid, stiff wingbeats and quicker wheeling in windy conditions.

Murphy's Petrel (subtropical waters) slightly smaller but longer tailed and fatter-bodied, with higher wing-loading; thus, in windy conditions, Murphy's has faster and more bounding flight, with steeper wheeling. Murphy's is glossy gray above in fresh plumage, typically with dark hood and fairly distinct dark M pattern; underwings have more diffuse, reflective flash across primary bases, with no second flash on primary coverts.

Solander's Petrel (subtropical waters) larger with longer, narrower wings and bigger bill; flight often with longer-wavelength arcs, but wheels high in windy conditions. Plumage grayer overall (glossy gray above in fresh plumage) with contrasting dark hood, dark M pattern on upperparts; white underwing flash on primaries typically narrows on outer primaries (where typically broadest on Kermadec).

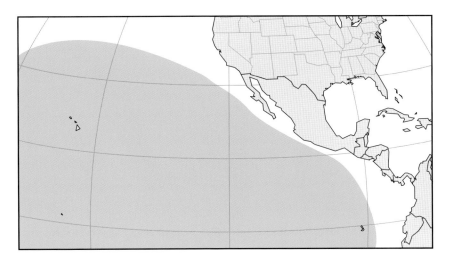

Light morph. See jaegers (above) and Herald Petrel. Some light morphs are so white-headed they can suggest White-headed Petrel (*P. lessoni*) of temperate Southern Ocean, but that species has whitish rump and tail, lacks white wing flashes, and gray upperparts have dark M pattern recalling Mottled Petrel.

Habitat and Behavior Pelagic over warmer offshore waters. As likely to be found alone as associating with mixed-species feeding flocks of other petrels, such as over schooling fish or dolphins. Taking advantage of their jaeger-like plumage, Kermadecs sometimes pirate other large petrels and shearwaters (Spear & Ainley 1993).

In light winds, flight relatively heavy and leisurely, usually low over the water with deep, powerful wingbeats and low, wheeling glides on flexed wings; in moderate to strong winds flight faster, with prolonged gliding and long-wavelength, relatively low wheeling arcs, the wings often more crooked; also towers high and easily in strong winds. Pursuit flight of other petrels and large shearwaters is fairly agile, changing easily in a single stroke from wheeling gadfly flight to deep, powerful, steady wingbeats much like a large jaeger.

Description Medium-large, fairly thickset gadfly petrel with long, relatively broad wings and relatively short, squared tail. Fairly low wing-loading. Ages similar.

Dark morph. Dark sooty brown to brown overall, the head and underbody of some birds contrastingly paler and warmer, medium-brown. Upperwings with white primary shafts forming variable white flash, noticeable at moderate range. Underwings dark with bold, skua-like white flash across primary bases, and often a narrow white crescent on dark-tipped primary coverts. White bases to rectrix shafts rarely visible at sea. Exceptionally, undersides of primaries can be silvery gray, lacking skua-like flashes (Spear et al. 1992). Paler birds in particular can have a narrow strip of whitish mottling on greater and median underwing coverts. Some birds have whitish on throat or around base of bill, often forming a "noseband" across the lores. Bill black; legs and feet blackish overall, or bicolored pale pinkish and black.

Light morph. On lightest birds, whitish head and underparts contrast with dark brown to gray-brown upperparts, dark underwings, and dark distal undertail coverts; often the head and chest are mottled dusky, with variable chest band, and flanks are mottled gray-brown. Darker birds have dark brown head and chest, white throat and underbody, or underbody can be washed dusky. Wing pattern resembles dark morph but usually with more whitish mottling on median and greater coverts. Legs and feet bicolored pale pinkish and black.

On the water. Dark morphs brown overall or with head and neck paler than back (recalling South Polar Skua); light morphs whitish headed or with variable whitish on throat, chest, and undertail coverts. Sides whitish with variable brown mottling.

Hybrids On Round Island, Indian Ocean, appears to be hybridizing extensively with Trinidade Petrel (Brown et al. 2010).

Molt Given potential year-round breeding, wing molt may occur in any month.

P34.1. Dark morph Kermadec Petrel. Note stocky shape, bright white primary shafts. CC. Pitcairn Islands, Central South Pacific, 15 Jun 2006.

P34.2. Light morph Kermadec Petrel with very dark brown upperparts (most are somewhat paler above; cf. P34.3). Note stocky shape, bright white primary shafts. CC. Pitcairn Islands, Central South Pacific, 11 Jun 2006.

P34.3. Light morph Kermadec Petrel with typical, dark gray-brown upperparts (cf. P34.2). CC. Pitcairn Islands, Central South Pacific, 11 Jun 2006.

P34.4. Plumage pattern of Kermadec Petrel recalls a skua or jaeger; resemblance to a jaeger enhanced here by tail molt. At a distance, white primary shafts only visible on old, bleached outermost primary (cf. P34.5). SNGH. Western Pacific, 26°S 167°E, 7 Apr 2008.

P34.5. Light morph Kermadec Petrel with bleached whitish head and mid-primary molt (shafts to older, faded primaries much more striking than on fresh feathers; cf. P34.4). SNGH. Western Pacific, 21°N 145°E, 28 Apr 2008.

P34.6. Underparts of dark morph Kermadec Petrel often slightly paler than underwings. Note relatively short broad tail (cf. P35a.5, P35b.4). White flash on primaries relatively broad on p10 (cf. P32.6–P32.8). AJ. Easter Island, Chile, 16 Feb 2009.

P34.7. Dark morph Kermadec Petrel with relatively pale body. Compared to South Polar Skua, note relatively long narrow wings and slender body. SNGH. Western Pacific, 30°N 141°E, 23 Apr 2007.

P34.8. Body of light morph Kermadec Petrel sometimes washed dusky. Note stocky shape, bold white primary flash. CC. Pitcairn Islands, Central South Pacific, 13 Jun 2006.

P34.9. (Below) Light morph Kermadec Petrel. Plumage pattern much like a jaeger, from which best distinguished by flight manner and, at close range, tubenose bill. SNGH. Western Pacific, 31°S 170°E, 29 Mar 2007.

P34.10. (Below right) Some light morph Kermadec Petrels, like this, have a contrastingly dark head and chest (cf. P34.11–P34.13). SNGH. Western Pacific, 31°S 170°E, 29 Mar 2007.

P34.11. Underwing of light morph Kermadec Petrel variable in terms of whitish on coverts (cf. P34.10, P34.12–P34.13). AJ. Easter Island, Chile, 16 Feb 2009.

P34.12. Plumage tones of light morph Kermadec Petrel vary with lighting (cf. P34.11). CC. Pitcairn Islands, Central South Pacific, 15 Jun 2006.

P34.14. Light morph Kermadec Petrel on the water can appear strikingly similar to light morph South Polar Skua but is appreciably smaller; also note tubenose bill. DLW. Hawaii, 28 Oct 2009.

P34.13. Some light morph Kermadec Petrels, like this, have extensive whitish on underwing coverts (cf. P34.10–P34.12). AJ. Easter Island, Chile, 16 Feb 2009.

P35A. HERALD PETREL *Pterodroma [heraldica] heraldica*
P35B. HENDERSON [HERALD] PETREL *Pterodroma [h.] atrata*

L 34.5–37 cm, WS 90–97 cm, tail 97–114 mm (graduation 20–25 mm)
Figures 130, P35a.1–P35a.5, P35b.1–P35b.5

Identification Summary Tropical Pacific. Herald Petrel is a medium-sized, lightly built gadfly petrel with fairly narrow wings, medium-long tail, and low wing-loading. It has an easy, buoyant flight. Some dark morph populations may comprise a separate species, Henderson Petrel (see Taxonomy). Because no criteria are known for at-sea separation of this cryptic taxon, it is combined here with Herald Petrel. Upperwings all-dark without white primary shafts. Darkest morph Herald (and Henderson Petrel) dark sooty brown overall with little or no paler flash under primary bases. Light morph Herald has white underparts with variable dark chest band, variable white wing flashes.

Taxonomy Vexed. Most authors treat Trinidade Petrel of Atlantic and Indian oceans as a separate species, *P. arminjoniana*. Within Pacific populations, specific status (as Henderson Petrel [*P. atrata*]) has been suggested for dark morph birds breeding on Henderson Island in the Pitcairn group, e Pacific (Brooke & Rowe 1996). Measurements between these proposed species overlap completely, vocalizations also overlap, and the only visible difference is the dark underbody of Henderson Petrels (simply dark tipping to the distal third of the feathers) (Brooke & Rowe 1996). Whether all dark morph Pacific birds are Henderson Petrels, or whether true dark morph Herald Petrels exist, are questions that remain unresolved.

Names *Pterodroma* means "winged runner"; *heraldica* and the English name commemorate the British ship HMS *Herald*, during whose explorations in the Pacific (1845–1851) the type specimen was collected; *atrata* means "clothed in black, as in mourning," in reference to the very dark plumage of Henderson Petrel.

Status and Distribution Herald Petrel (Least Concern) breeds (year-round, perhaps mainly Feb–Sep) in tropical South Pacific, ranges n at least to 25°N in cen Pacific. Henderson Petrel (Endangered) breeds (mainly May–Dec) at least on Henderson Island in Pitcairn Islands; at-sea range unclear.
   Pacific. Probably a rare nonbreeding visitor off Middle America n to around 15°N (recorded only in Oct, but may occur year-round; Howell & Webb 1995). Both light and dark birds have occurred, the latter perhaps most likely Henderson Petrels.

FIELD IDENTIFICATION

Similar Species Herald Petrel is a medium-sized, lightly built petrel with a medium-length tail, low wing-loading, and a distinctly buoyant, easy flight. Henderson Petrel not known to be distinguishable from darkest morph Herald Petrel (indeed, all darkest morph "Herald Petrels" may simply be Henderson Petrels; see Taxonomy); however, some observers suggest Henderson Petrel appears narrower winged than Herald Petrel (C. Collins, pers. comm.). Most likely to be confused with larger and bulkier Kermadec Petrel. Also cf. Christmas Shearwater, Murphy's and Solander's petrels. Some light morph Heralds are similar to Phoenix Petrel (*P. alba*, unrecorded in e Pacific).
   Jaegers (particularly immatures with little or no tail projection) wheeling high in windy conditions might be mistaken for Herald Petrel, and a steadily flapping petrel well above the water (usually in calm conditions) could be taken for a jaeger. Jaegers have relatively shorter and broader wings, with white flashes on upperside of primaries, head and neck projection more tapered (or pin-headed), and wingbeats typically more gull-like.
   Dark morph (and Henderson Petrel). *Kermadec Petrel* (mainly subtropical waters) larger and heavier (mean mass 370 g vs. 275 g of Herald; Spear et al. 1992) with relatively broader wings and shorter, less graduated tail creating a stockier overall appearance; flight of Kermadec also less buoyant, wheeling lower and less steeply across the wind in longer-wavelength arcs. Upperwings of Kermadec have white primary shafts (recalling jaegers), and upperparts lack subtle darker M pattern sometimes apparent on Herald. Underwings of darkest Heralds have dark to dull silvery bases of primaries and primary coverts (rarely appearing bright); conversely, underwings of darkest Kermadecs typically have bold white flashes

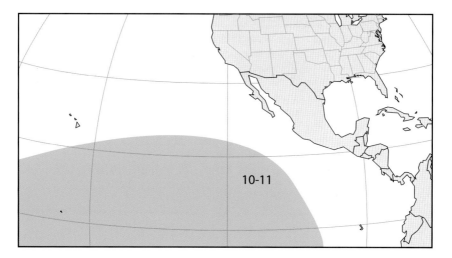

on primaries and primary coverts (exceptionally dark overall; Spear et al. 1992). Many Kermadecs paler and warmer brown on head and underparts than dark Herald, and some have whitish around base of bill, including a "noseband" across the lores (whitish on dark Herald less extensive, typically limited to chin and throat). Herald Petrels in molt can show white wing flashes, on secondary bases or coverts, or limited to one white stripe in the primaries.

Christmas Shearwater (tropical waters) somewhat similar in size, shape, and color but note thinner bill. Flight generally lower with bursts of rapid, stiff wingbeats and quicker, less graceful wheeling in windy conditions.

Murphy's Petrel (subtropical waters) fatter bodied, bigger headed, and heavier (mean mass 375 g vs. 275 g of Herald; Spear et al. 1992); thus, in windy conditions, Murphy's has faster flight with steeper wheeling. Upperparts glossy gray in fresh plumage, with distinct dark M pattern, typically with dark hood and more extensive white around base of bill, mainly on chin; underwings have reflective flash across primary bases.

Solander's Petrel (subtropical waters) larger and heavier bodied with longer, broader wings and bigger bill; flight lacks easy buoyancy of Herald Petrel and across the wind flies with lower, long-wavelength wheeling. Plumage resembles Murphy's Petrel, thus grayer overall with dark hood, dark M pattern on glossy gray upperparts, and bold white underwing flashes on primaries and primary coverts.

Light morph. *Kermadec Petrel* larger and heavier with broader wings and shorter, less graduated tail; flight less buoyant, wheeling lower and often less steeply across the wind. Upperwings of Kermadec have white primary shafts (recalling jaegers). Plumages of Herald largely parallel those of Kermadec but some light Keramdecs are whitish headed and lack a chest band (a plumage apparently not found in Herald), and Kermadec's chest band often diffuse and dusky (typically darker and more solid on Herald, although patterns overlap).

Phoenix Petrel (L 36–38 cm, WS 90–96 cm, tail 106–120 mm [graduation 30–35 mm]) of tropical w and cen Pacific (unrecorded e Pacific) much like Herald Petrel in flight manner, size, and shape, although tail averages longer. Phoenix has a solidly dark brown head and chest (white chin patch rarely visible at sea), and overall white undertail coverts (blackish brown vermiculations visible mainly in hand).

Habitat and Behavior Pelagic, well offshore over warm tropical waters. As likely to be seen alone as in association with mixed-species feeding flocks that include Juan Fernandez and other petrels, Wedge-tailed Shearwaters, and Sooty Terns.

In calm to light winds, flight almost delicate, but easy and controlled, with prolonged buoyant glides interspersed with loose clipped wingbeats, the flexed wings pressed forward and slightly crooked. In moderate to strong winds, flies with fairly high and steep but buoyant wheeling arcs, at times almost flipping back on itself at the top of a climb; at other times wheels fairly low, especially into the wind.

Description Medium-sized, lightly built gadfly petrel with long, fairly narrow wings and medium-long tail. Low wing-loading. Plumage variation also linked to taxonomy (see above). Age similar.

Dark morph Herald. Blackish brown to chocolate-brown overall; in bright light rarely shows indistinct darker M pattern above. Underwings dark overall, usually with variable reflective silvery flash across primary bases, sometimes a contrasting white flash and a whitish crescent on the under primary coverts; narrow whitish patagial bar rarely visible and perhaps not always present. Some birds have whitish on throat or around bill base, visible at closer ranges. Paler dark morphs have paler brownish underbody and variable whitish mottling on median and greater underwing coverts. Bill black; legs and feet blackish overall, or bicolored pale pinkish and black.

Henderson Petrel resembles darkest morph Herald and perhaps not distinguishable by plumage; undersides of primaries dark overall or with a variable (usually dull) reflective gray to silvery flash across bases. Legs and feet bicolored pale pinkish and black (Brooke & Rowe 1996).

Light morph. Head, chest, and upperparts gray-brown to dark brown, with variable whitish throat patch (often extending through lores and over bill as a "noseband") set off by dark chest band, which varies from narrow to broad and from grayish and vermiculated to solidly dark brownish; upperparts can show a subtle darker M pattern; whitish bases to outer rectrices unlikely to be visible at sea. Underparts white with dusky distal undertail coverts, sometimes dark mottling on flanks. Underwings dark overall with white flashes on primaries and primary coverts, variable whitish mottling along greater secondary coverts, and white patagial bar typically broader than dark morph. Legs and feet bicolored pale pinkish and black.

On the water. Dark brown overall or with variable whitish on throat, chest, and undertail coverts. Sides of light morphs whitish with variable brown mottling.

Molt Given potential year-round breeding, wing molt may occur in any month.

P35a.1. Light morph Herald Petrel appears all-dark from above, often with whitish blaze on lores. Note light build, long slender wings without white primary shafts (cf. P34.1–34.3). CC. Pitcairn Islands, Central South Pacific, 15 Jun 2006.

P35a.3. (Right) Plumage of light morph Herald Petrel can be similar to light morph jaegers, with bold white flash on underside of primaries. Herald lacks white primary shafts on upperwing and typically has different flight manner. CC. Pitcairn Islands, Central South Pacific, 15 Jun 2006.

P35a.4. (Below) Variation in light morph Herald Petrel parallels bulkier and broader-winged Kermadec Petrel (cf. P34.9–P34.12) but white primary flashes average less extensive on Herald, and extreme white-headed types occur only in Kermadec (cf. P34.5, P34.14). PH. Henderson Island, Central South Pacific, 3 Oct 2005.

P35a.2. Underwing of light morph Herald Petrel rather variable; some birds, like this, have dull silvery undersides to primaries and greater coverts (cf. P35a.3–P35a.5). Note slender build, long tail, narrow wings (cf. P34.2–P34.3). CC. Pitcairn Islands, Central South Pacific, 11 Jun 2006.

P35a.5. A typical light morph Herald Petrel. Compared to Kermadec Petrel, note slim build, long tapered tail, reduced white primary flashes. AJ. Easter Island, Chile, 16 Feb 2009.

P35b.1. Henderson Petrel appears identical in size and shape to Herald Petrel but is dark chocolate-brown overall and lacks light morph. Christmas Shearwater has smaller head, slender bill. CC. Pitcairn Islands, Central South Pacific, 11 Jun 2006.

P35b.2. (Above right) Plumage tones of Henderson Petrel vary with lighting (cf. P35b.1) but rarely if ever appear grayish. CC. Pitcairn Islands, Central South Pacific, 11 Jun 2006.

P35b.3. (Right) Henderson Petrel. Note slender build, long narrow wings, lack of white primary flashes. PH. Henderson Island, Central South Pacific, 2 Oct 2005.

P35b.4. Underwings of Henderson Petrel dark overall, but remiges can reflect dull silvery and narrow whitish patagial stripe often present (cf. P35b.5). PH. Henderson Island, Central South Pacific, 2 Oct 2005.

P35b.5. Henderson Petrel. Note slender build, long narrow wings, muted silvery underwing markings. CC. Pitcairn Islands, Central South Pacific, 11 Jun 2006.

P36. TAHITI PETREL *Pseudobulweria rostrata*

L 37–42 cm, WS 101–108 cm, tail 109–121 mm (graduation 35–40 mm)
Figures P36.1–P36.10

Identification Summary Pacific, over warm tropical waters. A medium-large gadfly petrel with long narrow wings, fairly long tapered tail, and very thick black bill. Dark chocolate-brown with sharply contrasting white lower chest to undertail coverts, dark underwings with variable whitish median stripe. Languid, wheeling flight.

Taxonomy Two subspecies recognized, following de Naurois and Erard (1979), probably not separable at sea. Beck's Petrel (*P. becki*) resembles Tahiti Petrel in plumage pattern but much smaller and usually treated as a separate species (Birdlife International 2010a, Onley & Scofield 2007). Tahiti and Beck's petrels, together with Fiji Petrel (*P. macgillivrayi*) and Mascarene Petrel (*P. aterrima*), have been placed in the genus *Pterodroma*. Genetic studies confirm, however, that these taxa are not closely related to *Pterodroma*, and they form the genus *Pseudobulweria* (Bretagnolle et al. 1998).

P. r. rostrata breeds cen tropical Pacific, ranges to waters off Middle America. Bill slightly smaller and less stout.

P. r. trouessarti breeds New Caledonia, ranges (presumably) in w tropical Pacific. Bill slightly larger and stouter.

Names *Pseudobulweria* indicates perceived similarity to the genus *Bulweria*; *rostrata* refers to the species' formidable beak.

Status and Distribution Near Threatened. Breeds (mainly Sep–Feb) in tropical sw and s cen Pacific, ranges to waters off Middle America.

Pacific. Fairly common to common nonbreeding visitor (May–Dec at least, likely year-round) off Middle America, n to around 10°N, uncommon to fairly common (late May–Nov at least) n to around 21°N (Oct 2008; M. Sadowski, photos).

FIELD IDENTIFICATION

Similar Species A distinctive, medium-large petrel with very long, albatross-like wings, a fairly long tapered tail, and a long neck with relatively small head and stout black bill. Plumage pattern might suggest some light morph Herald and perhaps Kermadec petrels (which see), but shape and flight of Tahiti Petrel are distinct from *Pterodroma*.

Smaller *Phoenix Petrel* (L 36–38 cm, WS 90–96 cm, tail 106–120 mm [graduation 30–35 mm]) of tropical w and cen Pacific (unrecorded e Pacific) much like Herald Petrel in size and shape but plumage similar to Tahiti Petrel. Phoenix has slightly darker head and upperparts (its white chin patch is rarely visible at sea) and lacks paler uppertail coverts; underwings lack a paler central stripe (except when white feather bases are exposed by molt) but have inconspicuous white patagial bar. Buoyant flight much like Herald Petrel.

Habitat and Behavior Pelagic over warm tropical waters, ranging widely in search of dead squid, which it scavenges (Spear & Ainley 1998, Spear

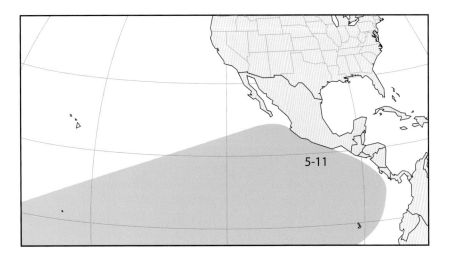

5-11

et al. 2007). Found singly or in small groups, often separate from other species, but frequently joins briefly or inspects the periphery of mixed-species feeding flocks over marine mammals.

In calm to light winds, flies low with long shearing glides on slightly bowed wings interspersed with languid, easy, powerful flapping, the wings when gliding held fairly straight out from the body with the tips often curled up slightly. In moderate to strong winds, flight fast and powerful with little or no flapping and often relatively low wheeling arcs, the wings held fairly straight or slightly crooked. Across strong winds can wheel and tower fairly high and steeply, but lacks buoyant bounding ease of smaller and lighter gadfly petrels.

Description A medium-large petrel with long narrow wings, a fairly long and tapered tail, long neck, and relatively small head with a very stout bill. Fairly high wing-loading.

Ages similar. Head, chest, and upperparts dark brown, the uppertail coverts and tail base often contrastingly paler. White underbody contrasts with dark chest and dark underwings; long tail usually appears as a dark point beyond white undertail coverts. Whitish median stripe often apparent on underwing is formed by exposed bases of greater coverts. Bill black, legs and feet bicolored pale pinkish and black.

On the water. Dark brown overall with long neck, relatively small head, thick bill, white undertail coverts, and white chest at waterline.

Molt Wing molt in the region noted Mar–Oct (pers. obs., M. P. Force, unpubl. data).

P36.1. Tahiti Petrel (here nominate *rostrata*) is a distinctive gadfly petrel with very long narrow wings, long head/neck projection, and very stout bill; also note long tail with paler rump. CC. Pitcairn Islands, Central South Pacific, 9 Jun 2006.

P36.2. Tahiti Petrel (here subspecies *trouessarti*) has a long neck, relatively small head but thick bill, and long tapered tail, all typical of genus Pseudobulweria and unlike typical Pterodroma. SNGH. Western Pacific, 21°S 164°E, 4 Apr 2007.

P36.3. (Above) Nominate subspecies of Tahiti Petrel (presumably shown here) averages smaller-billed than western subspecies *trouessarti* (cf. P36.4). Prebasic molt completing with growth of p10, inner secondaries, and rectrices. SNGH. Oaxaca, Mexico, 1 Oct 2009.

P36.4. (Above right) Western populations of Tahiti Petrel (subspecies *trouessarti,* shown here) average heavier billed than nominate subspecies (cf. P36.3). Apparent darkness of upperparts varies with lighting and wear (cf. P36.3). SNGH. Western Pacific, 26°S 167°E, 7 Apr 2008.

P36.5. (Right) Tahiti Petrel completing molt (same bird as P36.3). White underparts contrast strongly with blackish-brown underwings and hood; also note very stout bill, long tail. SNGH. Oaxaca, Mexico, 1 Oct 2009.

P36.6. As well as its contrasting plumage pattern, Tahiti Petrel is distinctive by virtue of very long narrow wings (almost albatross-like), small head, very stout bill, and long tapered tail. CC. Pitcairn Islands, Central South Pacific, 9 Jun 2006 (nominate *rostrata*).

P36.7. Underwing of Tahiti Petrel often shows broad whitish central stripe. SNGH. Western Pacific, 21°S 164°E, 4 Apr 2007 (subspecies *trouessarti*).

P36.8. Tahiti Petrel. Note small head, very long narrow wings, bold plumage pattern. SNGH. Western Pacific, 26°S 167°E, 7 Apr 2008 (subspecies *trouessarti*).

P36.9. In moderate to strong winds, Tahiti Petrel (here nominate *rostrata* in outer primary molt) can sail high with ease, like other gadfly petrels; note distinctive shape. SNGH. Oaxaca, Mexico, 1 Oct 2009.

P36.10. Tahiti Petrel often scavenges dead squid floating near the surface; on the water, note the long neck, relatively small head, and massive bill. SNGH. Western Pacific, 23°S 166°E, 8 Apr 2008 (subspecies *trouessarti*).

Other Petrels

These other petrel species, in the genera *Fulmarus, Procellaria,* and *Bulweria,* comprise one breeding resident of cold n seas off both coasts (Northern Fulmar), one regular nonbreeding visitor off the Pacific coast of Middle America (Parkinson's Petrel), and two exceptional or very rare visitors recorded in both oceans (White-chinned Petrel and Bulwer's Petrel).

Fulmarus petrels are part of a primarily s hemisphere group of medium-sized to very large petrels that inhabit polar and temperate waters; one representative occurs in the n hemisphere. The Northern Fulmar is a fairly large, stocky, and polymorphic petrel with a stout pale bill, fairly broad and stiffly held wings, and a medium-short, slightly graduated tail. Fulmars are surface nesters that visit their colonies in daylight, and they often scavenge at fishing boats.

Procellaria petrels are five species of large petrels that breed in the s hemisphere; four species (including those recorded in North American waters) have predominantly blackish plumage and blackish legs and feet, and are sometimes called "black petrels." Bills are pale yellowish overall with well-defined plates and tend to be slightly stouter than shearwater bills; wings are long and fairly broad, and tails medium-short and graduated (the toes can project in flight). Black petrels often accompany ships and scavenge readily. For species identification note bill size and pattern, overall size (relative to other species), and any white markings on the chin or head (see Howell 2006).

Bulweria petrels are two distinctive tropical species (one recorded in the region, the other endemic to the Indian Ocean) of small to medium-sized petrels with stout black bills, long narrow wings, and long, strongly graduated tails usually held closed in a point. Bulwer's Petrel is usually indifferent to boats but can be attracted to fish-oil slicks. Its plumage is all-dark with a paler ulnar band, a pattern recalling some of the large northern storm-petrels.

P37. NORTHERN FULMAR *Fulmarus glacialis*

L 40.5–45.5 cm, WS 95–115 cm, tail 100–135 mm (graduation 15–25 mm)
Figures P37a.1–P37a.19, P37b.1–P37b.8

Identification Summary Pacific and Atlantic. A large, stocky, polymorphic, and rather gull-like petrel of cold and temperate waters. Bill stout and pale pinkish to pale grayish overall with darker orange tip. Dark morph (common Pacific, scarce Atlantic) smoky gray overall. Light morph has white head and underparts, white flashes on primary bases.

P37a.1. Rafts of nonbreeding Northern Fulmars often group fairly loosely. Off California, as here, most fulmars are dark morphs; note the light morph on the left, plus two Buller's Shearwaters (third from left and back right). SNGH. Off Bodega Bay, California, 30 Sep 2007.

Taxonomy Geographic variation complex. Two subspecies recognized here, differing slightly in size and in relative frequency of plumage morphs; differences between the two are comparable to those between some species of petrels, and it may be that two species of "Northern Fulmar" should be recognized. Low Arctic and boreal breeders (n to nw Greenland) sometimes separated as subspecies *auduboni* but variation in Atlantic populations is complex (van Franeker & Wattel 1982), and *auduboni* not recognized by Cramp and Simmons (1977) or Boertmann (1994). Interestingly, light morphs in the Pacific breed n of dark morphs, but the opposite tendency pertains in Atlantic populations. Measurements from Cramp and Simmons (1977), Hatch and Nettleship (1998).

F. g. rodgersii (Pacific Fulmar) averages smaller (wing chord 280–328 mm, mass 445–787 g); bill relatively long and slender (L 34–42 mm); dark and light morphs common. Tail darker, smoky gray to sooty gray, on light morphs usually contrasting with paler uppertail coverts.

F. g. glacialis (Atlantic Fulmar) averages larger (wing chord 312–348 mm, mass 560–1050 g); bill varies in size, smallest in High Arctic (L 33–40 mm), larger in boreal populations (L 36–44 mm). Light morphs common, dark morphs scarce except locally in high Arctic. Tail paler, ashy gray to pale gray, usually concolorous with, or barely darker than, uppertail coverts.

Names *Fulmarus* comes from fulmar, an old Norse name meaning "foul gull" in reference, presumably, to the stomach oil that fulmars can projectile-vomit; *glacialis* means "icy," in reference to the species' high-latitude n breeding range.

P37b.1. Light morph Atlantic Northern Fulmar. Like other fulmarine petrels, fulmars typically nest above ground and visit their nest sites during the daytime. BM. Copeland Island, Northern Ireland, 22 Apr 2007.

Status and Distribution Least Concern. Breeds (May–Sep) in North Pacific and North Atlantic, n to Bering Sea and high Arctic, winters at sea (mainly Oct–Mar) off the Americas s to California and the mid-Atlantic coast, off Asia s to w Europe and Japan.

Pacific. Locally common breeder (late May–Sep) from islands off Alaska Peninsula through Aleutians, and n locally into Bering Sea to Pribilof and St. Matthew islands, ranging in summer (May–Oct) n into Chukchi and Beaufort seas. In Alaska, 99% of population breeds at only 4 colony locations, each with more than 50,000 birds (dark morphs at Semidi and Chagaluk islands, light morphs at Pribilof and St. Matthew islands). Rare and local breeder (May–Sep) in se Alaska, probably also Triangle Island, British Columbia. Bering Sea breeding population 100% light morph in 1960s, but with 5–10% dark morph by mid-1980s, possibly linked to warming trend in 1970s and 1980s (Shuntov 1993); conversely, n Pacific breeding population 80% dark morph (Hatch 1993). Within Bering Sea, birds foraging over the continental shelf are mainly light morphs, but dark morphs more frequent over deeper waters beyond the shelf.

Remains common to fairly common in Bering Sea through Sep, but most withdraw s by late Oct; winters n to edge of pack ice, which varies in location from year to year. In winter (Oct–Mar), generally common from Aleutians and Gulf of Alaska s to British Columbia (where 80% are dark morph), and common to fairly common s to cen California (n of Point Conception). Irregularly uncommon to fairly common (mainly late Nov–Mar) from s California to Baja California Peninsula; very rare in Gulf of California and exceptionally s (Dec–Jan) to Nayarit (NAB 57:263, 2003). Numbers off West Coast generally lowest Apr–Jun, increasing again in Jul–Oct. Invasions of birds inshore (mainly Oct–Dec) often include die-offs, with birds entering harbors and bays, and washing ashore dead in hundreds or thousands. Some birds oversummer s to w Mexico, especially after invasion years. Exceptional inland (Dec) in Oregon.

Off the West Coast, there is marked interannual variation in the abundance of fulmars as viewed from or near shore; Briggs et al. (1987) concluded this was largely an artifact of regional redistributions (e.g., reflecting water conditions and the location of fishing fleets) of a population that may not vary much in size between years.

Atlantic. Locally common breeder (Jun–Sep) in Canadian Arctic and w Greenland, from around 76°N in n Baffin Bay (Devon Island, formerly Ellesmere Island) s to se Baffin Island. Southward

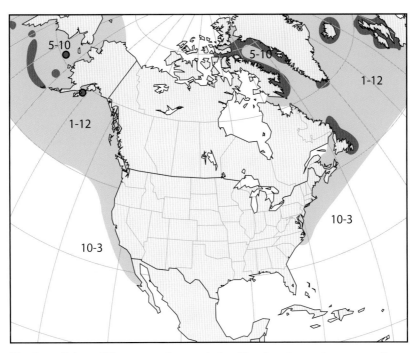

Northern Fulmar. Winters north to pack-ice. Numbers in southern parts of winter range vary greatly between years; occasional south to northwest Mexico and Florida.

breeding since late 1960s and 1970s in Labrador and Newfoundland apparently a belated continuum of exponential population increase documented in ne Atlantic since mid-1700s. In summer, common to fairly common (Apr–Oct) in Canadian Arctic, ranging w rarely to Banks Island, n to Ellesmere Island (around 85 N), s to waters off Newfoundland; absent Hudson Bay, accidental (Nov) on James Bay.

Wintering numbers off Atlantic coast have increased greatly since 1970s, with most birds there originating in nw Europe and Greenland. Generally occurs out of sight of land but can be seen from shore in windy conditions. Fall movement off New England apparent in Sep, with main influxes Oct–Dec. Common to fairly common in fall and winter (Oct–Mar, with maximum numbers southward in Dec–Mar) from Atlantic Canada (n to ice edge) s to Georges Bank, Massachusetts, thence irregular s to North Carolina, occasionally reaching South Atlantic Bight, exceptionally Bahamas and Florida (Oct–Apr; NAB 59:426, 2005; NAB 63:65, 2010). Northward migration mainly Feb–Apr, but in invasion years some linger into May off North Carolina, and hundreds (thousands in invasion years) remain locally off Massachusetts into May–Jun. Ranges into Gulf of Maine in winter (uncommon

except in invasion years), where some linger into Jun–Jul, exceptionally Aug. Northward shift of nonbreeding birds noted from Scotia Shelf (where commonest May–Jun) into Labrador Sea (commonest Jul–Aug) (Brown 1988).

Very rare inland (mainly Nov–Dec) in e North America, mainly along St. Lawrence and Ottawa rivers, exceptionally to e Great Lakes and s to Pennsylvania. A report from Alabama (AOU 1998) is not accepted by the state committee (S. McConnell, pers. comm.).

FIELD IDENTIFICATION

Similar Species A distinctive species, perhaps as likely to be mistaken for a gull as for any other tubenose in the region. Note the stocky shape, stout pale bill, stiffly held wings, gray rump and tail, and (on light morphs) white primary flashes. Rafting fulmars away from the nesting grounds tend to swim in scattered groups, whereas shearwaters often group into fairly tight rafts.

In almost any light, *Sooty and Short-tailed shearwaters* appear darker than most fulmars, but in gloomy conditions the darkest North Pacific fulmars can appear as dark as shearwaters. Note that shearwaters have slimmer bodies, smaller heads, slender dark bills, and narrower, more pointed wings; they lack the distinctive, slightly floppy shallow wingbeats of stiffly held wings, which identify a fulmar at almost any distance. Fulmars in heavily worn plumage, however (mainly Mar–Aug), have deeper and quicker wingbeats that can suggest Sooty Shearwater.

At long range or on the water, some white-bodied *gulls* might suggest a fulmar, but adult or near-adult gulls have a white rump and tail (usually gray on light fulmars, rump rarely white), typical gull flight, and a different bill. At a distance, and usually in windy conditions, dark morph fulmars might be confused with dark gadfly petrels by overeager observers; fulmars have straighter wings, less graceful flight.

Antarctic Fulmar (*F. glacialoides*, circumpolar in s hemisphere, ranging n off w South America to around 10˚S; L 45.5–48 cm, WS 96–104 cm) is an unlikely vagrant to n hemisphere. Resembles Northern Fulmar in size and shape, but lacks a dark morph: head and underparts white with smoky gray clouding on crown and hindneck, upperparts pale gray with blackish remiges and contrasting white primary flashes; bill pink with blue tubes and black tip.

Habitat and Behavior Pelagic away from breeding islands, favoring cool saline waters. Can been seen from shore in storms, especially during invasions or "wrecks" (mainly Oct–Dec off West Coast). At-sea distribution colored by the distribution of fishing fleets, where fulmars scavenge readily. Off West Coast, commonest over outer shelf and shelf break, but also ranges far offshore. Found singly or in groups, locally in thousands (such as scavenging at fishing boats, or rafting near the breeding islands); associates readily with gulls, shearwaters, albatrosses, and other scavengers, and can be quite bold and aggressive among larger gulls. Nests mainly on cliffs or steep ledges; diurnal at colonies, which range from a few pairs to hundreds of thousands.

In calm to light winds, flight low to the water, with fairly shallow and quick, slightly floppy wingbeats of stiffly held wings interspersed with glides on slightly bowed wings; first-cycle birds in heavily worn plumage (mainly Mar–Aug) have deeper and quicker wingbeats that can suggest Sooty Shearwater. In moderate to strong winds, flight steady and strong, with frequent glides on wings held stiffly and straight out from body; at times wheels high and fairly steeply, recalling gadfly petrels. Hoarse chuckling and cackling calls given mainly around nest and in feeding interactions.

Description A large, stocky petrel with fairly thick neck, slightly rounded wings, broad, slightly rounded tail, and thick bill with well-defined plates. Polymorphic (see Taxonomy).

Pacific Fulmar (*F. g. rodgersii*). Ages similar but note differences in wing molt timing. **Dark morph.** Varies from dark sooty gray overall to distinctly paler, smoky blue-gray overall, usually with a black smudge forward of eyes; plumage browner overall when worn. Upperside of flight feathers dark gray with paler flash (often dull or virtually absent) on bases of inner primaries and primary coverts; underside of primaries and greater coverts reflective, appearing dull silvery in some lights. Some first-summer birds can be very worn and faded with incoming feathers contrastingly dark; bleached (at times creamy) juvenile feathers retained last on the mantle and belly, creating quite striking piebald patterns. Bill pale pinkish to greenish yellow with variable black subterminal ring (perhaps broadest on immatures; absent on some birds) and deeper-colored orangeish tip; legs and feet pale pinkish overall. **Light morph.** Variable. Typical birds have head, neck, and underparts clean white with blackish smudge forward of eye; underwings white overall with narrow dark margins broadest on primary coverts; and upperparts smoky blue-gray with dark gray flight feathers (tail often darker than uppertail coverts), white flashes on bases of inner primaries and primary coverts. Bleached first-summer birds (into Oct–Nov) can have rump, uppertail coverts, and bands of lesser coverts bleached almost white, contrasting with "dark" incoming gray feathers. Lightest birds have head and underparts snowy white; upperwings snowy white overall (blackish mainly on primary tips, outer primary coverts, and trailing edge), and contrasting slightly with smoky blue-gray back; and rump and uppertail coverts pale gray to whitish, contrasting with darker tail. Duller birds have head and underparts dingy white, sometimes with dusky smudging; blackish underwing margins can be thick, surrounding a broad whitish median panel. Dullest birds ("intermediate morphs") have head and underparts dingy whitish to pale smoky gray, often smudged dusky gray, but still contrastingly pale relative to overall dark underwings. Bill and feet similar to dark morph but bill averages paler pinkish, less greenish, and black subterminal bill ring usually reduced or absent.

Atlantic Fulmar (*F. g. glacialis*). Overall much like Pacific Fulmar, but light and dark morphs less extreme; tail paler gray; latericorn usually blue-gray to greenish gray, and nostril tubes darker, often blackish. **Light morph.** Resembles typical light morph of *rodgersii*, but tail paler gray, usually not contrastingly darker than uppertail coverts; head and neck sometimes suffused yellow. **Dark morph.** Smoky blue-gray overall, often slightly paler on head and underparts.

Molt (see Fig 48, p. 38) Adult wing molt mid-Jun/Sep–Dec/Feb, starting earlier (mid-Jun to Aug) in failed and nonbreeders; may end later in food-poor years (especially in Pacific?). Tail molt occurs at or after completion of primary molt. PB2 wing molt Apr/May–Sep/Nov (mainly May–Sep); at least in Pacific populations, p10 or p9-p10 can be retained through following summer, often worn and bleached to a whitish spike.

P37a.2. Dark morph Northern Fulmar with primary molt completing, on this date presumably second cycle (adult Western Gull below). Note stocky shape, stout pale tubenose bill. SNGH. Off Bodega Bay, California, 1 Aug 2008.

P37a.3. Broad wings, blocky head, and relatively pale, milky plumage tones distinguish dark morph Pacific Northern Fulmar from dark-bodied shearwaters; tail molt presumably represents end of second prebasic molt. SNGH. Off Fort Bragg, California, 10 Aug 2007.

P37a.4. (Above) On dark morph Pacific Northern Fulmar, tail often contrastingly darker than rump (cf. P37b.4–P37b.5). SNGH. Off Bodega Bay, California, 9 Oct 2006.

P37a.5. (Above right) Some dark morph Pacific Northern Fulmars have tail concolorous with rump (cf. P37a.4). TMcG. Off Fort Bragg, California, 18 Oct 2009.

P37a.6. (Right) Some dark morph Northern Fulmars oversummering off the West Coast can become very bleached. Faded greater coverts relative to fresher secondaries and timing of wing molt (recently started) indicate a bird in at least its second summer (cf. P37a.2–P37a.3). SNGH. Off Santa Barbara, California, 25 Jul 2009.

P37a.7. Molting Northern Fulmars in summer and fall often appear blotchy (cf. P37a.11); primary molt completing on this date suggests second cycle (cf. P37a.6). SNGH. Off Monterey, California, 28 Sep 2007.

P37a.8. Light morph Pacific Northern Fulmar characteristically has contrasting dark tail (cf. P37b.2). Uniform-looking plumage on this date suggests juvenile. SNGH. Off Monterey, California, 15 Oct 2006.

P37a.9. Light morph Northern Fulmar more variable in Pacific than Atlantic populations (cf. P37a.8, P37a.10, P37b.2). EWP. Off Bodega Bay, California, 4 Dec 2005.

P37a.10. (Above) Whitest light morph Pacific Northern Fulmar has no counterpart in Atlantic populations. EWP. Off Bodega Bay, California, 4 Dec 2005.

P37a.11. (Left) Light morph Pacific Northern Fulmar. Some first-summer birds are heavily worn and reluctant to fly. SNGH. Off Bodega Bay, California, 20 Jun 2007.

P37a.12. Dark morph Pacific Northern Fulmar. Note stocky shape with broad, relatively rounded wings, thick neck, large head, and stout pale bill. SNGH. Off Santa Barbara, California, 15 Nov 2009.

P37a.13. Most dark morph Pacific Northern Fulmars are appreciably paler than dark-bodied large shearwaters; also note big head and stout bill. EWP. Off Bodega Bay, California, 4 Dec 2005.

P37a.14. (Above) Whitest-bodied light morph Pacific Northern Fulmars have mostly clean white underwings. EWP. Off Bodega Bay, California, 4 Dec 2005.

P37a.15. (Above right) Light morph Northern Fulmar more variable in Pacific than Atlantic populations (cf. P37a.9–P37a.10, P37a.14, P37b.2). SNGH. Off Bodega Bay, California, 7 Sep 2007.

P37a.16. (Right) Dark morph Pacific Northern Fulmar. Even disappearing into the fog can be distinguished from dark-bodied shearwaters by large fat body, relatively short wings. SNGH. Off Bodega Bay, California, 24 Sep 2006.

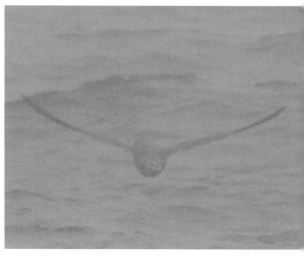

P37b.2. Typical light morph Atlantic Northern Fulmar. Note concolorous pale-gray rump and tail, creamy tinge to hindneck. BM. Newfoundland, Canada, 14 Aug 2006.

P37b.3. Typical light morph Atlantic Northern Fulmar in mid-primary molt. Note superficially gull-like plumage aspect but stout tubenose bill, pale gray rump and tail. BM. Newfoundland, Canada, 15 Aug 2009.

P37b.4. (Above left) Most "dark morph" Atlantic Northern Fulmars seen off the East Coast are paler than typical Pacific birds; note concolorous rump and tail. BM. Newfoundland, Canada, 4 Aug 2007.

P37b.5. (Above right) Dark morph Atlantic Northern Fulmar with outer primary molt; note concolorous rump and tail. BM. Newfoundland, Canada, 30 Jul 2009.

P37b.6. (Left) Light morph Atlantic Northern Fulmar (behind) with Great Shearwater. Note stocky body, big head, and stout bill of fulmar relative to lighter build and slender bill typical of large shearwaters. BM. Newfoundland, Canada, 13 Aug 2007.

P37a.17. Dark morph Pacific Northern Fulmars vary in intensity of darkness. Compare pinkish bill with gray-green of Atlantic birds (cf. P37b.4, P37b.8). SNGH. Off Bodega Bay, California, 30 Sep 2007.

P37a.18. Light morph Pacific Northern Fulmar. Note dark tail and bill color (cf. P37b.21, P37b.7). EWP. Off Bodega Bay, California, 4 Dec 2005.

P37a.19. Whitest light morph Pacific Northern Fulmar has no counterpart in Atlantic populations. EWP. Off Bodega Bay, California, 4 Dec 2005.

P37b.7. Light morph Atlantic Northern Fulmar in outer primary molt. Note greenish bill tones and blackish nostril tubes relative to Pacific birds (cf. P37a.18). BM. Newfoundland, Canada,

P37b.8. Dark morph Atlantic Northern Fulmar. Note greenish bill tones and pale tail (cf. P37a.17). BM. Newfoundland, Canada, 4 Aug 2009.

P38. PARKINSON'S PETREL *Procellaria parkinsoni*
L 41–46 cm, WS 112–123 cm, tail 93–106 mm (graduation 25–35 mm)
Figures P38.1–P38.7

Identification Summary Pacific, in warm waters off Middle America. A large, long-winged, blackish petrel with a dark-tipped, pale yellowish bill (plates outlined neatly in black), blackish feet. On the water, note long wing projection past tail.

Taxonomy Monotypic.

Names *Procellaria* connotes a creature of the storm; *parkinsoni* and the English name commemorate Sydney Parkinson (1745–1771), a British explorer on James Cook's first voyage. In New Zealand known simply as Black Petrel.

Status and Distribution Vulnerable. Breeds (Nov–May) in n New Zealand, nonbreeding visitor to e Pacific, from s Mexico to Peru (mainly 15°N to 5°S; Pitman & Ballance 1992).
    Pacific. Uncommon to locally fairly common nonbreeding visitor (year-round, mainly Mar/Apr–Oct) from Gulf of Tehuantepec s to Gulf of Panama (Pitman & Ballance 1992), occasionally n to Guerrero (Jehl 1974). Exceptional n to cen California (Oct 2005; Stallcup & Preston 2006). A report from Oregon (Oct 2005; NAB 60:127, 2006) is unverified.

FIELD IDENTIFICATION

Similar Species Seen well this is a distinctive species, albeit one unfamiliar to many observers. As likely to be passed off as a Flesh-footed Shearwater as it is to be confused with larger *Procellaria* petrels (see Howell 2006 for details).

Flesh-footed Shearater (Pacific) more lightly built and longer tailed (toes do not project beyond tail in flight, and wing projection past tail relatively short on swimming birds), with a more slender bill that is pink with a black tip, lacking neat black outlines to the plates; pink feet diagnostic, but in flight these are often tucked in and not visible. Flesh-footed slightly paler and browner overall, less blackish, but this can be difficult to judge.
    White-chinned Petrel (vagrant off both coasts) larger and bulkier, appreciably larger than a large shearwater. Lacks dark bill tip, and note that white chin patch often very difficult to see.
    Westland Petrel (*P. westlandica*) of temperate South Pacific (L 48–53 cm, WS 135–145 cm, tail 120–135 mm [graduation 25–30 mm]; P38a.1–P38a.2) essentially identical in plumage and bill pattern to Parkinson's, but larger with a thicker neck, blockier head, bigger bill, and relatively shorter wing projection past tail. Nonjuvenile Westlands are in wing molt Oct–Mar (Parkinson's mainly Mar–Aug), but molt timing of vagrants could be atypical.

Habitat and Behavior Pelagic, over warmer waters of e tropical Pacific. Associates only loosely with mixed-species feeding flocks, and more often found singly or in small groups of its own species; feeding flocks exceptionally up to 300 birds

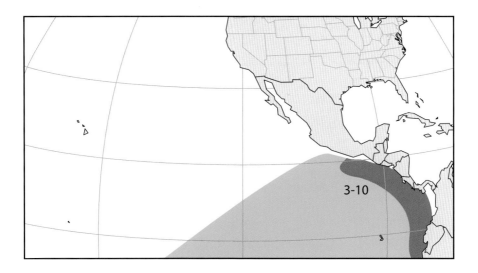

(Pitman & Ballance 1992). Feeds mainly by scavenging, and dives readily. Often attracted to fishing boats discarding offal and associates with schools of cetaceans, notably Melon-headed Whales (*Peponocephala electra*) and False Killer Whales (*Pseudorca crassidens*), where the petrels scavenge scraps (Pitman & Ballance 1992).

In calm to light winds, flies with easy, smooth wingbeats and buoyant glides; often appears a little heavier than large shearwaters such as Flesh-footed; in light to moderate winds, flies with languid, leisurely glides and occasional bouts of loose flapping, wheeling low over the water. In moderate to strong winds holds wings more crooked, and high, wheeling flight may recall larger gadfly petrels.

Description Large petrel with fairly rounded head, long wings, and medium-length, slightly graduated or wedge-shaped tail; toes can project beyond tail but often pulled in. At rest, wings project well past tail tip.

Ages similar but juveniles fresh in May–Aug when older ages worn or in wing molt. Plumage brownish black overall. Undersides of primaries and greater coverts often flash silvery, noticeable even at moderate to long range. Worn and molting birds show paler and exposed white patches on upperwings. Bill pale ivory to greenish yellow with black culminicorn, naricorn, sulcus, and variable dark tip: ungues tipped blackish on all birds (but can be poorly contrasting such that bill looks all-pale at a distance), and all-black on some birds (probably immatures); legs and feet blackish. In bright light, bill can look wholly pale pinkish at moderate to long range.

On the water. Blackish overall with dark-tipped pale bill.

Molt Wing molt mainly Mar–Aug, earlier in immatures and nonbreeders.

P38.1. Parkinson's Petrel. Note blackish-brown plumage, pale yellowish bill with dusky tip. SNGH. North Island, New Zealand, 31 Mar 2008.

P38.2. Parkinson's Petrel with inner primary molt and extensively dusky bill tip. Toes often project beyond tail tip but can be pulled in (cf. P38.1). SNGH. North Island, New Zealand, 26 Mar 2007.

P38.3. Parkinson's Petrel in worn plumage, apparently starting body molt. In bright light, especially at a distance, bill can appear wholly pale, inviting confusion with larger White-chinned Petrel. SNGH. Western Pacific, 30°S 169°E, 5 Apr 2008.

P38.4. Parkinson's Petrel (left) with Flesh-footed Shearwater. Besides its blacker plumage, Parkinson's has shorter tail (toes often project) and shorter, blockier head projection with stouter, greenish-yellow bill. SNGH. North Island, New Zealand, 31 Mar 2008.

P38.5. Parkinson's Petrel (behind) with Flesh-footed Shearwater. Parkinson's is stockier with blacker plumage, stouter and yellowish bill, and long wing projection past tail tip. SNGH. North Island, New Zealand, 31 Mar 2008.

P38.6. Parkinson's Petrel has smaller head and slimmer bill relative to larger Westland Petrel (P38a.1). SNGH. North Island, New Zealand, 1 Apr 2008.

P38a.1. Westland Petrel, shown here, is larger than Parkinson's with thicker head/neck projection and stouter bill. SNGH. South Island, New Zealand, 28 Mar 2008.

P38.7. Parkinson's Petrel. Relative to larger Westland Petrel (P38a.2), note smaller, more rounded head, slimmer bill, and longer wing projection past tail tip. SNGH. North Island, New Zealand, 1 Apr 2008.

P38a.2. Westland Petrel, shown here, has larger, blockier head, thicker bill, and shorter wing projection past tail tip than Parkinson's. SNGH. South Island, New Zealand, 28 Mar 2008.

P39. WHITE-CHINNED PETREL *Procellaria aequinoctialis*

L 50–57 cm, WS 132–145 cm, tail 113–132 mm (graduation 15–20 mm)
Figures P39.1–P39.5

Identification Summary Vagrant from subantarctic oceans. A large, brownish-black petrel with contrasting pale yellowish bill (plates outlined neatly in black) and blackish feet. Small white chin patch visible only at close range. Sometimes known as Shoemaker.

Taxonomy Monotypic.

Names *Procellaria* connotes a creature of the storm, an appropriate name for the family as a whole; *aequinoctialis* refers to stormy waters commonly associated with the equinox off the Cape of Good Hope.

Status and Distribution Vulnerable. Breeds (Nov–Apr) on subantarctic islands, ranges at sea mainly 30–60°S, and in winter (mainly Apr–Oct) n to 6°S in cooler waters off w South America.

Pacific. Accidental off cen California (mid-Oct 2009; NAB 64:147–148, 189, 2010).

Atlantic. Accidental. A weak individual found in the surf on the Gulf coast of n Texas (late Apr 1986; Lockwood & Freeman 2004) is considered of controversial origin (AOU 1998). A White-chinned Petrel was seen (description examined by SNGH) and a poor photo taken (perhaps since lost; H. LeGrand, pers. comm.) off North Carolina on two dates in mid-Oct 1996 (Brinkley 1997, R. Fraker, unpubl. data). This record has not been accepted by regional committees (LeGrand et al. 2001), but it is difficult to imagine what else the bird could have been (the photo supported identification as a dark *Procellaria* petrel; E. S. Brinkley and J. B. Patteson, pers. comm.). Recently, one was found off the Maine coast (Aug 2010; L. Kennedy, J. McCordic, pers. comm., photos).

FIELD IDENTIFICATION

Similar Species Within North American waters, White-chinned Petrel would stand out as something different, being blackish overall, pale-billed, and distinctly larger than large shearwaters or Northern Fulmar. With any record, however, other species of all-dark *Procellaria* petrels should be considered (Howell 2006), namely, Spectacled (*P. conspicillata*), Westland, and Parkinson's.

Spectacled Petrel of subtropical South Atlantic (L 50–55 cm, WS 130–140 cm, tail 105–115 mm [graduation 20–25 mm]) much like White-chinned in size and shape (tail averages more strongly graduated) but has diagnostic white ring on head sides, joined across forehead; usually has dark bill tip.

Westland Petrel of temperate South Pacific (L 48–53 cm, WS 135–145 cm, tail 120–135 mm [graduation 25–30 mm]) much like White-chinned in size and shape but head slightly blockier, wings and tail proportionately slightly longer, and tail more strongly graduated. Lacks white chin, and bill usually has a distinct blackish tip (rarely almost absent). Nonjuvenile Westlands are in wing molt during Oct–Mar (White-chinneds molt mainly Feb–Aug), but molt timing of vagrants may be atypical.

Parkinson's Petrel (subtropical and tropical Pacific) smaller and more lightly built, about the size of a large shearwater. Lacks white chin, and bill usually has distinct blackish tip. On the water, note relatively long wing projection past tail.

Immature *giant-petrels* (genus *Macronectes*) of Southern Ocean (unrecorded, but possible vagrants to the region) are also blackish overall with pale bills but are huge (the size of a small albatross) with a massive pale yellowish bill (tipped greenish on Southern Giant-Petrel [*M. giganteus*], pinkish on Northern Giant-Petrel [*M. halli*]).

Habitat and Behavior Pelagic, favoring cooler waters. A proficient scavenger, attracted to chum or to fishing boats cleaning their catch; associates readily with large shearwaters, gulls, and albatrosses. Often accompanies ships, following in the wake.

Flight appears heavy relative to large shearwaters, but wheels confidently and easily in moderate to strong winds. In calm to light winds, flies with steady smooth wingbeats and short glides; in light to moderate winds holds its wings straight out or pressed forward, and slightly bowed, and flies with leisurely glides and occasional bouts of loose flapping, wheeling low over the water; in moderate to strong winds, wings held more crooked, and high wheeling arcs may recall larger *Pterodroma*.

Description A large petrel with fairly large, rounded head, long and fairly broad wings, and medium-length, slightly graduated or wedge-shaped tail; toes can project beyond tail but often pulled in. At rest, wings project a moderate distance past tail tip.

Ages similar but juveniles fresh in May–Aug when older ages worn or in wing molt. Plumage brownish black overall. White chin rarely visible except at close range, averages more extensive in Atlantic than Pacific populations. Undersides of primaries and greater coverts often flash silvery, noticeable even at moderate to long range. Worn and molting birds show paler and exposed white patches on upperwings. Bill pale ivory to greenish yellow with black culminicorn, naricorn, and sulcus, very occasionally with a fine dusky tip; legs and feet blackish. In bright light, bill can look pale pinkish at moderate to long range.

On the water. Blackish overall with a pale yellowish bill.

Molt Wing molt mainly Feb–Aug, exceptionally starting Nov (Howell 2006).

P39.1. White-chinned Petrel. Note blackish-brown plumage, pale yellowish bill (including tip); small white chin patch often not visible. SNGH. South Island, New Zealand, 27 Mar 2008.

P39.2. White-chinned Petrel with mid-primary molt. White chin patch often relatively large on Atlantic (and Indian) Ocean birds (cf. P39.1). SNGH. South Africa, 34°S 17°E, 17 Apr 2009.

P39.3. White-chinned Petrel. Small white chin patch of Pacific populations best seen from below (cf. P39.1, P39.4). SNGH. Valparaíso, Chile, 31 Oct 2006.

P39.4. White-chinned Petrel. A typical head-on view; note pale bill tip. SNGH. South Island, New Zealand, 29 Mar 2008.

P39.5. White-chinned Petrel. Besides pale bill tip, note relatively small rounded head, relatively short wing projection past tail tip (cf. P38.7, P38a.2). SNGH. South Island, New Zealand, 28 Mar 2008.

P40. BULWER'S PETREL *Bulweria bulwerii*

L 27–29 cm, WS 63–68 cm, tail 100–122 mm (graduation 40–45 mm)
Figures P40.1–P40.10

Identification Summary Pacific and Atlantic. Exceptional or very rare visitor. A small, all-dark petrel with long, narrow, and pointed wings, fairly long tapered tail, pale ulnar band, and thick black bill. Flight buoyant and weaving, low to the water.

Taxonomy Considered monotypic, despite wide geographic range.

Names The genus and species names commemorate James Bulwer (1794–1879), a Scottish naturalist who collected the type specimen in Madeira.

Status and Distribution Least Concern. Breeds (mainly May/Jun–Aug/Sep) in tropical and subtropical w and cen Pacific, e to Hawaii; in w Indian Ocean; and in e and cen Atlantic. Ranges widely in tropical and subtropical oceans.

Atlantic. Perhaps a very rare nonbreeding visitor (late Apr–Aug) over warmer Atlantic waters n at least to South Atlantic Bight, with three well-documented records (early May–early Aug) from Florida n to North Carolina (Haney & Wainright 1985, Hass 1995, LeGrand et al. 1999). Also reported casually (late Apr–Jun) since 2003 off the Lesser Antilles (Levesque & Yésou 2005; NAB 60:589, 2007). Exceptional (Sep 2006) from shore in Virginia, following Tropical Storm Ernesto (Brinkley 2007).

Pacific. Exceptional (late Jul–early Sep) off cen and s California (Sep record not accepted by state committee). Perhaps a rare but regular nonbreeding visitor (mainly May–Sep?) to warm waters well off Middle America, but no documented records from the region.

FIELD IDENTIFICATION

Similar Species Bulwer's Petrel really doesn't look much like any other tubenose. Its size (larger than all-dark storm petrels, slightly smaller than small gadfly petrels), shape, and buoyant weaving flight are all distinctive. Large all-dark storm petrels similar in coloration, but all are smaller with relatively shorter, forked tails (beware effects of molt) and different flight (although some can wheel and bank in windy conditions).

Jouanin's Petrel (*Bulweria fallax*) of Indian Ocean (vagrant to cen n Pacific, unrecorded North America) is appreciably larger (L 32–35.5 cm, WS 76–80 cm, tail 104–113 cm), about the size of a small shearwater such as Manx (although its all-dark plumage often makes it appear larger than Manx; K. Mullarney, pers. comm.), whereas Bulwer's is appreciably smaller than Manx. Jouanin's is bulkier with a proportionally bigger head and bill, shorter and broader tail, broader wings, and often has a much duller pale upperwing band (to the point where it may be hard to discern at all); Jouanin's has more length and weight forward of the wings, which contributes to a more shearwater-like appearance at times; flight of Jouanin's is powerful and steady, but surprisingly agile given its large size, and often includes sudden switchback turns when foraging (K. Mullarney, pers. comm.)

Black Noddy (*Anous minutus*) and Brown Noddy (*A. stolidus*) share similar shape, all-dark plumage, and often fly low over the water. Both noddies are larger (although Black is close in size to Bulwer's) with a variable whitish cap, and their flight is tern-like—although in windy conditions they can bank and wheel, suggesting a petrel.

Another pitfall could be migrating nighthawks at a distance or in low light (a recent review of Bulwer's Petrel claims from Spain involved rejection of several reports that may have involved distant nightjars migrating over the sea; Gutierrez 2006).

Habitat and Behavior Pelagic. In many areas inhabits oceanic deserts—warm and generally dead tropical waters, where few other birds live. Likely to be encountered singly, not in association with other species, but is attracted to chum slicks. Does not typically accompany ships but not shy, often appearing indifferent or oblivious until nearby, when may fly off with spectacular freak-out flight. Normal flight low over the water with a buoyant, weaving, and switchback progression: in transiting flight, fairly quick bowed wingbeats typically interspersed with prolonged, buoyant glides and sometimes low wheeling, the wings held bowed, pressed forward, and crooked at the carpals. In moderate winds, can wheel higher, recalling a small *Pterodroma*, but generally does not bank steeply and tends to stay low to the water, befitting its low wing-loading. Foraging birds can fly into the wind with loose, fairly deep, and quick wingbeats, alighting briefly to seize food near the surface, at times pattering like a storm petrel, with wings raised, and at times sitting on the water. Freak-out flight (such as when disturbed by a ship) involves crazed-looking back-flips, manic swerving, and high, sweeping loops; much more demonstrative and powerful than storm petrels under similar circumstances.

Description A small petrel with long pointed wings, long tapered tail that is typically held closed in a point, and very low wing-loading.

Ages similar (probably differ in molt timing). Dark sooty brown overall (often looking black at any distance, warm brown below in some lights), slightly paler below and sometimes with contrasting pale grayish throat; contrasting paler brown ulnar band on upperwing tapers slightly toward body and palest on tips to greater coverts; can look pale grayish in some lights. Ulnar band can be difficult to see at moderate to long range; palest in worn plumage, when bleached tips to greater coverts can be pale buffy (mainly first-cycle birds?). Undersides of primaries and greater coverts reflect silvery in some lights. Bill black, legs and feet pinkish to dark grayish.

On the water. All-dark with long wings and tail; often hunches down and appears short necked.

Molt Adult wing molt occurs away from breeding grounds, thus Oct–Apr for most populations; PB2 probably starts 1–2 months earlier (needs study).

P40.1. Bulwer's Petrel in fresh plumage. Note distinctive shape, pale upperwing bands. SNGH. Madeira, eastern Atlantic, 16 May 2010.

P40.2. Bulwer's Petrel in mid-primary molt; white wingstripe is formed by bases of secondaries exposed by shed greater coverts. SW. East Pacific, 19°N 170°W, 27 Sep 2005.

P40.3. Bulwer's Petrel. Note long tapered tail; prominence of pale upperwing band varies with lighting and wear; plumage can appear relatively pale and ashy in fog, as here (cf. P40.4–P40.5). SNGH. Western Pacific, 20°N 146°E, 20 Apr 2007.

P40.4. Bulwer's Petrel. Prominence of pale upperwing band varies with lighting (cf. P40.3, P40.5). SNGH. Madeira, eastern Atlantic, 15 May 2010.

P40.5. Bulwer's Petrel. Prominence of pale upperwing band varies with lighting (cf. P40.3–P40.4). SNGH. Madeira, eastern Atlantic, 14 May 2010.

P40.6. Foraging Bulwer's Petrel sometimes patters like storm-petrels; note long tapered tail, stout bill, dirty pinkish legs. SNGH. Madeira, eastern Atlantic, 15 May 2010.

P40.7. Bulwer's Petrel. Note slim, tapered body and long tail offset by big wings, which give Bulwer's Petrel the lowest wing-loading of any petrel. SNGH. Madeira, eastern Atlantic, 15 May 2010.

P40.8. Bulwer's Petrel often holds head slightly raised, and stout bill can be emphasized by paler gray throat on some individuals, as here. SNGH. Madeira, eastern Atlantic, 14 May 2010.

P40.9. Size of Bulwer's Petrel can be appreciated here with Cory's Shearwater for comparison. SNGH. Madeira, eastern Atlantic, 15 May 2010.

P40.10. Bulwer's Petrel. Note hunched posture, long wings and tail, stout bill. SNGH. Madeira, eastern Atlantic, 16 May 2010.

ALBATROSSES: DIOMEDEIDAE

lbatrosses are very large seabirds characteristic of the windy Southern Ocean, with three species nesting in the North Pacific (Fig 135). Ages differ in appearance (slightly or markedly), while sexes usually look similar, although males average larger than females, with broader heads and longer bills. Plumages are colored in black, white, browns, and grays, often boldly patterned and mostly dark above and white below. In general, species of sunnier lower tropical latitudes are darker (such as Galapagos and Black-footed albatrosses), whereas those of higher latitudes have more extensive white in their plumage (a correlation that holds even for foraging ranges of different ages and sexes of Wandering Albatrosses and Steller's Albatross, in which the darker-hued females and immatures range into lower latitudes than the whiter adult males). Bills vary in color and pattern from dark overall to brightly patterned; legs and feet are pale pinkish in most species. Molts, especially of immatures, are not well known, and in most species and individuals not all remiges are replaced in a single molt cycle, such that some species can be aged up to 6–9 years by patterns of feather retention and bill color (e.g., Prince & Rodwell 1994, Prince et al. 1997, Howell 2010b).

Fig 135. Albatrosses are ostensibly unmistakable, given their large size and very long narrow wings. Black-footed Albatross is the commonest species seen off the West Coast, often within sight of shore, as here off Santa Cruz, California. SNGH. 12 Oct 2008.

Robertson and Nunn (1998) recommended that 24 albatross species be recognized, a leap from the 12–13 species traditionally recognized and one that has yet to be universally accepted. Although most if not all of these "new" species are probably valid, it is not always possible to distinguish them at sea. In the region, 3 species are regular nonbreeding visitors off the n Pacific coast (with 2 having started nesting off Mexico since the 1980s), 8–9 are vagrants to the North Pacific, and 2 are vagrants to the North Atlantic.

North Pacific Albatrosses

Three species of albatross occur regularly in the North Pacific, all in the genus *Phoebastria*: Black-footed, Laysan, and Steller's (or Short-tailed) albatrosses. These are fairly small to medium-large albatrosses with relatively short wings (with 25–30 secondaries), relatively short tails (the feet project in flight unless pulled in), and relatively plain-patterned bills. They often accompany ships and readily scavenge around fishing boats (Fig 136). Ages differ slightly in three species, but strongly in Steller's Albatross. Unlike most s hemisphere albatrosses, *Phoebastria* molt their outer primaries (plus some inner and middle primaries) annually. For species identification check overall color patterns, and bill size and color.

Fig 136. Albatrosses often scavenge around fishing boats, such as these Laysan (left) and Black-footed (right) albatrosses with Northern Fulmars and an adult gull. MJI. Aleutian Islands, Alaska, 12 Sep 2006.

A1. BLACK-FOOTED ALBATROSS *Phoebastria nigripes*
L 71–82 cm, WS 200–220 cm, bill 10–11 cm
Figures 1, 5, 13–14, 25, 60, 135–136, A1.1–A1.15, A2a.1–A2a.2, A3.1

Identification Summary North Pacific. Common off the West Coast, uncommon Alaska; favors warmer and more inshore waters than Laysan Albatross. All-dark with variable whitish band around base of bill; adults have white tail coverts. All ages have dusky to dull pinkish bill, blackish feet.

A1.1. Black-footed Albatrosses often gather with gulls to scavenge around boats. Extensively white uppertail coverts indicate an older adult, perhaps a male. SNGH. Off Monterey, California, 11 May 2008.

Taxonomy Monotypic.

Names The derivation of *Phoebastria* is unclear; *nigripes* refers to the black feet.

Status and Distribution Endangered. Breeds (Nov–Jun/Jul) on Hawaiian Islands, Wake Island, several islands s of Japan, and (since 2000) off nw Mexico. Ranges at sea in n Pacific (mainly n of 20˚N).
    Pacific. Starting around the year 2000, one or more pairs have nested off w Mexico, on Isla San Benedicto and possibly Isla Guadalupe (Pitman & Ballance 2002).
    Offshore nonbreeding visitor (year-round) from Alaska to Baja California, with latitudinal shift of population northward in summer to fall; commonest off West Coast in Apr–Oct. Rarely seen from shore, but can be seen off cen California in summer, mainly on windy days. During Nov–Feb (when most of population is closer to breeding grounds), generally uncommon to rare (mostly immatures) offshore from Baja California to cen British Columbia, very rare n to se Gulf of Alaska. With Mar–May dispersal from breeding grounds becomes fairly common to locally common off West Coast, with a slight northward shift from peak numbers off s California in Mar to off n California in May; rare in Gulf of Alaska by Mar. During Jun–Aug, numbers off s California decrease, but remains common off cen and n California; peak numbers off Washington to British Columbia are Aug–early Sep, when fairly common to common from Gulf of Alaska (peak numbers in Sep) to cen Aleutians, with low numbers ranging to w Aleutians

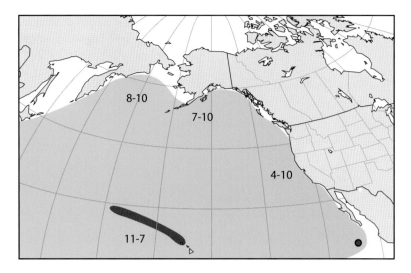

and into Bering Sea (mainly Sep–Oct). Numbers off n California to British Columbia decline late Sep–Oct as breeders withdraw, and irregular in Aleutians and s Bering Sea into Nov.

FIELD IDENTIFICATION

Similar Species A distinctive species, although confusion possible with stage 1 Steller's Albatross, which is dark overall (with white teardrop but lacking distinct white noseband). Steller's is larger (especially in body and bill), with a big pale pinkish bill, tipped pale bluish, and pinker legs and feet (see A3.1). Some Black-footeds have pinkish bills but these are duller overall, the bill of Black-footed is smaller and shorter than that of Steller's, and Black-footed has blackish legs and feet. Also see discussion of hybrid Black-footed x Laysan in the Laysan Albatross account.

Habitat and Behavior Nests on level or gently sloping ground near areas that offer sufficient wind for take-off; egg laid in a shallow scrape. Otherwise pelagic over deep waters, especially over the shelf break, but locally can be seen from shore (e.g., off Point Pinos, California, especially in Apr–Jul; Roberson 2002). Scavenges readily at fishing boats, where hundreds of birds may gather, associating readily with gulls and other species. Flight labored in calm to light winds and low to the water, but sails high and easily in strong winds.

Description A fairly small but stocky albatross with a fairly short thick bill and relatively short tail (toes often project in flight but can be pulled in). Bleached whitish head can occur on all ages, perhaps especially on immatures in sunnier latitudes, and on breeding adults that spend long periods incubating.

Despite a large population of known-age birds, plumage sequences in this species remain poorly known, compounded by potential differences between the sexes. The three-stage plumage index proposed by Hyrenbach (2002) was flawed in its characterization of class 1 and class 2 plumage aspects (fresh head and body plumage of postjuvenile immature plumages is, in fact, often darker than juvenile plumage; cf. A1.2–A1.3, A1.10–A1.13), and in its assumptions of age relating to white on the tail coverts; conclusions about the distribution of age classes off s California based on such criteria are thus fallacious. The age/sex categories proposed by Pyle (2008) are contradicted by small samples of known age/sex. For example, some birds age 4 years have white on the undertail coverts (Oikonos, unpubl. data[1]), and birds age 13 years can still have virtually all-dark undertail coverts (see A1.9). Interested observers can collect plumage data (for future analysis, if and when meaningful age/sex keys are developed) by scoring the amount of white on the tail coverts (Fig 137). At-sea observations indicate that white develops first on the undertail coverts (starting at age 4 on some males; Oikonos, unpubl. data) but that white does not appear on the uppertail coverts before the undertail coverts have a score of 4 (Table 8).

Five plumage stages of Black-footed Albatross are distinguished here as follows (see Fig

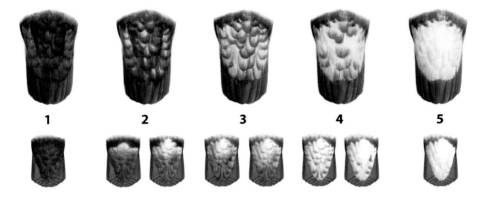

Fig 137. Scoring system for extent of white on tail coverts of Black-footed Albatross (as developed for surveys at Cordell Bank National Marine Sanctuary; Pyle and Howell, unpubl. data). Score 1: all-dark, 2: some white (< 50%), 3: about 50:50 white/dark, 4: mostly white (> 50%); 5: ostensibly (> 95%) all-white (small-dark areas can be difficult to see in the field). © Ian Lewington.

Table 8. Scores (see Fig 137) for uppertail coverts (UPTC) and undertail coverts (UNTC) of 236 Black-footed Albatross (expressed here as percentages) observed off cen California during May–Oct 2006–2008. Note how undertail coverts become mostly white before white develops on uppertail coverts, and how most birds are presumed immatures (score 1/1).

UPTC =	1	2	3	4	5
UNTC =					
1	59				
2	7				
3	1				
4	3	3	0.5	0.5	
5	1	3	3	9	10

137). Stage 1: all-brown (uppertail coverts score 1/undertail coverts score 1); 2: all-dark uppertail coverts, some white on undertail coverts (1/2–4); 3: all-dark uppertail coverts, all-white undertail coverts (1/5); 4: some white on uppertail coverts, mostly to all-white undertail coverts (2–4/4–5); 5: all-white uppertail and undertail coverts (5/5). Relating these five stages to birds of known age and sex could quickly generate a huge database to help determine at-sea distributions of different age and sex classes, and thus provide data to aid in conservation. Careful observation of stage 1 birds also can allow first-cycle, second-cycle, and sometimes third-cycle birds to be distinguished (see A1.2–A1.4 and Molt, below).

"Adult" (Stages 2–5, see below and Fig 137). Dark sooty brown overall (paler when worn), paler and grayer on underbody, with a variable whitish "noseband" around base of bill, white teardrop, and variable white on tail coverts; white primary shafts on upperwing. White on undertail coverts can start to appear at 4–6 years of age (at least in males; Oikonos, unpubl. data), whereas some birds 10 and older (females?) have dark undertail coverts. White on uppertail coverts starts to appear only after undertail coverts are mostly white (see Table 8), and may be more typical of males (Pyle 2008); confirmation needed from birds of known sex. Underwings dark overall, although bases of remiges and greater coverts reflectively pale in some lights. **Bill** dull dark purplish to dusky pinkish with blackish ungues and base of culminicorn (appears dark overall at any distance); legs and feet blackish (often with purplish or dark pinkish tones); eyes dark. Rarely, bill mostly dull pink, relatively bright (for a Black-footed) but much duller (and dark-tipped) than pale pinkish and pale-tipped bill of Steller's Albatross. **On the water.** Dark brown overall with white noseband offsetting dusky bill; undertail coverts with variable white.

Stage 1 (1/1; see Fig 137). Held at least 4–6 years, which may vary with sex (study needed). Plumage dark brown overall, paler and grayer on underbody; no white on tail coverts. Overall the commonest stage off cen California (59% of birds; see Table 8). **Juvenile/first cycle.** Fledges in Jun–Jul. Dark sooty brown overall, paler on underbody; subocular teardrop dull pale grayish (becomes white in first winter); lacks white on tail coverts. Primaries uniform in wear and relatively fresh. Underwings dark overall, although bases of remiges and greater coverts reflectively pale in some lights. By Apr–May, darker second-cycle feathers on head and body can contrast with faded juvenile feathers. **Bill** typically darker and duller than adult. **Second cycle.** Brown overall with whitish teardrop and noseband. PB2 primary molt involves outer 2–5 (usually 3) primaries; hence, e.g., birds with blacker and fresher-looking p8-p10 but otherwise uniform and relatively worn brown (juvenile) middle and inner primaries are in their second cycle. **Bill** much like adult but may average duller. Aging of third-cycle birds sometimes possible (cf. A1.4 and Molt, below). **On the water.** Dark brown overall with white noseband and dusky bill; undertail coverts brown.

Stage 2 (1/2–4; see Fig 137). As stage 1 but undertail coverts with some to extensive white feathering; uppertail coverts remain all-brown (beware of mistaking pale feather bases exposed during molt for actual white or whitish feathers). Fifth-cycle birds (males, at least) can have some white on undertail coverts (Oikonos, unpubl. data). On stage 2 and older birds, bill may average paler and pinker, and underbody paler and grayer, than on stage 1 birds. **On the water.** White on undertail coverts can be hard to see.

Stage 4 (2–4/4–5; see Fig 137). Undertail coverts mostly to all-white, uppertail coverts partly white. **On the water.** White on undertail coverts obvious (but uppertail coverts often hidden).

Stage 5 (5/5; see Fig 137). Undertail coverts and uppertail coverts white (may show a few dark

feather tips). Uncommon off cen California (10% of birds; see Table 8); perhaps mainly older adult males? **On the water.** White undertail coverts obvious (but uppertail coverts often hidden).

Hybrids With Laysan Albatross (McKee & Pyle 2002).

Molt Adult wing molt of breeding birds is at sea away from nesting grounds, mainly Jun–Sep. Adults replace p8-p10 between breeding seasons, and usually a variable number of middle and inner primaries (Langston & Rohwer 1995). Adults with most restricted primary molt presumably successful breeders, and replace only p8-p10 during Jul–Sep; nonbreeding adults can start inner or mid-primary molt Apr–May and can replace all primaries in one cycle. Adult body molt mainly Apr–Oct; can start on nesting grounds.

Young fledge in Jul, and presumed PB2 starts with head and body in Oct–Dec; wing molt (mainly Jul–Sep, about 12–15 months after fledging) involves outer 2–5 primaries, commonly only p8-p10. Subsequent wing molts of immatures and nonbreeders start late Apr–early Jul (with inner or mid-primaries), end late Aug–early Oct (pers. obs.), and include outer primaries (mainly Jul–Sep) and usually some middle and inner primaries. Molts of nonbreeders (including immatures and adults that skip a breeding season) can include all primaries, usually starting with p7 and progressing inward (Howell 2006, Rohwer & Edwards 2006); p8-p10 are typically replaced fairly rapidly in Jul–Aug, and sometimes all three feathers grow simultaneously.

Typical PB2 includes p8-p10 and sometimes a few outer and inner secondaries; PB3 includes most or all primaries (including p5-p10) but a large block of juvenile secondaries is commonly retained; PB4 commonly involves p7-p10 plus inner primaries, but with p5-p6 retained, and remaining juvenile secondaries replaced.

Note 1. Oikonos, unpubl. data (bird number 521 tagged in summer 2007, fledged summer 2003 and thus age 4 years; male with some white undertail coverts, sexed genetically).

A1.2. Fresh juvenile Black-footed Albatross. Note evenly fresh plumage and pointed outer primary. SNGH. Off Bodega Bay, California, 16 Sep 2009.

A1.3. Second-cycle Black-footed Albatross. Note contrast between fresh blacker (second basic) outer primaries and faded brown (juvenile) middle and inner primaries, plus large block of juvenile secondaries. Whitish patches on the uppertail coverts are bleached juvenile feathers, not incoming adult feathers. SNGH. Off Bodega Bay, California, 17 Oct 2008.

A1.4. Third-cycle Black-footed Albatross. All primaries and some secondaries were renewed in third prebasic molt (Apr–Oct of previous year); note long block of (shorter and browner) retained juvenile secondaries. SNGH. Off Monterey, California, 11 May 2008.

A1.5. "Adult" Black-footed Albatross (uppertail covert score 3; see Fig 137). Age and sex of birds in this plumage unknown. SNGH. Off Bodega Bay, California, 30 Sep 2007.

A1.6. Adult Black-footed Albatross (undertail covert score 5; see Fig 137). Contrasting paler and grayer underbody is typical of adults, but age (beyond "adult") and sex of birds in this plumage unknown. SNGH. Torishima, Japan, 1 May 2008.

A1.7. Adult Black-footed Albatross (undertail covert score 5; see Fig 137). Compare worn and faded plumage of molting fall birds with fresh plumage (A1.6). SNGH. Off Bodega Bay, California, 9 Sep 2008.

A1.8. Black-footed Albatross (undertail covert score 1; see Fig 137). Dark plumage like this has been suggested to indicate juvenile (Hyrenbach 2002; but cf. A1.2–A1.4). However, wing molt patterns (p1 and p7-p10 new, no juvenile secondaries) indicate at least fourth molt cycle, and color band (A959, white on blue) reveals this bird fledged in summer 2001, thus in its sixth cycle. SNGH. Off Bodega Bay, California, 13 Oct 2006.

A1.9. Black-footed Albatross (undertail covert score 1; see Fig 137). This bird's color band (E451, black on yellow; image here flipped 180°) reveals it fledged in summer 1994, and thus is 13 years old. All-dark undertail coverts at this age may indicate a female (study needed). SNGH. Off Monterey, California, 11 Feb 2007.

A1.10. "Adult" Black-footed Albatross (undertail covert score 4, uppertail score 3; see Fig 137). Age and sex of birds in this plumage unknown. Note p7 on near wing has been shed at start of prebasic primary molt. SNGH. Off Monterey, California, 11 May 2008.

A1.11. Juvenile Black-footed Albatross (same bird as A1.2). Note uniformly fresh scapulars and upperwing coverts. Pale flecking on neck may represent start of protracted second prebasic molt. SNGH. Off Bodega Bay, California, 16 Sep 2009.

A1.12. "Immature" (front) and "adult" (behind) Black-footed Albatrosses (undertail covert score 5; see Fig 137). Compare mottled scapulars and upperwing coverts with fresh juvenile (A1.11). SNGH. Off Bodega Bay, California, 14 Aug 2007.

A1.13. Immature Black-footed Albatross. In fresh basic plumage, head and body can be very dark sooty brown (cf. A1.11–A1.12). SNGH. Off Bodega Bay, California, 30 Sep 2007.

A1.14. Some Black-footed Albatross (usually adults) have strong pink tones to the bill. SNGH. Off Bodega Bay, California, 28 Sep 2008.

A1.15. Viewed head-on, white facial blaze of Black-footed Albatrosses is often striking, as is white head and body of Laysan Albatross (center bird). SNGH. Off Bodega Bay, California, 11 Aug 2010.

A2. LAYSAN ALBATROSS *Phoebastria immutabilis*
L 71–79 cm, WS 195–215 cm, bill 10–11 cm
Figures 5, 60, 136, A1.15, A2.1–A2.13, A2a.1–A2a.2

Identification Summary North Pacific. Uncommon off the West Coast, common Alaska; favors cooler and more offshore waters than Black-footed Albatross. Striking black-and-white plumage (with black back) distinctive among North Pacific albatrosses, might suggest a giant dark-backed gull. Note pinkish bill and lack of appreciable age-related variation.

A2.1. In the 1980s, Laysan Albatross started nesting on some islands off western Mexico. Note large chick with left-hand adult. SNGH. Isla San Benedicto, Mexico, 25 Apr 1992.

Taxonomy Monotypic.

Names The derivation of *Phoebastria* is unclear; *immutabilis* refers to the similarity of all plumages, which thus appear unchanging, or immutable. The English name refers to Laysan Island in Hawaii, where this species breeds in large numbers.

Status and Distribution Near Threatened. Breeds (Nov/Dec–Jun/Jul) on Hawaiian Islands and Wake Island, also (since 1970s) on Bonin Islands and (since 1980s) off nw Mexico. Ranges at sea in North Pacific (mainly n of 20°N).

Pacific. Population has expanded noticeably in past 40 years, reflected in colonization of islands off w Mexico since 1980s (Howell & Webb 1992, Gallo-R. & Figueroa-C. 1996). Increasing numbers now breed (Nov–Jul/Aug) on Isla Guadalupe (increased from 4 pairs in 1983/1984 to 193 pairs in 2000/2001 and 245 pairs in 2002/2003; Pitman et al. 2004, Luna Mendoza et al. 2005), Rocas Alijos, Isla Clarión (since 1987/1988; 46 pairs in 2002/2003, Wanless et al. 2009), and Isla San Benedicto (since 1990/1991, 12 pairs in 2000/2001; Pitman & Ballance 2002).

Offshore nonbreeding visitor year-round from Alaska to Baja California, with latitudinal shift of population northward in summer; commonest off West Coast Oct–Mar. Rarely seen from shore except in Aleutians. During Nov–Mar (when

288

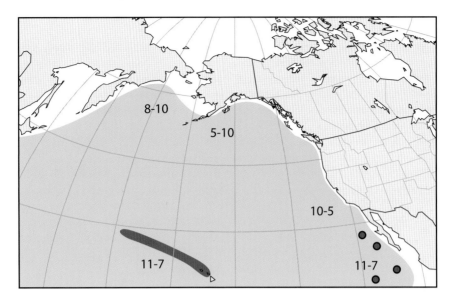

FIELD IDENTIFICATION

most of population is closer to breeding grounds) uncommon (mainly nonbreeders) offshore from Baja California n to cen British Columbia, rare to Gulf of Alaska and Aleutians. In Mar–May, becomes rarer off West Coast as birds move n, and commoner in Gulf of Alaska as birds head toward the Aleutians. In Jun–Aug, rarest off West Coast, common from w Gulf of Alaska to Aleutians (peak numbers Jun–Sep in e Aleutians); smaller numbers range into s Bering Sea (mainly Aug–Oct). Most birds return to colonies Sep–Oct, and become commoner off British Columbia and Washington at this time, with southward movement of (mainly) nonbreeders back to waters off West Coast. Breeding birds from Hawaii mainly range n toward the Aleutians for foraging; those breeding off Mexico presumably range n to the offshore California Current.

Increased sightings since 1990s off s California (mainly Oct–May) and juveniles off cen California in Aug–Oct reflect growing Mexican population. Ranges s rarely (mainly Apr–May) to waters off Jalisco and into Gulf of California. Casual (May–Jun) inland in the Southwest (all records since 1976, including four from Salton Sea). Birds occasionally land on ships and ride into West Coast ports, mainly in late winter and spring, and 1 bird has returned to Point Arena, Mendocino Co., California (late Nov–early Apr) for 17 winters (through 2009/2010).

Similar Species A distinctive, relatively small albatross with plumage pattern recalling an adult dark-backed gull, swimming individuals of which a hopeful observer might mistake, at least momentarily, for an albatross. Laysan is much larger and longer-necked, with a hunched back, long pinkish bill, and dark tail. Note superficial similarity of Laysan to some mollymawks (genus *Thalassarche*), which could occur as vagrants to North Pacific. Mollymawks are relatively longer tailed (their toes do not project in flight) and all have plumage patterns and bill colors distinct from Laysan.

Hybrid Laysan x Black-footed Albatross are variable in appearance (McKee & Pyle 2002) but generally rare, and even more rarely reported at sea. Most (presumed F1 hybrids) have head and neck grayish (smoky gray to sooty brownish gray) with white noseband similar to Black-footed; underparts pale gray to whitish. A few (perhaps F2 backcrosses with Laysan) resemble Laysan but have darker face and dusky markings or dusky wash on neck and underparts. Some hybrids have dark body and whitish head and neck, a pattern superficially suggesting Galapagos Albatross, which has much bigger and longer yellow bill, pale vermiculations in dark plumage. Rump and uppertail coverts of hybrids tend to be extensively dark, with *U*-shaped white band on distal tail coverts (McKee & Pyle 2002).

Habitat and Behavior Nests on level or gently sloping ground near areas that offer sufficient wind for take-off; egg laid in a shallow scrape. Otherwise pelagic over cooler offshore waters, with a more northerly distribution than Black-footed Albatross. Feeds mainly on squid and scavenges readily at fishing boats, where tens of birds may gather, associating readily with other albatrosses, fulmars, and gulls. Flight labored in calm to light winds and low to the water, but sails high and easily in strong winds.

Description A relatively small and lightly built albatross with a relatively short tail (toes often project in flight but can be pulled in) and fairly slender bill.

Adult. White head and neck contrast with slaty blackish back and upperwings (browner when worn), which have white primary shafts; black brow and smoky gray clouding on sides of head; uppertail coverts and sides of rump white; tail slaty blackish (paler and frostier when fresh) with whitish shafts. Underparts white, the underwings with variable and irregular black margins thickest along leading edge on primary coverts and humerals. Lightest marked birds have overall white underwings, with narrow black margins expanded on primary coverts but little or no black on humerals (McKee & Pyle 2002); on the darkest birds, especially at long range and in dull light, underwings appear dark overall with white restricted to a central panel (darkest birds may be hybrids with Black-footed Albatross; McKee & Pyle 2002). **Bill** pale pinkish, often flushed orange (especially at base), with gray-blue ungues and fine black tip; legs pale pinkish; eyes dark.

Juvenile/first cycle (Jul–Jun). Nestling has dark bill but this quickly changes to adult-like in color by fledging in Jun–Jul. Plumage adult-like but gray face muted or messily defined, and (especially in sunny conditions) often appears white headed with goggle-like black eye patch; also, greater secondary underwing coverts often relatively small and narrow, producing finely serrated, or comb-like, effect on dark trailing edge of underwing. **Bill** pale pinkish with little or no orange, and may retain dusky traces (e.g., on base of culminicorn) for a few months. Primaries uniform in wear and relatively fresh. Variable molt of head and body feathers in first winter presumed to be start of PB2, perhaps sometimes producing adult-like gray face (study needed; see A2.12). Some birds completing PB2 wing molt, about 14 months after fledging, still have juvenile-like face (e.g., A2.5), which may be retained for second year. PB2 primary molt involves outer 2–5 (usually 3) primaries; hence, e.g., birds with blacker and fresher-looking p8-p10 but otherwise uniform and relatively worn brown (juvenile) middle and inner primaries are in their second cycle. Aging of third-cycle and older birds may be possible by wing molt patterns (see Molt, below), but good views/photos or in-hand examination required.

Hybrids With Black-footed Albatross (McKee & Pyle 2002).

Molt Adult wing molt at sea away from nesting grounds, mainly Jul–Oct. Adults replace p8-p10 between breeding seasons, and usually a variable number of middle and inner primaries (Langston & Rohwer 1995). Young fledge in Jun–Jul and start (presumed PB2) head and body molt in first winter; much of juvenile head and body plumage replaced by first spring (e.g., A2.12). PB2 primary molt (mainly Jul–Sep) includes outer 2–5 primaries, usually only p8-p10. Subsequent annual wing molts include outer primaries and some middle and inner primaries; wing molt more extensive in prebreeders and also in adults that skip a year of breeding to catch up on molt (Langston & Rohwer 1996).

Patterns of PB2 through PB4 wing molts overall similar to Black-footed Albatross (which see), allowing some birds to be aged through their fourth cycle. It has been reported that Laysan typically replaces fewer wing feathers per molt than Black-footed (Langston & Rohwer 1995), but at least in some years Laysan can replace more feathers than Black-footed; this may reflect Laysans skipping a year of breeding, perhaps related to food supply and the different foraging ranges of the two species (P. Pyle and T. McKee, unpubl. data for 1998–2000 on Midway Atoll).

A2.2. Postjuvenile plumages of Laysan Albatross show smoky-gray cheeks offsetting a whiter crown. Primary molt patterns (with the outer five primaries fresher) indicate a bird at least 4–5 years old. TMcG. Off Santa Barbara, California, 22 Apr 2006.

A2.3. Evenly fresh plumage of back and upperwings, together with overall white face lacking distinct gray cheeks (cf. A2.2), identify this Laysan Albatross as a juvenile (fledged summer 2010 from Guadalupe Island, Mexico, based on color band read in field). SNGH. Off Monterey, California, 6 Aug 2010.

A2.4. (Above) First-winter Laysan Albatross in slightly worn juvenile plumage, starting to renew some back feathers. SNGH. Off Bodega Bay, California, 20 Nov 2010.

A2.5. (Above right) Second-winter Laysan Albatross completing PB2 molt of outer primaries (new p7-p10 contrast with uniformly worn and browner juvenile inner primaries and secondaries); note juvenile-like face pattern. BLS. Off Monterey, California, 27 Aug 2010.

A2.6. (Right) Typical end-on view of Laysan Albatross (same juvenile as A2.11); the white area is more extensive than Black-footed Albatross; note toes projecting beyond tail tip, ruling out mollymawks. SNGH. Off Bodega Bay, California, 30 Sep 2007.

A2.7. Extent of black underwing markings on Laysan Albatross highly variable (cf. A2.8–A2.10), this adult being at the whiter end of the spectrum. TMcG. Off Los Angeles, California, 16 Apr 2005.

A2.8. Adult Laysan Albatross with moderately heavy black underwing markings (cf. A2.7, A2.9). TMcG. Off San Diego, California, 9 May 2009.

A2.9. Juvenile Laysan Albatross with extensive black underwing markings; also note finely serrated pattern of relatively narrow greater secondary coverts (cf. A2.7–A2.8). SNGH. Off Monterey, California, 26 Sep 2008.

A2a.1. Hybrid Laysan x Black-footed Albatross with classically intermediate features. RLP. Aleutians, Alaska, 2 Jun 2002.

A2.10. Adult Laysan Albatross with chick. KL. Isla Guadalupe, Mexico, 13 Mar 2003.

A2.11. Juvenile Laysan Albatross. Compare black "goggle-eyes" in white head with gray-faced adult plumage (A2.10). SNGH. Off Bodega Bay, California, 30 Sep 2007.

A2.12. First-year Laysan Albatross in active head and body molt. Over first winter and spring, may attain smoky gray cheeks like adult. KP. Off Monterey, California, 8 May 2010.

A2.13. Juvenile Laysan Albatross with fourth-cycle Western Gull. SNGH. Off Monterey, California, 6 Aug 2010.

A2a.2. Hybrid Laysan x Black-footed Albatross (same bird as A2a.1). RLP. Aleutians, Alaska, 2 Jun 2002.

A3. STELLER'S (SHORT-TAILED) ALBATROSS *Phoebastria albatrus*
L 80–90 cm, WS 220–240 cm, bill 13–14 cm
Figures 42–43, A3.1–A3.25

Identification Summary North Pacific. Rare. All ages have a very big, pale pinkish bill, tipped pale blue. Older adults striking and unmistakable, with golden hindneck, white back and inner half of upperwings. Younger immatures dark sooty brown overall, whitening first on face and underbody. Immature and sub-adult plumages have dark-brown cowl from crown to hindneck.

A3.1. Second-cycle Steller's Albatross (right) with adult Black-footed Albatross. The huge pink bill of an immature Steller's renders it unmistakable. SNGH. Off Bodega Bay, California, 16 Sep 2009.

Taxonomy Monotypic.

Names The derivation of *Phoebastria* is unclear; *albatrus* may refer to "white-clothed" in reference to the adult plumage. It has been noted that Georg Steller (1709–1746) worked hard for his albatross and deserves to be remembered; "short-tailed" is not especially appropriate, or memorable.

Status and Distribution Vulnerable. Breeds (late Oct to mid-Jun) s of Japan on Torishima and Senkaku retto, with a few adults also visiting Hawaii in the breeding season. Ranges widely in North Pacific, mainly n of 30°N. Breeding is annual, like other *Phoebastria* (H. Hasegawa, pers. comm., *contra* Pyle 2008).

Pacific. Rare to locally "common" nonbreeding visitor (Mar–Oct, mainly May–Sep) in w and cen Aleutians (where gatherings of more than 100 birds can occur at fishing boats), ranging into s Bering Sea and e to Gulf of Alaska. Rare to casual but increasing (most recent records since 1980s) offshore from British Columbia to s California (mainly Aug–Apr, but records year-round). All ages occur in the Aleutians, but recent West Coast records have been stage 1 immatures; some older ages reach British Columbia. Also an anomalous report of an adult off w Mexico, Apr 1990. Among adults, males average higher-latitude foraging ranges than females (Suryan et al. 2007).

Prior to 1900, numerous off Pacific coast of North America from Bering Sea and Aleutians s to Baja California, although details of historic distribution and abundance in some areas clouded by confusion with Laysan and Black-footed albatrosses. Exploitation of birds on the nesting islands

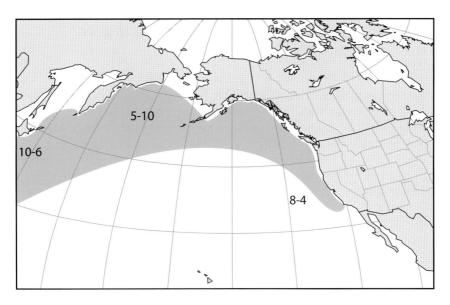

brought Steller's Albatross close to extinction by the 1930s, when the last known breeding adults were killed for their feathers. However, prebreeding immatures remained at sea and slowly recolonized Torishima in the late 1940s and 1950s. Increased conservation awareness and protective legislation dating from the 1950s helped the population grow to around 2460 birds (418 breeding pairs) by the 2008/2009 season (H. Hasegawa, pers. comm.). Records from North American waters have increased in tandem.

FIELD IDENTIFICATION

Similar Species A distinctive species if seen well; note large pale pinkish bill at all ages. All-dark immatures could be confused with smaller Black-footed Albatross, which has a relatively short dark bill offset by a whitish noseband, blackish legs and feet. Very rare aberrant Laysan Albatross might superficially resemble Steller's (McKee & Pyle 2002), but are smaller with smaller bills.

A vagrant Wandering Albatross (see that species) might be overlooked as a Steller's, and all-dark plumages of giant-petrels (genus *Macronectes*) could also be mistaken for an immature Steller's. Giant-petrels have a massive pinkish-yellow bill with prominent nostril tubes on the culmen, dark grayish legs and feet, and bill tip pale greenish (Southern Giant-Petrel) to pinkish (Northern Giant-Petrel).

Habitat and Behavior Pelagic, but might be seen from shore, especially in the Aleutians; occurs over shelf, shelf break, and offshore waters. Singles off West Coast associate readily with Black-footed Albatrosses and other birds around fishing vessels; tends to dominate the smaller Black-footed (pers. obs.). Exceptional recent concentrations of more than 100 birds have been seen around fishing boats in the Aleutians, where Steller's associate mainly with fulmars. Flight labored in calm to light winds and low to the water, but sails high and easily in strong winds, often towering higher than Black-footed Albatrosses in similar conditions.

Description A fairly large albatross with a massive body, long stout bill, and relatively short wings and tail (toes often project in flight but can be pulled in). Despite a reasonably large population of known-age birds, no age-based plumage key has been developed that could aid in gathering at-sea data. Plumage sequences thus remain poorly known, compounded by differences between and within sexes. Some males are mostly white at 8 years, whereas others still have a brown back with white mottling at 10 years (H. Hasegawa, pers. comm.). From a known breeding pair, the male attained full "adult plumage" by age 10, but the female had not done so by age 14 (H. Hasegawa, pers. comm.), suggesting a parallel with the complex plumage changes in Wandering Albatross taxa.

Seven plumage stages are provisionally distinguished here, from 1 (all-brown immature) to 7 (whitest "adult"), while accepting that these are lines of convenience drawn on a potential continuum of patterns. Relating these stages to birds of known age and sex could generate a database to determine at-sea distributions of different age/sex classes, and thus provide data to aid in conservation.

"Adult" (Stage 7). Whitest plumages may be developed more quickly by males. Head and body snowy white with golden-yellow crown and hindneck (cowl), black subscapulars and tail. Upperwings: inner third extensively snowy white with mostly black median and greater humerals, black middle secondaries (forming a narrow trailing edge), and narrow black leading edge; outer two-thirds black with whitish primary shafts. Underwings white with a narrow black margin, most distinct on trailing edge and on leading edge to primaries and primary coverts. **Bill** pale pink with pale bluish ungues; legs and feet bluish pink to pale pink; eyes dark. **On the water.** White overall with a golden-yellow cowl; black subscapulars, humerals, and wingtips.

Stage 1 (ages 1–2). Plumage dark brown overall, with blacker head and neck, paler and grayer underbody, especially chest. **Juvenile/first cycle.** Fledges in June. Blackish brown overall, darkest on head and neck, palest on underbody, with contrast between blacker hood and paler chest accentuated by fading; underwings dark overall, often with reflectively paler remiges, especially primaries. Lacks whitish subocular teardrop on fledging, but this develops through molt and fading by first winter. Primaries and secondaries fresh or slightly worn, uniform in wear, and relatively tapered. Dark bill of nestling becomes pink with pale bluish ungues within 2 months but can retain fine blackish tip for 2+ years; legs and feet dark with variable pink or purplish tones. **Second cycle.** PB2 molt apparently starts on head and body in first winter, with p8-p10 molted Jul–Sep, about 13–15 months after fledging. Appears much like first cycle but outer primaries fresher, relatively rounded at tips in contrast to worn and tapered middle and inner primaries; a small bleached whitish elbow patch usually distinct. Underparts often paler in contrast to blackish brown head and neck, which have a whitish subocular crescent. Some birds (ages 2–3?) may develop a small whitish area ("bridle") around base of bill and under eyes. Legs and feet dark pinkish to pink.

Stage 2 (ages 3–5 and older). Face and foreneck become extensively white, with golden suffusion bordering dark brown cowl from crown to hindneck. Underbody becomes mostly white, with brown remaining last on lower belly; underwings become extensively white, but still with obvious dark tips to lesser coverts. Upperparts remain brown overall, with little or no white mottling on distal tail coverts; whitish elbow patch fairly small. Some presumed third-cycle birds (males?) develop large white bridle plus white foreneck, whitish median underbody, extensive white on underwing (with broad dark tips to coverts), and some white on distal uppertail coverts. Conversely, some presumed fourth-cycle birds (females?) have only a small white bridle, dirty whitish foreneck and median underbody, and extensively dark underwings. Bill can retain fine dusky tip into fourth cycle; legs and feet pale bluish pink to pink.

Stage 3 (ages 4–6 and older). Relative to stage 2, lower back, rump, and uppertail coverts develop extensive white mottling, and distal uppertail coverts become whiter; back and upperwings paler overall, often with a grayish sheen, such that dark cowl contrasts more strongly with brown mantle; some birds (males?) become golden on forecrown. Underparts clean white; underwings white overall, with dark tips to some coverts. White elbow patch larger (especially males?) and brighter, usually obvious on swimming birds. Bill can have fine dark tip, perhaps mainly on fourth- and fifth-cycle birds (males?) in this plumage.

Stage 4. Relative to stage 3, back becomes mostly white, but still with some brown mottling, so that dark cowl contrasts with white mantle; lower back and rump mostly white to wholly white; scapulars start to show white. Underwings still with dark tips to some coverts, especially a narrow dark bar across tips of primary coverts. On some birds (males?) crown and nape become golden, with dark collar limited to lower hindneck, and lesser upperwing coverts become frostier.

Stage 5. Relative to stage 4, back and scapulars clean white or with only scattered dark marks. Some birds (males?) have crown and nape golden, above a narrow dark-brown hindcollar. Other birds (females?) have an extensive dark-brown cowl. Underwings with few or no dark tips to coverts.

Stage 6. Crown and hindneck golden with reduced or no dark brown hindcollar. Variable white to silvery gray develops on humeral coverts.

Underwings with few or no dark tips to coverts. White elbow patch large.

Stage 7. See adult description above. Relative to stage 6, no dark brown on hindneck; white scapulars, humeral coverts, and large elbow patch form large white upperwing panel, although on some birds dark outer edges to scapulars create a narrow diagonal bar that splits the white; underwings white, without dark tips to coverts.

Molt Breeding adults molt between breeding cycles (although some molt of body feathers may start toward end of breeding season), with wing molt mainly Jun–Sep and outer primaries molted annually, like other *Phoebastria* (pers. obs.). Young fledge in Jun and retain juvenile plumage into winter. Head and body molt on some birds in Oct–Dec presumed to be start of PB2 but might be PF molt (needs study); PB2 wing molt typically includes p8-p10 (mainly Jul–Sep, about 13–15 months after fledging), but may well vary (with 2–4 outer primaries renewed) as in other *Phoebastria*. Subsequent wing molts of immatures and nonbreeders start Apr–Jun (with inner or mid-primaries), usually end by late Sep, and include outer primaries (mainly Jul–Sep) and usually some middle and inner primaries (pers. obs.; M. J. Iliff, photos).

PB3 apparently can include all primaries but large blocks of juvenile secondaries are retained (see A3.8–A3.9); PB4 usually replaces all remaining juvenile secondaries plus outer (usually p7-p10 or p8-p10) and some inner primaries (pers. obs.); extent of PB2-PB4 wing molts are thus much like Black-footed and Laysan albatrosses. Occasional juvenile secondaries, and exceptionally an inner primary (such as p3), may be retained by some fourth-cycle birds.

A3.2. Adult (stage 7) Steller's Albatross. Whitest adults have unbroken white upperwing panel (cf. A3.3). SNGH. Torishima, Japan, 1 May 2008.

A3.3. Adult (stage 7) Steller's Albatross. Compare black markings in white upperwing panel with A3.2. SNGH. Torishima, Japan, 1 May 2008.

A3.4. Adult (stage 7) Steller's Albatross. Full adult has almost completely white underwings. SNGH. Torishima, Japan, 1 May 2008.

A3.5. First-winter (stage 1) Steller's Albatross, aged by freshly uniform upperwings with pointed p10 (visible clearly in other photos of same bird). Molt of head and body feathers under way, apparently start of second prebasic molt (cf. A3.21, A3.6). SNGH. Off Bodega Bay, California, 20 Nov 2010.

A3.6. Second-winter (stage 1) Steller's Albatross, renewing p8-p10, p1, and rectrices toward end of protracted second prebasic molt (cf. A3.5). SNGH. Off Bodega Bay, California, 16 Sep 2009.

A3.7. Second-/third-cycle (stage 1) Steller's Albatross in faded plumage (p8-p10 renewed in second prebasic molt the previous fall; cf. A3.6), probably starting third prebasic molt (cf. A3.23 of same bird). SNGH. Torishima, Japan, 1 May 2008.

A3.8. Third-cycle (stage 1/stage 2) Steller's Albatross, aged by retained block of juvenile secondaries and uniform (third basic) primaries. CC. Torishima, Japan, 15 Apr 2009.

A3.9. Third-cycle (stage 2) Steller's Albatross, aged by retained block of juvenile secondaries and uniform (third basic) primaries. CC. Torishima, Japan, 15 Apr 2009.

A3.10. Stage 2 Steller's Albatross, perhaps completing fourth prebasic molt. Note fresher p7-p10 (p10 still growing) compared to older middle primaries (rounded and not overly worn, thus not juvenile feathers), presence of one very worn (juvenile?) middle secondary, and relatively retarded plumage aspect. MJI. Aleutians, Alaska, 12 Sep 2006.

A3.11. Immature (stage 2) Steller's Albatross, perhaps fourth cycle; note contrastingly worn (third cycle?) middle primaries and long block of evenly fresh secondaries, corresponding to block of juvenile secondaries typically retained in third cycle (cf. A3.8–A3.9). SNGH. Torishima, Japan, 1 May 2008.

A3.12. Immature (stage 3) Steller's Albatross, possibly fourth cycle; note heavily abraded and faded p3 and s4 on near wing, perhaps retained juvenile feathers now four years old. SNGH. Torishima, Japan, 1 May 2008.

A3.13. Immature (stage 3) Steller's Albatross, possibly fourth cycle (male?); note contrastingly worn (third basic?) middle primaries and long block of evenly fresh secondaries, corresponding to block of juvenile secondaries typically retained in third cycle (cf. A3.8–A3.9). SNGH. Torishima, Japan, 1 May 2008.

A3.14. (Above) Steller's Albatross (early stage 4). Note white hindneck offsetting dark cowl, cf. stage 3 birds (A3.12–A3.13). SNGH. Torishima, Japan, 1 May 2008.

A3.15. (Above right) Steller's Albatross (later stage 4). Age and sex of birds in older "immature" plumages like this needs study; some may be breeding-age females. SNGH. Torishima, Japan, 1 May 2008.

A3.16. (Right) Immature (stage 3) Steller's Albatross. Patterns of whitening on the underwing coverts are poorly known, but relatively advanced state (for stage 3) may indicate a male. SNGH. Torishima, Japan, 1 May 2008.

A3.17. Steller's Albatross (stage 4, possibly male because of reduced dark hindneck cowl). After body has become mostly white, upperwing covert panel starts to become paler. SNGH. Torishima, Japan, 1 May 2008.

A3.18. Steller's Albatross (stage 4, possibly male because of reduced dark hindneck cowl). Underwing mostly white but with dark tips to primary coverts. SNGH. Torishima, Japan, 1 May 2008.

A3.19. Steller's Albatross (stage 5). Age and sex of birds in "subadult" plumage stages like this needs study. SNGH. Torishima, Japan, 1 May 2008.

A3.20. Steller's Albatross (stage 6). Head and body have adult aspect, but note black tips to underprimary coverts, reduced white upperwing panel. Next plumage stage fully "adult" (A3.2–A3.4). SNGH. Torishima, Japan, 1 May 2008.

A3.21. First-winter Steller's Albatross (stage 1). Much of head and body feathering has been renewed, perhaps as start of protracted second prebasic molt; note narrow dull eye crescents. EWP. Off Bodega Bay, California, 4 Dec 2005.

A3.22. Second-winter Steller's Albatross (stage 1, same bird as A3.6). Pale areas of face and foreneck may represent molt as well as bleaching of feathers renewed almost a year ago (cf. A3.21). SNGH. Off Bodega Bay, California, 16 Sep 2009.

A3.23. Second-/third-cycle Steller's Albatross (stage 1, same bird as A3.7). Pale blotching on neck indicates molt (likely start of third prebasic molt). SNGH. Torishima, Japan, 1 May 2008.

A3.24. Presumed third-cycle (stage 2) Steller's Albatross, aged from other photos by retained block of juvenile secondaries and uniform generation (third basic) primaries. CC. Torishima, Japan, 15 Apr 2009.

A3.25. Steller's Albatross (stage 5). Age and sex of birds in "subadult" plumage stages like this need study. SNGH. Torishima, Japan, 1 May 2008.

Vagrant Albatrosses

Some 10–11 taxa of albatrosses have occurred as vagrants to North American waters from the s hemisphere. Vagrant albatrosses in the North Atlantic have been almost annual in recent years, but only involve two species of mollymawks (genus *Thalassarche*): Western Yellow-nosed and Black-browed albatrosses. Vagrants to the Pacific region are exceptional, with most taxa represented in North American waters by only single records. Pacific vagrants comprise 4 species of mollymawks (Tasmanian Shy, Auckland Shy, Salvin's, and Chatham albatrosses), 2–3 taxa in the Wandering Albatross complex (Antipodes and Gibson's, at least), and single species in the genera *Phoebastria* (Galapagos Albatross; see genus introduction on p. 280), and *Phoebetria* (Light-mantled Sooty Albatross).

Mollymawks: Genus *Thalassarche* Six of the 11 taxa in this genus have occurred as vagrants in the region: 2 in the Atlantic, 4 in the Pacific. Mollymawks are small to fairly large albatrosses with relatively short wings (24–30 secondaries), relatively long tails (with feet not projecting in flight), and brightly patterned bills. They often accompany ships and scavenge readily around fishing boats. Ages differ in appearance; most species attain adult-like plumage aspect in 2–3 years, with fully adult bill pattern taking 4–5 years or longer to develop. For species identification check head and neck patterns, bill color and pattern, underwing pattern, and degree of contrast between hindneck and back (Figs 138–139).

Fig 138. As well as differing in bill and plumage patterns, mollymawks can also differ appreciably in structure. Compare the short neck and stocky body of the immature Black-browed Albatross (left) with the lighter build, slimmer wings, and longer bill of the adult Western Yellow-nosed Albatross (right). SNGH. South Atlantic, 45°S 21°W, 7 Apr 2009.

Fig 139. Mollymawks range in size from the small and lightly built Western Yellow-nosed Albatross (right) to the relatively large and broad-winged Shy Albatross (immature, left). Also note the dark bill and thicker black wing margins of the Yellow-nosed. SNGH. Tristan da Cunha, South Atlantic, 1 Apr 2002.

As an aging guideline, mollymawks about 6 months after fledging are in slightly worn juvenile plumage, perhaps with a little head and body molt apparent; birds at about 12 months have slightly worn outer primaries and often are undergoing obvious body molt and tail molt (their PB2 molt); birds at about 18 months have fresh head, body, and tail plumage contrasting with obviously worn juvenile upperwings (sometimes with a few fresh coverts); and birds at about 24 months after fledging have new outer primaries (usually p8-p10) and some new upperwing coverts. Mollymawks molt their primaries in two phases, which alternate between years (see Fig 140, p. 312): the outer primaries and often some inner and middle primaries are molted in one year (phase 1), and the middle and some inner primaries in the next year (phase 2). Body molt and wing molt are offset in timing so they don't overlap in the PB2 and PB3 molts, perhaps so that primary molt is not compromised. In Shy and Yellow-nosed albatrosses, head coloration of immatures in their second through fourth cycles varies from dusky gray to messy whitish, perhaps reflecting hormone levels at the time of molt, in combination with fading. Conversely, in Salvin's and Chatham albatrosses, head coloration of immatures in these same age classes appears consistently to be dusky gray.

A4. WESTERN YELLOW-NOSED ALBATROSS
Thalassarche [chlororhynchus] chlororhynchus
L 70–76 cm, WS 188–215 cm, bill 11–12 cm
Figures 138–139, A4.1–A4.9

Identification Summary Atlantic. Very rare off e North America (mainly May–Aug). The smallest mollymawk, with relatively light build and long slender bill. All ages have white underwing with black leading edge. Juvenile bill dark, becoming black with yellow culminicorn stripe in 1–2 years; adult bill black with yellow culminicorn stripe and orange nail. Also known as Atlantic Yellow-nosed Albatross.

Taxonomy The two taxa of Yellow-nosed Albatross are variably treated as subspecies or species, and differ slightly in bill structure, face pattern, and adult head color.

T. [c.] chlororhynchus (Western, or Atlantic, Yellow-nosed Albatross) breeds and ranges in s Atlantic Ocean, very rare e to Australia. Yellow culminicorn stripe slightly broader and more rounded at forehead, with slightly convex sides; outer edges of naricorn convex; eye patch larger and triangular. Adult has smoky gray head and neck.

T. [c.] carteri (Eastern, or Indian, Yellow-nosed Albatross) breeds and ranges in s Indian Ocean, w to South Africa, rarely e to New Zealand. Yellow culminicorn stripe slightly narrower and more tapered at forehead, with straighter sides; outer edges of naricorn straight; eye patch smaller, less triangular. Adult has gray clouding on head and neck. Also called *T. [c.] bassi* (see Robertson 2002).

Names *Thalassarche* means "ruler of the sea," *chlororhynchos* refers to yellow on the bill.

Status and Distribution Endangered. Breeds (Sep–Apr) and ranges in South Atlantic Ocean, mainly 25–50°S.

Atlantic. Very rare nonbreeding visitor (mainly May–Aug, but records year-round) to inshore waters of e North America. North American records presumably all refer to Western Yellow-nosed (adult or subadult Westerns have been recorded in Texas, Florida, North Carolina, New York, and Maine). Records are spread from Newfoundland s to Florida and in Gulf of Mexico from Florida w to Texas. Records in the Northeast (s to New England) mainly late Mar–late Aug; from mid-Atlantic coast s to Florida, mainly late Nov to mid Apr; and from Florida and Gulf of Mexico, mainly May–Oct. Some records may pertain to individuals returning in subsequent years.

FIELD IDENTIFICATION

Similar Species Great Black-backed Gull and Northern Gannet have been mistaken for albatrosses, especially with birds viewed at a distance or in poor conditions. A real albatross, however, should be unmistakable as such. *Gulls* have steadier, less labored wingbeats in calm or light winds but they can sail and bank in strong winds, although with the wings typically crooked at the carpals (vs. held straighter on an albatross); an albatross has a long head and neck projection, a long bill, dark tail, and longer wings with a longer inner arm. *Gannets* have a more tapered and pointed front end and rear end, broader-based wings usually held slightly crooked, and they glide on slightly arched wings.

The only other mollymawk confirmed to date from the North Atlantic is Black-browed, but other species should be considered if you are lucky enough to see any albatross. Note the distinctive underwing pattern of Western Yellow-nosed, consistent in all ages: white overall with a narrow black leading edge.

Black-browed Albatross stockier overall with relatively shorter and thicker bill, broader wings. All ages have more-extensive black on underwing, and adults have clean white head, orange bill. First-cycle Black-browed can have dusky, black-tipped bill approaching pattern of juvenile Western Yellow-nosed, and both species can have variable dusky hindneck shawl; note all-dark underwings of Black-browed. With birds seen only from above, or on the water, note rounded culmen base (squared on Yellow-nosed) and narrow, dark browline (vs. thicker black triangular eye patch of juvenile Western Yellow-nosed or smaller beady eye of older immatures).

Eastern Yellow-nosed Albatross not always safely distinguished at sea. Note smaller black eye patch (eye typically looks small and beady, vs. set in a large black triangle on Western Yellow-nosed, but immature Western can show small beady eye much like Eastern); adult has paler gray clouding on head and neck, which often look white overall in bright sun (apparent intensity of gray greatly affected by wear and lighting); given exceptional views of adult or subadult, note shape of yellow culminicorn stripe at base: averages narrower and more pointed on Western, broader and more rounded on Eastern.

Gray-headed Albatross (*T. chrysostoma*) of subantarctic s oceans (unrecorded n hemisphere) much like Black-browed in size (L 79–86 cm, WS 205–230 cm, bill 10–12 cm), shape, and underwing pattern (underwings thus with much more black than Yellow-nosed). Adult has gray head (deeper gray than Yellow-nosed and without strongly contrasting whitish forecrown, smaller and less contrasting black eye patch) and black bill with orange-tipped yellow culminicorn stripe and yellow ramicorn stripe; yellow culminicorn stripe broad and rounded at base (narrower and more tapered on Yellow-nosed), culmen base broadly rounded (squared on Yellow-nosed), and naricorn broad and wedge-shaped (visible at close range).

Shy Albatross (ranging to s Atlantic; see pp. 317–320) larger and bigger billed. Faded first cycle can have white head and dusky hindneck shawl recalling Yellow-nosed, but bill pale grayish with contrasting black tip; underwings whiter overall with narrower black margins and often a black preaxilliary notch.

Northern and Southern Buller's Albatrosses (*T. platei* and *T. bulleri*, respectively) of s Pacific Ocean (unrecorded Atlantic or n hemisphere) slightly larger (L 76–84 cm, WS 198–225 cm, bill 11–13 cm) and less rangy overall. Underwings of all ages have slightly thicker black leading edge than Yellow-nosed, and adult and older immature have bold yellow culminicorn and ramicorn stripes; faded first-cycle Buller's can have white head and gray shawl but bill pale (grayish and creamy) with contrasting black naricorn lines and black subterminal band.

Salvin's Albatross (unrecorded n Atlantic; see pp. 321–324) larger and broader winged with stouter bill; all ages typically have grayish hood; immature bill typically dusky grayish with black tip, soon develops paler culminicorn and ramicorn lines; adult bill pale grayish green with yellowish culmen, black subterminal band.

Habitat and Behavior Favors inshore shelf waters. Several records are from shore or even slightly inland from the coast, with birds found flying around buildings or resting on beaches and sandy islets in coastal sounds, sometimes in association with other birds such as Great Black-backed Gulls. Scavenges readily at fishing boats and sometimes accompanies ships. Flight fairly labored in calm to light winds, deep wingbeats interspersed with short glides; sails and wheels easily in moderate to strong winds.

Description Relatively small and lightly built with a fairly long neck and slender bill; culmen base squared, naricorn reduced to a line.

Adult. Head and neck smoky gray with whitish crown and triangular black eye patch; gray hood distinct in overcast conditions but bleaches paler in bright sunlight. Back and upperwings slaty blackish, the back slightly paler and grayer, the wings darker and browner with white primary shafts; rump and uppertail coverts white, tail slaty blackish (paler and frostier when fresh) with whitish shafts. Underparts white, the underwings with a distinct but fairly narrow black leading edge, narrow dark trailing edge, and dark primaries. **Bill** black with bright yellow culminicorn stripe leading into orange-red nail, narrow yellow mandible gape line; legs and feet pale pinkish, eyes dark.

Juvenile/first cycle. Fledges in Apr–May with white head, blackish eye patch, and variable dusky gray hindneck shawl; rest of plumage adult-like but black leading edge to underwing often messier and perhaps slightly wider. **Bill** dull dark brownish to blackish overall with black tip and dull paler brownish culminicorn stripe visible at closer range. Culminicorn stripe becomes dull pale yellowish in first year.

Second cycle. Not well known. Birds presumed about 18 months of age (in Aug–Oct) can have heavily abraded (i.e., juvenile) outer primaries, white head and neck with beady eye (black eye patch smaller than on juvenile), reduced or no hindneck shawl. **Bill** blackish (or subtly paler slaty on basal half) with pale yellow stripe on basal two-thirds of culmen, reddish-orange tinge to nail.

Older immature. Not well known. May attain gray head by PB3 molt, and bill pattern then resembles adult but with duller and reduced color, probably adult-like by age 4 or 5.

Molt (see Fig 140, p. 312). Adult wing molt mainly May–Sep, away from breeding grounds, when only about half of the primaries are replaced in a given season (Furness 1988). As with other mollymawks, apparently does not molt primaries until PB3 molt (in Jan–Apr, about 20–23 months after fledging), when juvenile outer primaries are replaced, and subsequent primary molts alternate inner and middle primaries in phases.

A4.1. As well as the relatively slim build, note the gray hood, white crown, and "yellow-nosed" bill pattern of this Western Yellow-nosed Albatross. SNGH. Tristan da Cunha, South Atlantic, 26 Mar 2005.

A4.2. Active stage 2 primary molt (see p. 304) of this Western Yellow-nosed Albatross may be fourth pre-basic molt (about 35 months after fledging) given how worn the old inner (juvenile?) primaries appear to be. Messy white and gray-mottled hood and distal dark smudge in yellow culmen stripe also indicate "subadult." SNGH. South Atlantic, 34°S 17°E, 17 Apr 2009.

A4.3. Apparent tone of gray hood on adult Western Yellow-nosed Albatross varies greatly with lighting; hood can be quite washed out in strong sun (cf. A4.5). SNGH. Inaccessible Island, South Atlantic, 10 Apr 2009.

A4.4. Immature Western Yellow-nosed Albatross (about 11 months after fledging), with typical "messy" underwing margins (cf. A4.5). Bill starts to develop traces of yellow, and black eye patch reduced, at times suggesting black beady eye of Eastern Yellow-nosed Albatross. SNGH. South Atlantic, 35°S 12°E, 16 Apr 2009.

308

A4.6. Immature Western Yellow-nosed Albatross (about 11 months after fledging). Underwing pattern messier than adult; also note whitish head and black bill. SNGH. South Atlantic, 35°S 12°E, 16 Apr 2009.

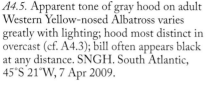

A4.5. Apparent tone of gray hood on adult Western Yellow-nosed Albatross varies greatly with lighting; hood most distinct in overcast (cf. A4.3); bill often appears black at any distance. SNGH. South Atlantic, 45°S 21°W, 7 Apr 2009.

A4.8. Adult Western Yellow-nosed Albatross. Several North American records have been of adults on shore, often in loose association with other waterbirds. Note distinctive albatross posture and shape, diagnostic head and bill colors. SNGH. Nightingale Island, South Atlantic, 29 Mar 2005.

A4.9. Juvenile Western Yellow-nosed Albatross, within about a month of fledging. Fresh juveniles have variable gray clouding on hindneck and usually a dull pale culmen stripe. SNGH. Nightingale Island, South Atlantic, 29 Mar 2005.

A4.7. Immature Western Yellow-nosed Albatross, possibly third cycle (about 35 months after fledging) about to start fourth prebasic primary molt (cf. A4.2). Relative to adult, bill duller, hood mottled whitish, and underwing margins messier. SNGH. Gough Island, South Atlantic, 8 Apr 2009.

A5. BLACK-BROWED ALBATROSS *Thalassarche [melanophris] melanophris*

L 79–86 cm, WS 205–230 cm, bill 11.5–12.5 cm
Figures 138, A5.1–A5.14

Identification Summary Atlantic. Very rare off e North America. A fairly small and stocky albatross. On immatures, white underbody contrasts with dark underwings; adults have white central underwings with broad black leading and trailing edges. First cycle has dusky bill with black tip; bill becomes orange with reddish-orange tip by 5–6 years of age.

Taxonomy The two taxa of Black-browed Albatross are variably treated as subspecies or species, and differ primarily in adult eye color and underwing pattern.

T. [m.] melanophris (Black-browed Albatross) breeds and ranges widely in subantarctic latitudes from s South America e to New Zealand. Adult eyes dark brown, underwing averages less extensive black. Population structure differences within *melanophris* have also been reported, with Falkland birds being distinct from other populations (Burg & Croxall 2001).

T. [m.] impavida (Campbell Albatross) breeds Campbell Island, New Zealand, ranges to Australia. Adult eyes pale yellowish, underwing averages more extensive black.

Names *Thalassarche* means "ruler of the sea," *melanophris* means "black-browed."

Status and Distribution Endangered. Circumpolar in s oceans, breeding (mainly Sep–Apr) from s South America e to New Zealand. Ranges n (mainly Apr–Nov) in Humboldt Current to Peru, and in Atlantic to s Brazil. Casual in w Europe, with more than 30 records including birds building nests in Northern Gannet colonies and returning for many years.

Atlantic. Very rare nonbreeding visitor (mainly Jun–Oct) off Atlantic coast, with records from Labrador (Aug 2009, NAB 64:34, 2010), Newfoundland (Jun 2009, NAB 64:34, 2010), Nova Scotia (Aug 2009, NAB 64:34, 2010), Maine (Jul 2009, NAB 63:570, 2009), Massachusetts (Jun–Sep), and Virginia (Feb), plus a Nov specimen from Martinique, West Indies (AOU 1998). Additional sightings from Newfoundland s to Florida (see Patteson et al. 1999) are not accepted, but some may be correct. Also two Jul–Aug specimens from w Greenland. Latitudinal distribution of these records mirrors the species' higher-latitude summer distribution and lower-latitude winter distribution in s hemisphere.

FIELD IDENTIFICATION

Similar Species See under Western Yellow-nosed Albatross for distinguishing albatrosses from Great Black-backed Gull and Northern Gannet. Black-browed is a distinctive species: adult has white head and orange bill, thick black underwing margins; immature has dark underwings, dusky to pinkish bill with black tip.

Yellow-nosed Albatross rangier overall with relatively longer and more slender bill, narrower wings. All ages have overall white underwings with black leading edge, mostly black bill (with yellow culminicorn stripe and reddish tip on older immatures and adult); adult has smoky gray head and neck. First-cycle Yellow-nosed can have dark bill similar to juvenile Black-browed, and both can have variable dusky hindneck shawl; note all-dark underwings of Black-browed. With birds seen only from above, or on the water, note the squared culmen base (rounded on Black-browed), and note narrow dark browline of Black-browed vs. the thicker black triangular eye patch of juvenile Western Yellow-nosed or smaller beady eye of older immature.

Gray-headed Albatross (of subantarctic s oceans, unrecorded n hemisphere; A5a.1) much like Black-browed in size (L 79–86 cm, WS 205–230 cm, bill 10–12 cm), shape, and underwing pattern, although averaging a little stockier. Adult distinctive, with gray head and neck, black bill with bright yellow culmen and ramicorn stripes. Immature Gray-headed at age 1–3 years can appear quite similar to Black-browed. Note that Gray-headed's bill is blackish to black with no distinct darker tip, may show a trace of yellow culminicorn and ramicorn stripes, and has diagnostic broad, wedge-shaped naricorn visible at close range.

Shy Albatrosses (ranging to s Atlantic) larger and bigger billed, although size of a lone bird hard to judge. Faded first-cycle Shy can have white head and dusky hindneck shawl similar to Black-browed but bill usually paler, grayish with more contrasting black tip, broader and squarer culmen base, and neat black naricorn lines; underwing of Shy very different from immature Black-browed, being white overall with narrow black margins.

Salvin's Albatross of s Pacific slightly larger and bigger billed with broader wings. A few very faded first-cycle Salvin's Albatrosses might show dusky shawl but most have grayish hood. Salvin's has bigger and grayer bill with narrow black strip around its broader and squarer culmen base; underwing of Salvin's white overall with narrow black margins.

Northern and Southern Buller's Albatrosses of s Pacific Ocean similar in size (L 76–84 cm, WS 198–225 cm, bill 11–13 cm) to Black-browed but less stocky, recalling Yellow-nosed in build; some faded first-cycle Buller's can have whitish head and gray shawl recalling Black-browed but bill typically paler (pale grayish and creamy), with contrasting black naricorn lines and black subterminal band; underwing of Buller's white overall with broad black leading edge (see Howell 2009).

Habitat and Behavior Pelagic, but might be seen from shore. In s oceans, a professional ship follower that often scavenges from fishing boats where it occurs with other albatrosses, petrels, shearwaters, gulls, etc. Birds in ne Atlantic have joined Northern Gannet colonies, built nests, and returned for many years. Flight fairly labored in calm to light winds, deep wingbeats interspersed with short glides; sails and wheels easily in moderate to strong winds.

Description Relatively small and stocky with a thick neck and fairly large head; culmen base rounded, naricorn reduced to a line.

Adult. White head and neck contrast with slaty blackish back and upperwings (browner when worn) which have white outer primary shafts; black brow visible at closer range; rump and uppertail coverts white; tail slaty blackish (paler and frostier when fresh) with whitish shafts. Underparts white, the underwings with bold black wing margins thickest along leading edges; at long range, and especially in bright light, underwings can appear white overall with black restricted to a relatively narrow (but still distinct and quite thick) black leading edge. **Bill** pinkish orange with dark orange to orange-red tip; legs and feet pale pinkish; eyes dark.

Juvenile/first cycle. Fledges in Apr–May with variable gray wash to head and hindneck, this soon fading to white with variable gray hindneck shawl; black brow usually poorly defined. Rest of plumage adult-like except for all-dark underwings, which often show variably paler central panel on greater coverts. **Bill** dark brownish olive to dusky flesh with black tip usually set off by narrow paler subterminal band; often develops variable paler areas and small pale tip toward end of first year. Primaries uniform and relatively fresh. Limited molt of head and body feathers on some birds may be PF molt or start of protracted PB2 molt.

Second cycle. PB2 molt involves head, body, and probably tail, but no primaries. Looks overall similar to first cycle but gray shawl often reduced; fresh gray hindneck and back contrast with worn and variably faded browner upperwings; outer primaries can be frayed at tips. **Bill** variegated in pattern, varies from fairly dark overall, typically with small pale tip, to dusky pale orangeish with a broad dark tip.

Third cycle. PB3 molt includes outer primaries (in Jan–Apr, about 20–23 months after fledging; see Fig 140). Whiter headed with small black brow, gray shawl reduced or absent; outer primaries (usually p8-p10) blacker and fresher in contrast to faded and worn inner and middle primaries (which are still juvenile feathers); upperwing coverts mostly gray (often mixed with faded brown juvenile feathers); underwings with variable whitish median panel (mainly on greater secondary coverts). **Bill** variable, typically paler and more orangeish overall, usually with extensive blackish on tip and dusky sides, but some still dark overall with paler patches.

Fourth cycle. PB4 molt includes some middle and inner primaries (molted Apr–Sep) but not outers, which thus appear somewhat faded. Resembles adult overall but underwings average more-extensive and messier blackish margins; **bill** variable in color and pattern, usually with some blackish on tip and dusky on sides.

Fifth cycle. PB5 molt includes outer primaries. Much like adult and some birds perhaps not distinguishable; **bill** typically duller and paler orange, often with some dark near tip and duskier sides. Following this age, resembles adult but some sixth-cycle birds may be distinguishable by limited dusky on bill, faded outer primaries.

Molt (Fig 140). Adult wing molt mainly Apr/May–Aug/Sep, between breeding seasons, includes some but not all primaries. PB2 molt (mainly Jan–Sep) involves head and body, probably tail, but no primaries. PB3 molt includes outer primaries (molted Jan–Apr, about 20–23 months after fledging; Howell 2010b). Subsequent PB molts include some but not all primaries, with outer three primaries replaced every other year (mainly Apr–Sep) (Prince et al. 1993, Prince & Rodwell 1994). If birds switch hemispheres, however, their molt can also switch in timing, as with nonmolting adult Black-browed Albatrosses in the northern summer (Apr–Sep) at Northern Gannet colonies in nw Europe.

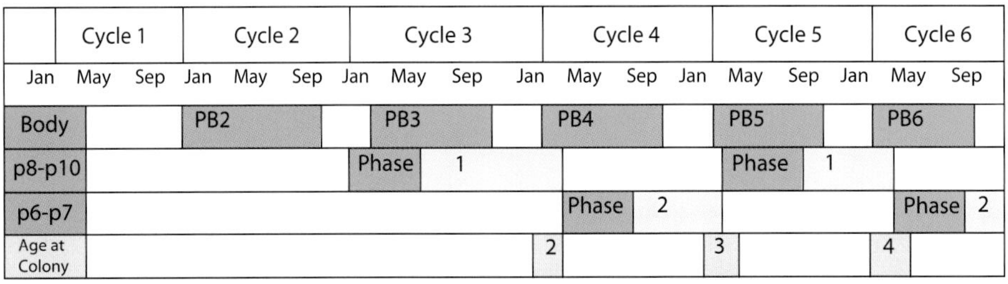

	Cycle 1			Cycle 2			Cycle 3			Cycle 4			Cycle 5			Cycle 6		
	Jan	May	Sep	Jan	May	Sep	Jan	May	Sep	Jan	May	Sep	Jan	May	Sep	Jan	May	Sep
Body				PB2			PB3			PB4			PB5			PB6		
p8-p10						Phase	1						Phase	1				
p6-p7									Phase	2						Phase	2	
Age at Colony								2			3			4				

Fig 140. Provisional molt schedules for Black-browed Albatross (other mollymawks appear similar) in first few years of life (from Howell 2010b); fledging date assumed as 1 May. Dark orange blocks represent molt of body feathers, outer primaries (p8-p10), and middle primaries (p6-p7), starting with complete first prebasic (= prejuvenile) molt in the nest. Pale orange blocks indicate periods when phases of primary molt can be distinguished. Second prebasic molt involves no primaries, but subsequent molts involve alternating renewal of outer and middle primaries in phases. "Age at colony" correlates molt schedules here with data from Prince et al. (1993).

A5.1. (Left) Adult Black-browed Albatross. A fairly stocky mollymawk, with white head (black brow variable, often inconspicuous) and diagnostic pale orange bill with deeper-colored tip. SNGH. South Atlantic, 34°S 17°E, 17 Apr 2009.

A5.2. (Below left) First-year Black-browed Albatross (about six months after fledging). Note uniformly fresh juvenile back and upperwings, solidly black-tipped bill, slightly worn tail (cf. A5.3). SNGH. Valparaíso, Chile, 3 Nov 2009.

A5.3. (Below) Second-cycle Black-browed Albatross (about 18 months after fledging). Note contrastingly fresh postjuvenile back and tail (cf. A5.2); bill often develops a pale tip at this age (cf. A5.7). SNGH. Valparaíso, Chile, 3 Nov 2009.

A5.4. Third-cycle Black-browed Albatross (about 23 months after fledging). Note recently renewed (blacker) p8-p10 (and coverts) contrasting with juvenile middle and inner primaries and coverts. Extent of first wing molt variable, as is bill pattern at this age (cf. A5.5). SNGH. South Atlantic, 45°S 21°W, 7 Apr 2009.

A5.5. Advanced third-cycle Black-browed Albatross (about 23 months after fledging) with extensive wing molt. Note fresh p7-p10 (p10 not quite full grown) and p1-p2 contrasting with browner juvenile middle primaries (cf. A5.4). SNGH. South Atlantic, 35°S 12°E, 16 Apr 2009.

A5.7. Second-cycle Black-browed Albatross (about 18 months after fledging). Note dark underwings, white head, and bill color (cf. A5a.1); aged by pale bill tip, heavily frayed tips to outer primaries, fresh tail (cf. A5.2–A5.3). SNGH. Valparaíso, Chile, 31 Oct 2006.

A5.6. Adult Black-browed Albatross. Note thick black leading edge to underwing, white head, orange bill. SNGH. South Atlantic, 35°S 12°E, 16 Apr 2009.

A5a.1. Third-cycle Gray-headed Albatross (about 23 months after fledging; p10 growing). Plumage of immature Gray-headed often very similar to immature Black-browed but note even stockier shape, blackish bill without contrasting dark tip (cf. A5.2–A5.3, A5.7). SNGH. South Atlantic, 45°S 21°W, 7 Apr 2009.

A5.8. (Right) Third-cycle Black-browed Albatross (about 23 months after fledging). Underwing often develops extensive, but highly variable, white areas in third cycle; note relatively fresh outer primaries (cf. A5.9). SNGH. South Atlantic, 34°S 17°E, 17 Apr 2009.

A5.9. (Far right) Fourth-cycle Black-browed Albatross (about 35 months after fledging). Note frayed tips to outer primaries and more adult-like underwing pattern than third cycle (cf. A5.8). SNGH. South Atlantic, 35°S 12°E, 16 Apr 2009.

A5.10. Adult Black-browed Albatross. Note white head, black brow, orange bill. SNGH. South Atlantic, 45°S 21°E, 7 Apr 2009.

A5.11. Third-cycle Black-browed Albatross (about 23 months after fledging) can have mostly dark bill with pale culmen stripe, suggesting immature Yellow-nosed Albatross. Note rounded culmen base, dark brow, stocky shape, extensive dark on underwings. SNGH. South Atlantic, 45°S 21°E, 7 Apr 2009.

A5.12. Adult Black-browed Albatross. Dark eye distinguishes Black-browed from pale-eyed but otherwise similar Campbell Albatross. SNGH. South Island, New Zealand, 27 Mar 2008.

A5.13. First-cycle Black-browed Albatross (about six months after fledging; adult Salvin's Albatross behind), apparently in juvenile plumage. Not known to be distinguishable at this age from Campbell Albatross. SNGH. South Island, New Zealand, 5 Nov 2008.

A5.14. Immature Black-browed Albatross, probably a third-cycle bird (about 34 months after fledging) undergoing first wing molt. SNGH. South Island, New Zealand, 27 Mar 2008.

The Shy Albatross complex comprises four taxa, breeding in Australia and New Zealand. All have been united as a single species, the Shy Albatross (as by AOU 1998), despite striking differences between some of the taxa (Fig 141). They are increasingly treated as four species on the basis of differences in morphology, genetics, and breeding chronology (Chambers et al. 2009, Robertson & Nunn 1998).

The white-necked Tasmanian Shy (*T. [c.] cauta*) and Auckland Shy (*T. [c.] steadi*) albatrosses look very similar and are rarely distinguishable at sea (even as adults). The smaller gray-necked Salvin's (*T. salvini*) and Chatham (*T. eremita*) albatrosses are distinctive as adults, and are usually identifiable at all ages (Howell 2006, 2009). Salvin's and Chatham are treated here as distinct species. Tasmanian Shy and Auckland Shy are treated provisionally as distinct species, but are lumped into one account because of their overall similarities in terms of identification. Remarkably, all four Shy Albatross taxa have been recorded off the Pacific coast of North America.

Fig 141. The Shy Albatross complex comprises two white-necked species (including Auckland Shy Albatross, left) and two gray-necked species (including Salvin's Albatross, right). Also note the very different bill patterns of these adults. SNGH. South Island, New Zealand, 9 Dec 2005.

A6A. TASMANIAN SHY ALBATROSS *Thalassarche [cauta] cauta*
L 87–96 cm, WS 229–251 cm, bill 12–14 cm
A6B. AUCKLAND SHY ALBATROSS *Thalassarche [cauta] steadi*
L 90–100 cm, WS 240–265 cm, bill 12.5–14 cm
Figures 139, 141, A6.1–A6.9

Identification Summary Pacific. Exceptional off the West Coast. Medium-large albatrosses. On all ages, underwings white overall with narrow black margins. Adults and subadults have a white cap and hindneck with smoky gray clouding on cheeks; bill pale gray-green with a yellow tip and, on typical adult Tasmanian, a yellow base to culminicorn. Immatures have variable gray on head and neck; bills pale grayish with contrasting black tip.

Taxonomy See introduction to the Shy Albatross complex (p. 316).

Names *Thalassarche* means "ruler of the sea," *cauta* means "wary, or shy," which is not a particularly appropriate name; *steadi* commemorates New Zealand ornithologist E. F. Stead.

Auckland Shy Albatross usually known as White-capped Albatross in New Zealand, while Tasmanian Shy Albatross usually known simply as Shy Albatross in Australia. I prefer the unambiguous names proposed by Tickell (2000).

Status and Distribution Both taxa Near Threatened. Tasmanian Shy breeds (Sep–Apr) around Tasmania, while Auckland Shy breeds (Nov–Jul/Aug) in New Zealand, mainly on Auckland Islands. Both taxa range w to South Africa and s Atlantic Ocean; casual or very rare off w South America (taxon unknown).

Pacific. Exceptional nonbreeding visitor (Aug–Jan) off West Coast: first North American record an adult Auckland Shy (see Cole 2000) collected off Washington in Sep 1951 (Slipp 1952). Subsequent records may all refer to one individual: a subadult (unidentified to taxon) off Oregon (Oct 1996), and an adult Tasmanian Shy off California (Aug–Sep 1999), Washington (Jan 2000), and Oregon (Oct 2001).

FIELD IDENTIFICATION

Similar Species As adults, Tasmanian Shy and Auckland Shy are distinctive as a species-pair. Note white hindneck and crown, smoky clouding to cheeks, pale gray-green bill with yellow tip. Immatures can be confused with Salvin's and other albatrosses; note underwing pattern, bill color, and head/neck pattern. Tasmanian averages smaller than Auckland, but all measurements overlap and only extremes can be identified, aided by knowledge of a bird's sex (Double et al. 2003). Unknown proportion of adult Tasmanian have obvious yellow on basal third of culmen, absent in apparently all adult Auckland.

Salvin's Albatross (accidental n Pacific) has gray head and neck, but some first-cycle (mainly fairly fresh juvenile) Shy can have gray hood similar to Salvin's. Note bill colors: paler gray to olive-gray with contrasting black tip on Shy, vs. dusky grayish to dark pinkish gray with less contrasting black tip on Salvin's. Underwings of Shy typically have narrower black margins (lacking Salvin's broad fan of black on primary coverts), and paler primary bases, which are often whitish (dusky on immature Salvin's).

Chatham Albatross (accidental n Pacific) differs in much the same ways as does immature Salvin's, but immature Chatham bill dull yellowish (pale grayish on Shy).

Black-browed Albatrosses (casual n Atlantic) smaller and stockier, although size of lone bird hard to judge. Immature Black-browed can have white head and dusky hindneck shawl similar to first-cycle Shy, but bill dark dull brownish or dusky pinkish with black tip and narrower and rounded culmen base; underwing dark overall.

Yellow-nosed Albatross (casual n Atlantic) smaller and slimmer billed. Immature can have white head and dusky hindneck shawl recalling immature Shy, but bill dark overall, usually appearing blackish or with narrow paler culminicorn stripe; underwing has broader black leading edge.

Northern and Southern Buller's Albatrosses of s Pacific smaller (L 76–84 cm, WS 198–225 cm, bill 11–13 cm) and slimmer billed, usually with grayish head and neck; underwing white overall with broad black leading edge. First-cycle has distinctive bill pattern with well-defined black naricorn lines and black subterminal band; pale creamy culminicorn and ramicorn stripes contrast slightly with pale gray latericorn. Older ages have mostly black bill with yellow culminicorn and ramicorn stripes.

Habitat and Behavior Pelagic, but might be seen from shore as it often forages over shelf waters. In s oceans, a professional ship follower that often scavenges from fishing boats where it occurs with other albatrosses, petrels, shearwaters, gulls, etc. Birds in ne Pacific have usually been in areas where other albatrosses congregate, and have associated readily with Black-footed and Laysan albatrosses. Flight fairly labored in calm to light winds, deep wingbeats interspersed with short glides; sails and wheels easily in moderate to strong winds.

Description A relatively large and broad-winged mollymawk.

Adult. Smoky-gray clouding to head sides offsets well-defined white crown and white hindneck; black brow usually stops short of culmen base; back and upperwings slaty blackish (browner when worn) with white outer primary shafts; rump and uppertail coverts white; tail slaty blackish (paler and frostier when fresh) with whitish shafts. Underparts white, the underwings with very narrow black wing margins that taper on leading edge near body, accentuating a black preaxilliary notch; primaries white based with blackish tips. **Bill** pale gray-green with yellow tip, narrow orange mandible gape line, and black culmen base and naricorn (perhaps broader on Tasmanian; needs study); many Tasmanian Shy (breeding adults at least) have distinct yellow patch on basal third of culminicorn. Legs and feet pale pinkish; eyes dark.

Juvenile/first cycle. Fledges in Apr–Aug with variable gray wash or mottling to head and hindneck (lacks contrast between white hindneck and blackish back), whitish crown; head often fades to whitish within first year except for variable gray hindneck shawl; black brow less striking than adult. Rest of plumage adult-like but black underwing margins slightly broader and messier, preaxilliary notch less distinct or lacking. **Bill** pale to medium grayish with a contrasting black tip. Primaries uniform and relatively fresh.

Second cycle. PB2 molt involves head, body, and perhaps tail, but no primaries. Plumage adult-like or with variable trace of gray shawl, underwing margins cleaner but average broader than adult. Fresh hindneck and back contrast with worn and variably faded browner upperwings; outer primaries noticeably frayed at tips. **Bill** pale gray with black tip or subterminal band and small pale tip, sometimes a paler yellowish culminicorn.

Older immature. Plumage mostly adult-like. Bill typically paler and more adult-like overall but with variable blackish subterminal band or marks retained for two or more years; subadults much like adult but yellow bill tip duller, dark subterminal marks remain on mandible.

Molt (see Fig 140, p. 312) Adult wing molt presumably between breeding seasons, thus mainly Apr–Sep in Tasmanian and Jul–Nov in Auckland, including some but not all primaries. PB2 molt (timing needs study) involves head and body, probably tail, but no primaries. Subsequent PB molts include primaries, apparently in two phases as in other mollymawks; outer primaries renewed every other year starting with PB3 molt. Although Auckland Shy fledges about three months later than Tasmanian Shy, both may undergo PB3 molt of outer primaries during Jan–Apr, in austral fall, rather than Auckland Shy molting in winter, which may be a less favorable season for molt. Birds spending time in n hemisphere might exhibit modified molting schedules.

A6.1. Adult Shy Albatross (presumed Auckland Shy). Note white hindneck and bill color (some Tasmanian Shy have yellow on base of culmen but otherwise indistinguishable in the field). Prominence of gray face varies with lighting (cf. A6.3). SNGH. South Island, New Zealand, 26 Mar 2008.

A6.2. First-year Shy Albatross (species unknown, 8–12 months after fledging depending on species). Note solid black bill tip, medium-gray bill (cf. A7.2–A7.3), and white primary bases. Gray hood rarely darker or more extensive than this (cf. A7.2–A7.3). SNGH. South Atlantic, 34°S 17°E, 17 Apr 2009.

A6.3. Adult Shy Albatross (presumed Auckland Shy). Note extensively white underwing and black preaxillary notch. Gray face rarely appears darker than this (cf. A6.1). SNGH. South Island, New Zealand, 28 Mar 2008.

A6.4. Third-cycle Shy Albatross (species unknown). Head at this age can be mostly whitish; contrastingly fresh p8-p10 indicate age. Bill pattern at this age variable, and may vary with species (cf. A6.5–A6.6). SNGH. South Atlantic, 35°S 12°E, 16 Apr 2009.

A6.5. Third-cycle Shy Albatross (species unknown). Note p10 growing; bill pattern more advanced than A6.4. SNGH. South Atlantic, 45°S 21°W, 7 Apr 2009.

A6.6. Presumed third-cycle Shy Albatross (species unknown), with p10 growing. Head and bill pattern relatively advanced (cf. A6.4–A6.5), perhaps individual variation or perhaps indicative of species-level differences (study needed). SNGH. South Atlantic, 34°S 17°E, 17 Apr 2009.

A6.7. (Right) Adult Shy Albatross (presumed Auckland Shy). Note head and bill pattern. SNGH. South Island, New Zealand, 26 Mar 2008.

A6.8. (Below) First-year Shy Albatross (presumed Auckland Shy, thus about four months after fledging). Note whitish face, bill color (cf. A7.1–A7.2, A7.6). SNGH. South Island, New Zealand, 11 Dec 2005.

A6.9. (Below right) Immature Shy Albatross (presumed Auckland Shy). Note adult-like head pattern but extensive dark on bill. Fresh outer primaries (phase 1 primary molt) likely indicate third cycle (cf. A6.5–A6.6), or perhaps retarded fifth cycle. SNGH. South Island, New Zealand, 26 Mar 2008.

A7. SALVIN'S ALBATROSS *Thalassarche salvini*
L 87–96 cm, WS 235–255 cm, bill 12–13.5 cm
Figures 141, A5.13, A7.1–A7.10

Identification Summary Pacific. Exceptional off Alaska. A medium-sized albatross. On all ages, head and neck gray with white forecrown, underwings white overall with narrow black margins. Adult and subadult have dusky pale gray-green bill with pale yellow culminicorn, black subterminal mark on mandible. First cycle has dark grayish bill with black tip, developing adult-like pattern in 3–5 years.

Taxonomy Monotypic. See introduction to Shy Albatross complex (p. 316).

Names *Thalassarche* means "ruler of the sea," *salvini* and the English name commemorate British zoologist Osbert Salvin (1835–1898).

Status and Distribution Vulnerable. Breeds (Sep–Apr) on islands off New Zealand (mainly Bounty Islands), ranges at sea to w South America; recently found breeding on Crozet Islands, Indian Ocean (Jouventin 1990); exceptional in Hawaii (Apr 2003; Robertson et al. 2005).
  Pacific. Exceptional nonbreeding visitor (Aug 2003) off Alaska: an immature Salvin's in the Aleutians appeared to be undergoing PB3 or PB5 molt, including outer primaries (Benter et al. 2005).

FIELD IDENTIFICATION

Similar Species Note gray head and neck with white forecrown, mostly white underwings, and overall dark or relatively dull bill pattern of all ages. In some lights, pale yellow culminicorn stripe of adult can contrast strongly with dusky bill sides.
  Chatham Albatross (accidental n Pacific) similar in immature plumages (through third cycle at least) but bill typically shows distinct yellow or orange tones lacking in Salvin's, immatures of which have bill dark grayish overall; gray of Chatham's hood averages darker, but often bleaches on head and shows whitish crown. By third cycle, yellowish bill of Chatham usually obvious. Some adult Salvin's have relatively pale and yellowish bill overall, but this is distinct from adult Chatham, which has bright orange-yellow bill and deeper blue-gray hood without contrasting white crown.
  Shy Albatross (accidental n Pacific) usually has white hindneck, but some first-cycle birds (mainly fairly fresh-plumaged juveniles) have extensive gray hood similar to Salvin's. Note bill colors:

paler gray to olive-gray with contrasting black tip on Shy, vs. dusky grayish to dark pinkish gray with less contrasting black tip on Salvin's. Underwings of Shy typically have narrower black margins (lacking Salvin's broad fan of black on primary coverts), and paler primary bases often whitish (dusky on immature Salvin's).
  Northern and Southern Buller's Albatrosses of s Pacific smaller (L 76–84 cm, WS 198–225 cm, bill 11–13 cm) with slimmer bill, underwing of all ages has broad black leading edge. First-cycle Buller's distinguished from first-cycle Salvin's also by paler bill (pale grayish and creamy) with well-defined black naricorn lines and black subterminal band; older ages have mostly black bill with yellow culminicorn and ramicorn stripes (Howell 2009).
  Gray-headed Albatross of subantarctic s oceans (unrecorded n hemisphere) smaller and stockier (L 79–86 cm, WS 205–230 cm, bill 10–12 cm). Immature underwing all-dark and adult underwing with much thicker black margins. Gray-headed immature plumages usually lack neatly contrasting white forecrown, bill blackish overall or with variable yellowish culminicorn stripe. Adult has gray head without white forecrown, black bill with bright yellow culminicorn and ramicorn stripes. At close range note broadly rounded culmen base (squared on Salvin's) and diagnostic broad, wedge-shaped naricorn.
  Yellow-nosed Albatross (very rare n Atlantic) smaller and slimmer billed, underwing of all ages has slightly thicker black leading edge. Immature mostly white headed, adult has paler gray hood. Bill darker in all ages and after age 2–3 years has yellow culminicorn stripe.
  Black-browed Albatross (very rare n Atlantic) smaller and stockier, although size of lone bird hard to judge. Immature Black-browed typically white headed with dusky hindneck shawl, smaller bill dark dull brownish or dusky pinkish with black tip and rounded culmen base; underwing

dark overall; older ages have clean white head. Salvin's has bigger and grayer bill.

Habitat and Behavior Much like Tasmanian Shy and Auckland Shy albatrosses; the Alaska bird was associating with other albatrosses on the water.

Description A medium-large mollymawk with fairly broad wings.

Adult. Head and neck gray with white forecrown set off by black brow from eye to culmen base; back and upperwings slaty blackish (browner when worn) with white outer primary shafts; black brow usually merges with culmen base; rump and uppertail coverts white; tail slaty blackish with whitish shafts. Underparts white, the underwings with narrow black wing margins and usually a black preaxilliary notch; primaries dusky with blacker tips, rarely with white basal tongues (< 1% of adults; pers. obs.); at a distance, underwings appear all-white with neat black tip. **Bill** pale olive-gray with contrasting pale yellow culminicorn and nail, mostly black mandibular unguis, pale yellow ramicorn stripe, narrow orange mandible gape line, and black culmen bridge and naricorn lines; legs and feet pale pinkish; eyes dark.

Juvenile/first cycle. Fledges about Apr with dusky gray head and neck, dull whitish forecrown; black brow less striking than adult. Rest of plumage adult-like but black underwing margins broader and messier, preaxilliary notch lacking or indistinct. **Bill** dark grayish to purplish gray with black tip often offset by a narrow paler subterminal band. Primaries uniform and relatively fresh.

Second cycle. PB2 molt involves head, body, and perhaps tail, but no primaries. Plumage adult-like but black brow less striking, underwing margins may average broader. Fresh hindneck and back contrast with worn and variably faded browner upperwings; outer primaries noticeably frayed at tips. **Bill** dusky gray with black tip or subterminal band and small pale tip, sometimes a paler culminicorn and hint of orange mandible gape line.

Third cycle. PB3 molt includes outer primaries (probably in Jan–Apr, about 20–23 months after fledging; see Fig 140, p. 312). Plumage adult-like overall. Outer primaries (usually p8-p10) blacker and fresher in contrast to faded and worn juvenile inner and middle primaries. **Bill** dusky gray with black subterminal band, variable traces of adult-like pattern.

Older immature. Resembles adult but bill duskier overall (especially on sides) with blackish subterminal band bleeding onto maxilla.

Molt (see Fig 140, p. 312). Adult wing molt mainly Apr/May–Aug/Sep, includes some but not all primaries. PB2 molt (perhaps mainly Jan–Sep) involves head and body, apparently tail, but no primaries. PB3 molt includes outer primaries (probably molted Jan–Apr). Subsequent PB molts apparently include outer primaries every other year, as in Black-browed Albatross (pers. obs.). Birds spending time in n hemisphere might exhibit modified molting schedules.

A7.1. Adult Salvin's Albatross. Note pale gray hood, whitish forecrown, diagnostic bill pattern. SNGH. West-southwest of Antipodes Island, New Zealand, 20 Nov 2008.

A7.2. First-year Salvin's Albatross (about seven months after fledging). Note solid black bill tip, pinkish-gray bill tones, underwing pattern. SNGH. Valparaíso, Chile, 30 Oct 2007.

A7.3. First-year Salvin's Albatross. Note solid black bill tip and characteristic dark bill tones (cf. A6.2). Some gray postjuvenile feathers are coming in on back. SNGH. Valparaíso, Chile, 4 Nov 2003.

A7.4. Adult Salvin's Albatross. Note pale gray hood, bill pattern, dusky primaries (cf. A6.3). SNGH. Northeast of Bounty Islands, New Zealand, 21 Nov 2008.

A7.5. Adult Salvin's Albatross. Some adults have relatively contrasting bill pattern with dark latericorn setting off pale yellowish stripes above and below. SNGH. Bounty Islands, New Zealand, 21 Nov 2008.

A7.6. In first year Salvin's Albatross, dark leading edge to underwing often extensive and messy (cf. A7.4–A7.5, A7.8). Also note head and bill pattern. SNGH. Valparaíso, Chile, 4 Nov 2003.

A7.7. First-year Salvin's Albatross (about seven months after fledging). Note solid black bill tip, messy dark leading edge to underwing, unworn primary tips (cf. A7.8). SNGH. Valparaíso, Chile, 31 Oct 2006.

A7.8. Second-cycle Salvin's Albatross (about 19 months after fledging). Note small, pale bill tip, fairly clean black underwing margins, worn outer primaries (cf. A7.7). SNGH. Valparaíso, Chile, 31 Oct 2006.

A7.9. Adult Salvin's Albatross. Note pale gray hood, whitish forecrown, diagnostic bill pattern. SNGH. South Island, New Zealand, 29 Mar 2008.

A7.10. Second-cycle Salvin's Albatross. Note small, pale bill tip, and contrast between faded juvenile wing coverts and fresh second basic feathers on wings and back (cf. A7.2–A7.3). SNGH. Valparaíso, Chile, 30 Oct 2007.

A8. CHATHAM ALBATROSS *Thalassarche eremita*

L 86–95 cm, WS 230–250 cm, bill 11–12.5 cm
Figures A8.1–A8.9

Identification Summary Pacific. Exceptional off California. A fairly small albatross. On all ages, head and neck gray, underwings white overall with narrow black margins. Adult and subadult have yellow-orange bill with black subterminal spot on mandibular unguis. Immature has dusky yellowish bill with black tip, developing adult-like pattern in 3–5 years.

Taxonomy Monotypic. See introduction to Shy Albatross complex (p. 316).

Names *Thalassarche* means "ruler of the sea," *eremita* means "hermit," perhaps an allusion to this species' very limited breeding range—on a small rock in the Chatham Islands.

Status and Distribution Vulnerable. Breeds (Sep–Apr) on Chatham Islands, off New Zealand, ranges at sea to w South America (Spear et al. 2003).

Pacific. Exceptional nonbreeding visitor (Jul–Sep) off cen California. An immature in Sep 2000 was likely the same as an older-looking immature seen Jul 2001 in the same area (pers. examination of California Bird Records Committee files).

FIELD IDENTIFICATION

Similar Species Note gray head and neck, mostly white underwings, and yellow bill tones of all ages. Criteria for separating Chatham from other species much the same as for Salvin's (which see), with the exception of bill color differences (Howell 2009).

Salvin's Albatross (exceptional n Pacific) similar in immature plumages (through third cycle at least) but bill darker, dull grayish or purplish gray, lacking distinct yellow or orange tones; gray of Chatham's hood averages darker but often bleaches and shows whitish crown. By third cycle, yellowish bill of Chatham usually obvious. Some adult Salvin's have relatively pale and yellowish bill overall, but this is distinct from adult Chatham, which has bright orange-yellow bill and deeper blue-gray hood without contrasting white crown.

Habitat and Behavior Much like Tasmanian Shy and Auckland Shy albatrosses; the California bird associated at times with Black-footed Albatrosses on the water.

Description A medium-sized mollymawk but the smallest member of the Shy Albatross complex, not much larger than Black-footed Albatross.

Adult. Head and neck blue-gray with black brow from eye to culmen base; back and upperwings slaty blackish (browner when worn) with white outer primary shafts; black brow merges with culmen base; rump and uppertail coverts white; tail slaty blackish with whitish shafts. Underparts white, the underwings with narrow black wing margins and usually a black preaxilliary notch; primaries dusky with blacker tips; at a distance, underwings appear all-white with neat black tip. **Bill** bright orange-yellow (slightly duller on sides) with mostly black mandibular unguis, narrow orange mandible gape line, and black culmen bridge and naricorn lines; legs and feet pale pinkish; eyes dark.

Juvenile/first cycle. Fledges about Apr with dusky gray head and neck, forecrown often fades to whitish; black brow less striking than adult. Rest of plumage adult-like but black underwing margins broader and messier, preaxilliary notch lacking or indistinct. **Bill** dull pale yellowish with black tip. Primaries uniform and relatively fresh.

Second cycle. PB2 molt involves head, body, and perhaps tail, but no primaries. Plumage adult-like but black brow less striking, underwing margins may average broader. Fresh hindneck and back contrast with worn and variably faded browner upperwings; outer primaries noticeably frayed at tips. **Bill** ochre-yellow to orange-yellow, usually with duskier sides, and with black tip or subterminal band and small pale tip, sometimes a hint of orange mandible gape line.

Third cycle. PB3 molt includes outer primaries (probably in Jan–Apr, about 20–23 months after fledging; see Fig 140, p. 312). Plumage adult-like overall. Outer primaries (usually p8-p10) blacker and fresher in contrast to faded and worn juvenile inner and middle primaries. **Bill** ochre-yellow to orange-yellow, often with duskier sides, and with black subterminal or distal band.

Older immature. Resembles adult but bill duskier overall (especially on sides) with blackish subterminal band bleeding onto maxilla.

Molt Probably much like Salvin's Albatross (pers. obs.); birds spending time in n hemisphere might exhibit modified molting schedules.

A8.1. Adult Chatham Albatross. Note solid dusky blue-gray hood, striking orange-yellow bill. SNGH. SW of Chatham Islands, New Zealand, 22 Nov 2008.

A8.2. First-year Chatham Albatross (about seven months after fledging). Note dirty orangeish bill tones (cf. A7.2–A7.3). Whether contrasting gray head represents juvenile or postjuvenile feathering needs study. SNGH. Valparaíso, Chile, 30 Oct 2007.

A8.3. First-year Chatham Albatross (about seven months after fledging). Note dirty yellowish bill tones (cf. A7.2–A7.3). Forehead often fades to whitish; also note some gray postjuvenile feathers on back. SNGH. Valparaíso, Chile, 30 Oct 2001.

A8.4. Second-cycle Chatham Albatross (about 19 months after fledging). Note heavily worn juvenile upperwings compared to fresher head, neck, scapulars, and tail (cf. A8.2–A8.3). At this age, underwing pattern variable (cf. A8.7), yellow bill tones obvious. SNGH. Valparaíso, Chile, 4 Nov 2003.

A8.5. Adult Chatham Albatross. Note solid dusky blue-gray hood, striking orange-yellow bill, mostly white underwings. SNGH. SW of Chatham Islands, New Zealand, 22 Nov 2008.

A8.6. First-year Chatham Albatross. Note dirty orangeish bill tones; black leading edge to underwing and pale tip to bill relatively advanced for this age (cf. A8.4). SNGH. Valparaíso, Chile, 30 Oct 2007.

A8.8. Adult Chatham Albatross. Note evenly dusky blue-gray hood, bright orange-yellow bill. SNGH. Chatham Islands, New Zealand, 26 Dec 2005.

A8.7. Second-cycle Chatham Albatross. Crown can fade to whitish at this age. Note very worn (juvenile) primary tips, bill color. SNGH. Valparaíso, Chile, 4 Nov 2003.

A8.9. Second-cycle Chatham Albatross. Note same features as A8.4, and cf. A7.10. SNGH. Valparaíso, Chile, 4 Nov 2003.

THE WANDERING ALBATROSS *(Diomedea exulans)* COMPLEX

The Wandering Albatross complex comprises five taxa (three described formally only since 1983) breeding on islands of the Southern Ocean. These five taxa are variably treated as subspecies or, perhaps more realistically, as 4–5 species (Burg & Croxall 2004, Chambers et al. 2009, Robertson & Nunn 1998, Robertson & Warham 1992, Tickell 2000), but are here lumped into one account because many birds seen at sea cannot be safely attributed to taxon. Northern hemisphere records are exceptional, comprising three from the e Pacific (including presumed Antipodes Albatross and Gibson's Albatross) and a few from the ne Atlantic (including a Gough Albatross; Haas 2009, Soldaat et al. 2009).

The five taxa of Wandering Albatross differ slightly in average size and average adult plumage patterns, but with appreciable overlap compounded by complex age/sex variation (Fig 142). As a rule, more northerly breeding taxa are smaller and darker overall, whereas more southerly breeding taxa are larger and whiter overall. Within taxa, adult males are usually whiter overall than females and immatures.

Fig 142. Up to a point, all Wandering Albatross taxa become whiter with age, but the extent and sequence of plumage whitening varies with sex, as well as with taxon. Both these birds exhibit phase 1 primary molt (outer three primaries renewed in preceding molt); remaining primaries and most or all secondaries are still juvenile feathers, indicating both birds are in their third plumage cycle (see Fig 143, p.334). Based on location, both may be Snowy Wanderers, the white-bodied bird perhaps a male, the brown-bodied bird a female. SNGH. Drake Passage, 59°S 58°W, 26 Mar 2009.

D. [e.] antipodensis (Antipodes, or Antipodean, Albatross) breeds (Jan–Jan; Walker & Elliott 2005) s of New Zealand, primarily on Antipodes Islands; ranges in s Pacific to w South America (Robertson & Warham 1992). Adults variable but rarely very white (upperwings and scapulars mostly to solidly dark), usually with a dark cap. Averages smaller than Snowy Albatross.

D. [e.] gibsoni (Gibson's, or Auckland, Albatross) breeds (Jan–Jan) s of New Zealand, primarily on Auckland Islands; ranges at least in sw Pacific (Robertson & Warham 1992). Adults highly variable, some (presumed males) extensively white like whitest Snowy (pers. obs.), others (presumed females) extensively dark like Gough Albatross. Size similar to Antipodes Albatross.

D. [e.] exulans (Snowy Albatross) breeds (Dec/Jan–Dec/Jan) from s Atlantic Ocean (South Georgia) e to sw Pacific Ocean (Macquarie Island); at-sea range circumpolar. Adults average larger, bigger-billed, and whiter than other taxa, but with much variation. Sometimes called *D. e. chionoptera* (Robertson & Nunn 1998).

D. [e.] dabbenena (Gough, or Tristan, Albatross) breeds (Dec/Jan–Dec/Jan; Jouventin et al. 1989) on Gough and Tristan da Cunha islands, s Atlantic Ocean; ranges at least to se Australia (Ryan et al. 2001); accidental in Italy (Haas 2009). Adults variable, with males resembling Gibson's Albatross males, females resembling Antipodes or Gibson's Albatross females. Averages smaller and shorter-billed than Snowy Albatross, shorter-winged than Gibson's Albatross (Robertson & Warham 1992). Sometimes called *D. e. exulans* (Robertson & Nunn 1998).

D. [e.] amsterdamensis (Amsterdam Albatross) breeds (Feb–Feb; Jouventin et al. 1989) on Amsterdam Island, Indian Ocean; at-sea range unknown. A small-dark taxon (upperwings, back, and chest typically all-dark), but many female Gough and Antipodes birds look similar; dark cutting edge to greenish-tipped bill of adult Amsterdam also found on some immature female Gough Albatrosses. Size similar to Gibson's Albatross.

A9A. ANTIPODES [WANDERING] ALBATROSS *Diomedea [exulans] antipodensis*
L 110–117 cm, WS 280–335 cm, bill 14–16 cm
A9B. GIBSON'S [WANDERING] ALBATROSS *Diomedea [exulans] gibsoni*
L 110–117 cm, WS 280–335 cm, bill 14–16 cm
A9C. SNOWY [WANDERING] ALBATROSS *Diomedea [exulans] exulans*
L 115–122 cm, WS 290–350 cm, bill 15–18 cm
Figures 142, A9.1–A9.9, A9a.1–A9a.7, A9b.1–A9b.8, A9c.1

Identification Summary Pacific; exceptional in North America. A huge albatross with a pale pink bill and dark-tipped white underwings. Juvenile dark brown overall with large white face patch. Older ages have variable white on underparts, back, and upperwings, and usually some black on tail. Oldest males of some taxa white overall with black trailing edge and tips to wings. In whiter birds (which can resemble Southern Royal Albatross [*Diomedea epomophora*]) bill lacks dark line on cutting edge, and neck sides often have a pink or tawny stain (lacking on Royal). Given poorly understood plumage variation among taxa in the Wandering Albatross complex, all taxa are treated here in a single species account. Some features, or combinations of features, appear to be diagnostic of various taxa, however, and provisional at-sea identifications can sometimes be made (see Description and photo captions).

Taxonomy See introduction to Wandering Albatross complex.

Names *Diomedea* refers to the Greek warrior Diomedes, whose companions transformed into seabirds; *exulans* means "to be exiled," and with Wandering alludes to this species' far-ranging movements at sea. Antipodes refers to the main breeding island of this taxon; Gibson honors Australian ornithologist J. D. "Doug" Gibson (1929–1984), who developed an index to score plumage variation in Wandering Albatrosses; Snowy refers to this being the whitest taxon of Wandering Albatross.

Status and Distribution Vulnerable. Circumpolar in s oceans. Biennial breeder on various islands (see introduction to Wandering Albatross complex). Ranges n regularly to around 40°S, rarely 30°S. Gough and Snowy albatrosses seem most likely candidates to occur in n Atlantic; Gibson's and Antipodes albatrosses may be most likely to reach the n Pacific; given tiny population size of Amsterdam Albatross, it seems unlikely to occur in North America.

Pacific. Exceptional in North American waters, with three records all in austral winter. A first-year bird (taxon unknown) captured in Panama Bay, Aug 1937 (Murphy 1938); a female or immature male (probably an immature Gibson's Albatross) photographed on shore in cen California, mid-Jul 1967 (Paxton 1968); and a presumed female Antipodes Albatross photographed off Oregon,

mid-Sep 2008 (Anon 2009), seen again in late Sep 2008 about 510 km off cen California coast (37°N 128°W; L. Ballance et al., unpubl. data).

FIELD IDENTIFICATION

Similar Species Huge size, especially massive body and very long narrow wings, should preclude confusion with all except similarly sized Royal Albatrosses (unrecorded in n hemisphere). Beware superficial resemblance of smaller adult *Steller's Albatross*, which has bluish bill tip, golden-yellow to brown cap and hindneck, lacks neat black tip to underwing. Juvenile and younger immature Wandering with extensive brown on head and body are distinctive (as are adults of taxa that do not become white-bodied). Wanderers with extensive white on upperwings and tail (mainly older adult males of Snowy, Gibson's, and Gough albatrosses) can look similar to Southern Royal Albatross, and some plumages may suggest Northern Royal Albatross (*D. [epomophora] sanfordi*). See under Description, below, for features to help distinguish among Wandering Albatross taxa.

Southern Royal Albatross (L 112–122 cm, WS 305–350 cm, bill 16–19 cm) and *Northern Royal Albatross* (L 110–120 cm, WS 290–340 cm, bill 15.5–17 cm) both a little slimmer with slightly longer neck and bill, whereas Wandering is stockier and thicker necked with broader rump and wider tail. At close range, dark cutting edges to bill of Royal may be visible (Wandering has pink bill without a black line) as may upward-pointing nostrils and dark orbital ring. Black on tail of Royal (when present) limited to fairly narrow tipping and edging, whereas Wandering usually has one or more extensively black rectrices (whole tail black on many birds), but this can be hard to see clearly, and oldest and whitest Wanderings can have all-white tails, like adult Royal.

Northern Royal Albatross has solidly black upperwings, white back (variably barred blackish on juveniles), and white tail (narrowly tipped black on immature), a combination of features not found in Wandering (those with solidly black upperwings usually have black tail, and often some dark markings on head and chest). At long range, when details of tail pattern are not visible, note that the white back of Northern Royal (and immature Southern Royal) forms narrower, oval-shaped patch between black upperwings (scapulars black overall), whereas on white-backed and black-winged Wandering the white back patch is broader and wedge-shaped, fanning out toward the rear (scapulars white overall).

Southern Royal Albatross with extensively white upperwings distinguished from whitest Wandering by overall shape and bill pattern (see above), and also by two aspects of upperwing pattern helpful at long range. First, Royal has broader black tips to scapulars and less black on longest humerals, so black trailing edge to inner section of wing thicker and more even in width; Wandering usually has a step between narrow black scapular tips and a broad black patch on longest humerals. Second, black/white border across upperwing coverts usually a more even diagonal on Wandering, vs. stepped on Royal from wider on innerwing to narrower on outer lesser coverts. At closer ranges, note that black/white border on Southern Royal is typically neater, looking like rows of dark bricks dusted with white, vs. blacker and more coarsely spotted on Wandering. Also, many Wanderings (especially broader-headed males) show diagnostic pink or tawny patch on sides of their neck; this may be a stain derived from food solution blowing back from forward-pointing nostrils (nostrils of Royal point up slightly, and presumably any food solution blows past the narrower head without hitting the neck).

Habitat and Behavior Pelagic in areas with persistent wind. Mainly over offshore waters, but California vagrant was found on land! A professional ship follower that accompanies ships for hours, even days, and scavenges readily at fishing boats. Flight labored in calm or light winds (when birds usually sit on the water), but birds sail almost effortlessly in strong winds.

Description A huge albatross with a big bill, relatively short tail (toes often project in flight), and extremely long and narrow pointed wings. Plumage sequences for different taxa in need of study and, as noted by Marchant and Higgins (1990:275), "except for juveniles and downy young, no two Wandering Albatrosses look alike." Following descriptions are of "typical" birds (also see photos for comments on different taxa). "Male-types" and "female-types" refer to differences that often correlate with sex but may not be consistent because of age variation. Helpful features to note are any molt contrasts among the primaries, extent and pattern of white on the body (especially scapulars), extent and distribution of any brown mottling (especially on upperparts), extent and nature (coarse vs. fine) of any dusky vermiculations, and extent of any white on upperwing. See Shirihai (2007) for additional information.

Adult. Highly variable. All taxa. Underwings white with a neat black tip; narrow black trailing edge rarely visible other than at close range. Bill pink (varies from deep pink to pale yellowish pink), tip usually slightly paler and sometimes with bluish or greenish patch on mandibular unguis; orbital ring pale pinkish to bluish; legs and feet pale pinkish.

Antipodes Albatross. Male-type develops mostly white head and body with dark cap and variable brown mottling on upperparts by 5–6 years of age, but scapulars mostly dark overall, and upperwings solidly dark, with no white on elbow; uppertail coverts often whiter than rump and back, the reverse of immature Snowy and Gough albatrosses. Female-type Antipodes retains immature-like plumage, with mostly brown upperparts and brown chest band, solidly dark upperwings. Oldest male-types may lose dark cap and develop some white on elbow, but may be distinguished from Gibson's and immature Snowy by mostly dark longest and "outer" scapulars; tail usually blackish overall. Oldest female-types have mostly white head and body with dark cowl or cap; upperwings and tail blackish overall.

Gibson's Albatross. Male-type develops mostly white head and body (including scapulars) in 5–6 years but often retains a mottled dark cap; upperparts and chest have coarse dark vermiculations; white elbow patch obvious on older immatures. Female-type has brown cowl, brown mottling and coarse dusky vermiculations on upperparts and chest through at least 7–8 years of age, by which time usually has some white at elbow; tail mostly black. Relative to Antipodes Albatross, immature Gibson's distinguished by extensively white scapulars (with coarse vermiculations), and white on elbow. Adult male and female Gibson's distinguished from adult Antipodes by mostly white scapulars and extensive white on upperwing. Many Gibson's Albatrosses appear rather similar to adult Gough Albatross, and, pending study, may not be identified other than on grounds of geographic probability. Oldest and whitest male Gibson's perhaps not distinguishable from oldest and whitest Snowy Albatross (pers. obs.).

Snowy Albatross. Averages largest and whitest. In general, males are whiter than females (such that a 5-year-old male can resemble a 20-year-old female) and s breeders are whiter than n breeders (Prince et al. 1997). Male-type develops white head and body in 3–4 years, but female can retain brown cap or cowl through breeding age; dusky vermiculations on upperparts and chest usually apparent at close range but finer than typical Gibson's immatures; scapulars mostly white, forming broad "fan" on back; white patches develop on upperwings of males 4–5 years of age, but female-types at this age have dark upperwings; tail becomes partly white only after white patches develop on upperwings. Fully adult male-type has head and body snowy white overall, often with a pink or tawny stain on neck sides; head, neck, chest, and upperparts sometimes with variable dusky vermiculations and dark smudging; upperwings with variable white on humerals and coverts, typically with at least a large white elbow patch; tail mixed black-and-white or, on oldest birds, all-white. Oldest and whitest males perhaps not distinguishable from oldest and whitest Gibson's males, but probably have more white on upperwing than whitest Gough males.

Gough Albatross. Male-type apparently develops mostly white head and body (including scapulars) by 4–5 years of age but may retain a mottled dark cap, and chest and upperparts vermiculated dusky, often with brownish mottling (similar to immature female Snowy) heaviest on uppertail coverts; upperwings may still be solidly dark

at 4–5 years of age (needs study); dark vermiculations more similar to Snowy Albatross than to very coarse markings of Gibson's Albatross. Older males have clean creamy-white head and body but may be slower to develop extensive white on upperwings and tail than Snowy, and apparently do not become as extensively white as oldest male Snowy and Gibson's albatrosses. Female Gough Albatross through at least 3–4 years of age has mostly brown upperparts and brown chest band, solidly dark upperwings similar to female Antipodes Albatross. Subsequent female plumages have whiter head with dusky cap, brownish upperparts (including scapulars) whiten progressively and can have coarse dark vermiculations like Gibson's Albatross.

Amsterdam Albatross. All adults resemble dark female Antipodes and Gough albatrosses; bill has black cutting edge to maxilla, visible at close range.

Juvenile fledges Dec–Feb. All taxa similar. Dark sooty brown overall with a large white face patch; white underwings resemble adult but also have a dark preaxillary notch. Following juvenile plumage, birds develop different patterns depending on taxon and sex.

Immature Snowy Albatross. Juvenile plumage fades appreciably in first year. By ages 3–6 (when Snowies first return to colonies), males are already much whiter than females (Prince et al. 1997). Based on at-sea observations and photos of birds aged by wing molt, the following is a provisional summary of immature plumage development for ages 1–3 (cf. A9.1–A9.8). Males may attain mostly whitish head and body (the white feathers vermiculated dusky and mottled brown) by 3 years of age, becoming white lastly on crown, rump, and tail covert; upperwings develop white only after body has become mostly white, and tail becomes white only after upperwings develop extensive white. Females attain a mostly white belly by 3 years of age, but crown, neck sides, chest, flanks, and tail coverts variably mottled and vermiculated with brown and dusky. Patterns of subsequent plumage aspect development remain to be elucidated, and the relationship (if any) of whitening in adults to social and sexual maturity has not, to my knowledge, been investigated. For those birds (mainly male Snowy and Gibson's) that develop extensively white upperwings, the white develops in variable and typically spotty white patches on the coverts, which show white first on the elbow.

Other taxa. Sequences of plumage aspect development not well known, but immature male Gibson's and Gough albatrosses may be intermediate between male and female Snowy in their whitening progress. Immature female Gough and Antipodes (and some Gibson's?) albatrosses have a distinct "brown bodied" (but white-bellied) plumage apparently not found in Snowy but much like adult Amsterdam and some adult female Antipodes Albatrosses.

Molt (Fig 143) Following summary based on Prince et al. (1997) and analysis of photos. Prebreeding immatures molt outer 2–3 primaries (phase 1 molt) and middle primaries (phase 2 molt) in alternate years, starting with molt of p8-p10 in PB3 molt about 2.5 years after fledging. Adults in their year between breeding usually renew 6–8 primaries in total, including the all-important outers. Most molt of flight feathers occurs during Feb/Apr–Sep/Nov. In prebreeding birds these wing molts are annual, whereas in breeders they are by necessity biennial.

Given fledging in January, start of body molt at about 6 months after fledging may represent PF molt or start of protracted PB2 molt of head and body feathers, which may occur mainly at about 11–20 months after fledging; thus, birds 1–2 years after fledging show faded juvenile plumage with variable signs of body molt, plus uniform generation juvenile upperwings. Incomplete PB3 (phase 1) molt includes head, body outer 3–4 (usually 3) primaries, and probably tail; thus, birds 2–3 years after fledging show contrastingly new outer primaries (probably molted Apr/May–Sep/Oct, at 27–33 months) but remaining primaries and secondaries are faded juvenile feathers. Such birds sometimes visit breeding grounds in Feb–Apr at about 3 years after fledging.

Subsequent molts include most head and body feathers, tail, and variable number of primaries and secondaries. Incomplete PB4 (phase 2) molt includes variable number of middle and inner primaries (especially p5-p7 and p1-p2) and 6–10 secondaries. PB5 (phase 1) molt includes p8-p10 plus some inner and middle primaries (usually p2-p5) and 20–25 secondaries. Retention of juvenile secondaries, and occasionally 1–2 worn juvenile primaries, makes it possible to age birds up to about 5 years of age. Subsequent molts of prebreeding birds alternate replacement of middle (plus some inner) primaries (phase 2 molt) and outer (plus some inner/middle) primaries (phase 1 molt).

	Cycle 1			Cycle 2			Cycle 3			Cycle 4			Cycle 5			Cycle 6			Cycle 7		
	Jan	May	Sep	Jan	May	Sep	Jan	May	Sep	Jan	May	Sep	Jan	May	Sep	Jan	May	Sep	Jan	May	Sep
Body				PB2			PB3			PB4			PB5			PB6			PB7		
p8-p10								Phase	1					Phase	1					Phase	1
p6-p7										Phase	2					Phase	2				
Age at Colony									3			4			5			6			

Fig 143. Provisional molt schedules for Wandering Albatross in first few years of life; fledging date assumed as 1 Jan (limited body molt can start at about 6 months of age). See Fig 140 (p.312) for key. "Age at colony" correlates molt schedules here with data from Prince et al. (1997).

A9a.1. Female/immature Antipodes Albatross. A classic individual with immature-like plumage aspect, cf. A9a.5 of same bird. SNGH. West-southwest of Antipodes Island, New Zealand, 20 Nov 2008.

A9a.2. Immature Antipodes Albatross, possibly male starting fifth prebasic molt, with p8 shed in phase 1 molt. Note dark cap, extensive white mottling on upperbody, mostly dark scapulars. SNGH. New Zealand, 33°S 172°E, 3 Apr 2008.

A9a.3. Male-type Antipodes Albatross. Classic individual with well-defined dark cap, mostly white body but mostly dark scapulars; also note solidly dark upperwings and tail. SNGH. West-southwest of Antipodes Island, New Zealand, 20 Nov 2008.

A9a.4. Presumed Antipodes Albatross, possibly second cycle (about 27 months after fledging) with solidly dark chest contrasting sharply with white belly, a pattern not seen in Snowy (or Gibson's?) wanderers. SNGH. New Zealand, 33°S 172°E, 3 Apr 2008.

A9a.5. Female-type Antipodes Albatross (same bird as A9a.1). Note mottled brown chest contrasting sharply with white belly, a pattern not seen in Snowy (or Gibson's?) wanderers. SNGH. West-southwest of Antipodes Island, New Zealand, 20 Nov 2008.

A9a.6. Male-type Antipodes Albatross. Note well-defined dark cap, ghosting of dark chest band. SNGH. West-southwest of Antipodes Island, New Zealand, 20 Nov 2008.

A9b.1. Female/immature male presumed Gibson's Albatross. Too much white on elbow and humerals for an Antipodes Albatross with this much of a dusky cowl; relatively slender bill suggests female (cf. A9b.6). SNGH. South Island, New Zealand, 6 Nov 2008.

A9b.2. Presumed Gibson's Albatross; relatively slender bill suggests female. Distinguished from Antipodes Albatross by extensively white scapulars, white elbow patches. Perhaps an older immature or even breeding age "adult," given dark cowl but white elbow patches (cf. A9b.3–A9b.4, presumed immature males with whiter heads, darker wings). SNGH. South Island, New Zealand, 6 Nov 2008.

A9b.3. Presumed Gibson's Albatross; relatively heavy bill suggests male. Distinguished from Antipodes Albatross by mottled (vs. solid) dark cap, extensive white on scapulars. SNGH. South Island, New Zealand, 27 Mar 2008.

A9b.4. Presumed Gibson's Albatross; relatively heavy bill suggests male. Vestigial dark cap and extensively white scapulars rule out Antiopodes Albatross. SNGH. South Island, New Zealand, 27 Mar 2008.

A9b.5. Possible Gibson's Albatross, presumably male. Old males of both Auckland and Snowy albatrosses can be extensively white like this and may not be separable by plumage. Distinguished from Southern Royal Albatross by coarse spotting on outer wing coverts, narrow black tips to longest scapulars, tawny neck stain. SNGH. West-southwest of Campbell Island, New Zealand, 17 Nov 2008.

A9c.1. Adult male Snowy Albatross (banded Jan 2003 as an adult on Kerguelen Island, subantarctic Indian Ocean, and estimated here to be 15–20 years old; H. Weimerskirch, pers. comm.). Note snowy white plumage lacking distinct dark vermiculations. SNGH. South Island, New Zealand, 27 Mar 2008.

A9.1. Immature Wandering Albatross (species unknown; same bird as A9.7). Uniformly juvenile wings indicate a bird 1–2 years after fledging. Whether this extent of fading and molt of white body feathers occurs at only 10 months after fledging is unknown, but body appreciably darker than A9.2 and extent of fading similar to A9.6. SNGH. Northeast of Macquarie Island, Australia, 14 Nov 2008.

A9.2. Second-cycle Wandering Albatross (species unknown; uniformly juvenile wings and degree of fading on scapulars suggest about 22 months, rather than 10 months, after fledging; cf. A9.1). Whitening of head and body at this age suggest male, perhaps Snowy Albatross. SNGH. West-southwest of Antipodes Island, New Zealand, 20 Nov 2008.

A9.3. Second-cycle Wandering Albatross (species unknown), about 26 months after fledging (note frayed outer primary tips). Whitening of head and body at this age probably indicate male, likely Snowy Albatross (cf. A9.2). SNGH. South Atlantic, 45°S 21°W, 7 Apr 2009.

A9.4. Wandering Albatross (species unknown) in phase 1 primary molt, perhaps following fifth prebasic molt and thus about 50 months after fledging. Previous wing molt included p8-p10 and p2-p5 (which contrast with browner and older p6-p7) but a few middle secondaries are very worn (perhaps juvenile feathers). White plumage aspect (for this inferred age), large head, and relatively stout bill suggest male, most likely a Snowy or Gough albatross. SNGH. Northeast of South Georgia Island, South Atlantic, 3 Apr 2009.

A9.5. First-year Wandering Albatross (species unknown), presumed about four months after fledging. Belly and hindneck have faded from dark chocolate-brown of fresh juvenile plumage. SNGH. South Atlantic, 45°S 21°W, 7 Apr 2009.

A9.6. First-year Wandering Albatross (species unknown), presumed about 11 months after fledging. Underparts and hindneck have faded from dark chocolate-brown of fresh juvenile plumage. SNGH. South of Snares Islands, New Zealand, 11 Nov 2008.

A9.7. Immature Wandering Albatross (species unknown; same bird as A9.1), perhaps only 10 months after fledging (cf. A9.2, A9.6). Note direct transition to whitish chest, presumably indicating a male, perhaps Snowy Albatross. SNGH. Northeast of Macquarie Island, Australia, 14 Nov 2008.

A9.8. Presumed third-cycle Wandering Albatross (other photos show fresh p8-p10 on otherwise juvenile wings; thus about 38 months after fledging). Extensive brown mottled chest at this age may indicate female Snowy Albatross. SNGH. Drake Passage, 59°S 58°W, 26 Mar 2009.

A9a.7. Male-type Antipodes Albatross. Note well-defined dark cap, extensively dark scapulars, ostensibly no white on upperwing. SNGH. South Island, New Zealand, 6 Nov 2008.

A9b.6. Female Gibson's Albatross, 9 years after fledging (banded as fledgling, Dec 1996 on Auckland Islands); at age 8 this bird looked similar but lacked the bright white (incoming?) white neck feathering (pers. obs.). Note immature-like plumage aspect but relatively limited dark on scapulars. SNGH. South Island, New Zealand, 12 Nov 2005.

A9b.7. Male (in front) and female presumed Gibson's Albatross (with Pintado Petrels [*Daption capense*]). Relatively small head and slim bill of female can be appreciated in direct comparison with larger-headed and stouter-billed male. SNGH. South Island, New Zealand, 27 Mar 2008.

A9.9. Male presumed Gibson's Albatross (in front, note stout bill) and male Snowy Albatross (same bird as A9c.1). Ages of these birds unknown, but Snowy whitens more rapidly and thus might be younger than presumed Gibson's. SNGH. South Island, New Zealand, 27 Mar 2008.

A9b.8. Male-type presumed Gibson's Albatross. Extensive coarse vermiculations in combination with extensive white on upperwing may be diagnostic of Gibson's Albatross (study needed). SNGH. South Island, New Zealand, 6 Nov 2008.

A10. GALAPAGOS ALBATROSS *Phoebastria irrorata*

L 80–90 cm, WS 220–250 cm, bill 13–16 cm
Figures A10.1–A10.5

Identification Summary Pacific (exceptional or very rare off Panama). This striking albatross is unlikely to be mistaken; note its very long yellowish bill and overall dark plumage with contrasting creamy-white head and neck.

Taxonomy Monotypic.

Names The derivation of *Phoebastria* is unclear; *irrorata* means "bedewed," and alludes to the vermiculated body plumage, to which the alternate English name, Waved Albatross, also refers. This is the only species of albatross breeding in the Galapagos Islands.

Status and Distribution Critically Endangered. Breeds (Apr/Jun–Nov/Dec) mainly on Isla Española in Galapagos Islands, also on Isla de la Plata, Ecuador. Ranges in Humboldt Current from Ecuador to cen Peru, irregularly s to n Chile (mainly during El Niño events) and n to Gulf of Panama.

Pacific. Exceptional (or very rare and irregular?) nonbreeding visitor (Feb–Mar at least) n to Gulf of Panama, perhaps most likely to occur during El Niño events. One was seen off e Panama, 26 Feb 1941, and one collected off adjacent Colombia, 8 Mar 1941 (Ridgely & Gwynne 1989). Another report from Panama (Sep 1964; Ridgely & Gwynne 1989) is unverified.

FIELD IDENTIFICATION

Similar Species Galapagos Albatross is a distinctive species unlikely to be mistaken. Note the very long yellow bill, overall dark plumage with a creamy-white head and neck.

Some *hybrid Laysan x Black-footed Albatross* have superficially similar plumage pattern, with dark body and whitish head and neck; note much smaller and pale pinkish bill of such birds, also their overall dark sooty plumage without pale vermiculations.

Aberrant or very bleached *Black-footed Albatross* unlikely to show such a neatly demarcated white head and neck; Black-footed smaller with dark underwings and shorter bill that is usually dark or dull pinkish.

Giant-petrels (genus *Macronectes*) of s oceans (unrecorded in North America) can appear superficially similar (some adult Southerns have contrasting whitish head and neck on otherwise dark plumage) but overall stockier and shorter necked, bills stouter and shorter with prominent tubes on top, and pale pinkish yellow overall with the tip greenish (Southern Giant-Petrel) or pinkish (Northern Giant-Petrel).

Habitat and Behavior Pelagic, typically over shelf-break waters. Like most albatrosses, scavenges readily at fishing boats and sometimes accompanies ships. Flight fairly labored in calm to light winds, deep wingbeats interspersed with short glides; sails and wheels easily in strong winds.

Description A medium-sized albatross with a fairly long neck, long bill, and relatively short tail (toes often project in flight but can be pulled in).

Adult. White to creamy-white head and neck contrast with dark slaty-brown back and dusky-looking underparts; golden-yellow suffusion to crown and hindneck most apparent under cloudy skies; rump and uppertail coverts white with dark bars and vermiculations sparser on distal coverts, which often appear as a white band at base of tail. Upperwings and tail dark slaty brown to blackish, flight feathers with white primary shafts. Lower neck, chest, and underparts densely vermiculated whitish and dark, appearing dusky overall and washed darker and browner on flanks; undertail coverts whitish with dark vermiculations. Underwings whitish, vermiculated dark, with variable broad dark margins including a blackish humeral panel (pattern suggests muted Laysan Albatross or stage 2 Steller's Albatross); can appear dark overall with a broad whitish central panel across greater and median coverts. Bill ochre-yellow, often with dusky cutting edges to ungues; legs and feet blue-gray to bluish flesh; eyes dark.

Juvenile fledges Nov–Dec. Similar to adult but head whiter overall, with buff wash mainly on crown (SDNHM specimen), plumage uniform in wear. Bill may average duller. Subsequent molts and plumages undescribed.

Molt Breeding adult wing molt at sea mainly Dec–Apr, away from nesting grounds. All adults replace p6-p10 between breeding seasons, and about 50% replace all primaries (Harris 1973), with p1-p3 most commonly retained. Outer primaries of breeders freshest and, exceptionally, p9-p10 still growing on birds incubating in May. Young fledge in Nov–Dec, may undergo first molt of outer primaries at 13–15 months after fledging like other *Phoebastria* (needs study).

A10.1. Adult Galapagos Albatross. Unmistakable; note golden cowl and very long yellow bill. GLA. Galapagos Islands, Ecuador, 27 Jul 2005.

A10.2. Adult Galapagos Albatross. Underwing pattern resembles that of congeneric Laysan. GLA. Galapagos Islands, Ecuador, 27 Jul 2005.

A10.3. Adult Galapagos Albatross. Unmistakable; juvenile would have little or no trace of golden cowl. AJ. Galapagos Islands, Ecuador, 13 Aug 2009.

A10.4. Adult Galapagos Albatrosses. Often looks long-necked when on water. CC. Piura, Peru, 3 Nov 2005.

A10.5. Adult Galapagos Albatross. Unmistakable; huge bill of this individual indicates male. GLA. Galapagos Islands, Ecuador, 24 Jul 2009.

A11. LIGHT-MANTLED SOOTY ALBATROSS *Phoebetria palpebrata*
L 89–93 cm, WS 208–232 cm, bill 10–11.5 cm
Figures A11.1–A11.7

Identification Summary Pacific. Exceptional off California. A fairly small but spectacular albatross with long angular wings and long tapered tail, this striking seabird of cold subantarctic waters is unlikely to be confused if seen well.

Taxonomy Monotypic.

Names *Phoebetria* means "prophet," perhaps an allusion to the qualities associated with albatrosses by early mariners; *palpebrata* indicates furnished with eyelids, a reference to this species' bold white eye crescents. Sometimes known simply as Light-mantled Albatross, an insipid name coined, no doubt, by emotionally castrated landlubbers.

Status and Distribution Near Threatened. Circumpolar in s oceans. Biennial breeder (Oct/Nov–May/Jun) on islands in South Atlantic and South Indian oceans and off New Zealand, ranging n mainly in austral winter (May–Aug) to subtropical latitudes (around 40˚S).

    Pacific. Exceptional off cen California, mid-Jul 1994 (Stallcup & Terrill 1996).

FIELD IDENTIFICATION

Similar Species A striking species, only likely to be confused with congeneric Sooty Albatross of subtropical s Atlantic and s Indian oceans but unrecorded in n hemisphere.

    Sooty Albatross slightly smaller (L 86–91 cm, WS 204–225 cm, bill 10–12 cm; A11a.1–A11a.2) and overall similar in shape but subtle differences can be helpful at long range: Light-mantled Sooty often deeper chested and shorter necked with larger, more domed head accentuated by more concave culmen (flat-crowned Sooty often looks relatively pin-headed, its forehead merging with a straighter culmen), and tail usually held mostly closed (more often fanned into a broader wedge on Sooty, accentuating small-headed front end). Sooty Albatross generally fairly uniform dark chocolate-brown overall but, especially in bright light, back can appear slightly but noticeably paler than the upperwings, with an ashy sheen. Most Light-mantled Sooties distinguished readily by their paler, ashy-gray body contrasting

sharply with dark upperwings and, especially, with blackish hood; at close range, note pale-blue sulcus stripe (cream to yellow sulcus stripe of Sooty tends to be more conspicuous). Faded first-year Sooty and Light-mantled Sooty (in Feb–Apr, at least) can appear quite similar. Besides structural clues, on Sooty the pale-mottled saddle may be less clean-cut and the underbody not as pale as the upperparts, which tends to be the case with bleached Light-mantled Sooty; also look for incoming feathers (ashy gray on Light-mantled Sooty, sooty brown on Sooty) and sulcus stripe color, although diagnostic color differences typically do not show until 2 years of age. Distant or briefly seen birds may be unidentifiable to species.

Habitat and Behavior Pelagic and unlikely to be seen from shore. Favors cold waters and readily associates with feeding aggregations of other albatrosses (the California bird was with Black-footed Albatrosses). Flight in moderate to strong winds often spectacular, sailing high and maneuvering easily relative to the lower-flying and heavier-looking Black-footed. Often approaches ships quite closely, although usually makes only one or two passes before losing interest and flying off; less often accompanies ships for an hour or two.

Description A fairly small albatross with long angular wings and a long tapered tail.

    Adult. Dark overall with a pale ashy-gray saddle that offsets a blackish hood (with white postocular crescent) and contrasts along a straight-edged division with the dark upperwings; back/upperwing contrast typically strong but relatively dull on some birds, perhaps mainly fresh-plumaged adults. From below, gray body contrasts less strongly with dark underwings. Outer primaries and rectrices have white shafts, often conspicuous on outer primaries. Bill black with a pale-blue sulcus stripe, visible at close range; legs and feet pale pinkish, eyes dark.

Juvenile/first cycle. Fledges May–Jun. Head and body paler than adult, with less extensive dark hood, duller and narrower postocular crescent; body plumage prone to fading over first year. By Oct–Nov some birds are very pale bodied (creamy or even whitish), with dark hood reduced to a mask. Molting immatures in Feb–Apr often show patchy upperparts (incoming ashy-gray feathers appearing contrastingly dark) and can have an extensive pale collar offsetting blackish mask. Some adults may also show these bleached plumages (Eades et al. 1994) but confirmation needed. **Bill** black overall with dull brownish or grayish sulcus stripe. Molt of head and body feathers in Nov–Apr may be PF molt or start of protracted PB2 molt.

Second cycle. PB2 molt involves head, body, tail, and probably outer primaries. Plumage resembles adult but upperwings relatively brown and faded except for fresher outer primaries. **Bill** develops pale grayish sulcus stripe.

Third cycle. PB3 molt probably includes middle but not outer primaries. Plumage resembles adult; outer primaries (usually p8-p10) faded and worn in contrast to fresher middle (and some inner) primaries; upperwing coverts mostly gray (often mixed with faded brown juvenile feathers). **Bill** like adult, but pale blue sulcus stripe may average duller.

Fourth cycle. Some birds may be identifiable by combination of phase 1 primary molt (with fresher outer primaries) and a few retained and very worn ("eaten away") juvenile secondaries. Following this age, not distinguishable from adult.

Molt (Fig 144) Adult wing molt mainly Jun–Oct (Marchant & Higgins 1990), although how molt relates to the 16–18 months between breeding attempts remains to be clarified; I have seen no molting adults during Nov–Apr, suggesting that primaries may be renewed in two (Jun–Oct?) periods rather than gradually throughout a single protracted molt. At-sea observations indicate outer primaries are molted every other year, as in mollymawks (pers. obs.), but that PB2 apparently includes outer primaries (usually p8-p10) in Jul–Oct (at about 13–16 months after fledging); confirmation from known-age birds desirable.

	Cycle 1		Cycle 2			Cycle 3			Cycle 4			Cycle 5		
Jan	May	Sep	Jan	May	Sep	Jan	May	Sep	Jan	May	Sep	Jan	May	Sep	Jan
Body			PB2			PB3			PB4			PB5		
p8-p10			Ph.	1					Phase	1				
p6-p7						Phase	2					Phase	2	

Fig 144. Provisional molt schedules for Light-mantled Sooty Albatross in first few years of life; fledging date assumed as 1 Jun. See Fig 140 (p.312) for key. Whether PB2 includes outer primaries requires confirmation. Marchant and Higgins (1990) suggest a late Jul bird molting outer primaries may be first-year; moreover, unlike mollymawks, I have seen no Light-mantled Sooties in Nov with worn juvenile outer primaries, only juveniles and birds with faded juvenile upperwing coverts and new outer primaries.

A11.1. Adult Light-mantled Sooty Albatross in phase 2 primary molt. Unmistakable, with blackish hood and clean-cut silvery-gray back (contrast varies with light angle and plumage fading; cf. A11.3–A11.4). SNGH. West-southwest of Antipodes Island, New Zealand, 20 Nov 2008.

A11.2. Juvenile Light-mantled Sooty Albatross (about five months after fledging?). In first year, dark hood typically reduced in extent, body often ashy white overall, and bill blackish overall with no obvious paler sulcus stripe. SNGH. East-northeast of Macquarie Island, Australia, 16 Nov 2008.

A11.3. Presumed second-cycle Light-mantled Sooty Albatross in phase 1 primary molt (about 17 months after fledging?). Faded juvenile greater coverts and remiges contrast with fresh outer primaries; pale sulcus stripe duller and narrower than adult. SNGH. West-southwest of Campbell Island, New Zealand, 17 Nov 2008.

A11.4. Presumed third-cycle Light-mantled Sooty Albatross in phase 2 primary molt (about 29 months after fledging?). Note contrast between new middle primaries and older outer primaries, plus a large block of juvenile secondaries. SNGH. West-southwest of Campbell Island, New Zealand, 17 Nov 2008.

A11.5. Adult Light-mantled Sooty Albatross. As well as plumage features, relative to Sooty Albatross (A11a.1–A11a.2) note bulbous head and neck accentuating slightly smaller bill (with slightly concave culmen). SNGH. East-northeast of Campbell Island, New Zealand, 19 Nov 2008.

A11.6. Juvenile Light-mantled Sooty Albatross (same bird as A11.2). Note reduced dark hood, ashy-white body; bill blackish overall . SNGH. East-northeast of Macquarie Island, Australia, 16 Nov 2008.

A11a.1. (Above) First-year Sooty Albatross (same bird as A11a.2). As with Light-mantled Sooty, juvenile plumage of Sooty often fades strikingly over first year (cf. A11.7). Note head and bill shape plus incoming dark-sooty feathers on head and body. SNGH. South of Gough Island, South Atlantic, 6 Apr 2009.

A11.7. (Above right) First-year Light-mantled Sooty Albatross (about 10 months after fledging?). Can be difficult to distinguish from corresponding plumage of Sooty Albatross (A11a.1–A11a.2). Note subtle structural clues, paler underbody, incoming ashy-gray feathers. SNGH. Northeast of South Georgia Island, South Atlantic, 29 Mar 2002.

A11a.2. (Right) First-year Sooty Albatross. Juvenile body plumage often fades strikingly over first year, inviting confusion with Light-mantled Sooty (cf. A11.7). Note overall structure, plus incoming dark-sooty feathers on head and body. SNGH. South of Gough Island, South Atlantic, 6 Apr 2009.

347

STORM-PETRELS: OCEANITIDAE AND HYDROBATIDAE

Storm-petrels are found over the world's oceans and comprise two families (see Introduction, pp. 20–21), which are combined here for identification purposes. These very small pelagic birds can suggest swallows or even bats, and often look improbably small as they fly low to the waves amid vast expanses of open water. Ages and sexes appear similar, and plumages are predominantly hued with blackish brown, gray, and white, usually with a paler diagonal band on the upperwing. Several species have white patches on the uppertail coverts, often called rump patches for convenience. Molts are typically complete, but with timings and sequences often poorly known.

Species limits are in a state of flux, and 40 or more species may be recognized worldwide when careful studies have been made. Learning how to identify some of these nascent species at sea is one of the most challenging frontiers in modern birding. Storm-petrels found in the region are considered here in three groups: white-rumped, dark-rumped, and distinctive (Fig 145).

Fig 145. Storm-petrels are tiny pelagic birds that flit and patter low over the ocean surface, and, like this group, they can often be attracted to fish-oil slicks. Among these Wilson's Storm-Petrels (a white-rumped species) is the slightly larger (and dark-rumped) Swinhoe's Storm-Petrel, just right of center. SNGH. Off Hatteras, North Carolina, 2 Jun 2008.

Identifying Storm-Petrels at Sea

Identifying storm-petrels at sea is frequently difficult—after all, most are small, similar-looking birds that fly low and are usually seen not that close and not that well from a moving observation platform. But, like almost all birding, the main stumbling block is an observer's lack of familiarity with the birds. For example, beginning birders usually take a while to appreciate the differences between Wilson's and Leach's storm-petrels, but after a few trips these two very different species usually look just that—very different (Fig 146). Considerably more trips are needed to feel comfortable separating Leach's Storm-Petrel from Grant's [Band-rumped] Storm-Petrel, and even experienced observers don't identify all birds.

Fig 146. This Wilson's Storm-Petrel (left) and this Leach's Storm-Petrel (right) are both white-rumped species but exhibit a number of differences. Typical of the southern storm-petrels (family Oceanitidae) the Wilson's has longer legs and straighter-held wings with a shorter arm; typical of northern storm-petrels (family Hybrobatidae) the Leach's has shorter legs (the feet, visible under the tail, fall well short of the tail tip) and more angled wings with a longer arm. In addition to the family-level differences, Wilson's is smaller and blacker with a duller and less extensive upperwing band and a small bill, whereas Leach's is bigger and browner with a bold pale upperwing band, a steely gray cast to the head and back, and a longer bill. With birds in the field, differences in flight manner and tail shape would also be apparent. SNGH. Off Hatteras, North Carolina, 26 May 2009.

Important things to note with storm-petrels are flight manner, overall size and shape, and the main patterns of contrast; looking for small-scale field marks is rarely helpful in picking out different species. Often it is best to watch the common species (such as Ashy Storm-Petrel off cen California, or Wilson's Storm-Petrel off the East Coast) simply with the naked eye, subconsciously absorbing flight behavior and structure, rather than focusing on one bird through binoculars and wondering about where the white goes, or exactly what shape the tail is, or how bold the upperwing band is. Then, when a different storm-petrel flies into the picture it should stand out by virtue of its flight manner, size, and shape. Perhaps more so than with other tubenoses, the naked-eye approach helps greatly for picking out different species of storm-petrels. When you really do see a different species then you can look for conventional field marks, but often they won't be easy to see. Just accept that the whole bird is a field mark.

In terms of seeing storm-petrels at sea, three regions with good diversity are cen California, w Mexico, and North Carolina. The large flocks of storm-petrels that gather at Cordell Bank and Monterey Bay in fall mainly comprise Ashy and Black storm-petrels, but Fork-tailed, Wilson's, and, in some years, Least storm-petrels can also be found, and these flocks provide a good opportunity to study different species together (Figs 147–148). Off w Mexico, all three species in the genus *Halocyptena* can be seen together (Fig 149). Off North Carolina from spring through fall, small numbers of Grant's (and perhaps other species in the Band-rumped complex) and Leach's storm-petrels can be seen in association with large numbers of Wilson's Storm-Petrels (Fig 150), offering a rare opportunity to study these three (or more) species together (Fig 151).

Fig 147. The large storm-petrel flocks that gather in fall off the California coast can be both exciting and frustrating—with so many tiny birds milling around, where do you start? Most if not all of the birds in this photo are Ashy Storm-Petrels, the commonest species and a good place to start. Become familiar with the size, shape, color tones, and flight manner of Ashy and then scan with the naked eye to look for something different. SNGH. Monterey Bay, California, 22 Sep 2007.

Fig 148. Among these Ashy Storm-Petrels, the larger, blacker, and long-necked bird on the water left of center near the back is a Black Storm-Petrel. Can you find the two Fork-tailed Storm-Petrels? SNGH. Cordell Bank, California, 7 Sep 2007.

Fig 149. Among flocks of Least Storm-Petrels flushed off the water, the gleaming white rumps of Wedge-rumped Storm-Petrels stand out like beacons, and Black Storm-Petrel (one bird, center right) is distinguished readily by its large size. SNGH. Baja California Sur, Mexico, 22 Aug 2010.

Fig 150. These white-rumped storm-petrels are Wilson's—except for one. Look for the larger and longer-winged bird with shorter legs (right center). On this date, the obvious wing molt on this "large storm-petrel" (large relative to Wilson's, the default reference species) indicates a Grant's [Band-rumped] Storm-Petrel. SNGH. Off Hatteras, North Carolina, 25 May 2008.

Fig 151. Storm-petrels on the water offer different challenges to those posed by flying birds. The two smaller and blacker front birds with bold white patches visible are typical Wilson's Storm-Petrels. The back center bird is larger, paler, and browner, and shows almost no white (the small white strip under the wings is often not visible in the field); together with the grayer head and back and the relatively long slender bill these features all indicate Leach's Storm-Petrel (some Pacific populations show more white than this). The right-hand back bird is a Grant's [Band-rumped] Storm-Petrel, which is also larger and browner than Wilson's, with a bigger bill. Relative to Leach's, Grant's shows more white, often looks shorter necked and sootier brown overall, and has a stouter bill. SNGH. Off Hatteras, North Carolina, 31 May 2008.

White-rumped Storm-Petrels

In the region, eight or more species in four genera (and in both n and s families) share mostly dark plumage relieved by a bold white rump patch, suggesting that this pattern is ancestral or has evolved independently several times. Wilson's Storm-Petrel is a nonbreeding visitor, common in the Atlantic, rare in the Pacific; European Storm-Petrel is a very rare nonbreeding visitor to North Atlantic waters; Leach's Storm-Petrel breeds in both the North Atlantic and North Pacific; Ainley's [Leach's] Storm-Petrel and Townsend's [Leach's] Storm-Petrel breed only on Guadalupe Island, in the Pacific Ocean off Mexico; Wedge-rumped and Darwin's [Band-rumped] storm-petrels are nonbreeding visitors to Pacific waters; and Grant's [Band-rumped] Storm-Petrel is a nonbreeding visitor to Atlantic waters. Madeiran [Band-rumped] Storm-Petrel and other species in the Band-rumped Storm-Petrel complex may also visit Atlantic waters.

In the Pacific region, an underappreciated problem is the separation of Townsend's [Leach's] and Wedge-rumped storm-petrels (Figs 152–153). In the Atlantic region, the most familiar identification challenge involves separating Leach's from Grant's [Band-rumped] (Figs 154–158), but other problems exist (see Figs 159–164). Distinguishing species within the Leach's complex in the Pacific (Leach's, Ainley's, and Townsend's), and species within the Band-rumped complex in the Atlantic (Grant's, Madeiran, and perhaps Monteiro's and Cape Verde) are problems that still require critical study (Howell et al. 2010a, 2010b).

Fig 152. Variation in Wedge-rumped Storm-Petrel remains poorly understood (see Fig 164), and some individuals, like this presumed *kelsalli*, have a relatively short white rump patch. Under at-sea conditions confusion is possible with Townsend's [Leach's] Storm-Petrel (see Fig 153). SNGH. Baja California Sur, 22 Aug 2010.

Fig 153. The little-known Townsend's [Leach's] Storm-Petrel is smaller and blacker than Leach's, with a broader white rump band and shorter, less deeply forked tail—all features that might invite confusion with Wedge-rumped Storm-Petrel (see Fig 152). More study is needed of this underappreciated pitfall. SNGH. Off San Diego, California, 20 Jul 2008.

354

Fig 154. Most Leach's Storm-Petrels off the East Coast in spring are not in wing molt, although some first years start inner primary molt during Jun–Jul. Relative to Grant's Storm-Petrel (see Fig 155), note broad white rump band not extending much on lateral tail coverts, relatively long rump/tail projection (forked tail could be apparent at different angles), bold pale upperwing band, and gray cast to head. SNGH. Off Hatteras, North Carolina, 21 May 2009.

Fig 155. Most Grant's [Band-rumped] Storm-Petrels off the East Coast are in obvious wing molt during spring, when Leach's Storm-Petrels are not molting or only starting wing molt. As well as obvious wing molt, note relatively narrow white rump band wrapping around to lateral tail coverts, relatively short notched tail, dull upperwing band, and overall sooty plumage tones. SNGH. Off Hatteras, North Carolina, 26 May 2009.

Fig 156. From below, Leach's Storm-Petrel (at least in the Atlantic) shows less white on the lateral tail coverts than Band-rumped. Also note forked tail, relatively long bill, and brown plumage tones with a grayer head. SNGH. Off Hatteras, North Carolina, 25 May 2009.

Fig 157. Band-rumped Storm-Petrel (taxon unknown) banking away (cf. Fig 156). Note big "cottony" white patch on lateral tail coverts, notched tail (tail notch often accentuated at such angles, and tail of this bird would probably appear square-tipped if viewed from above). SNGH. Off Hatteras, North Carolina, 2 Jun 2007.

Fig 158. Wing molt timing can be a useful clue for separating Grant's [Band-rumped] Storm-Petrel from Leach's Storm-Petrel, and also may prove useful in distinguishing among species in the Band-rumped complex. Although it wasn't noticed when this group of storm-petrels was on the water, the Grant's Storm-Petrel (second from left) can be picked out readily at this season from the surrounding Leach's by its obvious wing molt (cf. Figs 154–155). SNGH. Off Hatteras, North Carolina, 26 May 2008.

Fig 159. Wilson's Storm-Petrel (nominate *oceanicus*). Note fairly straight-held and relatively paddle-shaped wings with distinct pale upperwing band limited to greater coverts, obvious toe projection past slightly scooped-out tail tip, and generally sooty or blackish plumage tones. SNGH. Off Hatteras, North Carolina, 6 Jun 2009.

Fig 160. Presumed Grant's [Band-rumped] Storm-Petrel. Note slightly angled wings, stout bill, dull upperwing band not reaching wing bend, bold white rump band wrapping around under the body, notched tail tip (notch accentuated by angle), and generally sooty plumage tones. KS. Off Hatteras, North Carolina, 26 Jul 2009.

Fig 161. Leach's Storm-Petrel (nominate *leucorhoa*). Note pushed-forward and angled wings, bold pale upperwing band reaching to near wing bend, messy white rump patch, relatively long forked tail (fork reduced here by wear and molt), steely gray tones to head and back, and relatively slender bill. SNGH. Off Hatteras, North Carolina, 23 May 2009.

Fig 162. European Storm-Petrel (presumably nominate *pelagicus*). Note narrow and fairly straight-held wings with no distinct upper-wing band, overall blackish plumage, and squared tail tip. SNGH. Off Hatteras, North Carolina, 28 May 2007.

Fig 163. Possible Madeiran [Band-rumped] Storm-Petrel. Relative to presumed Grant's Storm-Petrel (Fig 160), note slighter build, narrower-looking wings, smaller head, and blacker plumage tones. Also note dull upperwing band not reaching wing bend, dark marks in white rump band (suggesting Leach's). SNGH. Off Hatteras, North Carolina, 7 Jun 2009.

Fig 164. Wedge-rumped Storm-Petrel (nominate *tethys*). Note long narrow wings, pale upperwing band not extending to wing bend, relatively short tail projection past long white rump patch, notched tail tip, and dark sooty plumage tones. Peruvian subspecies (species?) *kelsalli* may differ in having broader wings and shorter white rump patch, but more study needed (cf. Fig 152). GLA. Galapagos Islands, Ecuador, 27 Jul 2006.

S1. WILSON'S STORM-PETREL *Oceanites oceanicus*
L 16–20 cm, WS 34–42 cm, tail 55–73 mm
Figures 3, 15, 49, 55–58, 145–146, 148, 150–151, 159, 165, S1.1–S1.13, S2.1, S2.11, S3.1, S3.10

Identification Summary Atlantic (common) and Pacific (rare) transequatorial migrant from s hemisphere. A medium-sized to fairly small species with short arms and fairly broad wings not strongly crooked, a squared tail, and long, stilt-like legs; toes project beyond the tail tip in direct flight. Flight typically low and fluttering, swallow-like. Patters with legs dangling; often follows ships in the Atlantic region. Plumage blackish with a contrasting paler ulnar band not extending to bend of wing. Broad white rump patch extends conspicuously to lateral undertail coverts.

S1.1. Pattering flocks of Wilson's Storm-Petrels, many in obvious wing molt, are a common sight on East Coast pelagic trips in summer. SNGH. Off Hatteras, North Carolina, 24 May 2008.

Taxonomy Two well-marked taxa (see Murphy 1936), differing distinctly in size and perhaps best considered full species. Birds breeding around Antarctica sometimes separated as the subspecies *exasperatus*, averaging larger than birds breeding on subantarctic islands such as South Georgia.

O. [o.] oceanicus (Wilson's Storm-Petrel) breeds Antarctic region n to Scotia Arc islands, migrates to North Atlantic and North Pacific. Larger overall (L 18.5–20 cm, WS 36–42 cm); fresh plumage lacks distinct pale tips to greater underwing coverts.

O. [o.] chilensis (Fuegian Storm-Petrel) breeds Cape Horn region of Chile, ranges in Humboldt Current n to Peru, rarely Panama. Smaller overall (L 16–18 cm, WS 34–38 cm); fresh plumage has distinct pale tips to greater and median underwing coverts, and sometimes a small whitish belly patch.

Names *Oceanites* are the children of the Greek sea god Okeanos; *oceanicus* refers to the ocean. The English name commemorates Alexander Wilson (1766–1813), a Scottish-born poet who became one of the pioneers in American ornithology. Sometimes known simply as Wilson's Petrel.

Status and Distribution Least Concern. Breeds (Dec–Apr) Antarctic region (*oceanicus*) and Cape Horn region (*chilensis*); ranges at sea (mainly May–Oct) n to around 40°N in Pacific and 50°N in Atlantic.

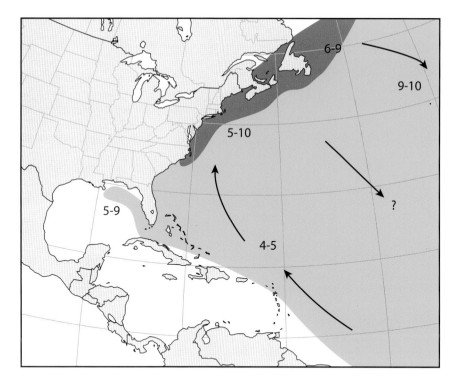

Atlantic. Nominate *oceanicus* is a common to locally abundant nonbreeding visitor (mainly May–Sep) from mid-Atlantic states n to Atlantic Canada, with smaller numbers s to Florida (where commonest May–Jul). Early migrants appear in Apr (perhaps mainly first-cycle birds in fresh formative plumage; NCSM specimens) but main numbers off North Carolina arrive in May (with juveniles appearing from mid-May onward; NCSM specimens), New York in late May, Massachusetts in Jun (day counts of 1000–5000 birds frequent on summer pelagic trips), and Atlantic Canada by mid-Jun, with return migration mainly Sep–Oct (later southward), and small numbers (mainly first-cycle birds) into Nov–Dec, very rarely Jan off North Carolina. Off Bermuda occurs late Mar–early Sep, with peak numbers late Apr–late May. Very rare inland in the East after tropical cyclones (mainly Aug–Sep), mainly e of the Adirondacks, exceptionally reaching e Great Lakes.

In Caribbean region, recorded off Guadeloupe mid-Feb to early Aug, with a peak in Apr, and seasonally fairly common around Bahamas (late Apr to mid-Jun), but generally uncommon (mainly Apr–Jun) within the Caribbean. Rare to locally fairly common (Apr–Sep, mainly late May–Aug) in n Gulf of Mexico, w to waters s of Mississippi

River mouth (Dittmann & Cardiff, unpubl. data), very rare w to Texas and exceptional inland after storms to Alabama (NAB 60:85, 2005).

Pacific. Rare to locally uncommon nonbreeding visitor (May–Nov, mainly Aug–Oct) off cen California (nominate *oceanicus*, see below), casual (late May to mid-Sep) n to Washington, and rare (mainly Sep–Oct) s to s California and n Baja California. Found mostly in areas of local upwelling, especially Cordell Bank, California (daily counts exceptionally 50–80 birds). Migration in North Pacific may follow clockwise path typical of many species in the region (study needed).

Few well-documented records off Middle America; reportedly "regular but sporadic" (Apr–Aug) off Costa Rica (Stiles & Skutch 1989), perhaps pertaining to northward incursions of *chilensis*, which has been collected (late Aug) in Gulf of Panama.

Two specimens from California have been attributed to *chilensis* (Grinnell & Miller 1944) but both are probably *oceanicus*. MVZ specimen 18742 appears to have a wing chord of 144 mm but this is the length of p8 (p9 and p10 are growing, and shorter than p8, which itself may not be full length); p8 on 5 Antarctic specimens of *oceanicus* at MVZ measures 144–151 mm, whereas on the 1 *chilensis* specimen there it measures 132

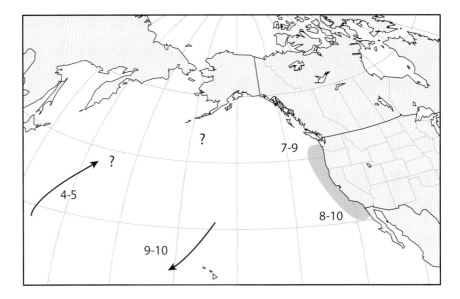

mm. UCLA specimen 37976 has a wing chord of about 145 mm (outer primaries worn) (K. C. Molina, pers. comm.), which falls in overlap range (*chilensis* wing chord 130–146 mm vs. 136–155 mm for *oceanicus*; Murphy 1936).

FIELD IDENTIFICATION

Similar Species Note medium size, short-armed wings, fluttery swallow-like flight, blackish plumage with a bold white rump patch, and long legs.

Atlantic. Distinctive, but cf. larger and longer-winged *Leach's and Grant's storm-petrels*, which have stronger wingbeats and different flight manners (see those species accounts for identification criteria). Also see *European Storm-Petrel*, a very rare visitor to North American waters.

Pacific. Off the West Coast cf. *Leach's Storm-Petrel*, *Ainley's Storm-Petrel*, and particularly *Townsend's Storm-Petrel* (see those species accounts for detailed identification criteria).

Wedge-rumped Storm-Petrel has longer-armed, narrower, and more crooked wings; flies with strong deep wingbeats in a more erratic, bounding manner; and has extensive wedge-shaped white rump patch covering much of cleft tail. Feeding Wedge-rumped, however, patters much like Wilson's and has relatively long legs and big feet. Wedge-rumped noticeably smaller than Wilson's Storm-Petrels found off West Coast (nominate *oceanicus*) but overlaps in size with

chilensis population of Wilson's that occurs off s Central America.

Congeneric *Elliot's Storm-Petrel* (L 14–15.5 cm, WS 30.5–37 cm; perhaps a casual visitor n to Panama Bight from Humboldt Current; see S1a.1–S1a.3 and Appendix B) similar in shape to Wilson's, with broad-based wings, squared tail, and toes projecting beyond tail tip. Viewed from above, Elliot's looks much like Wilson's but is slightly smaller, and best distinguished by its large whitish belly patch (often visible); it also has whitish tips to greater and median underwing coverts (often hard to see, and some Fuegian Storm-Petrels similar). White rump patch of Elliot's slightly less extensive on distal undertail coverts, hence Elliot's resting on the water typically shows less white than Wilson's (see S13.10). Elliot's tends to have slightly more fluttery flight than Wilson's, which may be apparent if the species are seen together.

As viewed from above (such as from high on a ship), *Black-bellied (and White-bellied) Storm-Petrel* in direct flight can appear similar to Wilson's; both are larger with longer and broader wings, and have a narrower, less distinct pale ulnar band; watch for diagnostic white on the underbody.

Habitat and Behavior Inshore and offshore waters; regularly seen from land off e North America, where ranges into bays and other coastal waters. Occurs singly or in loose aggregations, locally in concentrations of hundreds, even thousands, such as scavenging at fishing boats or marine mammal carcasses; often follows ships, seeking food in the wake. Off Pacific coast, readily associates with other storm-petrels, such as rafting flocks of Ashy, Black, and Fork-tailed, and more often at the edges of flocks than in the middle.

Transiting flight usually fairly low and direct over the water, with no banking or weaving and only short glides, the wings held straight out and not strongly crooked. Wingbeats usually quick, stiff, and fairly shallow (recalling a Barn Swallow), the upstroke looking quicker and flicking, the downstroke stronger. In calm conditions, sometimes sustains direct flapping flight 3–5 m above the sea for hundreds of meters. In strong winds, can glide hundreds of meters with little or no flapping, flying in low, long-wavelength arcs much like larger tubenoses; also "kicksails" like larger *Fregetta* storm-petrels, especially when transiting into and across the wind. Birds in heavy wing molt need to flap quicker and appear even more fluttery in contrast to full-winged birds that glide and sail strongly and more easily. When foraging, flies with stiff, shallow wingbeats interspersed with brief glides on slightly bowed wings, stalling to drop to the surface where patters with feet dangling, the quivering or fluttering wings held raised in a *V*. Feeding groups seem to dance like puppets, their feet held by some invisible force to the sea surface, and birds in feeding interactions utter high, slightly shrill piping whistles, audible at close range.

Description Medium-sized to fairly small (see Taxonomy) with a relatively short arm, broad wings not strongly crooked, and a broad, squared to slightly notched, medium-length tail (usually looks rounded when spread). Legs long, and toes typically project noticeably beyond tail in flight (can be held pulled in, and thus not projecting).

Ages similar but first-cycle birds in fresh plumage May–Jun when older birds worn and molting, and juveniles of *oceanicus* often have some whitish mottling on belly (Murphy 1936).

Slaty blackish overall (browner when worn), appearing black at any distance and sometimes with a pale grayish throat patch; *chilensis* often has a small whitish belly patch. Flight feathers blackish; upperwings with contrasting pale gray (tipped silvery when fresh) to pale brownish (when worn and faded) upperwing panel largely restricted to greater coverts and not reaching wing bend. Underwings of *oceanicus* sometimes show a broad but diffuse, reflective pale band on greater and median coverts; *chilensis* often has distinct whitish tips to greater underwing coverts, most distinct in fresh plumage. Clean-cut white rump patch extends conspicuously to lateral undertail coverts, and visible from below like a bulge of cotton wool (usually obvious on resting birds); white basal shafts and inner webs of outer rectrices usually not visible at sea. Bill, legs, and toes black, with pale yellow foot webbing visible under good conditions.

On the water. Appears all-dark or with a variable paler ulnar band sometimes visible; white rump patch usually apparent as bold white patch under folded wings.

Molt (Fig 49, p. 38) Adult (and PB2) wing molt relatively rapid in North Atlantic, starting mid-Apr to early Jun, completing mid-Aug to late Sep before southward migration; tail molt mainly Sep–Oct (NCSM specimens). Complete PF molt indicated by a second wave of birds that start primary molt mid-Jul to early Sep, completing late Oct–Dec or later (perhaps suspending on some transequatorial migrants, which may finish outer primary molt in s hemisphere); tail molt mainly Oct–Jan (NCSM specimens). A similar pattern of prebasic molt in May–Aug/Sep and of presumed PB wing molt starting in Aug also occurs in North Pacific migrants off California and Baja California (pers. obs.). Some birds in South Atlantic, presumed nonbreeders and perhaps birds not migrating to n hemisphere, start primary molt in Mar or earlier (pers. obs.).

S1.2. Wilson's Storm-Petrel has stiff wings with a short arm, and its toes typically project beyond the tail tip in direct flight. SNGH. Off Hatteras, North Carolina, 23 May 2008.

S1.3. Wilson's Storm-Petrel. Freshly molted greater coverts can have contrasting silvery edgings that fade by fall; note inner primary molt, with primary coverts molted in tandem with primaries. SNGH. Off Hatteras, North Carolina, 23 May 2008.

S1.4. Wilson's Storm-Petrel in mid-primary molt. Blended pattern to greater coverts apparently represents individual variation (cf. S1.3). SNGH. Off Hatteras, North Carolina, 26 May 2009.

S1.5. Wilson's Storm-Petrel in fresh plumage, possibly a juvenile. Pale upperwing band can be quite muted in some lights. SNGH. Off Hatteras, North Carolina, 30 May 2007.

S1.6. Occasionally Wilson's Storm-Petrels fly with their legs pulled in, which can produce a disconcertingly compact appearance. SNGH. Off Hatteras, North Carolina, 1 Jun 2009.

S1.7. Juvenile Wilson's Storm-Petrel. Note uniform wear to upperwings (cf. S1.8), which already appear relatively brown and faded after the bird's transequatorial odyssey. SNGH. Off Hatteras, North Carolina, 26 May 2009.

S1.8. Wilson's Storm-Petrel. Note subtle contrast between browner (and older) inner primaries and fresher blacker outer primaries and secondaries, indicating this bird is not a juvenile. SNGH. Off Hatteras, North Carolina, 23 May 2008.

S1a.1. Elliot's Storm-Petrel (shown here) averages smaller than Wilson's but, as viewed from above, these species are probably not safely separable by plumage or structure. SNGH. Lima, Peru, 16 Sep 2007.

S1.9. In some lights, greater underwing coverts on Wilson's Storm-Petrel appear as a paler stripe, but not as bold as the contrasting white stripe on European Storm-Petrel. SNGH. Off Hatteras, North Carolina, 29 May 2007.

S1.10. Among inshore flocks of dark-rumped Pacific storm-petrels (here mainly Ashy, with single Black at top right and Fork-tailed on far left) the white-rumped Wilson's (bottom right) really stands out. SNGH. Cordell Bank, California, 7 Sep 2007.

S1.11. Fuegian [Wilson's] Storm-Petrel. This smaller, Humboldt Current taxon has whitish tips to greater and median underwing coverts, sometimes a small white belly patch (cf. S1.12). AJ. Tarapacá, Chile, 21 Nov 2006.

S1.12. Presumed Fuegian [Wilson's] Storm-Petrel. Strongly patterned individuals like this may not always be distinguishable from Elliot's Storm-Petrel, but note extensive white wrap-around on lateral undertail coverts. SNGH. Valparaíso, Chile, 30 Oct 2007.

S1a.2. Elliot's Storm-Petrel has variable white belly patch (often best seen as birds turn away like this) and variable whitish tips to underwing coverts (cf. S1a.3). White on lateral undertail coverts less extensive distally than Wilson's (S1.11–1.12); thus, resting birds show less white than Wilson's (cf. S1.13, S13.10). SNGH. Lima, Peru, 16 Sep 2007.

S1a.3. Elliot's Storm-Petrel has variable whitish tips to greater and median underwing coverts, which can be matched by Fuegian Storm-Petrel (cf. S1a.2, S1.11–S1.12), and white belly patch variably visible on pattering birds. SNGH. Tarapacá, Chile, 23 Oct 2009.

S1.13. Wilson's Storm-Petrel. Resting birds typically look blackish (but can be browner when faded, and tones are light dependent) with a large puffy white patch on tail coverts. SNGH. Off Hatteras, North Carolina, 28 Jul 2007.

S2. EUROPEAN STORM-PETREL *Hydrobates pelagicus*
L 15–17 cm, WS 35–37 cm, tail 48–60 mm
Figures 162, S2.1–S2.10

Identification Summary Atlantic. This diminutive, almost moth-like storm-petrel is a very rare nonbreeding visitor to waters off e North America. Besides its small size (looking about 70% the size of Wilson's), note the rounded wings, overall black plumage aspect with a large white rump patch, broad white underwing stripe, slightly rounded tail (with no toe projection), and rapid, fluttery flight.

S2.1. European Storm-Petrel (left) and Wilson's Storm-Petrel. Relative to Wilson's, European is smaller and blacker with much shorter legs, more rounded wings, and a bold white underwing stripe. SNGH. Off Hatteras, North Carolina, 31 May 2010.

Taxonomy Birds breeding in Mediterranean have been described as subspecies *melitensis*, which differs vocally and morphologically from birds breeding in nw Europe. Mediterranean birds considered specifically distinct by some authors (Robb et al. 2008) but may not be identifiable in the field. Birds off North America are most likely British Storm-Petrels.

H. [p.] pelagicus (British Storm-Petrel) breeds nw Europe, winters off sw Africa. Averages smaller and slightly less blackish, with slightly paler upperwing bar, slighter and shallower bill.

H. [p.] melitensis (Mediterranean Storm-Petrel) breeds (and mostly resident?) in the Mediterranean; may range to waters off nw Europe. Averages larger and slightly blacker, with slightly duller upperwing bar, stouter and deeper bill.

Names *Hydrobates* means "water dweller or water treader"; *pelagicus* refers to the open sea. In Britain, sometimes known simply as Storm Petrel.

Status and Distribution Least Concern. Breeds (May–Oct) w Europe (mainly British Isles) and w Mediterranean, winters (Oct–Apr) off w and s Africa; ranges to w North Atlantic.

Atlantic. Very rare nonbreeding visitor (late May–Aug, at least). First authenticated North American record a bird mist-netted on Sable Island, Nova Scotia, 10 Aug 1970 (McNeil & Burton 1971). No further confirmed records for more than 30 years, but small numbers (1–6 birds per year) have been found almost annually from mid-May to early Jun since 2003 off North Carolina (Patteson et al. 2009a), suggesting that

European Storm-Petrels may have been overlooked in other years. Should be sought in summer off Atlantic Canada and the Northeast, especially in areas where Wilson's Storm-Petrels gather to molt.

FIELD IDENTIFICATION

Similar Species Distinctive, but can be overlooked among masses of Wilson's Storm-Petrels. Relative to *Wilson's Storm-Petrel*, European is noticeably smaller and blacker with a faster flight, and it often buzzes quickly around groups of relatively leisurely looking Wilson's as they flutter and sail with long, stilt-like legs dangling; tail rounded and toes do not project past tail tip in flight. European has narrower, blunter-tipped wings with longer arm and stronger crook at wrist; rarely glides in light winds and does not patter and kick off the water as Wilson's often does. Wilson's flying hard into the wind can look hurried and purposeful, suggesting European, but wingbeats of Wilson's are stiff, unlike deeper and slightly looser wingbeats of European. Upperwing of European has narrow, inconspicuous pale line unlike broad pale panel on Wilson's, and underwing has diagnostic, clean-cut white central stripe.

Habitat and Behavior Offshore, although often seen from land in Europe. Most likely to be found singly, in association with other storm-petrels, especially Wilson's. Flight usually rapid and fluttery, looking small and quick among a mass of Wilson's, with infrequent glides in light winds, more frequent sailing in strong winds. Patters and alights on water with wings raised when feeding, often slightly separate from groups of the stilt-like Wilson's but sometimes "sinks" among them and is lost easily. Likely to be silent at sea.

Description Very small. Tail slightly rounded and with no foot projection; wings slightly rounded and evenly broad or with slightly narrower arm and broader hand, not strongly crooked.

Ages similar but juveniles fresh in fall (Sep–Oct) when older ages worn, and first-cycle birds have worn wings in spring (Apr–Jun) when older ages in fresh plumage. Blackish brown overall (often looking black) with blacker flight feathers (white bases to outer tail feathers rarely visible unless tail widely spread); head and back with a gray sheen in fresh plumage; narrow pale gray edgings to subscapulars in fresh plumage. Large white rump patch relatively even-width and fairly squared off, wrapping around to lateral tail coverts; longest feathers tipped black, sometimes showing as narrow black subterminal crescents or bars within white patch. White underwing stripe conspicuous, formed by mostly white greater coverts, variable whitish mottling on median coverts, and broad white tips to axillars; pale gray (fresh) to pale brownish (worn) tips to greater upperwing coverts form inconspicuous line on upperwing. Bill, legs, and feet black.

On the water. Appears all-dark with white rump patch often visible under folded wings.

Molt Adult wing molt protracted, mainly Oct–Apr but inner primaries may start during incubation; prebreeders likely start earlier (Jul–Sep?). A variable PF molt, including head, body, and possibly tail, may occur in first winter to spring (pers. obs.), but this might be first stage of protracted PB2 molt (study needed); PB2 wing molt mainly Jun–Oct/Nov.

S2.2. European Storm-Petrel. Besides very small size (not apparent in a photo) note overall blackish plumage aspect with only narrow paler tips to greater coverts; closed tail can look quite wedge-shaped (cf. S2.4 of same bird). SNGH. Off Hatteras, North Carolina, 28 May 2007.

S2.3. In some lights, like this, European Storm-Petrel can appear relatively pale and brown above, rather than more typical blackish plumage aspect. SNGH. Madeira, eastern Atlantic, 15 May 2010.

S2.4. European Storm-Petrel. Compare squared-off tip of slightly spread tail tip with S2.2. SNGH. Off Hatteras, North Carolina, 28 May 2007.

S2.5. European Storm-Petrel flies with strong, deep wingbeats very different from the typical flight of Wilson's. SNGH. Off Hatteras, North Carolina, 28 May 2007.

S2.6. European Storm-Petrel. Heavily worn primaries and early onset of wing molt (p1 appears to have been shed on both wings) indicate a first-summer bird. SNGH. Off Hatteras, North Carolina, 29 May 2007.

S2.7. European Storm-Petrel. White underwing stripe on fairly long narrow wings is variable in extent, but usually obvious with a reasonable view. SNGH. Off Hatteras, North Carolina, 28 May 2007.

S2.8. European Storm-Petrel. White bases of outer rectrices rarely visible unless tail is widely spread. SNGH. Madeira, eastern Atlantic, 15 May 2010.

S2.9. European Storm-Petrel. Note how pattern of white underwing stripe, plus details of wing wear, can be matched with S2.7, of same bird. SNGH. Off Hatteras, North Carolina, 28 May 2007.

S2.10. European Storm-Petrel feeds by pattering, but legs much shorter than Wilson's; note bold white underwing stripe. SNGH. Off Hatteras, North Carolina, 31 May 2010.

S2.11. European Storm-Petrel (right) with Wilson's Storm-Petrel. Note distinct differences between these species in shape as well as plumage tones (blackness of European accentuated here by lighting) and upper-wing pattern. SNGH. Off Hatteras, North Carolina, 28 May 2007.

The Band-rumped Storm-Petrel complex comprises an undetermined number of taxa whose relationships remain vexed; all breed in tropical and subtropical latitudes. Up to five subspecies of Band-rumped Storm-Petrel have been recognized traditionally, although many recent authors have considered this species monotypic (Austin 1952, Harris 1969b). Another study suggested that Band-rumped Storm-Petrels comprise an old lineage distinct enough from typical *Oceanodroma* storm-petrels to be placed in their own genus, *Thalobata* (Penhallurick & Wink 2004, but see Rheindt & Austin 2005). Recent studies of genetics and vocalizations have found considerable diversity within Band-rumped Storm-Petrels, which comprise at least nine distinct populations, at least five in the Atlantic and four in the Pacific (Smith et al. 2007, Smith & Friesen 2007). Several, if not all, of these populations are distinct enough to be recognized as species (more study is needed in several cases), but identification criteria for birds at sea are still in their infancy (Howell et al. 2010b, Robb et al. 2008; see Figs 165–169).

In the ne Atlantic, at least four species-level taxa in the Band-rumped Storm-Petrel complex breed on various islands (Bolton 2007, Friesen et al. 2007, Monteiro & Furness 1998, Robb et al. 2008): the widespread winter-breeding Grant's Storm-Petrel (which has yet to be described formally), the little-known Cape Verde Storm-Petrel (*O. jabejabe*) of the Cape Verde Islands (which apparently comprises two genetically distinct populations; Smith et al. 2007), the local summer-breeding Monteiro's Storm-Petrel (*O. monteiroi*) of the Azores (described formally only in 2008; Bolton et al. 2008), and the summer-breeding Madeiran Storm-Petrel (*O. castro*) of Madeira and the Canaries. Farther s in the Atlantic, two or more additional populations of Band-rumped Storm-Petrels breed in equatorial and tropical

Fig 165. Unidentified Band-rumped Storm-Petrel (right) and Wilson's Storm-Petrel. A few spring Band-rumpeds off the East Coast (such as this individual) appear smaller, slighter, and blacker than the majority of presumed Grant's, and also differ in wing molt timing. These birds are more similar in size to Wilson's than the relatively large and bulky Grant's and more often have dark marks in the white rump band, sometimes forming a narrow central stripe, as here; they may be Madeiran Storm-Petrels but further study is needed. SNGH. Off Hatteras, North Carolina, 16 Aug 2009.

southern latitudes on the islands of Ascension and St. Helena (Bennett et al. 2009), and Band-rumps may also breed on islets off São Tomé, in the Gulf of Guinea (Williams 1984). In the Pacific, there are distinct (but unnamed) cool-season and hot-season populations on the Galapagos Islands, plus distinct summer-breeding populations in Hawaii and Japan (Smith et al. 2007, Smith & Friesen 2007). As a measure of nomenclatural convenience, I propose here the name Darwin's Storm-Petrel for the Galapagos populations—it has the benefit of ready association with geographic locality.

Of these nine or so populations, Grant's Storm-Petrel has been certainly recorded in North American waters (Woolfenden et al. 2001) and the wing molt schedule of most Gulf Stream and Gulf of Mexico birds is consistent with Grant's (Fig 166). Other Atlantic species of Band-rumps apparently also occur (Figs 167–169), including Madeiran Storm-Petrel (Howell et al. 2010b), which is provisionally included here as a component of the North American avifauna. Genetic analysis of (mainly hurricane-driven) specimens from e North America might yield further information on which taxa occur (Howell et al. 2010b). In the Pacific, Darwin's Storm-Petrels range n, at least rarely, to waters far off s Central America.

Fig 166. Around 80–90% of spring Band-rumped Storm-Petrels off North Carolina are in wing molt, like this, and presumed to come from winter-breeding populations, most likely Grant's Storm-Petrel (cf. Fig 167). SNGH. Off Hatteras, North Carolina, 30 May 2010.

Fig 167. Around 10–20% of spring Band-rumped Storm-Petrels off North Carolina are in fresh plumage, like this (and Figs 163, 165); these birds may come from summer-breeding populations, most likely Madeiran Storm-Petrel; also note the relatively fine bill (cf. Fig 166). SNGH. Off Hatteras, North Carolina, 22 May 2010.

Fig 168. Specimens of Band-rumped Storm-Petrel collected off North Carolina. From left to right, NCSM 9536 (male, 5 Jul 1983; wing molt completed, tail molt completing), NCSM 10369 (female, 31 Jul/9 Aug 1984; p9-p10 growing), NCSM 13860 (female, 21 Jun 1985; p8-p10 old), and NCSM 13861 (male, 24 Jun 1985; p8-p10 old). Besides its different molt schedule, left-hand bird (possibly Madeiran?) appears smaller and blacker than the other three (presumed Grant's). SNGH.

Fig 169. Unidentified Band-rumped Storm-Petrel. This bird appears to be starting wing molt, with p1 shed on both wings, at a season when the winter-breeding Grant's are not molting. The fairly stocky shape and notched tail may point to Monteiro's Storm-Petrel but further study is needed. SNGH. Off Hatteras, North Carolina, 16 Aug 2009.

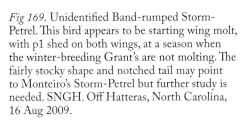

S3A. GRANT'S [BAND-RUMPED] STORM-PETREL *Oceanodroma [castro]* undescribed
L 19.5–21.5 cm, WS 45–51 cm, tail 66–79 mm (fork 0–7 mm)
S3B. MADEIRAN [BAND-RUMPED] STORM-PETREL *Oceanodroma [castro] castro*
L 18.5–20.5 cm, WS 42.5–48 cm, tail 62–71 mm (fork 5–10 mm)
Figures 150–151, 155, 157–158, 160, 163, 165–169, S3.1–S3.11

Identification Summary Atlantic. Offshore over deep, warm pelagic waters. Medium-large white-rumped storm-petrels best known from the Gulf Stream. Flight buoyant with measured wingbeats and a fairly deep downstroke; long wings bluntly pointed and crooked, tail squared to slightly notched. Plumage blackish with poorly contrasting paler upperwing band not extending to wing bend. Rump patch bright white, wrapping around tail base as an even-width band that extends to lateral undertail coverts. Grant's and Madeiran rarely separable in the field except by molt timing and plumage wear.

S3.1. Presumed Grant's Storm-Petrel (top) with Wilson's Storm-Petrels. Relative to Wilson's, Grant's is obviously big with long angled wings, short legs, and usually duller upperwing bands. SNGH. Off Hatteras, North Carolina, 1 Jun 2008

Taxonomy See introduction to Band-rumped Storm-Petrel complex. Both Grant's and Madeiran are considered monotypic, although populations breeding on different islands may exhibit slight mensural differences (cf. Bolton et al. 2008, Nunes 2000, Robertson & James 1988).

Names *Oceanodroma* means "ocean runner," *castro* refers to the "Roque de Castro" on Madeira, from which Edward Harcourt (1825–1891) described the first-known taxon of Band-rumped

Storm-Petrel. The English name of the cryptic and as yet formally undescribed winter-breeding taxon commemorates British birder Peter Grant (1943–1990), who led the way in challenging identification forums.

Status and Distribution Least Concern. Grant's breeds (Oct–Mar) in the e Atlantic on the Azores, Berlangas, Canary Islands, Madeiran archipelago, and Selvagens, and ranges at sea (mainly May–Aug) to warm waters of w Atlantic and Gulf of

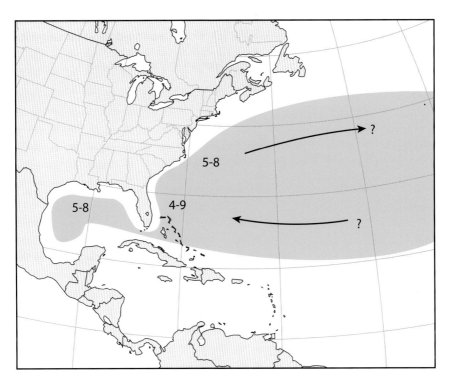

Mexico. Madeiran breeds (Jun–Oct) from the Madeiran archipelago s to the ne Canary Islands; its at-sea range is not well known.

Atlantic. Presumed Grant's Storm-Petrels are uncommon to locally or seasonally fairly common nonbreeding visitors (extreme dates Apr–Oct, rare before May and after Aug) to Gulf Stream waters off e U.S. from Florida (mainly late Apr–early Sep) n to Cape Hatteras, North Carolina (mainly late May–Aug), rare or casual (mainly Aug) n to warm offshore waters s of Cape Cod, Massachusetts. Presumed Grant's also ranges (May–Sep) to deep offshore waters in Gulf of Mexico, where Band-rumps are uncommon to locally fairly common late May–Aug. Presumed Madeiran Storm-Petrels are uncommon to rare nonbreeding visitors (probably May–Aug, at least) to Gulf Stream waters off North Carolina (Howell et al. 2010b) and may occur elsewhere through the North American range of Band-rumped Storm-Petrel.

Band-rumps (taxon or taxa unknown) are very rare onshore and inland in e North America (Jun–Sep, mainly Aug–Sep) after tropical cyclones (especially hurricanes), mostly e of the Appalachians, but have reached the e Great Lakes and n along Mississippi watershed to Missouri, Indiana, Kentucky, and Tennessee. Poorly known (taxon or taxa unknown) in Caribbean with few

documented records; may be expected as a rare visitor (Jun–Aug, at least).

FIELD IDENTIFICATION

Similar Species Note medium-large size with fairly pointed wings and squared to slightly notched tail, buoyant flight with emphasis on downstroke, and blackish plumage with white rump band wider than long.

Atlantic. *Leach's Storm-Petrel* frequently difficult to distinguish from Band-rumped under at-sea conditions, and even experienced observers leave many birds unidentified at moderate range or if not seen well, and log them as "large storm-petrel sp." (large relative to Wilson's Storm-Petrel). See under Leach's Storm-Petrel for identification criteria.

Relative to Grant's Storm-Petrel, Madeiran averages slighter in build with a smaller head and finer bill, and it may be blacker overall with a relatively short white rump band, broadly tipped (and often spotted) black; tail fork averages deeper (5–10 mm, BM specimens); adult wing molt likely spans Sep–Jun (Howell et al. 2010b). Flight of Grant's and Madeiran appears rather similar, but Grant's (at least molting birds in May–Jun) often have stronger and higher wing strokes that recall Leach's. Other taxa in the *Band-rumped Storm-Petrel* complex may occur in North America but no certain identification criteria have been established for birds at sea; wing molt timing, overall structure and bulk, bill size, shape and prominence of upperwing band, length of white rump band, and depth of tail notch are features that may repay study (Bolton et al. 2008, Howell et al. 2010b, Robb et al. 2008). Note, though, that wing molt timing of prebreeding immatures likely differs from breeding adults. *Monteiro's Storm-Petrel* has a moderately long white rump band, narrowly tipped black, and a cleft tail (tail fork 1–14 mm; Bolton et al. 2008); adults undergo wing molt mainly during Aug–Mar. *Cape Verde Storm-Petrel* not well-known but appears rather similar to Grant's, perhaps averaging smaller but relatively long billed (Murphy 1924, Robb et al. 2008); adults could be in wing molt during Mar–Dec.

Wilson's Storm-Petrel occurs throughout the Atlantic range of Band-rumped and provides a useful comparison. Wilson's is smaller and blacker with a shorter arm and broader-based, more triangular wings; its tail is slightly shorter and squared but can look cleft, an effect sometimes enhanced by long toes, which project beyond the tail tip. Usually distinguished readily from Band-rumped by flight manner, even at long range: Wilson's flies with shallower and quicker, swallow-like wingbeats in a fairly level and direct progression; Band-rumped flies faster and more buoyantly but with smoother, deeper, and stronger wingbeats, and longer glides on slightly arched wings. However, a purposefully beating Wilson's can more than momentarily suggest a Band-rumped, and a Wilson's flying across the wind can bank and glide without flapping, much like a "textbook" Band-rumped. Also beware of Grant's in wing molt, which has a more fluttery flight than full-winged birds and could suggest Wilson's. In direct comparison, Grant's is appreciably larger, but a pattering bird can disappear easily among a feeding flock of Wilson's. Madeiran Storm-Petrel averages smaller and blacker than Grant's, and thus can appear more similar to Wilson's.

Habitat and Behavior Offshore pelagic waters, typically over deep and warm "blue water" beyond the continental shelf, and often in dynamic areas of localized upwelling (Haney 1985); storm-blown birds may be seen from land. Usually found singly or in small aggregations, and associates readily with Wilson's and Leach's storm-petrels, both while rafting on the water and while feeding; also often rafts with shearwaters and Black-capped Petrels.

In calm to light winds, flight more buoyant than Leach's, with slightly looser and less springy wingbeats, usually with about two-thirds of the wingbeat arc appearing to be below the body plane and with emphasis on the downstroke. Wingbeats vary from fairly shallow and quick to deeper and looser, at times almost floppy, with glides on slightly arched wings. In light to moderate winds, flies with lower, longer-wavelength arcs and longer glides vs. steeper, shorter-wavelength arcs and shorter glides of Leach's. Prolonged shearing glides and low banking and weaving across moderate winds can recall Bulwer's Petrel and lack the steeper, bounding component often exhibited by Leach's. Foraging flight often into the wind, with bursts of wingbeats interspersed with short buoyant glides, and birds circling widely over a slick or food source before dropping to patter briefly or alight, with wings raised in a *V*. When alarmed, such as close to ships or when flushed off water, flight much more erratic, with strong, deep wingbeats and a higher upstroke, recalling Leach's Storm-Petrel.

Description Medium-large with fairly long, rather broad, and bluntly pointed wings somewhat crooked at wrist; tail medium length and cleft. Toes do not project beyond tail in flight.

Ages similar but note differences in molt timing (below). Sooty blackish brown overall, often appearing black at any distance; head and back with a variable gray sheen when fresh; narrow whitish edgings to subscapulars in fresh plumage. Flight feathers blacker and upperwings with a paler, usually poorly contrasting grayish (fresh) to pale brownish (faded) ulnar band often broadest toward carpal joint but overall fairly even in width, and not usually reaching wing bend. Clean-cut white rump band extends conspicuously to lateral undertail coverts; bases of outer rectrices white. Black tips to longest tail coverts and occasional dusky barring on central uppertail coverts rarely visible at sea. Bill, legs, and feet black.

On the water. Appears all-dark or with variable paler ulnar band; white rump patch often apparent as white wedge under folded wings.

Molt Wing molt of adult Grant's spans Feb–Aug (Bolton et al. 2008), and surely takes longer for an individual bird than the 9–10 weeks suggested by Lee (1984). Wing molt of adult Madeiran may span Sep–Jun but study needed; PB2 wing molt probably slightly earlier, perhaps Dec–Jun in Grant's, Jul–Feb in Madeiran (Howell et al. 2010b). Gulf Stream birds off North Carolina in late May–Jun include about 10–20% of fresh nonmolting birds per year, and about 80–90% of birds with p6-p9 growing (most still with 3–4 old outer primaries); primary molt of most birds in Gulf Stream completes Jul–Aug, with tail molt mainly during Jul–Sep (NCSM specimens, Howell et al. 2010b).

S3.2. Presumed Grant's Storm-Petrel with p1-p6 new, p7 shed, and p8-p10 old. As molt progresses past the middle primaries it can be harder to see in the field (cf. S3.1, S3.3–S3.4). Note lack of bold pale upperwing bands. SNGH. Off Hatteras, North Carolina, 23 May 2009.

S3.3. Presumed Grant's Storm-Petrel with mid-primary molt and unusually bold pale upperwing bands (cf. S3.2, S3.4–S3.5). SNGH. Off Hatteras, North Carolina, 23 May 2007.

S3.4. Unidentified Band-rumped Storm-Petrel. Advanced primary molt on this date, with p9-p10 growing, may indicate completion of second prebasic wing molt in winter-breeding Grant's or adult prebasic molt of summer-breeding Madeiran. SNGH. Off Hatteras, North Carolina, 28 May 2009.

S3.5. Presumed Grant's Storm-Petrel in fresh plumage. By Aug, most Band-rumpeds off the East Coast have finished wing molt, at which time some first-summer Leach's are in obvious wing molt (cf. S5.10). Note fairly stocky shape, straight-winged posture relative to Leach's. SNGH. Off Hatteras, North Carolina, 4 Aug 2007.

S3.6. Presumed Grant's Storm-Petrel in fresh plumage. Note overall shape, obvious wrap-around of white rump band, dull upperwing band. SNGH. Off Hatteras, North Carolina, 15 Aug 2009.

S3.7. Presumed Grant's Storm-Petrel. Concave tail surface and going-away angle accentuate any tail notch—seen from above this bird's tail appeared ostensibly square-tipped (cf. S3.8). Note obvious wing molt and big white wrap-around of rump band. SNGH. Off Hatteras, North Carolina, 27 May 2009.

S3.8. Presumed Grant's Storm-Petrel. A typical spring bird in mid-primary molt. Note squared tail tip and big white wrap-around of rump band. SNGH. Off Hatteras, North Carolina, 23 May 2007.

S3.9. Possible Madeiran Storm-Petrel completing pre-basic molt (note old faded hindneck feathers). SNGH. Off Hatteras, North Carolina, 7 Jun 2009.

S3.10. Presumed Grant's Storm-Petrel. As well as being larger and longer-winged than Wilson's Storm-Petrels (below), molting spring Band-rumps often appear browner above. SNGH. Off Hatteras, North Carolina, 24 May 2008.

S3.11. Presumed Grant's Storm-Petrel. Atypically, the white rump band is largely cloaked by the closed wings (see Fig 151). Distinguished from Wilson's by longer shape, bigger and heavier bill, paler brownish tones (and Wilson's usually shows a bold white rump patch); from Leach's by overall sooty plumage tones (especially head and back), shorter neck, stouter bill. SNGH. Off Hatteras, North Carolina, 23 May 2007.

S4. DARWIN'S [BAND-RUMPED] STORM-PETREL *Oceanodroma [castro] bangsi*

L 17.5–19.5 cm, WS 44–49 cm, tail 63–74 mm (fork 4–14 mm)

Figures S4.1–S4.4

Identification Summary Pacific. Rare nonbreeding visitor to deep offshore waters of s Central America. A medium-sized, white-rumped storm-petrel. Flight buoyant with measured wingbeats and a fairly deep downstroke; long wings bluntly pointed and crooked, tail cleft. Plumage blackish with poorly contrasting paler upperwing band not extending to wing bend. Rump patch bright white, wrapping around tail base as an even-width band that extends to lateral undertail coverts.

Taxonomy See introduction to Band-rumped Storm-Petrel complex. Galapagos birds include two populations that breed at opposite seasons and differ morphologically, genetically, and vocally (although a full vocal analysis has not been made). Some authors consider differences between these seasonal populations insufficient to warrant species status for both (Smith & Friesen 2007), although the case for two species could equally well be made. Critical studies linking vocalizations and genetics might be illuminating. The name Darwin's Storm-Petrel is proposed here, and should convey ready geographic association given Darwin's iconic status in the Galapagos Islands. Should two species be recognized, a new name will be needed for the second species, perhaps Wallace's Storm-Petrel… Band-rumped Storm-Petrels from the Galapagos have been described as subspecies *bangsi* (Nichols 1914), used here as the species' scientific name. The type specimen was collected at sea (1˚N 93˚W) in early Feb, and to which seasonal breeding population it pertains is uncertain.

Names *Oceanodroma* means "ocean runner," *castro* refers to the "Roque de Castro" on Madeira, from which Edward Harcourt described the first-known taxon of Band-rumped Storm-Petrel; *bangsi* refers to American zoologist Outram Bangs (1863–1932). The English name commemorates Charles Darwin (1809–1882), the British naturalist who changed our view of the natural world.

Status and Distribution Not recognized by Birdlife International (2010a). Breeds on Galapagos Islands (mainly May–Oct and Dec–May) and ranges at sea in equatorial Pacific, mainly e of 100˚W and between 10˚N and 10˚S (Spear & Ainley 2007).

Pacific. Probably a rare nonbreeding visitor (year-round?) to warmer offshore waters of s Central America n to at least 12˚N (Spear & Ainley 2007), but no well-documented records from Mexico (Howell 1996, *contra* Howell and Webb 1995); reports n to 25˚N off Baja California Sur (Crossin 1974) are unsubstantiated. Only confirmed Pacific region record is a specimen in wing molt (Jun 1898) from vicinity of Cocos Island, Costa Rica.

FIELD IDENTIFICATION

Similar Species Note medium size with fairly pointed wings and cleft tail, buoyant flight with emphasis on the downstroke, and blackish plumage with the white rump band wider than long.

Pacific. Most similar species probably Townsend's Storm-Petrel. Darwin's also likely to occur in same areas as Wedge-rumped Storm-Petrel. Wilson's Storm-Petrel might occur in same waters, and differences from Darwin's much as those described for Grant's Storm-Petrel. Also cf. Leach's and Ainley's storm-petrels; see under Leach's Storm-Petrel for identification criteria relative to Darwin's.

Townsend's Storm-Petrel slightly smaller and shorter-winged with a deeper tail fork (11–17 mm vs. 4–14 mm on Darwin's), longer white rump band, and somewhat jerkier flight with less gliding. White rump band of Townsend's does not extend to lateral undertail coverts.

Wedge-rumped Storm-Petrel appreciably (*kelsalli*) to slightly (*tethys*) smaller than Darwin's but shares blackish plumage (darker than Leach's), bright white rump patch, and cleft tail. Note different overall structure, with smaller head, longer legs and bigger feet, generally quicker and often more erratic flight with deeper wingbeats; also much longer, wedge-shaped white rump patch (beware birds molting longest uppertail coverts),

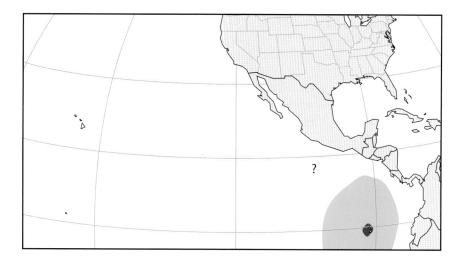

which does not wrap around as much on undertail coverts.

Habitat and Behavior Warm offshore waters, especially over the continental slope in Costa Rica Current (Spear & Ainley 2007). Flight manner has not been studied critically but may be most similar to Grant's Storm-Petrel (which see). Associates readily on the water with Wedge-rumped Storm-Petrel, perhaps also with Leach's Storm-Petrel.

Description Medium-sized with fairly long, rather broad, and bluntly pointed wings somewhat crooked at wrist; tail medium length and cleft. Toes do not project beyond tail in flight.

Ages similar. Sooty blackish brown overall, often appearing black at any distance; head and back with a gray sheen when fresh; narrow whitish edgings to subscapulars in fresh plumage. Flight feathers blacker and upperwings with a paler, usually poorly contrasting, grayish (fresh) to pale-brownish (faded) ulnar band often broadest toward carpal joint but overall fairly even in width, and not usually reaching wing bend. Clean-cut white rump band extends conspicuously to lateral undertail coverts; bases of outer rectrices white. Broad black tips to longest tail coverts (and occasional dusky barring on central uppertail coverts) rarely visible at sea. Bill, legs, and feet black.

On the water. Appears all-dark or with a variable paler ulnar band; white rump patch often apparent as a white wedge under the folded wings.

Molt Given different breeding cycles and potential age-related differences in timing, some birds might be found in wing molt year-round (study needed).

S4.1. Darwin's Storm-Petrel. Note blackish plumage tones with dull upperwing band, even-width white rump band extending well on to lateral tail coverts. AJ. Galapagos Islands, Ecuador, 19 Jun 2007.

S4.2. Darwin's Storm-Petrel. Note same features as S4.1, with slight tail notch apparent here. Faint dusky median strip on white rump band may be typical (cf. S4.1; A. Jaramillo, pers. comm.). AJ. Galapagos Islands, Ecuador, 23 Jun 2007.

S4.3. Darwin's Storm-Petrel. Not readily separated in this photo from Atlantic populations in Band-rumped Storm-Petrel complex. GLA. Galapagos Islands, Ecuador, 23 Jul 2009.

S4.4. Darwin's Storm-Petrel readily distinguished from Leach's and Wedge-rumped storm-petrels by extensive wrap-around of white from rump band, squared to slightly notched tail. AJ. Galapagos Islands, Ecuador, 19 Jun 2007.

The Leach's Storm-Petrel complex comprises at least four taxa, one breeding in both the North Pacific and North Atlantic, and three breeding on islands off the Pacific coast of Mexico (Ainley 1980, Ainley 1983, Bourne & Jehl 1982, Howell et al. 2010a, Power & Ainley 1986; Fig 170). Within birds of the North Pacific there is a cline from smaller, shorter-winged, and dark-rumped breeding populations in the s (where the complex may have originated) to larger, longer-winged, and white-rumped breeding populations in the n. The prevailing view is to recognize two "mainland" subspecies: *O. l. chapmani* (Chapman's Storm-Petrel), breeding on the Coronado and San Benito islands, Mexico, is smaller and usually dark-rumped, while nominate *O. l. leucorhoa* (Leach's Storm-Petrel), breeding from California n to Alaska, is larger and usually white-rumped. However, West Coast populations average smaller than Aleutian (and North Atlantic) Leach's, and three other subspecies (from n to s, *beali, beldingi,* and *willetti*) have been described from se Alaska to n Baja California. These three differ subtly, but seemingly not consistently, in size and rump pattern, and have been combined as the subspecies *beali* (Austin 1952, Crossin 1974). In recent years, *beali* and *beldingi* have been merged with nominate *leucorhoa,* and *willetti* with *chapmani* (Power & Ainley 1986). Further study of these West Coast populations is desirable.

Fig 170. Comparison of Leach's Storm-Petrel (left) and presumed Townsend's Storm-Petrel (right). Townsend's is smaller, less rangy, and blacker overall than Leach's, with a bolder white rump patch and shorter, less deeply forked tail. SNGH. Off Santa Barbara, California, 21 Jul 2007.

In addition, two distinct taxa breed on Guadalupe Island, offshore of Mexico's Baja California Peninsula (Figs 171–172): the relatively small *socorroensis* in summer (which is white rumped and dark rumped), and the slightly larger *cheimomnestes* in winter (which is white rumped). A scoring system of rump patterns, grading from all-white (1) to all-dark (11) was devised by Ainley (1980) and a simplified version of five steps is used here (Fig 173; Howell et al. 2010a).

The four taxa in this complex traditionally have been treated as subspecies. The taxon *cheimomnestes* was described as a subspecies of Leach's Storm-Petrel (Ainley 1980:849), when it was noted that "on Guadalupe [Island], the two populations of *O. leucorhoa* [= winter-breeding *cheimomnestes* and summer-breeding *socorroensis*] are morphologically and behaviorally distinct" and "so different are their songs that, if they met, it is questionable that interbreeding would occur." Ainley (1980) drew parallels between these Guadalupe storm-petrels and the "Soft-plumaged Petrel" complex, then considered a single species. Bretagnolle et al. (1991) showed *socorroensis* to be as morphologically and vocally distinct from Leach's as Swinhoe's Storm-Petrel, which is usually treated as a separate species. That Leach's Storm-Petrels from the North Atlantic and North Pacific s to Mexico all sound similar, but that both of the morphologically distinct Guadalupe populations sound different, argue that the latter are more realistically treated as separate species (Howell et al. 2010a), as has been done in recent years with "Soft-plumaged" Petrels (now considered as three or four species in two clades: Soft-plumaged, Cape Verde, Desertas, and Zino's petrels).

The two Guadalupe populations are here considered as separate species: the winter-breeding population is called Ainley's Storm-Petrel (*Oceanodroma cheimomnestes*), and the summer-breeding population is called Townsend's Storm-Petrel (*O. socorroensis*); the name Socorro Storm-Petrel would be inappropriate for the latter, since this species does not breed on Socorro Island.

Fig 171. Comparison of fresh-plumaged adult Townsend's Storm-Petrel (left; SDNHM 17672, 13 Jul; rump score 1) and fresh-plumaged juvenile Ainley's Storm-Petrel (right; SDNHM 37473, 14 Apr; rump score 2). Despite overlap in most conventional measurements between these two species, the larger bulk of Ainley's is usually readily apparent when the two are compared directly. SNGH. Specimens from Guadalupe Island, Mexico.

Fig 172. Comparison of fresh-plumaged adult Townsend's Storm-Petrel (left; SDNHM 17672, 13 Jul) and fresh-plumaged adult Ainley's Storm-Petrel (right; SDNHM 30177, 2 Nov). Collected at corresponding points in their breeding cycles, these specimens with comparable plumage wear illustrate the darker plumage aspect of Townsend's. Also, as in Fig 171, note greater bulk of Ainley's. SNGH. Specimens from Guadalupe Island, Mexico.

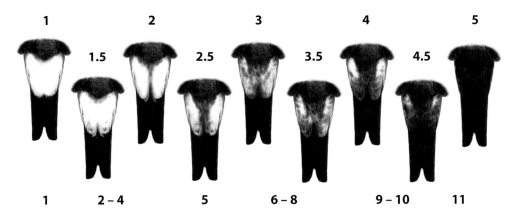

Fig 173. Scoring system for uppertail-covert ("rump") patterns in the Leach's Storm-Petrel complex, with corresponding Ainley scale values across the bottom. 1 = white, or with a few dusky flecks not likely to be visible at sea; 2 = mostly white, with some obvious dusky; 3 = about 50:50 dark/white; 4 = mostly dark; 5 = dark, or with a few pale marks not likely to be visible at sea; half-scores can be used for intermediate patterns. In the field, scores 1–2 usually appear as "white-rumped," 3 as "intermediate," and 4–5 as "dark-rumped." Scores 1 and 2 are typical of white-rumped Townsend, scores 1.5 and 2.5 of Leach's, 2.5–3.5 of Ainley's, and 4–5 of Chapman's and dark-rumped Townsend's. Extent of rump patches and depth of tail forks shown here are not intended to convey any taxonomic significance. © Ian Lewington.

S5. LEACH'S STORM-PETREL *Oceanodroma [leucorhoa] leucorhoa*

L 19–21.5 cm, WS 43.5–49.5 cm, tail 75–86 mm (fork 15–25 mm)

Figures 45, 50, 146, 151, 154, 156, 158, 170, 173, S5.1–S5.15

Identification Summary Atlantic and Pacific, usually well offshore. A medium-large storm-petrel with relatively pointed wings and moderately forked tail. Confident bounding flight in combination with rangy and angular shape can recall Common Nighthawk. White rump patch rather *U*-shaped, usually with variable dusky median stripe (uppertail coverts rarely mostly dark), and not extending much to lateral undertail coverts. For identification purposes, dark-rumped s populations of Leach's are treated in a separate account as Chapman's Storm-Petrel (pp. 423–426).

S5.1. Leach's Storm-Petrel. Strongly crooked wings, bold pale upperwing bands, and a contrasting gray head and back are all good field marks of this common offshore species. Also note the relatively long slender bill, forked tail, limited wrap-around of white rump band. SNGH. Off Hatteras, North Carolina, 23 May 2009.

Taxonomy Two subspecies provisionally recognized here (see introduction to Leach's Storm-Petrel complex), differing in size and rump color, and intergrading between Farallon and Coronado islands (38–32°N).

O.[l.] leucorhoa (Leach's Storm-Petrel) breeds (May–Oct) North Atlantic and North Pacific, s to California. Larger and longer-winged (L 19–22 cm, WS 43–50 cm, tail 70–86 mm [fork 13–25 mm]). Uppertail coverts mostly white, but a few are darker (Atlantic score 1–4, mainly 2–3; Pacific score 1–5, mainly 2–3; Ainley 1980, Flood 2009; see Fig 173). White rump patch relatively short (typically 15–25 mm) and usually about one-third of rump/tail projection beyond trailing edge of wings.

O. [l.] chapmani (Chapman's Storm-Petrel) breeds (May–Oct) on Coronado and San Benito islands, Mexico. Averages smaller (L 17.5–19.5 cm, WS 42–46 cm, tail 69–82 mm [fork 14–24 mm]). Uppertail coverts usually dark (rump score 3–5, mainly 4–5; see Fig 173). See separate account on pp. 423–426.

Names *Oceanodroma* means "ocean runner," *leucorhoa* refers to the white rump. The English name commemorates William Leach (1790–1836), a world authority on crustaceans at the British

384

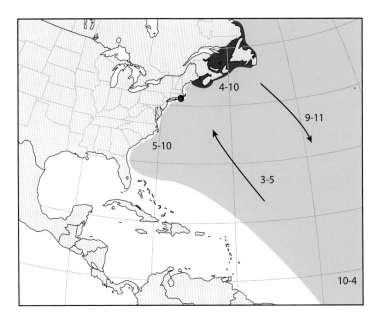

Museum. In Britain, sometimes known simply as Leach's Petrel.

Status and Distribution Least Concern. Breeds (May–Oct) in North Pacific and North Atlantic oceans; winters (Nov–Apr) in equatorial and tropical Pacific and Atlantic oceans. Recently found nesting (Oct–Mar) in South Africa and prospecting in New Zealand (Whittington et al. 1999). See separate account for dark-rumped birds under Chapman's [Leach's] Storm-Petrel (pp. 423–426).

Atlantic. Fairly common to very common but local breeder (mid-May/mid-Jul to Sep/Nov) from s Labrador to Maine, and one small colony off Massachusetts. Fairly common to common (mainly Apr–Oct) from Atlantic Canada s to Massachusetts, foraging in pelagic waters beyond the continental shelf and locally over the shelf; rare visitor (mainly Oct–Nov) n to w Greenland. Fairly common to locally common migrant offshore (mainly Mar–May, Sep–Nov; casual off New England in Dec–Jan) from cen Atlantic and Bermuda to New England and Atlantic Canada. Uncommon to very rare off mid-Atlantic coast and se U.S. (mainly Apr–Oct) where most frequent Apr–Jul (presumably immatures); very rare (May–early Dec, mainly late May–early Sep) in Gulf of Mexico, and (mainly Nov–Jun) in Caribbean region. Very rare inland in e North America, mainly storm-blown individuals (Jul–Oct) in coastal states and provinces, exceptionally w to Ontario.

Pacific. Fairly common to very common but local breeder (May/Jun–Aug/early Nov) from Aleutians to California (Farallon and Channel islands). Fairly common to common well offshore (Mar–Nov) in breeding latitudes, foraging mainly in warmer pelagic waters beyond continental shelf (thus very rare over nearshore waters such as Monterey Bay); rarely ranges in summer into s Bering Sea, exceptionally n to Seward Peninsula. Migrants move n off West Coast in Feb–Apr (later northward), and last southbound migrants mostly in Nov, with stragglers into Dec, exceptionally Jan; storm-blown birds, probably mostly fledglings, occasionally seen from shore or slightly inland (mainly Oct–Nov).

Status off Mexico and Central America confounded by presence there of similar taxa. Leach's appears to be fairly common to locally and seasonally common well off Pacific coast from Mexico s (mainly Oct–Apr, with smaller numbers of nonbreeders May–Sep), wintering mainly s of 20˚N (Crossin 1974); no well-documented records within Gulf of California.

White-rumped birds exceptionally found inland in the Southwest (usually associated with tropical cyclones, late Jun–late Sep) may be Leach's, Townsend's, or Ainley's storm-petrels.

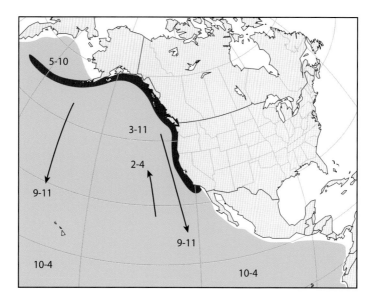

FIELD IDENTIFICATION

Similar Species Note medium-large size with pointed wings and forked tail, bounding flight with high upstroke, dark-brownish plumage with white rump patch often split by dusky stripe. A few Atlantic Leach's have limited whitish or pale grayish feathering on rump patch, mainly at the sides, and can appear all-dark at moderate range or if seen poorly (see under Swinhoe's Storm-Petrel). See Chapman's [Leach's] Storm-Petrel (pp. 423–426) for discussion of dark-rumped birds.

Atlantic. *Wilson's Storm-Petrel* (widespread) usually distinguished readily from Leach's by flight style even at long range: Wilson's flies with shallower and quicker, swallow-like wingbeats in a fairly level and direct progression; Leach's flies faster with powerful, jerky wingbeats of crooked wings, with a high upstroke; typically has a more bounding, erratic progression. In direct comparison, Leach's is appreciably larger and longer winged, but a pattering bird can disappear in a feeding flock of Wilson's. Wilson's has a shorter arm and broader-based, more triangular wings not strongly crooked; its tail is squared but can look notched, an effect sometimes enhanced by long toes, which project beyond the tail tip; its plumage is blacker overall with a squarer and brighter white rump patch that extends to the lateral undertail coverts; and upperwings have a more even-width pale panel that does not reach wing bend. On the water, Leach's does not usually show white at rump sides, but this is conspicuous on

Wilson's. Many spring Wilson's (May–Jun) show heavy wing molt, when most Atlantic Leach's are not in wing molt.

Grant's Storm-Petrel (Gulf Stream waters) similar in size and plumage to Leach's, and frequently difficult to distinguish under at-sea conditions; even experienced observers leave many birds unidentified at moderate range or if not seen well, and log them as "large storm-petrel sp." (large relative to Wilson's). These species best distinguished by combination of flight manner, structure, plumage features, and wing molt timing. Many Grant's show conspicuous molt of middle and outer primaries in May–Jul, when Leach's are not molting or have just started molt of inner primaries; this can make wingtips of Grant's look uneven, or broader and more paddle-shaped, less pointed. Beware of heavily worn first-summer Leach's with ragged middle-outer primaries that can suggest molt.

Typical flight manners of Grant's and Leach's in light to moderate winds differ, but evaluating differences requires critical experience, and flight manner often rather similar in calm conditions. Band-rumped generally has deeper and smoother, looser, and more measured wingbeats (two-thirds of wingbeat arc appears to be below body plane, vs. two-thirds above in Leach's), lacking high, jerky upstroke typical of Leach's, which helps contribute to latter's bounding, more confident-looking flight. Grant's thus has less impetuous, less three-dimensional flight, often with lower and more predictable progression that includes buoyant and more prolonged glides. However, Leach's can fly with prolonged shearing glides, and Grant's in purposeful flight (e.g., when flushed from the water or when avoiding a boat) can have deep jerky wingbeats much like Leach's. Leach's generally glides with the wings arched higher above body plane, Grant's with only slightly arched wings. In calm conditions, flight of foraging Leach's often relatively leisurely and floppy, much like Grant's.

Grant's generally blacker, less brownish, and more similar in tone to Wilson's, whereas Leach's is browner overall except on the head, which often has a noticeable gray sheen even in worn plumage (worn Grant's usually has a brown head). Grant's has shorter, less contrasting ulnar band more even in width and usually not reaching wing bend; slightly broader looking and less pointed wings; and squared to slightly notched tail. In comparison, Leach's has longer, more tapered, and more contrasting ulnar band that usually reaches wing bend; narrower and more pointed wings; and distinctly forked tail (outer rectrices can be heavily worn or molting in first-summer Leach's, reducing tail fork depth). Rump patch of Grant's usually looks brighter white (lacking distinct dusky median stripe typical of Leach's) and wraps around tail base as an even-width band (looking wider than long, the opposite of Leach's), which extends to lateral undertail coverts (thus often showing on birds on the water, unlike Leach's). Especially in bright sun, however, white rump patch of Leach's can look solid and bright white, without a dusky median stripe, and some Grant's have dusky scalloping in the white, forming a faint dark median line.

Pacific. White-rumped Leach's distinct from Wilson's (see above) but similar to *Darwin's Storm-Petrel* (unrecorded off West Coast); features to distinguish Darwin's from Leach's are similar to those listed above under Grant's Storm-Petrel, although Darwin's is smaller and averages a deeper tail notch than Grant's. Also be aware of the (slim) possibility of finding Guadalupe Storm-Petrel (presumed extinct; see Appendix A), which resembles a large, intermediate-morph Leach's with a deeply forked tail.

Ainley's Storm-Petrel (winter breeder on Guadalupe Island, may range n to s California) looks much like light morph Leach's Storm-Petrel in plumage (rump score 2–4, mainly 2–3; see Fig 173) and at-sea identification criteria unknown.

Ainley's is slightly smaller with shorter, slightly less pointed wings and shallower tail fork (12–20 mm vs. 13–25 mm on Leach's). Flight manner undescribed but likely similar to Leach's. Wing molt timing of adult Ainley's probably Apr–Oct, vs. Aug–Apr in adult Leach's.

Light morph *Townsend's Storm-Petrel* (summer breeder on Guadalupe Island, Mexico, ranges n to s California in late summer) is smaller with shorter, less pointed wings and a shorter, less deeply forked tail (tail projection beyond white tail coverts 30–40 mm, vs. 36–45 mm in Leach's; tail fork 11–17 mm vs. 13–25 mm on Leach's). Size differences readily apparent when the two species are seen together. Townsend's often appears blacker and has relatively long and bright white rump patch (score 1–2; cf. Fig 173) that typically comprises about half of the rump/tail projection behind the wings (vs. one-third on Leach's); dusky central stripe weakly defined on many Townsend's and rump patch often solidly white. Flight slightly quicker and steadier, less confident and bounding than Leach's, although Townsend's still generally a strong flier with fairly clipped wingbeats.

Wedge-rumped Storm-Petrel (Middle America, casual California) distinctly smaller (looking half the size of Leach's when the two are seen together), with thicker bill, longer legs and bigger feet, shallower tail fork, and (when not molting) a longer, wedge-shaped white rump patch covering much of tail. Flight of Wedge-rumped in light winds usually with deep wingbeats, much like Least Storm-Petrel, but flight into and across moderate winds can be much like Leach's. Birds with longest uppertail coverts molting strongly suggest Leach's in rump pattern but distinctly smaller and usually blacker; note shape and flight manner.

Habitat and Behavior Pelagic waters, usually beyond the continental shelf, but storm-blown birds may be seen from land, mainly in fall. Usually found singly or in small aggregations, and associates readily off the East Coast with Wilson's and Grant's storm-petrels, both while rafting and feeding. Note that birds in wing molt (mainly in winter) can have a more fluttery flight than confident bounding flight of full-winged birds.

In calm to light or moderate winds, erratic bounding flight varies from fairly fast and "aggressive" to leisurely, with fairly deep, jerky wingbeats, short glides, and about two-thirds of wingbeat arc apparently above the body plane. Generally glides on arched wings. Transiting flight, such as migrants on a set heading, can be fairly steady, with bursts of wingbeats interspersed with banking glides. In moderate to strong winds, transits across the wind with prolonged banking glides interspersed with bursts of quick, fairly shallow wingbeats, wheeling up to 3 m above the sea surface like a small shearwater; sometimes transits with a persistent low-wavelength progression, not banking steeply, especially with the wind astern. Foraging flight more varied, often weaving back and forth into the wind or beating up and down over a slick, then sweeping up to drop and patter briefly, or settle, at food. At times, foraging birds fly with steady, fairly quick, and slightly fluttery wingbeats and occasional glides, quite different from "textbook" bounding flight of transiting birds and almost suggestive of Wilson's Storm-Petrel. In calm to light winds over tropical seas, foraging can be unhurried, wingbeats relatively languid and shallow, though still with a slightly jerky rhythm. At such times, wings can look relatively rounded and cupped as a bird meanders, pauses, and circles with short glides, but this Grant's-like flight is usually not prolonged, and sooner or later a Leach's changes to jerkier and more purposeful wingbeats. In calm conditions, sometimes flies 3–5 m above the sea surface with steady wingbeats and no gliding. When alarmed, such as close to big ships or when flushed off water, flight can be much more erratic, almost frenetic, with deep wingbeats and no gliding that can suggest Wedge-rumped Storm-Petrel.

Nocturnal at colonies, which range from a few pairs to tens or hundreds of thousands, nesting in burrows dug in soil (mainly in the wetter n) or in rock crevices and talus (mainly in drier s). Often nests alongside Fork-tailed Storm-Petrel in the n and alongside Ashy Storm-Petrel in California. Burrow call a hard, rolled purring, or chatter (15–23 notes/second), typically given in rapid bursts of 2–4 seconds' duration and punctuated by abrupt, plaintive, gulping inhalations, with the first note after the inhalation only slightly louder than the following chatter (Ainley 1980): *urrrr..., ieh'urrrrr...* Flight calls are gruff, chuckling chatters, typically a clipped introductory note followed by two accelerating, chuckling phrases, *krruh tit-ti-krruh-kuh kuh-huh-huh-huh*, or *krrih pih-pih-pih-pih pyuh piupiupiu*, and variations. Flight call comprises 9–12 notes (usually

11), with emphasis on 3 notes, 1 at the start and 2 in the middle (Ainley 1980).

Description Medium-large with fairly long and pointed wings usually held crooked; tail medium length and forked. Toes do not project beyond tail in flight.

Ages similar but juveniles fresh in fall (Sep–Nov) when older birds worn or molting, and first-summer birds (May–Aug) worn or in wing molt when adults are fresher. Dark sooty brown overall, often appearing black at any distance and browner when worn, with a slaty-gray sheen to the head and back strongest in fresh plumage; narrow whitish edgings to subscapulars in fresh plumage. White rump patch longer than wide, usually with a variable dusky median stripe; a few birds (mainly in Pacific) have mostly dark uppertail coverts with pale gray or whitish ovals on the sides, others have bright white uppertail coverts with dusky median stripe reduced or absent; white rump patch does not wrap around to undertail coverts in northern birds but does to some extent in California birds. Some white uppertail coverts tipped finely with dusky in fresh plumage, forming faint barring visible in the hand. Flight feathers blacker and upperwings with pale brownish gray to pale buff ulnar band broadest at carpal joint and usually extending to wing bend; ulnar band can be fairly dull (and grayer) in fresh plumage but often quite bright (and buffy) when faded; exposed bases of primary shafts sometimes whitish (rarely visible at sea). Bill, legs, and feet black.

On the water. Appears all-dark or with variable paler ulnar band visible; white rump patch sometimes shows as a small sliver under folded wings (more conspicuous on California birds) but usually not apparent until birds take flight.

Molt (see Fig 50, p. 38) Adult wing molt starts Aug/Oct and completes Feb/Apr, often with suspension for fall migration; tail molt in Pacific reported Jul–Sep, usually completed before departure from breeding areas (Ainley et al. 1976). PB2 wing molt starts May/Jul, ends Oct/Dec; tail mainly Jun–Oct (Crossin 1974). Birds of unknown age off North Carolina in tail molt late May–early Jun (pers. obs.; S5.6) presumably nonbreeders.

S5.2. Leach's Storm-Petrel. Note bold pale upperwing bands, gray head and back, forked tail. White rump patch variable in pattern and extent (cf. S5.3–5.4), with this individual being fairly typical of East Coast birds. SNGH. Off Hatteras, North Carolina, 26 May 2009.

S5.3. Leach's Storm-Petrel. Under at-sea conditions, particularly in dull light or at distance, plumage looks blackish overall, lacking brown and steely gray tones apparent in good light (cf. S5.1–S5.2). Although "textbook" Leach's has a dusky median rump stripe, many birds are essentially white-rumped and show no dusky at sea. BM. Newfoundland, Canada, 23 Jul 2009.

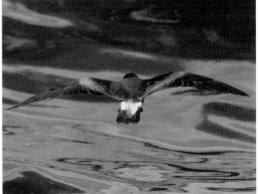

S5.4. Leach's Storm-Petrel. A few North Atlantic birds have reduced white on the rump patch and, at a distance or in poor light, such birds can appear dark-rumped. KS. Off Hatteras, North Carolina, 23 May 2009.

S5.5. Leach's Storm-Petrel. At least in the western Atlantic, some birds (perhaps mainly first- and second-year individuals) are heavily worn in summer. The tail fork can be lost by wear and molt, size and shape of the rump band can be atypical, and such birds might be confused with Grant's Storm-Petrel. Overall structure and flight manner are the best clues in such cases. SNGH. Off Hatteras, North Carolina, 1 Jun 2007.

S5.6. Leach's Storm-Petrel. This bird shows tail molt, contrast between fresh gray and older brown scapulars, and fairly fresh-looking wings. Adults in Pacific populations molt their tail in fall, before wing molt in winter (Ainley et al. 1976). Study is needed on differences in molt timing and sequence relative to breeding status, or might there be differences between ages or between Atlantic and Pacific birds? SNGH. Off Hatteras, North Carolina, 23 May 2009.

S5.7. Leach's Storm-Petrel. Readily identified by crooked wings, forked tail, and limited white visible from below. Note lack of obvious wing wear, although tail may be slightly worn, having likely been molted a few months earlier than the outer primaries (cf. S5.8–5.9). SNGH. Off Hatteras, North Carolina, 21 May 2009.

S5.8. Leach's Storm-Petrel. Abraded inner primaries and tail suggest these were molted earlier than relatively unworn (presumably newer and fresher) outer primaries. Because second prebasic molt occurs earlier (in first summer and fall) than subsequent prebasic molts (in fall and winter), heavily worn flight feathers in spring suggest this is a second-summer bird. SNGH. Off Hatteras, North Carolina, 23 May 2007.

S5.9. Leach's Storm-Petrel. Abraded outer primaries and tail, which are the most exposed flight feathers, in combination with relatively unworn inner primaries, suggest these may all be of the same age and thus juvenile feathers. Therefore, this is likely a first-summer bird (cf. S5.7–S5.8, S5.10). SNGH. Off Hatteras, North Carolina, 28 May 2007.

S5.10. Leach's Storm-Petrel. Mid-primary molt on this date indicates a first-summer bird (older ages typically start primary molt in mid-late fall). Tail looks fresh and may have been molted during Jun–Jul. Grant's Storm-Petrels show a similar stage of wing molt in spring but by this date are in fresh plumage. SNGH. Off Hatteras, North Carolina, 15 Aug 2009.

S5.11. Leach's Storm-Petrel. Rump pattern among Pacific Leach's is more variable than on Atlantic birds, particularly in California Current region. This white-rumped bird shows a "textbook" rump pattern, with an obvious dusky median stripe. SNGH. Off Santa Barbara, California, 25 Jul 2009.

S5.12. Presumed Leach's Storm-Petrel. Birds like this, with an "intermediate" rump pattern (score 3, Fig 173), are far less numerous off California than white-rumped birds. This rump pattern is typical of the enigmatic Ainley's Storm-Petrel, and identification here as a Leach's is tentative. SNGH. Off Santa Barbara, California, 21 Jul 2007.

S5.13. Presumed Leach's Storm-Petrel. White rump patch on West Coast Leach's often appears more extensive than on Atlantic and North Pacific birds, especially on lateral tail coverts (cf. S5.14). This pattern is also typical of white-rumped Townsend's Storm-Petrel, which confounds the identification of Leach's off southern California. SNGH. Off San Diego, California, 20 Jul 2008.

S5.14. Presumed Leach's Storm-Petrels (a white-rumped bird flanked by two dark-rumped birds, presumably Chapman's Storm-Petrels). White rump patch on West Coast Leach's often shows up more on sitting birds than it does on Atlantic and North Pacific birds (cf. Fig 151). SNGH. Off San Diego, California, 25 Aug 2009.

S5.15. Specimens of Leach's Storm-Petrel collected off Oregon in summer. From left to right, SDNHM 7380 (score 1), SDNHM 19466 (score 1.5), SDNHM 19500 (score 2), SDNHM 19490 (score 2), SDNHM 19497 (score 3). These birds show the typical variation in rump pattern of "white-rumped" Leach's off the West Coast. SNGH.

S6. AINLEY'S [LEACH'S] STORM-PETREL *Oceanodroma [leucorhoa] cheimomnestes*

L 17.5–19 cm, WS 42–46 cm, tail 70–80 mm (fork 12–20 mm)

Figures 171–173, S6.1

Identification Summary Pacific. Poorly known endemic, breeding in winter on Guadalupe Island, Mexico, pelagic range not well known. A medium-sized cryptic species, described in 1980 as a subspecies of Leach's Storm-Petrel. Plumage dark sooty brown with a contrasting paler ulnar band extending about to wing bend; tail moderately forked. Uppertail coverts white with messy dusky median markings (rump score 2–4, mainly 2–3; cf. Fig 173, S6.1); white rump patch typically more than one-third of rump/tail projection beyond trailing edge of wings.

S6.1. Specimens of Ainley's Storm-Petrel collected at Guadalupe Island, Mexico. Fvrom left to right, SDNHM 30016 (score 2), SDNHM 50806 (score 2), SDNHM 30172 (score 2), SDNHM 30176 (score 3), SDNHM 30276 (score 4). These birds exhibit the range of variation in rump pattern of Ainley's Storm-Petrel; fully white-rumped and fully dark-rumped birds are unknown in this species. SNGH.

Taxonomy Monotypic. Has been considered a subspecies of Leach's Storm-Petrel (see introduction to Leach's Storm-Petrel complex [pp. 381–382]).

Names *Oceanodroma* means "ocean runner," *cheimomnestes* means "winter suitor," in reference to this species' winter-breeding regime. The English name commemorates U.S. marine ornithologist David Ainley, who described this taxon.

Status and Distribution Not recognized by Birdlife International (2010a). Endemic breeder. Breeds (mainly Nov/Dec–Apr/May) on three islets (Islote Negro, Islote Afuera, and Gargoyle Rock) off the s end of Guadalupe Island, Mexico (Ainley 1980, 1983, Crossin 1974, Jehl & Everett

1985); population may not be in excess of a few thousand birds.

Pelagic distribution poorly known, presumed to range over waters off the Baja California Peninsula during breeding season and apparently southward in the nonbreeding season (May–Oct). A female (SDNHM #29925) collected 360 km sw of Isla Guadalupe on 21 May and a worn juvenile (SDNHM #29924) collected 550 km w of Isla Clarion, Mexico, on 24 May (about 18°S) suggest a southward dispersal after breeding, as does a specimen in wing molt collected on 11 Jun at 4°S 93°W (CAS #484), which is about 400 km sw of the Galapagos Islands. A specimen completing wing molt on 9 Oct (CAS #471), about 500 km sse of Revillagigedo Islands, may have been a northbound migrant.

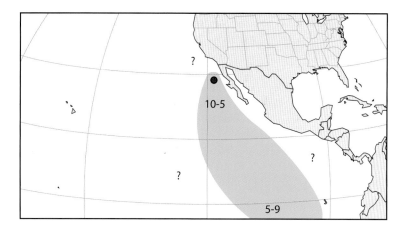

FIELD IDENTIFICATION

Similar Species Note medium size with bluntly pointed wings and moderately forked tail, white rump patch with messy dusky median stripe. Separation from light morph Leach's Storm-Petrel may not be possible except perhaps under exceptional circumstances (see under that species). Also cf. Wedge-rumped and Wilson's storm-petrels.

Light morph *Townsend's Storm-Petrel* (summer breeder on Guadalupe Island, ranges n to s California in summer) averages smaller (slighter build likely to be apparent when the two species are seen together) with shorter, slightly less pointed wings, and slightly shorter tail. Townsend's darker in fresh plumage and has relatively broader and more solidly white rump patch (rump score mainly 1–2 vs. 2–3 on Ainley's; see Fig 173). Flight manner of Townsend's may differ, but flight manner of Ainley's remains to be described.

Habitat and Behavior Presumably ranges over pelagic waters but essentially unknown at sea; habits likely similar to Leach's Storm-Petrel. Specimens of Ainley's appear bulky relative to those of Townsend's Storm-Petrel, suggesting these species have different wing-loadings and thus different flight manners (study needed).

Nests in crevices and burrows; nocturnal at colonies. Burrow call a relatively fast-paced, rough purring, or chatter, punctuated by a barely audible inhalation every 4–5 seconds, with first note after inhalation much louder than following chatter (Ainley 1980); this call is similar to Townsend's Storm-Petrel but differs distinctly from Leach's, which is slower paced and not as gruff. Flight call slightly rasping or scratchy (with little or no chuckling quality typical of Leach's) consisting of about 14 notes, with emphasis on 1 note at the start, 3 at the end (Ainley 1980).

Description Medium-sized with fairly long and bluntly pointed wings probably held crooked at wrist; tail medium length and moderately forked. Toes do not project beyond tail in flight.

Ages similar but juveniles fresh in early summer (Apr–Jul) when older birds worn or molting, and first-year birds (Nov–Jan) likely to be worn or in wing molt when adults are fresh. Dark sooty brown overall, often appearing black at any distance and browner when worn; head and back with slaty blue-gray sheen when fresh; narrow whitish edgings to subscapulars in fresh plumage. White rump patch slightly *U*-shaped with a variable and often messy dusky median stripe or smudging (rump score 2–4, mainly 2–3; see Fig 173); white wraps around slightly to lateral undertail coverts. Some white feathers tipped finely with dusky in fresh plumage, forming faint barring visible in the hand. Flight feathers blacker, and upperwings with paler, brownish gray to pale buff ulnar band broadest at carpal joint and usually extending to, or slightly short of, wing bend; ulnar band can be fairly dull in fresh plumage but often quite bright when faded; exposed bases of primary shafts sometimes whitish. Bill, legs, and feet black.

On the water. Presumably much like Leach's Storm-Petrel.

Molt Needs study, but timing likely the opposite of summer-breeding populations; thus adult wing molt mainly Mar–Oct, PB2 wing molt may be mainly Nov–Jun.

S7. TOWNSEND'S [LEACH'S] STORM-PETREL *Oceanodroma [leucorhoa] socorroensis*
L 16.5–17.5 cm, WS 41–45 cm, tail 66–77 mm (fork 11–17 mm)
Figures 170–173, S7.1–S7.6

Identification Summary Pacific. Breeds in summer on Guadalupe Island, Mexico, ranges at sea n to s California, s to waters off Middle America. A medium-small, polymorphic storm-petrel that has been considered a subspecies of Leach's Storm-Petrel. Plumage blackish brown with a contrasting paler ulnar band extending to or near wing bend; tail moderately forked. Uppertail coverts variable, bright white on some birds (rump score 1–3, mainly 1–2; cf. Fig 173, S7.1), mostly dark on others (rump score mainly 4; cf. Fig 173, S7.1). Tail relatively short, hence white rump patch typically about half or more of rump/tail projection beyond trailing edge of wings. See under Similar Species (below) for identification criteria.

S7.1. Specimens of Townsend's Storm-Petrel collected at Guadalupe Island, Mexico. From left to right, SDNHM 12630 (score 1), SDNHM 17249 (score 2), SDNHM 14962 (score 2), SDNHM 8869 (score 3.5), SDNHM 8868 (score 4), SDNHM 8889 (score 4.5). These birds exhibit the typical range of variation in rump pattern of Townsend's Storm-Petrel; most birds are white-rumped (score 1–2) or dark-rumped (around score 4); few birds are wholly dark-rumped. SNGH.

Taxonomy Monotypic. Has been considered a subspecies of Leach's Storm-Petrel (see introduction to Leach's Storm-Petrel complex [pp. 381–382]).

Names *Oceanodroma* means "ocean runner," *socorroensis* refers to Socorro Island, Mexico, the nearest land to where the type specimen was collected at sea. The English name commemorates Charles H. Townsend (1859–1944), the U.S. ornithologist who described this species.

Status and Distribution Not recognized by Birdlife International (2010a). Endemic breeder. Breeds (late May/Jun–Oct/Nov) on islets off s end of Guadalupe Island, perhaps also locally on the main island but most storm-petrels there have been killed by feral cats (Ainley 1980, Ainley 1983, Crossin 1974, Jehl & Everett 1985). Population on Islote Negro estimated at 4000 birds (80–90% dark-rumped; score 4–5; see Fig 173) population on Islote Afuera estimated at 3000 birds (70–90% white-rumped; score 1–3; see Fig 173) (Ainley 1983, Crossin 1974).

Pelagic range not well known but has been found offshore in the e Pacific between 35˚N and 10˚N (Crossin 1974), and at least in some years uncommon to fairly common (Jun–early Nov, mainly Jul–Sep) off s California (Howell et al. 2010a).

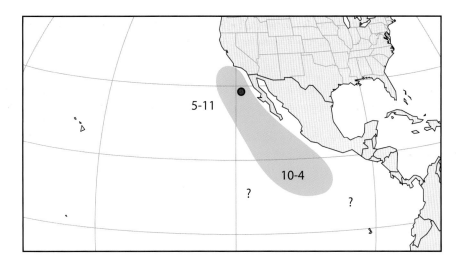

FIELD IDENTIFICATION

Similar Species Note medium-small size with bluntly pointed wings and moderately forked tail, rather bounding flight, and blackish-brown plumage with variable white rump patch (some birds all-dark). Main problem lies with distinguishing Townsend's from Leach's and Ainley's storm-petrels. Furthermore, relatively small size and relatively bold black-and-white plumage of light morph Townsend's could invite confusion with Darwin's [Band-rumped], Wedge-rumped, and Wilson's storm-petrels. Dark morph Townsend's can be confused with Ashy and even Least storm-petrels.

Light morph. *Leach's Storm-Petrel* (occurs throughout range of Townsend's) larger with longer, more pointed wings and longer, more deeply forked tail (tail fork 13–25 mm vs. 11–17 mm on Townsend's). Size differences appreciable when the two species are seen together. Leach's often appears browner overall, with a duller and narrower white rump patch that typically comprises about one-third of rump/tail projection behind wings (about one-half on Townsend's). Flight of Leach's stronger and more bounding.

Ainley's Storm-Petrel (winter breeder on Guadalupe Island) averages larger (may be apparent when the two species are seen together) with longer, slightly more pointed wings and slightly longer tail. Ainley's looks much like Leach's, and is thus generally browner overall than Townsend's, with a duller white rump patch that usually has a distinct dusky median stripe or messy dusky markings. Flight manner may differ from Townsend's, but undescribed.

Wedge-rumped Storm-Petrel (Middle America, exceptional n to California) slightly to distinctly smaller, with thicker bill, longer legs and bigger feet, shallower tail fork, and (when not molting) a longer, wedge-shaped white rump patch covering much of tail. Flight of Wedge-rumped in light winds usually with deep wingbeats, much like Least Storm-Petrel, but flight into and across moderate winds can be much like Townsend's.

Darwin's Storm-Petrel (s Central America, unrecorded off West Coast) larger and longer-winged with shallower tail fork (4–14 mm vs. 11–17 mm in Townsend's), narrower white rump band, and more buoyant flight with fairly loose wingbeats and frequent gliding. Pale upperwing band of Darwin's usually duller, more even in width, and does not reach wing bend, and white extends to lateral undertail coverts.

Wilson's Storm-Petrel (mainly cooler waters) has shorter arm and broader based, more triangular wings not strongly crooked, and usually flies low and directly with stiff, swallow-like wingbeats; its tail is squared but can look cleft, an effect sometimes enhanced by long toes, which project beyond tail tip in direct flight. Wilson's is blacker overall with squarer and brighter white rump patch that extends to the lateral undertail coverts, and upperwings have a more even-width pale panel that does not reach wing bend.

Dark morph. *Chapman's [Leach's] Storm-Petrel* (offshore Mexico) averages larger and longer tailed with slightly deeper tail fork (14–24 mm vs. 11–17 mm), but note that Chapman's are often molting tail feathers in fall and thus appear short-tailed. Chapman's slightly paler and browner over-all, upperwing band often brighter and slightly longer. Flight of Townsend's tends to be a little quicker and more direct than Chapman's, but critical study needed.

Ashy Storm-Petrel (California Current region) is a bird of cooler waters, but some occur in range of Townsend's. Ashy averages larger with longer, deeply forked tail and proportionately larger, puffier head. Ashy is slightly paler and grayer over-all with silvery stripe on underwing coverts, and a more even-width upperwing band that does not usually reach wing bend. Ashy probably has higher wing-loading and flight generally more fluttery, with shorter glides and quicker wingbeats.

Least Storm-Petrel (inshore waters) smaller and usually blacker with a graduated tail, narrower and more rounded wings, and deep jerky wingbeats. On occasion, however, Townsend's can appear disconcertingly Least-like, having somewhat rounded wings and a fluttery flight with deep wingbeats relative to larger Leach's and Chapman's storm-petrels. Note Townsend's longer, moderately forked tail (beware molting birds) and more angular wings; in direct comparison, Least is noticeably smaller with a faster, more erratic flight and only brief glides.

Habitat and Behavior Pelagic waters, usually beyond the continental shelf. Habits overall much like Leach's Storm-Petrel, and Townsend's can be found rafting or feeding with Leach's, Black, and Least storm-petrels off s California. Flight manner requires critical study but in calm to light winds Townsend's is a fairly fast, strong flier, with fairly deep, clipped wingbeats and a more direct and steadier flight than the jerkier, more confident, bounding flight of Leach's.

Nests in crevices and burrows; nocturnal at colonies. Burrow call much like Ainley's Storm-Petrel, a relatively fast-paced, rough purring, or chatter, punctuated by a barely audible inhalation

every 4–5 seconds, with the first note after the inhalation much louder than the following chatter (Ainley 1980). Flight call has little or no chuckling quality typical of Leach's, and consists of 11–20 notes (usually 17), with emphasis placed only on 1 note, about two-thirds through the sequence (Ainley 1980).

Description Medium-small with fairly long and bluntly pointed wings usually crooked at wrist; tail medium length and moderately forked. Toes do not project beyond tail in flight.

Ages similar but juveniles fresh in fall (Sep–Nov) when older birds likely to be worn or molting. Blackish brown overall, appearing black at any distance and browner when worn; head and back with slaty blue-gray sheen when fresh; narrow whitish edgings to subscapulars in fresh plumage. Uppertail coverts range from bright white (with fine, dark shaft streaks and dusky subterminal marks usually only visible in hand; rump score 1–3 (mainly 1–2; see Fig 173) to dark sooty brown overall, usually with some pale gray or whitish at sides (rump score 4–5, mainly 4; see Fig 173). Some white uppertail coverts tipped finely with dusky in fresh plumage, forming faint barring visible in the hand. Flight feathers blacker and upperwings with paler, brownish gray to pale buff ulnar band broadest at carpal joint and extending to, or slightly short of, wing bend; ulnar band can be fairly dull in fresh plumage but often quite bright when faded. Bill, legs, and feet black.

On the water. All-dark or with variable paler ulnar band visible; white rump patch may sometimes show as a sliver under folded wings.

Molt Needs study. Assuming molt relates to breeding as in Leach's Storm-Petrel (and given that Townsend's is smaller and may require less time for its complete molt), adult wing molt of Townsend's may start Aug/Oct and complete Feb/Mar; PB2 wing molt may start Jun/Aug, end Oct/Dec.

S7.2. Presumed Townsend's Storm-Petrel. Small, dark, and compact relative to Leach's, with an extensive white rump patch and short forked tail. SNGH. Off Santa Barbara, California, 21 Jul 2007.

S7.3. Possible Townsend's Storm-Petrel. Relative to northern Leach's, upperwing bands average duller and white wraps around more on lateral tail coverts, but these features may be matched by some West Coast Leach's; more study is needed on this identification problem. SNGH. Off Santa Barbara, California, 20 Jul 2008.

S7.4. Possible Townsend's Storm-Petrel. A different view of the same individual as in S7.3. SNGH. Off Santa Barbara, California, 20 Jul 2008.

S7.5. Presumed Townsend's Storm-Petrel. Extensive white rump patch and relatively short tail (fork foreshortened in this photo) may invite confusion with Wedge-rumped Storm-Petrel. SNGH. Off Santa Barbara, California, 21 Jul 2007.

7.6. Presumed dark morph Townsend's Storm-Petrel. This bird's small size and quick flight manner among Leach's Storm-Petrels momentarily suggested Least Storm-Petrel. Note relatively rounded wingtips, typical of Townsend's and southern populations of Leach's. SNGH. Off Santa Barbara, California, 7 Sep 2006.

S8. WEDGE-RUMPED STORM-PETREL *Halocyptena (Oceanodroma) tethys*

L 14.5–16.5 cm, WS 33.5–40 cm, tail 52–67 mm (fork 7–11 mm)
Figures 149, 152, 164, S8.1–S8.10, S10.10

Identification Summary Pacific (exceptional n to California). A small white-rumped storm-petrel with relatively pointed wings and notched tail. Flight often fairly quick with deep wingbeats and short glides. Plumage blackish overall with pale brownish upperwing band and large, wedge-shaped white rump patch.

Taxonomy Two subspecies described, differing in size and proportions, likely representing two species. Here placed in the genus *Halocyptena*, together with Least and Black storm-petrels (Nunn & Stanley 1998).

H. [t.] tethys (Galapagos Storm-Petrel) breeds Galapagos Islands (mainly Apr–Sep; Harris 1969b), ranges n to Mexico over pelagic waters. Averages larger (clearly larger than Least Storm-Petrel) and longer winged (L 15–16.5 cm, WS 36–40 cm, tail 56–67 mm) with slightly stouter bill but with relatively shallower tail fork (5–9 mm) and shorter tail projection (11–21 mm) beyond longer white rump patch (BM, CAS specimens, n = 20). May average narrower wings, higher wing-loading, and less extensive white wrap-around on lateral undertail coverts than *kelsalli* (study needed).

H. [t.] kelsalli (Peruvian Storm-Petrel) breeds Peru (Mar–Aug, at least; Murphy 1936), ranges s to Chile, n to Mexico over shelf waters. Averages smaller (only slightly larger than Least Storm-Petrel) and shorter winged (L 14.5–15.5 cm, WS 33–37 cm, tail 52–62 mm) with slighter bill but with relatively deeper tail fork (7–10 mm) and longer tail projection (17–24 mm) beyond shorter white rump patch (BM, CAS specimens, n = 20). May average broader wings, lower wing-loading, and more extensive white wrap-around on lateral undertail coverts than *tethys* (study needed).

Names *Halocyptena* means "speedy or swift wing of the sea," *tethys* refers to the Greek goddess of the sea. Sometimes known as Galapagos Storm-Petrel.

Status and Distribution Least Concern. Breeds (mainly Mar–Sep) on Galapagos Islands and along coast of Peru, ranges at sea n to Mexico, s to n Chile.

Pacific. Fairly common to locally and seasonally common nonbreeding visitor (year-round) off Middle America n to 23˚N, uncommon to rare

to 25˚N off Pacific coast of Baja California, and uncommon to locally fairly common in s Gulf of California (May–Aug at least); very rare n to Guadalupe Island (nominate *tethys* found in burrow, late Jan; Huey 1952) and exceptional to cen California (Jan specimen of *kelsalli* found inland; also a few late Jul–early Oct reports at sea). Nominate *tethys* tends to occur farther offshore (where collected Mar–Sep in the region), mainly > 100 km from land (Spear & Ainley 2007), whereas *kelsalli* is commoner inshore (regular May–Nov inshore off Panama and Costa Rica), and occurs mainly < 400 km from land (Spear & Ainley 2007).

FIELD IDENTIFICATION

Similar Species Fairly distinctive by virtue of small size (similar to, or slightly larger than, Least Storm-Petrel), structure, and long, wedge-shaped white rump patch, but under at-sea conditions can be confused with Leach's Storm-Petrel complex. See differences noted under *Leach's, Townsend's, and Darwin's storm-petrels*.

Pacific. *Wilson's Storm-Petrel* has broader, more triangular wings, fluttery, swallow-like flight with shallower, stiff wingbeats, squarer white rump patch, and long legs with toes often projecting beyond tail tip in direct flight. S-breeding Wilson's larger than both taxa of Wedge-rumped, but Fuegian [Wilson's] Storm-Petrel similar in size to Galapagos [Wedge-rumped] Storm-Petrel.

Habitat and Behavior Pelagic, but also ranges to within a few km of shore and occasionally seen from land. Occurs singly or in small groups, at times in fairly dense flocks up to a few hundred birds, especially when scavenging marine mammal carcasses; associates readily with other storm-petrels (especially Least and Black inshore, and Leach's offshore) on the water and when feeding. Sometimes follows ships.

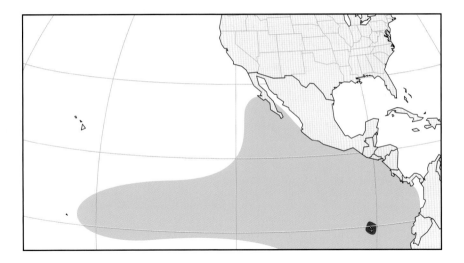

In calm to light or moderate winds, flight fairly low with a slight side-to-side rocking and deep, slightly floppy, fairly quick wingbeats, overall progression fairly direct to weaving, with pauses or short glides on slightly bowed wings. Flight manner of *kelsalli* in calm to light winds much like Least Storm-Petrel but with longer and more frequent glides. Glides longer in moderate winds, especially when flying across the wind. Across and with the wind can also fly with steady, fairly deep, but not hurried wingbeats and fairly long glides on bowed to slightly arched wings, rather similar to Leach's and Townsend's storm-petrels. Often forages into the wind, stalling upward and dropping to the surface where it foot-patters while picking at prey, holding wings raised. Also feeds while swimming. When alarmed, such as close to big ships or flushed off water, flight can be much more erratic and manic, with much swerving and looping.

Description Small, with relatively pointed wings, notched tail; feet do not project beyond tail tip.

Ages similar. Sooty blackish brown overall, often appearing black at any distance but with warmer brown tones in sunlight. Flight feathers blacker and upperwings with paler, fairly even-width gray-brown to pale buff ulnar band not reaching wing bend. Bright white rump patch long and wedge-shaped (shorter on *kelsalli*), often with a dark medial notch distally, and at times imparting a gleaming white-ended appearance (strikingly shorter when longest coverts molting); white wraps around slightly to lateral undertail coverts on *tethys*, apparently more so on *kelsalli*. Bill, legs, and feet black.

On the water. Appears all-dark with variable paler upperwing band; white rump patch usually apparent as white wedge under folded wings.

Molt Given different breeding cycles and potential age-related differences in timing, some birds might be found in wing molt year-round (study needed). Of 30 birds photographed off s Baja California Peninsula in mid-late Aug 2010 (pers. obs.), 25% still with p9–p10 or p10 old, 60% with p10 growing or wings fresh, 15% full-winged but worn, some apparently first-cycle birds. These observations of wing molt completing Aug–Oct (around the end of the breeding seasons described for both taxa) suggest breeding seasons may be variable; also see comments by Spear and Ainley (2007:35) on anomalous seasonal distributions of *kelsalli* relative to reported breeding season (more study needed).

S8.1. Wedge-rumped Storm-Petrel (nominate *tethys*). Note long white rump patch, notched tail, extent of pale upperwing band. GLA. Galapagos Islands, Ecuador, 25 Jul 2009.

S8.2. Wedge-rumped Storm-Petrel (presumed *kelsalli*) in fresh plumage. Note long white rump patch, large feet typical of genus. SNGH. Baja California Sur, Mexico, 22 Aug 2010.

S8.3. Wedge-rumped Storm-Petrel (presumed *kelsalli*) in fairly worn plumage, probably first cycle based on uniform-looking upperwings. SNGH. Baja California Sur, Mexico, 22 Aug 2010.

S8.4. Wedge-rumped Storm-Petrel (taxon unknown). Prominence of pale upperwing band varies with wear (cf. S8.1–S8.3) and extent of white rump patch varies with taxon and molt. SW. Eastern Pacific, 2°S 89°W, 26 Sep 2006.

S8.5. Wedge-rumped Storm-Petrel (presumed *kelsalli*) molting uppertail coverts can have reduced white rump patch, at times even with apparent dusky central stripe. Note bill shape, big feet, extent of pale upperwing band, all typical of *Halocyptena*. TMcG. Baja California Sur, Mexico, 22 Aug 2010.

S8.6. Wedge-rumped Storm-Petrel (nominate *tethys*). Wings tend to be held straighter than on Leach's Storm-Petrel, closed tail can appear almost squared; also note limited wrap-around of white rump (cf. S8.7). AJ. Galapagos Islands, Ecuador, 21 Jul 2008.

S8.7. Wedge-rumped Storm-Petrel (presumed *kelsalli*). White wrap-around on undertail coverts variable (cf. S8.6, S8.8). Best distinguished from Leach's and Band-rumped complexes by small size, flight manner; also note lack of gray sheen to head. SNGH. Baja California Sur, Mexico, 22 Aug 2010.

S8.8. Wedge-rumped Storm-Petrel (subspecies *kelsalli*) is barely larger than Least Storm-Petrel (left). Note similarities in overall structure, bill shape, and large feet typical of genus *Halocyptena*. SNGH. Baja California Sur, Mexico, 22 Aug 2010.

S8.9. Wedge-rumped Storm-Petrel (presumed *kelsalli*) often scavenges with congeneric but all-dark Least Storm-Petrel (lower left) and Black Storm-Petrel (right two birds). Note diagnostic shape and extent of white rump patch (tail may be in molt). SNGH. Baja California Sur, Mexico, 20 Aug 2010.

S8.10. Wedge-rumped Storm-Petrel (nominate *tethys*). cf.58.6 Extent of white visible on resting birds greatly affected by how wings are held, and may vary with taxon. GLA. Galapagos Islands, Ecuador, 27 Jul 2006.

Dark-rumped Storm-Petrels

The dark-rumped storm-petrels comprise eight species worldwide in the genera *Oceanodroma* and *Halocyptena*, with seven species recorded in North America. They occur mainly in the North Pacific, and six have been found in Pacific waters of the region: Black, Least, Ashy, and Chapman's [Leach's] are breeding species, Markham's is a nonbreeding visitor, and Tristram's is a vagrant; Swinhoe's is a nonbreeding visitor to the North Atlantic and is the only dark-rumped species known from the North Atlantic. An identification review of dark-rumped, fork-tailed storm-petrels was provided by Howell and Patteson (2008c), and some identification pitfalls are illustrated here (Figs 174–187).

Off the West Coast, the commonest dark-rumped species are Ashy and Black storm-petrels, which are usually fairly easy to distinguish, at least given experience with one or both species (Figs 174–175). An underappreciated pitfall is the separation of Black and Least storm-petrels (Figs 176–178); despite differing markedly in size these two species share similar structure and flight manner. Separating Ashy from dark-rumped Chapman's [Leach's] Storm-Petrels off s California can be challenging under some conditions. The flight manner of these two is similar at times, and, besides structural differences, Ashy is best distinguished by its pale underwing stripe and longer, more deeply forked tail (Figs 179–182). Any solidly dark-rumped storm-petrel in the Atlantic is almost certainly the little-known Swinhoe's Storm-Petrel (Fig 183); wholly dark-rumped Leach's are unknown in the Atlantic. Over the warm offshore waters of Middle America, care should be taken distinguishing Black and Markham's storm-petrels (Figs 184–187), which is actually fairly easy; a greater challenge lies in distinguishing Markham's and Chapman's storm-petrels because these species can fly in a fairly similar manner.

Fig 174. Black and Ashy storm-petrels are usually distinguished readily by size and flight manner. Black (front left, and three birds at back right) is appreciably larger (a large storm-petrel) and blacker with deep, languid wingbeats, whereas Ashy is smaller (a medium-sized storm-petrel) and grayer with a quicker, more fluttery flight. Other features are the long legs and big feet of Black, and the small fine bill and pale underwing stripe of Ashy. SNGH. Off Monterey, California. 12 Sep 2008.

Fig 175. Relative to Ashy Storm-Petrel (left two birds), the much larger size, bigger wings, and blacker plumage of Black Storm-Petrel is obvious in direct comparison. SNGH. Off Monterey, California, 22 Sep 2007.

Fig 177. The larger size, slightly broader wings, and forked tail of Black Storm-Petrel distinguish it from Least Storm-Petrel (Fig 176), but the two can appear surprisingly similar at times. SNGH. Oaxaca, Mexico, 1 Oct 2009.

Fig 176. Least Storm-Petrel can be difficult to separate in a photo from Black Storm-Petrel (Fig 177) other than by tapered tail (which molting Black can have). Both share dark sooty plumage, big feet, a fairly thick bill, and deep wingbeats. Least flies more quickly and glides less, but a lone bird at close range from a small boat, or over the ocean with nothing for scale, can be disconcertingly similar to Black. SNGH. Baja California Sur, Mexico, 22 Aug 2010.

Fig 178. Least Storm-Petrel (upper three birds) and Black Storm-Petrel (lower four birds) often associate when feeding (as here) or when resting, when they tend to form fairly tightly packed rafts (unlike the more open rafts of Ashy Storm-Petrel). Note the similar plumage tones of these two species, both in the genus *Halocyptena*. SNGH. Baja California Sur, Mexico, 20 Aug 2010.

Fig 179. Ashy Storm-Petrel. Relative to dark-rumped Chapman's [Leach's] Storm-Petrel (Fig 180), note Ashy's narrower wings and fatter body, plus its bigger head and deeper tail fork (Ashy also has a longer tail, not apparent at this angle). Given reasonable lighting, the paler and ashier plumage tones of Ashy and its contrasting underwing pattern are usually apparent. SNGH. Off Monterey, California, 14 Sep 2008.

Fig 180. (Above right) Presumed Chapman's [Leach's] Storm-Petrel. Relative to Ashy Storm-Petrel (Fig 179), note Chapman's broader wings and slimmer body (resulting in a lower wing-loading and more buoyant flight), plus its smaller head and shallower tail fork. Given reasonable lighting, darker and browner ventral plumage tones of Chapman's are usually apparent, as well as fairly even-toned underwings. Many Chapman's have some whitish on the lateral tail coverts, as here; others are all-dark. SNGH. Off San Diego, California, 7 Sep 2006.

Fig 181. Ashy Storm-Petrel. Note ashy-gray plumage tones, long and deeply forked tail, reduced pale upper-wing band. SNGH. Off Monterey, California, 13 Sep 2008.

Fig 182. Chapman's [Leach's] Storm-Petrel. Relative to Ashy note shallower, slightly lobed tail fork, brown-ish (vs. ashy-gray) rump, longer pale upperwing band. SNGH. Off Santa Barbara, California, 21 Jul 2007.

Fig 183. Swinhoe's Storm-Petrel. Relative to Leach's note white bases to outer primary shafts, lack of back/rump contrast, more even tail fork, slightly blunter wingtips, thicker bill. SNGH. Off Hatteras, North Carolina, 2 Jun 2008.

Fig 184. Black Storm-Petrel has somewhat rangy build typical of genus *Halocyptena*, with relatively long neck, somewhat rounded head, and stout bill. Also note dark sooty-brown head and back, pale upperwing bands limited largely to greater coverts (cf. Fig 185). TMcG. Baja California Sur, Mexico, 20 Aug 2010.

Fig 185. Markham's Storm-Petrel. Relative to Black Storm-Petrel (Fig 184), shape and plumage patterns of Markham's are similar to dark-rumped Leach's. Note bold pale upperwing bands, relatively slender bill, steely gray cast to head. SNGH. Tarapacá, Chile, 23 Oct 2009.

Fig 186. Black Storm-Petrel. In some lighting, plumage tones can resemble Markham's, but should be readily separable in the field by structure and flight manner. Note very big feet, stout bill (cf. Fig 187). SNGH. Oaxaca, Mexico, 3 Oct 2009.

Fig 187. Markham's Storm-Petrel. Note very deeply forked tail, small feet, ashy-gray head, and long slender bill (cf. Fig 186). SNGH. Tarapacá, Chile, 23 Oct 2009.

S9. BLACK STORM-PETREL *Halocyptena (Oceanodroma) melania*

L 21.5–23 cm, WS 50–55 cm, tail 80–90 mm (fork 20–31 mm)
Figures 148–149, 174–175, 177–178, 184, 186, S8.9, S9.1–S9.11, S10.9

Identification Summary Pacific, over warmer waters. This large all-dark storm-petrel of inshore and shelf waters might better be called "Great-winged Storm-Petrel" for its long and big wings, which are typically slightly crooked and which make the forked tail look relatively small. Flight powerful and unhurried with deep wingbeats and frequent glides.

S9.1. Flocks of Black Storm-Petrel often pack tightly, creating a dense "slick" not usually seen with flocks of Ashy Storm-Petrels (cf. S11.1). Note overall blackish plumage tones, big long wings, and, on several birds, long dangling legs with big feet. A few Ashy Storm-Petrels are mixed in, mainly at the back of the group. SNGH. Off Monterey, California, 22 Sep 2007.

Taxonomy Monotypic. Has been placed in the monotypic genus *Loomelania*, but here placed with Least and Galapagos storm-petrels in the genus *Halocyptena* (Nunn & Stanley 1998).

Names *Halocyptena* means "speedy or swift wing of the sea," *melania* (blackness) and the English name refer to this species' black plumage aspect. Sometimes known simply as Black Petrel.

Status and Distribution Least Concern. Endemic breeder. Breeds (May–Oct) off s California and nw Mexico, ranges s to Peru (around 15°S) and n to cen California.

Pacific. Local breeder on islands off Pacific coast (mid-May/Jun–late Aug/Oct) from California Channel Islands (where uncommon and local; Ainley 2008) to San Benito Islands (common), and locally common in n Gulf of California (breeding cycle earlier than Pacific coast, perhaps Apr–Aug), where known from Islas Cardinosa (= Partida), Isla San Luís, and Roca Consag; other nesting islands probably remain to be discovered.

Generally fairly common to common (Mar–Sep) over inshore waters from Gulf of California s to Central America, arriving later (Apr–May) to s California waters. Peak numbers off s California occur Aug–Oct (when generally common),

406

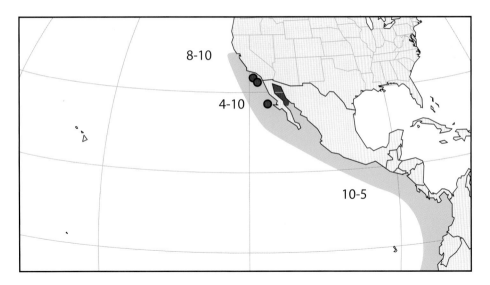

corresponding to warmest waters and postbreeding dispersal, most depart s by Nov, and casual Dec–Jan. Regular fall visitor n to Monterey Bay, especially in warm-water years (mainly Aug–Oct, casually from late May and into Dec, exceptionally early Jan), where rafts usually number 4000–8000 birds (annual maxima 200–10,000 birds). Very rare n in warm-water years (mainly Aug–Oct), and mainly since 1983, to Cordell Bank, Marin Co. (tens of birds in some years; pers. obs.), exceptionally to Oregon. Occurs year-round (commonest Oct–May, with marked influxes of migrants in Oct–Nov) off Central America, with nonbreeding concentrations in Gulf of Nicoya and Panama Bight.

Casual inland (mid-Aug to early Nov) in the Southwest after tropical cyclones (sometimes tens of birds; Jones 1999), exceptionally (Oct 1994) one in Tulare Co., California (AFN 49:95–99, 1995). Can be seen from shore off s California, seasonally common from shore in Gulf of California (mainly Apr–Aug), and sometimes visible from shore off Middle America (mainly Nov–May). Occasional birds onshore or slightly inland in s California (mainly Sep–Oct in San Diego Co.) are probably fledglings disoriented by lights.

FIELD IDENTIFICATION

Similar Species Several other all-dark storm-petrels occur in the range of Black and are best separated by structure and flight style. Also see Swinhoe's Storm-Petrel, not known to overlap in range. Black has characteristics of the genus *Halocyptena*, which set it apart from *Oceanodroma*: long and "big" wings, which make the tail look relatively small, a long neck and relatively small rounded head, and relatively long legs that often dangle slightly.

Ashy Storm-Petrel (California Current region) appreciably smaller and shorter winged with shorter neck, bigger and puffier head, and proportionately longer tail (Black looks about twice the size of Ashy when the two are seen flying together). Ashy has a different flight manner, with quicker, more fluttery wingbeats and usually only short glides. When seen together, the two species are usually separated readily by size and flight manner (often best appreciated by scanning flocks with the naked eye) but, without the benefit of comparison, Ashies can suggest Blacks, especially to inexperienced observers. Ashy usually looks paler overall, often with paler and grayer uppertail coverts (vs. the darker and more uniformly blackish Black), bolder pale upperwing bands, and silvery-gray underwing-covert panels. Most Ashies on Monterey Bay in fall are in wing and tail molt whereas many Blacks there in fall are not molting. Resting groups of Blacks are often fairly tightly bunched vs. the wider spacing typical of rafts of Ashies.

Chapman's [Leach's] Storm-Petrel (mostly offshore waters) appreciably smaller (readily apparent in direct comparison) and shorter winged with relatively longer tail, shallower tail fork, slightly shorter neck, and proportionately larger and squarer head with a fine bill. Plumage slightly paler and browner overall with bolder pale upperwing bands, and typical flight quicker and more bounding, with confident jerky wingbeats and shorter glides on arched wings.

Markham's Storm-Petrel (offshore tropical Pacific) similar in length but lighter bodied with longer, more deeply forked tail, shorter neck, slightly larger and squarer head with longer bill, shorter legs, and smaller feet. Plumage often slightly paler and browner overall with grayer (vs. dark sooty) head and more contrasting pale upperwing bands, which usually reach the wing bend. Typically flies with shallower wingbeats and buoyant glides different from the usual flight of Black. In hand, tarsus 23–26 mm in Markham's vs. 29–34 mm in Black.

Least Storm-Petrel occurs throughout the range of Black and, despite marked size differences (Black looks about three times the size of Least when the two are flying together), these two species share long wings, short tail, and similar plumage aspect, and fly with deep wingbeats. They can be confused surprisingly easily if only one species is seen, especially at long range such as from shore. Least is much smaller and proportionately shorter winged, with a quicker, jerky flight that includes little or no gliding.

Bulwer's Petrel (tropical waters) larger with a long tapered tail, and a quicker, lower, and more buoyant weaving flight with usually shallower wingbeats.

Habitat and Behavior Mainly inshore, especially over the continental slope, less often over deeper offshore waters (Spear & Ainley 2007). Associated with warmer waters off California, but may favor relatively cooler waters off Middle America (Jehl 1974). Often gregarious and seen in tight to loose aggregations scattered over feeding areas, sometimes in groups of hundreds and locally thousands; also found singly and in small groups. Associates readily with other storm-petrels, particularly inshore with Least and Wedge-rumped, also with Chapman's [Leach's] off s California and Baja California; often with rafts of Ashy Storm-Petrels off cen California. Can be seen from shore, especially in Gulf of California during spring and summer, and after storms along the Mexican mainland coast. Often accompanies ships, scavenging in the wake.

Flight typically powerful and unhurried, more languid than other storm-petrels in region, often with prolonged gliding on slightly arched or slightly bowed wings; often holds head slightly raised, accentuating long neck, and long legs often dangle slightly. In calm to light or moderate winds direct flight unhurried with easy, deep, and fairly quick but slightly floppy wingbeats, and often prolonged sailing glides. In moderate winds, wheeling glides suggest Leach's Storm-Petrel but generally lower and less bounding; wingbeats measured and fairly deep. Foot-patters when feeding, the long legs obvious when dangled, and also eats while sitting or picks food from the surface in flight and flies off with it. When alarmed, such as disturbed from the water, strong, deep wingbeats can appear almost hurried and flight soon breaks into short, weaving glides.

Nocturnal at colonies, which range from a few pairs to tens of thousands, nesting in crevices, among boulders, and under large rocks. Often nests alongside Least Storm-Petrel and (on the San Benito Islands) Chapman's [Leach's] Storm-Petrel, both of which use smaller crevices. Burrow call a strong, prolonged, rapid-paced rattled churr up to 10–12 seconds' duration, swelling from a soft start and ending abruptly, with pauses of 1 second or longer between churrs. Flight calls rough and screechy with an accelerating, often emphatic ending, and with emphasis usually on 2 notes near the start: *kreeih kreehr kree-kree-kree-kreehr*, or *kriih krri, krri ki-ki-kihr*, etc. Flight calls can suggest Least Storm-Petrel but stronger, more emphatic, and often with a shriekier quality.

Description Large and fairly heavy bodied with a relatively long neck, small rounded head, and thick bill. Wings long ("great-winged") and pointed, usually somewhat crooked at wrist; tail long and forked. Toes do not project beyond tail in flight.

Ages similar. Blackish brown overall, often looking simply blackish at any distance and browner overall on underparts, especially when faded (underparts can even appear warm brown in low-angle sun); head and upperparts blacker, with a dull gray sheen in fresh plumage; uppertail coverts blackish brown, not contrastingly paler. Flight feathers slightly blacker, often with bases of primary shafts creamy-whitish; upperwings with pale brownish or gray-brown (fresh, when can show fine whitish tips to greater coverts) to pale-buff (worn) upperwing band, which is mostly even in width and approaches or just reaches wing bend. Upperwing band can be poorly contrasting in fresh plumage (mainly Mar–Jul in adults) but often striking when bleached (perhaps mainly first-summer birds), and also can become dull again if faded pale tips wear off. Bill, legs, and feet black.

Molt Adult wing molt mainly Aug/Oct–Mar/Apr, perhaps averaging a month earlier in Gulf of California breeders (pers. obs.), and may be suspended over southward migration; presumed PB2 wing molt may be mainly Jun/Aug–Oct/Nov, again perhaps averaging earlier in Gulf birds (study needed).

S9.2. Black Storm-Petrel in fresh juvenile plumage. Note lack of distinct gray gloss above, extent of pale upperwing band, big toes projecting into base of tail fork, dark sooty head, stout bill. SNGH. Baja California Sur, Mexico, 22 Aug 2010.

S9.3. Black Storm-Petrel in mid-primary molt. Note relatively small head and stout bill, long legs, and big feet. SNGH. Baja California Sur, Mexico, 20 Aug 2010.

S9.4. A classic pose of Black Storm-Petrel, with relatively small rounded head slightly raised, big wings deeply beating, and big feet dangling. Also note fairly stout bill, extent of pale upperwing band. SNGH. Oaxaca, Mexico, 2 Oct 2009.

S9.5. Note classic pose as well as contrastingly dark sooty head. Some Blacks, like this individual, show distinct white flashes on the primary bases. MD. Lima, Peru, 17 Nov 2007.

S9.6. With tail held closed, and in molt like this, Black Storm-Petrel might invite confusion with Bulwer's Petrel, but at sea note very different flight manners of these two species and appreciably larger size of Bulwer's. SNGH. Off Monterey, California, 22 Sep 2007.

S9.7. Black Storm-Petrel in fresh plumage. Note dark sooty brown plumage tones, stout bill, forked tail. SNGH. Baja California Sur, Mexico, 21 Aug 2010.

S9.8. A classic pose of Black Storm-Petrel, with long neck, relatively small rounded head slightly raised, deep chest, and big feet dangling. Also note stout bill. SNGH. Oaxaca, Mexico, 1 Oct 2009.

S9.9. A typical view of Black Storm-Petrel crossing the wake as it follows a boat. Note relatively small head, stout bill, big wings, forked tail. SNGH. Off San Diego, California, 26 Aug 2009.

S9.10. The large size of Black Storm-Petrel (or small size of Galapagos Shearwater!) can be appreciated with the two species together. Note relatively small, dark sooty head and thick bill of the storm-petrel (cf. S13.10). SNGH. Oaxaca, Mexico, 1 Oct 2009.

S9.11. Black and Ashy storm-petrels rafting together. Besides the larger size of Black Storm-Petrel, note the darker plumage, especially the dark head, relative to the paler and grayer Ashies. SNGH. Off Monterey, California, 22 Sep 2007.

S10. LEAST STORM-PETREL *Halocyptena (Oceanodroma) microsoma*

L 13.5–15 cm, WS 32–36 cm, tail 51–59 mm (graduation 8–14 mm)
Figures 149, 176, 178, S8.8, S8.9, S10.1–S10.11

Identification Summary Pacific, over warmer continental shelf waters. A tiny all-dark storm-petrel of inshore and shelf waters; endemic as a breeder to Mexico. Wings relatively long and bluntly pointed, tail tapered. Flight quick and erratic with deep jerky wingbeats and no or little gliding.

S10.1. The fairly dense rafts of Least Storm-Petrel are much like those of Black Storm-Petrel, and with nothing for scale these two species can appear similar at a distance. BLS. Baja California, Mexico, 27 Sep 2005.

Taxonomy Monotypic, although birds breeding on San Benito Islands may average larger than birds breeding in Gulf of California (CAS, MVZ specimens; more study needed): San Benito wing chord = 120.5 mm (115–126 mm, n = 12 male, 10 female); Gulf wing chord = 117.5 mm (113–121 mm, n = 4 male, 4 female). Sometimes placed in genus *Oceanodroma*, but here retained in genus *Halocyptena*, which also includes Black and Wedge-rumped storm-petrels (Nunn & Stanley 1998).

Names *Halocyptena* means "speedy or swift wing of the sea," *microsoma* (small-bodied) and the English name refer to this species' tiny size. Sometimes known simply as Least Petrel.

Status and Distribution Least Concern. Endemic breeder. Breeds (May–Oct) off Baja California, ranges s to Peru (around 10˚S), n irregularly to cen California.

Pacific. Common breeder on Islas San Benitos, off Pacific coast of Baja California (laying late Jun–Jul, probably fledging Sep–Oct), and locally in n Gulf of California (laying May–Jun, fledging Aug–Sep), where known from Islas Cardinosa (= Partida), Isla San Luís, and Roca Consag; other nesting islands probably remain to be discovered.

Generally fairly common to common (Mar–Sep) over inshore waters from Gulf of California s to Central America, probably arriving later (late Apr–May) to vicinity of San Benito Islands. Most birds move s from n Mexico and Gulf of

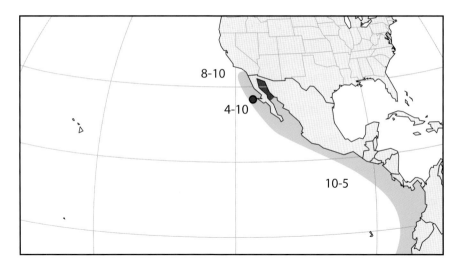

Least Storm-Petrel. Irregular (about every 2–3 years) and generally rare in late fall north to central California.

California during Oct–Mar, when commonest off Central America. Occurs year-round off Central America, with nonbreeding concentrations in Gulf of Nicoya and Panama Bight augmented by migrants in Sep–Nov and, especially, in Feb–May.

Irregular visitor n to California, mainly Aug–Oct, casually from Jul and into Nov. Recorded most frequently off San Diego Co. (max. counts of 3000–3500 birds), thence less frequent n to Monterey Bay (max. 500–1400 birds), mainly in warmer-water years and occurring on average every other year; casual in very small numbers n to Cordell Bank, Marin Co. (pers. obs., photos). Very rare inland (late Aug–Oct) in the Southwest after storms, exceptionally hundreds of birds at Salton Sea, California, and Lake Havasu, Arizona. Very rarely seen from shore off California but seasonally common from shore in Gulf of California (mainly Apr–Aug) and sometimes from coasts of Middle America (mainly Nov–May).

FIELD IDENTIFICATION

Similar Species Generally distinctive by virtue of small size, graduated tail, and all-dark plumage. Nonetheless, picking out a Least among swarms of Ashy Storm-Petrels can be challenging, and molting Ashies are often logged as Leasts by incautious and inexperienced observers. Underappreciated problems are distinguishing Least from Black Storm-Petrel (when only one species is viewed from shore, far out in a heat haze, such as occurs in the Gulf of California) and from dark morph Townsend's Storm-Petrel. Also cf. Chapman's [Leach's] Storm-Petrel.

Ashy Storm-Petrel (California Current region) larger but not always strikingly so (Least looks about three-quarters the size of an Ashy in tail molt) with longer tail (even when molting) and broader wings. Ashy has a more fluttery, less erratic, and less jerky flight than Least. The best way to spot Leasts with Ashy flocks is by using your naked eye, scanning the fluttery Ashies for a smaller, darker bird with strong deep wingbeats and a quicker, more erratic flight.

Black Storm-Petrel (occurs throughout range of Least) much larger and longer winged (appears three times the size of Least when the two are flying together) but has similarly black plumage and deep wingbeats. Black's flight is powerful and unhurried, with frequent shearing glides, and lacks the quick, fairly hurried flight of Least as viewed in the distance; tail of Black forked but rarely apparent at long range, when Black can look fairly short tailed, an effect enhanced by its big wings.

Chapman's [Leach's] Storm-Petrel (mainly farther offshore) has relatively rounded wings and more fluttery flight than nominate Leach's. Compared to Least, note Chapman's longer forked tail (beware molting birds), slightly broader and more angular wings, and fairly buoyant flight with more frequent glides; in direct comparison, Least is noticeably smaller and darker with faster and more weaving flight that involves little or no gliding.

Dark morph *Townsend's Storm-Petrel* (mainly farther offshore) can sometimes appear disconcertingly Least-like, having somewhat rounded wings and a fluttery flight relative to larger Chapman's [Leach's] Storm-Petrel. Note Townsend's longer, moderately forked tail (beware molting birds) and more angular wings; in direct comparison, Least noticeably smaller with a faster, more weaving flight and only brief glides.

Habitat and Behavior Mainly inshore, over continental shelf and slope waters, less often over deeper offshore waters (Spear & Ainley 2007). Associated with warmer waters off California, but may favor relatively cooler waters off Middle America (Jehl 1974, Spear & Ainley 1999b). Often gregarious and seen in tight to loose aggregations scattered over feeding areas, sometimes in groups of hundreds; also found singly and in small groups. Associates readily with other storm-petrels, most often with congeneric Black and Wedge-rumped; off cen California occurs with rafts of Ashy Storm-Petrels. Can be seen from shore, especially in Gulf of California during spring and summer, and after storms along Mexican mainland coast. Sometimes follows ships.

In light winds, flight quick with a slight side-to-side rocking or bounding rhythm, the deep and high wingbeats slightly clipped yet floppy, and with only brief pauses between flapping; in stronger winds may glide briefly, and foraging into moderate to strong winds can glide or "kite" low to the water with wings outstretched, feet occasionally dangling. Deep clipped wingbeats not especially quick, which can make birds appear deceptively large when no frame of reference is available. When feeding in calm to light winds, flight often erratic with dashing changes of direction, sharp turns, and quick stalls, rising slightly with moth-like fluttering (vs. the more pronounced upward sweeps and stalls of bigger and faster-flying species) before dropping to foot-patter or settle with wings raised and fluttered.

Nocturnal at colonies, which range from a few pairs to tens of thousands, nesting in crevices and among talus. Often nests alongside Black Storm-Petrels and (on San Benito Islands) Chapman's [Leach's] Storm-Petrels, both of which use larger crevices.

Burrow call a relatively soft, rapid-paced, rattling or snoring churr, bursts of 3–4 seconds' duration punctuated by abrupt, plaintive inhalations. Flight calls are rough, burry, and relatively low-pitched rhythmic chatters, often accelerating toward a slightly emphatic ending, *krrih krrih krrih-krri-krri-krri*, or *krruh kuh-uh krr-krr-krr-krr*, and variations; they can suggest Black Storm-Petrel but lack the strong and often screechy quality typical of Black.

Description A tiny storm-petrel with narrow, bluntly pointed wings; tail medium-length and graduated. Toes do not project beyond tail.

Ages similar. Sooty blackish brown overall, appearing black at a distance but in sunlight often has warm brown cast at closer range. Upperwing band formed mainly by paler edges to greater coverts, which are dull pale brownish to gray-brown when fresh, fading to dull pale brownish, often with pale buffy tips by late summer (Jun–Jul), the tips sometimes wearing off so upperwing can appear dark overall by late fall (Sep–Nov). Bill, legs, and feet black.

Molt Details not well known, and timing probably differs between Gulf and Pacific coast populations (study needed). Wing molt of some birds (perhaps mainly Pacific coast breeders?) starts Dec–Feb on nonbreeding grounds, completes Mar–May, with tail molt Feb–Apr (BM, SDNHM, USNM specimens). Many birds in Gulf of California start wing molt Jul–Sep (pers. obs., B. L. Sullivan, photos), perhaps concluding Nov–Dec or suspending for migration to complete in mid-late winter; this molt perhaps PB2 but presence of numerous fresh juveniles in Aug suggests that postbreeding adults could start wing molt in Aug.

Birds off s Central America starting wing molt in Mar–May (USNM specs.) presumably would complete Jun–Aug; age and natal origin of these birds unknown. Other birds off s Baja California starting wing molt in Aug 2010 had relatively fresh primaries (pers. obs.), suggesting little time since completion of previous wing molt.

S10.2. Least Storm-Petrel is dark sooty brown overall with a relatively dull upperwing band. Note tapered tail and relatively small head with fairly stout but long bill. As in most tubenoses, wing shape varies with flight manner (cf. S10.3). SNGH. Oaxaca, Mexico, 1 Oct 2009.

S10.3. Least Storm-Petrel. Contrast between fresher secondaries (blackness enhanced by light angle) and faded greater coverts and primaries indicate this is not a juvenile. Note sooty-brown plumage tones, big feet, stout bill. TMcG. Baja California Sur, Mexico, 20 Aug 2010.

S10.4. Although many field guides consider Least Storm-Petrel "short tailed," this seems more an effect created by contrast with its relatively big wings, as often also occurs with Black Storm-Petrel. At some angles, Least can appear quite long tailed. SNGH. Oaxaca, Mexico, 3 Oct 2009.

S10.5. Least Storm-Petrel in mid-primary molt. Tail also probably in molt, thus appearing relatively short and blunt. SNGH. Oaxaca, Mexico, 3 Oct 2009.

S10.6. Least Storm-Petrel in outer primary molt, showing a classic flight pose with deep wingbeats and tapered tail. SNGH. Oaxaca, Mexico, 1 Oct 2009.

S10.7. Least Storm-Petrel in fresh plumage, perhaps a juvenile. Note dark sooty head contrasting with brown body, fairly heavy bill. SNGH. Oaxaca, Mexico, 3 Oct 2009.

S10.8. Note distinctive shape, with projecting, "jaeger-like" central rectrices and fairly big bill. SNGH. Oaxaca, Mexico, 1 Oct 2009.

S10.9. Note overall similarities in shape and plumage tones between these two Least Storm-Petrels and much larger Black Storm-Petrel (behind). BLS. Baja California, Mexico, 27 Sep 2005.

S10.10. Off western Mexico, Least Storm-Petrels (four right-hand birds) often feed with slightly larger Wedge-rumped Storm-Petrels (two left-hand birds). SNGH. Baja California Sur, Mexico, 22 Aug 2010.

S10.11. Shape of resting Least Storm-Petrel rather similar to congeneric Wedge-rumped Storm-Petrel (S8.10), but Least shows no white on tail coverts. SNGH. Baja California Sur, Mexico, 20 Aug 2010.

S11. ASHY STORM-PETREL *Oceanodroma homochroa*
L 18.5–19.5 cm, WS 40–45 cm, tail 73–85 cm (fork 21–27 cm)
Figures 24, 147–148, 174–175, 179, 181, S9.1, S9.11, S11.1–S11.11, S14.7, S16.8–S16.11

Identification Summary Pacific, over cooler continental slope and offshore waters. A medium-sized, all-dark, and large-headed storm-petrel endemic to the California Current region. Note the long, deeply forked tail, ashy-gray plumage, and pale underwing panel. Flight fairly direct and fluttery with fairly deep wingbeats and short glides.

S11.1. Rafting Ashy Storm-Petrels tend to be rather openly spaced, unlike denser and blacker-looking "slicks" often formed by Black and Least storm-petrels (cf. S10.1). Note the relatively pale gray tones, accentuated here in diffuse sunlight, distinct from black or blackish-brown tones of roosting Black Storm-Petrels. Can you spot the single Fork-tailed Storm-Petrel with this group? SNGH. Off Bodega Bay, California, 19 Sep 2010.

Taxonomy Monotypic.

Names *Oceanodroma* means "ocean runner," *homochroa* refers to the uniform (ashy) coloration.

Status and Distribution Endangered. Endemic. Breeds (Apr–Nov) and ranges from California s to Baja California.
  Pacific. Local breeder (mainly late Apr/mid-Jul to late Aug/Nov), with most of population on Farallon Islands and Channel Islands. Small numbers also breed on rocky islets along the coast from at least Marin Co. (and probably n to Mendocino Co.; Carter et al. 2008) s to Monterey Co.,

and on the Coronado Islands and Todos Santos Islands, Baja California (Carter et al. 2008).
  Fairly common to locally abundant year-round over continental slope and adjacent offshore waters of the California Current in cen California, s to vicinity of Channel Islands, typically ranging farther offshore in winter (Nov–May), and nearer to shore in summer and fall. Notable rafting concentrations occur at Cordell Bank, Marin Co. (mainly late Jul–early Sep, regularly 500–1500 birds, rarely up to 5000) and in Monterey Bay (Aug–Nov, peaking in Sep–early Oct with 4000–7000 birds most years, rarely up to 10,000 or more). Uncommon to rare off southernmost

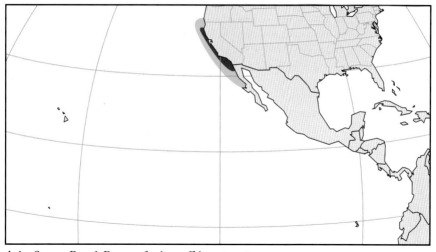

Ashy Storm-Petrel. Ranges farther offshore in winter.

California and Baja California, s to 28°N (reports from farther s, e.g., Crossin 1974, require verification). Small numbers (rarely hundreds) range n to Cape Mendocino, California (mainly Aug–Oct), very rarely to s Oregon (Oct 2005; Pyle 2006) and exceptionally to Washington (Apr–Jun, at least; NAB 60:570, 599, 2007; NAB 62:469, 2009). Occasional birds onshore or slightly inland in cen and s California (mainly Sep–Nov) are probably mainly fledglings disoriented by lights.

FIELD IDENTIFICATION

Similar Species Several all-dark storm-petrels occur in the range of Ashy and are best separated by size, structure, and flight manner. Note Ashy's long tail, large head, pale underwing panels, and fluttery flight. Also see Markham's and Swinhoe's storm-petrels, not known to overlap in range.

Black Storm-Petrel (inshore waters, often with rafts of Ashies) appreciably larger and longer winged with relatively shorter tail, longer neck, smaller and more rounded head, and heavy bill. Black looks about twice the size of Ashy when flying in direct comparison, and also appreciably larger on the water. Black usually looks darker overall and has powerful, unhurried flight with strong deep wingbeats and longer, more frequent glides.

Least Storm-Petrel (inshore waters, sometimes with rafts of Ashies) smaller but not always strikingly so (Least looks about three-quarters the size of an Ashy in tail molt) with a shorter, graduated tail and narrower wings. Ashies in tail molt, with outer rectrices shed or growing (mainly Aug–Oct, when Leasts arrive in cen California), invite confusion with Least but still relatively longer tailed. Least's flight is quicker and more erratic, with deep clipped wingbeats (Ashy's flight looks weaker and more fluttery, less purposeful). Leasts typically look darker overall and are not usually in wing molt when in cen California.

Chapman's [Leach's] Storm-Petrel is a bird of warmer offshore waters, but can be seen alongside Ashy off s California and perhaps responsible for many s or extralimital reports of Ashy. Chapman's slightly rangier overall with slightly lower wingloading and proportionately longer, more pointed wings, a shorter, less deeply forked tail, and a relatively smaller head but longer bill. Chapman's usually has a more bounding and confident-looking flight, like Leach's, but flight manner can be very similar to Ashy, especially in light winds. Under such conditions, note that Chapman's tends to have relatively clipped wingbeats and more frequent glides, vs. slightly weaker-looking, more fluttery flight of Ashy. Upperwing band of Chapman's often more contrasting, tapered overall, and usually reaches wing bend. Given comparable lighting and plumage wear, Chapman's appears browner overall. Underwings of Chapman's lack broad silvery central panel of Ashy but remiges and greater coverts can reflect silvery. Rump patterns of Chapman's and Ashy similar, although Ashy tends to have a pale-gray rump overall, vs. duller sooty brown, or mixed with whitish, as on Chapman's.

Dark morph *Townsend's Storm-Petrel* (s California and Mexico) a bird of warmer offshore waters, but some occur in the range of Ashy. Townsend's averages smaller with proportionately smaller head and shorter tail that is less deeply forked. Townsend's is blacker overall, without a silvery underwing panel. Townsend's probably has a lower wing-loading and its flight is generally more buoyant, with stronger, clipped wingbeats and longer glides.

Fork-tailed Storm-Petrel is a distinctive, pearl-gray species that should not be confused with Ashy if seen well. However, in low-level light the plumage of Fork-tailed can appear dull or dusky grayish, inviting confusion with Ashy (which tends to look blackish under such conditions); conversely, faded Ashies in bright sun may appear disconcertingly pale, almost milky gray-brown, and have been mistaken for Fork-tailed by incautious observers (in bright sun, Fork-tailed looks strikingly pale, silvery gray, and is more likely to be confused with a Red Phalarope). Fork-tailed is larger and bulkier with broader wings and a more confident, heavy-bodied flight.

Habitat and Behavior Ranges year-round over cooler California Current waters, with concentrations often over the continental slope and adjacent offshore waters (Spear & Ainley 2007); rafts often gather over submarine canyons off the cen California coast. Usually found singly or in loose aggregations scattered over feeding areas, sometimes in rafts numbering thousands. Rafts often include smaller numbers of other storm-petrel species (mainly Black, Least, Fork-tailed, and Wilson's, but very rarely Leach's); in Monterey Bay, rafts in warm-water years often comprise a few thousand of both Ashy and Black storm-petrels. Rarely seen from shore.

In light to moderate winds, flight rather even-tempered to slightly weaving and generally low over the water, with fairly steady wingbeats that vary from slightly fluttery to deeper and jerkier (a little over half the wingbeat arc appearing to be above the body plane), interspersed with short sailing glides on slightly bowed wings. In calm conditions, sometimes flies 3–5 m above the sea surface with steady wingbeats and no gliding. Conversely, in moderate to strong winds can glide for longer periods. When food is spotted, birds swoop up, stall, and drop, usually pattering or alighting briefly with wings raised above the body plane. Also feeds into the wind, pattering on the surface and holding its wings raised, remaining in or near

one place for several seconds. Progression across, and especially with, the wind is usually fairly fast and direct, following the contours of crests and swells but typically without bounding or weaving. When alarmed, such as disturbed from the water, deeper wingbeats can recall Black Storm-Petrel but slightly quicker and more clipped, with a higher upstroke.

Nocturnal at colonies, which range from a few pairs to thousands, nesting in rock crevices and areas generally devoid of vegetation. Well-studied at Southeast Farallon Island (Ainley et al. 1974), where species present year-round. First arrivals of breeding birds late Dec, reaching a peak by early Feb and remaining at that level for several months; first young fledge late Aug, most by late Nov, but some not until Jan. Prebreeding immatures visit the colony starting early Apr and continuing through early Jul.

Burrow call a prolonged series of hard clicking and purring churrs, usually 1.5–3.5 seconds' duration, punctuated by abrupt, plaintive, gulping inhalations; drier and more rattled than churr of Leach's. Flight calls shrieky and slightly gruff, with emphatic barking or yelping phrases, often ending with a gruff phrase: *kri-ih whee-pu', ki-krr,* or *krieh whii pi-pi-peu' k'k'kirr;* cadence may recall Leach's but lower and gruffer overall.

Description Medium-sized with relatively short neck, large puffy head, and small bill; medium-long and pointed wings usually somewhat crooked at wrist; tail relatively long and deeply forked, often looking slightly upswept at the tip when viewed in profile. Toes do not project beyond tail in flight. Moderate wing-loading. Leucistic birds are occasionally seen, such as with white patches on the belly and head, or on the rump and back.

Ages similar. Dark ashy gray overall, often appearing black at any distance; head and back with a slaty blue-gray sheen when fresh (mainly in spring); more brownish overall when worn (can look warm milky brown above in bright sun); narrow whitish edgings to subscapulars in fresh plumage. Uppertail coverts usually contrastingly paler gray, often with a partial or complete darker median stripe. Flight feathers slightly blacker and upperwings with pale dusky gray (fresh, when can show fine whitish tips to greater coverts) to pale buff (worn) ulnar band, which is mostly even in width and does not extend to wing bend (can approach wing bend on molting birds); exposed bases of primary shafts can be creamy-whitish (mainly in fall, when bleached). Underwings have reflectively silvery-gray greater and median coverts that often appear as a contrasting pale median band or, in some lights, merge into reflectively pale remiges to give the appearance of silvery-gray underwings with a broad dark leading edge. Bill, legs, and feet black.

Molt Adult molt spans mid-Jun to Mar: molt of body feathers starts mid-Jun, around time of egg-hatching, tail molt mainly Aug–Sep, and wing molt Aug/Sep–Jan/Mar (Ainley et al. 1976). PB2 wing molt probably May/Jun–Sep/Oct.

S11.2. A typical Ashy Storm-Petrel, showing well the long, deeply forked tail, head and bill shape, and extent of pale upperwing bands. Compare with S11.3. SNGH. Off Bodega Bay, California, 7 Sep 2007.

S11.3. Molting Ashy Storm-Petrels in fall can have "sawn-off" rear ends that invite confusion with Least Storm-Petrel. Besides being paler and grayer overall than Least, note obvious wing molt (most Leasts reaching central California are not molting) and blocky head with small, slender bill. SNGH. Off Bodega Bay, California, 19 Sep 2010.

S11.4. Ashy Storm-Petrels. Note ashy-gray rump contrasting with long forked tail, squared head and small fine bill, extent of pale upperwing band; also note underwing contrast on far bird. SNGH. Off Bodega Bay, California, 7 Sep 2007.

S11.5. In fall, Ashy Storm-Petrels are worn and often relatively brown toned, like this. The glossy gray tones of fresh plumage are best seen in late winter and spring. SNGH. Off Bodega Bay, California, 19 Sep 2010.

S11.6. Many Ashy Storm-Petrels off California in fall are in molt, which can create odd tail shapes; note contrast between gray rump and black tail. Most if not all species of dark-rumped storm-petrels can show variable white flashes on primary bases. SNGH. Off Bodega Bay, California, 7 Sep 2007.

S11.7. Ashy Storm-Petrel can show a contrasting pale rump patch, especially when worn and faded, as here. Note overall structure, pale underwing stripe, extent of pale upperwing band. SNGH. Off Bodega Bay, California, 19 Sep 2010.

S11.8. Ashy Storm-Petrel. Pale upperwing band appears more extensive than usual, and rump sides show as contrastingly paler ovals, two features suggesting Chapman's [Leach's] Storm-Petrel. Note contrasting underwing pattern, gray-toned rump. SNGH. Off Bodega Bay, California, 28 Aug 2009.

S11.9. Even in diffuse fog, as here, pale underwing stripe of Ashy Storm-Petrel usually apparent (but see S11.11). Also note long tail, which often appears to sweep slightly upward. SNGH. Off Bodega Bay, California, 5 Sep 2009.

S11.10. The normally pointed wings of Ashy Storm-Petrel can appear quite rounded when the inner primaries are shed, as here. Silver leg band suggests origin on Farallon Islands, where large numbers of Ashies are banded in long-term monitoring program. SNGH. Off Monterey, California, 13 Sep 2008.

S11.11. Ashy Storm-Petrel (below) with two Fork-tailed Storm-Petrels. In dense fog, Ashy tends to look solidly dark (but ashy black rather than jet black), with no plumage contrast apparent. Note long, slender, forked tail, and, in comparison to Fork-tailed, slightly smaller size and lighter build. SNGH. Off Bodega Bay, California, 1 Aug 2008.

S12. CHAPMAN'S [LEACH'S] STORM-PETREL *Oceanodroma [leucorhoa] chapmani*

L 17.5–19.5 cm, WS 44–48 cm, tail 69–82 mm (fork 14–23 mm)

Figures 13, 180, 182, S12.1–S12.6

Identification Summary Pacific; mainly Mexico and southward, offshore. A medium-sized all-dark storm-petrel (some birds have pale on the rump sides). Shape and flight manner like nominate Leach's Storm-Petrel but averages smaller overall.

The smaller and generally dark-rumped s-breeding subspecies of Leach's Storm-Petrel is treated here in a separate account, as Chapman's Storm-Petrel (*O. [l.] chapmani*). These all-dark birds present different identification challenges to those of the larger and white-rumped n-breeding populations of Leach's.

S12.1. Variation in rump pattern among Chapman's [Leach's] Storm-Petrels collected at the Coronado and San Benito Islands, Baja California, Mexico (SDNHM specimens). From left to right scoring 3, 4, 4.5, 5, and 5 (see Fig 173, p. XX); scores of 4–5 are typical of Chapman's SNGH.

Taxonomy See under Leach's Storm-Petrel, plus introduction to Leach's Storm-Petrel complex (pp. 381–382).

Names *Oceanodroma* means "ocean runner," *chapmani* and the English name commemorate American ornithologist Frank Chapman (1864–1945).

Status and Distribution Least Concern. Endemic breeder. Breeds (mainly May–Oct) on islands off the Pacific coast of Baja California, ranges at sea mainly off Middle America and s California. Small numbers of dark-rumped "Leach's" (taxon or taxa unclear) occur n to the Farallon Islands, where up to 6% of birds are dark-rumped and may breed (Ainley 1983).

Pacific. Fairly common to very common but local breeder (May–Oct) from Coronado Islands south to San Benito Islands, Baja California, Mexico; taxonomic status of birds breeding on Alijos Rocks (Everett & Pitman 1996) and California Channel Islands unclear. Common off Pacific coast of Baja California and s California in summer (mainly Apr–Oct), ranging in smaller numbers n to cen California but generally rare n of Point Conception. Fairly common to common nonbreeding visitor s off Middle America (Oct–Apr, with smaller numbers of nonbreeders May–Sep), generally nearer the continental slope than white-rumped northern Leach's, and ranging rarely s to around 10˚S (Crossin 1974, Pitman 1986, Spear & Ainley 2007). Status at sea confounded by possible confusion with dark

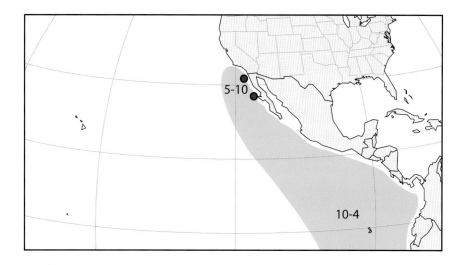

morph Townsend's Storm-Petrel. A dark-rumped "Leach's Storm-Petrel" at the Salton Sea (Sep 1976) was thought to be Chapman's.

FIELD IDENTIFICATION

Similar Species Note medium size with bluntly pointed wings and forked tail, bounding flight with high upstroke, and all-dark plumage (little or no pale on rump). Can be confused with Ashy, Townsend's, Black, and even Least storm-petrels.

Ashy Storm-Petrel (California Current region) a bird of generally cooler waters but occurs alongside Chapman's off s California where the two species can at times be difficult to distinguish under at-sea conditions. Ashy is less rangy overall than Chapman's with slightly higher wingloading, proportionately shorter wings, a longer, more deeply forked tail, and proportionately larger, puffier head. Ashy grayer overall (browner when worn) with silvery underwing panel, and more even-width pale upperwing band that does not usually reach wing bend; often has mostly pale gray rump, rather than dusky brown or mixed with whitish on Chapman's. Ashy's flight generally more direct and slightly fluttery with shorter glides and quicker wingbeats. However, Chapman's flapping into the wind can strongly suggest Ashy, but still has stronger, more clipped, and less fluttery wingbeats, shorter tail (beware molting birds), and relatively smaller head; Chapman's glides on more strongly arched wings.

Dark morph *Townsend's Storm-Petrel* (breeds Guadalupe Island in summer) averages smaller and shorter tailed with a slightly shallower tail fork (11–17 mm vs. 14–23 mm), but beware that Chapman's are often molting tail feathers in fall and thus appear short-tailed. Townsend's slightly darker overall, often with duller and slightly shorter upperwing band. Flight of Townsend's tends to be a little quicker and more direct than Chapman's, but critical study needed of at-sea differences.

Black Storm-Petrel (mainly shelf and shelf break waters) appreciably larger (obvious in direct comparison) with longer and bigger wings, longer neck, relatively smaller and more rounded head, appreciably thicker bill, and long legs that often dangle. Black's plumage darker overall and flight powerful but unhurried, with slower, deeper wingbeats and frequent, often prolonged glides, unlike quicker, more bounding flight of Chapman's; at times, though, Black can fly at least briefly in bounding manner much like Chapman's.

Markham's Storm-Petrel (warmer offshore waters) appreciably larger (obvious in direct comparison, but size can be hard to judge on lone birds) with longer wings and longer, more deeply forked tail. Upperparts do not have paler uppertail coverts and often appear slightly paler and browner overall than Chapman's, with more contrasting pale buff upperwing bands and black remiges, but depending on light can look darker overall, similar to Chapman's. Wingbeats more measured, often shallower and looser, without high, jerky upstroke of Chapman's; flight generally fairly low, direct to slightly weaving but without bounding often shown by Chapman's; prolonged glides on arched wings similar in both species.

424

Least Storm-Petrel (inshore waters) smaller and blacker with a shorter, graduated tail, narrower and more rounded wings, and deep, clipped wingbeats. Molting Chapman's might suggest Least but on Chapman's note more angular wings, flight manner, and usually bolder pale upperwing bands; in direct comparison, Least noticeably smaller with faster, more weaving flight and only brief glides.

Habitat and Behavior Offshore waters, usually around or beyond the continental slope (Spear & Ainley 2007). Usually found singly or in small aggregations, at times in loose concentrations associated with Cook's Petrels off cen Baja California. Flight averages less confident, with slightly quicker wingbeats and slightly less creative use of three-dimensional space than northern Leach's Storm-Petrel, such that Chapman's is easier to track with a camera, but still generally a strong flier with fairly clipped wingbeats.

Nocturnal at colonies, which range up to tens or hundreds of thousands on the San Benito Islands, nesting in burrows dug in soil and in rock crevices. Voice much like northern Leach's Storm-Petrel (p. 388), and distinct from Black and Least storm-petrels, which nest alongside Chapman's on San Benito Islands.

Description Medium-sized with fairly long and pointed wings usually crooked at wrist; tail medium length and moderately forked. Toes do not project beyond tail in flight. Fairly low wing-loading.

Ages similar but juveniles fresh in fall (Sep–Nov) when older birds are worn or molting, and first-summer birds (May–Jul) are worn or in wing molt when adults are fresh. Dark sooty brown overall, often appearing black at any distance and browner when worn; head and back have a slaty blue-gray sheen when fresh; narrow whitish edgings to subscapulars in fresh plumage. Flight feathers blacker and upperwings with paler, brownish gray to pale buff ulnar band broadest near carpal joint and usually extending to wing bend; ulnar band can be fairly dull in fresh plumage but often quite bright when faded; exposed bases of primary shafts sometimes whitish (rarely visible at sea).

Uppertail coverts typically gray-brown overall, often with slightly paler or whitish patches on the sides, and often appearing slightly paler in contrast to blacker tail (at any distance, upperparts usually appear all-dark). On the Coronado Islands, rump scores = 3–5 (mainly 4–5); on the San Benito Islands, 4–5 (mainly 5) (see Fig 173; p.383 Ainley 1980). Bill, legs, and feet black.

Molt Given a summer-breeding schedule, molt timing probably similar to n-breeding Leach's Storm-Petrel, but study needed. Adult wing molt probably starts Aug/Oct and completes Feb/Apr, perhaps with suspension for fall migration; tail molt Jul–Sep, perhaps completed before departure from breeding areas. PB2 wing molt probably starts May/Jul, ends Oct/Dec; tail mainly Jun–Oct.

S12.2. Presumed Chapman's [Leach's] Storm-Petrel. Many birds have contrasting whitish ovals at rump sides; also note bold pale upperwing bands, and, relative to Ashy, relatively short tail with shallower fork. SNGH. Off San Diego, California, 25 Jul 2009.

S12.3. Presumed Chapman's [Leach's] Storm-Petrel. Relative to Ashy Storm-Petrel note extensive pale upperwing bands, relatively short tail with shallower, slightly lobed fork, relatively small head but heavier bill, brown-toned rump. SNGH. Off Santa Barbara, California, 21 Jul 2007.

S12.4. Presumed Chapman's [Leach's] Storm-Petrel. Many birds in fall off southern California are in tail molt, making the tail appear both short (inviting confusion with Townsend's Storm-Petrel) and squared. SNGH. Off Santa Barbara, California, 31 Jul 2010.

S12.5. Typical view of presumed Chapman's [Leach's] Storm-Petrel. Compared to Ashy, note larger wing area and relatively short, notched tail. Generally, rump/tail projection on Chapman's about equal to wing width at body, whereas on Ashy it is longer than width of relatively narrower wings. Also note extensive pale upperwing bands. SNGH. Off San Diego, California, 20 Jul 2008.

S12.6. Presumed Chapman's [Leach's] Storm-Petrel. Relative to Ashy Storm-Petrel note larger wing area, shorter and less deeply forked tail, smaller head. Many Chapman's off southern California have some whitish on lateral tail coverts, like this individual. SNGH. Off San Diego, California, 20 Jul 2008.

S13. MARKHAM'S STORM-PETREL *Oceanodroma markhami*

L 21–23 cm, WS 49–54 cm, tail 87–98 mm (fork 27–37 mm)
Figures 185, 187, S13.1–S13.10

Identification Summary Pacific. A large all-dark storm-petrel of warm offshore waters. Wings long, pointed, and slightly crooked at wrist, tail long and deeply forked. Flight buoyant with easy wingbeats and fairly prolonged sailing glides on slightly arched wings.

Taxonomy Monotypic.

Names *Oceanodroma* means "ocean runner," *markhami* and the English name commemorate British admiral Albert Markham (1841–1918), who collected the type specimen of this species off Peru.

Status and Distribution Data Deficient. Humboldt Current endemic: breeds (mainly Jun/Jul–Nov/Dec) in deserts of Peru and n Chile (J. Jahncke & C. Pickens, unpubl. data, Johnson 1965, Murphy 1936, Spear & Ainley 2007), ranges n to Middle America.

   Pacific. Uncommon to rare (but probably overlooked) nonbreeding visitor (late Apr–Oct, at least) over warmer offshore waters n at least to around 17°N (pers. obs., M. P. Force, pers. comm.). Unsubstantiated reports off Baja California (Crossin 1974) are likely in error, and one was reported (late Jul 1991) about 540 km off s California (Pyle 1993).

FIELD IDENTIFICATION

Similar Species Although Markham's is more similar in size to Black Storm-Petrel, it is more similar in coloration and flight manner to Chapman's [Leach's] Storm-Petrel. In particular, note Markham's deeply forked tail, relatively brown plumage, and contrasting pale upperwing bands. Also see Ashy, Swinhoe's, and Tristram's storm-petrels, not known to overlap in range.

   Black Storm-Petrel (inshore waters) blacker overall with heavier body, shorter and less deeply forked tail, longer neck, and smaller, rounded head with shorter, thicker bill, and longer legs (which often dangle visibly). Usually flies with strong deep wingbeats and languid glides different from the typical flight of Markham's. Upperwing bands of Black usually duller and fade out before wing bend, and upperwing does not show strong tricolored pattern (brown coverts, creamy upperwing bands, blackish primaries) often apparent on Markham's. In hand, tarsus of Black 29–34 mm (23–26 mm on Markham's).

   Chapman's [Leach's] Storm-Petrel (widespread in range of Markham's) smaller (Markham's looks about one-third larger in direct comparison, but size hard to judge on lone birds) and shorter winged with shorter, less deeply forked tail. Chapman's often has slightly paler uppertail coverts, which contrast with black tail. Chapman's often flies in a somewhat bounding manner, with deeper and slightly jerkier wingbeats most pronounced on the upstroke, vs. shallower and slightly floppier wingbeats on Markham's; but flight manner of both species can be similar depending on wind conditions and behavior, and both species glide on slightly arched wings.

   Bulwer's Petrel (tropical waters) larger with long tapered tail, overall blacker plumage with duller upperwing bands, and quicker, lower, and more buoyant weaving flight.

Habitat and Behavior Pelagic over warm offshore waters, unlikely to be seen from shore in the region. Singly or in small groups, which may associate loosely with other storm-petrels; does not habitually follow ships but sometimes stays in the wake of larger vessels for some minutes. Flight generally fairly low, direct to slightly weaving, with buoyant wingbeats and glides, the wings held slightly arched. In calm to light or moderate winds, transiting flight unhurried with short bursts of fairly shallow, flicking wingbeats interspersed with low-wavelength glides on slightly arched wings; foraging birds can switch to floppy, loose, and fairly deep wingbeats interspersed with short glides and abrupt swoops up over food. In calm conditions, also flies with steady flapping up to 3 m above the sea surface. In moderate to strong winds, weaves across the wind buoyantly with bursts of loose, fairly deep, and quick flaps interspersed with

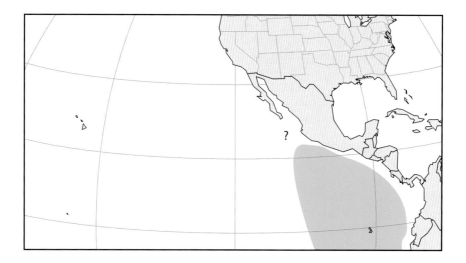

banking and often prolonged, low-wavelength glides, thus recalling Chapman's [Leach's] Storm-Petrel; with the wind astern, sometimes flies with more prolonged bouts of fairly quick flaps and short glides, at other times alternates a few quick flaps with long shearing glides. Forages into the wind with steady wingbeats, occasional pauses, and short glides, swooping up to drop on food and patter briefly, the wings raised in a *V* and bowed slightly at the wrist; also picks at food while on the water, with wings raised and fluttered.

Description A large but fairly light-bodied storm-petrel with long, bluntly pointed wings crooked at wrist; tail long and deeply forked. Toes do not project beyond tail in flight. Fairly low wing-loading.

Ages similar. Dark sooty brown overall, often appearing black at any distance and browner overall when worn and faded; head and back with slaty-gray sheen strongest in fresh plumage; uppertail coverts concolorous with back but distal uppertail coverts can be slightly paler, contrasting slightly with blackish tail; narrow whitish edgings to subscapulars in fresh plumage. Remiges blackish, often with creamy-white exposed bases of the primary shafts; upperwings with pale dusky gray (fresh, when can show fine pale ashy-gray to gray-brown tips to greater coverts) to pale buff (faded) upperwing band, which typically extends to or near wing bend where it is broadest. Upperparts often look tricolored, with brown back and coverts, broad pale buff ulnar bands, and blackish remiges. Pale upperwing bands usually bold on both fresh and molting (worn) birds, typically quite bright and contrasting, and can even look like "headlights" when viewed head-on from slightly above; at other times, with high-angle sun, contrast is reduced overall and bands appear relatively dull. Bill, legs, and feet black.

Molt Based on breeding cycle and at-sea observations, adult wing molt probably starts Dec–Jan, completes Apr–May. PB2 can be expected Sep–Mar (study needed). In late Apr 1995, of 100 birds between 14˚S and 10˚N, 52 (possibly adults) had from p5 to p9 growing; 48 showed no molt and looked fresh (presumed juveniles and perhaps birds with PB2 recently completed); hundreds in late Jul–early Nov (1995–2009) showed no wing molt (pers. obs.).

S13.1. A classic Markham's Storm-Petrel with deeply forked tail, bold pale upperwing bands, concolorous rump and back, white primary flashes, steely gray head with relatively long bill; relatively short outermost primary contributes to bluntly pointed wingtip. SNGH. Tarapacá, Chile, 23 Oct 2009.

S13.2. White primary flashes of Markham's Storm-Petrel are variable, and sometimes absent as here. Otherwise, note same features as S13.1. SNGH. Tarapacá, Chile, 23 Oct 2009.

S13.3. Often considered similar to Black Storm-Petrel, Markham's is actually more similar to smaller Chapman's [Leach's] Storm-Petrel. Relative to Black, note *Oceanodroma* structure of Markham's, paler plumage tones, bold pale upperwing bands, small feet, steely-gray head, long bill. Relative to Chapman's, note very deep tail fork, concolorous rump and back, long bill. SNGH. Tarapacá, Chile, 23 Oct 2009.

S13.4. As with all storm-petrels, lighting affects perception of plumage tones and contrasts. The pale upperwing bands on this Markham's Storm-Petrel are muted here, as are any whitish primary flashes. Note the long, deeply forked tail, concolorous rump and back, and long bill. SNGH. Tarapacá, Chile, 23 Oct 2009.

S13.5. Plumage tones of Markham's Storm-Petrel appear much blacker in overcast conditions; note deeply forked tail, concolorous back and rump, long bill. CC. Arequipa, Peru, 8 Nov 2005.

S13.6. Markham's Storm-Petrel. In this image, distinguished from smaller Chapman's Storm-Petrel by longer tail, even brown tones to back, rump, and tail, and big long bill. Relative to smaller Swinhoe's Storm-Petrel, perhaps best distinguished in this image by big long bill. SNGH. Tarapacá, Chile, 23 Oct 2009.

S13.7. Markham's Storm-Petrel. Note bold pale upperwing band, plumage tones, long bill, deeply forked tail. CC. Arequipa, Peru, 9 Nov 2005.

S13.8. Markham's Storm-Petrel. Typical gliding posture in light winds, with wings slightly cupped. Even at this angle long bill is apparent; also note even brown plumage tones, bold pale upperwing bands. SNGH. Tarapacá, Chile, 23 Oct 2009.

S13.9. Very long wings and tail of Markham's Storm-Petrel on the water are often held together in a point. Relative to Black Storm-Petrel (S9.10), Markham's appears smaller bodied and bigger headed, with an obviously longer bill. SNGH. Tarapacá, Chile, 23 Oct 2009.

S13.10. Markham's Storm-Petrel (front) and two Elliot's Storm-Petrels (behind). Note fairly large, grayish head and long bill of Markham's. Elliot's differs from sitting Wilson's Storm-Petrel in having less white on lateral tail coverts. SNGH. Tarapacá, Chile, 23 Oct 2009.

S14. TRISTRAM'S STORM-PETREL *Oceanodroma tristrami*
L 24.5–27 cm, WS 52–57 cm, tail 100–110 mm (fork 32–40 mm)
Figures S14.1–S14.7

Identification Summary Pacific. Exceptional or very rare visitor from w subtropical Pacific. A very large, all-dark storm-petrel with a deeply forked tail, bold pale upperwing bands, and a variably paler gray upper rump patch. Flight often fairly direct with relatively shallow wingbeats and short glides, tending to a more bounding flight with prolonged wheeling glides in windy conditions.

Taxonomy Monotypic.

Names *Oceanodroma* means "ocean runner," *tristrami* and the English name commemorate Henry Tristram (1822–1906), an English naturalist.

Status and Distribution Near Threatened. Breeds (Dec–May) in nw Hawaiian Islands and off Japan, ranges in w subtropical and temperate Pacific.

    Pacific. Exceptional or very rare: one bird mist-netted (Apr 2006) on Southeast Farallon Island, California, and one seen at sea off s California (Jul 2007) (Warzybok et al. 2009).

FIELD IDENTIFICATION

Similar Species Very large size of Tristram's (appreciably larger than Black Storm-Petrel) likely to draw attention, especially if seen with other storm-petrels; also note deeply forked tail, bold pale upperwing bands, paler gray rump patch (variable and often hard to see). Also cf. much smaller Ashy and Chapman's [Leach's] storm-petrels.

    Black Storm-Petrel smaller and blacker with a longer neck, smaller head, relatively thicker bill, shorter and less deeply forked tail, and relatively long legs that often dangle. Black typically flies with strong, deep wingbeats unlike shallower wingbeats of Tristram's.

    Markham's Storm-Petrel (offshore tropical Pacific) smaller and more lightly built, with a more buoyant flight. Markham's often appears browner above, lacks the paler grayish upper rump patch of Tristram's, and often has whitish flashes on the primary-shaft bases.

    Matsudaira's Storm-Petrel (*O. matsudairae*; unrecorded in e Pacific; S14a.1–S14a.2) also very large and all-dark (L 24–26.5 cm, WS 53–56 cm, tail 98–107 mm [fork 28–37 mm]), and should be considered if a suspected Tristram's is seen. Matsudaira's has lighter build and smaller head, tail fork not as deep (and tail often held fairly closed so fork is inconspicuous), wings often less crooked, and flight more buoyant overall, with prolonged glides on slightly arched wings in light to moderate winds. Matsudaira's plumage darker and browner overall with duller upperwing bands but conspicuous white flashes on primary-shaft bases. In the w Pacific, Matsudaira's often follows ships (much like Black Storm-Petrel), but Tristram's rarely follows ships for long, if at all (pers. obs.).

    Bulwer's Petrel (tropical waters) larger with long tapered tail, overall blacker plumage with duller upperwing bands, and quicker, lower, and more buoyant weaving flight.

Habitat and Behavior Pelagic, unlikely to be seen from shore but one California record involved a bird visiting an island at night. Might associate with other storm-petrels, or could be found singly; does not habitually follow ships. Flight fairly heavy bodied, not buoyant, recalling a giant Fork-tailed Storm-Petrel, another largely resident, heavy-bodied species of the windy North Pacific.

    Into and across light to moderate winds, flight fairly direct and usually low, with fairly quick but measured stiff wingbeats and short glides; across moderate to strong winds, flies with fairly prolonged wheeling or slightly bounding glides on slightly crooked and arched wings, interspersed with bursts of fairly quick wingbeats, at times wheeling to 10 m or more above the sea like a miniature gadfly petrel. Foraging birds often patter briefly and alight on the sea to pick at food, the wings held slightly raised.

Description A very large, heavy-bodied storm-petrel with fairly long wings crooked at wrist; tail long and deeply forked. Toes do not project beyond tail in flight. High wing-loading.

    Ages similar but juveniles fresh in May–Aug when older ages worn or molting. Dark sooty brown overall, often appearing black at any distance, with a strong blue-gray sheen to head and back in fresh plumage; narrow whitish edgings to subscapulars in fresh plumage. Broad paler band on basal uppertail coverts varies from dull ashy brownish gray (difficult to see other than at close range), to fairly distinct pale grayish. Remiges blackish, and upperwings with a distinct pale brownish-gray to ashy gray-brown ulnar band reaching to or near wing bend; upperwing band usually obvious but duller in fresh plumage, paler and buffier when worn; faded bases of upper primary shafts can be pale grayish (rarely visible at sea), but not strikingly whitish. Bill, legs, and feet black.

Molt Based on breeding cycle, adult wing molt mainly May/Jun–Oct/Nov; PB2 can be expected Mar–Sep (study needed).

S14.1. Tristram's Storm-Petrel. The largest and heaviest-bodied dark-rumped storm-petrel, with bold pale upperwing bands, long deeply forked tail, and variably paler rump patch. SNGH. Western Pacific, 26°N 142°E, 22 Apr 2007.

S14a.1. Unrecorded in the region, Matsudaira's Storm-Petrel should be considered if confronted with a very large dark storm-petrel out of range. More lightly built than Tristram's, with darker and sootier plumage overall, duller upperwing bands, bold white primary flashes, concolorous rump and back; long tail often held more closed than Tristram's. SNGH. Western Pacific, 26°N 142°E, 22 Apr 2007.

S14.2. Tristram's Storm-Petrel in worn plumage. Pale upperwing bands vary in prominence with lighting and wear, as does the variable rump patch (cf. S14.1). SNGH. Western Pacific, 26°N 142°E, 22 Apr 2007.

S14.3. Tristram's Storm-Petrel. Note stout body, large head, and long tail. SNGH. Bonin Islands, Japan, 30 Apr 2008.

S14.4. Tristram's Storm-Petrel. Note stocky, chesty body, and very deeply forked tail. SNGH. Western Pacific, 26°N 142°E, 22 Apr 2007.

S14.5. Tristram's Storm-Petrel. From below note bulky body and long, very deeply forked tail. SNGH. Bonin Islands, Japan, 30 Apr 2008.

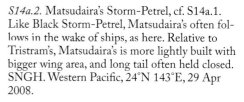

S14a.2. Matsudaira's Storm-Petrel, cf. S14a.1. Like Black Storm-Petrel, Matsudaira's often follows in the wake of ships, as here. Relative to Tristram's, Matsudaira's is more lightly built with bigger wing area, and long tail often held closed. SNGH. Western Pacific, 24°N 143°E, 29 Apr 2008.

S14.6. Tristram's Storm-Petrel. Note stocky shape and fairly large head with stout bill. SNGH. Bonin Islands, Japan, 30 Apr 2008.

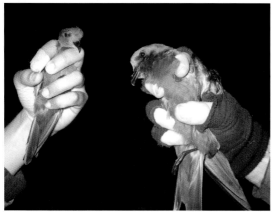

S14.7. Tristram's Storm-Petrel (right) and Ashy Storm-Petrel (left). Mist-netted at night on Southeast Farallon Island, California, this Tristram's constituted the first North American record. Note its massive bulk (dwarfing Ashy), steely gray head, stout bill. PW. 22 Apr 2006.

434

S15. SWINHOE'S STORM-PETREL *Oceanodroma monorhis*

L 18–20 cm, WS 45–50 cm, tail 74–83 cm (fork 14–22 mm)
Figures 145, 183, S15.1–S15.5

Identification Summary Atlantic (and Pacific?). Very rare visitor to Gulf Stream waters off East Coast; perhaps exceptional off se Alaska. A medium-large, all-dark storm-petrel of warmer waters. Wings long and bluntly pointed, slightly crooked at wrist, tail fairly long and forked. Flight loping and unhurried, with fairly deep wingbeats and buoyant glides. Rump not paler than back, and upperwings have white shafts to exposed bases of outer primaries, visible at closer range.

Taxonomy Monotypic. Sometimes considered a subspecies of Leach's Storm-Petrel (Bretagnolle et al. 1991).

Names *Oceanodroma* means "ocean runner," *monorhis* refers to the single nostril tube atop the bill. The English name commemorates Robert Swinhoe (1836–1877), a British diplomat and naturalist who in 1866 collected the type specimen of this species in China.

Status and Distribution Least Concern. Breeds (mainly May–Dec) on islands in s Sea of Japan and Yellow Sea, ranges to n Indian Ocean. Recently found (since 1983) in North Atlantic (Bretagnolle et al. 1991, James & Robertson 1985, Robb et al. 2008), perhaps an invasion of misplaced migrants from the Indian Ocean or perhaps a previously overlooked breeding population.

Atlantic. Very rare nonbreeding visitor (Jun–Aug) to Gulf Stream waters off North Carolina, with four records, all since 1993 (Brinkley 1995, O'Brien et al. 1999, NAB 63:408, 2009, Patteson et al. 2009b).

Pacific. A dark-rumped, fork-tailed storm-petrel considered to be Swinhoe's was video-taped off se Alaska, 5 Aug 2003 (S. and L. Terrill, pers. comm.); record considered unsubstantiated by Alaska Checklist Committee (D. D. Gibson, pers. comm.).

FIELD IDENTIFICATION

Similar Species Swinhoe's is similar in size to Leach's Storm-Petrel, although shape and flight manner can suggest a larger storm-petrel.

Atlantic. *Leach's Storm-Petrel.* Solidly dark-rumped Leach's is unknown from Atlantic (Flood 2009), but some birds have so little whitish on lateral tail coverts that they can appear dark-rumped under at-sea conditions. Leach's typically shows some pale on uppertail coverts (which contrast with darker back and black tail) and lacks distinct white bases to exposed outer primary shafts. Leach's has more pointed wings and more bounding, erratic flight with slightly quicker wingbeats that rise higher above body plane. Leach's further differs in its relatively slender bill, bolder pale upperwing bands that tend to be wider at the carpal joint, and in having a more double-rounded or lobed shape to the tail fork (Howell & Patteson 2008c).

Pacific. Potential confusion species of about the same size are Chapman's [Leach's] and Ashy storm-petrels (neither of which occurs n to Gulf of Alaska). Black, Markham's, and extralimital Tristram's and Matsudaira's storm-petrels are all markedly larger than Swinhoe's, although Markham's and especially Matsudaira's are similar in plumage.

Chapman's [Leach's] Storm-Petrel (mainly Mexico south) similar in size, but Swinhoe's looks larger because of its broader wings and slower, deeper wingbeats and loping flight. Chapman's usually has slightly paler gray uppertail coverts, and bases of outer primaries lack distinct white shafts. Flight quicker and more erratic than Swinhoe's, with more-clipped wingbeats and stronger upstroke.

Ashy Storm-Petrel (mainly California) slightly smaller with proportionately longer, more deeply forked tail. Ashy grayer overall and uppertail coverts often have some pale gray, especially at the sides; bases of outer primaries lack distinct white shafts; and underwings have a broad silvery central panel. Flight quicker and more fluttery than Swinhoe's, with short glides.

Markham's Storm-Petrel (offshore tropical Pacific) distinctly larger with a longer, more deeply forked tail, squarer head, and longer bill. Markham's often shows whitish bases to outer primary shafts but these typically do not form such a bold, jaeger-like panel as on Swinhoe's. Markham's has a more buoyant flight with fairly shallow wingbeats and frequent glides on slightly arched wings.

Matsudaira's Storm-Petrel (w North Pacific, unrecorded in region) much larger and rangier (L 24–26.5 cm, WS 53–56 cm, tail 98–107 mm [fork 28–37 mm]) but very similar in plumage to Swinhoe's. Matsudaira's has a slightly squarer, proportionately smaller head (accentuated by bigger wings) and longer bill, and a longer, narrower-looking tail that is usually held closed. It has generally duller upperwing bands and an easy, measured flight with fairly shallow wingbeats and prolonged glides.

Habitat and Behavior Pelagic, unlikely to be seen from shore. Not well known at sea. Single birds associate readily with other storm-petrels; the North Carolina birds were with Wilson's, Leach's, and Grant's storm-petrels, the Alaska bird with Fork-tailed Storm-Petrels at a slick.

In light to moderate winds, flight generally unhurried, fairly direct to slightly weaving. Wingbeats loping but not especially deep, interspersed with sailing glides on slightly bowed wings. More of the wingbeat arc appears to fall below the body plane than above it, and the slightly floppy downstroke can recall Grant's [Band-rumped] Storm-

Petrel in calm conditions. Flight manner can bring to mind a Black Tern, but Swinhoe's wingbeats are stiffer and shallower than the tern's. Tail often held mostly closed in direct flight but spread in maneuvers and while pattering. Patters to pick at the sea surface with wings raised, legs dangling.

Description Medium-sized with long, bluntly pointed wings usually somewhat crooked at wrist; tail fairly long and forked. Toes do not project beyond tail in flight. Moderate wing-loading?

Ages similar. Dark sooty brown overall, often appearing black at any distance and browner overall when worn and faded or when viewed in strong sunlight; head and upperparts with a slaty-gray sheen in fresh plumage; uppertail coverts not contrastingly paler; narrow pale gray edgings to subscapulars in fresh plumage. Flight feathers blackish, with white bases of primary shafts typically forming a jaeger-like crescent visible at moderate range; upperwings with pale dusky gray (fresh, when can show fine whitish tips to greater coverts) to pale buff (worn) ulnar band, which is mostly even in width and does not extend to wing bend. Bill, legs, and feet black.

Molt Undescribed (?). Based on breeding cycle in Pacific, adult wing molt may be Oct/Dec–Apr/May, with PB2 Aug/Sep–Feb/Mar.

S15.1. Swinhoe's Storm-Petrel. Compare brown plumage tones and bold pale-buff upperwing bands with S15.2 of same bird in cloudy conditions. Note white primary flashes (accentuated in bright light), concolorous brown rump and back, forked tail. SNGH. Off Hatteras, North Carolina, 2 Jun 2008.

S15.2. Swinhoe's Storm-Petrel. Compare cold dark plumage tones and muted pale upperwing bands with S15.1 of the same bird taken in sunny conditions. Note white primary flashes, concolorous brown rump and back, forked tail, thick bill. SNGH. Off Hatteras, North Carolina, 2 Jun 2008.

S15.3. Relative to Leach's Storm-Petrel, Swinhoe's often holds its wings straighter, less crooked. Also note fairly angular tail fork, slightly different from lobed fork typical of Leach's. SNGH. Off Hatteras, North Carolina, 2 Jun 2008.

S15.4. Pale upperwing bands of Swinhoe's Storm-Petrel (here with Wilson's Storm-Petrels) tend to be fairly even in width and do not widen nearer the wing bend, as is typical of Leach's. SNGH. Off Hatteras, North Carolina, 2 Jun 2008.

S15.5. Swinhoe's Storm-Petrel is similar in size to Leach's and Grant's [Band-rumped] storm-petrels, which can be appreciated here with Wilson's Storm-Petrel for comparison. SNGH. Off Hatteras, North Carolina, 2 Jun 2008.

Distinctive Storm-Petrels

Four species of storm-petrels recorded in North American waters are distinctive enough that they can be identified fairly readily: Fork-tailed is a North Pacific resident, White-faced is a nonbreeding visitor off the Atlantic Coast, and Hornby's and Black-bellied are vagrants from the s hemisphere to the North Pacific and North Atlantic, respectively.

S16. FORK-TAILED STORM-PETREL *Oceanodroma furcata*

L 20.5–24 cm, WS 43–52 cm, tail 80–94 mm (fork 24–33 mm)
Figures 61, 148, S11.1, S16.1–S16.11

Identification Summary North Pacific, offshore to inshore over cooler waters. A distinctive, medium-sized, and fairly thickset storm-petrel. Smoky blue-gray plumage blends well with the rainy and foggy weather that predominates in this species' range. Note contrasting black underwing coverts, darker upper-wings with pale ulnar band.

S16.1. Gray plumage tones of Fork-tailed Storm-Petrel often blend well with its gray North Pacific habitat. Note contrasting blackish shoulders and lesser underwing coverts. SNGH. Off Bodega Bay, California, 1 Aug 2008.

Taxonomy Two subspecies described, differing in size and color (Grinnell & Test 1939). Somewhat clinal differences correlated to latitude, and many specimens perhaps difficult to assign; breeding populations in Gulf of Alaska not assigned to subspecies but likely *furcata* (Boersma & Silva 2001).

 O. f. furcata breeds from Kurile Islands in nw Pacific through Aleutians to Alaska Peninsula. Averages larger (L 22–24 cm, WS 45–52 cm) and paler, overall silvery blue-gray, often with contrasting whitish undertail coverts.

 O. f. plumbea breeds se Alaska to n California. Averages smaller (L 20.5–22.5 cm, WS 43–49 cm) and darker, overall dusky blue-gray, undertail coverts average paler but often concolorous with underparts.

Names *Oceanodroma* means "ocean runner," *furcata* refers to the forked tail.

Status and Distribution Least Concern. Breeds (Apr–Oct) and ranges in the North Pacific, from Bering Sea s to California and Japan.

 Pacific. Fairly common to very common breeder (Apr/Jun to mid-Jul/Oct; earlier to the s, later to the n) from Aleutians to n Washington, thence uncommon and local (mid-Mar/Apr to mid-Jul/Aug) s to n California (Humboldt Co.; Harris 1974). Fairly common to common (Mar–Oct) at sea in this region, mainly foraging in cooler waters over the continental shelf and, especially, the shelf break; ranges commonly in summer into s Bering Sea (s of 58°N), casually (Jul–Oct) to n Bering Sea. Also ranges rarely

439

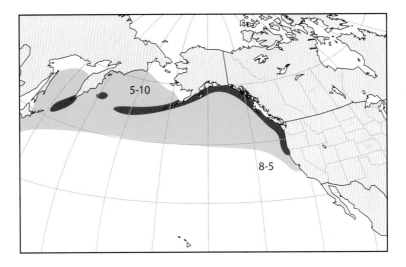

Fork-tailed Storm-Petrel. Ranges farther offshore in winter. Rare and irregular south to southern California.

into channels and tidal convergences of inland marine waters of British Columbia and Washington. Gatherings of 3000–6000 birds off Oregon in Aug 2009 (M. P. Force, pers. comm., NAB 63:144, 2009) parallel occasional fall gatherings off cen California (see below), and may represent nonbreeding birds.

In winter (Sep/Nov–Mar/May) fairly common to common offshore to well offshore over cooler and deeper waters of North Pacific from s and sw Alaska s to n California; n subspecies *furcata* recorded s at least to Washington. Perhaps most frequent from shore off Washington to California during Oct–Dec and Mar–May, and accidental inland in British Columbia (late Sep–early Jan) and California (Apr). Most coastal birds are associated with strong onshore winds, but other inshore incursions (mainly Jun–Nov) may be driven by food shortages (Roberson 2002).

Seasonal status complex at s end of range. Year-round presence off cen California suggests birds there are mainly nonbreeders (Ainley 1976), and largest numbers generally occur in cold-water years. Cordell Bank, Marin Co., is s limit of (irregular) occurrence in any numbers (mainly Aug–Oct), with rafts exceptionally up to 5650 birds (Sep 1999; NAB 54:100, 2000); smaller numbers irregular (year-round) s to vicinity of Monterey Bay, and casual (Sep–Jun, mainly Feb–May) off s California s to San Diego Co, exceptionally to Baja California, Mexico (Nov 2009; NAB 64:158, 2010).

FIELD IDENTIFICATION

Similar Species A distinctive species, perhaps more likely to be confused with nonbreeding Red Phalarope than with other storm-petrels. *Red Phalarope* is white below and has a quicker flight typical of small sandpipers, but it can glide in windy conditions, causing more than a passing resemblance to a storm-petrel. Conversely, high-wheeling Fork-tailed at medium to long range can even be confused, at least for a second or two, with Mottled Petrel or Cook's Petrel.

A brightly sunlit or molting *Ashy Storm-Petrel* might invite confusion with larger Fork-tailed, but Ashy is darker overall and less thickset, with a longer, more deeply forked tail, narrower wings, and a weaker, more fluttery flight. Among rafts of Ashy Storm-Petrels, Fork-tailed often stands out by virtue of its paler coloration and also its larger size and bulkier shape, which may be accentuated by its sitting higher on the water. In silhouette compared to *Leach's Storm-Petrel*, Fork-tailed is heavier bodied with broader, relatively short-looking wings; and note flight manner.

Habitat and Behavior In summer, ranges over cooler shelf and even inshore waters (at least in Aleutians), with concentrations often over the shelf break; summer birds seen well offshore over deeper waters perhaps mainly nonbreeding immatures (as indicated by wing molt timing;

pers. obs.). Usually found singly or in loose aggregations scattered over feeding areas, sometimes in rafts that can number thousands. Follows fishing boats and ships, sometimes joining with gulls, fulmars, and other species scavenging offal. In s of its range, associates readily in rafts with Ashy and other storm-petrels. In winter, favors shelf-break and cooler offshore waters. Storm-blown birds may be seen from land in s parts of range, mainly in late winter and spring.

In calm to light or moderate winds, flight generally low and direct or slightly weaving with fairly quick, stiff, and fluttery wingbeats interspersed with short glides on arched wings. In moderate to strong winds can whip around easily and wheel in arcs, rising to 10 m or higher, alternating bursts of quick stiff wingbeats with buoyant glides on slightly arched wings, banking and sailing like a small petrel. Foraging flight tends to be low and fairly direct, into the wind, with stiff fluttery wingbeats and short glides, stalling to drop and patter briefly, or settle, at prey. Also feeds while swimming, picking food from the surface. When alarmed, such as close to big ships or when flushed off water, flight can be much more erratic, with deeper wingbeats and sweeping arcs.

Nocturnal at colonies, which range from a few pairs to tens of thousands, nesting in burrows dug in soil or in rock crevices. Nesting islands, usually with grass or shrub cover and often wooded, are commonly shared with Leach's Storm-Petrels. Brevity of darkness at high latitude, coupled with diurnal predators and length of season of ice-free productive waters, may set n limit for breeding (Boersma et al. 1980). Calls at breeding islands (in flight and from burrow) are hoarse and screechy, often including slightly accelerating series and distinct from jerky emphatic chuckling of Leach's Storm-Petrel; lacks a churring burrow call. Main calls are a drawn-out, shrill screech followed by one to several (commonly three) shorter, slightly rasping notes, *krreíh kieh-kieh-kieh*; a less scratchy, high screeching *krieh krieh krieh*, given by males; and varied longer series, such as *kreeíh kyi-kyi-kyi-kyi-kyi keihr-kyi*, which are fairly fast-paced, almost with a warbling cadence.

Description Medium-large and heavy bodied with a fairly large head and relatively stout bill (appreciably slimmer on juveniles in fall); wings fairly broad and slightly crooked at wrist; tail medium length and forked. Toes do not project beyond tail in flight.

Ages similar but first-summer birds worn and molting in May–Jul, when older ages fresher or not in wing molt. Plumage smoky blue-gray overall (see Taxonomy), slightly paler below, with whitish throat and black eye patch. Pale-gray ulnar band contrasts with blackish lesser and median coverts, distal scapulars, and outer primaries; white-tipped subscapulars and inner secondaries form contrasting frosty-white trailing edge to innerwing in fresh plumage. Underwings gray with black axillars and lesser and median coverts. Tail gray with darker tips to outer rectrices, whitish outer web to r6. Bill, legs, and feet black.

Molt Adult wing molt starts Jul–Sep, probably completes Dec–Apr, perhaps suspending over winter in late-molting birds; tail molted mainly Jul–Sep in adults (Harris 1974). PB2 wing molt probably starts May–Jun, completes Aug–Oct.

S16.2. Fork-tailed Storm-Petrel does not always complete its prebasic molt. Here, 1 inner secondary on the near wing and 2–3 on the far wing are contrastingly brown and old, probably not renewed in the preceding molt. RLP. Aleutians, Alaska, 23 Jul 2005.

S16.3. In some lights, handsome plumage pattern of Fork-tailed Storm-Petrel can appear strongly contrasting (cf. S16.1). MJI. Aleutians, Alaska, 10 Sep 2006.

S16.4. Fork-tailed Storm-Petrel with outer primary molt. In bright sun, upperparts can appear pearly gray (cf. S16.1–S16.3). SNGH. Off Bodega Bay, California, 1 Aug 2008.

S16.5. In bright light, black underwing coverts of Fork-tailed Storm-Petrel contrast strongly. Note white undertail coverts, typical of northern subspecies *furcata* (cf. S16.6). MJI. Aleutians, Alaska, 9 Sep 2006.

S16.6. Fork-tailed Storm-Petrel. Undertail coverts only slightly paler than belly, as is typical of smaller and slightly darker southern subspecies *plumbea* (cf. S16.5). SNGH. Off Bodega Bay, California, 5 Sep 2009.

S16.7. In foggy conditions, underwing contrast of Fork-tailed Storm-Petrel can be muted. Note obvious tail molt, occurring toward end of (presumed) second prebasic molt. SNGH. Off Bodega Bay, California, 1 Aug 2008.

S16.8. In bright overcast conditions, Fork-tailed Storm-Petrels (such as these two birds) often blend well with the sea surface and can be difficult to detect among flocks of Ashy Storm-Petrel (cf. S16.9). SNGH. Off Bodega Bay, California, 7 Sep 2007.

S16.9. In bright sun, Fork-tailed Storm-Petrels stand out as starkly silvery among flocks of Ashy Storm-Petrel (cf. S16.8); also note Black Storm-Petrel (upper left). SNGH. Off Monterey, California, 21 Sep 2007.

S16.10. As well as being obviously paler than these Ashy Storm-Petrels, Fork-tailed Storm-Petrel (front right) is larger and bulkier. SNGH. Off Monterey, California, 14 Sep 2008.

S16.11. In thick fog, differences in plumage tones between Fork-tailed and Ashy storm-petrels are reduced (cf. S16.10). As well as larger bulk and paler overall plumage, note Fork-tailed's contrasting dark shoulder bar. SNGH. Off Bodega Bay, California, 1 Aug 2008.

S17. WHITE-FACED STORM-PETREL *Pelagodroma marina*

L 18.5–21 cm, WS 38–45 cm, tail 70–83 mm (fork 3–14 mm)
Figures 38–39, S17.1–S17.6

Identification Summary Atlantic (rare) and Pacific (casual). This medium-sized and striking storm-petrel is a sought-after late-summer visitor to waters off the ne U.S. Brownish gray above, white below, with black mask in white face. Flight low with much kicking off the water and prolonged, sailing glides. Wings fairly broad and paddle-shaped, feet project well beyond tail tip.

S17.1. A typical view of White-faced Storm-Petrel is of a bird kicking and sailing low over the water, where it may even be mistaken for a flyingfish, and vice versa. SNGH. Off Hatteras, North Carolina, 28 Jul 2007.

Taxonomy Six taxa recognized, differing slightly in size, depth of tail fork, rump coloration, and amount of white in face (Bourne 1953, Imber 1984, Murphy & Irving 1951). Critical study may reveal that White-faced Storm-Petrel comprises more than one species. In general, southern taxa (*maoriana, marina*) have longer, cleft tails and shorter tarsi, whereas subtropical taxa (*eadesi, hypoleuca, dulciae*) have shorter, notched tails and longer tarsi.

P. m. eadesi breeds (Jan–Jul) on Cape Verde Islands, ranges (Jul–Oct) to w Atlantic (L 18.5–21 cm, WS 40–45 cm); white of forecrown and face more extensive.

P. m. hypoleuca breeds (Mar–Sep) on Selvagens, may range to w Atlantic. Size similar to *eadesi* but bill averages shorter (16–19 mm vs. 18–20.5 mm;

Bourne 1953); white of forecrown and face less extensive.

P. m. maoriana breeds (Nov–Feb) New Zealand, ranges (Apr–Sep) to e tropical Pacific (L 19–20.5 cm, WS 38–42 cm). Relative to North Atlantic subspecies, shorter winged and longer tailed, with shorter bill (14.6–16.7 mm) and legs (38–43 mm vs. 42–48 mm in North Atlantic taxa), deeper tail fork (9–14 mm vs. 3–8 mm, in adults).

Names *Pelagodroma* means "sea running," *marina* refers to the marine realm. Sometimes known as White-faced Petrel or Frigate Petrel.

Status and Distribution Least Concern. Breeds (Jan–Sep) in North Atlantic on Selvagens and Cape Verde Islands, and (Nov–Feb) in s oceans

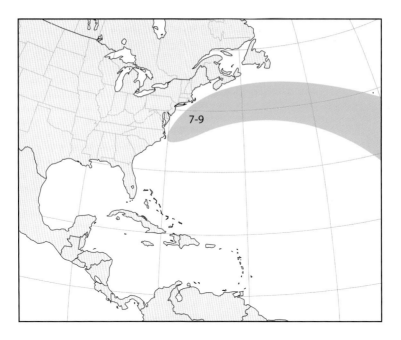

7-9

in South Atlantic and on islands off Australia and New Zealand. Ranges at sea into Indian Ocean, e tropical Pacific, and w Atlantic.

Atlantic. *P. m. eadesi* is a low-density, nonbreeding visitor (late Jul–early Oct, rarely from early Jul) to offshore waters from New England s to North Carolina, possibly n to waters s of Sable Island, Nova Scotia (Buckley 1997), mainly inshore of the Gulf Stream and over submarine canyons. A report from late May (AB 30:318, 1976) is not credible. Exceptional onshore after storms (Aug–early Oct) from North Carolina n to New England. Some North American records may pertain to *P. m. hypoleuca* (but see Watson et al. 1986).

Pacific. *P. m. maoriana* probably a rare nonbreeding visitor (Apr–Sep) to waters far offshore s Central America, with one late May specimen 100 km s of Cocos Island, Costa Rica.

FIELD IDENTIFICATION

Similar Species Size, plumage pattern, and flight manner render White-faced Storm-Petrel essentially unmistakable. In flight it is as likely to be confused with a large flyingfish as with any bird species in its range. On the water, black mask in white face suggests nonbreeding Red and Red-necked phalaropes, which have straight bills and often allow close approach; storm-petrels tend to flush at a distance and have a very different flight manner from that of phalaropes, which have the strong fast flight typical of small sandpipers.

Habitat and Behavior Pelagic, well offshore. Found singly or in sparse aggregations, sometimes in loose association with much more numerous Wilson's Storm-Petrel but also found in areas otherwise seemingly devoid of bird life; does not usually follow ships. Transiting flight in calm to low winds often steady and direct to slightly weaving, but not hurried, with shallow fluttering wingbeats, infrequent sailing glides on fairly level wings, and occasional foot-splashing or kicking off the surface. In light to moderate winds, flight can be more erratic, with fluttery, flicking wingbeats and short weaving glides; rarely seems to travel far without kicking off the sea surface with one or both feet, the kicks followed by a veering glide that adds a jerky, scything rhythm to flight progression. Often flies with legs dangling so that toes do not project beyond tail tip. When foraging, wingbeats often floppier, interspersed with glides as birds make frequent direction changes and kick off the surface; also travels by a bounding progression of two-footed hops and short, sailing glides. Aggregations of birds (an unlikely sight in the region) suggest a field of animated ping-pong balls. Feeds by picking at the surface with legs dangling, the wings fluttered stiffly and raised in a *V*.

Description Medium-sized with broad, slightly paddle-shaped wings pointed at the tips; tail broad and cleft to notched. In direct flight (without legs dangling), toes project well beyond tail tip, perhaps more so in North Atlantic than New Zealand populations.

Adult. Face and underparts white with slaty to slaty-brown crown and blackish eye mask, broad slaty patch at neck sides; white underwing coverts contrast with dark remiges. Back and upperwings gray (fresh) to gray-brown with a narrow pale gray (fresh) to pale brown or buffy white (worn) bar across tips of greater coverts, and blackish remiges; hindneck can fade to a paler (rarely whitish) hindcollar setting off the dark hood; narrow white tips to fresh inner primaries and secondaries lost through wear. Pale gray uppertail coverts contrast with black tail. Bill, legs, and toes black, feet with creamy webs rarely visible at sea.

Juvenile has inner primaries and secondaries more broadly tipped whitish (lost through wear). In *maoriana* at least, tail notch on fledglings shallower (4–7 mm vs. 9–14 mm on adult; BM, USNM specimens).

Molt Adult wing molt of *eadesi* fairly rapid, starts Jul–Aug, ends Sep–Oct. adult wing molt of *maoriana* also fairly rapid, mainly May–Aug. No data on first-cycle molts, but juveniles occur off North America in Aug–Oct.

S17.2. White-faced Storm-Petrel in slightly worn plumage; compare with fresh-plumaged juvenile (Figs 38–39). SNGH. Madeira, eastern Atlantic, 15 May 2010.

S17.3. White-faced Storm-Petrel lacks a bright white rump patch, making it easy to lose against the water. Many birds seen in the region are in wing molt, as here (presumed subspecies *maoriana*). SNGH. Western Pacific, 26ºS 167ºE, 24 Apr 2011

S17.4. Populations of White-faced Storm-Petrel ranging into the eastern Pacific have a distinctly notched tail. SNGH. North Island, New Zealand, 8 Nov 2009.

S17.5. Underparts of White-faced Storm-Petrel are as distinctive and striking as the upperparts. SNGH. North Island, New Zealand, 8 Nov 2009.

S17.6. Large wings and long tail of White-faced Storm-Petrel can bunch up into a big rear end on resting birds; also note striking face pattern. SNGH. North Island, New Zealand, 8 Nov 2009.

S18. HORNBY'S STORM-PETREL *Oceanodroma hornbyi*

L 20–21.5 cm, WS 48–51 cm, tail 78–83 mm (fork 22–32 mm)
Figures S18.1–S18.5

Identification Summary Pacific. This essentially unmistakable large storm-petrel is an exceptional vagrant to California from the Humboldt Current of South America.

Taxonomy Monotypic.

Names *Oceanodroma* means "ocean runner," *hornbyi* and the English name commemorate Phipps Hornby (1785–1867), a British admiral stationed in the Pacific. Sometimes known as Ringed Storm-Petrel.

Status and Distribution Data Deficient. Humboldt Current endemic, ranging offshore from Ecuador to cen Chile but breeding grounds unknown (presumed in Atacama Desert of s Peru and n Chile, with breeding probably during Dec–Jul).

   Pacific. Accidental (Aug 2005) off s California (Pyle et al. 2006), with molt timing suggesting an immature or prebreeding individual. A report of this species off Oregon (May 2007; NAB 61:500, 2008) is not credible.

FIELD IDENTIFICATION

Similar Species This striking species should be unmistakable, but cf. Fig 24 (p. 24).

Habitat and Behavior Pelagic. Might occur in association with other storm-petrels, although the California bird was alone. In light to moderate winds, flight distinct from other storm-petrels and may suggest a hurried Black Tern: mainly steady and fairly direct with fairly deep but quick and fluttery, or slightly floppy, wingbeats and only brief glides (P. Fraser, video); in moderate to strong winds tilts more and flight progression may be less direct, but still only glides or shears for brief periods (R. L. Flood, pers. comm.).

Description A fairly large storm-petrel with fairly long, broad, and pointed wings, and forked tail. Toes do not project beyond tail in flight.

   Ages similar. Slaty-blackish cap and broad slaty chest band offset white lores, lower face, and throat; underparts white with contrasting dark underwings; white often extends up behind cap as a narrow hindcollar. Back ashy gray (browner when worn) with slightly darker rump and paler uppertail coverts; tail blackish gray. Upperwings blackish with contrasting pale-grayish ulnar band (browner when worn) reaching wing bend, where broadest.

Molt Not well known. Adult wing molt can be expected Jun–Dec, PB2 wing molt perhaps Mar–Aug (needs study).

S18.1. Hornby's Storm-Petrel is a large and strikingly patterned storm-petrel endemic to the Humboldt Current region off western South America. CC. Arequipa, Peru, 8 Nov 2005.

S18.2. Hornby's Storm-Petrel in outer primary molt, which is less obvious than mid-primary molt (cf. S18.1). CC. Arequipa, Peru, 8 Nov 2005.

S18.3. Hornby's Storm-Petrel. Uniform-looking upperwings suggest a juvenile, or perhaps an older bird that recently completed wing molt. CC. Arequipa, Peru, 8 Nov 2005.

S18.4. Strikingly patterned underparts of Hornby's Storm-Petrel suggest a gadfly petrel rather than a storm-petrel. CC. Arequipa, Peru, 8 Nov 2005.

S18.5. Hornby's Storm-Petrels are often in later stages of primary molt at this season, suggesting a breeding season concentrated in Jan–Jun (the species' breeding grounds remain unknown). CC. Arequipa, Peru, 8 Nov 2005.

S19. BLACK-BELLIED STORM-PETREL *Fregetta tropica*
L 19.5–21 cm, WS 42–46 cm, tail 72–77 mm
Figures S19.1–S19.9

Identification Summary Very rare visitor to North Atlantic from Southern Ocean. A fairly large, strikingly patterned storm-petrel, suggesting Wilson's Storm-Petrel in shape but larger and broader winged, with a narrower and duller upperwing bar. From below, black hood contrasts with white body, which is split by a variable black median stripe from chest to undertail coverts. Often kicks one-footed off the water and splashes into the surface with a jerky, scything progression.

Taxonomy Monotypic. *Fregetta* storm-petrels on Gough Island, South Atlantic, sometimes treated as white-bellied subspecies (*melanoleuca*) of Black-bellied Storm-Petrel (Marchant & Higgins 1990; see Howell 2010a).

Names *Fregetta* is a diminutive form of frigate-bird, or of frigate, a small ship, perhaps an allusion to this species' oceanic range; *tropica* refers to the tropics where, ironically, this species occurs only rarely.

Status and Distribution Least Concern. Largely circumpolar, nesting locally (Dec–Apr) on subantarctic islands. Ranges n (mainly May–Sep) to subtropical waters, exceptionally to Peru.

Atlantic. Very rare nonbreeding visitor (late May to mid-Aug) to Gulf Stream waters off North Carolina, with four records, all since 2004 (Guris et al. 2004, NAB 60:517, 2007; NAB 61:574, 2008; K. Sutherland & J. B. Patteson, pers. comm. and photos).

FIELD IDENTIFICATION

Similar Species Larger and broader winged than Wilson's Storm-Petrel, with striking white belly and underwing coverts, and frequently eye-catching flight style. Vagrants should be distinguished with care from congeneric White-bellied Storm-Petrel of subtropical South Atlantic (and South Pacific), which is similar to Black-bellied in size, structure, plumage, and flight manner.
White-bellied Storm-Petrel (L 18–22.5 cm, WS 41–49.5 cm; S19a.1–S19a.6; see Appendix B) realistically comprises several species, with perhaps two in South Atlantic (Howell 2010a). Atlantic populations (L 19–22 cm, WS 41–46 cm) appear to have slightly smaller, rounder head and shorter neck than Black-bellied, accentuated by less extensive black hood;

lack black median stripe on white underparts; some (< 5%, n = 100) have uppertail coverts spotted dark gray, very rarely (< 1%, n = 100) wholly dusky grayish (pers. obs.). Some Black-bellied (at least in Pacific) lack black belly stripe and distinguished by more extensive black hood. Toe projection past tail tip has been suggested as a useful field mark in Pacific but overlaps in Atlantic (Howell 2010a). In fresh plumage, White-bellied has broader whitish tips to upperparts, often imparting a frosty look not known in Black-bellied; in worn plumage, however, Atlantic White-bellied identical on upperparts to Black-bellied.

Habitat and Behavior Pelagic, offshore. Likely to be found in association with Wilson's Storm-Petrels, when larger size of Black-bellied should be apparent. Direct flight across wind often low and direct, with fairly quick, stiff, and fluttery wingbeats interspersed with short glides, recalling Wilson's Storm-Petrel but wingbeats a little looser, not so quick and fluttering. At other times flies into or across the wind with eye-catching "kick-sail" progression, alternating bursts of flapping with one-footed kicks off the sea surface and veering glides, at times skipping low over the waves on stiff flattish wings, breaking into bursts of jerky, scything motions, and splashing belly-down into waves. Feeds into the wind by pattering, alternated with kicks and glides, often with its belly resting on the water, the outstretched wings raised in a *V* and fluttered.

Description Fairly large with relatively short arm and broad wings not strongly crooked; squared tail medium length and broad, usually looks rounded when spread. Legs long, toes often project noticeably beyond tail tip in flight (but can be pulled in). A 5-stage scoring system for belly pattern (score 1 = all-white, score 5 = maximum black median stripe) was proposed by Howell (2010a) and is referenced in the photo captions.

Ages similar but juveniles fresh (Apr–Jul) when older ages worn or molting. Head, neck, and upperparts sooty blackish overall, appearing black at any distance, and browner when worn; throat sometimes paler, or mottled whitish; back and rump with narrow whitish tipping when fresh (often hard to see and soon wears off). Flight feathers blackish, and upperwings with narrow, often inconspicuous pale gray (fresh) to pale brownish (faded) line across tips of greater coverts not reaching wing bend; underwings with broad, contrasting white panel on coverts; bases of outer rectrices white. From below, black hood contrasts with white body, which is split by a variable black median stripe from chest to undertail coverts; black stripe can be surprisingly hard to see (often most obvious on birds veering away). Some individuals, at least in sw Pacific, have black belly stripe broken, rarely lacking (Howell 2010a). Clean-cut white rump patch extends conspicuously to lateral undertail coverts, exceptionally marked with a few small dusky spots. Bill, legs, and feet blackish.

Molt Poorly known; wing molt of breeding adults presumably mainly Jun–Oct; timing of PB2 molt likely earlier (study needed).

S19.1. Black-bellied Storm-Petrel in fairly fresh plumage (cf. S19.2). A classic individual (cf. S19.5 of same bird), with relatively plain upperparts (cf. S19.3b), toe projection, pale chin. West-southwest of Campbell Island, New Zealand, 17 Nov 2008.

S19.2. Black-bellied Storm-Petrel (belly score 4.5) in worn plumage (cf. S19.1). Faded upperwing coverts can show as a pale panel, and toes often do not project beyond tail. SNGH. Drake Passage, 59°S 58°W, 26 Mar 2009.

S19.3. Black-bellied Storm-Petrel (belly score 4). Incoming fresh back feathers have paler tips that typically soon wear off (cf. S19.1), and which are narrower and less distinct than fresh-plumaged White-bellied Storm-Petrel (S19a.2). Note how angle of photo affects apparent shape, cf. S19.1–S19.2. SNGH. S Atlantic, 51°S 30°W, 4 Apr 2009.

S19a.1. White-bellied Storm-Petrel (taxon unknown) in worn plumage (belly score 1), with toe projection; not readily separable from Black-bellied in this photo. Taxonomy of South Atlantic populations vexed (Howell 2010a). SNGH. South Atlantic, 45°S 21°W, 6 Apr 2009.

S19.4. Black-bellied Storm-Petrel. Foraging birds often drag their feet in the water. Note how black belly stripe is not apparent at this angle. SNGH. West-southwest of Campbell Island, New Zealand, 17 Nov 2008.

S19a.2. White-bellied Storm-Petrel (likely *segethi*, cf. Spear & Ainley 2007) in heavy molt, with boldly white-tipped fresh back feathers (cf. S19.3). Toes fall well short of tail tip, as is typical of Pacific populations. SW. East Pacific, 13°S 90°W, 11 Oct 2006.

S19a..3. White-bellied Storm-Petrel (likely *segethi*, cf. Spear & Ainley 2007). Evenly fresh plumage on this date indicates juvenile, cf. molting adult in S19a.2. Extensive pale edgings to upperparts not shown by Black-bellied. SW. East Pacific, 13°S 90°W, 11 Oct 2006.

S19.5. Black-bellied Storm-Petrel (belly score 4); here, toes barely project past tail tip (cf. S19.1 of same bird). SNGH. West-southwest of Campbell Island, New Zealand, 17 Nov 2008.

S19.6. Black-bellied Storm-Petrel (belly score 3). Extent of white underwing panel varies (cf. S19.5, 19.7). SNGH. South Atlantic, 51°S 30°W, 4 Apr 2009.

S19.7. Black-bellied Storm-Petrel (belly score 5) with classic toe projection. SNGH. East-northeast of Campbell Island, New Zealand, 19 Nov 2008.

S19.8. Black-bellied Storm-Petrel (belly score 1.5). Very few birds lack a black belly stripe; note extensively black vent (cf. S19a.4); extensive black chest was noted in field. SNGH. West-southwest of Campbell Island, New Zealand, 17 Nov 2008.

S19a.4. White-bellied Storm-Petrel (likely *segethi*, cf. Spear & Ainley 2007). Note reduced black chest area (cf. S19.5–19.7), white projecting into vent, lack of toe projection. SW. East Pacific, 11°S 92°W, 12 Oct 2006.

S19a.5. White-bellied Storm-Petrel (taxon unknown). Note reduced black chest area (cf. S19.5–S19.7) but black in vent, obvious toe projection. Taxonomy of South Atlantic populations vexed (Howell 2010a). SNGH. South Atlantic, 45°S 21°W, 6 Apr 2009.

S19a.6. White-bellied Storm-Petrel (taxon unknown). Note reduced black chest area, lack of toe projection (cf. S19a.5). Taxonomy of South Atlantic populations vexed (Howell 2010a). SNGH. South of Gough Island, South Atlantic, 8 Apr 2009.

S19.9. Black-bellied Storm-Petrel. Resting birds usually show some white on sides; white rump visible on back bird, taking off; note relatively pale back. SNGH. Scotia Sea, 58°S 40°W, 30 Mar 2009.

Adult. A bird in adult plumage, i.e., a plumage whose appearance does not change appreciably with age, other than seasonally. Does not necessarily reflect sexual maturity.

Albino. Lacking in pigmentation; i.e., with completely white plumage and pink eyes, bill, and legs. Patches of white plumage, or even all-white birds with normal bare-part coloration, are better termed leucistic.

Auriculars. Feathers covering the ear region on the side of the head, also known as ear coverts.

B1, B2, etc. Immature basic plumages, i.e., first basic, second basic, etc.

Basal. Toward the base, e.g., basal undertail coverts refers to the visible portion of the undertail coverts nearest to the base of the tail.

Basic plumage. The plumage attained by the prebasic molt (which is complete, or nearly so) and presumed homologous among all birds (see Molts, Plumages, and Aging, pp. 38–45).

Bleaching. Whitening, fading, or becoming colorless as a result of exposure primarily to sunlight.

BM. British Museum of Natural History, Tring, U.K.

CAS. California Academy of Sciences, San Francisco.

Clade. A group of organisms distinguishable from other groups by shared characteristics and thus presumably of common ancestry.

Continental shelf. The relatively shallow seabed bordering large land masses and geologically part of the continental crust.

Cookilaria. Small gadfly petrel in the genus *Pterodroma*, including Cook's and Stejneger's petrels.

Coriolis force. The tendency of a moving object, such as an ocean current or a wind, to drift sideways from its original path because of the Earth's rotation.

Culmen. The dorsal ridge of the maxilla, which curves down distally and may project over the tip of the mandible as a hook.

Culmen base. The base of the bill where it meets the forehead.

Culminicorn. The horny plate covering the upper edge of the bill distal to the nostril tubes, contrastingly colored on some albatrosses.

Cycle. A regularly repeated phenomenon, such as a molt cycle. A basic molt cycle extends from the start of one prebasic molt to the start of the next prebasic molt.

Distal. Toward the tip; e.g., dark distal undertail coverts refers to the visible portion of the undertail coverts farthest from the base of the tail.

Flight feathers. The remiges and rectrices collectively, i.e., the main feathers of the wings and tail; in some literature (as in Britain) used only for the remiges.

Formative plumage. Any first-year plumage (attained by a preformative molt) that lacks a counterpart in the adult plumage cycle (see Molts, Plumages, and Aging, pp. 38–45).

Gadfly petrel. Mainly used for petrels in the genus *Pterodroma*, but also including genus *Pseudobulweria*; derives from their often impulsive and impetuous flight.

Hindcollar. A dark half-collar on the lower hindneck.

Humerals. A group of feathers on the inner wing of long-winged birds (such as albatrosses), associated with the humerus, or inner arm bone.

Immature. A general term for any nonadult plumage, including juvenile.

LACM. Natural History Museum of Los Angeles County, California.

Latericorn. The horny plate covering the side of the maxilla on a tubenose bill.

Leucistic. Milky-colored or white plumage due to deficiency of pigmentation; see albino.

LNS. Macaulay Library of Natural Sounds, Cornell Laboratory of Ornithology, Ithaca, New York.

M pattern. A contrasting dark pattern on the upperwings, formed by dark outer primaries and primary coverts joined to a dark ulnar band, sometimes connected across the rump.

Mandible. The lower half of the bill (also called the lower mandible).

Mandible gape line. On mollymawks, a narrow, brightly colored strip along the base of the cutting edge of the mandible.

Maxilla. The upper half of the bill (also called the upper mandible).

MCZ. Museum of Comparative Zoology, Harvard University, Massachusetts.

Molt. A period of normal and regular growth of feathers (i.e., molting), by which plumages are attained; feather loss is a passive by-product of molting.

Monophyletic. Sharing common ancestry, usually in terms of a group of clearly related species or genera that are distinct from other groups.

Monotypic. Literally, of one type. A monotypic species is one for which no subspecies are recognized, usually indicating that geographic variation is absent or poorly defined.

MVZ. Museum of Vertebrate Zoology, University of California, Berkeley.

NAB. The journal *North American Birds*.

Naricorn. The lateral border to the nostril tubes, contrastingly black on some albatrosses.

NCSM. North Carolina State Museum, Raleigh.

Nominate. Refers to a subspecies bearing the same scientific name as the species; e.g., *Oceanodroma furcata furcata* is the nominate subspecies of Fork-tailed Storm-Petrel, usually written *Oceanodroma f. furcata*.

PB2, PB3, etc. Second, third, and subsequent prebasic (PB) molts, by which second basic, third basic and subsequent basic plumages are attained.

Pelagic. Waters beyond the continental shelf. Also an abbreviation for pelagic trip, a broad term for any birding trip in a boat going offshore in search of seabirds (whether or not it reaches pelagic, vs. shelf, waters).

Polymorphic. Having two or more plumage morphs, such as dark morph and light morph.

Preformative. The molt producing formative plumage, which is a plumage unique to the first cycle.

Primaries. The wing feathers attached to the hand bone, or manus, their bases protected by primary coverts. Tubenoses (like most birds) have 10 visible primaries, numbered from p1 (innermost) to p10 (outermost).

Ramicorn. The horny plate covering the side of the mandible on tubenoses, sometimes contrastingly colored on albatrosses.

Rectrices (singular: rectrix). The main tail feathers, numbering 12 in most tubenoses (6 pairs each side of the central point; r1 is the central rectrix, r6 the outer rectrix).

Remiges (singular: remex). The main flight feathers of the wing, collectively referring to the primaries and secondaries.

Saddlebags. Informal term for white "flank patches" (actually feathers of the femoral tract) behind the wings on flying small shearwaters (and as on Violet-green Swallow).

Scapulars. A group of feathers that originate from a point at the base of the humerus and fan out to protect the base of the wings at rest; they form a seamless join between the wings and body in flight.

SDNHM. San Diego Natural History Museum, California.

Secondaries. The secondary wing feathers attached to the forearm (ulna) bone (numbering 11–38 in tubenoses), their bases protected by secondary coverts (often simply called wing coverts).

Shelf break. Where the continental shelf ends and the seabed starts to slope off into deeper waters, can be steep in places and often an area of productive upwelling.

Subscapulars. The longest underlying scapulars, often tipped whitish on *Oceanodroma* storm-petrels.

Subspecies. A taxonomic category below the level of species, referring to populations that can be distinguished by differences in plumage, measurements, etc., but which are not considered distinct enough to be treated as species.

Sulcus. A groove along the side of the ramicorn, contrastingly colored on sooty albatrosses.

Taxon (plural: taxa). A general taxonomic category, helpful when referring to populations whose taxonomic status is unresolved—e.g., taxa can be subspecies or species.

Tertials. Used here for the inner secondaries, which act as coverts on the closed wing.

Ulnar band. A diagonal band (pale on the upperwings of storm-petrels, dark on the underwings of gadfly petrels) mainly across the secondary coverts, roughly tracing the path of the underlying ulna bone.

Ungues (singular: unguis). The plates (maxillary unguis and mandibular unguis) covering the bill tip of tubenoses, sometimes contrastingly colored.

USNM. National Museum of Natural History, Washington D.C.

Wear (or plumage wear). The abrasion of feather tips and edgings through day-to-day exposure with the elements and such; compounded by weakening due to bleaching.

Wingtip. At rest, the exposed tips of the outer primaries. In flight, the outer portion of the wing (largely formed by the tips of the outer primaries).

GEOGRAPHIC TERMS

Atlantic Canada. Newfoundland and the Maritime Provinces.

East Coast. The Atlantic coast of North America from Newfoundland south to Florida.

Mid-Atlantic coast. From Long Island, New York, south to the Outer Banks, North Carolina.

New England. The six northeastern states of the U.S., from Maine southwest to Connecticut.

Northeast. From the Maritime Provinces south to New York.

South Atlantic Bight. From Atlantic coast of central Florida north to Cape Hatteras, North Carolina.

Southwest. The interior region including southeast California, southern Nevada, southern Utah, Arizona, New Mexico, and west Texas.

West Coast. From southern British Columbia to northern Baja California, Mexico; i.e., the area best known to pelagic birders and corresponding roughly to the productive waters of the California Current.

Tubenoses nest on or in the ground, often on small islands originally free from predators. Thus they are particularly vulnerable to being killed and eaten by introduced mammals, especially rats and cats, but also dogs, pigs, and mongooses. Further problems can be caused by goats, rabbits, and sheep that trample burrows and overgraze vegetation holding together soil. Hunting by humans (for food and feathers) is another factor that has affected, and continues to affect, some species. Add to this pollution, oceanwide food depletion by overfishing, and drowning on baited hooks as incidental catch during fishing operations, and it is safe to state that few if any tubenoses have lived free from deleterious human impact.

About half of the tubenose species worldwide were classified as vulnerable or endangered by Birdlife International (2010a), and two North American endemics are probably extinct, one in Mexico and one in the Caribbean. While there is faint hope these species may yet survive (seabirds, in particular nocturnal breeding species, can go undetected for many years), it is more sobering to list them here as extinct—and hope to be proven wrong.

JAMAICAN PETREL *Pterodroma caribbaea*
L 35–37 cm, WS 93 cm, tail 117–122 mm

See Collar et al. (1992) and Douglas (2000) for details of information summarized here.
This handsome-looking and distinctive species bred commonly through the mid-1800s (apparently Nov/Dec–May/Jun) in the mountains of Jamaica. Last recorded around 1890, its demise has been attributed to introduced mammals. Nonbreeding range unknown, but may have ranged to Gulf Stream waters off e U.S.

Plumage dark sooty brown overall with blacker upperparts and a broad pale buffy-gray band on the uppertail coverts; some birds paler and grayer with a ghosting of a black cap (Howell & Patteson 2008b). Similar in size to Bermuda Petrel (but stouter-billed than that species); flight characters likely similar to medium-sized petrels such as Bermuda and Fea's. Nocturnal at colonies, where bred in burrows in forests above 1600 m.

GUADALUPE STORM-PETREL *Oceanodroma macrodactyla*
L 22.5–24 cm, WS 50.5–52 cm, tail 88–92 mm (fork 27–30 mm)

This large storm-petrel nested (mainly Mar–Aug) on Isla Guadalupe, off the Pacific coast of Baja California, Mexico, but was never recorded away from the island. Common through the late 1800s, its demise was brought about by feral cats; the last record was in 1912 (Davidson 1928).

Blackish brown overall with slaty sheen to head and upperparts; upperwings with broad pale gray (fading to buffy?) ulnar band reaching near or to wing bend. White rump patch tipped black, mottled dark at base, and with a variable dusky median stripe; white extends to lateral tail coverts. Plumage thus suggests an intermediate morph Leach's Storm-Petrel, but appreciably larger than that species, with a longer and more deeply forked tail. Flight characters unknown, but relatively short wings and apparent bulk suggest a sedentary species or short-distance migrant. Nocturnal at colonies, where burrowed in soil under pine-oak and cypress groves that have been decimated by goats.

Tubenoses can be difficult to see well. They are even harder to photograph or document to the satisfaction of a records committee, the majority of whose members may rarely if ever go out to sea and often know less about the birds than do the observers themselves. Moreover, our knowledge of identification criteria is evolving at different speeds, such that some records accepted in the past may no longer withstand modern scrutiny. The result of all this is a number of records that have not been published or accepted into the body of records used for this guide. This appendix includes only records for which the species would be new for the area covered by this guide, not an evaluation of every record that has been reviewed but not accepted.

ELLIOT'S STORM-PETREL *Oceanites gracilis*

A very small storm-petrel resembling congeneric Wilson's Storm-Petrel, from which distinguished by smaller size and large white belly patch (see Similar Species section in Wilson's Storm-Petrel account, pp. 358–364, S1a.1–S1a.3). Perhaps a very rare (irregular?) visitor n to Panama Bight, where reported without details in Sep 1937 (Ridgely & Gwynne 1989). Not found in recent surveys of Panama Bight (Loftin 1991, Spear & Ainley 1999b).

WHITE-BELLIED STORM-PETREL *Fregetta grallaria*

A fairly large, strikingly plumaged storm-petrel resembling congeneric Black-bellied Storm-Petrel, from which distinguished by less extensive black hood, more extensive whitish edgings to upperparts in fresh plumage (see Similar Species section in Black-bellied Storm-Petrel account, pp. 450–454, S19a.1–S19a.6). Possibly a very rare visitor n to waters off s Central America but identification can be problematic and taxonomy of *Fregetta* is vexed (Howell 2010a). One was reported without details at 0°59'N 80°55'W on 21 May 1990 during an El Niño (Spear & Ainley 1999b), and a *Fregetta* storm-petrel photographed on 29 Nov 2006 at 15°N 112°W (some 450 km se of Clarión Island, Mexico) was likely White-bellied (Pagan et al. 2008).

LITTLE SHEARWATER *Puffinus assimilis*

This small shearwater of the s oceans has been reported from California waters (Hamilton et al. 2007) but review of the record indicates the bird in question was apparently a molting and bleached Manx Shearwater; the record is no longer accepted (Heindel & Garrett 2008). Reports from Alaska (e.g., Day 2006) are unsubstantiated and may also refer to Manx Shearwater. Little Shearwaters are not known to undertake long-distance migrations, and their occurrence in the n hemisphere would be exceptional.

LITERATURE CITED

ABBREVIATIONS

ABA: American Birding Association
AMNH: American Museum of Natural History
AOU: American Ornithologists' Union
BOC: British Ornithologists' Club
BOU: British Ornithologists' Union
CAS : California Academy of Sciences
ICBP: International Council for Bird Preservation

WORKS

Ainley, D. G. 1976. The occurrence of seabirds in the coastal region of California. Western Birds 7:33–68.

Ainley, D. G. 1980. Geographic variation in Leach's Storm-Petrel. Auk 97:837–853.

Ainley, D. G. 1983. Further notes on variation in Leach's Storm-Petrel. Auk 100:230–233.

Ainley, D. G. 2008. Black Storm-Petrel. Pp. 125–129 in W. D. Shuford & T. Gardali (eds.). California Bird Species of Special Concern. Studies of Western Birds 1. Western Field Ornithologists, Camarillo, CA, and California Department of Fish and Game, Sacramento, CA.

Ainley, D. G. 2009. Review of *Petrels Night and Day: A Sound Approach Guide.* Auk 126:227–228.

Ainley, D. G., & W. T. Everett. 2001. Black Storm-Petrel. No. 557 in A. Poole & F. Gill (eds.). The Birds of North America.

Ainley, D. G., T. J. Lewis, & S. Morrell. 1976. Molt in Leach's and Ashy storm-petrels. Wilson Bulletin 88:76–95.

Ainley, D. G., & B. Manolis. 1979. Occurrence and distribution of the Mottled Petrel. Western Birds 10:113–123.

Ainley, D. G., S. Morrell, & T. J. Lewis. 1974. Patterns in the life histories of storm-petrels on the Farallon Islands. Living Bird 13:295–312.

Ainley, D. G., T. C. Telfer, & M. H. Reynolds. 1997. Townsend's and Newell's Shearwater. No. 297 in A. Poole & F. Gill (eds.). The Birds of North America.

Alexander, W. B. 1928. Birds of the Ocean. Putnam, New York.

AOU. 1957. Checklist of North American Birds, 5th ed. AOU, Washington, DC.

AOU. 1998. Checklist of North American Birds, 7th ed. AOU, Washington, DC.

AOU. 2002. Forty-third supplement to the American Ornithologists' Union *Checklist of North American Birds.* Auk 119:897–906.

Austin, J. J. 1996. Molecular phylogenetics of *Puffinus* shearwaters: preliminary evidence from mitochondrial Cytochrome b gene sequences. Molecular Phylogenetics and Evolution 6:77–88.

Austin, J. J., V. Bretagnolle, & E. Pasquet. 2004. A global molecular phylogeny of the small *Puffinus* shearwaters and implications for systematics of the Little-Audubon's Shearwater complex. Auk 121:847–864.

Austin, O. L. 1952. Notes on some petrels of the North Pacific. Bulletin of Museum of Comparative Zoology 107:391–407.

Bailey, S. F., P. Pyle, & L. B. Spear. 1989. Dark *Pterodroma* petrels in the North Pacific: identification, status, and North American occurrence. American Birds 43:400–415.

Baker, K. 1993. Identification Guide to European Non-Passerines. British Trust for Ornithology Guide 24. British Trust for Ornithology, Tring, UK.

Bartle, J. A., D. Hu, J-C. Stahl, P. Pyle, T. R. Simons, & D. Woodby. 1993. Status and ecology of gadfly petrels in the temperate North Pacific. Pp. 101–111 in K. Vermeer, K. T. Briggs, & D. Siegel-Causey (eds.). The status, ecology, and conservation of marine birds of the North Pacific. Canadian Wildlife Service Special Publication, Ottawa.

Benter, R. B., H. M. Renner, & M. Renner. 2005. First record of a Shy Albatross in Alaska. Western Birds 36:135–137.

Bernal, M., A. Simeone, & M. Flores. 2006. Breeding of Wedge-rumped Storm-Petrels (*Oceanodroma tethys*) in northern Chile. Ornitologia Neotropical 17:283–287.

Binford, L. C. 1989. A distributional survey of the birds of the Mexican state of Oaxaca. Ornithological Monographs no. 43.

Birdlife International. 2010a. 2010 IUCN Red List. Downloaded from http://www.birdlife.org/datazone/species on 15 June 2010.

Birdlife International. 2010b. Species factsheet: *Puffinus auricularis*. Downloaded from http://www.birdlife.org on 15 June 2010.

Boersma, P. D., & M. C. Silva. 2001. Fork-tailed Storm-Petrel. No. 569 in A. Poole & F. Gill (eds.). The Birds of North America.

Boersma, P. D., N. T. Wheelwright, M. K. Nerini, & E. S. Wheelwright. 1980. The breeding biology of the Fork-tailed Storm-Petrel (*Oceanodroma furcata*). Auk 97:268–282.

Bolton, M. 2007. Playback experiments indicate absence of vocal recognition in temporally and geographically segregated populations of Madeiran Storm-Petrels *Oceanodroma castro*. Ibis 149:255–263.

Bolton, M., A. L. Smith, E. Gómez-Diaz, V. L. Friesen, R. Medeiros, J. Bried, J. L. Roscales, & R. W. Furness. 2008. Monteiro's Storm-Petrel *Oceanodroma monteiroi*: a new species from the Azores. Ibis 150:717–727.

Bonadonna, F., F. Hesters, & P. Jouventin. 2003. Scent of a nest: discrimination of own-nest odours in Antarctic Prions, *Pachyptila desolata*. Behavioral Ecology and Sociobiology 54:174–178.

Bourne, W. R. P. 1953. On the races of the Frigate Petrel, *Pelagodroma marina* (Latham) with a new race from the Cape Verde Islands. Bulletin of the BOC 73:79–82.

Bourne, W. R. P., & J. R. Jehl Jr. 1982. Variation and nomenclature of Leach's Storm-Petrels. Auk 99:793–797.

Bourne, W. R. P., E. J. Mackrill, A. M. Paterson, & P. Yésou. 1988. The Yelkouan Shearwater *Puffinus (puffinus?) yelkouan*. British Birds 81:306–319.

Bretagnolle, V., & C. Attié. 1996. Coloration and biometrics of fledgling Audubon's Shearwaters *Puffinus lherminieri* from Réunion Island, Indian Ocean. Bulletin of the BOC 116:194–197.

Bretagnolle, V., C. Attié, & E. Pasquet. 1998. Cytochrome-*B* evidence for validity and phylogenetic relationships of *Pseudobulweria* and *Bulweria* (Procellariidae). Auk 115:188–195.

Bretagnolle, V., M. Carruthers, M. Cubitt, F. Bioret, & J. P. Cuillandre. 1991. Six captures of dark-rumped, fork-tailed storm-petrels in the northeastern Atlantic. Ibis 133:351–356.

Bretagnolle, V., & B. Lequette. 1990. Structural variation in the call of the Cory's Shearwater (*Calonectris diomedea*, Aves, Procellariidae). Ethology 85:313–323.

Bried, J., & M. C. Magalhaes. 2004. First Palearctic record of the endangered Bermuda Petrel *Pterodroma cahow*. Bulletin of the BOC 124:202–206.

Bried, J., H. Fraga, P. Calabuig-M., & V. C. Neves. 2005. First two cases of melanism in Cory's Shearwater *Calonectris diomedea*. Marine Ornithology 33:19–22.

Brinkley, E. S. 1997. The Changing Seasons: Autumn 1996. National Audubon Society Field Notes 51(1):8–15.

Brinkley, E. S. 2007. Bulwer's Petrel (*Bulweria bulwerii*) new to Virginia. Raven 78(1):15–19.

Brinkley, E. S., & J. B. Patteson. 1998. Gadfly petrels in the western Atlantic. Birding World 11:341–354.

Brinkley, E. S., J. B. Patteson, & C. Tumer. 2001. Short-tailed Shearwater (*Puffinus tenuirostris*) at Norfolk Canyon. Raven 71:84–89.

Brinkley, W. S. 1995. Dark-rumped storm-petrels in the North Atlantic. Birding 27:95–97.

Brooke, M. 2004. Albatrosses and Petrels across the World. Oxford University Press.

Brooke, M. de L., M. J. Imber, & G. Rowe. 2000. Occurrence of two surface-breeding species of *Pterodroma* on Round Island, Indian Ocean. Ibis 142:154–158.

Brooke, M. de L., & G. Rowe. 1996. Behavioural and molecular evidence for specific status of light and dark morphs of the Herald Petrel *Pterodroma heraldica*. Ibis 138:420–432.

Brown, R. G. B. 1988. The wing-moult of Fulmars and Shearwaters (Procellariidae) in Canadian Atlantic waters. Canadian Field Naturalist 102:203–208.

Brown, R. G. B., W. R. P. Bourne, & T. R. Wahl. 1978. Diving by shearwaters. Condor 80:123–125.

Brown, R. M., R. A. Nichols, C. G. Faulkes, C. G. Jones, L. Bugoni, V. Tatayah, D. Gottelli, & W. C. Jordan. 2010. Range expansion and hybridization in Round Island petrels (*Pterodroma* spp.): evidence from microsatellite genotypes. Molecular Ecology 19:3157–3170.

Browne, R. A., D. J. Anderson, J. N. Houser, F. Cruz, K. J. Glasgow, C. N. Hodges, & G. Massey. 1997. Genetic diversity and divergence of endangered Galapagos and Hawaiian petrel populations. Condor 99:812–815.

Buckley, P. A. 1997. White-faced Storm-Petrel off Sable Island, Nova Scotia: Canada's first? Birders Journal 6:304–306.

Burg, T. M., & J. P. Croxall. 2001. Global relationships amongst Black-browed and Grey-headed albatrosses: analysis of population structure using mitochondrial DNA and microsatellites. Molecular Ecology 10:2647–2660.

Burg, T. M., & J. P. Croxall. 2004. Global population structure and taxonomy of the Wandering Albatross species complex. Molecular Ecology 13:2345–2355.

Carter, H. R., W. R. McIver, & G. J. McChesney. 2008. Ashy Storm-Petrel (*Oceanodroma homochroa*). Pp. 117–124 in W. D. Shuford & T. Gardali (eds.). California Bird Species of Special Concern. Studies of Western Birds 1. Western Field Ornithologists, Camarillo, CA, and California Department of Fish and Game, Sacramento, CA.

Catley, G. 2009. A Soft-plumaged Petrel in Arctic Norway—the first record for the North Atlantic region. Birding World 22:249–252.

Chambers, G. K., C. Moeke, R. Steel, & J. W. H. Trueman. 2009. Phylogenetic analysis of the 24 named albatross taxa based on full mitochondrial cytochrome *b* DNA sequences. Notornis 56:82–94.

Cole, L. 2000. A first Shy Albatross, *Thalassarche cauta*, in California and a critical re-examination of northern hemisphere records of the former *Diomedea cauta* complex. North American Birds 54:124–135.

Collar, N. J., L. P. Gonzaga, N. Krabbe, A. Madrono N., L. G. Naranjo, T. A. Parker III, & D. C. Wege. 1992. Threatened Birds of the Americas. ICBP, Cambridge, UK.

Cracraft, J. 1981. Toward a phylogenetic classification of the recent birds of the world (Class Aves). Auk 98:681–714.

Cramp, S., & K. E. L. Simmons (eds.). 1977. Handbook of the Birds of Europe, the Middle East, and North Africa. Oxford University Press.

Crochet, P. A. 2006. Little Shearwater: underwing pattern. Birding World 19:19–20.

Crossin, R. S. 1974. The storm-petrels (Hydrobatidae). Pp. 154–205 in W. B. King (ed.). Pelagic studies of seabirds in the central and eastern Pacific Ocean. Smithsonian Contributions to Zoology 158.

Davidson, M. E. McL. 1928. On the present status of the Guadalupe Petrel. Condor 30:355–356.

Davis, J. W. F., & I. Packer. 1972. Melanistic Manx Shearwater. British Birds 65:527.

Day, R. H. 2006. Seabirds in the northern Gulf of Alaska and adjacent waters, October to May. Western Birds 37:190–214.

de Naurois, R., & C. Erard. 1979. L'identité subspécifique des populations néo-calédoniennes de *Pterodroma rostrata* Peale 1848. L'Oiseau et la Revue Francaise d'Ornithologie 49:235–239.

Double, M. C., R. Gales, T. Reid, N. Bothers, & C. L. Abbott. 2003. Morphometric comparison of Australian Shy and New Zealand White-capped Albatrosses. Emu 103:287–294.

Douglas, L. 2000. Status of the Jamaican Petrel in the West Indies. Pp. 19–24 in E. A. Shreiber & D. S. Lee (eds.). Status and conservation of West Indian seabirds. Society of Caribbean Ornithology, special publication no. 1.

Dwight, J., Jr. 1897. A species of shearwater (*Puffinus assimilis* Gould) new to the North American fauna. Proceedings of the Biological Society of Washington 11:69–70.

Eades, D. W., P. Scofield, & T. Reid. 1994. Sorting out Sooties. Wingspan 15:11, 36–39.

Einoder, L. D., B. Page, & S. D. Goldsworthy. 2008. Sexual size dimorphism and assortative mating in the Short-tailed Shearwater *Puffinus tenuirostris*. Marine Ornithology 36:167–173.

Everett, W. T., & R. L. Pitman. 1996. Avian specimens from Rocas Alijos. Pp. 359–362 in R. W. Schmeider (ed.). Rocas Alijos. Kluwer Academic Publishers, Norwell, MA.

Faulkner, D. 2007. A Streaked Shearwater (*Calonectris leucomelas*) in Wyoming. North American Birds 60:324–326.

Finsch, O. 1872. *Puffinus auduboni*. Pp. 111–112 in G. Hartlaub & O. Finsch. On a fourth collection of birds from the Pelew and Mackenzie Islands. Proceedings of the Zoological Society of London 1872:87–114.

Flood, R. L. 2009. "All-dark" *Oceanodroma* storm-petrels in the Atlantic and neighboring seas. British Birds 102:365–385.

Force, M. P., S. W. Webb, & S. N. G. Howell. 2007. Identification at sea of Hawaiian and Galapagos petrels. Western Birds 38:242–248.

Friesen, V. L., A. L. Smith, E. Gómez-Diaz, M. Bolton, R. W. Furness, J. Gónzales-Solis, & L. R. Monteiro. 2007. Sympatric speciation by allochrony in a seabird. Proceedings of the National Academy of Sciences 104:18589–18594.

Furness, R. W. 1988. Influence of status and recent breeding experience on the moult strategy of the Yellow-nosed Albatross *Diomedea chlororhynchos*. Journal of Zoology 215:719–727.

Gallo-R., J. P., & A. L. Figueroa-C. 1996. The breeding colony of Laysan Albatrosses on Isla de Guadalupe, Mexico. Western Birds 27:70–76.

Gantlett, S. 2007. The Western Palearctic year. Birding World 20:26–43.

Garrett, K. L. 1990. Leucistic Black-vented Shearwaters (*Puffinus opisthomelas*) in southern California. Western Birds 21:69–72.

Gibson, D. D., & G. V. Byrd. 2007. Birds of the Aleutian Islands, Alaska. Series in Ornithology number 1.

Gill, F. B., C. Jouanin, & R. W. Storer. 1970. Notes on the seabirds of Round Island, Mauritius. Auk 87:514–521.

Gochfeld, M., J. Burger, J. Saliva, & A. Gochfeld. 1988. Herald Petrel new to the West Indies. American Birds 42:1254–1258.

Godfrey, W. E. 1986. The Birds of Canada, rev. ed. National Museums of Canada, Ottawa.

Gould, P. J., D. J. Forsell, & C. J. Lensink. 1982. Pelagic distribution and abundance of seabirds in the Gulf of Alaska and eastern Bering Sea. USFWS Biol. Serv. Program FWS/OBS-82/48. Anchorage.

Gould, P. J., & J. F. Piatt. 1993. Seabirds of the central North Pacific. Pp. 27–38 in K. Vermeer, K. T. Briggs, & D. Siegel-Causey (eds.). The status, ecology, and conservation of marine birds of the North Pacific. Canadian Wildlife Service Special Publication, Ottawa.

Granadeiro, J. P. 1993. Variation in measurements of Cory's Shearwater between populations and sexing by discriminant analysis. Ringing & Migration 14:103–112.

Grinnell, J., & A. H. Miller. 1944. The distribution of the birds of California. Pacific Coast Avifauna 27.

Grinnell, J., & F. H. Test. 1939. Geographic variation in the Fork-tailed Petrel. Condor 41:170–172.

Guicking, D., W. Fiedler, C. Leuther, R. Schlatter, & P. H. Becker. 2004. Morphometrics of the Pink-footed Shearwater (*Puffinus creatopus*): influence of sex and breeding sites. Journal of Ornithology 145:64–68.

Guris, P. A., M. D. Overton, M. H. Tove, & R. Wiltraut. 2004. First North American record of Black-bellied Storm-Petrel (*Fregatta tropica*). North American Birds 58:618–621.

Gutierrez, R. 1998. Flight identification of Cory's and Scopoli's Shearwaters. Dutch Birding 20:216–225.

Gutierrez, R. 2004. Identification of Yelkouan, Balearic, and Manx Shearwaters. Birding World 17:111–122.

Gutierrez, R. 2006. Bulwer's Petrels in the Mediterranean and the risk of confusion with nightjars. Dutch Birding 28:297–299.

Gutierrez, R., & J. González-Solis. 2009. Aberrantly dark Fea's Petrel trapped in Cape Verde Islands in March 2007. Dutch Birding 31:32–34.

Haas, M. 2009. Tristan Albatross collected in Sicily, Italy, in October 1957. Dutch Birding 31:180.

Hamilton, R. A., M. A. Patten, & R. A. Erickson (eds.). 2007. Rare Birds of California. Western Field Ornithologists, Camarillo, CA.

Haney, J. C. 1985. Band-rumped Storm-Petrel occurrences in relation to upwelling off the coast of the south-eastern United States. Wilson Bulletin 97:543–547.

Haney, J. C. 1987a. Ocean internal waves as sources of small-scale patchiness in seabird distribution on the Blake Plateau. Auk 104:129–133.

Haney, J. C. 1987b. Aspects of the pelagic ecology and behavior of the Black-capped Petrel (*Pterodroma hasitata*). Wilson Bulletin 99:153–168.

Haney, J. C., C. A. Faanes, & W. R. P. Bourne. 1993. An observation of Fea's Petrel, *Pterodroma feae* (Procellariiformes: Procellariidae), off the southeastern United States, with comments on the taxonomy and conservation of Soft-plumaged and related petrels in the Atlantic Ocean. Brimleyana 18:115–123.

Haney, J. C., & P. A. MacGillivray. 1985. Aggregations of Cory's Shearwaters (*Calonectris diomedea*) at Gulf Stream fronts. Wilson Bulletin 97:191–200.

Haney, J. C., & S. C. Wainright. 1985. Bulwer's Petrel in the South Atlantic Bight. American Birds 39:868–870.

Harper, P. C. 1978. The plasma proteins of some albatrosses and petrels as an index of relationship in the Procellariiformes. New Zealand Journal of Zoology 5:509–548.

Harris, M. P. 1969a. Food as a factor controlling the breeding of *Puffinus lherminieri*. Ibis 111:139–156.

Harris, M. P. 1969b. The biology of storm petrels in the Galapagos Islands. Proceedings of CAS 37:95–166.

Harris, M. P. 1973. The biology of the Waved Albatross *Diomedea irrorata* on Hood Island, Galapagos. Ibis 115:483–510.

Harris, S. W. 1974. Status, chronology, and ecology of nesting storm-petrels in northwestern California. Condor 76:249–261.

Harrison, P. 1983. Seabirds: An Identification Guide. Houghton Mifflin, Boston.

Harrison, P. 1987. Seabirds of the World: A Photographic Guide. Helm, London.

Harrop, A. H. J. 2004. The "Soft-plumaged Petrel" complex: a review of the literature on taxonomy, identification, and distribution. British Birds 97:6–15.

Hass, T. 1995. An additional record of Bulwer's Petrel *Bulweria bulwerii* off the southeastern United States of America. Marine Ornithology 23:161–162.

Hatch, S. A. 1993. Ecology and population status of Northern Fulmars *Fulmarus glacialis* of the North Pacific. Pp. 82–92 in K. Vermeer, K., K. T. Briggs, & D. Siegel-Causey (eds.). The status, ecology, and conservation of marine birds of the North Pacific. Canadian Wildlife Service Special Publication, Ottawa.

Hatch, S. A., & D. N. Nettleship. 1998. Northern Fulmar. No. 361 in A. Poole & F. Gill (eds.). The Birds of North America.

Hazevoet, C. J. 1995. The Birds of the Cape Verde Islands. BOU Checklist No. 13.

Heindel, M. T., & K. L. Garrett. 2008. The 32nd report of the California Bird Records Committee. Western Birds 39:121–152.

Heintzelman, D. S. 1961. Kermadec Petrel in Pennsylvania. Wilson Bulletin 73:262–267.

Hellmayr, C. E., & B. Conover. 1948. Catalogue of birds of the Americas and the adjacent islands. Field Museum of Natural History Publications, Zoological Series 13, part 2, no. 2.

Hess, P. 1997. The "Hawk Mountain Petrel": first Pennsylvania record, but which species? Pennsylvania Birds 11(1):2–5.

Hooker, S. K., & R. W. Baird. 1997. A Fea's Petrel off Nova Scotia: the first record for Canada. Birders Journal 6:245–348.

Howell, S. 2007a. Don't be afraid of two-thirds of the planet: pelagic birding. Pp. 79–83 in L. White (ed.). Good Birders Don't Wear White. Houghton Mifflin.

Howell, S. N. G. 1996. A Checklist of the Birds of Mexico. Golden Gate Audubon Society, Berkeley, CA.

Howell, S. N. G. 2002. A Black-capped Petrel off the Bay of Biscay: the fourth for the Western Palearctic. Birding World 15:219–220.

Howell, S. N. G. 2004. Further observations of birds from Colima and adjacent Jalisco, Mexico. Cotinga 21:38-43.

Howell, S. N. G. 2006a. Immature Shy Albatrosses. Birding 38(3):56–59.

Howell, S. N. G. 2006b. Identification of "black petrels," genus *Procellaria*. Birding 38(6):52–64.

Howell, S. N. G. 2006c. Primary molt in the Black-footed Albatross. Western Birds 37:241–244.

Howell, S. N. G. 2007b. The short tale of a melanistic Black-vented Shearwater. Western Birds 38:235–237.

Howell, S. N. G. 2009. Identification of immature Salvin's, Chatham, and Buller's Albatrosses. Neotropical Birding 4:19–25.

Howell, S. N. G. 2010a. Identification and taxonomy of White-bellied Storm Petrels, with comments on WP report in August 1986. Dutch Birding 32:36–42.

Howell, S. N. G. 2010b. Moult and ageing of Black-browed Albatross. British Birds 103:353–356.

Howell, S. N. G., C. Corben, P. Pyle, & D. I. Rogers. 2003. The first basic problem: a review of molt and plumage homologies. Condor 105:635–653.

Howell, S. N. G., C. Corben, P. Pyle, & D. I. Rogers. 2004. The first basic problem revisited: reply to commentaries on Howell et al. (2003). Condor 106:206–210.

Howell, S. N. G., & S. J. Engel. 1993. Seabird observations off western Mexico. Western Birds 24:167–181.

Howell, S. N. G., T. McGrath, W. T. Hunefeld, & J. S. Feenstra. 2010a. Occurrence and identification of the Leach's Storm-Petrel (*Oceanodroma leucorhoa*) complex off southern California. North American Birds 63:540–549.

Howell, S. N. G., & B. Patteson. 2007. Moult and Fea's Petrel identification. Birding World 20:201–202.

Howell, S. N. G., & J. B. Patteson. 2008a. Variation in Cory's and Scopoli's shearwaters. Alula 14:12–21.

Howell, S. N. G., & J. B. Patteson. 2008b. Variation in the Black-capped Petrel—one species or more? Alula 14:70–83.

Howell, S. N. G., & J. B. Patteson. 2008c. Swinhoe's Petrel off North Carolina and a review of dark storm-petrel identification. Birding World 21:255–262.

Howell, S. N. G., J. B. Patteson, K. Sutherland, & D. T. Shoch. 2010b. Occurrence and identification of the Band-rumped Storm-Petrel (*Oceanodroma castro*) complex off North Carolina. North American Birds 64:196–207.

Howell, S. N. G., L. B. Spear, & P. Pyle. 1994. Identification of Manx-type Shearwaters in the eastern Pacific. Western Birds 25:169–177.

Howell, S. N. G., & S. Webb. 1989. Additional notes from Isla Clarión, Mexico. Condor 91:1007–1008.

Howell, S. N. G., & S. Webb. 1995. A Guide to the Birds of Mexico and Northern Central America. Oxford University Press.

Howell, S. N. G., S. Webb, & L. B. Spear. 1996. Identification at sea of Cook's, de Filippi's, and Pycroft's petrels. Western Birds 27:57–64.

Huey, L. M. 1952. *Oceanodroma tethys tethys*, a petrel new to the North American avifauna. Auk 69:460–461.

Huler, S. 2004. Defining the Wind. Three Rivers Press, New York.

Humphrey, P. S., & K. C. Parkes. 1959. An approach to the study of molts and plumages. Auk 76:1–31.

Huntington, C. E., R. G. Butler, & R. A. Mauck. 1996. Leach's Storm-Petrel. No. 233 in A. Poole & F. Gill (eds.). The Birds of North America.

Hyrenbach, K. D. 2002. Plumage-based ageing criteria for the Black-footed Albatross *Phoebastria nigripes*. Marine Ornithology 30:85–93.

Imber, M. J. 1984. Migration of White-faced Storm-Petrels *Pelagodroma marina* in the South Pacific and the status of the Kermadec subspecies. Emu 84:32–35.

Imber, M. J. 1985. Origins, phylogeny, and taxonomy of the gadfly petrels, *Pterodroma* spp. Ibis 127:197–229.

Imber, M. J. 2004. Kermadec Petrels (*Pterodroma neglecta*) at Ilha da Trinidade, South Atlantic Ocean and in the North Atlantic. Notornis 51:33–40.

James, P. C., & H. A. Robertson. 1985. First record of Swinhoe's Storm-Petrel *Oceanodroma monorhis* in the Atlantic Ocean. Ardea 73:105–106.

Jehl, J. R., Jr. 1974. The near-shore avifauna of the Middle American West Coast. Auk 91:681–699.

Jehl, J. R., Jr. 1982. The biology and taxonomy of Townsend's Shearwater. Gerfaut 72:121–135.

Jehl, J. R., Jr., & W. T. Everett. 1985. History and status of the avifauna of Isla Guadalupe, Mexico. Transactions of San Diego School of Natural History 20(17):313–336.

Jesus, J., D. Menezes, S. Gomes, P. Oliveira, M. Nogales, & A. Brehm. 2009. Phylogenetic relationships of gadfly petrels *Pterodroma* spp. from the northeastern Atlantic Ocean: Molecular evidence for specific status of Bugio and Cape Verde petrels and implications for conservation. Bird Conservation International 19:199–214.

Johnson, A. W. 1965. The Birds of Chile, and Adjacent Regions of Argentina, Bolivia, and Peru, vol. 1. Platt, Buenos Aires.

Jones, R. M. 1999. Seabird carried inland by tropical storm Nora. Western Birds 30:185–192.

Jouventin, P. 1990. Shy Albatross *Diomedea cauta salvini* breeding on Penguin Island, Crozet Archipelago, Indian Ocean. Ibis 132:126–127.

Jouventin, P., J. Martinez, & J. P. Roux. 1989. Breeding biology and current status of the Amsterdam Island Albatross *Diomedea amsterdamensis*. Ibis 131:171–182.

Keitt, B. S., B. R. Tershey, & D. R. Croll. 2000a. Dive depth and diet of the Black-vented Shearwater (*Puffinus opisthomelas*). Auk 117:507–510.

Keitt, B. S., B. R. Tershey, & D. R. Croll. 2000b. Black-vented Shearwater. No. 521 in A. Poole & F. Gill (eds.). The Birds of North America.

Kennedy, M., & R. D. M. Page. 2002. Seabird supertrees: combining partial estimates of Procellariiform phylogeny. Auk 119:88–108.

King, W. B. (ed.). 1974a. Pelagic studies of seabirds in the central and eastern Pacific Ocean. Smithsonian Contributions to Zoology 158.

King, W. B. 1974b. Wedge-tailed Shearwater (*Puffinus pacificus*). Pp. 53–95 in W. B. King (ed.), Pelagic studies of seabirds in the central and eastern Pacific Ocean. Smithsonian Contributions to Zoology 158.

King, W. B., & P. J. Gould. 1967. The status of Newell's race of the Manx Shearwater. Living Bird 6:163–186.

Kratter, A. W., & D. W. Steadman. 2003. First Atlantic Ocean and Gulf of Mexico specimen of Short-tailed Shearwater. North American Birds 57:277–279.

Kuroda, N. 1967. Note on the whitish underparts of *Puffinus tenuirostris* and a supposed hybrid between *P. griseus*. Miscellaneous report of the Yamashina Institute of Ornithology 5:84–87.

Langston, N. E., & S. Rohwer. 1995. Unusual patterns of incomplete primary molt in Laysan and Black-footed albatrosses. Condor 97:1–19.

Langston, N. E., & S. Rohwer. 1996. Moult-breeding tradeoffs in albatrosses: life history implications for big birds. Oikos 76:498–510.

Lee, D. S. 1984. Petrels and storm-petrels in North Carolina's offshore waters: including species previously unrecorded for North America. American Birds 38:151–163.

Lee, D. S. 1987. December records of seabirds of seabirds off North Carolina. Wilson Bulletin 99:116–121.

Lee, D. S. 1988. The Little Shearwater (*Puffinus assimilis*) in the western North Atlantic. American Birds 42:213–220.

Lee, D. S. 1995. The pelagic ecology of Manx Shearwaters *Puffinus puffinus* off the southeastern United States of America. Marine Ornithology 23:107–119.

Lee, D. S. 2000. Status and conservation priorities for Black-capped Petrels in the West Indies. Pp. 11–18 in E. A. Shreiber & D. S. Lee (eds.). Status and conservation of West Indian seabirds. Society of Caribbean Ornithology, special publication no. 1.

Lee, D. S., & J. C. Haney. 1996. Manx Shearwater. No. 257 in A. Poole & F. Gill (eds.). The Birds of North America.

Lee, D. S., & N. Viña. 1993. A re-evaluation of the status of *Pterodroma hasitata* in Cuba. Ornitologia Neotropical 4:99–101.

LeGrand, H. E., Jr., P. Guris, & M. Gustafson. 1999. Bulwer's Petrel off the North Carolina coast. North American Birds 53:113–115.

LeGrand, H., et al. 2001. 1999–2000 report of the North Carolina Bird Records Committee. Chat 65:83–89.

Lesson, M. R. P. 1839. Description de treize oiseaux nouveaux, suivies de rectifications sur quelques espèces déjà publiées. Revue Zoologique (Paris) 2:100–104.

Levesque, A., & P. Yésou. 2005. Occurrence and abundance of tubenoses (Procellariiformes) at Guadeloupe, Lesser Antilles, 2001–2004. North American Birds 59:672–677.

Lewington, I., P. Alstrom, & P. Colston. 1991. Rare Birds of Britain and Europe. HarperCollins.

Lockwood, M. W., & B. Freeman. 2004. The TOS Handbook of Texas Birds. Texas A&M Press, College Station.

Loftin, H. 1991. An annual cycle of pelagic birds in the Gulf of Panama. Ornitologia Neotropical 2:85–94.

Loomis, L. M. 1918. Expedition of the California Academy of Sciences to the Galapagos Islands, 1905–1906, part 12. A review of the albatrosses, petrels, and diving petrels. Proceedings of CAS, 4th series, vol. 2, part 2, no. 12:1–187.

Luna Mendoza, L. M., D. C. Barton, K. E. Lindquist, & R. W. Henry. 2005. Historia de la avifauna anidante de Isla Guadalupe y las oportunidades actuales de conservación. Pp. 115–133 in G. K. S. d. Prado & E. Peters (eds.). Isla Guadalupe Restauración y Conservación. Instituto Nacional de Ecología, Mexico, D.F.

Marchant, S., & P. J. Higgins (eds.). 1990. Handbook of Australian, New Zealand, and Antarctic Birds, vol. 1. Oxford University Press.

Martin, J., & A. Rowlands. 2001. Small wonders. Birdwatch (December 2001):22–25.

Mathews, G. M. 1934. A Check-list of the Order Procellariiformes. Novitates Zoologicae 39:151–206.

McChesney, G. J., H. R. Carter, & M. W. Parker. 2000. Nesting of Ashy Storm-Petrel and Cassin's Auklet in Monterey County, California. Western Birds 31:178–183.

McKee, T., & P. Pyle. 2002. Plumage variation and hybridization in Black-footed and Laysan albatrosses. North American Birds 56:131–138.

McNeil, R., & J. Burton. 1971. First authentic North American record of the British Storm Petrel (*Hydrobates pelagicus*). Auk 88:671–672.

Mlodinow, S. G. 1999. Southern Hemisphere albatrosses in North American waters. Birders Journal 8:131–141.

Mlodinow, S. G. 2004. Manx Shearwaters in the North Pacific Ocean. Birding 36:608–615.

Mlodinow, S. G. 2005. Manx Shearwater update. Birding 37:348–349.

Monteiro, L. R., & R. W. Furness. 1995. Fea's Petrel *Pterodroma feae* in the Azores. Bulletin of the BOC 115:9–14.

Monteiro, L. R., & R. W. Furness. 1998. Speciation through temporal segregation of Madeiran storm petrel (*Oceanodroma castro*) populations in the Azores? Philosophical Transactions of the Royal Society of London B 353:945–953.

Monteiro, L. R., J. A. Ramos, R. W. Furness, & A. J. del Nevo. 1996. Movements, morphology, breeding, molt, diet, and feeding of seabirds in the Azores. Colonial Waterbirds 19:82–97.

Murphy, R. C. 1915. The bird life of Trinidad Islet. Auk 32:332–348.

Murphy, R. C. 1924. The marine ornithology of the Cape Verde Islands, with a list of all the birds of the archipelago. Bulletin of the AMNH 50:211–278.

Murphy, R. C. 1927. On certain forms of *Puffinus assimilis* and its allies. AMNH Novitates 276.

Murphy, R. C. 1936. Oceanic Birds of South America. 2 vols. AMNH, New York.

Murphy, R. C. 1938. The Wandering Albatross in the Bay of Panama. Condor 40:126.

Murphy, R. C. 1951. The populations of the Wedge-tailed Shearwater (*Puffinus pacificus*). AMNH Novitates 1512.

Murphy, R. C. 1952. The Manx Shearwater, *Puffinus puffinus*, as a species of world-wide distribution. Novitates 1586.

Murphy, R. C., & S. Irving. 1951. A review of the frigate-petrels (*Pelagodroma*). AMNH Novitates 1506.

Murphy, R. C., & J. M. Pennoyer. 1952. Larger petrels of the genus *Pterodroma*. AMNH Novitates 1580.

Nichols, J. T. 1914. An undescribed Galapagos race of *Oceanodroma castro*. Auk 31:388–390.

Nunes, M. 2000. Madeiran Storm-Petrel (*Oceanodroma castro*) in the Desertas Islands (Madeira archipelago): a new case of two distinct populations breeding annually? Arquipelago. Life and Marine Sciences Supplement 2(Part A):175–179.

Nunn, G. B., J. Cooper, P. Jouventin, C. J. R. Robertson, & G. G. Robertson. 1996. Evolutionary relationships among extant albatrosses (Procellariiformes: Diomedeidae) established from complete Cytochrome-*B* sequences. Auk 113:784–801.

Nunn, G. B., & S. E. Stanley. 1998. Body size effects and rates of Cytochrome *b* evolution in tube-nosed seabirds. Molecular Biology and Evolution 15:1360–1371.

O'Brien, M., J. B. Patteson, G. L. Armistead, & G. B. Pearce. 1999. Swinhoe's Storm-Petrel: first North American photographic record. North American Birds 53:6–10.

Oedekoven, C. S., D. G. Ainley, & L. B. Spear. 2001. Variable responses of seabirds to change in marine climate: California Current 1985–1994. Marine Ecology Progress Series 212:265–281.

Olson, S. L. 1985. The Fossil Record of Birds. Pp. 79–238 in D. S. Farner, J. R. King, & K. C. Parkes (eds.). Avian Biology, vol. 8. Academic Press.

Olson, S. L. 2010. Stasis and turnover in small shearwaters on Bermuda over the last 400,000 years (Aves: Procellariidae: *Puffinus lherminieri* group). Biological Journal of the Linnaean Society 99:699–707.

Olson, S. L., & P. C. Rasmussen. 2001. Miocene and Pliocene birds from the Lee Creek Mine, North Carolina. Pp. 233–364 in C. E. Ray & D. J. Bohaska (eds.). Geology and Paleontology of the Lee Creek Mine, North Carolina, III. Smithsonian Contributions to Paleobiology 90.

Onley, D., & P. Scofield. 2007. Albatrosses, Petrels, and Shearwaters of the World. Princeton University Press, Princeton, NJ.

Pagan, R., P. Pyle, & L. T. Ballance. 2008. A *Fregetta* storm-petrel off western Mexico. Western Birds 39:225–227.

Patten, M. A., P. Unitt, & G. McCaskie. 2003. Birds of the Salton Sea: Status, Biogeography, and Ecology. University of California Press.

Patteson, J. B., & G. L. Armistead. 2004. First record of Cape Verde Shearwater (*Calonectris edwardsii*) for North America. North American Birds 58:468–473.

Patteson, J. B., & E. S. Brinkley. 2004. A petrel primer: the gadflies of North Carolina. Birding 36:586–596.

Patteson, J. B., M. A. Patten, & E. S. Brinkley. 1999. The Black-browed Albatross in North America: first photographically documented record. North American Birds 53:228–231.

Patteson, J. B., K. Sutherland, & S. N. G. Howell. 2009a. Recent records of European Storm-Petrel (*Hydrobates pelagicus*) off North Carolina. North American Birds 62:512–517.

Patteson, J. B., S. N. G. Howell, & K. Sutherland. 2009b. Swinhoe's Storm-Petrel (*Oceanodroma monorhis*) off North Carolina. North American Birds 62:518–520.

Paxton, R. O. 1968. Wandering Albatross in California. Auk 85:502–504.

Pearce, J. M. 2002. First record of a Greater Shearwater in Alaska. Western Birds 33:121–122.

Penhallurick, J., & M. Wink. 2004. Analysis of the taxonomy and nomenclature of the Procellariiformes based on complete nucleotide sequences of the mitochondrial cytochrome *b* gene. Emu 104:125–147.

Peters, J. L. 1924. A second North American record for *Puffinus assimilis*. Auk 41:337–338.

Pitman, R. L. 1986. Atlas of seabird distribution and relative abundance in the Eastern Tropical Pacific. Nat. Marine Fisheries Service Admin. Report LJ-86-02C.

Pitman, R. L., & L. T. Ballance. 1992. Parkinson's Petrel distribution and foraging ecology in the eastern Pacific: aspects of an exclusive feeding relationship with dolphins. Condor 94:825–835.

Pitman, R. L., & L. T. Ballance. 2002. The changing status of marine birds breeding at San Benedicto Island, Mexico. Wilson Bulletin 114:11–19.

Pitman, R. L., W. A. Walker, W. T. Everett, & J. P. Gallo-R. 2004. Population status, foods, and foraging of Laysan Albatrosses *Phoebastria immutabilis* nesting on Guadalupe Island, Mexico. Marine Ornithology 32:159–165.

Poole, A., & F. Gill (eds.). 1992–2002. The Birds of North America (numbers 1–716). The Birds of North America, Inc. Philadelphia.

Porter, R., D. Newell, T. Marr, & R. Joliffe. 1997. Identification of Cape Verde Shearwater. Birding World 10:222–228.

Power, D. M., & D. G. Ainley. 1986. Seabird geographic variation: similarity among populations of Leach's Storm-Petrel. Auk 103:575–586.

Prince, P. A., & S. P. Rodwell. 1994. Ageing immature Black-browed and Grey-headed Albatrosses using moult, bill, and plumage characteristics. Emu 94:246–254.

Prince, P. A., S. Rodwell, M. Jones, & P. Rothery. 1993. Moult in Black-browed and Grey-headed Albatrosses *Diomedea melanophris* and *D. chrysostoma*. Ibis 135:121–131.

Prince, P. A., H. Weimerskirch, N. Huin, & S. Rodwell. 1997. Molt, maturation of plumage, and ageing in the Wandering Albatross. Condor 99:58–72.

Pyle, P. 1993. A Markham's Storm-Petrel in the northeastern Pacific. Western Birds 24:108–110.

Pyle, P. 2006. Offshore Pacific highlights in summer–fall 2005: just another year. North American Birds 60:4–13.

Pyle, P. 2008. Identification Guide to North American Birds, part 2. Slate Creek Press, Bolinas, CA.

Pyle, P., G. Friedrichsen, T. Staudt, C. Oedekoven, & L. T. Ballance. 2006. First record of Ringed [= Hornby's] Storm-Petrel (*Oceanodroma hornbyi*) for North America. North American Birds 60:162–163.

Radamaker, K., & G. McCaskie. 2006. First verifiable record of the Flesh-footed Shearwater for Mexico. Western Birds 37:51–52.

Randi, E., F. Spina, & B. Massa. 1989. Genetic variability in Cory's Shearwater (*Calonectris diomedea*). Auk 106:411–417.

Ratcliffe, N., & 8 co-authors. 2000. The status and distribution of Fea's Petrel *Pterodroma feae* in the Cape Verde Islands. Atlantic Seabirds 2:73–86.

Rheindt, F. E., & J. J. Austin. 2005. Major analytical and conceptual shortcomings in a recent taxonomic revision of the Procellariiformes—a reply to Penhallurick and Wink (2004). Emu 105:181–186.

Robb, M., K. Mullarney, & The Sound Approach. 2008. Petrels Night and Day. The Sound Approach, Poole, Dorset.

Roberson, D. 2002. Monterey Birds, 2nd ed. Monterey Peninsula Audubon Society, Carmel, CA.

Roberson, D., & S. F. Bailey. 1991a. *Cookilaria* Petrels in the eastern Pacific Ocean: identification and distribution, part 1. American Birds 45:399–402.

Roberson, D., & S. F. Bailey. 1991b. *Cookilaria* Petrels in the eastern Pacific Ocean: identification and distribution, part 2. American Birds 45:1067–1081.

Roberts, C. 2007. The Unnatural History of the Sea: The Past and Future of Humanity and Fishing. Octopus Publishing, London.

Robertson, C. J. R. 2002. The scientific name of the Indian Yellow-nosed Albatross *Thalassarche carteri*. Marine Ornithology 30:48–49.

Robertson, C. J. R., J. Klavitter, & R. McCarthy. 2005. Salvin's Albatross (*Thalassarche salvini*) on Midway Atoll. Notornis 52:236–237.

Robertson, C. J. R., & G. B. Nunn. 1998. Towards a new taxonomy for albatrosses. Pp. 13–19 in G. Robertson, & R. Gales (eds.). Albatross Biology and Conservation. Surrey Beatty & Sons, Chipping Norton.

Robertson, C. J. R., & J. Warham. 1992. Nomenclature of the New Zealand Wandering Albatrosses *Diomedea exulans*. Bulletin of the BOC 112:74–81.

Robertson, G. J. 2002. Current status of the Manx Shearwater (*Puffinus puffinus*) colony on Middle Lawn Island, Newfoundland. Northeastern Naturalist 9:317–324.

Robertson, H. A., & P. C. James. 1988. Morphology and egg measurements of seabirds breeding on Great Salvage Island, North Atlantic. Bulletin of the BOC 108:79–87.

Rohwer, S., & A. E. Edwards. 2006. Reply to Howell on primary molt in albatrosses. Western Birds 37:245–248.

Ryan, P. G., J. Cooper, & J. P. Glass. 2001. Population status, breeding biology, and conservation of the Tristan Albatross *Diomedea [exulans] dabbenena*. Bird Conservation International 11:35–48.

Sangster, G., J. M. Collinson, A. J. Helbig, A. G. Knox, & D. T. Parkin. 2005. Taxonomic recommendations for British birds: third report. Ibis 147:821–826.

Santaella, L., & A. M. Sada. 1991. The avifauna of the Revillagigedo Islands, Mexico: additional data and observations. Wilson Bulletin 103:668–675.

Seto, N. W. H. 2001. Christmas Shearwater. No. 561 in A. Poole & F. Gill (eds.). The Birds of North America.

Shaffer, S. A., & 10 co-authors. 2006. Migratory shearwaters integrate oceanic resources across the Pacific Ocean in an endless summer. Proceedings of the National Academy of Sciences 103:12799–12802.

Sharpe, R. B. 1904. Report on the birds obtained by the National Antarctic Expedition at the Island of South Trinidad. Ibis 4:214–217.

Shearwater, D. L. 2004. A brief history of pelagic birding in North America. Birding 36:634–638.

Shirihai, H. 2007. A Complete Guide to Antarctic Wildlife, 2nd ed. A&C Black, London.

Shirihai, H., V. Bretagnolle, & F. Zino. 2010a. Identification of Fea's, Desertas, and Zino's Petrels at sea. Birding World 23:239–275.

Shirihai, H., M. San Román, V. Bretagnolle, & D. Wege. 2010b. Petrels of the Caribbean: the Jamaica Petrel pelagic expedition (a pelagic expedition off Jamaica, and off the islands of Guadeloupe and

Dominica). Unpublished report for the Tubenoses Project and BirdLife's Preventing Extinction Programme (available for download at <outbind://61/index.html> http://www.birdlife.org/news/news/2010/05/Jamaica-Petrel-expedition-report_Nov09.pdf).

Shuntov, V. P. 1993. Biological and physical determinants of marine bird distribution in the Bering Sea. Pp. 10–17 in K. Vermeer, K. T. Briggs, & D. Siegel-Causey (eds.). The status, ecology, and conservation of marine birds of the North Pacific. Canadian Wildlife Service Spec. Publ., Ottawa.

Sibley, C. G., & J. E. Alquist. 1990. Phylogeny and Classification of Birds. Yale University Press, New Haven, CT.

Sibley, C. G., & B. L. Monroe Jr. 1990. Distribution and Taxonomy of Birds of the World. Yale University Press, New Haven, CT.

Simons, T. R., & C. N. Hodges. 1998. Dark-rumped Petrel. No. 334 in A. Poole & F. Gill (eds.). The Birds of North America.

Slipp, J. W. 1952. A record of Tasmanian White-capped Albatross, *Diomedea cauta cauta*, in American North Pacific waters. Auk 69:458–459.

Slotterback, J. W. 2002. Band-rumped Storm-Petrel and Tristram's Storm-Petrel. No. 673 in A. Poole & F. Gill (eds.). The Birds of North America.

Smith, A. L., & V. L. Friesen. 2007. Differentiation of sympatric populations of the Band-rumped Storm-Petrel in the Galapagos Islands: an examination of genetics, morphology, and vocalizations. Molecular Ecology 16:1593–1603.

Smith, A. L., L. Monteiro, O. Hasegawa, & V. L. Friesen. 2007. Global phylogeny of the Band-rumped Storm-Petrel (*Oceanodroma castro*; Procellariiformes: Hydrobatidae). Molecular Phylogenetics and Evolution 43:755–773.

Snow, D. W. 1965. The breeding of Audubon's Shearwater (*Puffinus lherminieri*) in the Galapagos. Auk 82:591–597.

Soldaat, E., M. F. Leopold, E. H. Meesters, & C. J. R. Robertson. 2009. Albatross mandible at archeological site in Amsterdam, the Netherlands, and WP records of *Diomedea* albatrosses. Dutch Birding 31:1–16.

Souto, L. R. A., R. Maia-Nogueira, & D. C. Bressan. 2008. Primero registro de *Puffinus tenuirostris* (Temminck, 1835) para o Oceano Atlântico. Revista Brasileira de Ornitologia 16(1):64–66.

Spear, L. B., & D. G. Ainley. 1993. Kleptoparasitism by Kermadec Petrels, jaegers, and skuas in the Eastern Tropical Pacific: evidence of mimicry by two species of *Pterodroma*. Auk 110:222–233.

Spear, L. B., & D. G. Ainley 1997. Flight behaviour of seabirds in relation to wind direction and wing morphology. Ibis 139:221–233.

Spear, L. B., & D. G. Ainley 1998. Morphological differences relative to ecological segregation in petrels (family: Procellariidae) of the Southern Ocean and Tropical Pacific. Auk 115:1017–1033.

Spear, L. B., & D. G. Ainley 1999a. Migration routes of Sooty Shearwaters in the Pacific Ocean. Condor 101:205–218.

Spear, L. B., & D. G. Ainley. 1999b. Seabirds of the Panama Bight. Waterbirds 22:175–198.

Spear, L. B., & D. G. Ainley. 2007. Storm-petrels of the eastern Pacific Ocean: species assembly and diversity along marine habitat gradients. Ornithological Monographs no. 62.

Spear, L. B., D. G. Ainley, N. Nur, & S. N. G. Howell. 1995. Population size and factors affecting at-sea distributions of four endangered procellariids in the tropical Pacific. Condor 97:613–638.

Spear, L. B., D. G. Ainley, & W. A. Walker. 2007. Foraging dynamics of seabirds in the eastern tropical Pacific Ocean. Studies in Avian Biology no. 35.

Spear, L. B., D. G. Ainley, & S. W. Webb. 2003. Distribution, abundance, and behaviour of Buller's, Chatham Island, and Salvin's albatrosses off Chile. Ibis 145:253–269.

Spear, L. B., S. N. G. Howell, & D. G. Ainley. 1992. Notes on the at-sea identification of some Pacific gadfly petrels (genus: *Pterodroma*). Colonial Waterbirds 15:202–218.

Stallcup, R. 1990. Ocean Birds of the Nearshore Pacific. Point Reyes Bird Observatory, Stinson Beach, CA.

Stallcup, R., & E. W. Preston. 2006. First record of Parkinson's Petrel (*Procellaria parkinsoni*) for the continental United States. North American Birds 60:166–169.

Stallcup, R., & S. B. Terrill. 1996. Albatrosses and Cordell Bank. Birding 28:106–110.

Steele, J. 2006. Do we know what British "Soft-plumaged Petrels" are? British Birds 99:404–419.

Stiles, F. G., & A. F. Skutch. 1989. A Guide to the Birds of Costa Rica. Cornell University Press, Ithaca, NY.

Sullivan, B. L. 2009. First documented record of Black-vented Shearwater (*Puffinus opisthomelas*) for Costa Rica. North American Birds 63:202–205.

Suryan, R. M., K. S. Dietrich, E. F. Melvin, G. R. Balogh, F. Sato, & K. Ozaki. 2007. Migratory routes of short-tailed albatrosses [*sic*]: use of exclusive economic zones of North Pacific rim countries and spatial overlap with commercial fisheries in Alaska. Biological Conservation 137:450–460.

Thibault, J. C., & V. Bretagnolle. 1998. A Mediterranean breeding colony of Cory's Shearwater *Calonectris diomedea* in which individuals show behavioural and biometric characters of the Atlantic subspecies. Ibis 140:523–528.

Tickell, W. L. N. 2000. Albatrosses. Yale University Press, New Haven, CT.

Tomkins, R. J., & B. J. Milne. 1991. Differences among Dark-rumped Petrel (*Pterodroma phaeopygia*) populations within the Galapagos archipelago. Notornis 38:1–35.

Tove, M. H. 1997. Fea's Petrel in North America: documentation. Birding 29:309–315.

Tove, M. H. 2005. Kermadec Petrels (*Pterodroma neglecta*) in the Atlantic Ocean—a rebuttal. Notornia 52:56–58.

Tuck, G. B., & H. Heinzel. 1978. A Field Guide to the Seabirds of Britain and The World. Collins, London.

Unitt, P. 2004. San Diego County Bird Atlas. Proceedings of the San Diego Society of Natural History Memoir No. 39.

Unitt, P., M. A. Faulkner, & C. Swanson. 2009. First record of Newell's Shearwater from the mainland of North America. Western Birds 40:21–28.

Van den Berg, A. B. 2006. Dutch Birding's Names: List of Western Palearctic Bird Species 2006. Dutch Birding Association, Amsterdam.

Van Franeker, J. A., & J. Wattel. 1982. Geographical variation of the Fulmar *Fulmarus glacialis* in the North Atlantic. Ardea 70:31–44.

Veit, R. R., J. A. McGowan, D. G. Ainley, T. R. Wahl, & P. Pyle. 1997. Apex marine predator declines ninety percent in association with changing oceanic climate. Global Change Biology 3:23–28.

Viot, C. R., P. Jouventin, & J. Bried. 1993. Population genetics of some southern seabirds. Marine Ornithology 2:1–25.

Wahl, T. R. 1985. The distribution of Buller's Shearwater (*Puffinus bulleri*) in the North Pacific Ocean. Notornis 32:109–117.

Wahl, T. R., D. G. Ainley, A. H. Benedict, & A. R. DeGange. 1989. Associations between seabirds and water-masses in the northern Pacific in summer. Marine Biology 103:1–11.

Wahl, T. R., & B. Tweit. 2000. Seabird abundances off Washington, 1972–1998. Western Birds 31:69–88.

Walker, K., & G. Elliott. 2005. Population changes and biology of the Antipodean Wandering Albatross (*Diomedea antipodensis*). Notornis 52:206–214.

Wanless, R. M., A. Aguirre M., A. Angel, J. K. Jacobsen, B. S. Keitt, & J. McCann. 2009. Birds of Clarion Island, Revillagigedo Archipelago, Mexico. Wilson Journal of Ornithology 121:745–751.

Warham, J. 1990. The Petrels. Academic Press, London.

Warham, J. 1996. The Behaviour, Population Biology, and Physiology of the Petrels. Academic Press, London.

Warzybok, P., R. Bradley, & S. N. G. Howell. 2009. First North American record of Tristram's Storm-Petrel (*Oceanodroma tristrami*). North American Birds 62:634–636.

Watson, G. E., D. S. Lee, & E. S. Backus. 1986. Status and subspecific identity of White-faced Storm-Petrels in the western North Atlantic Ocean. American Birds 40:401–408.

Wetmore, A. 1965. The Birds of the Republic of Panama, part 1. Smithsonian Miscellaneous Collections, vol. 150.

White, A. W. 2004. Seabirds in the Bahamian archipelago and adjacent waters: transient, wintering, and rare nesting species. North American Birds 57:436–451.

Whittington, P. A., B. M. Dyer, R. J. M. Crawford, & A. J. Williams. 1999. First recorded breeding on Leach's Storm-Petrel *Oceanodroma leucorhoa* in the southern hemisphere, at Dyer Island, South Africa. Ibis 141:327–330.

Williams, A. J. 1984. Breeding distribution, numbers, and conservation of tropical seabirds on oceanic islands in the south Atlantic ocean. Pp. 393–402 in J. P. Croxall, P. H. G. Evans, & R. W. Schreiber (eds.). Status and Conservation of the World's Seabirds ICBP Technical Publication No. 2.

Wilson, E. A. 1904. The birds of the Island of South Trinidad. Ibis 4:208–213.

Wingate, D. B. 1972. First successful hand-rearing of an abandoned Bermuda Petrel chick. Ibis 114:97–101.

Wingate, D. B., T. Hass, E. S. Brinkley, & J. B. Patteson. 1998. Identification of Bermuda Petrel. Birding 30:18–36.

Wink, M., P. Heidrich, U. Kahl, & I. Swatschek. 1993. Inter- and intraspecific variation of the nucleotide sequence of the cytochrome b gene in Cory's Shearwater (*Calonectris diomedea*), Manx Shearwater (*Puffinus puffinus*) and the Fulmar (*Fulmarus glacialis*). Zeitschrift für Naturforschung 48c:504–509.

Woolfenden, G. E., L. R. Monteiro, & R. A. Duncan. 2001. Recovery from the northeastern Gulf of Mexico of a Band-rumped Storm-Petrel banded in the Azores. Journal of Field Ornithology 72:62–65.

Zino, F., R. Brown, & M. Biscoito. 2008. The separation of *Pterodroma madeira* (Zino's Petrel) from *Pterodroma feae* (Fea's Petrel) (Aves: Procellariidae). Ibis 150:326–334.

Zino, P. A., & F. Zino. 1986. Contribution to the studies of the petrels of the genus *Pterodroma* in the archipelago of Madeira. Boletim do Museo Municipal do Funchal 38:145–165.

GEOGRAPHIC REFERENCES
Canada and Greenland

Boertmann, D. 1994. Meddelelser om Gromland. An annotated checklist to the birds of Greenland. Bioscience 38:1–63.

Campbell, R. W., N. K. Dawe, I. McT.-Cowan, J. M. Cooper, G. W. Kaiser, & M. C. E. McNall. 1990. The Birds of British Columbia, vol. 1. Royal British Columbia Museum, Victoria.

James, R. D. 1991. Annotated Checklist of the Birds of Ontario, 2nd ed. The Royal Ontario Museum.

Kenyon, J. K., K. H. Morgan, M. D. Bentley, L. A. McFarlane Tranquilla, & K. E. Moore. 2009. Atlas of pelagic seabirds off the west coast of Canada and adjacent areas. Technical Report Series No. 499. Canadian Wildlife Service, Pacific and Yukon Region, British Columbia.

Peters, H. S., & T. D. Burleigh. 1951. The Birds of Newfoundland. Dept. of Natural Resources, Province of Newfoundland, St. John's.

Squires, W. A. 1976. The Birds of New Brunswick, 2nd ed. The New Brunswick Museum, Monographic Series No. 7.

Tufts, R. W. 1986. The Birds of Nova Scotia, 3rd ed. Nimbus Publishing and Nova Scotia Museum, Halifax, Nova Scotia.

United States

ABA. 2008. ABA Checklist: Birds of the Continental United States and Canada, 7th ed. ABA, Colorado Springs, CO.

Ainley. D. G. 1976. The occurrence of seabirds in the coastal region of California. Western Birds 7:33–68.

Beaton, G., P. W. Sykes Jr., & J. W. Parrish Jr. 2003. Annotated Checklist of Georgia Birds. Georgia Ornithological Society, Occasional Publication No. 14.

Briggs, K. T., W. B. Taylor, D. B. Lewis, & D. R. Carlson. 1987. Bird communities at sea off California. Studies in Avian Biology 11.

Day, R. H. 2006. Seabirds in the northern Gulf of Alaska and adjacent waters, October to May. Western Birds 37:190–214.

Finch, D. W., W. C. Russell, & E. V. Thompson. 1978. Pelagic birds in the Gulf of Maine. American Birds 32:140–155.

Gabrielson, I. N., & F. C. Lincoln. 1959. Birds of Alaska. Stackpole Company, Harrisburg, PA, & Wildlife Management Institute, Washington, DC.

Garrett, K., & J. Dunn. 1981. Birds of Southern California, Status and Distribution. Los Angeles Audubon Society, Los Angeles, CA.

Gibson, D. D., & G. V. Byrd. 2007. Birds of the Aleutian Islands, Alaska. Series in Ornithology number 1.

Hamilton, R. A., & D. R. Willick. 1996. The Birds of Orange County, California: Status and Distribution. Sea and Sage Audubon Society, Irvine, CA.

Hamilton, R. A., M. A. Patten, & R. A. Erickson (eds.). 2007. Rare Birds of California. Western Field Ornithologists, Camarillo, CA.

Hess, G. K., R. L. West, M. V. Barnhill III, & L. M. Fleming. 2000. Birds of Delaware. University of Pittsburgh Press.

Iliff, M. J., R. F. Ringler, & J. L. Stasz. 1996. Field List of the Birds of Maryland, 3rd ed. Maryland Ornithological Society, Maryland Avifauna No. 2.

Imhoff, T. A. 1976. Alabama Birds, 2nd ed. University of Alabama Press, Tuscaloosa.

Kessel, B., & D. D. Gibson. 1978. Status and Distribution of Alaska Birds. Studies in Avian Biology No. 1.

Lee, D. S., & J. Booth Jr. 1979. Seasonal distribution of offshore and pelagic birds in North Carolina waters. American Birds 33:715–721.

Lehman, P.E. 2005. Fall bird migration at Gambell, St Lawrence Island, Alaska. Western Birds 36:2–55.

Levine, E. 1998 (ed.). Bull's Birds of New York State. Cornell University Press, Ithaca, NY.

Lockwood, M. W., & B. Freeman. 2004. The TOS Handbook of Texas Birds. Texas A&M Press, College Station.

Lowery, G. H., Jr. 1974. Louisiana Birds, 3rd ed. Louisiana State University Press, Baton Rouge.

Marshall, D. B., M. G. Hunter, & A. L. Contreras (eds.). 2003. Birds of Oregon, a General Reference. Oregon State University Press, Corvallis.

McWilliams, G. M., & D. W. Brauning. 2000. Birds of Pennsylvania. Cornell University Press, Ithaca, NY.

Mumford, R. E., & C. E. Keller. 1984. The Birds of Indiana. Indiana University Press, Bloomington.

Murphy, R. C. 1936. Oceanic Birds of South America. 2 vols. AMNH, New York.

Patten, M. A., P. Unitt, & G. McCaskie. 2003. Birds of the Salton Sea: Status, Biogeography, and Ecology. University of California Press.

Peterjohn, B. G. 2001. The Birds of Ohio. Wooster Book Co., Wooster, OH.

Post , W., & S. A. Gauthreaux, Jr. 1989. Status and Distribution of South Carolina Birds. Contributions of Charleston Museum, No. 18.

Pulich, W., Jr. 1982. Documentation and status of Cory's Shearwater in the western Gulf of Mexico. Wilson Bulletin 94:381–385.

Pyle, R. L., & P. Pyle. 2009. The Birds of the Hawaiian Islands: Occurrence, History, Distribution, and Status. B. P. Bishop Museum, Honolulu, HI, version 1 (31 December 2009). http:/hbs.bishopmuseum.org/birds/rlp-monograph/.

Robbins, M. B., & D. A. Easterla. 1992. Birds of Missouri. University of Missouri Press, Columbia.

Roberson, D. 2002. Monterey Birds, 2nd ed. Monterey Peninsula Audubon Society, Carmel, CA.

Rottenborn, S. C., & E. S. Brinkley. 2007. Virginia's Birdlife, an Annotated Checklist, 4th ed. Virginia Society of Ornithology, Virginia Avifauna No. 7.

Stevenson, H. M., & B. H. Anderson. 1994. The Birdlife of Florida. University Press of Florida, Gainesville.

Turcotte, W. H., & D. L. Watts. 1999. Birds of Mississippi. University Press of Mississippi, Jackson.

Unitt, P. 2004. San Diego County Bird Atlas. Proceedings of the San Diego Society of Natural History Memoir No. 39.

Veit, R. R., & W. R. Peterson. 1993. Birds of Massachusetts. Massachusetts Audubon Society.

Walsh, J., V. Elia, R. Kane, & T. Halliwell. 1999. Birds of New Jersey. New Jersey Audubon Society.

Zeranski, J. D., & T. R. Baptist. 1990. Connecticut Birds. University Press of New England.

West Indies, Mexico, and Central America

Amos, E. J. R. 1991. A Guide to the Birds of Bermuda. Published by author, Warwick, Bermuda.

Binford, L. C. 1989. A distributional survey of the birds of the Mexican state of Oaxaca. Ornithological Monographs no. 43.

Bradley, P. E. 2000. The birds of the Cayman Islands. BOU Checklist No. 19.

Buden, D. W. 1987. The Birds of the Southern Bahamas. BOU Checklist No. 8.

Crossin, R. S. 1974. The storm-petrels (Hydrobatidae). Pp. 154–205 in W. B. King (ed.), Pelagic studies of seabirds in the central and eastern Pacific Ocean. Smithsonian Contributions to Zoology 158.

Erickson, R. A., & S. N. G. Howell (eds.). 2001. Birds of the Baja California Peninsula: status, distribution, and biogeography. Monographs in Field Ornithology 3. ABA.

Garrido, O. H., & A. Kirkconnell. 2000. A Field Guide to the Birds of Cuba. Cornell University Press, Ithaca, NY.

Howell, S. N. G., & S. J. Engel. 1993. Seabird observations off western Mexico. Western Birds 24:167–181.

Howell, S. N. G., & S. Webb. 1990. The seabirds of Las Islas Revillagigedo, Mexico. Wilson Bulletin 102:140–146.

Howell, S. N. G., & S. Webb. 1995. A Guide to the Birds of Mexico and Northern Central America. Oxford University Press.

Jehl, J. R., Jr. 1974. The near-shore avifauna of the Middle American coast. Auk 91:681–699.

Jones, H. L. 2003. Birds of Belize. Texas University Press, Austin.

Keith, A. R. 1997. The Birds of St. Lucia. BOU Checklist No. 15.

Keith, A. R., J. W. Wiley, S. C. Latta, & J. A. Ottenwalder. 2003. The Birds of Hispaniola. BOU Checklist No. 21.

King, W. B. (ed.). 1974a. Pelagic studies of seabirds in the central and eastern Pacific Ocean. Smithsonian Contributions to Zoology 158.

Levesque, A., & P. Yésou. 2005. Occurrence and abundance of tubenoses (Procellariiformes) at Guadeloupe, Lesser Antilles, 2001–2004. . North American Birds 59:672–677.

Pitman, R. L. 1986. Atlas of seabird distribution and relative abundance in the Eastern Tropical Pacific. Nat. Marine Fisheries Service Admin. Report LJ-86-02C.

Pitman, R. L., & L. T. Ballance. 2002. The changing status of marine birds breeding at San Benedicto Island, Mexico. Wilson Bulletin 114:11–19.

Raffaele, H., J. Wiley, O. Garrido, A. Keith, & J. Raffaele. 1998. Birds of the West Indies. Princeton University Press.

Ridgely, R. S., & J. A. Gwynne Jr. 1989. A Guide to the Birds of Panama, 2nd ed. Princeton University Press.

Spear, L. B., & D. G. Ainley. 1999. Seabirds of the Panama Bight. Waterbirds 22:175–198.

Spear, L. B., & D. G. Ainley. 2007. Storm-petrels of the eastern Pacific Ocean: species assembly and diversity along marine habitat gradients. Ornithological Monographs no. 62.

Stiles, F. G., & A. F. Skutch. 1989. A Guide to the Birds of Costa Rica. Cornell University Press, Ithaca, NY.

van Halewyn, R., & R. L. Norton. 1984. The status and conservation of seabirds in the Caribbean. Pp. 169–222 in J. P. Croxall, P. G. H. Evans, & R. W. Schreiber (eds.). Status and Conservation of the World's Seabirds ICBP Tech. Publ. No. 2.

Wetmore, A. 1959. Description of a race of the shearwater *Puffinus lherminieri* from Panama. Proceedings of the Biological Society of Washington 72:19–22.

White, A. W. 2004. Seabirds in the Bahamian archipelago and adjacent waters: transient, wintering, and rare nesting species. North American Birds 57:436–451.

INDEX

Page numbers in italics indicate images; species in parentheses indicate mention (usually under discussions of similar species) and sometimes photos, but no full treatment.